MUHAMMAD ﷺ

THE MESSENGER OF ISLAM

His Life & Prophecy

compiled from traditional sources
in Ottoman Turkish by

Hajjah Amina Adil

Preface by Shaykh Nazim Adil Al-Haqqani

Foreword by Shaykh Muhammad Hisham Kabbani

The author, Hajjah Amina (right), and her daughter, Hajjah Naziha Adil.

Published and Distributed by:

Islamic Supreme Council of America (ISCA)
1400 Sixteenth Street NW, #B112, Washington, DC 20036 USA

Publishing Office:

17195 Silver Parkway, #201, Fenton, MI 48430 USA
Tel: (888) 278-6624
Fax: (810) 815-0518
Email: staff@islamicsupremecouncil.org
Web: www.islamicsupremecouncil.org
Please visit us on the Web for more titles in Islamic spirituality and traditional scholarship.

ISBN: 1-930409-11-7

Front cover photo: Entrusted to the Ottoman Sultan through the succession of caliphs dating back to 7th century, this exquisite tableau in many ways summarizes the life of Prophet Muhammad. The first flag of Islam is preserved within the closed box, representing the Prophet's spiritual authority. The Quran -- the divine book which he brought -- rests open, symbolizing the never-extinguished light of his guidance. The sheathed swords represent the Prophet's struggle, primarily against the ego (the greater jihad) and against religious oppression (the lesser jihad).

Back cover photos: The blessed footprint of Prophet Muhammad; golden keys to the Kaba in Mecca, bestowed upon the Ottoman Sultans as caretakers of the sacred site.

All items are part of a permanent display at Topkapi Museum, Istanbul.

Table of Contents

Preface

Muhammad: The Messenger of Islam has been published at a time when people around the world, particularly those who are unfamiliar with the Islamic faith, are searching for understanding of this great religion, its adherents, its holy book the Quran, and the life examples of its ultimate leader, Muhammad, unto him be peace.

This esteemed work arrives as crucial questions are being asked. What is so appealing about Islam that nearly one-fourth of the world's inhabitants claim it as their religion? How does Islam regard human life, women, education and literacy, democracy, military pursuits and, in general terms, the life we have come to know in the West? What is the Islamic view of other religions?

In fact Islam is a religion that engages its adherents at every level of life, going beyond the walls of the mosque. Islamic teachings are based on the divinely revealed Quran, on the Hadith (examples of the Prophet Muhammad 鑫), and on the legal judgments of trained jurists. It is also a religion largely open to interpretation, which allows for consensus, discussion, and disagreement.

However, everyone who is familiar with Islam will certainly agree it offers guidance for every aspect of our lives, with the goal of serving Allah subhana wa ta'ala, The Almighty in the best manner. Therefore, to be a servant of God is the highest goal of humankind, which encompasses respect for all creation and humility.

To achieve this goal or "station", one must be cognizant of what Allah subhana wa ta'ala truly expects from His creatures. One must seek guidance and the ability to distinguish what is right, and to stand for it even in the face of opposition. One must certainly remain open to Truth.

And thus we find in Islam the guidance in the form of the textual sources, but also practices that feed the soul, to keep it in tune with The Divine. Just as our physical bodies cannot survive without food and drink, being from Heavens, our souls have specific needs to survive in this earthly sphere of life. It is this spiritual connection with The Divine that actually allows us to carry the burden of life in this physical world.

To view humanity as mere physical beings - as evolved, more sophisticated animals - reduces us to a limited, one-dimensional, material level. History is replete with countless examples of the failure of humanity to resolve its miseries and challenges through material means. Currently there are more resources in the world than ever before, and yet poverty and hunger have reached unprecedented levels, prisons are bursting from overcrowding, the volume of refugees has surpassed all predictions, wars have not subsided, and fatal diseases and illnesses pervade every region. We live in a time when financial success and the material life does not solve our problems; in fact in most cases it drives us to excessive behaviors. As a people, these circumstances are spiritually killing us, across all social and religious boundaries, wiping out true humanity from the face of the earth.

Islam categorically refutes the materialist approach to life by raising the status of human beings to representatives of Allah subhana wa ta'ala on earth, equipped with faculties of reason, but similarly equipped with powers to develop as superior beings through acts of kindness, humility, and intervention against what is wrong. By following the divine guidance of Allah's prophets and saints, we are granted access to a spiritual world through which we are perpetually fed, gaining the crucial abilities we need to survive this material world.

Muhammad: The Messenger of Islam embodies the timeless teachings of holy souls through the ages, whom Allah subhana wa ta'ala has endowed with immense wisdom. May we benefit from what they offer, that these lessons help us evolve to higher stations, becoming truly in tune with the spiritual dimension of life, achieving a state of genuine peace – with ourselves and the world around us.

Wa min Allah at Tawfiq - and Allah knows best.

Shaykh Nazim Adil al-Haqqani, Cyprus, January 2002

Foreword

Praise be to Allah subhana wa ta'ala (The Almighty, glorified and exalted) that He created us and sent His messengers to teach us, and sent His message of the Unity of God through many prophets, including Noah, Abraham, Moses, Jesus and our master Muhammad ﷺ. To fill all peoples with love and peace, and to provide us wisdom and guidance, Allah subhana wa ta'ala sent the heavenly books: the Psalms of David, the Torah of Moses (Old Testament), the Injil of Jesus (New Testament), and the Holy Quran of Prophet Muhammad ﷺ.

We find in His infinite wisdom and mercy, Allah subhana wa ta'ala has sent divine knowledge much as the sun fills the horizon, illuminating the hearts of humankind as they navigate and face the challenges of this earthly life. He made his prophets role models for all humanity, for all times to come. May His blessings come on all messengers, especially on the Last Messenger, Sayyidina Muhammad ﷺ, the Chosen One from among all prophets, sent as a mercy for all humanity and a rainbow of divine light and revelation for the entire world. Blessings be upon his companions ؓ who are the stars of that universe of knowledge, and forgiveness be upon those who follow them until the Day of Judgment.

A prophet (nabi) is a human being to whom Allah subhana wa ta'ala has revealed a criterion of disciplinary law (Shari`a) but whom He did not ask to deliver it as a message.

A messenger (rasul) is a human being to whom Allah subhana wa ta'ala has revealed the disciplinary law as a prophet, but on top of that, sent him to deliver the message; thus he is both a prophet and a messenger.

Prophets, as they have been described in the sayings of Ibn `Abbas ❀ in the work of commentary *Ruh al-bayan*, specifically of the chapter of Quran entitled *Surat al-`Araaf*, it is stated that the prophets number around 124,000, and the prophet-messengers are twenty-five. Further, Imam Ahmad narrated that Abi Dharr al-Ghifari ❀ said, "Oh Messenger of Allah, who was the first Prophet?" He ❀ said, "Adam". ... And I asked, "Oh Messenger of Allah, how many are the messengers?" He said, "310 and a few more."

And in another narration of Imam Ahmad, from the narration of Abi Umaama, Abu Dharr asked, "Oh Messenger of Allah, how many are the prophets?" He said, "120,000 and between them 315 messengers."

The Holy Quran mentions twenty-five of these messengers, namely: Adam, Noah, Abraham, Ishma`il, Isaac, Jacob, David, Solomon, Job, Joseph, Moses, Aaron, Zacharia, John (the Baptist), Idris, Jonah, Hud, Shu`ayb, Salih, Lot, Ilyas, Ilya`sa, Dhul-kifli, Jesus and Sayyidina Muhammad, peace be upon them all. These are the messengers of Allah who came with holy books containing the divine message. The others are prophets who received divine revelation but who were not ordered to deliver it to anyone; it was for them. For example, all Jacob's sons were prophets, but Joseph was the only messenger from among them.

Muhammad: The Messenger of Islam proves a very great resource for Muslims and people of other faiths. It expounds intimate details of the life of Prophet Muhammad ❀, highlighting his love and respect for all humanity, the depth of his compassion and mercy for all creation, and his perfect example as a role model for anyone who seeks the ultimate proximity to Allah subhana wa ta'ala and perfection as a human being.

What he brought was revolutionary: enlightenment and education that immediately ushered people out of wayward darkness into guiding light, from unrealistic life to realistic life, from evil to good. The life examples of the Last Messenger Muhammad ❀ are a vast reservoir of examples from

xi

which we can draw deeply at any point in time, to quench the thirst for self-improvement and true guidance.

Laboriously compiled from rare manuscripts, traditional Islamic texts, and other printed source material (including sahih hadith and others*), painstakingly translated from Ottoman Turkish to English, *Muhammad: The Messenger of Islam* accurately depicts the perfected, blessed character and refined manners that Allah subhana wa ta'ala bestowed on His beloved prophet ﷺ. This illustrious work examines the greatness Prophet Muhammad ﷺ showed throughout his life. It depicts the great lengths to which he went - many times risking his own life, suffering humiliation, torment and abuse from his own tribe, leaving the only home he knew, always tolerant of his attackers and seeking peace - to guide the entire world with practical lessons on living a successful life. These lessons can be applied in any culture, place, or era, and miraculously remain as current today as they were fifteen centuries ago.

From Prophet Muhammad's life examples (sunnah) we find elaborate guidelines on all aspects of society building, from infrastructure development and establishing relations with foreign nations, to building academic, economic and welfare systems, and establishing the judiciary body and ministry of defense. To this day, he is known as a superior statesman who built a solid nation, able to face countless challenges. In fact over time, many of the Prophet's nation-building tactics have been applied and proven in various regions of the world.

In the glorious Quran, Allah subhana wa ta'ala said:

Muhammad is not the father of any of your men, but (he is) the Messenger of Allah, and the Seal of the Prophets, and Allah has full knowledge of all things.   [33:40]

Tirmidhi (hasan) and Ibn Maja:

> *Abu Sa`id al-Khudri narrated that the Prophet said: "I am the leader of human beings and I say this without pride."*

At-Tirmidhi narrated:

> *"The Prophet said: I heard your words, and everything you said is indeed true, and I myself am the Beloved of Allah (habibullah) and I say this without pride, and I*

carry the flag of glory (liwa ul-hamd) on the Day of Judgment, and am the first intercessor and the first whose intercession is accepted, and the first to stir the circles of Paradise so that Allah will open it for me and I shall enter it together with the poor among my Community, and I say this without pride. I am the most honored of the First and the Last, and I say this without pride."

And thus we lovingly present *Muhammad: The Messenger of Islam* in our humble attempt to bring light where there is darkness, to bring peace to troubled minds, and to restore love to battered hearts.

Wa min Allah at Tawfiq - and Allah knows best.

Shaykh Muhammad Hisham Kabbani, Washington D.C., January 2002

* According to a sound ruling in Islamic jurisprudence in reference to matters of worship, even a weak tradition (hadith) is acceptable in order to encourage people to a better way of life and self-improvement. In *Seerat ibn Hisham* and *at-Tabari* and in other Islamic historical sources, there appear numerous hadith from Bukhari and Muslim, but still you find weak narrations are included. This book has been compiled from all these sources: from the sahih hadith to the good, the fair to the weak, all of which serve to encourage people to live more pious lives and to clarify the details of the life of the Prophet ﷺ.

About the Author

Hajjah Amina Adil is a renowned author, lecturer and spiritual advisor who, for more than forty years, has devoted herself to help people of all walks of life better understand Islam. In addition, she has played a pivotal role in helping Muslim women understand and apply the many distinguishing rights God Almighty set forth for women in the Islamic faith.

Married for fifty years to Shaykh Muhammad Nazim Adil al-Haqqani, the spiritual head of the Naqshbandi-Haqqani Sufi Order, Hajjah Amina has traveled the world. A scholar of Shari`ah and shaykha, she has thousands of disciples throughout North and South America, Europe, the Middle and Far East, Southeast and Central Asia, and Africa.

She studied under many scholars of the Middle East and Turkey, including Grandshaykh Abdullah ad-Daghestani an-Naqshbandi, among others.

Hajjah Amina is from the family of Prophet Muhammad ﷺ. She was born in Russia's Kazan Province during the early Communist era, which mandated a statewide purge of Jews, Christians and Muslims. With neighbors mysteriously disappearing and millions exiled to camps in Siberia where they either froze or starved to death, when she was a mere toddler the family fled on foot in the dark of night on a perilous journey that, for reasons of safety, could only be undertaken with the clothes on their backs.

Too young to recall the long journey that would eventually lead them to Turkey, family members have narrated her parents' bravery and deep sense of faith, young Amina's sense of adventure, and a tragic life-threatening fall that left her in a coma from which they feared she would not recover. After more than a year and with Communist officials in deadly pursuit, the family miraculously made their way to Arzurum in northeastern Turkey.

Thus, at such a tender age, Hajjah Amina was granted the high status of "muhajirah", which means one who migrated from tyranny and religious oppression to a place where they can openly practice their faith. It is said the reward for such an undertaking rests solely with God Almighty.

These early life experiences seem to have shaped Hajjah Amina's love of family, community and travel, her forthrightness in standing for justice, and her love of Islam. However, after twelve years in Turkey, Hajjah Amina's father had a vision in which he was instructed to relocate the family to "Sham" (Damascus), which had been their original destination upon leaving Russia. In Damascus they found the life they had been seeking, and settled on Jabal Qasiyun, a high mountain which overlooks the entire city.

It was here the family met Grandshaykh Abdullah al-Fa`iz ad-Daghestani of the Golden Chain of the Naqshbandi Sufi Order, who took particular care in overseeing Hajjah Amina's religious and spiritual development. Under Grandshaykh Abdullah she studied Tasawwuf (Sufism – Islamic spirituality) and she studied Fiqh (Islamic Jurisprudence) under such notable scholars as Shaykh Salih Farfour of Syria and Shaykh Mukhtar Alaily, then Secretary General of Religious Affairs of Lebanon. Hajjah Amina's teachers and mentors were always amazed with her acumen, with her high level of retention, and her ability to grasp and reason complex issues within the framework of Islamic Law, even at a young age.

At age twenty-three, upon the advice of Grandshaykh Abdullah she was engaged to the young Shaykh Nazim; they married a month later and have remained great companions for nearly fifty years. In fact Shaykh Nazim often remarks that his wife seems to him the same as when they first married. Together they have lived and raised their four children between Syria, Turkey and Cyprus, and at the time of this writing they have been blessed with sixteen grandchildren and six great-grandchildren.

As a young mother and wife of a shaykh in training, Hajjah Amina was often left alone to face the challenges of raising a family while her husband was either in spiritual retreat or traveling for months on end, visiting various regions to spread the word of the Unity of God. This, coupled with her early life experience, only strengthened her faith and reliance on God Almighty.

Hajjah Amina has thrice performed Hajj, the Islamic pilgrimage to Mecca. Known for her wise, practical approach to life and her problem-solving skills, over the years she has become a much-turned-to advisor of women on a host of issues. She speaks fluent Turkish and Arabic, and is proficient in English. She is uniquely beloved to heads of state and their ministers, to celebrities, as well as common folk.

Hajjah Amina currently resides in Cyprus in a comfortable "old world" farm house with a spacious garden, where she receives thousands of visitors each year from all over the world. She still occasionally accompanies Shaykh Nazim on his official visits to other countries and has been a keynote speaker at numerous conferences on Islam and Muslim women.

Hajjah Amina's other works include the three-volume series *Lore of Light*, her inimitable narration of stories of the prophets and miracles of the saints. All inquiries for Hajjah Amina may be directed to the publisher.

Acknowledgements

This brilliant work stands as tribute to the profound impact on religious and social development made by the *Rahmatun-lil `Alamin*, the "Mercy to all the Worlds", Prophet Muhammad ibn Abdallah (peace and blessing of God be upon him).

As one who grew up at the feet of renowned scholars thoroughly conversant in Islamic history and tradition, it is my distinct honor to acknowledge my mother's shining attempt to bring to life stories handed down over centuries on the unprecedented life of the Prophet of Islam.

In her inimitable style – which captivates the imagination much like in the pre-television era - renowned scholar and author, my mother Hajjah Amina Adil meticulously compiled this great *Seerah* (biography) in her native Ottoman Turkish, a classic language which inevitably suffers loss when translated to English. Thus, every care has been taken to capture the linguistic styles and finer meanings of ancient narrations, while presenting them to a contemporary, English-speaking audience.

It is deeply hoped *Muhammad* (❊): *The Messenger of Islam* will fill the current literary demand for titles on traditional Islam, and its much-discussed religious interpretations. This book is presented with a view to answer many contemporary questions and to help those unfamiliar with this great world religion in better understanding its tenets, history and culture which is shared by 1.5 billion adherents, roughly one-fifth of the world's inhabitants.

For the past year our editorial team has worked intensely to bring you this highly authoritative work, replete with textual references and a glossary of the many foreign terms, which have recently surfaced into the mainstream English language.

My deep gratitude goes to Ms. Radhia Shukrullah of Cyprus who labored to provide an accurate translation from the original Ottoman Turkish.

The following women have taken great pains to ensure the integrity of all textual references, and have provided extensive editing to present this work to mainstream audiences: Dr. Hedieh Mirahmadi, Director of Public Affairs, Islamic Supreme Council of America; Hajjah Talibah Jilani, National Executive Director, Kamilat Muslims Women's Association; and Ms. Jennifer McLennan, Executive Director, Islamic Supreme Council of America.

Muhammad: The Messenger of Islam is a work of enduring love, which comes to you from our hearts. The efforts of this sincere group of women – from the author and translator through the editors and publisher – is tribute to the high standards of women's and human rights, introduced in Arabia fifteen centuries ago by this greatest of God's prophets.

In these times, when we are inundated with news of religious radicalism, I pray the readers of this shining work will gain a deeper respect and understanding for traditional Islam, which has thrived peacefully for many centuries, and which supports religious tolerance, gender equality, social consciousness, and civil responsibility. Further, through centuries of influence of the Sufi mystics and their various spiritual practices, classical Islam is known to liberate souls from their earthly bondage.

If you complete this reading better informed, with a sounder view of Islam and its adherents, if it spurns discussion and debate, and challenges you to re-evaluate past perceptions of Islam, Muslims, and their place in world history, not one moment of our collective effort has been in vain.

With a combination of pride, humility, and awe, I salute the five decades of my mother's devotion to bringing light where there is darkness, and for instilling in me a deep love for Islamic tradition. May this valuable book be blessed, and may it reach those who may truly benefit from it.

Hajjah Naziha Adil
Chairwoman, Kamilat, April 2002

Notes

Quran translations are quoted from the Arberry English translation, *The Quran Interpreted* by Arthur J. Arberry, Oxford University Press, 1964.

Quotes from the Quran and Hadith, the two major source texts on Islam, are italicized and referenced by the chapter name and verse.

The following symbols are universally recognized by Muslims and have been respectfully included in this work:

The symbol ﷺ represents "sallAllahu alayhi wa sallam" (Allah's blessings and greetings of peace be upon him) which is customarily recited after reading or pronouncing the name of Prophet Muhammad.

It is intended that "alayhis-salam" (peace be upon him/her) be recited after the names of the other prophets, the Family of the Prophet, the pure and virtuous women in Islam, and the angels, represented by the symbol السلام.

It is also intended that "radiAllahu anh" or (may Allah be pleased with him/her) is recited after the names of Companions of the Prophet, represented by the symbol ﵁.

Creation of the Light of Muhammad ﷺ

One day Ali, *karam Allahu wajhahu*, the cousin and son-in-law of the Holy Prophet ﷺ asked, "Oh Muhammad, both my parents shall be my ransom, pray tell me what the Lord Almighty created before all other beings of creation?" This was his blissful reply:

Verily, before your Lord made any other thing, He created from His own Light the light of your Prophet ﷺ, and that Light rested *haithu mashaAllah*, where Allah willed it to rest. And at that time there existed aught else—not the Preserved Tablets, not the Pen, not Heaven nor Hell, not the Angelic Host, not the heavens nor the earth; there was no sun, no moon, no star, no jinn nor man nor angel—none was as yet created, only this Light.

Then Allah – glorified be He – by divine decree willed the Creation to be. He therefore divided this Light into four parts. From the first part He created the Pen, from the second the Tablets, from the third the Divine Throne.

Now it has become known that when the Lord had created the Tablets and the Pen, the Pen had on it one hundred nodes, the distance between two nodes being that of two years wayfaring. The Lord then commanded the Pen to write, and the Pen asked, "Oh Lord, what shall I write?" The Lord said, "Write: *la ilaha illAllah, Muhammadan Rasulullah*." Thereupon the Pen exclaimed, "Oh, what a beautiful, great name is that of Muhammad that it is to mentioned in one with Thy hallowed Name, oh Lord."

The Lord then said, "Oh Pen, mind your manners! This name is the name of My Beloved, from his Light I have created the Throne and the Pen and

1

the Tablets; you, too, are created from his Light. Had it not been for him, I would not have created a single thing." When Allah Almighty had spoken these words, the Pen split in two from awe of the Lord, and the place from which its speech issued became blocked, so that to this very day its nib remains cloven in two and clogged up, so it does not write, which is the sign of this great divine secret. Therefore, let no one fail in veneration and honoring of the Holy Prophet ﷺ, or become lax in following his shining example, or contravene the noble custom he has taught us.

Then again the Lord commanded the Pen to write. "What shall I write, oh Lord?" asked the Pen. The Lord of the Worlds then said, "Write that which will be until the Day of Judgment!" Said the Pen, "Oh Lord, with what shall I begin?" Said the Lord, "With these words you shall commence: *Bismillah al-Rahman al-Rahim.*" In perfect respect and deference, the Pen then set out to write these words upon the Tablets, and it completed writing them in seven hundred years.

When the Pen had written these words, the Almighty spoke and said, "It has taken you seven hundred years to write three of My Names; the Name of My Majesty, My Mercy and My Compassion. These blessed words I have made as a present to the nation of My Beloved Muhammad ﷺ. By My Majesty I pledge that whenever any servant from this nation pronounces the words of the Bismillah with a pure intention, I will write seven hundred years of countless reward for this servant, and seven hundred years of sins I will erase."

Now, the fourth part of this Light I have again divided into four parts: from one part I have created the Throne-bearing Angels *(hamalat al-`Arsh)*; from the second I have created the *Kursi*, the Divine court (the upper Heaven supporting the Divine Throne, the `Arsh)*; from the third I created all the other heavenly angels; and the fourth part I have partitioned once more into four: from its first part I made the skies, from its second I made the earths, from its third I made the Jinn and the fire. Its fourth part I have again divided into four parts: from one part I made the light upon the faces of the believers; from the second part I made the light within their hearts,

2

imbuing them with knowledge of the divine; from the third the light upon their tongues which is the light of Tawhid (the Unity of Allah), and from the fourth part I made the different lights of the soul of Muhammad ﷺ.

This lovely soul came into being 360 thousand years before the creation of the world, and it was shaped most beautifully and made of incomparable matter. Its head was made from guidance, its neck from humility, its eyes from modesty, its forehead from closeness (to Allah), its mouth from patience, its tongue from truthfulness, its cheeks from love and admonition, its belly from abstemiousness and other worldliness, its feet and knees from following the straight path, and its noble heart was filled with mercy. This much-honored soul was taught with mercy and equipped with all manner of wondrous powers. It was given its message and its prophetic qualities were installed. Then the Crown of Divine Proximity was placed upon its blessed head, eminent and exalted above all else, embellished with Divine Pleasure and given the pure, holy name of Habibullah (Beloved of Allah).

The Twelve Veils

After this the Lord Almighty, blessed be He, created twelve Veils. The first of these was the Veil of Power within which the Prophet's soul remained for twelve thousand years, reciting *Subhana rabbil-'ala* (Glory be to my Lord, the Lofty). The second was the Veil of Grandeur in which he was veiled for eleven thousand years, saying, *Subhanal 'Alim al-Hakim* (Glory be to my Lord, the All-Knowing, the Wise). Ten thousand years he remained shrouded in the Veil of Kindness, saying *Subhana man huwa da'im, la yaqta* (Glory to Him who is perpetual, who never ends). The fourth veil was the Veil of Mercy, therein the noble soul remained for nine thousand years, praising Allah, saying: *Subhana-rafi'-al-`ala* (Glory be to the Elevated, the High). The fifth veil was the Veil of Bliss, and therein he remained for eight thousand years, glorifying the Lord and saying, *Subhana man huwa qa'imun la yanam.* (Glory to Him who is ever existent, who sleeps not).

The sixth veil was the Veil of Munificence; he remained enfolded in it for seven thousand years, praising, *Subhana-man huwal-ghaniyu la yafqaru* (Glory be to Him who is rich, who never grows indigent). Then followed the seventh veil, the Veil of Rank. Here the enlightened soul remained for six thousand years, praising the Lord and saying: *Subhana man huwal Khaliq-an-Nur* (Glory to Him who is the Creator, the Light). Next, He veiled him in the eighth veil, the Veil of Guidance where he remained for five thousand years, praising Allah and saying, *Subhana man lam yazil wa la yazal.* (Glory to Him whose existence does not cease, who does not vanish).

Then followed the ninth veil, which was the Veil of Prophethood where he stayed for four thousand years, glorifying the Lord: "Subhana man taqarrab bil-qudrati wal-baqa." (Glory to Him who draws nigh to His Omnipotence and Immortality). Then came the Veil of Eminence, the tenth veil where this enlightened soul remained for three thousand years, reciting praises on the Creator of all Causes, saying, "Subhana dhil-'arshi 'amma yasifun." (Glory be to the Owner of the Throne, above all else attributed to Him). The eleventh veil was the Veil of Light. There he remained for two thousand years, praying, "Subhana dhil-Mulk wal-Malakut." (Glory to the Lord over the heavenly and earthly Kingdoms). The twelfth veil was the Veil of Intercession, and there he remained for one thousand years, saying "Subhana-rabbil-'azhim" (Glory to my Lord, the Sublime).

Creation of the Beloved ❀

Thereafter the Lord created a tree which is known as the Tree of Certainty. This tree has four branches. He placed this blessed soul upon one of its branches, and it continued to praise Allah for forty thousand years, saying, *Allahu dhul-Jalali wal-Ikram.* (Allah, Possessor of Might and of Kindness). After it had thus praised Him with many and varied praises, the Almighty created a mirror, and He placed it so as to face the soul of Habibullah, and commanded his soul to gaze into this mirror. The soul looked into the mirror and saw itself reflected as possessing the most comely and perfect form. He then recited five times, *Shukran lillahi ta'ala* (thanks be to Allah, Exalted be He), and fell down in prostration before his Lord. He remained in each sajda for one hundred years, saying *Subhanal-aliyyul-azhim, wa la yajhalu.* (Glory be to the High, the Sublime, who ignores nothing); *Subhanal-halim alladhi la yu'ajjalu.* (Glory be to the Mild One who hastens not); *Subhanal-jawad alladhi la yabkhalu.* (Glory be to the Generous who is unstinting). Therefore the Causer of all Being obliged the nation of Muhammad ﷺ to perform sajda (prostration) five times a day – these five prayers in the course of one day and night were a gift of honor to the nation of Muhammad ﷺ.

From the Light of Muhammad ﷺ

Next the Lord created a lamp of green emerald from the Light, and attached it to the tree by a chain of light. Then He placed the soul of Muhammad ﷺ inside the lamp and commanded it to praise Him with the Most Beautiful Names (Asma al-Husna). This it did, and it began to recite each one of the Names for one thousand years. When it reached the Name ar-Rahman (the Merciful), the gaze of Mercy fell upon it and the soul began to sweat from modesty. Drops of sweat fell from it, as many as there were to be prophets and messengers, each drop of rose-flavored sweat turning into the soul of a prophet.

They all assembled around that lamp in the tree, and the Almighty addressed the soul of the Prophet Muhammad ﷺ, "See here this multitude of prophets whom I have created from the pearl-like drops of your sweat." Obeying this command, he gazed upon them, and as the light of the eye enfolds the object, so the souls of all these prophets were suddenly engulfed in the light of Muhammad ﷺ, and they cried, "Oh Lord, who has wrapped us in light?" The Lord answered them, "This is the Light of My Beloved Muhammad, and if you will believe in him and confirm his prophetic message, I will grant you the honor of prophethood." Thereupon all the souls of the prophets declared their belief in his prophethood, and the Lord said, "I bear witness to your acknowledgment," and they all assented. As it is declared in the Holy Quran:

> *And when God took compact with the Prophets: That I have given you of Book and Wisdom; then there shall come to you a Messenger confirming what is with*

*you—you shall believe in him and you shall help him; do you agree? He said. And
do you take My load on you on that condition They said, 'We do agree.' God said,
'Bear witness so, and I shall be with you among the witnesses.'*

(The House of Imran, 3:75-76)

Then this pure, holy soul took up its recital of the Most Beautiful Names
again. When it came to the Name al-Qahhar, its head began to sweat once
more from the intensity of His Divine Majesty and Awe, and from these
beads of sweat the Almighty created the souls of the blessed angels. From
the sweat on his face, the Almighty created the Throne and the Divine
Court, the Tablets and the Pen, the sun, the moon and the stars. From the
sweat of his chest He created the scholars, the martyrs and the righteous
believers. From the sweat on his back were made the Bayt-al-Ma'mur (the
heavenly house), the Kabatullah (the Kaba), and the Bayt-al-Muqaddas (the
Haram of Jerusalem), and the Rauda-i-Mutahhara (the Tomb of the Holy
Prophet ﷺ at Madinah), as well as all other mosques in the world.

From the sweat on his brows were made the souls of all the believers, and
from the sweat of his lower back (the coccyx) were made the souls of all the
unbelievers, fire worshippers and idolaters.

From the sweat of his feet was made all the ground from east to west, and
all that is within it. From every drop of sweat the soul of one believer or
unbeliever was created. That is the reason the Holy Prophet ﷺ is referred to
as "Abu Arwah", Father of Souls. All these souls gathered round the soul
of Muhammad ﷺ, circling round him with praise and glorification for one
thousand years; then the Lord commanded these souls to look at the soul
of Muhammad ﷺ. The souls all obeyed.

Who Gazed at the Soul of Muhammad ﷺ

Now, those among them whose gaze fell upon his head were destined to
become kings and heads of state in this world. Those who gazed at his
forehead became just chiefs. Those who gazed at his eyes would become
hafiz of the Word of Allah (i.e. one who commits it to memory). Those

who saw his eyebrows became painters and artists. Those who saw his ears were to be of those who accept admonition and advice. Those who saw his blessed cheeks became performers of good and reasonable works. Those who saw his face became judges and perfumers, and those who saw his blessed lips became ministers.

Whoever saw his mouth was to be of those who fast much. Whoever looked at his teeth would be of comely appearance, and whoso saw his tongue was to become the ambassador of kings. Whoever saw his blessed throat was to become a preacher and mu'adhdhin (who calls the adhan). Whoever looked at his beard was to become a fighter in the way of Allah. Whoever looked at his upper arms was to become an archer or a diver in the sea, and whoever saw his neck became a merchant and a trader.

Whoso saw his right hand became a leader, and who saw his left hand became a dispenser (who holds the scales and measures out provisions). Whoso looked at the palms of his hands became a generous person; whoso looked at the backs of his hands became a miser. Whoso saw the inside of his right hand became a painter; who saw the fingertips of his right hand was to be a calligrapher, and who saw the tips of his left hand would be an ironworker.

Whoso saw his blessed chest would be of the learned, ascetic and scholarly. Whoso saw his back would be a humble person and obeying the laws of the Shari'a. Whoso saw his blessed sides would be a warrior. Whoever looked at his belly would be of the contented ones, and whoever looked at his right knee would be of those who perform ruk'u and sujud. Whoever looked at his blessed feet became a hunter, and who saw the bottom of his soles became one of those who take to the road. Who saw his shadow were to become singers and saz (lute) players. All those who looked but saw nothing were to become unbelievers, fire worshippers and idolaters. Those who didn't look at all were to become those who would declare themselves to be gods, such as Nimrod, Pharoah and his ilk.

Now all the souls lined up in four rows. In the first row stood the souls of the prophets and messengers, on whom be peace; in the second row were placed the souls of the holy saints, the Friends of God; in the third row stood the souls of the believing men and women; in the fourth row stood the souls of the unbelievers. All these souls remained in the world of spirits in the presence of Allah Almighty until their time had come to be sent into the material world. No one but Allah Almighty knows how much time elapsed from the time of the creation of the Prophet Muhammad's ﷺ blessed soul to his descent from the spiritual world into his physical form.

It is narrated that the Holy Prophet Muhammad ﷺ asked the angel Jibra'il ﷿, "How long is it since you were created?" The angel answered, "Oh Rasulullah, I don't know the number of years, all I know is that every seventy thousand years a tremendous light shines forth from behind the Canopy of the Divine Throne; since the time of my creation this light has appeared twelve thousand times." "Do you know what this Light is?" asked Muhammad ﷺ. "No, I don't know," said the angel. "It is the light of my soul in the world of the spirit," replied the Holy Prophet ﷺ. Consider then, how immense a number it must be if 70,000 is multiplied by 12,000!

Descriptions of the Prophets of God ﷺ
(from *Anwar-al-'Ashiqin* by Ahmet Bijan)

Know then, oh ye who wish to learn divine secrets that I have set forth herein the stories of the prophets as they have been transmitted to us through the traditions and commentaries, in the Torah, the Zabur, the Injil and the Holy Quran in clear language and most pleasing style. It is confirmed beyond doubt in the sublime verses of the Holy Quran, in convincing signs and with evident miracles that the Holy Prophet, Muhammad, peace and blessings be upon him, is the Seal of the Prophets and the Prince among the Messengers.

Let us now mention the decrees of divine ordinance as revealed to various prophets and explanations pertaining thereto; after which we shall discuss the law brought by the Prince of the Universe and the Essence of all Creation, Muhammad, on whom be peace, inshaAllah.

Adam

Let it be known that in the time of Adam ﷺ, the first man and the first Prophet, judgment was pronounced according to the following procedure: after a sacrificial offering was made, one had only to wait. If a fire came down from Heaven to consume the sacrifice, the claimant was in the right; if, however, he was wrong, no fire came down to consume his sacrificial offering, and thereby he was judged.

Noah

In the time of the Prophet Nuh ﷺ, judgment proceeded in this way: when two litigants appeared before a court, they were both placed within a fire. If the fire burned one of them, he was judged to be in the wrong; the one who was not burnt by the fire was judged to be in the right.

David

In Da'ud's ﷺ time, justice was achieved by the following means: a chain was hung suspended in court. The litigant who was able to reach up to the chain was thought to be in the right, the one who failed to reach it, was judged to be in the wrong.

Solomon

In the time of Sulayman ﷺ legal cases were decided as follows: there was a pit in King Sulayman's ﷺ retreat. If two people came before the king, they were led to the pit, and he whose foot sank into the pit was judged as being in the right, while the other was judged as being wrong.

Zachariah

In Prophet Zakaria's ﷺ time judgment was pronounced thus: Zakaria ﷺ had two iron pens. When two people came before him seeking a legal decision, he would write their names upon these pens and place them in a container of water. The pen that floated to the surface bore the name of the litigant, who won his case, while the pen that sank to the bottom bore the loser's name.

Moses

The Prophet Musa ﷺ was given the Torah and all judgment proceeded according to its law.

10

Jesus

The Prophet 'Isa ﷺ was given the Injil and justice was done according to its precepts.

Then dawned the time of the most perfect being of all creation, our noble Prophet Muhammad, peace and blessings be upon him, who brought us the highest and most complete law (Shari'a) that has ever existed, and who said:

> It is for the plaintiff to bring forward evidence (for his case), and for the defendant (who protests his innocence) to place himself under oath.

And praise be to Him who has made us to belong to the nation of the Prophet of the best of all religions. Truly, He, Allah is full of Mercy and Compassion.

Oh ye who are versed in holy knowledge! Oh ye who seek to meet your Lord Almighty! Ye who have attained your goal! Who have set out in quest of divine secrets! In this book you will find all the knowledge of truth and the source of divine knowledge, inasmuch as Allah Almighty – exalted be He – has made it plain to the people of perfection through emanations of both general and particular nature. However, it is not disclosed herein in which aspect any of the prophets may be superior to any other, be it from consideration of the spiritual essence or some other reason, but Allah knows best the truth of any matter and its hidden implications. This humble dervish, Ahmet Bijan, was thrown thereby into a state of confusion and entrusted himself entirely to the guidance of the Almighty and the pure soul of the Prophet Muhammad, on whom be peace. The Almighty then made clear to me some matters mentioned in the compiled works of the commentators.

Adam

Now it should be known that each of the prophets was distinguished by attributes from the attributes of Allah, and that emanations of His holy names were manifested in them and that each became known by an unmistakable spiritual flavor and a distinct revelation. Therefore, Adam ﷺ

was the original model, as it were, both in his physical form and his spiritual composition, and Allah willed it so that Adam ﷺ became the father of mankind.

As regards Adam's ﷺ inner truth and spiritual reality, it is from the light of the name of Allah's essence, and this is His proper name: Allah. His mind and heart are from the light of two divine attributes: one of them is the Merciful (ar-Rahim), and one is the Compassionate (ar-Rahman), inasmuch as Allah Almighty has spoken:

And for Mercy I have created you, oh Adam!

Therefore Adam ﷺ was distinguished from both high and low through mercy. Adam's ﷺ self was created from the light of Allah's action. Al-Badi', the Creator, the Originator, whereby the singularity of Adam's ﷺ creation is indicated: he was made unlike and not resembling any other created being: he is the original specimen.

Seth

When Seth ﷺ was given to Adam ﷺ as a "gift of God", he was made to resemble his father in form. As regards Seth's ﷺ inner truth and spiritual reality, it is made from the light of the Name of divine essence, and it is the name: Malik, the owner, inasmuch as Seth ﷺ became the owner of the world after his father Adam ﷺ. His mind and heart are from the light of the divine attribute: al-Barr, the Pious, the Good, and for that Seth ﷺ was extremely good and compassionate towards his parents. Allah sent Seth ﷺ to Adam ﷺ and Hawa to make up for the loss of their beloved son Habil (Abel). Seth's ﷺ self was from the light of two divine actions: one was al-Jami', the Gatherer, the other: al-Mughni, the Enriched, the Independent, for after his father it was Seth ﷺ in whom was gathered all the perfection of mankind, thus he can be said to be rich and independent of all but Allah Almighty.

Idris

The Prophet Idris ﷺ was granted ascension to the heavens during his lifetime where he mingled with the angels and the insubstantial spirits. For ten years he remained with them, during which time he never once ate, drank or slept at all, so that his mind became free and cut off from all ties of material existence. In this exclusive devotion he was the predecessor of the Prophet Nuh ﷺ, and such was his holy station in the divine presence. His inner truth and spiritual reality were of the light of Allah's essence, and this is al-Quddus, the Hallowed, the All-Holy. His mind and heart are from the light of the divine attribute al-Muta'al, the Elevated, the Supreme, which refers to the high station assigned to him by the Almighty, as it is written in the Holy Quran:

> *We raised him up to a high place.*   *(Maryam, 57)*

His self was from the light of two divine actions: one of them ar-Rafi', that is He who raises aloft, and al-Basit, that is He who spreads, extends, inasmuch as Idris ﷺ was raised up to the heavens and found his enjoyment in looking down upon the worlds spread out beneath him.

Noah

As for Nuh ﷺ: when his people began to ascribe human characteristics to Allah and to worship idols, Nuh ﷺ was sent as a prophet to call them to the Truth and to purify their beliefs, for essentially Allah's attributes and actions are free from any attribute of form or similitude. Nuh ﷺ was sent to heal them by proclaiming the message that Allah was free from any defect. His inner truth and spiritual reality are from the light of the name of Allah's Essence which is as-Salam, the Giver of Safety, for that he made them safe from idolatry (anthropomorphism) and from drowning (in the flood), as it is written in the Holy Quran:

> *It was said, 'Noah, get thee down in peace from Us, and blessings upon thee and on the nations of those with thee.*   *(Hud, 50)*

His heart and mind are from the light of the divine attributes as-Shakur, the Grateful, as it is written in the Holy Quran:

The seed of those We bore with Noah; He was a thankful servant.

(The Night Journey, 3)

His self is from the light of two divine actions: al-Muntaqim, the Avenger, and al-Hafiz, the Keeper, Protector; for Nuh ﷺ avenged himself on the enemies of Allah and sent them down to the lowest pits in Hell.

Hud

When Idris ﷺ through his veneration, and Nuh ﷺ through his belief in Allah's freedom from defect had established a true description of divinity, and Allah's Oneness had become manifest, the Prophet Hud ﷺ was sent to his people to invite them to the creed of unity; thus his inner truth and spiritual reality are from the light of the Name of Allah's Essence which is al-Mu'min, the Believer. For the path of righteousness lies solely in Iman (faith) and Islam (submission to the divine will).

His heart and mind are from the Light of the divine attribute al-Qahhar, the Overwhelming, the Crushing; thus Hud ﷺ crushed the pagans with a wasting wind. His self was from the Name of two divine actions: al-Hadi, the Guide and ad-Darr, He who sends harm, for that Hud ﷺ sought to guide his people upon Allah's paths, while they chose to persist in their stubbornness and Allah therefore punished them with harm, and they remain forever in the darkness of their unbelief.

Salih

After the divinity had manifested through devotion, through purity and unity, the appearance of a cause was decreed, created from the keys to the unseen world. As for Salih ﷺ, his inner truth and spiritual reality were from the light of the divine essence, al-Muhaymin, the Guardian, Protector which also means the Witness, for that Allah Almighty saw it fit to show him His creative power. His heart and mind were of the light of the divine attribute al-Muhsi, which is the Reckoner, for that Salih 🕸 counted three days for his people as the duration of their destruction.

His self is from the name of two divine actions: one is al-Fattah, the Opener, the other is al-Qabid, the Constrictor. His act of opening occurred when he brought forth the camel from the rock, and his constricting lay in his reproaching his people for their excessive love of this dunya and their complete absorption in its pleasures. In the end they perished and were deprived of all they had ever coveted.

Abraham

As for Ibrahim 🕸: after the divine perfection had shown itself through the manifestation of devotion, purity, unity and asceticism, divine love made its appearance in Ibrahim Khalil-ullah 🕸, the Friend of God. Nimrod, driven by his commanding self, engaged on a dispute with this prophet, and in order to test whether he was truly a prophet and not a liar or impostor, he had him thrown into the fire. Nimrod's fire, "Nar-i-Ibrahim", was turned into a garden of light for the Prophet. His inner truth and spiritual reality are from the light of the divine essence, al-Aziz, the Glorious, for that Allah made him great despite the unbelievers' insults. He attained great honor in the divine presence and was shown the heavenly worlds and spiritual kingdom. His heart and mind are from the light of the divine attribute al-Halim, the Clement, as it is written in the Holy Quran:

Abraham was compassionate, clement. (Repentance, 115)

Therefore, it was given to Ibrahim 🕸 to be forbearing towards all and everyone. His self was from the Name of two divine actions: ar-Razzaq, the Provider, and ar-Rashid, the Righteous. Allah Almighty gave to Ibrahim 🕸 the means for providing, and through him provision became manifest. Regarding his quality of righteousness, it is written in the Holy Quran:

We gave Abraham aforetime his rectitude, for We knew him when he said to his father and his people... (The Prophets, 53)

15

Ishmail

As for Ismail ﷺ: after the divine love had manifested in Ibrahim ﷺ, Ibrahim ﷺ gave away his life and soul on the path of love; consequently, by divine decree he fathered two prophets to be his successors. One of them was distinguished by his willingness to surrender his very soul, namely the Prophet Ismail ﷺ, while the Prophet Ishaq ﷺ was distinguished by his resistance to his carnal impulses.

As for Ismail ﷺ, his inner truth and spiritual reality were from the light of the name of the divine essence al-Jabbar, the Compelling, for that he mortified his flesh for the sake of divine love and for that he constrained his soul to comply with the divine will. Therefore, Allah Almighty sent a large ram to be sacrificed in his stead. His heart and mind were from the light of the divine attribute al-Halim, the Mild, Forbearing, for that he showed great forbearance in the face of the divine decree, as it is written in the Holy Book:

> *Then We gave him good tidings of a prudent boy....*　　　　*(The Rangers, 101)*

His self was of the names of three divine actions: one of them was al-Mujib, He who replies; another was al-Hasib, He who takes account; and finally there was ar-Raqib, He who is on guard, for Ismail ﷺ replied to the divine command and acquiesced; he bowed to his father's orders and controlled his lower self through watchfulness.

Isaac

As for Ishaq ﷺ: when Ibrahim ﷺ was flung into the ocean of love, his soul was transformed into the precious substance of which are made all the holy spirits. Therefore it was said that no prophet would come to the spiritual world except he be a descendant of Ishaq ﷺ, the sole exception being our Prophet Muhammad (on whom be peace and blessings) who was descended from Ismail ﷺ, and Allah Almighty alone knows the secret that lies hidden therein.

This much, however, can be said: Ibrahim's ﷺ soul was created from the secret of divine unity, while his carnal soul, his self, was made from the plurality of secrets of the divine decrees. Therefore, Allah's unity was manifested through Ismail ﷺ, while Ishaq ﷺ was made to be the wellhead of plurality, the father of multitudes. His inner truth and spiritual reality were from the light of the divine essence, al-Mutakabbir, the Proud. His heart and mind were from the light of the divine attribute ar-Ra'uf, the Clement, the Benign. Therefore he was of great mildness towards the believers. His ego was of the name of two divine actions: al-Wakil, the Deputy, the Representative; and al-Ba'ith, the Inspirer, the Awakener. Therefore he was made steward over the treasury of blessed souls (i.e. the prophets).

Jacob

As for Ya'qub ﷺ: When the souls of the prophets began to appear in the material world, the first to come was Ya'qub ﷺ, for he was made to be the storehouse for the ordinances of the majority of prophets that were yet to come, and he became the father of twelve sons. Allah Almighty deigned to create one of these as the mirror image of the beauty of divine light. Ya'qub ﷺ perceived this light and fell in love and remained in bewilderment before this divine beauty. When it was later removed from his sight, he fell into a state of grief at this separation, and was beset by an abiding melancholy. For love is the fruit of affection, and grief is one of its necessary adjuncts, wherefore the people of perfection have ever maintained that love requires beauty and beauty necessitates calamity, while calamity brings grief.

Yaqub's ﷺ inner truth and spiritual reality were from the light of the name of the divine essence al-Kabir, the Great, for that he was a begetter of prophets and thus a great treasure for his people, the sons of Israil. His heart and mind were of the light of the divine attribute al-Wadud, the All-Loving; therefore he fell in love when the divine beauty manifested in the person of his son Yusuf ﷺ. His self was of the names of two divine actions: al-Khaliq, the Creator, and al-Bari, the Maker; therefore he begat a large number of sons.

Joseph

As for Yusuf 🏵: when the love of Ya'qub 🏵 necessitated a manifestation of divine light, Yusuf 🏵 was born into the world as the perfection of beauty. His inner truth and spiritual reality were of the light of the name of the divine essence, and Yusuf 🏵 embodied this divine light. Therefore, whoever gazed upon him fell in love, even so his father, his mother and his brethren who all were enraptured by his beauty and fell down in prostration before him. His heart and mind were from the light of the divine attribute al-Qadir, the Powerful, wherefore he became powerful in the land of Egypt. His self was of the names of three divine actions: al-Musawwir, the Designer, He who forms, for he appeared in the most perfectly formed shape; al-Hafiz, the Protector, for he kept the storehouses of Egypt under his care; and al-Afuw, the Forgiving, for that he forgave his brethren (for their crime against him).

Job

As for Ayyub 🏵: If love had become manifest in Ya'qub 🏵, and beauty in his son Yusuf 🏵, the Divine Will thereupon decreed the appearance of another prophet who was to be subjected to trials and suffering, for love is necessarily associated with pain.

Therefore Ayyub 🏵 was born into this world and suffered all manner of affliction, as troubles are the prerogative of the Friends of God. It is transmitted to us that the Holy Prophet Muhammad (on whom be peace) once said:

> *Affliction is one of the whips of Allah with which He drives His servants towards Himself.*

Ayyub's 🏵 inner truth and spiritual reality was from the light of the name of the divine essence al-Ghani, the Wealthy, for after he had been stripped of all his wealth and family, Allah Almighty gave back to him what he had lost, and made Ayyub ﷺ rich not once, but twice. His heart and mind were of the light of the divine attribute as-Sabur, the Long-Suffering, the Patient, inasmuch as the Almighty proclaims in the Holy Quran:

> *Surely We found him a steadfast man. How excellent a servant he was! He* > *was a penitent.* *(Sa`ad, 44)*

Ayyub's ﷺ self was made from the light of two divine actions. One of them was al-Wasi', the Copious, the Comprehending, and the other at-Tawwab, the Oft-Returning, the Penitent. For he was able to carry the burden of so many afflictions, and returned always to his Lord, penitent.

Shu'ayb

As for Shu'ayb ﷺ: following the Prophet Ayyub ﷺ who had manifested all the trials of affliction on the path of love, Allah Almighty wished to send a prophet who was consumed by a fervent desire to be united in the meeting with his Lord.

Thus Shu'ayb ﷺ was sent to the material world. From his exceeding love of God he wept for three hundred years, and thrice he became blind. Once every hundred years his eyes opened and he saw again. His inner truth and spiritual reality were of the light of the name of the divine essence al-Majid, the Illustrious; therefore he became a chieftain of his people and earned the title of "preacher of the prophets". His heart and mind were of the light of the divine attribute al-Karim, the Generous, the Munificent, for his kindness toward his nation was great. His self was of the light of two divine actions: al-Hakam, the Ruler, and al-Muqsit, the Just, the Equitable, for he governed his people and judged them at all times, exhorting them to measure with just measure.

Moses

Regarding Musa ﷺ: when the love of Allah had manifested perfectly through the friendship of Khalilullah (Ibrahim ﷺ), the passionate ecstasy of Ya'qub ﷺ, the beauty of Yusuf ﷺ, the patience of Ayyub ﷺ and the ardent yearning of Shu'ayb ﷺ, the Almighty decreed that they be succeeded by a prophet embodying perfectly the Majesty of Allah, who would completely vanquish the misguided unbelievers. Therefore Musa ﷺ was sent to this world of material existence. His inner truth and spiritual reality were of the light of the name of the divine essence al-Jalil, the Mighty, Majestic, and al-'Ali, the High, the Lofty, for that he had vanquished the foes of the Lord and risen above them, as He Almighty says in the Holy Quran:

> *Fear not, surely thou art the uppermost.*   *(TaHa, 20)*

His heart and mind were of the light of the divine attribute al-'Alim, the Wise, the Knowing, for he was knowledgeable in the learning of the Torah, and the Torah was the book of law for all prophets up until the time of 'Isa ﷺ, the son of Maryam. His self was of the light of two divine actions: one al-Mu'izz, the Exalter, the other al-Mudhil, the Abaser, for that he exalted the station of the believers while abasing the unbelievers.

Aaron

As for Harun ﷺ: after the appearance of a majestic prophet, the Grace of God willed a prophet of Mercy to succeed him. Thus Harun ﷺ was sent to be a helpmate to Musa ﷺ, as Allah Almighty says in the Holy Quran:

> *Appoint for me of my folk a familiar, Aaron, my brother...*   *(TaHa, 30)*

His inner truth and spiritual reality were of the light of two names of the divine essence: az-Zahir, the Manifest, the Outward, and al-Batin, the Hidden, the Inward, for his kindness was manifest while his secret was unrevealed, hidden. His heart and mind were of the light of the divine attribute al-Ghafar, the Pardoner; thus Allah Almighty forgave the sins of his nation. His self was made of the light of two divine actions: one al-Ghafur, the All-Forgiving, the other al-Latif, the Fine, the Subtle. Therefore he covered the sins of his nation and showed them subtle kindness.

Ilyas

As for Ilyas ﷺ: when Allah Almighty had manifested His Majesty and His Mercy, the divine will ordained for these prophets to be succeeded by a prophet who would explain their works to the world. His inner truth and spiritual reality were from the light of the divine essence. Therefore his people needed him to give them various healing plants. His heart and mind were of the light of the divine attribute: al-Jamil, the All-Gracious. His self was of the light of two divine actions, al-Wahhab, the Bestower, and al-Muqtadir, the Powerful, the Mighty. It was given to him that he should ascend the mountain of the Lebanon and regard things on earth below and in the heavens above as the angels do.

David

As for Da'ud ﷺ: after the manifestation of divine majesty and divine mercy had reached completion, Allah Almighty willed a prophet to come into the world who was to suffer the affliction of love of Allah and many other troubles, and he was to be tried with the trials of beauty. Thus Da'ud ﷺ came into this world. His inner truth and spiritual reality were of the light of the name of the divine essence: al-Hakim, the Absolutely Wise, inasmuch as Allah Almighty has said:

> ...and We gave him wisdom and speech decisive....   (Sa`ad, 20)

His heart and mind were of the light of the divine attribute al-Qawwiy, the Strong, the Mighty One, wherefore he became a strong and mighty ruler, as it is written in the Holy Quran:

> We strengthened his kingdom...   (Sa`ad, 20)

His self was of the light of two divine actions: one was al-Muqaddim, He who causes to precede; the other was al-Muakhkhir, He who delays; wherefore he sent the commander Uriah out to battle in front of the Ark of the Covenant while he himself stayed behind. When he repented of his wrongful action, he was made to be Allah's representative on earth.

Solomon

As for Sulayman ﷺ: after Da'ud ﷺ had witnessed the wonders which Allah revealed to him, after he had endured the afflictions Allah tried him with and wept for a full forty years, the divine will decreed a prophet to succeed him whose kingdom should be even greater and stronger than that of Da'ud ﷺ, so that his sovereignty should attain a degree of perfection. Thus Sulayman ﷺ was born into a position of worldly power. His inner truth and spiritual reality were of the light of the name of the divine essence al-'Azim, the Magnificent, the Glorious; therefore he rose to eminence above the people of this world.

His heart and mind were of the light of the divine attribute al-Matin, the Firm, the Trustworthy, wherefore his kingship, his judgment and his knowledge were sound and firmly grounded. His self was of four divine actions: one was al-'Adl, the Just; the second was Malik-al-Mulk, the Lord over worldly and spiritual dominion; the third, al-Hafiz, the Protector, the Keeper, and the fourth: ar-Rafi', the Exalter. He was just because he practiced perfect equity towards anyone he met; he was a protector because he set anyone who raised his head against him firmly in his place, be he of mankind or of the Jinn; he was exalted because his throne, when he mounted it, rose up into the air with him; and he was Lord over all dominions because by divine decree he was made ruler over all peoples.

Ezra

As for 'Uzayr ﷺ: when the perfection of kingship had been achieved through the rule of Sulayman ﷺ, the divine will decreed that he be succeeded by another prophet who was to be witness to many workings of the other world, such as coming to life again after having been dead, and he was made to witness absolute certainty, as it is written in the Holy Quran:

So We would make thee a sign for the people.... (The Cow, 187)

Thus 'Uzayr ﷺ was born to the world. His inner truth and spiritual reality were of the light of two names of the divine essence, al-Awwal, the First,

22

and al-Akhir, the Last. He was the first because in his life he witnessed his former condition; then he died. And he was last, because after death he witnessed his own coming back to life a second time. His heart and mind were of the light of two divine attributes, as-Sami', the All-Hearing, and al-Basir, the All-Seeing. He was hearing because he heard the Word of the Lord, inasmuch as He speaks in the Holy Quran:

> Nay, thou hast tarried a hundred years.　　　　　　　　*(The Cow, 263)*

He was seeing because he perceived himself in his second life. His self was of the light of the divine action al-Wali, the Guardian, the Trusted Friend, as he was trusted to witness the perfection of divine power.

Jonah

As for Yunus ﷺ: after Allah Almighty had shown various aspects of His power, one example being the Prophet 'Uzayr ﷺ, His divine will caused another prophet to be sent to the world, who enjoyed divine protection, even though he was made to live in the depths of the sea and to make his home in the belly of a fish. Thus Yunus ﷺ was born into the world. His inner truth and spiritual reality were of the light of the name of divine essence: al-Wajid, He who brings into existence, the Creator, by reason of his light-filled existence in which there was no darkness. His heart and mind were of the light of the divine attribute: al-Ghafur, the Pardoner, for that he attained forgiveness from his Lord and was saved from drowning and rescued from his solitary confinement.

For Allah Almighty says in the Holy Quran:

> So We answered him and delivered him out of grief; even so do We deliver the believers.　　　　　　　　*(The Prophets, 86)*

His self was of the light of two divine actions: one was al-Muqit, the Nourisher, the other was an-Nafi', the Beneficial. Allah nourished him by spiritual fortification when he resided in the belly of the fish. He was helpful to people when he lived among them, and they benefited from him.

Zacharia

As for Zakaria ﷺ: when by the Grace of the Almighty the quickening of the dead had been achieved in 'Uzayr ﷺ, and by divine munificence His Protection had been extended, the divine will decreed the succession of two prophets who both willingly gave their lives in the way of union with the divine. Thus Zakaria ﷺ and Yahya ﷺ came into the world.

Zakaria's ﷺ inner truth and spiritual reality were from the light of the name of the divine essence al-Qayyum, the Eternal, Self-Existent. He became permanently established in the love of Allah and was so steadfast therein that even when he was hewn into two pieces he was able to persevere in patience.

His heart and mind were of the light of the divine attribute al-Hamid, the Praiseworthy, for through his actions he became worthy of praise. He even gave his life and soul in the way of Allah. His self was of the light of two names of the divine essence: one was al-Muhiy, the Life-Giver, the Quickener, the other was al-Majid, the Most Glorious, for his Lord called to him and spoke: "I have given you a son and I have called him Wali. His is to inherit his father's knowledge as well as to give new life to his father's name." That is how the names al-Muhiy and al-Majid came to be manifested.

John

As for Yahya ﷺ: when Zakaria ﷺ had given away his life and soul for the love of God, the divine will decreed for a prophet endowed with perfection to succeed him and so necessitated his appearance. Thus Yahya ﷺ came into the world. His inner truth and spiritual reality were of the light of the name of the divine essence al-Haqq, the Truth. This name was given to him for his great endurance in preaching and his outstanding spiritual vision. His heart and mind were of the light of three divine attributes: al-Warith, the Inheritor; ash-Shahid, the All-Witnessing, and al-Baqi, the Permanent, Remaining. He inherited his father's knowledge; therefore he is an inheritor, an heir. He witnessed the unseen world as well as being martyred in the way of Allah; therefore he is a full witness. Allah Almighty Himself bears witness to Yahya 🕌:

Yahya has never sinned against Me; therefore, I do also love him.

Therefore, it is inevitable that the lover who is slain on the path of the beloved becomes permanently united with his beloved.

His self was of the light of a divine attribute, al-Wali, the Saint, the Friend of God. For none of Yahya's 🕌 actions was ever rooted in any motivation of his lower soul.

Jesus

As for 'Isa 🕌: when the divine and universal order of things had reached its maturity, the divine will decreed the appearance of a prophet who would awake the dead and manifest many miracles and divine signs, so that knowledgeable and informed folk no longer could deny that Allah quickens the dead. For Allah has revealed:

That is how Allah brings the dead to life again.... (Baqara, 73)

Thus 'Isa 🕌 came to this world. `Isa's 🕌 inner truth and spiritual reality were from the light of the name of the divine essence, al-Ahad, the One, for that he came to be born without a father, and was living proof for the Unity of God. His heart and mind were of the light of the divine attributes al-Wahid and al-Khabir. He is al-Wahid, the Only, for that in both the physical and the spiritual world he is unique. As for al-Khabir, it is because he encompassed the knowledge of both the manifest and the hidden. As Allah has revealed in the Holy Quran:

...and I have taught you (to write) the book, and wisdom, the Torah and the Injil.

(The Table, 110)

The knowledge obtained from the Torah is outer knowledge, while that of the Injil is inner, spiritual knowledge. His self was of the light of three divine actions: al-Muhiy, the Life-Giver; al-Mumiyt, the Life-Taker; and al-

Khaliq, the Creator. He is Muhiy on account of his raising the dead to life again.

Muhammad

When the perfection of the divine had completed its manifestation in the realities of men, on earth as in the unseen world, the divine will necessitated the coming of yet another prophet in whom all qualities of perfection would be expressed, and he was to be a messenger and all signs would be manifested in his person. This prophet was to be Muhammad (peace and blessings be upon him), Habibullah, the Beloved of Allah. In him are gathered all the (achievable) stations of this base world and the spiritual world separately and collectively. His spiritual reality encompasses the entirety of spiritual realities; he is a prophet in this world, as he is also a prophet in the world of spirits, and in the world of the divine.

After 'Isa ﷺ departed from this world, nearly six hundred years went by before the Seal of the Prophets and Prince of all Messengers came to the world. Inasmuch as Allah Almighty has spoken in the Holy Quran:

> *People of the Book, now there has come to you Our Messenger, making clear to you many things You have been concealing of the Book, and effacing many things. There has come to you from God a light, and a Book manifest whereby God guides whosoever follows His good pleasure in the ways of peace, and brings them forth from the shadows into the light by His leave: and He guides them to a straight path.*
>
> (The Table, 17-18)

As Muhammad ﷺ was of Light, his station in the Lord's Presence was an exalted one. His inner truth is of the truth of all truths, and his name is the greatest name, it combines all divine names and attributes within itself. His spiritual reality is from the light of the divine essence itself. His mind is from the light of the names of the divine essence. His heart is from the light of all the divine attributes combined. His self is from the light of the names of all divine actions.

26

When Allah Almighty sent him to perform his prophetic mission, He made him the Prince of all divine messengers, and He sent him as a mercy to the worlds, as it is revealed:

We have not sent thee, save as a mercy unto all beings.   (The Prophets, 107)

And Allah gave him knowledge of the stories of all the prophets who had gone before him. Thereafter Allah spoke to him: "Be patient, practice the patience of Asiya (wife of Pharoah)!" As He says in the Holy Quran:

So be thou patient, as the Messengers possessed of constancy were also patient.

(The Sand Dunes, 35)

By the "Messengers possessed of constancy" (the "ulul-'azm") are meant the great prophets like Nuh 🕮 who was patient with the great troubles his people heaped upon him; and like Ibrahim 🕮 who was patient in the face of the fire of Nimrod; and Ismail 🕮 who was patient as he was about to be sacrificed; and as Ya'qub 🕮 was patient during his separation from Yusuf 🕮, and with the blindness that beset him on account of the pain he felt; as Yusuf 🕮 was patient when he was cast into a well and later thrown into prison; as Ayyub 🕮 showed patience in the midst of so very many trials, and as Musa 🕮 was patient with the injustice and violence of his people. Da'ud 🕮 patiently wept for forty years over the mistake he had made. Yunus 🕮 was patient when he was swallowed by the fish. Zakaria 🕮 was patient when he was sawn in half. Yahya 🕮 was patient when he was martyred in the way of Allah Almighty. 'Isa 🕮 was patient while laying brick upon brick, and he said:

Truly, the world is but a bridge; seek to pass over it, and do not try to repair it.

Therefore, should they ask you: how are the prophets able to perform their calling of inviting people to the Truth while they are aware of Him at every station? Then the answer is as follows: the Lord has placed a veil of light between His prophets and Himself. By means of these veils they are able to address their people.

Some have also said: In the world of spirits Allah Almighty counseled His prophets thus: "I have sent you to My servants living in the world of base matter: therefore, show them no anger by ascribing to them certain actions, and veil yourselves from Me. Likewise, show them no pleasure on account of certain actions which they ascribe to themselves, and remain veiled from them also through spiritual concealment, for it is upon you to perceive the Lord Almighty in people, and to discern the people in the Almighty."

Know then that no one may reach the inner secrets of the prophets, and no one may know their states but Allah Almighty. Oh ye who are seekers of the divine! Of this you must be mindful: to follow from beginning to end what I have made clear to you, without deviating into denial or falsehood, but by keeping to the path of moderation and admonition. So that, perhaps, in the end you will comprehend the highest form of wisdom, and maybe at the final outcome you will drink of the wine of knowledge. For I have made plain the code of Divine Law of the prophets, their spiritual realities and their exemplary conduct; you must hold them in highest respect and try to follow their example.

In their stories is surely a lesson to men possessed of minds. (Joseph, 111)

Insha'Allah, we will now attempt to complete our instruction, to inform of the outer and inner aspects of religious law, and of the attributes and qualities of the Prophet Muhammad, on whom be blessings and peace.

Created Through the Light of Muhammad ❀

Praise be to Allah, the Exalted, the Wise; He who created man for Himself, possesses the entire universe.

Oh ye wishing to apprehend the divine secrets! Know then that Allah Almighty laid in the Prophet Muhammad ❀ the base for the edifice of the prophets (on all of whom be peace), and that in him He would complete it; and to him He revealed the Glorious Book of the Quran. In it He has made plain his authority, and He has described him in all the holy books, the

Torah (Old Testament), the *Zabur* (Psalms), the *Injil* (New Testament)and the *Furqan* (the Quran).

He has made him perfect by giving him the *Liwa-al-Hamd*, the Banner of Praise, and the *Maqam-al-Mahmud*, the Station of the Praiseworthy, thereby making him the light of both worlds, messenger to both Jinn and men, and enabling him to attain the secrets of proximity to the divine station by two bows' lengths, and becoming the king of the world. Peace and blessings be upon his pure and meritorious family and his worthy companions who are pursuing the way of greatest righteousness.

Then Allah Almighty spoke thus:

> *Alif. Lam. Mim. Allah, there is no god but He, the Living, the Everlasting. He has sent down upon thee the Book with the truth, confirming what was before it, and He sent down the Torah and the Gospel aforetime, as guidance to the people and He sent down Salvation. As for those who disbelieve in God's Signs, for them awaits a terrible chastisement; God is Almighty, Vengeful.*
>
> *(The House of Imran, 1-4)*

And in a Hadith al-Qudsi He has said: "Were it not for you, I would not have created the universe."

It is related by Abdullah bin Abbas that the Holy Prophet ❀ said: "The very first thing that Allah Almighty ever created was my soul."

In another place he is reported to have said: "First of all things, the Lord created my mind."

In yet another place he is to have said: "I am from Allah, and the believers are from me."

How many proofs has He not brought to bear that all existent things are from Him, and that he ❀, is more excellent than all of creation!

The Qutb-al-Muhaqqiqin, the most eminent of those who verify, Sayyidina 'Ali, has said: Before the Lord Almighty created the divine throne and the divine court, Heaven and Hell, the worlds and the skies, He created the light of our Prophet Muhammad ﷺ. He created his soul three hundred twenty-four years before He created the soul of Adam عليه السلام.

Thereafter Allah Almighty created twelve veils, namely: the veils of power, grandeur, kindness, mercy, bliss, munificence, high station, guidance, prophecy, eminence, awe, and the veil of intercession. Thereafter the Prophet's ﷺ soul remained wrapped in the veil of power for twelve thousand years; and for eleven thousand years it remained within the veil of grandeur. For ten thousand years it remained in the veil of kindness; for nine thousand years in the veil of mercy; for eight thousand years in the veil of bliss; for seven thousand years in the veil of munificence; for six thousand years in the veil of high station; for five thousand years in the veil of guidance; for four thousand years in the veil of prophethood; for three thousand years in the veil of eminence; for two thousand years in the veil of awe; and for one thousand years his soul remained in the veil of intercession.

After this it stayed on the divine throne for six thousand years. Thereafter the Lord Almighty took it and brought it to the offspring of Adam's عليه السلام loins. From Adam's عليه السلام loins it passed to Seth عليه السلام, from Seth عليه السلام to Idris عليه السلام and from Idris عليه السلام to Nuh عليه السلام. Thus it was transferred all the way down to Abdullah bin Abdul-Muttalib. Finally it came to this world in the city of Mecca.

It is reported that the Lord Almighty created a tree from the light of him who is the pride of the world. This tree had four branches, and it was called the tree of certainty.

The light of Muhammad ﷺ was manifested as a veil made of white pearls. It was placed upon this tree shaped as a peacock, and there it remained for one thousand years, steeped in the remembrance of Allah Almighty. Then the Lord created the mirror of modesty and placed it opposite the peacock. When the peacock looked into the mirror, he beheld a most beautiful face and form in it, and it became shamed before its glorious aspect, and prostrated itself five times. Therefore, five daily prayers became incumbent upon us, from that prostration.

The Lord Almighty trained His gaze upon that light once more. From shame, that light began to perspire under the gaze of the Almighty. From the sweat upon his brow, the Almighty then created the angels. From the sweat upon his face, He created the throne, the divine court, the tablets and the pen, the sun, the moon and the stars. From the sweat upon his breast, He created the prophets and the messengers, the holy martyrs and the men of knowledge, and those of righteousness. From the sweat on his feet He then created the worlds and what is contained within them, up to the lowest of all stations of Hell and what is in it.

Then the Lord Almighty spoke: "Oh Muhammad, look before you!" Muhammad ﷺ did so and he saw that all was replete with light. The light before him was the light of Abu Bakr. The light behind him was the light of 'Umar. The light to his right was the light of 'Uthman, the light to his left was the light of 'Ali, may Allah be well pleased with them all. Then the light of Muhammad ﷺ began to praise the Lord for seventy thousand years. After this, the souls of the prophets were created.

When Allah had created the souls of the prophets, they all spoke *La ilaha illAllah, Muhammad-ur-Rasulullah.*

Then Allah created a lamp. He placed the soul of Muhammad ﷺ upon this lamp in the very same shape he was to appear in this world, and he was as if in prayer. The souls of all the prophets performed tawaf (circumambulation) around the soul of Muhammad ﷺ for two hundred thousand years. Then the Lord ordered them to look at Muhammad ﷺ. The souls then gazed upon him. Whoever gazed upon his head became a king in this world. He whose gaze fell upon his forehead became one of the just. He who espied his chest became a man of learning. In brief, whichever part of his blessed body the soul cast its gaze upon, it was endowed with just such an art or craft as corresponded to that member.

Thereafter Allah Almighty commanded the people to perform their ritual prayer in the shape of the name "Ahmed". That is to say: the prayer position of qiyam (standing upright) resembles the Arabic letter 'alif'. The ruk'u (bending from the waist) resembles the letter 'ha', the sajda (prostration) resembles the letter 'mim', and the final position of jalsa (kneeling) resembles the letter 'dal'. (In Arabic the name Ahmad contains these consonants: *alif, ha, mim, dal*).

Then the Lord Almighty created the prophets resembling in their forms the shape of the name "Muhammad". The head is round, like the letter 'mim'. The two hands resemble the letter 'ha', the belly again resembles a 'mim', and the feet resemble a 'dal'.

And now, oh ye desirous of learning divine secrets! I will now put forth to you the circumstances of the birth of the Holy Prophet ❀, his mission and the revelation of the Quran and its holy words, by the leave of the Almighty Lord, Allah.

Descent of Nur-i-Muhammad ﷺ

Narration of Ka'b al-Akhbar

This narration is from Ka`b al-Akhbar, who was known as Abu Ishaq. Ka`b was of the learned scholars of the Jews and during the blessed lifetime of the Holy Prophet ﷺ he lived in the land of Yemen. He did not accede to the honor of true faith during the Prophet's ﷺ lifetime, but only thereafter, during the Khalifa of Abu-Bakr as-Siddiq, or, according to other accounts, during the time of 'Umar. He is referred to in some of the hadith related by the honorable companions of the Holy Prophet ﷺ. One of these companions, Sahif bin 'Umar al-Ansari, claims to have heard from his father 'Amr:

During the Holy Prophet's ﷺ lifetime I became acquainted with Ka`b and I used to meet him in a number of assemblies. It was his intention to come and attend the association of the Holy Prophet ﷺ, and without yet having met him, he confirmed that he was indeed the Seal of the Prophets; he frequently describe dhis characteristics to us. One day he told us that this was going to be the Holy Prophet's ﷺ last year, and that he very much wished he could make ready and go to meet him on time. He hastened his preparations and set out on the journey. There came one night, however, when he was seen to dart in and out (of the tent) at frequent intervals during the night, gazing intently at the night sky and weeping copiously.

As it dawned, I addressed him and said: "Oh, Abu Ishaq, what has befallen you? How is it that you have spent the night gazing at the sky and weeping?

What hidden wisdom is there in your action?" He turned to me and answered, "During this night the Holy Prophet ﷺ at Madinah al-Munawwara was transported from this world to the next. I looked at the skies and saw that the gates of Heaven were opened wide to receive him, and I saw all the angels stand in attendance and celebrate his coming with songs of praise and honor. And on the whole earth there is no better place than that place where his blessed remains are to be buried; it is the choicest of all spots in this world." Thus he spoke and swore by Allah.

I was completely dumbfounded by this explanation and therefore took exact note of the very date and hour when he uttered these words. So when we actually arrived in Madinah, we heard that it was indeed on that very night that the Holy Prophet ﷺ had departed from this passing abode to that of permanence. But at that time, I did not meet Abu Bakr as-Siddiq; only later, after his death, during the Khalifa of 'Umar, when I went to see the Khalifa at Madinah, I heard that he was there. I met him and gave him Salams. He looked at me and recognized me, and he honored me by admitting me into his close company.

I then told him and all those assembled of what I had observed of Ka`b ul Akhbar. Everyone present marveled at this, saying he must be a sorcerer, a wizard. But Ka`b who was there with me spoke up and said: "God forbid, I am neither sorcerer nor wizard, Allahu Akbar!" and he took from beneath his seat a small box which resembled a white pearl, fastened by a golden lock which was sealed with a golden seal. He broke the seal and opened the box that revealed a piece of green silk folded up in many folds. "Do you know what this is?" he asked the assembly. "I don't know," I answered him. He said, "In this is wrapped (a volume) of the divinely revealed books of the Torah and the Injil (Old and New Testaments) in which the signs and characteristics of the Holy Prophet are set down by the revelation of the Almighty." Thereupon we all cried out: "Oh Abu Ishaq! May Allah Almighty have mercy on you! Do tell us of the very beginning of creation, when the Prophet was created!" We entreated him and he began to speak:

34

Verily, when Allah Almighty intended to create the most noble of all the sons of Adam ﷺ, He spoke to Jibra'il ﷺ, the trustworthy angel, ordering him to bring a sufficient quantity of clay from the purest and most exalted place on earth. Jibra'il ﷺ, being the highest in command of the sublime heavenly assembly, descended down to earth, and took a quantity of clay from the site of what is now the Holy Prophet's ﷺ fragrant resting place, as there can be no better place on earth than this site.

Allah then took this bit of clay and mixed it with the waters of the river Tasnim which flows in Paradise. He formed something akin to a white pearl. Subsequently, the pearl was dipped into all the various rivers and streams of Paradise and endowed with their outstanding properties. It was then shown to all the seven layers of the heavens and the earth, and amid showers of praise and glorification it was made known to all dwellers of Heaven and earth that this substance had found acceptance and high honor in the divine presence, and that it was the very best of all created materials.

Now, when the time had come for Adam ﷺ to be created, this light was placed upon his forehead, and the sound of a rushing river issued from it. Adam ﷺ asked his Lord: "Oh my Lord, praised be Thy very mention, what is this voice upon my forehead?"

The Lord answered him, "It is the sound of the praise and glorification of the light of the seal of the prophets, Sayyiduna Muhammad ﷺ! Be mindful of this light and hold it in high respect, and know that it will be passed on to your descendants. Therefore, enjoin them to take only pure and virtuous women for their wives, and to refrain from folly and frivolous conduct until the time has come for the owner of that light to enter the world." This he solemnly vowed to undertake, and from that time on the light of Muhammad ﷺ shone upon his blessed forehead.

It is also said that at the time Adam ﷺ was created that light was first placed at his back upon his shoulders. Wherever Adam ﷺ went, rows upon rows of angels followed him, gazing at his back, and when he stood still, they stood behind him, praising and celebrating this shining light. Adam ﷺ finally addressed the Lord and said, "Oh my Lord, why is it that there are always so many angels gathered at my back, what is the wisdom in this?" The Lord answered him, "Oh Adam ﷺ, on your back I have placed the light of Muhammad, and the angels are forever paying their respects to it."

Thereupon Adam ﷺ said, "Oh my Lord, do Thou place this blessed and revered light in front of me, so that the angels are not always behind me." The Lord granted him this favor and placed the light of Muhammad ﷺ upon Adam's ﷺ forehead. Now the angels always stood facing Adam ﷺ as they revered this blessed light. Adam ﷺ perceived the great love and devotion the angels held for this light, until at last he made supplication to his Lord, saying, "Oh my Lord, will You not grant me the privilege of once seeing this wonderful light which all these myriads of angels are incessantly adoring?"

The Lord heard his prayer and in answer to Adam's ﷺ supplication He placed the light of Muhammad ﷺ upon the index finger of his right hand (which is called the Shahada finger). The finger began ringing the praises of this most auspicious light, and Adam ﷺ along with all the angels heard it and named that finger 'sajah'. They then continued to praise the owner of that magnificent light, reciting Salawat upon the most noble and perfect of all prophets, upon whom be peace, and not only the angels, but all of creation began praising the light of Muhammad ﷺ.

At the time when Adam ﷺ and his wife Hawa were by divine command expelled from their blessed abode in the Garden of Eden, their Paradise clothing was stripped from them so that they grew aware of their nakedness and felt shame. They sought to conceal themselves from the blessed angels, and tried to hide behind the trees of Paradise. But the trees refused them, all except the 'Ud tree (the aloes). Allah Almighty addressed this tree and asked it why it had sheltered Adam ﷺ and Hawa whereas none of the other trees had done so. The 'Ud tree answered, "Oh gracious and merciful Lord! You have placed the light of Your beloved Muhammad ﷺ upon Adam's ﷺ forehead and You have commanded all of creation to praise this wonderful light as they gaze upon it. Adam ﷺ came to me with this light upon him, begging for shelter. For the sake of this hallowed light, how could I refuse him? I felt shame for this blessed light and accepted it into my shade, oh Lord!"

Allah Almighty replied, "Oh, 'Ud tree! For that you have so honored the light of My beloved, I will cause you to be more highly esteemed by My servants among men than any other tree, and I have made your leaves to be white; however, since you have acted as you did without My leave, you will not be able to give off your much-desired fragrance lest you are burnt to ashes."

According to another narration: when Adam ﷺ and Hawa were stripped of their robes of Paradise and ordered to go down to earth and leave their celestial abode, they looked about at all the marvels and heavenly splendor they were to leave behind, and began to weep bitterly for what they had lost. All the trees of Paradise wept along with them, all except for the 'Ud tree (the aloes). Allah Almighty addressed that tree, asking it, "Why are you alone of all trees in Paradise not weeping for Adam ﷺ and Hawa?"

The tree answered, "Oh my Lord, it is upon Thy command that they leave the Jannah (Paradise); out of respect for what Thou hast commanded I do not weep for them." The Lord then said, "For that you have shown respect for my divine command, I decree that on earth they will not benefit from your fragrant essence until they have put fire to your wood."

The tree then asked, "Oh my Lord, as You have willed me to be burnt, do tell me what is the wisdom of it?" The tree then received this reply: "It is because you have showed no compassion with My Prophet in his need that I have decree for you..."

When Adam ﷺ and Hawa stood naked they looked about from which tree they might take a few leaves to cover their nakedness. All the trees surrounding them lifted up their branches away from them and refused them even a single leaf. Desperately they searched, until they came to the fig tree. This tree took pity on them and gave them some of its leaves to cover themselves with. However, no sooner had they taken the leaves from this tree than they turned black and brittle and fell away from them, uselessly.

Upon this, they wept even more bitterly than before, and there came to them a call which they heard and understood: "Know that whomever the Lord has stripped of his covering, no one has the power to clothe! The servant forsaken by his Lord can receive no help from any quarter!"

Upon these words, Adam ﷺ turned to his Lord, the Almighty Source of All Things, and pleaded with Him to grant them the gift of covering their nakedness. Again they came to the fig tree, and it willingly gave them a few leaves. Adam ﷺ shook the tree, and three leaves fell from it. With these Adam ﷺ covered himself. He then shook the tree a second time, and this time five leaves fell from it. These Hawa used to cover herself with. From that time onwards, it has been the custom to wrap men's bodies for burial in three pieces of unstitched cloth, while women are wrapped in five pieces of cloth.

The Lord then said to the fig tree, "Oh fig tree, why did you make Adam ﷺ a gift of your leaves?" The tree replied, "Oh my Lord, You had not prohibited it, so I gave them some of my leaves." The Lord then spoke to the fig tree, "As you took pity on Adam ﷺ when My Wrath was upon him, I shall make you very brittle and hollow from within, so that men shall not climb upon you nor use your wood for any purpose, nor will they burn you for fuel. Your leaves I will make brittle and harsh, and no living creature on earth will find them tasty or sweet."

When the Lord of the Worlds issued His divine command for Adam ﷺ to go down from Paradise and settle upon the earth, Adam ﷺ in his distress called upon the souls of all the prophets who were to be his offspring, and he called upon the noble soul of Muhammad ﷺ, the seal of the prophets, to intercede with the Lord on his behalf, and he wept long and much. "What is the hidden meaning of this," he cried, "that my Lord has created me and placed me in these Paradise gardens, only to remove me now from this abode of bliss and making me to live in the lower world, upon the earth?"

The Lord Almighty answered his wailing thus: "Oh Adam! In My majesty and might, I have created you to be My representative on earth; the reason I first set you to live in these gardens of Paradise is this: so that from this day on until the Last Day you and all your descendants may look to this realm of bliss as to their real and true native land; that they may turn their hearts towards it full of longing and desire, and that they may believe in My unity and confirm the message of all My prophets and messengers, and respond in their words and works to My command. Thus they will exert themselves to regain their homeland of Paradise."

Therefore some of the learned in the scriptures have interpreted the saying of the prophet ﷺ: "Love of one's homeland is a part of faith" as referring to Paradise, the original home of man, and this saying is a sign and indication of this secret. Adam ﷺ, when he received his Lord's words, understood His intention and left Paradise behind him.

Adam ﷺ descended upon the mount of Sarandib (Sri Lanka) while Hawa came to earth at Jeddah. Shaytan was cast out also, but opinions differ as to where he landed: some say it was at Basra, some say at another place, but some even say he alighted at no particular place at all. Now, when Adam ﷺ and Hawa were expelled along with Iblis, Iblis conceived within himself an evil suggestion. "I have succeeded in driving Adam ﷺ and his mate out of Paradise," he thought to himself, "what damage can I do him now that he is coming to earth, what intrigue can I work against him there?"

Wondering about this, he called together all the wild beasts living on earth and told them that Adam's ﷺ advent would result in his progeny peopling the whole earth and hunting all the wild beasts to extinction. "Woe on us," they cried, "what are we to do?" Shaytan replied, "This is what you must do: gather all together at the spot where Adam ﷺ is to descend, and as soon as he arrives, attack him all of you and tear him to pieces. That will be the end of him for all times."

Thus Iblis excited the wild beasts against Adam ﷺ before he came to earth. When Adam ﷺ set foot on the ground he found all the animals gathered round him, prepared to attack. Adam ﷺ was bewildered at this reception and knew not what to do. The angel Jibra'il ﷺ came to him in less than an instant and told him, "Oh Adam, put out your hand and stroke the head of the dog, that you might witness the power of our Lord to effect the strange and wondrous." Adam ﷺ did as the angel counseled him, and no sooner had he touched the dog than it turned against its fellow creatures and fell upon them, so that they dispersed in confusion. Since that day the dog is the enemy of all other beasts of prey, and he attacks them wherever he chances upon them.

Adam ﷺ spent his first long years on earth weeping constantly, entreating the Almighty to forgive him and show him mercy. At long last he also prayed to the Lord to reunite him with his wife, Hawa. His prayer was then accepted, and it is written that the Lord Himself inspired in Adam ﷺ the words of supplication that made his prayer acceptable:

Thereafter Adam received certain words from his Lord, and he turned towards him...   *(The Cow, 35)*

The commentators have written much on this subject; here only two of their remarks shall be mentioned. One is transmitted from Sayyiduna 'Ali who relates that Adam's ﷺ prayer for forgiveness was this:

La ilaha illa anta, subhanaka, Rabbi, a'amiltu su'an wa zalamtu nafsi wa anta arham-ur-rahimin. (There is no God but Thou, Glory to Thee; my Lord, I have done wrong, I have wronged my own soul, and Thou art most merciful of those that show mercy).

The Holy Prophet ﷺ says that Allah Almighty will pardon him who entreats Him with these words, even if his sins be as numerous as the foam upon the waves of the ocean, or the grains of the desert sands.

Secondly, Hasan of Basra relates that the words given to Adam ﷺ were these verses of the Holy Quran:

...Lord, we have wronged ourselves, and if Thou dost not forgive us, and have mercy upon us, we shall surely be among the lost.   *(The Battlements, 23)*

When Adam ﷺ pleaded to the Lord in these words, Allah Almighty forgave him, and sent down to him from Heaven a house which had been made in Paradise, that was called the 'Bayt al-Ma'mur, the heavenly house.

Two doors it possessed, one of which opened to the east, the other to the west, and it was set down at the spot where today the Kaba stands at Mecca. Adam was then commanded through revelation to circumambulate this heavenly house, and he was taught the rites of the Hajj and the Sa'i by the angel Jibra'il himself.

After completing the Tawaf and Sa'i, he was led out to Arafat to be reunited with Hawa. She had spent the long years of separation looking for him in this place, and as it was the place of meeting and, as it were, re-acquaintance, it was known henceforth as 'Arafat' which means 'to get to know'. The angel then asked them what they hoped for from their Lord, and they answered, "We seek nothing but His pardon and forgiveness," wherefore this place is called Muna (hope, wish, desire).

Now every time Adam wished to consort with his wife Hawa, they would proceed by purifying themselves and by making preparations so that the sublime light that was housed in Adam's body might be transferred to his wife while in a state of purity, and they persisted in these efforts. Each time Hawa became pregnant, she would look at her husband Adam, and when she perceived the light of Muhammad upon his brow, she knew that she had not yet conceived his successor.

Hawa was pregnant twenty times, and each time she bore him twins, a boy and a girl. Until one day she conceived the father of the prophets, Seth: she then saw the light upon Adam's brow disappear from its place only to relocate upon her own. She greeted it with great joy and celebration. Allah Almighty created Seth as the only single birth in her womb, as an honor to the light of Muhammad. This was an omen to them that the owner of this illustrious light was about to be born into the world and that though he was of mankind, there was none like him and no one matched him in perfection. When the child was born, they named him Seth, and the meaning of this name is 'gift of God'.

When Hawa had born her son Seth, she looked at him and saw the light of Muhammad sparkling upon his brow. The Almighty also placed a veil between Seth and Shaytan, so that he was shielded and protected from his wiles. The angels circled round the child and honored him, and from the heavens on high a call was heard: "Good tidings to thee, oh earth, and all thy inhabitants! The proof of the light of Muhammad ﷺ has shone forth upon Seth ﷺ, it illuminates the heavens and the earth! This light will continue to pass from the pure to the pure, until such a time as its rightful possessor will appear in the world of men!"

This heavenly voice was heard every day until the boy Seth ﷺ had reached the age of puberty. Adam ﷺ then called his son to him, gazed at his forehead and said to him, "Oh my son, truly the Lord of might and glory has promised to me that this light of Muhammad ﷺ which is upon your brow shall not be taken from the world and shall not disappear. However you must take care that it is passed only to such women as are very chaste and pure, and of outstanding virtue."

Thereafter Adam ﷺ turned to the Lord and prayed: "Oh Allah! I have received a promise from this servant that he will carefully preserve this noble light, and I bear witness to this, his commitment. Oh Lord, wilt Thou not send a witness to confirm this solemn pledge?" The Lord then sent the angel Jibra'il ﷺ with a host of seventy thousand angels. They brought with them a piece of white silk from Paradise, as well as a pen from the heavenly pens.

They saluted Adam ﷺ and spoke to him, "The Lord Almighty says: Verily, the time is nigh for the light of My beloved Muhammad ﷺ to travel down through the generations; therefore, prepare and make your bequest to your son Seth. Let him swear a solemn oath that he too will pass this on to his sons, and they to theirs, until the time is ripe for the rightful possessor of this noble light to come into his own. The heavenly angels this day bear witness to this solemn pledge that you undertake, to ensure that this light is carried down through the generations only by those of pure and chaste comportment, who refrain from all manner of lewdness and sinful action and seek to keep the line of transmission untainted. Today this oath is witnessed by the angels and penned down upon this white silk from Paradise."

Jibra'il ﷺ had brought another object from Paradise: this was a box in which were kept the descriptions of the great prophets and messengers. The piece of white silk was placed therein. Next, two crimson robes were brought and Seth ﷺ was clothed in them. Then a contract of nikah (marriage) was drawn up for him with a woman by the name of Nahwailat al-Baida who in beauty and nature resembled his mother Hawa. The angel Jibra'il ﷺ performed the nikah ceremony and recited a khutba (sermon) for them and thus they were man and wife.

When this lady now became pregnant from Seth ﷺ, she heard a voice calling to her: "Oh Nahwailat-al-Baida! Good tidings to you, you have conceived the successor of that luminous light which is upon your husband's brow!" Thus she was cheered. When she bore the child, they named him Enush. The child was protected from the wiles of Shaytan the Accursed by this noble light. When the boy had grown, his father Seth ﷺ said to him, "Oh my son, when you marry, be mindful of selecting a pure and chaste woman, for you are to be my successor." Enush heeded his father's words, and in time he passed on the trust to his son Kan'aan, and he to his son Mahalalel, and he to Yered, his son.

Yered took to wife a woman named Birra who bore him a son, Enoch who is known to us as Idris ﷺ. Yered bequeathed to his son Enoch all the pledges that were written and recorded, and Enoch accepted them from him. He married a woman by the name of Barukhanan, and had a son by her. This son they named Methusalah; and he sired a son named Lamaq. Lamaq was as a lad extremely bright and gifted, and he also was very strong. Lamaq took to wife Kaswir and she became the mother of Nuh ﷺ. Lamaq bequeathed to Nuh ﷺ all he had; Nuh ﷺ married Na'ama and had a son named Sam by her. Upon his brow Nuh ﷺ perceived the light of Muhammad ﷺ, and he bequeathed to him the holy trust that had come to him from the time of Adam ﷺ.

Sam had a son by name of Arpachshad, and his son was named Shalach. Shalach married Marhana and had a son by her whom he named Abir. (He was to become the Prophet Hud ﷺ). Abir married a woman named

Munshaha and had a son by her whom he named Peleg. Peleg had a son named Arghu, and Arghu's son was named Saruq. Saruq's son was Nahor. Nahor had a son and called him Terah. Terah married a pure woman named Edna, and their son he named Ibrahim ﷺ.

When Ibrahim ﷺ came into the world two banners of light were set up, one in the east and one in the west. Ibrahim ﷺ grew and became aware of a voice coming from his hands that was praising the light of Muhammad ﷺ which he held in his blessed hands. He begged the Almighty to tell him about this voice, and the Lord answered him, "It is the voice of the light of My beloved Muhammad ﷺ, and it is reciting praises of My Glory and Unity. Now your turn has come to preserve this light; it has come down to you from the time of your father Adam ﷺ, you are the next in line to pass it on."

Ibrahim ﷺ told his wife Sarah what the Lord had told him, and for a very long time she expected the successor to that light to make his appearance through her. Until such a time as her maid Hagar conceived the intended heir to that blessed light; then Sarah was stricken with disappointment and jealousy, being deprived of the honor and happiness of bearing the Prophet Ibrahim's ﷺ sole and single heir. Her husband consoled her and said, "Don't give in to sorrow; our Almighty Lord is full of grace and bounty and does not rescind on His promise. It is His decree that you too will be blessed and made glad." So Sarah was patient until Allah's time was fulfilled and she bore her son Ishaq ﷺ.

When Ishaq ﷺ had reached the age of maturity, Ibrahim ﷺ called all his six children to him, gathered them round him and showed them the box which had come to him as inheritance from his forefather Adam ﷺ. He opened the box for them and in it they saw many small boxes, as many as there are prophets and messengers sent to this world. Each of the boxes contained a description of one of the prophets.

The very last box contained the description of the earthly form of the seal of prophets, Muhammad ﷺ. He was shown in the position of Qiyam (standing in prayer). On his right side stood Abu Bakr as-Siddiq, and upon his forehead were written these words: 'he was the first to believe in me'; on his left was depicted 'Umar ibn Khattab, upon whose forehead were written the words: 'in his righteousness he fears neither blame nor blamer.' Behind him, stood 'Uthman ibn 'Affan, and upon his forehead was written: 'Modesty is his virtue.' Before him stood 'Ali ibn Abi Talib, and upon his forehead was written: 'His virtue is generosity, and in faith he is the brother of the Prophet Muhammad ﷺ.' All around him stood the sainted uncles and companions and the elders of the community of Madinah, and their names were written upon their depictions.

Ibrahim showed all his children the family tree and this chain of succession of the Holy Prophets. They saw that henceforth all prophets were to be descended from their brother Ishaq, with one exception: the seal of the prophets was to be born of the line of Ismail. The Prophet Ibrahim spoke to his son Ismail, "As you can tell, the pride of all the worlds and seal of the prophets is to descend from your line; therefore, take the utmost care for yourself and enjoin upon your sons, to marry only the purest and most virtuous women of your age, so that this unrivalled light may come down through the ages to its rightful owner unsoiled."

Ismail married a woman by the name of Ri'lah and she conceived and bore him a son Qaydar. Qaydar grew into a strong and comely youth, the first and best among the spear throwers and a champion wrestler as well. Ismail perceived the light of Muhammad ﷺ upon his forehead and to him he bequeathed the box he had inherited from his father and made him his heir.

Qaydar, thinking it preferable to marry from the tribe of Ishaq, chose women from that line, and he married no less than one hundred times. For two hundred years he lived with them, but they bore him not a single child. One day, as he was returning from the hunt, the wild animals assembled round him and addressed him in distinct and eloquent speech. "Oh Qaydar," they said, "what is it with you? Already you have passed a large portion of your life on earth, how is it that the successor to the light upon

45

your forehead has not yet appeared? Could it be that you have been wasting your time? And what of the solemn pledge you made to your father."

Qaydar, upon hearing these words, felt hurt and fell into a mood of gloom and foreswore all worldly enjoyments, until he could solve this problem. As he was wandering about in his perplexity, Allah Almighty sent an angel to speak to him who assumed the shape of a man, and said to him, "Oh Qaydar, in a short while Allah Almighty will adorn you with new strength, and you will bring under your dominion great cities and towns. You will also deliver the holy light which is deposited in your safekeeping to a pure woman who is not of the tribe of Ishaq ﷺ. Allah demands a sacrifice of you, so that you may be directed towards that woman who is destined for you."

Qaydar then slaughtered seven hundred rams as a sacrifice to his Lord, and from Heaven descended a fire like a streak of white light and burned his sacrifices. A heavenly voice was heard saying: "Oh Qaydar! Your sacrifice is made and accepted, your prayer is granted. The box you have inherited is with you and guidance shall come to you through your dreams."

That night Qaydar saw a dream; in it he was told that the prophet who was to be the ultimate heir of the holy light was to come from the pureblooded Arab tribes of Arabia. He was told to go to those tribes and ask for the hand of one lady named Fakhira in marriage, so that through her he might attain his goal. Qaydar joyfully awoke from his dream, praised the Lord and thanked Him. He sent out his scouts and envoys forthwith to all the tribal chiefs of the Arabs to ask for the hand of such a woman. But no one could be found fitting the description.

At long last he himself set out to search among the Arab tribes. He came into the realm of Jurhum ibn Zuhri bin Amir bin Yaru' bin Qahtan, and learned that this king indeed had a daughter named Fakhira and that she was a woman of modesty and virtue. He asked for her and they were united in marriage. Qaydar traveled back with her to his home country and this lady conceived from him. Qaydar then wished to open the box that had been passed down to him, but a voice was heard coming from it, that said: "Beware and refrain! Only the hand of a prophet may open this chest! Desist, lest harm befall you!" Qaydar heeded the warning and took the box to the son of Ishaq عليه السلام who was Ya'qub عليه السلام.

His wife Fakhira meanwhile bore him a male child and they named him Hamil. Hamil grew up, and when he was old enough his father said to him, "Come with me, I will take you to the building which your grandfather Ibrahim has built at Mecca, and I will show the holy sites and teach you the rites." They set out for the holy house, the 'Baytullah', and when they had come to a place known as Sabil which is quite close by the holy house, they encountered the angel of death who had assumed a human form. "Where are you going?" he asked Qaydar. Qaydar answered, "We are going to the holy house of the Lord so that I might show my son the holy places and teach him the rites." The angel of death said to him, "Come up to me, I have something to tell you in private.." Qaydar stepped up to him, and the angel took from his soul while yet engaged in conversation with him. Hamil saw his father fall and rushed to attack the killer. But the angel of death addressed the young man, "Will you not check at least to see whether he is really dead..?" and while Hamil bent to do so, the angel vanished.

When Hamil looked up and found himself alone, he realized he had been speaking to an angel. Just then, by the grace of God, some people from the tribe of Ishaq came by that place. They attended to the dead man; they washed and prepared him for the funeral, prayed over him and laid him to rest.

Hamil then returned to his home. He grew up and married a woman, Javda by name, who bore him a son whom they named Lais. Lais in his turn had a son called Hamisa; Hamisa begat Adnan, and this is the chain of descent from our father Adam عليه السلام to Adnan and the Holy Prophet Muhammad ﷺ. However, there is no end to dissent and dispute concerning this genealogy. Our Holy Prophet ﷺ only confirmed the line of succession up until Adnan; he refrained from telling particulars of the family tree before that.

Ibn Abbas relates that from Ishaq to Adnan there were thirty generations, but he did not name them. He said, "If Allah Almighty had wished for these to be known, He would have made His Holy Prophet ﷺ instruct us about them." No real disagreement exists concerning the genealogical chain from Adnan to Muhammad's ﷺ father Abdullah. Adnan had a son Ma'add; Ma'add had Nizar. Nizar married Sauda bint Adnan. The sons of Nizar were four: Mudar, Rabi', Yaman and Ayar. Some sources claim that Sauda bint Adnan was the mother of all four, while others maintain that she was only the mother of Mudar, while his brothers were the sons of her sister, Shafiqa bint Adnan, Mudar was a great hunter and he read and recited with great reverence the scriptures that were handed down from the time of Adam ﷺ.

He took very seriously the task of passing on the light of Muhammad ﷺ, bequeathing it to his son. This he wrote down in the form of a solemn pledge, which he hung upon the Kaba. His sons after him married pure and worthy women to protect the sanctity of the light. Mudar belonged to the nation of Ibrahim ﷺ, and the light of Muhammad ﷺ upon him shone forth brightly so that whoever met him felt love for him in his heart. He also possessed a most beautiful voice.

When Nizar felt death approaching, he gathered his sons around him to give them his blessing and his last advice. To Mudar he bequeathed a tent of red leather, and willed that any other tents of this kind should be his. Thereafter he was known as Mudar the red. Nizar also had a gray horse; this one he gave to Rabi' and willed all similar horses to be given to Rabi'. Therefore he was called Rabi' of the horses. Nizar possessed a slave, him he gave to Yaman, and willed that all like him should belong to Yaman. Lastly, he had a black mattress, this he bequeathed to his last son, Ayar, willing all similar ones to be his. He recommended them to go to the seer Af'a who lived in Bahrain, in case any disagreement arose concerning their inheritance.

After Nizar had died, dissent arose between the brothers, and they set out towards Bahrain, each upon his camel. Af'a was known to be a great seer and soothsayer. As they traveled along their way, they came to a pasture which had been unevenly grazed, green in places, eaten away in others. Mudar remarked to his brothers, "A camel has pastured here; moreover a camel that is blind in one eye, its left eye, to be sure." To this Rabi' added, "And its right leg was lame." Yaman joined in, saying, "And its tail was clipped." Ayar concluded, "And it had run away from its owner."

After a little while they met an Arab mounted upon a camel. They asked him, "Who are you?" He replied, "I have lost my camel and I am looking for him." Mudar asked the man, "Perchance it was blind in its left eye?" "So it was," answered the Arab. Then Rabi' said, "And its right foot was lame?" "Indeed," said the Arab. Yaman then said, "And was its tail clipped?" "Yes, it was," said the Arab. Finally Ayar said, "And your camel had run away and was on the loose?" "To be sure, it was," said the Arab. Then they told him, "Your camel has passed by such-and-such a place, go and find it there." The man however said, "No, you must have stolen my camel and taken it away, how else could you know my camel so well?"

The brothers denied this and told him they knew all this from the signs of its grazing and they swore to that, but the man would not believe them. "No," he said, "you have told me all these details about my camel, it must be with you. I demand it back from you." "We have never set eyes on your camel," the brothers assured the man again and again. He then asked them where they were headed for. "We are going to Bahrain to see a certain soothsayer named Af'a," they said, so the man decided to join them, and they rode off together towards Bahrain.

When they had arrived at the soothsayer's, the Arab called out to him, "Oh Af'a, help me, for these four men have absconded with my camel that I lost in the desert." The wise man then turned to the brothers and asked them, "Since you claim never to have seen the camel, how is it you know so much about it?" Mudar answered, "I knew the camel was blind on its left eye because wherever it had grazed, the grass was eaten only on the right side." Rabi' then spoke, "I could tell from its tracks that it was a camel whose right foot was lame: its left footprint was very clear, while the right one was weak and indistinct." Next Yaman spoke and said, "I knew that its tail had been clipped because it is the habit of the camel to disperse its excrement as soon as it has defecated; this camel had not done so, therefore I knew it must have a clipped tail." Lastly, Ayar spoke up and said, "I noticed that this camel had been grazing here and there, as it pleased; therefore, I concluded that it had escaped from its owner."

The wise man Af'a listened to the brothers' testimony and marveled at their cleverness. He turned to the Arab and told him, "Go now and look for your camel, for these brothers have told the truth, they have not stolen your camel." Then he said to the four brothers, "Who are you and why have you come?" They answered, "We are the sons of Nizar, and we have a problem which we hoped you could help us with." Af'a invited them to stay with him the night as his guests, and he would look into their case in the morning.

The seer Af'a set before them a roast lamb to eat and a wineskin full of wine to drink. They sat down to eat and busied themselves with their meal. Their host did not sit down with them but concealed himself in a corner where he could overhear their conversation. He heard Mudar say, "This wine is excellent, but the grapes it is made from grew in a cemetery." His brother Rabi' spoke up next, "This lamb is nicely roasted, however the animal was fed on dog's milk." The next brother, Yaman, then said, "This is very good bread, only the dough was kneaded by a menstruating woman." At last Ayar also spoke and said, "Our host, the seer, is a good man, even though he is a bastard."

Hearing their words, Af'a went out to check the truth of their claims. He asked the man who had brought the wine where the grapes were grown. The man said, "There was no other wine left, so I gave you the wine made of the grapes that grow on your father's grave." Next he went to the shepherd and asked him about the lamb. The man told him, "It was a motherless lamb and there were no other ewes left in the herd to suckle it, so I gave it to a bitch who accepted it and suckled it on her own milk. I could have found no better lamb to give you when you asked me for one."

Next Af'a went to his kitchens and asked about the slave girl who had kneaded the bread dough that day. He found out that it was indeed as the son of Nizar had said. At last he went to his mother and asked about the circumstances of his own birth. "Tell me the truth," he said to her, "who was my father? Is it true that I am a bastard?" His mother answered him, "Your father was the governor of this province and he was a very rich and powerful man, but he was childless. I feared that after his death a new governor might take his place and that all our fortunes might be ruined. Therefore, one night a guest came to our house, and I spent the night with him. That is how I conceived you, my son."

Af'a went to a trusted friend and told him about all he had learned. He asked him to go to the strangers and ask them how they came to know all these hidden things. The man went and asked them, but they knew it was their host who had sent him. Nonetheless, they answered him. Mudar said, "Normally, when one drinks wine, all one's troubles and worries fade away; but with this drink, I found it brought trouble to my mind and it did not quench my thirst. From this I understood that the vine must be growing on a gravesite." Next Rabi' answered, "The fat of sheep and goats is found on the upper side of their meat, while the fat of the dog is found below. The fat of this lamb was below, therefore I knew it had been fed on dog's milk." Then Yaman spoke, "When you dip bread in gravy, it soaks up the liquid. This bread did not do so, hence I knew that the woman who had kneaded it was menstruating at the time." Lastly, Ayar said, "I knew that our goodly host must be a bastard, because a lawfully born son will sit and partake of the meal with his guests. This our soothsayer did not do, he kept apart from us and joined us not for the meal, therefore I knew he must be of illegitimate birth."

Af'a heard their explanations and he wondered much at their sharp wit and sagacity, went to them and expressed his admiration. The brothers then said, "Will you not now hear our case and help us decide our matter?" The seer said, "How can I be of assistance to the likes of you, who possess learning and wisdom in such great measure? Can there be anything you wouldn't be able to solve for yourselves?"

Then they told him, "Upon his deathbed, our father willed that we should go to you so that you might distribute among us justly what we have inherited from our father." Af'a then said, "What has your father left you then?" "To one of us he left a red leather tent, and to another a gray horse; to another a slave and to the last he left a black mattress." Af'a then said, "The message of this bequest is clear to me: as much as there is red gold in my possession, I leave it to Mudar; All the horses, cows, camels and sheep I own are to go to Rabi'. To Yaman I leave all the silver and brocade and costly cloth that I own, and Ayar shall have all my vineyards and fields." The brothers all accepted this decision and were glad, each with his portion.

Ibn Abbas relates that the Holy Prophet 🌿 said to his companions: *"Do not be against Mudar and Rabi', for they became Muslim."*

Following these events, Mudar married a woman named Karima who was also known as Umm Habib, and with her he had a son whom they called Iliyas. Iliyas, like his father, was a believer. In the book *Muntaqa*, it is related that often a sound akin to the buzzing of bees was heard when Iliyas passed by; this was the sound of the light of Muhammad 🌿 reciting Talbiya *(Labbayk allahumma labbayk).*

Iliyas married a woman, Fatha, and begat a son on her, Mudrika. Mudrika married Quz'a and their son was Khuzayma. Khuzayma saw in a dream that he married a certain Barra bint Adwin, who was also called Tabiha. He awoke and found this woman, married her and Kanana was born to them. Kanana in his turn married a lady named Rayhana and they called their son Nadhir. Later he came to be called Quraysh, on account of a dream his father Kanana had one night. In this dream he saw a tree growing out of his back. It had many, many branches and its foliage was green and abundant. The tree grew as high as the sky and spread out into the heavens. Suddenly men of pale countenance appeared and embraced the branches of the tree.

When Kanana awoke from this dream, he went straight to an interpreter of dreams, and told him about it. The wise man said, "Should your dream be a true vision, it means that you are destined to be the forebear of the prophet of the last times. People from all around the world will show him honor, venerate him and follow his religion."

His people heard about his dream and the interpretation the seer had given it, and all voiced their surprise and said, "Just look at him, this Kanana, he just wants to promote his son Nadhir's importance and standing among us, whereas he is only a Quraysh." The term "Quraysh" denotes a small sea fish that chases and eats up other, larger fish and sea creatures. This nickname stuck with Nadhir son of Kanana, pointing to his strength in overcoming obstacles.

Nadhir, who was henceforth called Quraysh, married Hint bint Adwan, and their son was Malik. Malik married Jedlaka bint Harith, and their son was named Fihr. Fihr married Selma bint Said and their son was Ghalib. Ghalib married Wahshia bint Madih, and their son was Lu'ayy. Lu'ayy married Selma bint Harith and they had Ka'b. Ka'b married the daughter of Shadwan and they had Murra. Murra married Nu'ma bint Sa'd, and they had a son, Kilab. Kilab married a woman, Fatima bint Sa'd, and their son was Qusayy. Qusayy married Atiqa bint Murra, and their son was named Hashim.

This was Hashim who is known to us as the felicitous great-grandfather of the Prophet of the last times ﷺ, was famed among the Arabs in his own time for his wealth and lordliness. All tribes wished to be connected through marriage to that purebloooded and powerful tribe. Many offered to him their daughters in marriage, even the Emperor of Byzanz, Constantine, sent his messengers to Hashim, saying, "I have one daughter whose grace and beauty is unrivalled among the women of this age. I will give him the hand of my daughter in marriage, if he will come to me." For he had probably learned from his study of the Injil that the Prophet of the last times, Muhammad ﷺ was to be born of the tribe of Hashim ibn 'Abdu-Manaf.

In order to secure the honor of being connected to that prophet he wished to marry into that tribe, and he sent out his envoys with many persuasive gifts and promises. But Hashim was mindful of the solemn pledge of his forefathers to marry only women of pure and chaste extraction, therefore he was not tempted or swayed by the Emperor's proposals. He refused, but he did wonder how to fulfill his pledge and whom to marry. While he was pondering this in a state of indecision, he was shown in a dream the daughter of 'Umra, Selma bint Zayd, of the tribe of Jurshum. In the dream he was commanded to ask for her hand in marriage. He promptly acted on this and the marriage contract was concluded.

This girl Selma was similar to Khadija al-Kubra in that she possessed wealth and dignity, and eloquence of speech and culture. She was married to Hashim and they had a son whom he called Shayba, but afterwards he came to be called Abdul-Muttalib. Abdul-Muttalib had great personal beauty and charisma. His eyes were 'mukahhal' from birth, that is to say, they were naturally rimmed with black as if with antimony by the Hand of the Almighty, and he carried himself with grace and dignity. When he was grown, his father Hashim married him to Wasifa bint Jundab from the tribe of Sa'sa. Abdul-Muttalib had a son with her named Harith (wherefore Abdul-Muttalib is also called Abu Harith).

When Abdul-Muttalib was twenty-five years of age, his father Hashim fell ill and called for his son. "Assemble all the chiefs of the tribe of Nadhir," he told his son, "the Abdu-Shams, the Bani Mahzum, the Bani Lu'ayni, the Bani Fahri and the Bani Ghalib, and invite them to come here." Abdul-Muttalib did as his father bade him, and when all were assembled, Hashim addressed them, "Oh ye tribal chiefs of Quraysh! You are directly descended from the Prophet Ismail and Allah Almighty has chosen you to be the custodians of the holy places, the Haram of Mecca. I am the leader of this tribe, so hear today my bequest: all the honorable offices of this custodianship I am passing on to my son Abdul-Muttalib: the banner of Ismail, the distribution of water to the pilgrims and the keys to the holy house, the shrine of the Kaba. Do you all accept my decision and pledge to abide by it?" "We hear and obey," replied the chiefs of the tribes. Then Hashim passed away and Abdul-Muttalib took his place as ruler and chief of Mecca, and he became a personality of rank and eminence. Many kings from far and near sent him their respects accompanied by gifts, excepting the Khosroe of Hormuz.

No rain had fallen in the lands of the Quraysh for a number of years, and there was a drought. Abdul-Muttalib joined his people filing up Mount Yasira to pray for rain, and Allah in His grace and boundless mercy sent rain upon the land, for the sake of the blessed light of Muhammad ﷺ which was present in Abdul-Muttalib. That year they had plentiful fruit and abundance. Due to the light which was with him at all times, Abdul-Muttalib was well loved and respected by everyone, and people hastened to show him courtesy and to do him favors.

In a dream it was shown to Abdul-Muttalib that one of the sons of Ismail ﷺ had hidden two deer-shaped ornaments in the well of Zamzam, made of red gold, as well as one hundred swords from the time of the prophet-king Sulayman ﷺ, and one hundred suits of mail from the time of the Prophet Da'ud ﷺ. Abdul-Muttalib was ordered to bring them out of the well in his dream.

When he came before the assembly of the Quraysh and told them what he had seen, they were not pleased and declined to assist him. Abdul-Muttalib at that time had only one son, Harith. He had no way to oppose the ranks of the Quraysh. He went to the holy house of the Kaba and prayed fervently to his Lord, Allah Almighty, invoking as intercessor the light of Muhammad ﷺ upon his forehead. He vowed at that time that were he to beget ten sons and live to see them grown, and should they be obedient and willing to dig up the old well of Zamzam despite the Quraysh's opposition; should they, furthermore, succeed in this task without losing one drop of holy Zamzam water and unearth the objects he had seen in his dream, then he would sacrifice one of his sons at the threshold of the Kaba, in the Name of the Almighty Lord.

Abdul-Muttalib then married Hala bint Wahhab bint Abdu Manaf, and she bore him Hamza. After her he married Lubba bint Hajari, and through her he became the father of Abu Lahab. His mother died and Abdul-Muttalib married Atila bint Hubaba and she bore him Abbas, and his two brothers.

Abbas relates: One day my father Abdul-Muttalib lay asleep in his chamber when he suddenly started and woke up trembling. Hurriedly he tied his loincloth around his waist and rushed from the house. Wondering where he was going in such a hurry, I followed him hastily, and saw him go to the house of a fortuneteller skilled in the interpretation of dreams. The fortuneteller saw in him the signs of intense fright and asked him what he had seen. Abdul-Muttalib then told him his dream.

"I saw a great white chain rise up at my back," he said, "which then divided into four branches, stretching to the east, to the west, up into the skies, and down into the ground. While I gazed at this vision, I saw it change into a great green tree of incredible beauty. All sorts of fruit were growing upon its boughs, as are found in all parts of the world. Such a tree of marvels has never been seen before. All peoples of the world bowed down before it, Arabs and non-Arabs alike, and performed prostration. From moment to moment its light grew stronger. Among the people, I saw also the tribe of Quraysh: one group clung to the branches of the tree, while another group gathered round, trying to cut down that beautiful tree. Someone I have never seen stepped forward to prevent them, and he was more beautiful than anyone I have ever set eyes upon.

"I stretched out my hand to take hold of that bit of light, and I ask that beautiful person whose portion of light that would be; he answered me that it would fall to those who were clinging to the branch of that tree. Then I just stood gazing at the beauty of that person, and as I looked on, I saw two great and venerable Sheikhs by the foot of the tree. They, too, were radiant with inner beauty. I asked them who they were, and one of them said, 'I am Nuh', the other one said, 'I am Ibrahim'."

When my father had finished telling him his dream, the soothsayer went pale. He said, "If your dream is a true one, it means that the Prophet of the last times will come to the world through you. The whole world, East and West, the earth and the heavens will testify to his prophethood and accept to be part of his nation. He will ascend to the heavens during his lifetime (Mi'raj), and in the end he will pass into the other world, and his body will remain to be buried. One faction of the Quraysh will accept his prophethood, while another will not, and they will be vanquished. The radiant person you saw is the religion of Islam; thereby they will be crushed and vanquished. The Prophet Nuh ﷺ standing at the foot of that tree means that those opposing that prophet to come will be drowned, as were the people of Nuh, in a flood of trials and affliction. The Prophet Ibrahim ﷺ standing at the foot of the tree means that those who follow the coming prophet will be honored by belonging to the nation of Khalil Ibrahim ﷺ and will attain their innermost desires. This prophet will bring with him a law that will be safe from later accretions and changes, and on the Last Day it will stand out as incontrovertible proof; this law and this nation will stand until the Last Day has come. This religion is true, and it is light and easy to bear." That is how the seer interpreted my father's dream.

After this Abdul-Muttalib married Fatima bint 'Umri bin A'izz, and he had further children with her. Her last child was a son, Abdullah, who was destined to become the father of the Holy Prophet Muhammad ﷺ. Abdullah was the youngest child of Abdul-Muttalib.

Scholars of the unbelievers of Sham knew that the father of the last Prophet had been born, for they possessed the blessed Prophet Yahya's ﷺ mantle in which he had been martyred, and his blood was upon it yet. Furthermore, in their scriptures they had found a prediction that told them that whenever this dried blood would flow afresh, it would be the sign that father of the last Prophet was born at Mecca.

Every morning they would inspect the robe for these traces. The night Abdullah, Muhammad's ﷺ father was born at Mecca, the blood on the cloak became fresh and began to flow anew, as if it has been shed just that night, hence they knew this sign was fulfilled. They took counsel with each other, for they saw this event as a threat to themselves. They said, "If we don't rid ourselves of this one while he is yet a child, he will grow up and become the father of this Arab prophet. He will then go forth and avenge the blood of Yahya ﷺ upon the unbelievers."

They discussed ways and means of doing away with this boy Abdullah while he was yet a child. In the end they agreed on a plan: under the pretext of a trade delegation, the unbelievers would travel to Mecca and keep a close watch over the boy Abdullah, until a good opportunity presented itself. Seventy of their strongest and bravest men set out, each one armed with a poisoned sword and they turned towards Mecca. Having set up their camp there, they were watchful day and night for an opportunity to slay the boy, but Allah Almighty, Exalted be He, kept the boy out of harm's way. The light of Muhammad ﷺ grew stronger with each passing day, and his beauty and virtue increased. It was a much-discussed fact that he was to be the father of the Prophet of the last times.

Abdul-Muttalib now had ten sons, including Abdullah. When they had all reached manhood, they stood by their father and represented an influential faction. Abdul-Muttalib himself was a man of eminence among all the tribes of Arabia, and Quraysh could not oppose him unaided. Abdullah one night had a dream that instructed him to unearth the precious objects that were hidden in the Zamzam well for such a long time, so Abdul-Muttalib and his ten sons began digging at the site. They eventually found all, as Abdul-Muttalib had been told in his own dream long ago. The swords of steel they melted down and made from them a pair of doors for the Kaba, and the golden deer figures they also melted and fashioned from this a golden ornament to place above those doors. Therefore, the first person to use gold on the doors of the Kaba was Abdul-Muttalib, the Prophet's ﷺ grandfather.

Now, Abdul-Muttalib was also mindful that he had vowed to Allah to sacrifice one of his ten sons, should he be able to complete his task. He therefore drew the lots three times to determine which one of his sons should be sacrificed. Thrice the lot fell upon Abdullah. So it was decided that he should be sacrificed in fulfillment of his father's vow.

The mother of Abu Talib was from the tribe of the Bani Mahzum. She went to her uncles to tell them of Abdul-Muttalib's intention. They put their heads together and discussed what was to be done. They took

Abdullah aside, and spoke to Abdul-Muttalib: "You are now the chief of the tribes of Quraysh, and if you institute such a practice, it will be done so ever after and become a custom. It is not a good thing to sacrifice your own son in fulfillment of a vow, we implore you not to do so." Abdul-Muttalib thought about their objections, then he asked them, "What do you suggest I do then?" They replied, "There lives a very wise man at Khaybar; go to him and ask what course you should take." Abdul-Muttalib went to the soothsayer at Khaybar who was known as Saja. He stated his case and Saja advised him, "Give ten camels for your son, then draw the lots once more. If the lot still falls on your son, increase the number of camels by ten, and keep on doing so until the lot you draw finally falls upon the camels. That number will then be the ransom for your son Abdullah. You will slaughter the animals in his stead."

Abdul-Muttalib was gladdened when he heard these words and he returned to Mecca and did as the wise man had told him. He took ten camels and drew the lots, and again the lot fell on his son Abdullah. He increased the number of camels by ten each time he drew the lot, until he had reached one hundred camels, and his son Abdullah was spared. Perhaps it is for this that in Islamic law the blood money paid in compensation for a murder is the equivalent of a hundred camels.

The Holy Prophet's word: "Ana ibn zabihayn", I am the son of the two (intended) sacrifices, refers to these events as well. One of those intended for sacrifice was his forefather Ismail, the other his own father Abdullah.

Abdullah saw many visions and experienced many strange things. One day he said to his father Abdul-Muttalib, "I came to a certain place in Mecca where I saw a light rise up from behind me; it divided in half and became two branches. One went to the east and one to the west. This light spread out all over the world, and yet in less than a second it returned, rolling itself up in a ball and hovering over my head. I saw the gates of Heaven open and this light rose up, and descended again into my back. Also, every time I sit down, I hear a voice coming up from the ground that says to me:

'Greetings of peace be with you! The light of Muhammad ❀ is with you and in your care!' Every time I sit down beneath a dry and barren fig tree, it comes back to life and springs again, sprouting leaves, so that I have shade. When I get up and leave, it instantly dies and withers away."

All these things Abdullah told his father when he was yet a child. Abdul-Muttalib told his son, "If your vision is true, it confirms the dream that I saw and had interpreted, according to which you are indeed the blessed child I was promised, and that you will engender the Prophet of the last times ❀.

Because of all the strange and wonderful events surrounding this child, many of the great and powerful wished to connect themselves through marriage to this family. Abdullah was offered the hand of many a princess. But his father Abdul-Muttalib said, "The girl he marries must be of the tribe of Quraysh," and he considered none of these proposals seriously. Abdullah reached his twenty-fifth year, and he was in his prime, a model of a youth, and the light of Muhammad ❀ shone upon his brow.

Many who saw him were infatuated with him, propositioning him with secret get-togethers and forbidden pleasures, but each time the angels showed themselves to him in their frightful aspect and prevented him from committing any unlawful act, by the grace of Allah Almighty. Abdullah never went to the house of idols, then housed in the Kaba. Each time he even thought of doing so, the idols within cried out with a voice of their own: "Oh Abdullah! Beware, do not come near us! The light of the Pride of all the Worlds ❀ is in your safekeeping, it is the light of the Prophet of the last times, and through his hand all idolatry will be wiped out–he will destroy us and all our worshippers!"

Abdul-Muttalib convened a family council and said to them, "My son Abdullah has now reached the age that he should get married. Already there have been many proposals, but I wish to discuss the question with you. Are there any daughters of the Quraysh who would make a suitable bride for my son?" They answered, "There lives in Madinah a judge named Wahb bin

Abdu Manaf bin Zuhra whose daughter Amina would make a suitable bride for your son. She is a model of beauty and modesty and good upbringing, unique among the girls of her generation. Moreover, the scholars insist that both father and mother of the last Prophet be descended from an ancestor named Abdu Manaf. Both grandfathers were named Abdu Manaf, so this condition is fulfilled thereby."

The family council agreed heartily, and Abdul-Muttalib said to them, "Your words ring good and true. The girl you have suggested is in all respects a perfect match. However, her father has not given her to anyone yet, even though she is known among the tribes for her excellence and virtue; great men of all descriptions, men of fabulous wealth and power have asked for her hand, yet her father has consented to none. We have not the means to match their precious gifts, and if we appear as paupers, he may refuse us, too."

Thus they held their counsel and were worried and in doubt as to what they should do. But Allah, the Creator of Causes, made the knowledge of the seers and sorcerers of Madinah known through the unbelievers, concerning that sun of comeliness and prodigy of virtue who was to become the father of the last Prophet ##, and it reached the ears of Wahb, the father of Amina. He received it with great joy in his heart and an immediate surge of affection. He was inspired to wish to marry his daughter Amina to Abdullah, and considered sending a message to this effect to Mecca. But being a man of prudence, he opted for a cautious course, and decided to leave a deputy in his place in Madinah, and personally travel to Mecca himself, thus performing a pilgrimage as well as viewing the prospective groom. He was prepared to draw up the marriage contract right there and then, should things turn out to his satisfaction.

Having thus made up his mind, he set out on his own from Madinah to Mecca, for he was a forthright and courageous man. Meanwhile in Mecca, Abdullah was sitting with his father one day, when a person came by with a fine Hijin camel. Seeing the camel, Abdullah asked leave of his father to take that camel and ride out hunting. Abdul-Muttalib permitted him to go out with a group of his friends, and they all picked their camels.

Word of their planned venture spread through the town, and it came to the ears of the seventy unbelievers who lay in wait for him. Instantly they left the city and went to a nearby hilltop to wait in ambush. Through the grace of the Almighty God, just that very night, Wahb arrived before the gates of Mecca, but as he was very tired, he decided to spend the night outside the gates. By divine providence it so happened that he chose as a resting place just that spot where the seventy unbelievers lay in wait. He dismounted from his camel and sat down to rest.

Abdullah had set out from Mecca on his swift Hijin camel, and was making straight for the hill where Wahb was resting and the unbelievers lay in ambush. Wahb saw him coming from afar, a handsome youth mounted on a beautiful Hijin camel, a radiant light upon his brow. Wahb said to himself, "This can be no other than Abdullah, the son of Abdul-Muttalib whom I have come to see, for the light of Muhammad 🕸 is shining on his brow. My doubt vanishes before this sight; he must be the destined father of the last Prophet, Muhammad 🕸. Quickly I will wed my daughter to him."

Thus he reflected, when suddenly he saw the seventy unbelievers emerging from hiding with swords drawn. They rushed upon Abdullah to surround him and strike him down. Wahb instantly rose to the occasion; he mounted his camel and ran to Abdullah's aid. But again he realized that there must be hidden wisdom in these events: if Abdullah was truly destined to be the father of the Holy Prophet 🕸, no one could harm him, even if whole armies gathered against him, let alone seventy men. Allah Almighty would make him safe from harm and secure him from all their wiles. If he were not that person, then surely, he would be slain. While these thoughts were still passing through Wahb's mind, he suddenly perceived a company of tall men on heavenly steeds descending out of the skies. These fighters of the Lord surrounded the attackers, and the unbelievers were struck down even as they raised their sabers, and their heads rolled—all seventy perishing in a mere moment. Abdullah rode on, unscathed. Wahb now mounted his camel and followed him into the city of Mecca.

Abdul-Muttalib and his kinsmen were still discussing how to ask Wahb for the hand of his daughter Amina when a messenger came in, announcing the arrival of Wahb himself. Abdul-Muttalib himself rose and went out to meet Wahb. When he had welcomed the guest and made him comfortable, Wahb began, "Oh my friend, Abdul-Muttalib! I have come to you with a far-reaching request. If you permit, I will speak to you of it in front of this honorable assembly."

"We are at your command," replied Abdul-Muttalib, "whatever it is, feel free to name it." Wahb then said, "As you may have heard, I have a daughter, Amina, who is a model of virtue and chastity, she is ranked among the best women of this age. Kings and princes have asked for her hand, yet I consented to none of their offers. Now, Abdul-Muttalib, my friend, I have come to you to tell you that I have decided to give my daughter Amina to your son Abdullah; if this is agreeable to you and if you accept, then let this assembly of nobles witness our agreement and the contract be drawn up forthwith."

Abdul-Muttalib consented joyfully and a marriage contract was concluded without delay. The wedding feast was prepared and both sides made ready. The wedding took place, congratulations were exchanged, and the couple entered their nuptial chamber on the eve of the first Friday (Thursday night) of the month of Rajab wherefore this night is called "Laylat-al-Raghaib," which means "night of desires".

That very night the pure elements composing the light-filled body of Muhammad ﷺ descended from Abdullah's loins and settled within Amina's womb, as a pearl will form in the shell of the sea. The scholars maintain that this event took place while their bodies were in a state of ritual purity.

Sahil ibn Abdullah reports: When the Lord Allah Almighty applied His Will to the creation of Muhammad ﷺ, He commanded the guardian of Paradise gardens to open wide its gates and to give all inhabitants of Paradise the glad tidings of the coming of the Prophet Muhammad ﷺ. Messengers were sent out to spread the good news to all who dwelt in the heavens and the earth that this very night the concealed light of Muhammad ﷺ was to descend into his mother's womb. Thus the Mercy to the Worlds would be conceived and born to earth.

It is related that at the time the precious elements of Muhammad's ﷺ physical existence were embedded in Amina's blessed body, a call went out in the spiritual kingdoms of the other world: "Oh blessed ones! Anoint your abodes with perfume and incense and prepare for a feast of holiness! Mark the coming of Muhammad ﷺ to the lower world with exuberant celebration and joyful festivity!"

In that same night innumerable strange and wondrous events took place of which we can only relate a small number here: the animals in Mecca all spoke fluently in human speech on that night of conception, and they said, "By the Lord of the Kaba! Tonight the Prophet Muhammad ﷺ is conceived in his mother's womb, the guiding light of all the world, the lodestar of the entire universe"!

That night the wild beasts and birds congratulated one another on the coming of the Mercy to the Worlds. That night the thrones of all the kings of the whole world shook and trembled, the idols fell down upon their faces and broke; the roofs of many churches collapsed and the seers and soothsayers became tongue-tied. All the sorcerers and soothsayers assembled and held counsel, debating the portent of these signs.

They concluded that all these signs heralded the coming of the Prophet Muhammad ﷺ, the long awaited prophet of the Arabs who that night was conceived in his mother's womb in the holy city of Mecca. Of this they informed their kings and potentates, and told them that they would be overcome and defeated, their sovereignty wrested from them and their code of law abolished. It was to be replaced by the divine law this messenger of light was to bring the world. They informed their kings that the revelation he would bring was to remain on earth until the last day of the world. It would supersede all previous revelations and invalidate them. Thereupon great fear and apprehension seized the hearts of the kings for the awesomeness of this divine envoy.

The mother of the blessed Prophet Muhammad ﷺ would hear a heavenly voice calling to her at the beginning of every month of her pregnancy that seemed to come from above as well as from below: "Blessings upon you and tidings of joy! The felicitous advent of Abu-Qasim to the world has indeed drawn nigh!"

It is related from Amina, the blessed mother of the Prophet ﷺ:

"I first became pregnant at the beginning of the month of Rajab. One night as I lay sleeping, I saw a very fair-faced man entering my chamber. He gazed at my heart and pointed to the unborn child in my belly, and said, 'As-salamu alaykum, ya Muhammad! Peace be upon you!' I asked this person, 'Who are you, sir?' He answered, 'I am the father of mankind, Adam Safiullah, and I have come to give you the glad news that you are now pregnant with the Crown of Creation, the Prince of the Worlds!'

"At the start of my second month of pregnancy, I saw another man enter my room. He was very calm and dignified and shone with great light and beauty. He gazed at my heart and spoke, 'Peace be upon you, oh much beloved, as-salamu alaykum, oh goal of all desires!' I asked this person who he was, and he answered, 'I am the Prophet Seth, oh Amina, and I have come to confirm the joyful auspicious prediction, for you are to become the mother of the most illustrious prophet of all!'

"At the beginning of my third month, again I saw a person of immense beauty and dignified bearing enter my abode, and he too gazed at my heart and spoke, 'Peace be upon you, oh thou enwrapped in thy robes, (ya ayyuhal Muzammil); as-salamu alaykum, oh thou shrouded in thy mantle, (ya ayyuhal Muddahthir)!' I then asked this person who he was, and he answered. 'I am the Prophet Idris, and I have come to bring to you the joyous news that you are pregnant with the prince of all prophets who is invested with Allah's mercy and compassion.'

"At the beginning of my fourth month of pregnancy a person of dark color appeared in my room who was of gentle gaze and luminous countenance. He looked at my heart and made a sign to the unborn child within me and greeted him thus: 'Peace be upon you, oh you choicest of created beings!' I asked this person who he was and he answered, 'I am the Prophet Nuh, good news and joyful tidings to you, oh Amina, who are to be the mother of the celebrated and victorious Prophet of the last times!'

"In my fifth month, I beheld another person entering my chamber whose perfect grace and enlightened features were awesome. He, too, gazed at my heart and signaled to the unborn innocent within me, greeting him, 'As-salamu alaykum, oh seal of the prophets!' I asked this person, 'And who are you?' He answered, 'I am the Prophet Hud, and I compliment you, Amina, on your good fortune of bearing the most praiseworthy of all prophets, who excels in generosity and munificence.'

"In the sixth month of my pregnancy, a person of illustrious aspect and radiant mien entered my room, gazed at my heart and addressed the unborn child within me, 'Peace be upon thee, oh Messenger of Allah, as-salamu alayk, ya Habibullah (oh Beloved of Allah)!' I asked this person who he might be, and he answered me, 'I am the Prophet Ibrahim, oh Amina, the Friend of God, and I give you tidings of your bright fortune: you are to become the mother of a mighty prophet fair to behold.'

"In my seventh month, another winsome person entered my chamber, whose features were gentle and pleasing. This man looked at my heart and addressed the child within me, 'As-salamu alayk, oh Prophet of Allah, peace be upon you, oh true friend of Allah!' When I asked this man who he was, he said, 'I am the Prophet Ismail, oh Amina, the Offering to Allah. I have come to give you the joyous news that you are to be the mother of a mild tempered prophet whose tongue excels in eloquence and whose portion is mercy.'

"My eighth month began, and a man came to my apartment who was of tall build and amiable expression. He gazed at my heart and spoke to the unborn child within me, 'Peace be upon you, oh Beloved of Allah, oh mighty prophet of the Almighty!' I asked him, 'Who might you be, oh noble lord?' I am Musa, the son of Imran, and I bring you the good news that you are to be the mother of the great prophet to whom will be revealed the holy book of the Quran.'

"At the beginning of the ninth month again a person entered my room whose undergarment was of pure wool. He gazed at my heart and spoke to my child, 'Peace be upon you, oh Messenger of Allah, as-salamu alayk, ya Rasulullah!' I asked this person, 'Who are you?' and he said, 'I am `Isa, the son of Maryam, the Messiah. Best of tidings to you, oh Amina, the time is near that you will give birth, so prepare yourself and make ready.'"

In that year when Amina became pregnant, the people endured great hardship from drought and famine, and there had been a great deal of tribal warfare. When Amina conceived, all these troubles suddenly ceased, the Almighty sent down from Heaven the blessing of rain, and their land was refreshed and food prices came down. Because of the relief they experienced in that year, the people took to calling it "the year of the solving of difficulties". So favorable was this year that all the women who were pregnant gave birth to a son.

When the Holy Prophet ﷺ was within his mother's womb for two months, Abdul-Muttalib spoke to his son Abdullah, "Oh my son, within this year you are to become the father of the Arabian prophet whose coming is foretold in all the holy scriptures and who is expected by all in this year of blessings. Both you and I have been shown the high rank and station of this blessed child in our dreams. Therefore, it is only right and proper that we make suitable preparations for the birth of this extraordinary child.

The best form of congratulation I can think of is this: now is the time of the date harvest, and there are no better dates than the ones that grow in Madinah. Hence, I see it fit that you repair to Madinah to gather the best dates you can find and bring them back to celebrate the birth of your son." So Abdul-Muttalib sent his son Abdullah to Madinah to fetch dates.

Abdullah set out on his journey, accomplished his errand and made to return. During the rest stop of the second night he passed away and was buried there. At this all the angels in Heaven became highly perturbed, and spoke to the Lord of the Worlds, "Oh, All-Powerful Lord! How is it that You have made him - who is the noblest of all Your creation and the Pride of the Worlds to whom all dwellers of Heaven and earth owe reverence and praise - how is it that You have chosen to make this superb being a weak and fatherless orphan before he has yet beheld the light of day? What secret significance is there to this?" Thus the angels mourned and wailed. The Almighty Lord Allah spoke to them, "A child has need of his father in this world for protection, training and education. My Beloved however has no need for anyone but Me to teach him all these things. I am his supreme protector, and through Me he is to learn all things he is needful of knowing. Other children will call to their fathers when they are in need of help; but My Beloved will call out only 'Oh my Lord,' when he needs assistance, he will ask support and succor from none but Me, Allah Almighty."

The Holy Prophet 🕮 himself points to this fact when he says:

Truly, Allah Almighty has taught me, and His was the most excellent teaching.

When Abdullah died, he left a flock of sheep and five camels, as well as an Abyssinian slave woman who was nursing a child at the time. Her name was Umm Ayman. When the Holy Prophet 🕮 came into the world, this woman, Umm Ayman, became his first wet-nurse. When he had grown up, he gave her freedom and even married her to his adopted son (another freedman) Zayd bin Harith, and she bore him `Usama.

There are differing opinions as to how long his mother carried the Holy Prophet 🕮. Some say it was six months, some say seven, or eight or nine months. Ibn Abbas says on this subject that it was nine months. It is also reported that his mother never experienced any of the discomforts of pregnancy, nor the pangs of childbirth that most women go through. The Prophet's 🕮 mother Amina says:

"The whole duration of my pregnancy I felt none of the weight or pressure that pregnant women often feel. I only realized that I was pregnant from the absence of my monthly courses.

"From my belly there always emerged a beautiful scent, and at night I would hear the voice of *dhikr and tasbih* (praise and invocation) coming from within. I heard angels' voices saying to me, "Oh Amina, you who are pregnant with the most excellent creature in all the universe, surely you are most favored of womankind!" In the sixth month of my pregnancy I saw in my dream a person who said to me, "When you have given birth, you must give the babe the name Muhammad and be sure to take the best care of this outstanding being.""

Ibn Abbas relates:

"The heavenly angels descended and surrounded the Prophet's ❀ mother Amina on all sides, so that she was placed in the middle and thus protected from the invidious gaze of the Jinn, and so no harm could befall her. Then one of the angels addressed her and spoke, 'Oh Amina, I bring you good news of the blessed boy you bear, for this son is meant to be the last and the seal of all prophets, and the prince of them all, and a leader of his people. Allah Almighty bears witness to this from his beginning up to the end.

When you have given birth to this blessed child, recite over him these words for his protection:

Bismillahi astar'ika rabbak, wa a'wwadhuka bil-wahid

(In the Name of Allah, I beseech Thy Lord for Thy protection and I place Thee in the keeping of the One.)

Min sharri kullu hasidin wa qa'imin wa qa'id

(From the evil of every invidious one, be he standing or seated.)

Wa kullu khalqin za'id (and whatever other creature)

wa 'an il-fasadi jahilin wa kullu khalafin fasid

(and from the mischief of the ignorant and every evil consequence) *min nafizhin au 'abithin wa kullu jinnin marid*

(from the meddler or disturber, and from every defiant Jinn)

ya'khudhu bil-murasidin bi-t-turuq-il-muwarid.

(who takes advantage of any easy way of access)

La yadurrahu wa la ya'tunahu fi yaqazhatin wa la manam wa la fi zha'ni wa la fi maqam

(that they may not approach with harm while he wakes or sleeps, in no circumstance or place)

Sajis-al-layali wa awakhar-al-ayyam Yad-allahi fauqa aydihim wa hijab-allahi fauqa 'adiyatihim.

(Allah's Hand is above theirs, and Allah's Shield over their misdeeds.)'"

This protective prayer is mentioned also by Muhammad bin Abdullah al Karim ibn Khalid al-Baghdadi, who reports that the Holy Prophet's 🕌 mother Amina said, "One night in a dream I heard a voice saying to me, 'Oh Amina, verily Amina, you are to be the mother of the most excellent of all beings and the prince of them all, the last and the seal of all the prophets of Allah. When you have born him, you are to name him Muhammad; and know that in the Torah his name is given as Ahmad. Attach this amulet to him..' Upon waking I found a page of silver at the head of my bedstead upon which was written: *Bismillahi astar'ika wa a'wwadhu bil-wahid....* etc."

As those versed in holy learning teach us: Any child that has this ta'wiz (amulet) placed upon him will be safe from interference and enmity of the Jinn, by the leave of Allah.

Abul-'Umar said: "Whoever carries upon his person this protective talisman of the Prophet, let him lie down to sleep wherever he wishes and fear not, for no harm can befall him then, for the sake of the blessed Prophet of Allah."

There is also dispute concerning the month the Holy Prophet 🕌 was born; most scholars agree that it was the month of Rabi' al-Awwal. There is also disagreement as to the exact day, but largely it is assumed to have been the twelfth night of the month, though there is dissent concerning even the time of day: some think it more correct to say he was born in daytime. Some, however say there is really no disagreement in this matter at all, but rather that both may be true, in that the hour of the noble and blessed birth of the Prophet Muhammad ﷺ may have been the early dawn, before the actual rising of the sun. Therefore, those claiming it was nighttime have justifiable point to argue, while those claiming it to have been day are also not wrong, depending on the point of view. At any rate, it seems certain to have taken place in the early hour of dawn.

There is dispute as well concerning which day of the week it was, but it seems most correct to say that it was a Monday. It was a Monday also when the Holy Prophet ﷺ set out on the Hijra (migration from Mecca to Madinah) and he entered Madinah on a Monday as well. The Sura al-Maida (The Table) was revealed on a Monday, he was blessed with the Mi'raj (the Ascension) on a Monday eve, and the victory of Mecca also took place on Monday, and finally, the Holy Prophet ﷺ exchanged this passing world for his eternal abode on a Monday also. Peace and Blessings be upon him and his blessed family and his noble companions, from now on until eternity, Amin.

The religious scholars ('Ulama) say that the decisive battle in the Year of the Elephant took place when nine days remained to the month of Muharram. Fifty days later was the twelfth of Rabi' al-Awwal, and it was a Monday. According to some authorities it was the twenty-first day of April, while others maintain it was the second day of that month that the Holy Prophet ﷺ was born to the world.

Because it was in the month of April that the Pride of Creation appeared in this world, the Lord Almighty blessed the water that rains from the sky during this month in a special way so that it is of particular benefit and usefulness to men, for the sake of His beloved prophet ﷺ. The sun stood at the end of the sign of Aries, and the moon in the sign of Libra, and all the planets stood in a place of exaltation at that hour. It was six hundred years

71

after 'Isa bin Maryam's ﷺ ascension to the heavens, two thousand years after the death of the Prophet Ibrahim ﷺ, and six thousand sixty-two years after Adam ﷺ was sent down to be the representative of Allah Almighty on earth.

People might ask why was the prophet ﷺ born during the month Rabi'-al-Awwal, rather than during Ramadan or one of the holy months; why was he born on a Monday rather than on the eve of Jum'a (the night of Thursday to Friday), or on Laylat-al-Qadr, or the fifteenth of Sha'ban, or any other holy night? Had the birth of Allah's Beloved ﷺ occurred on one of these blessed days or nights, ignorant people could easily have imagined that the Holy Prophet's ﷺ eminence and high spiritual station, his extraordinary gifts and special powers were due to his birthday falling on these dates.

However, quite the opposite is the case: any place or date is honored by its being associated with the Holy Prophet ﷺ. Muhammad ﷺ was born in the city of Mecca and spent most of his life there, being called to prophethood in his fortieth year; he then spent thirteen years in the city of his birth, preaching Islam to his people before he migrated to Madinah where he lived for another decade teaching his message.

Finally, he surrendered his noble soul and took up his station in the abode of permanence. His pure body was laid to rest in the soil of Madinah, not in Mecca, so that Madinah should be honored above other places by harboring his blessed remains in her soil. Perhaps it is that this place is especially distinguished by the Owner of the Throne on High, and He chose to honor this city by making it the burial site of His Beloved. May Allah grant us the visit to his fragrant tomb and make our way there easy, Amin.

The Year of the Elephant
(adapted from Abu Ishaq)

In the year that the Holy Prophet ﷺ was born, the following event took place. In Yemen there lived a Christian king, Abraha, who marched on Mecca with his elephants in order to destroy the Kaba. This came about in the following way: the Negus, the Christian Emperor of Abyssinia, was a friend and supporter of Abraha of Yemen and honored him in many ways. Abraha was very happy at this, and prepared a lavish feast for his subjects and made many sacrifices, gave food to the poor and the dervishes and had churches built in many cities of Yemen.

In the capital city of San'a he built the greatest church of all, in honor of the Negus. It was such a splendid and beautiful building that all who saw it were stricken with wonder and doubted that such a marvel could be the work of mere mortals. It took four years to complete, and the building was named al-Qullays. By the time it was finished it was already famed far and wide.

Abraha then sent the Negus of Abyssinia a letter, saying: "The Lord has forgiven the Emperor and pardoned Abraha for his failings; I have therefore built a cathedral in the name of the Negus the likes of which the world has never seen before." He included a drawing of this building with his letter and sent it to the Negus. The Negus received the letter and was very pleased, and praised Abraha for his good work. The fame of this church spread, and Christians from all over came to see it. Everyone was stunned, for they had never seen such a church. The Christians brought sacrificial animals, and gifts and donations came from neighboring lands.

73

Even the Byzantine Emperor heard of this marvelous building, and wishing to add a good deed to his name, he sent precious gifts for the decoration of the church: paints and gold and marble.

For Abraha he sent a Byzantine robe of honor; He also wrote a letter to the Negus in which he said: "There is a trustworthy subject living in the province of Yemen, and he has built a church in your name of such splendor as there is no other in the world. Let this church become a center of worship and pilgrimage for all Christians, and let Abraha be its caretaker and governor of the whole province of Yemen."

The Negus was extremely pleased when he received this letter, and he himself wrote to Abraha, congratulating him and expressing his pleasure through robes of honor and a crown for his head, as well as giving him his freedom and making him the future ruler upon the Yemeni throne. Abraha, full of joy, wrote back to the Negus, saying, "I have heard that the Arab tribes of Mecca have a building made of stone, and they call it the 'house of God'. They go there every year and perform the rites of pilgrimage and they pray there, and make their sacrificial offerings, and it is a great and busy center of worship, as it is of commerce.

"Now, the church I have built is ten, no, one hundred times better than that square building. I have a mind to order the people of Yemen to come to my church and perform all their worship and their sacrifices in it. I'm thinking also of ordering those Arab tribesmen to leave off their pilgrimage to that building at Mecca and come here instead, so that this building will be remembered by all the world as that of the Emperor, and his fame will last for all times to come."

When the Negus read these words, he was even more delighted and he ordered Abraha to tell all the people living in Yemen, whether they be Christians, Jews, or Arab tribesmen, to perform their worship in the new church from now on, and to conduct all their rites there.

Diverting the Pilgrimage to Yemen

Now, among the tribesmen of Arabs there were two brothers. The elder brother was named Muhammad Khuza'i, the younger brother Qays. They were both noble and esteemed among the Arabs. For some reason or other they traveled to the province of Hijaz. With kith and kin they entered the country of Yemen where Abraha received them with honors in a most friendly manner, and informed them of his wish to divert the annual pilgrimage from the sanctuary of Mecca to the grand cathedral at San'a.

He called Muhammad Khuza'i to him and showed him great favor, clothed him in a robe of honor and gave him a crown, declaring him king over Mecca and the Hijaz. With that he sent him to Mecca to tell the Arabs to make their Hajj to Abraha's great church in Yemen from now on, and to leave off worship of the Kaba. His church, he said, was much better than their house of worship, for they had filled it up with idols, thereby defiling it, while his church was unspoiled. In all it was a much more suitable place for making the pilgrimage to. "Go, and deliver this message to the Arabs," he said.

Muhammad Khuza'i and his brother and clan promptly set out for Mecca. Abdul-Muttalib was the chief of the tribes of Quraysh and Kinana at Mecca. When Muhammad arrived at Mecca, he went in to the Bani Kinana, and began telling them about his claim to be their chief. This proposal offended them. Now there was one person among the tribe of Hudhayl, by name 'Urwa bin Hayyad who was a very skilled marksman. Him they sent to meet with Muhammad Khuza'i. 'Urwa struck him down with an arrow, and Qays, his brother fled back to Yemen, and informed Abraha of what had happened. Abraha, enraged, said, "No need to send anyone there, I will go there myself with an army, and destroy the place, and whomever I find of the Bani Kinana, I will slay them all. Whether they like it or not, I will force them to come worship at my church!" So Abraha set about to array his troops.

Meanwhile, the Bani Kinana had sent one of their men to Yemen to have a look at that marvelous church. He arrived and stood gazing at the building from outside, but not going in. They could tell he was not a Christian, so they asked him, "Who are you and where are you from?" He told them, "I am a tribesman, and I have heard the news of a great church that was built here in Yemen, so I have come to see it for myself, so that I might bring the Arab tribes here for the pilgrimage." Abraha was informed of this, and he said, "Let the man inside the church and show him everything, don't prevent him from looking around."

So they took the Bedouin into the church, and here he saw things he had never seen before in all his life, such exquisite paintings set with precious gems, gilded crosses and crucifixes embellished with rubies, garnets and pearls, suspended from golden chains, sumptuously decorated and of priceless, inestimable wealth. The sight of this glory made him speechless, he stood still for a long while and at last began to weep. He then turned to the guardians of the church and said, "Please permit me to stay in this church overnight, I wish to spend the night therein, all by himself." Towards the morning he felt a need and emptied his bowels, and smeared the filth all along the altar and the pulpit of the church. Then he asked the doorkeepers to let him out, and he left and was quickly gone.

When the people assembled in the morning to pray, they saw what had happened in their church, and they sent word to Abraha, their king. "This Arab who stayed in the church last night, he did this, and he was sent by those Arabs in Mecca to do it." Abraha flew into a rage and swore a holy oath that he would not return to Yemen before he had not totally destroyed the holy house of the Arabs, and defiled it with filth.

Now, the Negus had an elephant whose name was Mahmud. It was battle-proven, and when placed amidst the troops it would never step on any of the soldiers. It was always victorious, and there was no greater and more sweet-natured elephant in all of Abyssinia than he. The other elephants feared him and weakened before him, and followed his lead. Wherever Mahmud the elephant turned to go, there all the other elephants would direct their course. Abraha possessed thirteen Abyssinian elephants that he had brought to Yemen. Abraha now wrote a letter to the Negus, explaining to him what the Arab had done to the church, and he asked the Negus to send him the elephant Mahmud. Abraha lined up the elephants, assembled his fighters and set out for Mecca with the intention of destroying the Kaba.

Abraha marched towards Mecca and when he entered the region of Hijaz, he was confronted by Dhu Nafr a very valiant fighter who had seen many battles. He was a native of the region of Hamir in the Kingdom of Yemen and he was a close friend of Abdul-Muttalib. He met Abraha's forces with an army of twelve thousand men and they engaged in battle. This time Abraha won the battle, and Dhu Nafr was taken prisoner. Abraha wanted to have him killed, but Dhu Nafr pleaded for his life. He said, "What good is it to you if you spill the cupful of blood coursing in my veins? As you know, my name is well-known among the Arabs – it is better if you spare me and keep me as your prisoner, I may yet be of use to you and render you valuable service." So Abraha spared him and set a watch over his prisoner of war, then he marched on towards Mecca.

Near to the city he came to a camp of tent dwellers. There was a man of the Bani Khath'am, Nufayl bin Habib. The tribe of Khath'am was divided into two groups, one of them Shahran and the other Nahis, and they were a tribe of 50,000 households. Their leader was Nufayl, and he led an army of 1,000 men against Abraha. Abraha won the upper hand and took Nufayl prisoner. He wanted to put him to death, but Nufayl pleaded with him and said, "Oh Abraha, as you know I am the leader of 50,000 households. If you spare my life, these 50,000 homes will be your faithful servants. The ways through this desert are difficult; you need a guide through this terrain. If you spare me, I will guide you to Mecca and on to the Kaba." Abraha saw that he had a point, and spared his life.

The heads of the tribes, hearing of the fate of both Dhu Nafr and Nufayl, grew afraid and nobody else dared stand in Abraha's way. Thus he advanced as far as the area of Ta'if. The leading tribe there was the Bani Thaqif, and their leader was Mas'ud bin Mu'attib. They welcomed Abraha with gifts and offerings, paying homage to him and submitting to his superiority. Abraha also presented them with gifts and asked for a guide to lead him to Mecca. They sent with him a man from the Bani Thaqif called Abu Righal and he went ahead of them, showing them the way to Mecca. Thus they arrived before the city and set up their camp at a place known as Mughammas. There Abu Righal died, and to this day his grave can be seen at Mughammas. It is a custom among all the Arabs to throw stones at his grave every time they pass by, so that there is a huge pile of stones over it.

The Wisdom of Abdul-Muttalib

When Abraha and his army were seen to be approaching Mecca, all the townspeople gathered round Abdul-Muttalib, Muhammad's ❀ grandfather. They said, "What shall we do? We cannot fight against Abraha; what shall we do?" Abdul-Muttalib answered them, "There is only one thing to be done: everyone betake himself and his sons and daughters into the hills surrounding Mecca and hide them there. This Kaba here is Allah's house: we will leave it in His care, for He is mightier than we are. Either He will let the enemies take and destroy it, or He will keep it from them, and defend it from their forces. It is in His hands, and He does as He pleases." So spoke Abdul-Muttalib.

While they were yet engrossed in their deliberations, Abraha selected an advance party of 5,000 men and sent them towards Mecca. He appointed al-Aswad bin Mafsud as their chief and Abraha ordered him to plunder and pillage the outskirts of Mecca, and to take what ever he pleased of men and animals, but on no account should he enter the city itself.

So, al-Aswad bin Mafsud took his men to the environs of the town. They rounded up whatever they found of horses, sheep, camels and cattle and took the shepherds hostage as well. Among the animals they drove off were 200 camels belonging to Abdul-Muttalib. They brought the captive shepherds before Abraha who asked them, "What preparations have the people of Mecca made? Are they intending to fight or are they going to ask for quarter?" The shepherds replied, "The people of Mecca are not intending to fight at all. They are giving up the city to the king, for this is what Abdul-Muttalib advised them to do."

Present among the Arab tribesmen in Abraha's army there was a man from among the nobles of Yemen, named Hunata. To him Abraha turned and said, "You go to the people of Mecca and tell them that I take no pleasure in spilling the blood of the Meccans. All I am interested in is destroying the Kaba, which is here. This is what I have come for, and to this end I have sworn a binding oath. Let them have no fear; they are safe. Bring to me their leader so that I might see what sort of person he is."

Hunata went then and informed Abdul-Muttalib of what Abraha wanted, and he brought him before the king. It was evening before the soldiery arrived, and Abdul-Muttalib spent that night together with the two prisoners. One of them, Dhu Nafr was Abdul-Muttalib's good friend. Abdul-Muttalib said to him, "Is there no way you can use your influence?" He answered, "I have no power over anything, I am a prisoner, and every day I must fear for my life. But there is one person I know although I have not told Abraha about this, but I am acquainted with one of the servants here, and he is a friend of mine, a good man, by name Unays. I will send to him and commend your case to him strongly, so that he will inform the king of your standing with the Arabs, and that he may treat you accordingly."

For Abdul-Muttalib was a very highly respected man, and none among the Arabs enjoyed greater regard than he; he was known to stand by his word, and he was a model of generosity. Every time he slaughtered a camel, he would distribute its meat among men, break up the bones and throw them to the dogs, and the offal he would take to the mountains where the birds and the wild beasts could feed on them. He therefore was called, 'he who feeds men and wild beasts'. Dhu Nafr told Unays about Abdul-Muttalib and his high reputation, and sent him to Abraha, so that he might inform him. Hearing about this noble Arab, Abraha sent for him, and in the morning Abdul-Muttalib was brought before Abraha.

Abraha was seated upon his royal throne. Now Abdul-Muttalib was most impressive and dignified in his person, and perceiving this, Abraha found it unsuitable for Abdul-Muttalib to be seated beneath him. He also thought it imprudent for him to sit beside him on his throne, so he descended from his throne and sat with him upon the carpet. He greeted him with all tokens of respect and looked him over. His dignity and appearance pleased him very much. He asked his interpreter to translate for him, and he was much taken by Abdul-Muttalib's conversation. In his heart he conceived the intention not to destroy the Kaba for the sake of Abdul-Muttalib, and not to raze the city.

He let the interpreter ask Abdul-Muttalib what favor he would ask of him, promising him to fulfill whatever it was. Abdul-Muttalib answered, "Yesterday they plundered and took away my two hundred camels; these I want returned to me." Abraha felt sad hearing these words from Abdul-Muttalib, and said to himself, "What a pity! This person apparently has not the wits to match his looks; his arrangements are not wise; here I am come with a mighty army to destroy that on which depends the whole fame and pride of Mecca. He could have asked for me to spare it, I would have granted it him for his sake; instead he asks me only for his 200 camels! If I went away and left the Kaba intact, he would get back his two hundred camels in any case!" This he told the interpreter to tell Abdul-Muttalib. To this Abdul-Muttalib answered, "This house does not belong to me. It has an owner, and He knows very well how to guard and defend it. He has no need of my protection, if He likes He will save it, if He likes He will let it be destroyed. That is none of my concern. All I want are my camels, they are my rightful property, let the king return them to me." So Abraha had the camels returned to him, and he led them back towards Mecca.

He said to the people of Mecca, "Go, go out and hide in the hills! Leave the city, and leave the (holy) house, leave it in the hands of Him who owns it!" So all the men took their families and went out into the hills. Abdul-Muttalib also took his sons and went to the hills. The next morning Abraha set out and approached the town. At Mina he stopped and enquired what the inhabitants of the city were up to. He was told that they had all left town, and no one was left. Then Abraha ordered the elephant Mahmud and the other elephants to march into the town and to tear down the Kaba, the houses of Mecca and to devastate the whole city without harming a single soul. Then they should retreat and go back to where they came from.

Divine Support Saves Mecca

They led the elephant Mahmud towards the city, but when it was about to set foot across the city limit, it stopped, and nothing they did could move it. They beat it about the head, stuck hooks into its belly; no force could sway him. Seeing the elephant Mahmud stopped, all the other elephants stopped dead in their tracks as well.

Then Allah ordered the Ababil birds to fly against them. They came down by the sea. Each one of the birds carried three little bits of mud or stone, like peas or lentils, one in its beak and one in each claw. They came flying towards Mecca and hovered over the army. By the leave of Allah, a wind rose up from Hell and turned those bits of mud into stone, as clay is baked. While these stones were red-hot and glowing, they pelted the army of Abraha. No sooner they fell upon a man that they burnt their way into his body, so that he swelled up and burst. Some were hit and died on the spot; others withdrew and fled in panic and disarray. Some made it back all the way to their country, there to die.

Only the ones who were not touched by these stones survived. Abraha was hit on his head by a stone, and his whole body swelled, and he suffered greatly the whole journey back to Yemen where he died, in terrible agony. As for the elephants, they too fled and Allah had mercy on them and spared them, leading them into safety. Abdul-Muttalib returned to Mecca and sent word to the Meccans to come back to their city, all danger now being over. On account of these events Abdul-Muttalib's reputation grew even more, and they now knew for sure that the Kaba was the house of the Lord, and that Allah destroyed any who dared to go against it.

This event is mentioned in the Holy Quran in these words:

Bismillahir-Rahmanir-Rahim. Hast thou not seen how thy Lord did with the Men of the Elephant? Did He not make their guile to go astray? And he loosed upon them birds in flights, hurling against them stones of baked clay and He made them like green blades devoured. (The Elephant)

The Blessed Birth

When the term was fulfilled and the moment of delivery approached, the holy house, the Kaba at Mecca all at once was seen to split in two. The Quraysh were appalled by this event, and everybody searched for an explanation. The Bani Hashim said, "This is on account of Abdullah, the son of Abdul-Muttalib's death that this has happened", while the Bani Zuhayr said, "This holy house has split asunder because the father of Amina, Wahb ibn Abdu Manaf has died, and he was one of the bravest men of Quraysh."

While they were thus engaged in finding explanations for this inexplicable happening, they heard a voice coming from inside the Kaba that said, "Oh men of Quraysh! This holy house has not come apart on account of the death of any, but rather because the time of birth has drawn nigh for the Light of this world, the Glory of the world to come, the shining Lamp of Paradise, Muhammad bin Abdullah 🌸 to emerge from his mother's womb. He is to be a great prophet, he will cleanse this holy house of the abominations and idols that are polluting my precincts, and he will make me pure and pristine once more with the light of true faith; I will become the Qibla of his entire nation and the annual pilgrimage will be held on my grounds. Know that it is in honor of his long desired advent that this edifice has cracked and split."

The night that Muhammad 🌸 was born, Allah Almighty, Exalted be He, commanded the angels to open wide all the gates of Heaven and of Paradise; on that day the sun shone with more brilliance, and greater was its light than on other days, and the whole world was gladdened.

Abdullah bin Salam reports: On the night the prophet 🕸 was born, I was sitting together with a learned Jew. He raised his face to Heaven and spoke to me, "Ya Ibn Salam! This very night at Mecca the Arabian prophet, Muhammad ibn Abdullah 🕸 is to be born who will illuminate the world." I said to him, "What do these words of yours mean, how do you know such a thing?" He answered me, "I have been watching the skies, and I see now such a light as has not been seen since the world began. That is how I come to know of this event."

I then entered a dark room, and I saw seventy candles burning in it so that it was brilliantly lit. I knew then that unusual things were happening. When I came to Mecca, I asked about that night, and I found that the Jewish scholar had told me the truth; it had indeed been the night in which the Prophet Muhammad 🕸 came into this world.

The Prophet's 🕸 blessed mother, Amina, relates: "At the time I was ready to give birth there was no one with me, neither man nor woman attended me (for everyone, including Abdul-Muttalib, had gone to make Tawaf of the Kaba.) I was all alone in the house. Suddenly there was a terrifying noise and I felt great fear. Then a white bird alighted upon my breast and my fear left me, I became calm and no trace of pain or anxiety remained. Next I was handed a cup of sweet white sherbet, and when I drank of it, my heart filled with peace and joy and light. After this, I beheld a number of tall women approaching me, tall and slender as cypress trees, and of astounding beauty. I took them to be the daughters of Abdu Manaf. They came and sat around me in a circle, and I was mostly surprised and wondered how they had come to know of my condition and who had informed them.

While I was yet pondering this question in my heart, one of the ladies spoke and said, 'I am Hawa, the wife of the Prophet Adam,' and another one of them said, 'I am Sarah, the wife of the Prophet Ibrahim.' Yet another said, 'I am Asiya, the wife of Fir'aun of Egypt'. And another said, 'I am Maryam, the daughter of 'Imran, the mother of 'Isa.' The others were introduced as the Huris of Paradise, all of whom had come to usher the Holy Prophet 🕸 into his earthly life and to welcome him with due veneration.

All the while the noises I had been hearing became stronger and louder and more fearful. Suddenly I perceived a white curtain being drawn from the skies down to the earth, so that I was veiled from the eyes of the Jinn. Then there was a flock of birds with beaks of green emerald and ruby red wings. These birds flew down and fluttered about me so closely that I could feel the beating of their wings upon my skin. They flew round and round me as if in Tawaf (circumambulation). The Lord Almighty then removed the veil from my eyes so that I beheld the whole world from east to west. Three flags I saw them bring down from Heaven: one they planted in the ground in the east, one in the west and one right atop the Kaba. In the heavens that were open to my eyes I beheld men bearing bejeweled vessels of gold, and they assisted at the birth of the blessed child, and I suffered neither pain nor trouble.

And when I looked again, I saw that the child was born circumcised, and that his umbilical cord was cut and he was wrapped in a piece of white silk. He touched the ground with his blessed head, lifted the forefinger of his right hand, and made humble supplication to Allah Almighty. I bent down to hear what he was saying, and these were the words I heard:

Ash-hadu an la ilaha ill'Allah wa inni Rasulullah; Allahu Akbar kabiran, wal-hamdu-lillahi kathiran, wa subhanallahi bukratan wa asilan. Allahumma, ummatiy, ummatiy...

There is a narration from Safiya, the daughter of Abdul-Muttalib:

"I was present the night the Prophet Muhammad # was born. At the very moment of birth I saw a great light appear. During the night, I beheld six signs. The first was that the instant the holy child was born. He bent down his head and performed a prostration. The second, that he lifted up his blessed head and spoke clearly and distinctly these words: La ilaha illAllah, inni Rasulullah. The third, that a great light was manifested. The fourth, that when I wished to wash the child, I heard a voice speaking to me that said: 'Oh Safiya, do not trouble yourself, we have already washed and cleansed him.' The fifth sign was that he was born already circumcised, and his umbilical cord was cut. The sixth sign was when I looked for something with which to swaddle the child, I noticed upon his back a certain mark. Looking at it closely, I was able to read the words: 'La ilaha illAllah, Muhammad Rasulullah."

Safiya also said, "When he prostrated himself, he spoke some words in secret. I bent my ear to his blessed lips to hear what he was saying, and I heard him say: '*Ummatiy, ummatiy* (my nation, my nation).'"

Now let us pause briefly to consider this point: this noble prophet of unequaled rank and highest station prayed to his Lord from the very moment he was born, entreating Him for our sake, for the sake of his nation, while we, who stand in dire need of his prayer and intercession in this world and the next are enveloped in heedlessness. We forsake the example of his radiant and honored Sunna (example) and are negligent in our observance of the Shari'a that we have the privilege of knowing. Day and night we are careless in the recital of Salawat (praises and prayers on the Holy Prophet ❀), being engulfed in our own sloth. How can we be worthy of such lofty intercession?

If we paused to consider this for a moment and reflected on the implications, we would realize that we are totally overcome by our heedlessness, whereas we should busy ourselves constantly with the application of the holy ways of the law, and try to make all our actions accord with the guidance it contains, and to tirelessly recite praises and prayers on the Holy Prophet ❀. May Allah–Exalted be He–effect betterment for us all and improve our state, and grant us success and favor, for the sake of the prince among all the Divine Messengers. Amin.

To continue our narration: Amina the mother of the Holy Prophet ❀ recounts: "I then beheld a white cloud in the sky moving towards me, and from it came as if the sounds of horses. This cloud descended and enveloped the little child Muhammad ❀ and carried him away out of my sight. I heard a voice calling: 'We are taking Muhammad ❀, to show him the whole world. We shall encircle it and dive into the depths of the oceans, so that all that lives in and under the earth may know of the advent of this noble being and shall have seen his face and learned of his arrival. Hereafter the world shall be filled with the light of faith; of unbelief and rebellion against the Lord Almighty nothing will remain.' Thus I heard the voices speak to me."

"After only a brief moment, that cloud alighted anew, and I saw my son Muhammad 🏵 again, wrapped now in a piece of green silk, dripping with milk. His face was radiant as the moon on her fourteenth night, and he exuded a fragrance sweeter than that of yellow musk. I then beheld three persons standing aside; one of them held in his hand a jug of silver, another held a bowl of green emerald, and the third held a piece of folded white silk. The latter unfolded this bit of silk and took from its folds a ring so bright it dazzled the eyes of the beholder.

"The first took the baby Muhammad 🏵 and washed him seven times from the silver jug; then the next person took a ring from the folds of silken cloth and impressed its bezel in a place between the baby's shoulders. After that he wrapped it up again in the bit of silk. He then took the baby Muhammad 🏵 from me and held him under his wing for a whole hour, all the while whispering many secrets into his ears. At last he kissed him upon both his eyes and said, 'Tuba laka, ya Muhammad 🏵, blissful tidings to you, oh Muhammad 🏵, in all Allah's creation, you are the most awesome and venerable of all that serve Him Almighty. Triumph and victory has been given to your companions and your nation. It is you who holds the keys to the castle of bliss.'"

It is related by Ibn Abbas: The night the Holy Prophet 🏵 was born, all the idols in the Kaba fell from their places and broke to pieces. At that time a voice was heard calling out from the unseen, and it said: "Woe and perdition on Quraysh, for the glorious and trusted prophet 🏵 has come in truth, embellished with adornments from the loftiest gardens of Paradise. Lat and Uzza and all other idols are now finished and done for, Iblis himself is imprisoned."

The Kaba itself was inwardly hung with golden lamps from Paradise, and all creatures of the heavens and the earth, the youths and the maidens from

Paradise, all created beings other than mankind rejoiced and gave each other the glad tidings. "Oh Muhammad," they wished, "may Allah make you happy and always pleased, for there is no creature born with greater honor than you, and none that is more excellent. Never have the angels celebrated the birth of any created being as they now celebrate your birth into this world!" Between Heaven and earth there were raised pillars of support, and all were made of precious stone, and not one of them was alike unto another.

It is reported by Ka'b-al-Akhbar: One of the miracles of that night was a fish that lived in the sea, and its name was Zalmusa. This fish had seventy heads and seventy tails, and a single scale on his back could have held seventy mountains and plains, the smallest of which would have been the size of Jabil Qubais (a hill in Mecca). Now you can picture the size of that tremendous fish! The night the Holy Prophet ❁ was born, by the Will of Allah Almighty this fish was so convulsed with mighty emotion that he caused the seven seas to heave from enthusiasm, so that all the sea creatures were instantly informed of the arrival of the Holy Prophet ❁ in the world of men.

The Holy Prophet's ❁ illustrious grandfather was at the Kaba when Amina gave birth, and she sent him word of the glad event, inviting him to come and see her newborn son. Abdul-Muttalib relates: "I was at the time within the building of the Kaba. There I witnessed how the walls of the building themselves began to shake and tremble with joy, calling out to each other: 'The Lord Almighty has bestowed great honor on us that we might see the coming of the prophet who will cleanse us of the filth of these idols!' I was amazed at hearing this, and I understood then that you must have given birth, and that these words heralded the importance of the child you had born."

Amina reports: Later, when he looked upon my son Muhammad ❁, he said, "Praise be to the All-Powerful Lord that He has granted me such an auspicious grandchild!" and he praised him with a great many praises, while from the child's blessed body such a beautiful scent issued forth that it filled the whole town of Mecca as if with the fragrance of musk and amber.

Voices of praise and rejoicing were heard throughout the town, even to the house of Abu Lahab, the Prophet's ﷺ uncle. While he lay sleeping, voices from the unseen filled his room and the smell of musk and amber pervaded the air. From this he awoke, greatly perplexed. A slave girl, Thauba, was sleeping by his side. To her he turned to ask what she made of these strange sounds and voices. Thauba answered, "Good news and tidings of joy to you, oh Abu Lahab! Your brother Abdullah's wife Amina has born a son. Muhammad ﷺ. From his blessed body issues this perfumed cloud and this wonderful fragrance. The sounds you hear are the voices of those who inhabit the regions between Heaven and earth, heralding the birth of this miraculous child."

Abu Lahab was pleased at the good news she gave him and he said to her, "Ya Thauba, for that you have given me joyful tidings, I shall give you your freedom. Go to the house of the mother of Muhammad ﷺ and offer your services as a wet-nurse, for you too, are nursing a child, named Masruj." So Thauba went and became the wet-nurse for Muhammad ﷺ. For seven days his mother Amina gave him milk, after that Thauba came and nursed him until he was given to Halima as-Sa'adia.

It is related that some people saw Abu Lahab in their dreams after he had died. When they asked him how he fared in the afterlife he replied, "Woe is me! Was I not the uncle of a great and distinguished prophet? Would that I had believed in him and become one of the blissful dwellers of Paradise gardens! Ah, but I chose to be his greatest enemy, persisting in error and disbelief, so that I am one of the damned of Hell.

However, there are two grants of mercy that I receive over and above all the other inmates of the Fire: from the night linking Sunday to Monday up to the following night, my punishment is alleviated; and when I place my two fingers in my mouth on that day, a cool drink of water issues forth from between my index and middle fingers that soothes my torment."

That blessed night all idols in the entire world fell from their pedestals and shattered to bits, and Shaytan's throne was overturned so that it hung downwards and he fell off it. The angels then caught hold of him and imprisoned him for forty days in the forty seas. Finally, he contrived his escape, and he came up to the Mount Abu Qubais and let out a mighty scream. Hearing him yell, all the devils and Ifrit came flying and gathered round, asking him, "What is it with you that you scream so loud?" He answered them, "Such a terrible destroyer has been sent down upon you as you have never known or seen before. What is more, against this plague there is no remedy."

The devils were all shocked, and asked, "Who is it?" Shaytan replied, "It is the Prophet Muhammad 🌸, mighty and glorious, the son of Abdullah, son of Abdul-Muttalib who is born in Mecca tonight. He has the power to demolish all idols and defeat all unbelief in the whole wide world. He will bring the Light of Islam and spread the faith from east to west; no place will remain on earth where the call of Unity has not been heard, and the unbelievers will be smitten and abased. No trick and no deception will prevail against his influence. The scripture he will bring will watch over his nation, and his religion and law will remain valid and in place until the Day of Judgment, his followers being assured of the Lord's forgiveness and grace." So he said and let out another terrible scream.

In that blessed night the fires of the fire worshippers that had been continuously burning for a thousand years went out, and not a trace remained of heat or fire—their hearths became cold as ice, colder than the fiercest winter's cold.

In the lands of Persia there flows a great stream, the Euphrates. In the region of Kasane there lies a place called Sawa by the banks of this great river, and formerly there lived in this town a large number of Christians and Jews. They had built their churches and monasteries there and were recognized and highly esteemed. Now the night the Holy Prophet 🌸 was born in Mecca, the whole river at Sawa suddenly ran dry, and the ground was cracked and arid when they awoke in the morning, as if there had never been a trace of water in this spot. Such a fierce heat arose in place of the water as if a fire had been burning there since uncounted days. Dust rose around the feet of the people as they walked about.

Now the king of the region was termed Khosroes, and the king in those days was Kaykubad Nushurevan. In that night, fourteen of his twenty-two palaces and domed mansions crumbled and fell, and there remained only eight standing. That night also his throne tumbled and fell, and the king himself had a terrifying dream. In the morning when he woke, he called for all his dream interpreters and diviners, and when they were assembled at his court, he asked them to tell him about the dream he had seen that night. He said to them, "I will not tell you what I dreamt, you will tell it to me. If you are not able to do this, what good is your interpretation to me? I will dismiss you all, if you fail me."

They answered, "Oh King, not one of us can know about your dream, but there lives a man called Satih, no one but he can inform you of it." This Satih lived in the land of Bahrain, and his name was really Rabi' bin Rabi'a. He was generally called Satih, which means 'plain, surface', because he could only lie flat on his back, unable to even sit up, for he had not a bone in his body, excepting his skull. The reason for this was that he was born of two women, and the bones of man are created from the seed of the male.

This Satih lived in Bahrain, and he had been in the world for a very long time already, some said for thirty generations, and one generation consists of thirty years. Thus Satih knew and had seen a great many things and was known to be a wise man and a seer. He had read all the heavenly revealed scriptures, and was well versed in the art of divination and fortune telling. Once a year he would be carried out in grand procession upon a golden tray, and all the learned would gather round him and listen to his predictions for the coming year. Of these they took note and recorded them with care.

Now, King Nushurevan was one of the very chosen servants, for he was the just king whom the Holy Prophet 🏵 referred to when he said, "I came to this world in the time of one very just king." Nushurevan decided to send an envoy to Bahrain to consult with this man Satih, and he chose as his messenger one Abdul-Massih. This man set out for Bahrain, and by the Almighty's providence he arrived just on the day that Satih was carried out on the golden tray to do his predictions. When he met with him, he told Satih about the events in his country: about the fires of the fire-worshippers being extinguished and the waters by Sawa drying up; about the toppling and the ruin of the king's palaces and domed mansions, and lastly about the dream the king had seen which he would tell to no one, but expected them to interpret for him.

To this Satih said, "The King Nushurevan has seen a frightful dream. In his dream he saw the approach of an army, riders of Arabian steeds and Hijin camels, filling the whole city of Mada'in. These riders then led all the camels they found out of the city."

"And this is the meaning of these signs: in the town of Mecca al-Mukarrama the unlettered Prophet Muhammad ❈ is born. He is descended from the line of Ibrahim Khalilullah, and he is to become the Seal of Prophets. In him all the signs and portents mentioned in the previous holy books, the Torah, the Injil and the Zabur will become manifest and revealed. From this day on all divinations and predictions will become invalid and unreal, for from now on the Jinn and Ifrit are prevented from eavesdropping on the heavenly council as they have been doing so far, spying out the secrets of the future, and unveiling them partially to the soothsayers of mankind."

(Still, certain ones among them would yet attempt to fly up and steal some secret knowledge, but the angels will chase them away with heavenly missiles called 'shihab', which are shooting stars, as we see up to this very day.)

"So," Satih continued, "the Lord of Knowledge has been manifested, and the meaning of King Nushurevan's dream is this: the Arabian horses and Hijin camels signify his companions, the companions of the prophet ❈ whom the Almighty is about to send. The camels being led out of the city means that the companions of this prophet ﷺ will come and take the city and expel them from within it."

Next Satih explained to him, "The meaning of the eight domed mansions that did not crumble, is this: King Nushurevan will be succeeded by eight kings, then his kingdom will be conquered by the armies of Islam. The dying down of the fires of the fire worshippers and the drying up of the waters around Sawa signifies that the light which is with unbelievers will be taken from them and their fount will run dry. The prophet who is to come will fill the whole world with his light and become a messenger to all peoples, and these dreams and happenings are signs of his advent."

When he had spoken these words, the seer Satih paused for a while and wept bitterly. He then said, "There remains only very little time for Satih to live, he will not live to see the coming of this light of a new age; so Satih weeps from longing, unfulfilled."

The king's emissary Abdul-Massih heard these words and took note of them; then he returned to his king, Nushurevan, and told him of what he had heard and seen.

There were a great many signs announcing the birth of the Holy Prophet Muhammad ﷺ. As the light of Muhammad ﷺ was passed from father to son from the time of Sayyiduna Adam ﷺ, each time a woman conceived a prophet to be, this light would appear on her forehead and linger there until the child was born. So also the mother of the Prophet Muhammad ﷺ experienced many strange and wonderful things during her pregnancy. She received revelations of the divine and angelic messages that would fill many books, and yet only a fraction would have been told, for these wonders are limitless.

The night of the Prophet's ﷺ birth was such a great and holy night that for all those who were wakeful during that night it was as if they had been awake for the Night of Power (Laylat al-Qadr).

Therefore it is recommended to make special celebrations and to light the lights on the minarets. All the lands of Islam are to rejoice and engage in festivities, for every Muslim should be glad to remember the birth of the Prince of Prophets ﷺ with love and devotion. The blessed companions of the prophet ﷺ made special celebrations and honors for the Prophet's ﷺ children. The learned scholars have thought it in order to make special arrangements for the descendants of the prophet ﷺ, by holding banquets in their honor, for the benefit of the poor and indigent, for widows, orphans and students (which is commendable on any other day as well.) For instance, a banquet could be held, a sermon read, Quran recited, a Mawlid held and the assembly treated to sweets or sherbet. All this is considered very meritorious, and our Lord rewards all our good deeds.

More Events Surrounding the Noble Birth of the Prophet ﷺ

In the kingdom of the West, al-Maghrib there lived a king. In that country, kings were called Emir, and as all Arabs of that age, this king, too, worshipped idols. It so happened that this Emir had a daughter who was born with a disturbing handicap, so that the king was ashamed to let this child be seen in public. He had her locked away and confined to underground chambers of the palace, where she was looked after by slave girls and never seen outside the palace. At night she would scream and rave and make such terrible sounds that the windows were always kept tightly shut, so nobody would hear this dreadful noise.

Nevertheless, the Emir was very sad and dispirited on account of his daughter's misery, and he tried with all his might and means to find help for her. He sacrificed to the idols, he fasted and prayed the whole night through, he lit candles in the temples, he vowed many a solemn vow, gave alms to the poor; he implored the idols to do something to heal his daughter and free her from this piteous condition—but what could the idols do?

One evening he retired with his wife to their apartments and they stepped out on their roof to look at the stars. Now this king had a small statue of an idol that he always carried around with him. As they were gazing at the night sky, it was as if the skies suddenly were rent asunder and a light shone forth, illumining all the world. They saw the trees and flowers of their garden even the stones bow down and prostrate themselves. *"La ilaha ill'Allah, Muhammad-ur-Rasulullah"*, everything was saying, and the king and queen witnessed it. They looked at one another and said, "Did you hear and see what I have heard and saw?" When they assured each other that they had both witnessed these strange things, the queen said, "This is exceedingly wondrous, let us ask the idol what this means." They turned to look at it and they found it hanging upside down, its head to the ground and its feet up in the air, for it was at this very moment that the idols in the whole world were reversed in their places and smashed to bits.

Next they heard a voice issue from that figure: "Between Safa and Marwa a child is born, our unbelief is cast down and done for."

> *The truth has come, and falsehood has vanished away, surely falsehood is ever certain to vanish.*   (The Night Journey, 81)

This voice caused them great consternation, for never had the idol spoken before this time, after all it was nothing but a stone, and this they knew well. But only now did they realize that this was no object to be worshipped, and together they called out, "Oh speaker whom we hear speaking from this dry stone, who is it?" Again the voice was heard, and it said, "It is Muhammad ✿, the Holy Prophet who has come to the world in the Last of Times; he is born this very night between the rocks of Safa and Marwa, at the holy house of the Lord, the Kaba, and it is for him that all eighteen thousand worlds were created, that the whole universe was called into being." The king then asked, "Why is this idol of mine standing on its head?" The voice explained that it was happening to all idols this night, for their time was over and the Truth had come and all falsehood was revoked.

The Emir then said to his spouse, "Oh wife, we must go out and find this prophet and accept his creed, so that he will pray for us and cure our unfortunate child." Before he had finished speaking, his wife turned around and said, "Oh, see here, this is our daughter!" The king turned to look, and there was his daughter standing behind him, a lovely young girl, without blame or blemish. The king was speechless with surprise, and when he could speak again, he said, "Oh my daughter! What is this? What has happened to you? Where have you left your chains, your ranting and raving, all the signs of your insanity? How is it you are no longer convulsed and tormented with pain, what has become of our hideous disease – how has it come about that you are entirely healed?"

The girl answered, "Oh my father, here I stand before you, just as I am and was meant to be. What happened to me is this: I had just fallen asleep when I beheld a person of radiant appearance enter my room. As soon as I espied him, I thought, 'Oh you who are so bright and beautiful, have you no healing power with which to treat my sorry condition?' This person then answered me and said, 'I will teach you a prayer; if you recite this, you will be healed.' 'What prayer is this prayer,' I asked, 'and who are you?' 'I am an angel,' he said, 'and I have just come from visiting a newborn child, together with all the other angels. The prayer I have come to teach you is this: Oh Allah, for the sake of Your Holy prophet who is born this night, make this affliction, this pain and plague go away from me! Then you must blow upon your hand, and wipe your whole body with your hand. Continue praying and wiping yourself until no more disease remains upon you.' Thereupon I awoke and looked about and saw that the whole room was filled with light; I remembered what the angel had said, so I did what he had told me. I prayed, then wiped my hands over my face and my whole body. My fetters fell off from me, my reason returned, I became whole and clean, and in this state I have come before you, oh my parents."

Her father, the king, heard her story and said, "We must quickly set out and find this miraculous prophet at once." So they each mounted a Hijin camel, taking only scanty provisions with them and set out, the three of them, telling no one of their destination. They didn't even know themselves where they were bound, as the distance between the Maghrib and Mecca is vast, but they were so impressed by the miracle they had experienced that this never crossed their minds, they just left their kingdom behind and set out for far away Arabia. When they had gone some way, all at once a heavy sleepiness came over them that left them no choice. While they slept, the angel Jibra'il ☙ came and took their camels' halters, and folded the earth up underneath them. Before noon of the next day they reached Mecca, whereas it is a camel journey of eighty and more days from the Maghrib to Mecca.

Arriving at Mecca, they began to ask whether any child had been born the night before. Yes, they were told, Amina the daughter of Wahb had given birth to her child the night before, and they were shown the way to her house. They came to the house and asked to see the newborn baby, but they were told that the child's grandfather had forbidden anyone to see the child, for it had many enemies. The unbelievers were still seeking to kill the child. The king and his family began to weep, and said, "We have left everything behind, our country, our lands, our kingdom, our palace—just to see this newborn child, and now you would deny us this favor! No, this we cannot accept, that we should go away without having seen him!" The mother finally relented and permitted them to come in and they spent an hour at her side. She uncovered her child's face and the light on it reached to the heavens. For one whole hour they regarded the child's unearthly beauty, kissed his hands and feet, until Amina said to them, "It is best that you leave now, for if his grandfather finds you here, he might be displeased that I have let in strangers." So they turned to leave and as they were leaving the house, the Emir put his hand on his breast and said, "Let me gaze on him once more, only one more time, and I will be gone."

At last they consented and let him in; he bent over the child, kissed his blessed feet, then let out one scream, before he fell senseless to the ground and expired.

For when he had perceived the first sign, his heart began to glow; then he saw the child once and longed to see him again. When he saw him the second time, his heart blazed with the fire of love and he surrendered his soul, which the angels carried off to Paradise without delay.

Muhammad bin Khatim reported:

"There once lived a man in Egypt who every year on the night of the Prophet's ☙ birthday used to arrange a great festivity, and invite the

97

poor and orphans and widows to his feast. There would be Quran readings, litanies of praise would be recited and Mawlids sung, and a banquet was prepared in honor of the Holy Prophet ❀.

"This pious man had a neighbor who was from *Ahl al-Kitab* (People of the Book). Once his wife asked him, 'I've been wondering what it means that our neighbor makes a great feast every year and invites all the destitute people he can find and treats them in such a magnificent way, what is the occasion?' Her husband answered, 'It is the night of the birth of their prophet which they always celebrate in gratitude and remembrance of the event.'

"That night this woman saw in her dream a person of very beautiful and light-filled aspect, he was awesome and his face radiant as the sun. He was surrounded by a great number of companions whose faces were like the morning star. All the shining people were headed for the house of the neighbor who always gave the feast. In her dream, the woman was irresistibly drawn to this beautiful appearance, and she asked one of the companions, 'Who is this person, I have never seen anyone so sweet and full of love?' The companion answered her, 'This noble being is the Pride of Creation, the Prince of all mankind, the Messenger of God, the Beloved of Allah, Muhammad ❀. All these companions have come to pay their respects and to show him honor.'

"The woman thought to herself, 'I will ask this companion whether I can wait for him, whether I can approach him when he comes out and ask him my question.' She asked the companion if she could address the Prophet ❀ when he came out, and ask him her question. He replied, 'No need to wait outside, just go on in. There is room enough, no one is going to prevent you from reaching his blessed presence. You may ask whatever you need to know, he will not turn you away, nor will he leave your questions unanswered.'

"The woman then went inside and beheld the blessed presence ❀, surrounded by his companions, may Allah be well pleased with them all. She then approached the Holy Prophet ❀ and said, 'Ya Muhammad!' The Holy Prophet ❀ turned towards her and answered, "*Labbayk*, I am here with you." She then said, 'How can it be that a great, much-honored personality such as you, the Prophet of Allah Almighty, deigns to speak to a plain and undistinguished person such as me, answering me with 'Labbayk', particularly as I am not even of your religion?'

"The Holy Prophet 🕸 then said to her, 'No sooner had I seen your face that I knew that the Lord has singled you out for the guidance of Islam. He has honored you with the light of Islam, therefore I answered you with Labbayk.' Again the woman said, 'You are a noble prophet and surely you hold high and lofty stations in the Divine Presence; what can be the wisdom and secret of your appearance in a place and neighborhood such as ours?'

"Again the Holy Prophet 🕸 spoke to her, 'Out of love for us the owner of this house has invited this gathering of people of good will and sound heart, from among the needy and indigent, as from among the readers and reciters of the Holy Quran. He has expended large sums of money in order to feed them all lavishly. He has shown largesse and generosity, therefore, by the leave of Allah Almighty, I too have come to visit him and have so entered his house. In recognition of my coming to this man's house, the Lord has vouchsafed to all its visitors safety and freedom from tribulations for a whole year, and He showers blessings and all manner of favors upon all those present at this time.'

"The woman then said, 'What would happen if I, too, entered your religion and prepared such a feast for you; would you consent to come to my house?' The Holy Prophet 🕸 smiled and said, 'Yes, I would come to your house also.' The woman then said, 'Hereby I renounce the religious creed I have clung to up till now, as it is obsolete, and I say: *Ash-hadu an la ilaha illAllah, wa ash-hadu annaka Rasulullah*', and thus she entered the fold of Islam. Similarly she vowed to prepare a great feast and to expend a large amount in the way of Allah. In the morning when she woke from this dream, she found herself bathed in light, her heart radiant with the faith she had found, and she waited for further manifestation of divine guidance.

"When her husband had gone out that morning, she went before a judge to make official her conversion to Islam. She was ready to hold a great celebration in honor of the Holy Prophet ﷺ and declared that she was prepared to follow his guidance from that day on. At this very moment she saw her husband coming to her, asking her how many sheep and chickens she required to be slaughtered, and what else she might need.

"The woman was confused and could not understand, until he explained to her that he had seen the same dream as she had that night, and that he too had been granted the honor of entering into Islam. The Holy Prophet ﷺ had said to him, 'You have no possessions of your own, so you may assist your wife in going out and buying what is needful for the Mawlid she intends to prepare; thus you will have the merit of the good deed.' Hearing this, the woman was even happier than before, and they both made their new faith openly known."

Therefore, if the mere presence of a pious neighbor who spends of his wealth for the love of the Prophet ﷺ is of such benefit to others who happen to live in the vicinity, if it is sufficient to bring to such a one the great favor of becoming Muslim and the mercy and guidance of Islam, how much more reward is coming to the person who hosts the Mawlid? How much unlimited favor will be bestowed on him! This story should serve as advice and as a reminder. May Allah Almighty guide us all to the love and veneration of His Holy Prophet ﷺ, and give all the Muslims who are yet to come their fair shares, Amin.

Allahumma salli wa sallim wa barik 'alayh.

Halima as-Sa'adia, the Prophet's ﷺ Nurse

After the Prophet's ﷺ mother Amina had been with her infant for some time, all the while witnessing all manner of miraculous events and signs, the time came when, according to custom, the child was to be given to one of the Bedouin women of the desert, so that he be nursed and weaned in the clean air outside the heat of the crowded city. Bedouin women would come from afar to the town, from their distant mountain pastures and desert dwellings, to look for infants to take home and nurse for a fee. The children would stay with them for up to four years, then they were returned to their parents. The Holy Prophet ﷺ also had a wet-nurse, and her name was Halima as-Sa'adia, Halima of the tribe of Sa'ad who came from the Najd.

The year of the Prophet's ﷺ birth had been a year of severe drought, and both men and animals suffered greatly, finding neither food nor drink. The animals gave no more milk, and many perished of thirst. When the time had come for the nursing women to go to town in search of suckling infants, her companions came to Halima to ask whether she would come with them to find a child, for she too was nursing a baby at the time. Halima was doubtful that she was able to make the journey, for her only donkey was so weak from deprivation that it could barely totter along. The other women had already departed by the time she made up her mind to make the journey after all, and she know longer could see them ahead of her on the road. When she finally did arrive in Mecca, she met up with the Bedouin women who already had found children to nurse, and who were well equipped with food and provisions, and were heading homewards.

Halima said to them, "So I have come too late, are there no more children left to be nursed?" They answered her, "So it is, there is no one left except this one baby which none of us wanted to accept. It is a fatherless child, and the family is not able to pay us our fees, so we left him there. Come back with us, and join us on the road." "No," said Halima, "I will go on, now that I have come this far, and I might as well have a look at that child nobody wanted."

So while the other women set out on their homeward journey, Halima went to the place where people would come to look for nurses. There she met Abdul-Muttalib who asked her who she was. She replied, "I have come late, all my friends have gone home already while I am still hoping to find a nursling. They say there is one child left." Abdul-Muttalib said, "Surely that can only be my grandson. His father has died, therefore we cannot afford to pay very much, so no one wanted to take him on, even though she would have been blessed eternally, had one of those women agreed."

"Well, let me look at him," said Halima, and she followed him to the house and beheld the sleeping child. She took him onto her lap and uncovered his face. He smiled at her and when he opened his eyes, their light flashed up to the heavens. Instantly she made up her mind. "Even if you give me nothing at all," she said, "I will take this child with me and nurse it." She uncovered her right breast and gave him to drink, and though she had only little milk, it was enough to satisfy the child. They gave her food and she ate; then she prepared to give him her left breast, but the child declined by raising his eyebrows, as if to say, "No, I will not drink this, another has the right to the milk of this breast." Halima understood from this sign what he was saying. His mother Amina said to Halima, "Go and take my child and look after him well; it may be that you will see many wonders and strange things while he is with you, but whatever you see, let no one know about it, tell no one what you have witnessed, for he has many enemies who seek to harm him."

They gave her what they could, and she took the infant in her arms. As she relates in her own words, "Even though I was so weak I could barely hold myself upright, I was so elated with joy when I held the child that I ran out like a lioness, back to my old donkey who was suddenly suffused with new strength and sped along like a Buraq. I even caught up with the caravan of my friends who already had gone ahead of me quite a while ago. They all wondered at the change that had come over me; whereas I was almost too weak to walk and my riding beast was ailing, now I came charging along like a lioness and my donkey had become as strong as a mule."

"We are waiting here for the fortune tellers to arrive to tell us of these children's destinies," they told her, so she took her place in line and waited with them. When the chief diviner came he looked the crowd of people over, then he looked up at the sky. All at once he let out a yell and cried, "Quick, over here, we have found him, right here in our midst!" For in reality, the diviner was one of the unbelievers who had slipped into a disguise, as it was known that the women would be passing by this place. Everyone looked to see who it was, and the crowd grew restive. A general confusion took hold of it during which Halima fled unnoticed into the hills, with the child and the donkey. She paused when she thought herself alone and in safety, when suddenly she realized that she was surrounded by one hundred warriors, all armed with poisoned swords. "What shall I do now," thought Halima and inwardly prayed while gazing at the child. She saw him raise his gaze to Heaven, as if giving a sign, and suddenly a sword came from above, and in no time they were all chopped to pieces.

Halima then continued on her homeward journey, and when at last she reached her house, she was extremely tired, so she fastened a cradle in a tree and laid the baby to sleep in it. Umm Habiba, a woman who was blind, came over and said to her, "Oh Halima, you have been to Mecca, haven't you? How is it that you were able to purchase such fine and costly perfume, despite your poverty—how did you manage to do such a thing?" "No," said Halima, it's no perfume at all, this fine scent is coming from the child I took in charge and brought home with me, it is his fragrance you are smelling." "Oh, do show me this wonderful child and let me fill my heart with his sweet scent," said the blind woman.

Halima led her to the tree from which she had strung up the cradle, and when Umm Habiba sniffed his lovely scent, she cried out and said, "Ah, if only I had eyes with which to behold this child!" The child Muhammad 🌸 raised his hands from his cradle, and as she bent over him, he touched the blind eyes of Umm Habiba with both his index fingers. No sooner had he touched them, that her blindness left her eyes and she could see. "Halima," she cried, "guard well the secret of this child, for now I can see with my own eyes!" From that day on she became a faithful servant to the household and helped with all the chores and duties around the house. She now knew this child was unlike all other children.

The whole time the holy child lived with her, she saw and heard many amazing things. She grew to love him exceedingly, more even than her own natural children. In time he began to speak, and his first words were these:

*La ilaha ill'Allah, wahdahu la sharika lak; lahul-mulk wa lahul-hamd wa huwa
'ala kulli shay'in qadir.*

Halima's children used to take the sheep and goats out to pasture and
Muhammad ❀ would go with them. But since the day he had come to them,
wherever they took the flock, a strip of fresh green pasture would appear all
around them, and the ground was always moist as if it had recently rained,
whereas all around them it was the same barren desert as before. Her sheep
and goats would return with bloated udders, and the household was blessed
as never before.

The other villagers would wait to see where she would lead her goats, then
they told the children to follow them so that they might also partake of this
miraculous sustenance. One day, when Muhammad ❀ had grown into a
little boy, he asked Halima, "Mother, where do my brothers and sisters go
every day? They go out every morning and I would like to go with them."
"Oh my son," she said, "they go out with the sheep and goats every day and
lead them to pasture." "Please let me go along," pleaded the child, until at
last Halima tied a belt around his middle, gave him a stick to hold in his
hand, strung a leather bag across his shoulder and sent him out with his
brothers to herd the flock. They led him out with the other children to the
edge of the fields and followed him with their eyes for as far as they could
see. Their hearts and minds were uneasy from love and care and worry
about him.

Around noon the children came running to the house, screaming that
something had happened and told the parents to come right away. A great
bird had swooped down, they said, and had taken their Quraysh-brother up
into the air and deposited him atop a great boulder. Anxious and alarmed
they ran to that place, where they found the child Muhammad ❀, on top of
the rock, as the children had said. As they were looking, he sat up and
rubbed his eyes, as if he had just woken from a deep sleep.

However, it was no bird that had taken him away, but the angel Jibra'il ﷺ
who had been ordered to take him and to wash his heart. The traces of the

operation were still visible as silken stitches upon his breast. This was the first operation on his heart; the second was to happen later, during his ascension to the heavens (Mi'raj). In every human heart there is a spot of black blood that is called the part of Shaytan, which consists of fear and evil suggestion. The angel had come to Muhammad ﷺ and told him that he must remove this spot, that it was not right for him, and he opened his heart and performed the operation.

The troubled parents took the boy home and resolved never to let him go out again with the other children. When they came home at nightfall, they told their parents of all the wonderful things they had seen and heard while their Quraysh-brother was out with them that day. All the rocks on the ground had given their greetings, they said, when he went by, saying, "as-salam alaykum, ya nabi-ullah", and all the trees bent their boughs low as he passed, as if in prostration.

They had gone as far as a certain valley, where all of a sudden a terrible mountain lion had sprung out before them. The children had run off in fright, calling to Muhammad ﷺ to hide himself as well, but Muhammad ﷺ had not moved from his spot, he just stood and watched. "The lion came up to him," they said, "and were afraid that this would be the end, that the lion would just devour him, but nothing of the sort happened. Instead, the lion kneeled down before him, bowing low, and began to lick his feet. It seemed to be telling him something, and then we saw it lift one of its paws, which we could tell was hurt, maybe broken.

The Quraysh-boy looked at the paw and set it straight, then he stroked it and it was healed. The lion then fell down at his feet again and kissed and licked them, and Muhammad ﷺ stroked its head, as if it were a great cat. Slowly the lion retreated, having expressed his gratitude and thanks, and when it was out of sight, we came out and saw that Muhammad ﷺ was unhurt. It was after this that the great bird swooped down and carried him away, it was then that we were afraid for him."

Halima then said, "If his enemies hear of these strange and wonderful happenings, they will surely trace him to our tents and take him from us by force. We have no way to protect him then." Therefore, they decided to take the boy back to his family in Mecca, even though it pained them to let him go, so dear had he grown to his foster family.

When Muhammad ﷺ was either two or four years old, according to varying narrations, his mother Amina suddenly fell ill and died. He was now completely orphaned and his grandfather, Abdul-Muttalib took him into his care. He took him along wherever he went, and never let him out of his sight. When Muhammad ﷺ was eight years old, Abdul-Muttalib fell ill and called for all his sons (ten in all, four of whom who were still living: Abu Lahab, Abu Talib, Hamza, Abbas), as well as for the dignitaries of Mecca, for Abdul-Muttalib was the head of the tribes of Mecca.

He said to them, "This is my bequest. It is clear to me that this is my final illness and that I will not rise from my sickbed again. My one worry is in whose care to leave Muhammad ﷺ, this fatherless child of your brother Abdullah." Hamza spoke and said, "Oh my father, leave him with me, I shall look after him better than after my own soul." But his father answered him, "Oh Hamza, you have no children of your own, hence you cannot know the value of a child." After that Abu Lahab spoke up and said, "I will look after him, father." Abdul-Muttalib said, "You already have too many children, you will not be able to look after him well." Abbas was still a young man and unmarried, so Abu Talib offered to take him in. His father then said, "Now my soul is at rest, I give you this boy as a trust. Treat him with more care than you treat your own children, and for the sake of my memory, do nothing to undermine his noble nature, and if you wish to please me, show him the same honor and respect that you have always shown me." He repeated this last wish several times until he passed away.

After his death, Abu Talib took the boy into his household and left nothing undone regarding his care and upbringing. He personally did not accept the faith of Islam during the lifetime of the Prophet ﷺ, but he never failed to show him respect and honor, he always shielded him from his enemies and did everything in his power to protect him whenever he could.

After Abdul-Muttalib's death, the Prophet Muhammad ﷺ lived with his uncle Abu Talib until his marriage to his wife, Khadija. When Muhammad ﷺ had been with him for about a year, Abu Talib planned to travel to Sham on a business trip. Muhammad ﷺ was then nine years old, and he begged his uncle to take him along, but Abu Talib refused, saying, "Your are only a boy, stay here at home with my brother, Abbas while I am away."

When the time of parting had come, Abu Talib was about to mount his camel, his whole household assembled round him, bidding him farewell. Among them stood also the boy Muhammad ﷺ, his nephew, and he wept bitterly. "Oh uncle," he cried, "please take me with you!" Abu Talib's heart burned when he heard the boy pleading, he relented and allowed Muhammad ﷺ to accompany him after all.

They traveled along until they came to the town of Basra, a town in the border region of Sham. Outside the settlement there was a hermitage where a Christian monk named Buhayra stayed. He was a very learned man who had read a great many books, and he had read about the signs of the prophet who was to come. At his place the caravan of Abu Talib stopped for the night. The next day they let the camels loose to pasture, while the men rested awhile. Everyone was pursuing his leisure, and the boy Muhammad ﷺ went to look at the loads and the bales of cloth they were carrying along.

Now the day was at its hottest, a scorching sun in a cloudless sky, however just above the boy's head, a small fluffy white cloud appeared that shaded him and little else. The monk Buhayra happened to open the door of his hermitage and looked the sleeping men over. He saw Muhammad ﷺ moving about, went to him and asked him about himself. He asked him his father's name and his mother's name, and Muhammad ﷺ told him all he knew. The monk Buhayra found everything he had read in his books confirmed. He then asked the boy to remove his shirt, and on his back, between the shoulder blades, he found the sign he was looking for, the seal of prophethood.

He returned to Abu Talib and asked him how the boy Muhammad ﷺ was related to him. Abu Talib said, "He is my son." Buhayra then said, "That cannot be, the boy's father cannot be among the living." Abu Talib then admitted that he was his deceased brother's son. The monk then asked, "Where are you going with him?" Abu Talib answered that he was taking him to Sham, to the merchants and market places. Buhayra then said, "This boy is worth more than all the crowds of the city, for he is destined to become one of Allah's Holy Prophets. We find revealed in the scriptures the description of his signs and marks. For seventy years I have been waiting for this prophet to appear. By God, do not take this boy to Sham, for the unbelievers will take him from you, since they dread his coming. But however much they try, they will not be able to kill him before his time, for I have read in my books that his death will be occasioned by his eating poisoned goat's meat, and that he will die several years after having eaten it. Still, take him back to Mecca now."

Abu Bakr was traveling in the same caravan with Abu Talib, and he sent Muhammad ﷺ back to Mecca with Abu Bakr and his slave Bilal. According to a different narration, Abu Talib himself gave up his trip and turned back towards Mecca.

Early Historical Events that Shaped the Islamic Community

Muhammad's Marriage to Khadija al-Kubra
(from Kara Da'ud)

It is related that Muhammad was twenty-five years old when he married Khadija who was forty years and some months at the time—his senior by fifteen years. Muhammad was either twenty or twenty-five years old. All of the Prophet's descendants, except for his son Ibrahim, the son of Marya Quptiya, were born of Khadija. She was his first wife, and it was in reference to her that this Quran verse was revealed;

Did He not find thee needy, and suffice thee? (The Forenoon: 9)

It is related that after the death of both her previous husbands, Khadija saw a dream: she saw the sun descending from the skies into her house, but it did not shine. During its stay in her house it began to shine, until there was not a house in Mecca where its light had not penetrated. When she awoke, she went to see her uncle's son, Waraqa bin Naufal who knew about dream interpretation, who had read all the ancient books and was known to be a man of knowledge.

He said to her, "Your dream means that you will marry the Prophet of the last times before his prophethood is revealed, and you will be his wife. In the course of your marriage his prophethood will be revealed, and all of Mecca will be cleansed of unbelief and idolatry, and the pure light of faith will shine forth." When he had told her this, she asked, "But where is he now?" Waraqa bin Naufal answered, "He is in Mecca," and she asked, "Which tribe does he belong to?" "He is of Quraysh," said her uncle's son. "And of which clan?" she asked. "Of the clan of Hashim." "Then tell me his name," said Khadija. "His name is Muhammad, oh Khadija," said Waraqa.

Having been told no more than this, without ever having set her eyes on him, Khadija began to love him with all her heart and soul. She asked Waraqa, "When and where will this sun rise?" and she began to wait night and day for these events to take place. Now, Khadija was a woman excelling in beauty and perfection, and her mind and manners were of great delicacy. She had no dearth of suitors among the Arab nobles and notables, but she inclined towards none and would accept no offer, despite the wealth and position it might have conferred. She waited patiently, burning with undisclosed passion.

One day Muhammad ﷺ was having a meal at his uncle's house. Abu Talib and his sister Atiqa watched him as he ate, and they remarked his good table manners and his fine style of eating. They said to each other, "Muhammad is now grown, he is a young man now, it is time he got married. What shall we do? He cannot marry just any woman; she should be a woman of rank and from a good family, who will make him a pure and decent wife. But to find such a woman is very costly, and we don't have the means..." For at that time, by divine wisdom, Abu Talib's affairs had foundered, and he was now a poor man.

Thus it was possible for Muhammad ﷺ to become Khadija's trading agent in her business with the merchants of Sham, and he had opportunity to prove his exceptional worth of character and high-mindedness. Had Abu Talib been as well off as he was aforetime, none of this would have transpired, Rasulullah ﷺ would have had no occasion to travel in business.

Abu Talib now answered his sister Atiqa, "I don't know how to go about this, what shall we do?" The Prophet's aunt Atiqa said, "I have an idea. You know of Khadija, and you know also the excellent reputation she enjoys;

whoever has had dealings with her, has profited by them, she is a very fortunate and auspicious lady. Besides, she is very wealthy. At this time, she is just getting ready to send a caravan to Sham, laden with all manners of goods, and she is employing people in her service. Why don't we send Muhammad along to accompany the caravan, in her employ; that way he will earn a little something, and with a little help from our side, he should be able to get married."

Abu Talib agreed with her, he thought this a very good and useful proposition. He approved and said, "Indeed, this is a very reasonable idea, only I am too shy to go up to Khadija and ask her to hire Muhammad to do her business for her in Sham." So Atiqa said, "I will go to her then, and talk to her."

First she went and informed Muhammad ﷺ of the talk she had had with his uncle. Muhammad ﷺ was agreeable to the idea and voiced no objections. When his uncle Abu Talib heard that he had accepted, he wept, for it hurt him to see his nephew sent on such a trip for wages. "No one of our tribe has ever had to travel for wages before, least of all such a pure bred, nobly born boy as Muhammad, with his honor, nobility and grace shining upon his forehead; yet, what can I do? We have fallen upon hard times, and situations may occur when dubious actions are permitted, some things become permissible through necessity. So if it has to be, go then and speak with the lady, Khadija."

So Atiqa went to Khadija and tried to explain things to her. As for Khadija, the coming of the Prophet's ﷺ aunt to her meant the advent of happiness, and she received her with honors and signs of great favor. When it came to stating her request, she felt ashamed to do so, considering the honor with which she had been received. Atiqa sat choking on her words, when Khadija herself broached the subject. "Oh Atiqa, noblewoman of the Arabs," she said, "your demeanor tells me that you have something on your mind that you wish to say, but are not quite happy to do so. Tell it to me, for whatever is your request, know, that I will be more than happy to oblige, it is an honor for me to comply with your wishes."

Then Atiqa felt easier and she said, "You must have heard of Muhammad ﷺ, my brother Abdullah's son who was orphaned before he was even born and brought up first by his grandfather, then by my other brother, Abu Talib. Now he is grown and it is time for him to get married. However, Abu Talib has fallen into straightened circumstances and has not the wherewithal to perform this important duty towards his nephew. Now we have heard that you are getting ready a trade caravan to travel to Sham these days, and if you see it fit to take my nephew along, you will gain the gratitude of the house of Hashim. Will you accept our young relative in your service, and send him on this trade mission to Sham?"

Khadija became thoughtful, thinking to herself, "This youth must be the man in my dream, all the descriptions that my uncle's son Waraqa gave me apply to him. He is of the Arabs of Mecca, of Quraysh, of the house of Hashim. His noble name is Muhammad ﷺ. He is known even now in the town as al-Amin, the trustworthy, he is always called Muhammad Amin. His purity and piety are the talk of the town. The Muhammad of my dream can be no other Muhammad than this man who is destined to become the Prophet of the last times."

She then turned to Atiqa and addressed her thus: "Oh noblewoman of the Quraysh! I have heard talk of this Muhammad, he is thought by all to be honest and truthful, and of exemplary piety. But I have never met him myself. Will he have the necessary strength to lead a caravan? For it is no easy task to look after such an assemblage of men and beasts, and to ensure their safety and protection. I ask you to please have him come to me, so that I might see him and judge for myself."

Khadija wished to see him so that she might be sure he bore all the signs mentioned in the holy books, and accorded to all the descriptions given therein. When Atiqa had gone, Khadija went to bathe and dressed herself in her finery, then she got her house ready and waited for her visitors to come. She had a thin curtain hung across the room, and she told all her servants to treat the arrivals with respect and to seat them in the place of honor. Then she sat down and perused the holy books until her visitors were announced.

When Rasulullah # and his aunt came, they were duly received and given every courteous attention. Khadijah compared Muhammad's # person with what she had read in the holy books concerning the prophet to come, and she found all the signs matching and in accordance with what was written of him. Now she was certain that he was the man of her dream. She knew this to be the truth and her heart beat with excitement.

She would have been happy to marry him at once, but being a very principled lady, she realized it was wiser to wait awhile; for were she to marry him at once, she would certainly encounter a lot of resistance from the people. She concluded that it would be much better if she first sent him to Sham as her business agent, and then arrange the marriage proposition. So she said to the Prophet's # aunt Atiqa, "Normally I give my caravan drivers twenty-five gold pieces for this journey. However, since Muhammad is such a nobly-born and high-ranking person, I agree to give him fifty pieces of gold, if he is willing to accept."

Atiqa was more than pleased with Khadija's handling of the affair, and she went to inform Abu Talib who was equally pleased. They both impressed on Muhammad # to accept the offer and to do whatever she asked him to do. Muhammad # then went to her house and offered his services, and Khadija was very glad for this outcome.

The leader of this caravan was a man by the name of Maysara. Khadija said to him, "Oh Maysara! Whatever you do, do not treat Muhammad as a simple laborer-for-wages in my employ! You are the leader of this caravan, but I ask you to regard him as my independent business agent. Serve him well, and make everything as easy and pleasant as possible for him. Obey him, don't oppose him, and do him no harm." After many such admonitions she added, "One more thing: until you have left the town behind, treat him as you would treat any ordinary man traveling with the caravan; only when you have passed out of the city, clothe him in this new suit of clothes and mount him upon this finely equipped camel. Do only as he orders and do your best for his protection. Lead him home by the shortest and safest route, and let no distractions of the road interfere. For know that he is a noble kinsman of Quraysh, and the best of them all. Let us not be shamed before them. If you do as I have bidden you, and all goes well, I will give you your freedom and reward you better than you have hoped for."

Then the caravan prepared and assembled to leave. The townspeople gathered round to watch it go, some just came to stare, others to bid farewell to their friends and relations. Muhammad's ❀ departure aroused a great deal of interest, and many of his relatives had come to see him off, among them the nobles of Quraysh and the Bani Hashim. When his aunt and uncle, Atiqa and Abu Talib saw Muhammad ❀ in the garb of a common hireling, they lost control and began to weep. Abu Talib even fainted from excessive emotion, and when he came to his senses, he clasped Rasulullah ❀ to his breast.

Tears more shining than pearls welled up in his blessed eyes and rolled down his cheeks, fairer than the petals of the rose, and he spoke, "Forget me not and forget not to pray for me in those distant lands and the hardships that await me there." Hearing these words from him, all his relatives began to sigh and weep. The heavenly angels wept as well and implored the Almighty, "Oh Lord, is this not Muhammad ❀ of whom You have spoken, 'Were it not for you, I would not have created the universe'; is it not he whom You have crowned with such honor?" Allah Almighty responded to them and said, "It is he who is My Beloved ❀. You, however, are ignorant of love and of being loved. Herein there is also hidden wisdom which is yet to appear."

After everyone had dispersed, the caravan set off for its distant destination. Now Muhammad ❀ was overcome with the pain of being a stranger in this world, so that he wept and spoke inwardly, "Oh my parents, oh beloved mother, oh my father whom I never knew! If only you could see what has become of your son, if only you could behold him in the attire of a lowly wayfarer! Oh exile, oh toil, come to me, now is your moment! Mecca, my homeland, shall I ever see you again, or shall I breathe my last, far from

114

home in a strange and foreign land?" Thus he was overcome by the pangs of homesickness and the loneliness of the road.

Oh Nation of Muhammad ﷺ! When you hear of the woeful events that befell your noble Prophet ﷺ, and the pain he experienced from feeling like a lonely and deserted stranger, it is incumbent upon you to weep for him in his plight! For whenever this Nation weeps for him in such moments as these, the angels register it and turn to the Lord Almighty, saying, "Oh Lord, what is it that they are now weeping?" The Almighty then answers them, "It is because they are following the story of their prophet, and they weep out of empathy and compassion for My beloved Prophet ﷺ and all that befell him. Oh My angels both in Heaven and upon the earth bear witness! I will free from the torment of Hell all those of my servants who weep for the sake of My beloved, My wrath and punishment shall be lifted from them!" This is another evidence of the compassionate Grace and Munificence of our Lord Almighty.

Thus the Holy Prophet ﷺ departed from his hometown Mecca-tul-Mukarrama, may Allah increase its renown and favor us with a sojourn at these holy places. After they had left the city behind, the leader of the caravan, Maysara, gave him the splendid robe to wear and he had him mount upon a lavishly adorned camel. Abu Bakr was also traveling with this caravan. Maysara and Abu Bakr said to Muhammad ﷺ, "Oh Muhammad ﷺ, you are our chief, and we will abide by your word. Inform us of your wishes, and of what is required." From then on till the end of the journey, they served Muhammad ﷺ and showed him honor in every way.

Allah Almighty sent a little cloud to accompany them which stood above the Holy Prophet ﷺ at all times, shielding him from the rays of a violent sun. The Almighty also ordered the wind to send a soft little breeze to accompany His beloved, that brought him cooling as from a fan, so that he felt neither the heat of the road nor the torridity of the desert round him. In this way the infinite Grace of the Almighty manifested and the caravan proceeded along its way.

At some point in the trip, two of the camels belonging to Khadija grew exhausted and could no longer go on. Maysara came and told Muhammad ❀ of this. The Holy Prophet ❀ went over to the animals and with his blessed hand he gently stroked the legs of the camels. Of an instant the camels rose and their strength was restored; they assumed their place in the string of camels and followed the lead. Seeing this, Abu Bakr and Maysara marveled and understood that Muhammad ❀ carried with him a special blessing and that he would one day be great.

The caravan moved along at a steady pace until it reached a certain church by Busra on the outskirts of the land of Sham. It was the same hermitage that Muhammad ❀ had visited with his uncle Abu Talib when he was a boy, and he had known the monk Buhayra. This old monk had meanwhile passed away, and in his place there lived a younger monk by the name of Nastura. He was renowned for his asceticism and for his great learning, and his knowledge of the scriptures was profound. The Prophet ❀ and his companions came up close to the church, wishing to dismount and rest awhile under the shade of the old trees. Rasulullah ❀ went and sat beneath a tree, leaning his back against its trunk. It was an old, dead tree, but as soon as he touched it, it came to life again, sprouting fresh green and even bearing fruit on its boughs.

The monk Nastura watched the approach of the caravan and emerged from his cell. He beheld a radiant person seated at the foot of the dead tree which had suddenly sprung to life and greened anew and now was laden with fruit. He also saw a small white cloud hovering in the sky that shaded him alone. Nastura realized instantly that this man must be either a prophet or a very holy man of God. He turned back and disappeared in his cell where he prepared a splendid meal for the wayfarers. He invited the entire caravan to his dwelling, for he wished to see up close that blessed person he had noticed at a distance, and to learn more about his mission with the caravan. By inviting them to his hermitage he could take a closer look at him and make his acquaintance.

Maysara responded gladly to the monk's invitation, while Muhammad ﷺ said, "You go ahead, I will stay here and guard our belongings and pack animals." Maysara was very pleased with this arrangement, for Muhammad ﷺ, as everyone knew, was the most trustworthy of all. So Maysara took his leave of him and went to have dinner at the hermitage. When all his guests were assembled, the monk went out and saw that the cloud had not moved from its place, so he came back to his guests and asked whether they had left anyone outside. They answered truthfully that they had left Muhammad ﷺ outside to keep watch over their belongings. The monk Nastura then said, "You have my word that your belongings will remain untouched; just ask this person to come in to me, for I have need to see him." Then he went out in person to invite the Holy Prophet ﷺ to come inside.

The Holy Prophet ﷺ rose when he saw the monk approaching him and shook his hand. Nastura said, "I have prepared this meal especially for you, my friend, it is quite important that you attend it in person." So, as Rasulullah ﷺ began to walk towards his hermitage, the monk observed that the little white cloud overhead followed him, and that as soon as he stood still, the cloud also stopped above him. They came to the church hall; the monk seated Muhammad ﷺ in the seat of honor, and went out again to look. He saw the cloud hovering over the entrance to the church, and he heard these words coming from it, "When our Holy Prophet ﷺ comes out again, I will again be his shade; therefore I am waiting here." Then Nastura went in and joined his guests.

When they had eaten, the monk addressed Muhammad ﷺ and asked him the following questions, and received these answers:

"Where are you from?"

"I am from Mecca."

"Of which tribe?"

"Of the tribe of Quraysh."

"Of which clan of Quraysh?"

"Of the clan of the Bani Hashim."

"What is your name?"

"My name is Muhammad."

Thereupon the monk rose and embraced Muhammad ﷺ and kissed him upon the forehead. Then he gave his testimony: "I testify that there is no god but Allah, and I testify that you are Muhammad, His Prophet." After showing him all the respect and honor he could, Nastura asked him, "There is one request I wish to make of your holy person which I beg you to accept." "What could your wish be?" asked Muhammad ﷺ. "I would ask you to show me the unmistakable mark of your prophethood so that my heart might have certainty and my mind be at peace and my conviction be strengthened.

The Prophet ﷺ answered him, "What is it you wish to see?" The monk said, "I wish to see the seal of prophethood which is stamped on your back between your shoulder blades, this is the stamp of your mission. I would so wish to behold it and kiss it and rub my eyes upon it, that my eyes might be filled with the light therefrom and I might delight in its heavenly scent." The Holy Prophet ﷺ in order to please his host then stripped off his upper garment so that the monk could see what he wished to see. Upon the seal was written:

Tawajjuh haithu shi'ta fa-innaka mansur

(turn wherever you will, you will be assisted.)

The monk rubbed his face and eyes on this seal, then he said with great deference and respect, "Oh Holy Prophet ﷺ, oh Beautification of the Judgment Day, oh Intercessor of your Nation, oh Amender of Troubles, oh Dissolver of Difficulties, oh Prophet of Mercy!" Having praised the Prophet in these words, the monk was honored with acceptance into Islam (before its time, as the prophethood of Muhammad ﷺ had not been revealed as yet).

After this, the monk turned to the whole caravan and told them that the Prophet ﷺ who had now appeared among them was the celebrated personality that had been anticipated and foretold in the words and scriptures of all prophets since the time of Sayyidina Adam ﷺ. He confirmed that all the prophets were of great worth and closeness to Allah Almighty, but that the long-awaited prophet the whole world had been expecting now dwelt in their midst, and he implored them not to stay for long in Sham. For just as he had been able to recognize him by his marks and signs, so could the unbelievers of Damascus who were his sworn enemies and wished to do him harm.

After the gathering had heard the admonition of the monk, they rose to resume their journey. When they reached Sham, their trading was accomplished in a very short time and yielded unexpectedly high profits, through the blessings carried by Muhammad ﷺ.

One day during their stay in Sham the Holy Prophet ﷺ said to and Abu Bakr, "Let us go to the unbelievers' house of worship and see what they do there." Neither Abu Bakr nor Maysara were too happy to go there, but they didn't feel right about refusing Muhammad's ﷺ request either. So, on a certain day they went to the unbelievers' house of prayer. There were a great many people assembling there, and the unbelievers manifested their disbelief. When Muhammad ﷺ entered the prayer house, the chains on which the great lamps were suspended began to swing under the impact of his holy gaze, until they snapped and broke, the lamps tumbling to the ground in broken shards. The unbelievers who were assembled in the building were stricken with horror and took to weeping and wailing, and they made a great commotion. The most learned among them however said, "Quick, shut all the gates, for the man who is to be the Prophet of the last times must secretly be among us! Let him not escape, for all this is written and described in our holy books. Let each one of us now be identified by his brethren, and he who is not of us, him let us seize and dispose of forthwith; in that way we shall have rid ourselves of the danger coming to us from this Arabian prophet who could destroy our religion once he takes up his calling."

119

So the gates were shut and all the unbelievers got together and looked at each other to discover who they did not know. Abu Bakr and Maysara now feared for their lives and began to weep, but Muhammad ﷺ said to them, "Have no fear, for they cannot see us; Allah's protective power will cover us, so that they cannot touch us." In this way Muhammad ﷺ reassured his friends. The unbelievers meanwhile gathered in one spot and began to search the premises.

Abu Bakr relates: "The three of us remained standing in one place. The unbelievers passed to the right and to the left of us, so close that they even touched us. Despite this, not one of them was able to see us. They passed by us in a confused and senseless manner. They took count of their own number and found no stranger among them. They checked all corners and window niches several times over, yet they found nothing. At long last they concluded that he must have stood outside the building and cast a glance at the lamp from there, causing it to crash. 'Now they have come and gone; where shall we look for them?' they wondered. So they opened the doors and gates again, and we left." Abu Bakr, Maysara and the Holy Prophet ﷺ went back to their caravan and prepared for immediate departure.

When seven days journey remained till they would reach Mecca - may Allah increase its luster and grant us easy access – Maysara wrote a letter to Khadija as was his custom whenever he reached this stage of the journey, informing her of their progress and the results of their trading. This time he wrote to her that they had fared far better than in previous years, and their trade had been far more profitable than before, and that he believed this had to do with the blessing of Muhammad ﷺ who had traveled with them for the first time this year. He then sealed the letter, looked at the Holy Prophet ﷺ and said, "Oh Muhammad, light of my eyes, will you do this letter the honor of taking and delivering it in person to the lady Khadija?" Muhammad ﷺ agreed and a fine Hijin camel was decked out for the journey. He set out at the break of dawn, proceeding towards Mecca, and they followed him with their eyes until he disappeared from view.

When they could no longer see him, the camel lost its way. The following narration tells of this: Shaytan took hold of the camel's halter and led it astray. Thereupon Allah Almighty in all His Might and Glory commanded the angel Jibra'il to descend to earth and set the Prophet and his camel back on the right way. Thus it is revealed in the Holy Quran:

Did He not find thee erring and guide thee? (The Forenoon, 7)

Then He commanded the angel to fold up the earth so that he might reach his destination speedily. The angel Israfil was commanded to stand by his right, and Mikhail by his left side, and in this way the Holy Prophet was protected and guided safely through the perilous desert. He felt sleepy and dozed off, and the angel Jibra'il folded up the earth beneath him, so that he reached Mecca by the time the sun rose again, though it was seven days distance from where he had set out.

After the Holy Prophet had departed for Sham, Khadija was beset by a great and passionate longing for him, which grew stronger with each passing day. When she awoke in the morning she would look out her window facing north, the direction of Sham, and wonder whether this day she would have any news. She waited. One day, she was again looking out for a messenger when in the distance she beheld a cloud of dust. She looked again carefully and managed to distinguish a rider approaching at the speed of an arrow shot from a bow. Two angels in the guise of birds were shading this rider with their wings, or according to a differing narration, she saw him being shaded by a white cloud. As soon as she saw him, she began to wonder who he might be and what urgent message he might bring, for he came on in great haste. Presently a servant girl entered and brought her the news.

"Good tidings to you, my lady," she said, "the rider we saw approaching is Muhammad." To this Khadija replied, "If it is really so, I will set free all the slave girls that I own." No sooner had she uttered these words that the Holy Prophet rode up to her gate.

All of a sudden Muhammad awoke from his slumber and found himself before Khadija's gate. He dismounted and entered the courtyard and was received with great courtesy and regard. Khadija then read the letter he handed her and noticed that it was written on the same day as it was delivered. "When did you set out?" she asked Muhammad 🏵. "This morning, at the break of dawn," answered the Holy Prophet 🏵. Then Khadija knew for certain that this man of miracles was the prophet to be, and from joy at his safe return she set free all her slave girls. Then she said to Muhammad 🏵, "The camel on which you have come, and all that is upon it shall be yours. Go now to see your relatives, then quickly return to me."

While he was gone, she prepared bread dough and baked the bread with her own hands. Nobody else could bake bread as she did. When the bread was done, Muhammad 🏵 returned from visiting his relatives. She asked him if he would be willing to return once more to the caravan if she asked him to. "Certainly," he said, and she wrote him an answering letter, gave him the warm bread and sent him off. The Holy Prophet 🏵 remounted his camel and took to the road again. As soon as he was gone out of sight, as before he was overcome by a great drowsiness and he fell into a deep sleep. Again the angel Jibra'il 🏵 folded up the ground ahead of him, Israfil 🏵 shielded him from the right and Mikhail 🏵 from the left, and a small white cloud traveled overhead, shading him. In this way he made his progress.

Meanwhile, when Muhammad 🏵 set out with Maysara's letter, Abu Bakr said to him, "You have committed a bad mistake. Muhammad 🏵 is inexperienced, he knows not the way through the desert and you have sent no one along to guide him. How easily he may go astray and get lost in this wilderness! How will you face the lady Khadija and the Bani Hashim?" Maysara became downhearted when he heard these words from Abu Bakr. He ordered the caravan to halt, and sent out Hijin riders in search of Muhammad 🏵. While the search party was yet roaming for him, they saw Muhammad 🏵 coming towards them from the direction of Mecca. It was the time of Duha, the late morning. When Maysara was told, he said, "You see, he missed the way and kept going round in circles until he ended up back where he started out from."

As they were yet talking of him, the Holy Prophet ﷺ strode in, and they could smell the scent of fresh bread, which took them greatly by surprise. "It smells just the same as the bread that Khadija bakes," they wondered, "how can that be? Where can he have found that?" Just then Muhammad ﷺ entered the tent, greeted them and handed them bread and letter from Khadija. It was obvious to all that indeed it had come from the hand of the lady Khadija, but no one could understand how. "When did you get there?" they asked Muhammad ﷺ. "I arrived just as the sun was rising," said Muhammad ﷺ, "I handed Khadija your letter and while she was baking the bread I went to see my relations. When I came back to her, the bread was ready and she wrote this letter and sent me back to deliver it."

They all marveled at this and murmured among themselves, "All that the monk has told us about him is true. It is a seven days journey from here to Mecca, and a seven days return. To cover such a distance in a space of a few hours is beyond the power of any human being, it can only be done through direct empowerment by the Almighty Lord of the Universe, which He confers only on His Holy Prophets."

Together they set out for Mecca, and in due time they arrived. Rasulullah ﷺ went to his uncle's house while Maysara went to report to the lady Khadija. She welcomed him back and said, "When Muhammad came here, I saw two birds hovering alongside, as well as a white cloud above his head." Maysara told her, "It's been like that ever since we departed from Mecca." Then he told her all that had occurred from the time they left to the present moment, and how everything confirmed what they had suspected already: that Muhammad ﷺ was destined to be the Prophet of the last times. Khadija also felt confirmed in her certitude as she listened to Maysara's tale, but she said to him, "Oh Maysara, tell no one about what you have seen and heard," and she repeated this over and over again for reasons of her own. For if the chiefs of Quraysh should hear about the exceptional gifts of this young man, they would all rush to marry their young daughters to him, and she would see herself deprived of happiness.

After the travelers had rested from their exertions for a few days, Abu Talib said to Muhammad 🌸, "Oh Muhammad 🌸, oh light of my eyes, it is time now to go to the lady Khadija and ask her for your wages. We will add to this whatever we can afford, and in this way we hope to find you a suitable match." So Muhammad 🌸 went to Khadija's house, but he was too shy to ask for what was his due. When at last he did ask her she said to him, "What will you do when I have paid you your wages?" Truthfully, Muhammad 🌸 answered her, "I will take the money to my uncle who intends to get me married." Khadija then said, "How much is this money going to buy you? I have found you a wife who possesses a lot more of it. Of good family she is, of clear lineage and excellent character, pure and chaste. Her beauty is renowned throughout the lands of the Arabs, and not a few of the Arab chieftains have asked for her hand in marriage. Plenty are the offers of gold and silver and gifts of great value; alone, she would consent to none of these worthy suitors. There is one thing only in which she is lacking, and that is that she has been married before and has been widowed. If you will accept her despite this flaw, all of her wealth will be your own, and she herself your loyal servant." In this manner Khadija made allusion to her own person. The Holy Prophet 🌸 heard and understood this proposal, and he blushed, and from bashfulness was unable to answer her.

When he returned to his uncle's house empty-handed, Abu Talib asked him, "So, what did she give you?" Muhammad 🌸 said, "She did not give me it, instead she made fun of me, by talking of unsuitable things that cannot possibly be." Alarmed, Atiqa went to Khadija and asked her about what had transpired between her and Muhammad 🌸, and why she had made fun of her nephew in such a way. Khadija swore solemnly that she had not thought to ridicule him at all, rather that she was completely convinced of his superior qualification, both by birth and by personal distinction, on account of his truthfulness and trustworthiness which had been amply proven during his journey to Sham, and that her heart inclined strongly towards him so that she wished him for herself.

Muhammad's ✿ aunt Atiqa was amazed to hear these words from the high-born lady and said, "If I go now and explain this matter to Abu Talib, and should he consent, will you surely not change your mind and shame me thereby? Truly, you are not speaking in jest?" Khadija replied, "By Him who holds my soul, never have I been more serious about anything in my entire life. Go directly to Abu Talib and give him my salams. Go also and invite my cousin Waraqa bin Naufal; give him plenty of wine to drink and when he is quite happily drunk, let Abu Talib ask him for my hand. The rest I will take care of when he comes to speak to me. In that way the match can be arranged."

Atiqa went back, jubilant in her heart and told all to Abu Talib. He too was glad and prepared to invite Waraqa bin Naufal, Abu Bakr and the chiefs of the Meccan clans. They gave Waraqa a lot of wine to drink, and when he was nicely in his cups, Abu Talib approached him and said, "Oh Waraqa, there is a favor I have to ask of you." "What may that be, ya Abu Talib?" asked Waraqa. Abu Talib then said, "You know for yourself what a fine young man my nephew Muhammad ✿ is, truthful, trustworthy and honorable as no other; for him I am asking the hand of your cousin Khadija." All the assembled chiefs and notables thought this a suitable proposal, and Waraqa answered, "Yes, it is a good idea, and my wish as well. As her guardian, I give her to your nephew in marriage. But I will speak to her first, then I will return."

So Waraqa proceeded to Khadija's house and spoke to her. He said, "All the dignitaries of Mecca and the heads of Quraysh have proposed that I marry you to Abu Talib's nephew Muhammad ✿. I, too, find this a suitable proposition, but I have come to you to discuss the matter with you and to obtain your consent, if indeed it is forthcoming. Should you find this acceptable, you need only appoint me as your representative, and the marriage contract will be concluded."

Khadija then pretended to know nothing of this matter and asked Waraqa to tell her about Muhammad ✿. "He is extremely pious," said Waraqa, "of excellent character, truthful and reliable. He is nobly born and his honor, kindness and good nature are undisputed. The only thing he lacks is money, of that he possesses none to speak of." Khadija then said, "Money, of that I have an ample supply myself, more than I can count. If this Muhammad is really as excellent as you say he is, I have no objection. Go then, and as my representative perform the ceremony of nikah."

Waraqa then returned to Abu Talib and the assembled Meccan dignitaries, and the nikah was performed and witnessed, and thus Muhammad ﷺ and Khadija were joined in the bond of holy matrimony. This ceremony took place on a Friday, and both Abu Talib and Waraqa bin Naufal made speeches at the wedding, but it was Khadija's uncle 'Amr bin Asad who gave her away.

There is disagreement concerning the matter of the marriage settlement (Mahr). Some authorities say it consisted of twelve okes of gold and five hundred dirhams of silver, some say it was twenty camels. When the marriage contract was concluded, Abu Talib slaughtered one camel in gratitude and invited all the nobles of Mecca to a feast. Muhammad ﷺ then said to Abu Bakr, "Will you go with me to the house of my bride, Khadija?" "With the greatest pleasure," replied his friend, and together they went there. Abu Bakr accompanied Muhammad ﷺ to Khadija's house where she had prepared a splendid welcome for him. After food and drink had been served and all the guests had departed, the couple finally remained alone. Khadija then kissed his hands and made over to him all she owned, even the robes she wore on her person, disassociating herself entirely from all material belongings.

Khadija was Muhammad's ﷺ first wife and he loved her dearly and always held her in the highest esteem. As long as she lived he married no other woman. For twenty-four years, five months and eight days she lived with him and served him. It was fifteen years before the revelation of his prophethood; when it was revealed, she believed in him and accepted his message and was the first woman to accept Islam, may Allah be well pleased with her.

Khadija passed away three years and four months before the Hijra from Mecca to Madinah and lies buried on the hill of Hajun in the Nam area of Mecca. Seven children were born to the couple, three sons and four daughters. Their first son was Qasim; therefore the Prophet ❀ is called Abu Qasim by the Arabs (meaning, "the father of Qasim"). The second son was Tahir, the third Tayyab; the first daughter was Zaynab, the second Ruqiyya, the third Umm Kulthum, and the fourth Fatima. All three sons died before the coming of the revelation, while the daughters still lived.

Through his marriage to Khadija, Muhammad ❀ had become a wealthy man, and he now began to work with her capital. He was known throughout Mecca as a reliable and eminently trustworthy personality. Still there were his enemies and detractors who were not idle in pointing out that he had become rich through his marriage to Khadija, and they spread vicious gossip about him, saying he would soon cause her bankruptcy and ruin.

When Khadija heard of these rumors, she made a public proclamation, saying that she had made over all her wealth and worldly goods to her husband Muhammad ❀, that she had done so at the time of their marriage and she was now repeating the act, with full conviction. "From now on I own nothing, I am his slave and his dependent," she said.

Muhammad ❀ was known as al-Amin, the Trustworthy, for he was known to be utterly reliable, and anyone could entrust his goods to him. If ever there was a disagreement, he would be called as peacemaker between two parties. He was Abu Talib's designated successor, for there was no one more highly esteemed than he.

When Muhammad ❀ had reached his thirty-fifth year, the Quraysh wished to dismantle the building of the Kaba and erect a new one on the same spot. Since the time of Ibrahim ❀ the Kaba had not been rebuilt. It stood between two mountains, and whenever it rained heavily, the water drained into the Kaba and dirtied it. Therefore the elders of Mecca had decided to rebuild the holy house in such a way as to make it safe from flood damage, but from fear and awe no one had dared to apply himself to the task. The problem presently arose who was to have the honor of placing the black stone (Hajar-al-Aswad) in its place. The great clans of Quraysh, the Bani Hashim, the Bani Umayya, the Bani Zuhra, and the Bani Mahzun all came together to combine their efforts. They split the task between them, each clan being assigned to one wall. For a long while they hesitated to tear down the venerated ancient structure, but at last one man from among them took it upon himself to breach the wall, and the work began. They had torn the walls down to about a man's height when they hit upon a green stone, which could not be split by any means. This was the stone mentioned by Allah in the holy verse:

"And when Abraham, and Ismail with him, raised up the foundations of the House..."

(The Cow, 127)

Then they knew they could dig no deeper, so they began to reconstruct the walls upon this foundation, using the original stones. When it came to resetting the Black Stone in its place, all four clans disagreed who should be given the honor of that supreme task. They sat down in the confines of the sanctuary and began to argue about the matter, each man praising the heroic deeds of his forefathers that entitled him to this honor rather than his rivals. Each accused the other of lying, tempers grew heated and soon it would have come to blows.

Finally they agreed to choose one man to perform the task, and they all agreed that it could be no other than Muhammad Amin 🌺, no one doubted that he was the right man. Muhammad 🌺 considered their problem, then he took his cloak from his shoulders and spread it upon the ground. He then lifted the Black Stone and set it upon his cloak. Then he called to the men of all four clans to come and each lift a corner of his cloak and to thus carry the stone to its intended place in the newly built Kaba. In this way each clan would have taken part in the honorable feat and they all could take pride in it. Everyone was highly satisfied with the wisdom of this decision as it saved them the trouble of protracted disputes and, possibly, even tribal warfare, so they happily did as Muhammad ﷺ had suggested. When they had brought the stone near to the house, the question still arose who was to actually lift it to its place, but now they all agreed that no one was more suitable than Muhammad ﷺ, so he himself placed it there with his blessed hands.

Now all was completed but the roof, which was to be of wood. But in all of Mecca there was no wood and no carpenter to be found. However, it so happened that just at that time a merchant ship had come into Jeddah with a cargo of wood. They bought it from this ship, and they also found a Coptic carpenter who built the roof for them. To this very day the roof that was built at that time is still in its place.

In the time of Hujjaj bin Yusuf one corner (rukn) of the building was damaged by a falling stone, and it was immediately repaired.

Revelation of Prophethood

When Muhammad ﷺ had reached the age of forty, Allah sent the angel Jibra'il ﷺ to him to bring him the revelation. According to a different narration, Muhammad ﷺ was forty-three, and another version by Muhammad ibn Jarid says he was only twenty, but that cannot possibly be correct, for the mind of man does not mature before he has reached his fortieth year. As the time of the first revelation approached, Muhammad ﷺ began to experience many curious signs. In his dreams at night he would see the angel Jibra'il ﷺ, but he did not know him. During the day, he would roam about, lost in thought, and all the stones and clods of earth along the road would greet him, saying, "as-salamu alaykum, ya Rasulullah". He would hear their voices and grow afraid of them.

At that time it was a custom among the Quraysh for the pious to retreat to a cave on the Mount of Hira during the month of Rajab and to spend this time secluded from their fellow men in solitary contemplation. Each group of the Bani Hashim had their own place there, side by side in adjacent caves.

129

One day the Holy Prophet ❀ came down from the mountain and said to his wife Khadija, may Allah be well-pleased with her, "I am afraid, for I have seen many strange signs with my eyes; by day I hear the stones and clumps of earth speaking to me with a voice of their own, and at night there are great creatures that appear to me. One of them in particular is so tremendous that its feet are on the ground while its head is in the heavens. It would approach me and take hold of me..."

Khadija comforted and reassured him, "Oh Muhammad, these happenings are all part of the momentous changes that are about to come over you. When this sort of thing comes on you again, let me know." So one day as they were sitting together, Muhammad ❀ had another visitation of this kind, and he told to Khadija what he was seeing. Khadija went around to his back and embraced him from behind, then she asked him, "Do you still see it?" "Yes," replied Muhammad ❀. Then she took off her head covering and asked, "So, do you see it still?" "No I do not; it has gone," said Muhammad ❀. Thereupon Khadija said, "Good tidings to you, for whatever you have seen, it is not from the evil one, it must have been an angel from Heaven. For had it been the accursed devil, he would not have shied away when I uncovered my hair."

Whenever the Holy Prophet ❀ felt low-spirited and downcast, he would retreat to the cave on Mt. Hira to spend time in reflection and contemplation. Even if he came home at night looking downhearted, Khadija would always welcome him warmly, praying for the day to come when Allah would reveal to him his destiny. The day did come, and it was on a Monday that Allah's mercy was revealed to him–just as the Holy Prophet ❀ was born on a Monday, and died on a Monday as well – and according to some it was the eighteenth day of Ramadan, while others maintain it was the twelfth day of Rabi' al-Awwal. Allah sent the angel Jibra'il ❀ to Muhammad ❀, commanding him to appear to him and to teach him the Sura 'Iqra' (The Blood Clot).

This was the first revelation of the Holy Quran. The angel descended upon Mt. Hira, appeared to the Prophet ❀ and greeted him, "As-salamu alaykum, oh Messenger of Allah!" The Holy Prophet ※ startled in surprise and would very nearly have fallen off the cliff from fright, had the angel of Allah not caught him in his wings, and held him so that he could move neither forward nor back. Then the angel said to him, "Oh Muhammad, read!" "How shall I read," asked Muhammad ※, "I do not know how." "*Iqra!* (Read!)," repeated the angel, "*Iqra! Bismi-rabbikal-ladhi khalaq.* Recite in the Name of thy Lord who created!" and the angel recited the first Sura to him.

When the apparition of the angel was over, and he had released Muhammad ※ from his wings' embrace, the Prophet ※ was in pain and left the mountain to go home. He reached his house trembling, repeating over and over to himself the Sura the angel had taught him, and he felt intensely afraid. He came to Khadija and said, "Now I have seen up close that person who has been appearing to me in the distance." "What did he say to you?" asked Khadija. "He told me that I was a Prophet of Allah, and that he was the angel Jibra'il ※. Then he made me recite after him this Sura -" and he repeated to Khadija what he had heard. Khadija had heard before that the prophets of old were instructed by the angel Jibra'il ※, and through him received revelation from the Lord. Muhammad ※ was shivering and felt cold from within. He lay down, saying to his wife Khadija, "Cover me up!" as he laid his blessed head upon the pillow. She covered him with his cloak, and he slept.

Khadija then went to see her relative Waraqa ibn Naufal who was a learned man and who knew a lot of things about the coming of the prophet of the last times. She asked him whether he had ever heard the name Jibra'il, and he said, "Jibra'il is the name of one of the great angels of Allah; he is the messenger-angel sent to the prophets. But why do you ask me this question?" Then Khadija told him what Muhammad ※ had experienced, and Waraqa replied, "If what you say is true, then Muhammad ※ is the Arabian prophet we are waiting for, whose advent is foretold in all the ancient scriptures. Oh Khadija, did this angel not command your Muhammad to do something?" She answered that he had ordered him to proclaim the Unity of Allah, and that he taught him a Sura, which she then recited (Sura: The Blood Clot). Waraqa then exclaimed, "If this is truly the anticipated prophet of the last times, then I will be the first to believe in him, for I have expected and waited for him to come for such a very long time."

Khadija returned to her house where she found the Prophet ﷺ still asleep. In his sleep the angel Jibra'il ؑ appeared to him again and addressed him:

Ya ayyuhal Mudaththir Oh thou shrouded in thy mantle;

The Holy Prophet ﷺ lifted his head to listen.

Qum fa-andhir. Arise and warn.

Wa rabbaka fa-takbir. Thy Lord magnify;

Fa-thiyabaka fa-tahhir. Thy robes purify,

(i.e. rid your heart from doubt and all other than God)

wa-r-rijza tahjur; and defilement flee!

wa la tamnan tastakthir Give not, thinking to gain greater,

wa li-rabbika fa-sbir and be patient unto thy Lord.

In these first verses Allah Almighty set forth to Muhammad ﷺ his prophethood and enjoined on him prayer, magnanimity, kindness and patience. The Holy Prophet ﷺ rose. Khadija saw him and said, "Oh Abu Qasim, why have you risen, why won't you rest some more?" "Khadija," he replied, "my time for rest has passed. Again the angel has come to me, this time commanding me to go out and proclaim my message and to teach people to believe in Allah and to pray to Him."

Khadija felt great joy when she heard these words, and said, "I believe in you, before anybody else; instruct me in your religion." Khadija was therefore the first to embrace Islam. The Holy Prophet ﷺ was very happy that his wife was his first follower. Jibra'il ؑ was present and instructed the prophet ﷺ. He told him to fetch water so that he might teach him the rites of ablution and show him how to pray. After teaching all these things to Muhammad ﷺ, they prayed together, and Jibra'il ؑ was the Imam.

How 'Umar bin Khattab Came to Islam

The revelations continued and after a time there were thirty-nine people who followed the new religion of Islam. The Quraysh however were opposed to the new cult, and because of this, the new Muslims could not pray openly at the Kaba. The Holy Prophet ﷺ then prayed to his Lord, "Oh Allah, make Islam openly known, and let it be through one of these two, You alone know which one is the best: either 'Umar bin Khattab or Abu Jahl bin Hisham." Allah Almighty heard his prayer and answered it through 'Umar bin Khattab.

At first 'Umar bin Khattab was a sworn enemy of Islam and of the new Prophet ﷺ. One day he made his way to the Prophet's house in order to kill him and to put an end to the 'disturbance', brandishing his sword. Abu Jahl had set out a reward on Muhammad's ﷺ head, promising one hundred camels and one hundred pieces of gold to his murderer.

'Umar was a man of fiery temperament. On his way to Muhammad's ﷺ house he ran into one of the Sahaba (Companions of the Prophet ﷺ) whom he knew, and he yelled at him, "So you too have become one of those Muslims?" and slapped him in the face. This man replied, "What is your concern with me, 'Umar, when your own sister and brother-in-law have entered the faith of Islam?" 'Umar refused to believe this and turned directly towards his sister's house to see if there was any truth to this. This sister was married to Talha ibn Zubayr.

As he approached the house, he could hear voices from inside reciting verses from the revelation. It was a Muslim named Habib who was teaching them the newly revealed verses. Enraged, 'Umar stormed in, and yelled, "Where is he?" Habib hid himself and hid also the piece of deerskin on which the holy verses were written. 'Umar in his rage began pushing and shoving his brother-in-law, even hitting him. His wife, 'Umar's sister, came between them to prevent the blows, and 'Umar's blows fell on her. Her cheek was split and blood ran down from her wound. Thereupon his sister also grew very angry, and cried, "Yes, we too have become Muslims, and it is the Truth, Allah and His Messenger Muhammad ﷺ are real and true. We worship no idols; we worship none but Allah Almighty, Allahu Akbar! If you don't like it, then you must kill us!"

Hearing his own sister utter these words, 'Umar came to his senses and regarded his sister's bleeding face and his brother-in-law knocked down on the floor, and he said, "Show me what it was that you were reciting!" The sister went to clean herself and make ablution; she then brought out the piece of skin on which were written these verses:

> *Bismillahir-Rahmanir-Rahim. TaHa. We have not sent down the Quran upon thee for thee to be unprosperous, but only as a reminder to him who fears, a revelation from Him who created the earth and the high heavens; the All-Compassionate sat Himself upon the Throne; to Him belongs all that is in the heavens and in the earth and all that is between them and all that is underneath the soil.* (TaHa. 1-5)

Hearing these divine verses, 'Umar was profoundly stirred, and he said, "If this be the truth, then what we have been worshipping so far is nothing. Take me to Muhammad!" They said to him, "We will take you to him only if you promise not to speak badly and to do him no harm." Now that 'Umar had calmed down, Habib also came out of hiding, and saying, "Allahu Akbar!" they set out for the Prophet's ❁ house.

Looking out of Khadija's house, Hamza saw them approaching. He had himself accepted Islam only three days before, and seeing 'Umar he now unsheathed his sword and said, "If 'Umar is coming with good intentions, he is welcome; but if he draws near in anger, then our swords shall do the talking." The Holy Prophet ❁ said, "Let him draw near, it appears a change has come over him."

So it was indeed: 'Umar came before the Prophet ❁ as a humble man, dragging his sword. The Prophet ❁ welcomed him, saying, "Alhamdulillah, Allah has answered my prayer regarding you, He has chosen you rather than Abu Jahl to enter into the fold of Islam." 'Umar then accepted Islam at his blessed hands and was taught the prayers and rites of the religion. He then learned that the Muslims were forced to pray in secret, because Quraysh were preventing them from praying publicly at the Kaba.

'Umar exclaimed, "What! Shall they pray to their false gods openly while we must worship the true God in secret? Come, we will go there right now!" So they set out, taking the Holy Prophet ﷺ in their midst, the whole flock of those first Muslims. Ahead of them strode 'Umar, brandishing his sword, Abu Bakr on his right, 'Uthman at his left, and Ali behind him, and all the other Sahaba grouped around and behind them. Thus they drew near to the sanctuary where the Quraysh were awaiting them, for they all knew of the price Abu Jahl had put on Muhammad's ﷺ head.

When they saw them approaching with 'Umar in the lead, they thought, "Ah, he has taken the lot of them prisoner!" But Abu Jahl was more observant than they and said, "By God, this does not resemble a line of prisoners, he seems to have embraced the new faith himself!"

When they had come up close 'Umar in a loud voice declared his faith for all to hear. He said, "Let everyone stand informed that I, 'Umar bin Khattab have become a Muslim, and this is my declaration of faith: Ash-hadu an la ilaha illAllah, wa ash-hadu anna Muhammadar-Rasulullah."

Hearing this declaration, all the Quraysh assembled there with Abu Jahl slunk away and dispersed, from fear of 'Umar who was fierce and known as a mighty warrior. Had it not been for him, they might have done all manner of cruelty to the small band of Muslims. From that day on they prayed openly at the Kaba, at all the times of prayer.

The Holy Prophet ﷺ preached Islam privately for three years, and instructed each Muslim individually, until the revelation of this holy verse:

> O Messenger, deliver that which has been sent down to thee from thy Lord; for if though dost not, thou wilt not have delivered His Message. God will protect thee from men; God guides not the people of the unbelievers.   (The Table, 72)

From that time onwards, he began to preach openly and in public.

Some Miracles of the Holy Prophet ❀

Allahumma la hawla wa la quwwata illa billahil-'aliyyil-'azhim.

These are some of the miracles that our Holy Prophet Muhammad ❀ performed.

The Prophet ❀ and the Deer

Once the Holy Prophet ❀ was out in the desert, when he heard a loud cry, "Stop, oh Prophet of Allah!" He followed the direction of the voice, and came across an Arab fast asleep, while a doe he had caught was tied up beside him. The Holy Prophet ❀ realized that it was this animal's voice that he had heard calling out to him. He approached it and asked, "What is it with you, what is your need?"

The deer answered, "Oh Prophet of Allah! I have left two of my young behind on yonder mountain, who are still too small to know which grasses to feed on; they are dependent on my milk. Please let me go so that I might nurse them and tell them what has happened to me. Let me take them to the pasture and show them what grasses to eat, so that they might not perish when I'm gone. I will be back after five hours have passed."

The Holy Prophet ❀ replied, "Will you keep your word? What if you don't show up?" The deer said, "Then let the punishment of the traitor come upon me."

Just at that very moment, the sleeping Bedouin awoke. He had heard the conversation of the deer with the Holy Prophet ❀, and now he said: "Have you ever heard of a wild animal that came back once it was set free?" "This one will come, inshaAllah," answered the Prophet Muhammad ❀. The Bedouin said, "If it doesn't come, I will kill you!" The Holy Prophet ❀ then smiled and asked, "And if it does come back, will you then accept Islam?" "Yes, I will," said the Bedouin.

So they set the deer free, and it ran off. After four hours had passed, the deer returned. The Holy Prophet ❀ asked it, "You promised to return after five hours, but only four have passed. How is that?" "Oh Holy Prophet," said the deer, "I went to find my fawns, and I told them of what had happened to me. They drank, but then withdrew so that you might not remain waiting in a tight situation. They said, 'Go back to him an hour ahead of time, so that this Bedouin in his ignorance might not speak untoward words against him.' That is how I arrived an hour ahead of time." Hearing these words, the Bedouin embraced Islam and set the deer free.

The Splitting Apart of the Moon

Although the pagan Quraysh had witnessed a great many true miracles by the Holy Prophet ❊, they still would not forego their denial and disbelief. They continued in their efforts to confuse people, so that they would not embrace the faith. Their main aim was to make difficulties for the Holy Prophet ❊. However, Allah Almighty never leaves His Beloved Prophet ҫ amidst difficulties in the face of the disbelievers and never withdraws His Protection from his side.

One day the accursed Abu Jahl who was one of the foremost of Quraysh saw that there were a great many people following Muhammad and professing their belief in his prophethood. He conceived of a devilish plan and immediately sent word to one tribesman, Habib ibn Malik. In his message he wrote: "There has risen one person among us who claims that the religion we have inherited from our forefathers is null and void. He has gathered a great following around himself, and we are incapable of containing him. Therefore, we ask you to come and find means against him."

As soon as Habib ibn Malik received and read Abu Jahl's letter, he grew very angry and came to Mecca with a sizeable following. Abu Jahl saw him coming and said, "Let somebody go and fetch Muhammad by force", but Habib said, "No, he merits a polite invitation; if he doesn't respond, then let him be brought by force," and he sent a messenger to invite Muhammad ❊. Together with eighty of the Sahaba, Muhammad ❊ set out to meet Habib ibn Malik. According to another narration, he came alone, his black turban wound about his noble head. Habib looked at him and saw that he shone with the Light of Divine Beauty. He turned to Abu Jahl and said, "Is this Muhammad who you speak about?" "Yes, it is he," replied Abu Jahl, may his name be cursed.

Habib's heart was filled with faith at the sight of the Holy Prophet ﷺ and he guided him to his tent and said to him, "If you are truly a prophet, then show us a miracle." The Holy Prophet ﷺ answered, "What is it you would like to see?" Habib said to him, "I would like to see the moon rise before nightfall to its highest point, then split in two; the two halves should descend and stand in front of you as witnesses; they should speak the words of the creed, be hidden beneath your robes and then emerge from your sleeves to ascend again to the high heavens. Thereafter the moon should return to the place of its arising, and it should be dark again; in its place let the sun shine forth anew. Secondly, there is something else I wish for in my heart: that you might have knowledge of that." Abu Jahl heard these words, and they pleased him. "Bravo, Habib," he said to him.

The Holy Prophet ﷺ climbed up to Jabel Abu Qubays and bowed down low in prayer. He entreated his Lord to help him in this matter, and instantly the angel Jibra'il ﷺ appeared to him, informing him of what Habib had in mind. The miracle Habib had requested was also made manifest. Before the moon rose, however, the Wardens of Hell opened a hole the size of a pinpoint through which the blackness of Hell seeped onto the earth. Of such intensity was this darkness that people's teeth began to chatter, and they fell all over each other in the lightless gloom. Then the moon rose in its usual fashion till it reached its peak position. Then, upon a sign from the Holy Prophet ﷺ it split into two halves that descended by his side. Both parts were heard to utter the Kalimat-u-Shahada, then they disappeared beneath the skirt of his robe and emerged from his sleeves, paused upon his head for a moment, from there to resume their heavenly station once more. The moon then returned to the place of its arising, and the sun shone out over the world again.

(According to another narration, it was Abu Jahl or the Quraysh who wished for this miracle. That night, the Holy Prophet ﷺ pointed his finger at the moon and it split into two, one half descending on the Jabel Hira, the other half in another place. Later the caravan coming from Sham was questioned as to this event and confirmed having witnessed it as well.)

This was the first miracle Habib had requested. As for his second request, the Holy Prophet ﷺ now turned to Habib and said to him, "What you hold in your heart is your daughter; for you have a daughter who is blind and who is lame of hand and foot. She will now behold me in a dream and she will be filled with health and faith." Upon these words, Habib also believed, but Abu Jahl was filled with unfathomable rage, and yelled at Habib, "I thought you were a reasonable person! We have held out for such a long time against this nonsense, not believing in any of the tricks he shows us! Yet you believe in the very first demonstration of his wizardry!" Habib replied, "Alhamdulillah, Allah be praised, I have believed and I am freed from error and misguidance. May you remain therein forever more, oh accursed one!"

According to one narration, Habib had hidden thirty thousand men behind the mountain, in order to fight the Prophet ﷺ if the need arose. When he embraced Islam, ten thousand of those men came forth every day and became Muslims. Jibra'il ﷺ descended and revealed the verses:

> When comes the help of God, and victory, and thou seest men entering God's religion in throngs, then proclaim the praise of thy Lord and seek His forgiveness; for He turns again unto men. (Help)

At this the Holy Prophet ﷺ wept so much that those standing by him asked him, "Our Prophet ﷺ, why do you weep? Is it from joy that you weep, as men are entering into Islam in throngs?" Thereupon the Holy Prophet ﷺ answered, "At the end of times my nation will thus depart in throngs from the religion of Islam; it is therefore that I weep."

Habib returned to his home and palace. At the gate, his daughter herself came out to welcome him. She told him of the dream she had had, in which she saw the Holy Prophet ﷺ and embraced Islam. Together father and

139

daughter repeated the holy words of the Shahada. Habib sent two camel loads of precious stones to the gates of the Kaba. The messengers bringing the gifts did not know Muhammad ❀ and asked for him. Abu Jahl intercepted them and said, "I am the chieftain here. Such gifts are sent from one chief to another, therefore they are due to me. Who is this Muhammad anyway?" Just then, Muhammad ❀ happened to come that way, and an argument rose. To cut it short, Muhammad ❀ said, "Let the camels decide the matter; whomever they choose, let the gifts be his."

Thereupon Abu Jahl asked for time until the next morning at sunrise. He spent all night in front of his idols, imploring them to help him in this matter. "If you help decide this in my favor and make the camels speak for me, I will bring you great sacrifices, and anoint you with precious oils and perfumes..." he said to them. Finally even his companions grew tired of his antics, and they said, "It is enough, Abu Jahl; have Muhammad ❀ called, so the matter can be decided."

Muhammad ❀ came and held his woolen cloak over the faces of the camels. He spoke to them and said, "Tell us now, where have you come from, and who has sent these gifts for whom?" The camels first pronounced the words of the Shahada so that all could hear them, then they said, "We have been sent with these gifts by Habib ibn Malik to Muhammad ❀".

Thereby the matter was decided beyond doubt, but now there was a lot of talk about how rich Muhammad ❀ had become all at once. He therefore led the camels to the other side of Jabel Abu Qubays and unloaded them there. He said, "I accept all of these gifts; may Allah reward the giver for them," and sent the camels back to where they had come from. Then he spoke the words: *"Kunu turaban juruza!* Be ye turned to barren dust!" and the precious stones and gems all turned to dust. The Prophet ❀ performed this miracle in order to demonstrate to the people that worldly wealth and earthly possessions meant nothing to him and were of no real value.

Migration to Abyssinia

Still, day-by-day conditions in Mecca worsened for the Muslims. They suffered more and more injustice and oppression at the hands of the pagan Meccans. One day in the fifth year of his prophethood, his closest friends came to Muhammad # and said, "Oh Muhammad #, we can bear it no longer, our patience is used up. Grant us permission to fight against them." But the Holy Prophet # had not yet received the divine command to fight the unbelievers, so he replied, "If you can stand no more, then you may migrate elsewhere." "But whereto?" they asked.

He pointed with his arm in the direction of Abyssinia. "Go to Abyssinia," he told them, "they are Christians there, believers in a holy book. They will not harm you; they will respect your beliefs. There you may find relief." (This became known as the first Hijra (migration). The second Hijra was the Prophet's # migration from Mecca to Madinah.) Eighty of the companions set out for Abyssinia then, though according to other narrations they were only twenty-three. Their names included 'Uthman bin 'Affan and his wife Ruqiyya; Zubayr bin Awwam; Abu Hudhayfa bin' Utba and his wife Sahla; Mus'ab bin' Umayr, Abdurrahman bin 'Auf; Abu and Umm Salama;' Uthman bin Maz 'un; Amir bin Rabi'a and Layla; Suhayl bin Bayda'; Abu Sabra bin Abi Ruhm and his wife Umm Kulthum.

Hamza Enters the Fold of Islam

The pagan Meccans continued to harass the Holy Prophet # and the Muslims in every way. One day `Utba came running up from behind and knocked the Prophet's # turban off his head. Another time Abu Jahl, standing on the hill of Safa, threw a stone at the Holy Prophet #, which hit and injured his head, but he said nothing. The Prophet's # uncle and milk-brother Hamza bin Abdul Muttalib was just returning from the hunt. As he was going from the hill of Safa towards the Kaba, he was met by the freedwoman of Abdullah bin Jud'an who called to him, "Had you seen what Abu Jahl and his louts have done to the son of your brother, you never would have stood for it!"

Hamza grew extremely angry when he heard this, and grasping his bow in his hand, he made straight for the Haram. He went up to Abu Jahl and hit him on the head a violent blow, hurting him. Abu Jahl began to protest, and seeking to defend himself, he said, "But it was he who insulted us, deeming us to be of no mind. He has insulted our gods and departed from the way of our forefathers." To this, Hamza replied in a firm manner, "You worship other than Allah Almighty, can there be anything more mindless than that? I hereby bear witness that there is no god but Allah and that Muhammad is His Messenger!"

Then Hamza went to the house of Khadija where he met the Holy Prophet ❀ and said, "Oh Muhammad, I have injured Abu Jahl on his head." To this the Holy Prophet ❀ answered, "You have caused him pain; of what use is that to me?" Hamza then said, "What would you rather have me do?" "I would wish that you became Muslim," said the Holy Prophet ❀. "That is my wish as well, therefore I have come to you, oh Muhammad, please accept me into the fold of Islam." The Holy Prophet ❀ accepted him and Hamza became Muslim. According to a different narration, Hamza had already entered Islam at the time that 'Umar became Muslim.

The Quraysh Send Envoys to the King of Abyssinia

The leaders of Quraysh sent envoys laden with gifts to the King of Abyssinia, demanding that he send back the emigrants. The messengers were 'Amr bin al-'As and Abdullah bin Abi Rabi'a. They came before the Negus and said, "Some mischief-makers from among our people have fled from us and sought refuge with you. They have come to carry out their mischief here among you, your religion, and your people. We have come to warn you of this."

The envoys hoped that the Negus would give them a favorable reply, but instead he flew into a rage and cried, "No, by God, I will not give them up to you! Having no other recourse, they have sought shelter here with me – never shall I surrender them, not without having spoken to them!" The Negus had the emigrants called before him and he listened to them. He understood that the messengers who had come for them bore them ill intentions, so he sent them back, rejecting their offerings and request. He said to them, "Why do you attribute lies to your own prophet? He is the Messenger of Allah, we have read his description in our holy books, he has been announced to us already by Isa, the son of Mary." In this way it was made known that the King of Abyssinia, the Negus was very close to Islam.

This Negus passed away five years after the Holy Prophet 🕌 had come to Madinah. The angel Jibra'il 🕌 withdrew the veil from the Holy Prophet's 🕌 eyes, so that he could see from Madinah all the way to Abyssinia. He prayed the funeral prayer for the Negus at Madinah. This is the origin of the custom of the "salat al-janaza 'alal-gha'ibin", the funeral prayer for absent or anonymous dead.

Once the people of Mecca suggested to the Prophet 🕌, "Oh Muhammad, we will worship your god, if you wish, but you must consent to worship our gods as well." Thereupon the following holy verse was revealed:

> *Say, 'Is it other than God you bid me serve, you ignorant ones?' It has been revealed to thee, and to those before thee, 'If thou associates other gods with God, thy work shall surely fail and thou wilt be among the losers.' Nay, but God do thou serve, and be thou among the thankful.* (The Companies, 64-66)

The Sura 'The Unbelievers' was also revealed on this occasion.

> *Say, 'O unbelievers, I serve not what you serve, and you are not serving what I serve, nor am I serving what you have served, neither are you serving what I serve. To you your religion, and to me my religion!* (The Unbelievers)

Then the pagan Quraysh came together and decided to write a document, which they did, and hung it up in the middle of the Kaba. The contents of their writ was this: there was to be a boycott on the Bani Hashim and the Bani Muttalib, that they should not marry their women nor give women to them to marry; that they should neither buy from them nor sell to them. These conditions were very difficult for the Muslims to carry, but they accepted them without complaint.

A space of about three years went by in this manner. One day a certain man Wahb bin Umayya came along and tore the piece of paper from its place. He asked who had written this page. Abu Jahl replied, "We attached it in its place in agreement with 'Umar." Allah Almighty sent a little worm to destroy this document, and by means of revelation He informed His Prophet ❁ of this. The only thing on this sheet of paper that the insect left untouched were the words: *"Bismika Allahumma"* (In Thy name, oh God).

It later became known through the Prophet's ❁ uncle Abu Talib that the hands of the writer of this page both withered.

The Deaths of Abu Talib and Khadija

In the tenth year of the Holy Prophet's ❁ prophethood, his uncle Abu Talib died. This year was the most difficult and sorrow-laden year for Muhammad ❁. For three days after the death of Abu Talib, in the month of Ramadan, his wife Khadija also left this world for the next, at the age of sixty-five. Even more than by the death of these beloved persons, the Holy Prophet ❁ was affected by certain rumors that cast doubt on whether his beloved uncle Abu Talib had died as a Muslim or not. At this point, a verse was revealed to the Prophet ❁ which addressed itself to all the Muslims in the person of the Holy Prophet ❁:

> *Thou guidest not whom thou likest, but God guides whom He wills, and knows very well those that are guided.* (The Story, 56)

In spite of all the Prophet's attempts to convince him, Abu Talib had not become Muslim. However, he is reported to have said, "Were it not that I feared that you would be abused after my death, and that Quraysh would think I had only said it in fear of death, I would have accepted what you call me to."

When Abu Talib lay dying, the Prophet ❁ sent Ali to him so that he might recite to him. When he passed from this life, the Holy Prophet ❁ wept for him and said to Ali, "Go, and place him in his grave."

After Abu Talib's death, the leadership of Quraysh passed on to 'Abbas, the son of Abdul Muttalib. 'Abbas was unable to extend his protection to the Holy Prophet ﷺ, and Quraysh persecuted him and sought to harm him at every step. One day the Holy Prophet ﷺ was in the mosque praying, and while he was bowing down in Sajda, the disbelievers came and dumped dirt upon his head. His long hair and beard were soiled with dust. Nobody would have dared do such a thing while Abu Talib was alive. The Prophet ﷺ was patient for another year, then this verse was revealed to him:

So if they turn their backs, say, 'God is enough for me. There is no god but He. In Him I have put my trust. He is the Lord of the Mighty Throne.' (Repentance, 129)

The Holy Prophet's ﷺ Visit to Ta'if

After Abu Talib's death, the Holy Prophet ﷺ was subjected to a great deal of insult and hostile persecution by the pagan Arabs of Mecca, and he was very much affected by this. People began turning away from him when he spoke and told them about Islam. He therefore decided to turn towards Ta'if for help.

Ta'if was a very important place in ancient Arabia. It was, as it were, a 'hill station', situated on the slopes of the higher and cooler mountains on the road to the Yemen, full of fruitful gardens and orchards. Because of the perpetual drought at Mecca, the Meccans were in need of the produce of Ta'if. At the time, a distance of three days' journey separated Ta'if from Mecca. The higher classes and dignitaries of Mecca used to spend the three summer months up in the hills.

The Holy Prophet ﷺ now set out secretly from Mecca towards Ta'if, in the company of Zayd ibn Harith. (According to other sources, he went all alone). At Ta'if, the main chiefs and leaders were at the time three brothers of Bani Thaqif: Habib, Mas'ud, and Abdu Yalayl.

The Holy Prophet ﷺ went to them with the intention of speaking to them about Islam, perchance they might accept it, and with the purpose of securing their aid and protection against the hostile idolaters of Mecca. But when he had spoken to them and made his intentions plain, they said, "If you are truly a prophet what need do you have of our help? If God sent you as His messenger, why doesn't He protect you? And if Allah wished to send a prophet, couldn't He have found a better person than you, a weak and fatherless orphan?"

Hearing their response, the Holy Prophet ❀ realized that it was hopeless to try to talk to these hard-hearted people, so he gave up and turned to leave. On account of the people of Ta'if this verse of the Holy Quran was revealed:

> *They say, 'Why was this Quran not sent down upon some man of moment in the two cities?' What, is it they who divide the mercy of thy Lord? We have divided between them their livelihood in the present life, and raised some of them above others in rank, that some of them may take others in servitude; and the mercy of thy Lord is better than that they amass.* (Ornaments: 31, 32)

The Holy Prophet ❀ feared that news of this encounter might embolden his Meccan enemies against him, so in parting he asked the Bani Thaqif of Ta'if to keep the matter secret. But they refused to comply even with this request, and they stirred up the rabble of Ta'if against him, who drove the Holy Prophet ❀ out of the walled town, pelting him with stones and injuring his hands and feet. He was compelled to take refuge in an orchard beyond the city limits, which belonged to `Utba bin Rabi'a and his brother Shayba of the Meccan tribe of Shams. There he sat down by the side of the road to rest from the heat of the sun and the pain in his foot. He prayed to Allah Almighty, complaining to Him of his own weakness, little resource and lowliness before men. He did not invoke against the people of Ta'if, fearing the Wrath of Allah that would descend upon them.

The two brothers `Utba and Shayba were in their gardens at the time. They witnessed what had happened to the man of Quraysh, and they were indignant at his treatment. Moreover, they were moved to compassion by his condition, so they sent their slave 'Addas, a Christian, to him, offering him a plate of grapes. The Holy Prophet ❀ accepted the refreshment, took a bunch of grapes and began eating them, after pronouncing over them the words *"Bismillah"* (In the name of Allah). The young slave looked at him carefully and said, "By Allah, I have not heard these words spoken since I left my country."

The Holy Prophet then asked him which place he came from, and what was his religion, and he answered him, "I am a Christian from Nineveh." "From the town of the righteous man Yunus, the son of Matta," said the Holy Prophet. 'Addas was surprised and asked, "How do you know about Yunus, and who are you?" The Holy Prophet then replied, "He is my brother, he was a prophet of Allah, and I am a prophet of Allah, too." 'Addas then bent over him and kissed his head, his hands and feet. The two brothers were watching this from afar, and when 'Addas came back to them, they reviled him for it. He answered his masters, saying, "There is no man in this country better than he; he has told me things that only a prophet can know."

Then the Holy Prophet returned to Mecca from Ta'if. News of what had transpired at Ta'if had already reached Abu Jahl and his henchmen, and he said, "They did not permit him to enter Ta'if, so let us also refuse him entry into Mecca." Late at night, the Holy Prophet reached the halfway halt between the two towns at the valley of Nakhlah. There he proposed to rest, and while he was engaged in prayer, a company of Jinn passed by, seven in number and from Nasibin. They witnessed the Prophet reciting the holy words of the Quran. They hearkened to these words and responded, believing in the Prophet's mission. They returned to their own people as Muslims. The Holy Quran mentions this incident:

And when We turned to thee a company of Jinn giving ear to the Quran; and when they were in its presence they said, 'Be silent!' Then when it was finished, they turned back to their people, warning. They said, 'Our people, we have heard a Book that was sent down after Moses, confirming what was before it, guiding to the truth and to a straight path. O our people. Answer God's summoner, and believe in him, and He will forgive you some of your sins, and protect you from a painful chastisement. Whosoever answers not God's summoner cannot frustrate God in the earth, and he has no protectors apart from Him; those are in manifest error.

(The Sand Dunes, 29-32)

This is mentioned in another Sura as well:

Say: "It has been revealed to me that a company of the Jinn gave ear, then they said, 'We have indeed heard a Quran wonderful, guiding to rectitude. We believe in it, and we will not associate with our Lord anyone.'" *(The Jinn, 1-3)*

The Sura ar-Rahman, the All-Merciful is addressed to the Jinn, as well as to men. The Holy Prophet was sent as a 'Mercy for the Worlds', again confirming his mission to both humankind and Jinn.

Now as the Holy Prophet ﷺ was approaching Mecca from Ta'if, he knew he would not be welcomed there. When a horseman bound for Mecca overtook him, he asked him to convey a message to a clansman of his mother's clan, Akhnas bin Shariq. He asked him to extend to him his protection, so that he might enter in safety. But Akhnas sent back a reply, declining, saying he was only a confederate to the home tribe of Quraysh. The Holy Prophet ﷺ had by now reached the cave of Hira, where he had received the first revelation.

From there he sent word to Suhayl bin 'Amr, asking him for protection, but Suhayl declined as well, also on the grounds of tribal principles. Then he sent the man to ask Mut'im ibn 'Adiy, the chief of Bani Nawfal. Mut'im agreed and having girt his weapons, he rode out in the morning with his sons and nephews to escort the Prophet ﷺ from Hira to Mecca. When Abu Jahl saw him, he asked, "Are you giving him protection, or have you entered his religion?" Mut'im replied, "Granting him protection, of course." Then Abu Jahl said, "We protect him to whom you give protection."

Thus the Holy Prophet ﷺ continued his life in Mecca for a time, praying and preaching inspire of the hostility of the pagan idol-worshippers. He endured much abuse and insult, yet he sought to spread the message he had been entrusted with. He would move among the tribesmen who came to Mecca on the occasion of various fairs and religious feasts, and he tried to set forth to them his view. More often than not he met with incomprehension and derision, all the more so as his own uncle Abu Lahab went round behind his back, telling people that he was crazy and advising them not to listen to his words. It was during this period that the Mi'raj of the Holy Prophet ﷺ took place.

The Holy Ascension of Prophet Muhammad ﷺ

(from the *Dalail-al-Khayrat Sharhi* of Kara Da'ud, d. 1541)

The 178th name of the Prophet, on whom be peace, is Sahib-al-Mi'raj (he who was granted ascent to Heaven). Oh Allah, Thy Benediction be upon the owner of this name. The word 'Mi'raj' signifies an instrument that facilitates ascent, such as a flight of stairs. Our Holy Prophet ﷺ ascended to the heavens on a stairway of precious gems beginning at al-Quds ('the holy', i.e. Jerusalem) during his lifetime and in his pure physical form. Among all the prophets and messengers, it was a privilege reserved for the Holy Prophet ﷺ alone to be granted such an experience. Therefore the appellation Sahib-al-Mi'raj was appended to his name.

Now we shall set forth in full the account of the Mi'raj that the Holy Prophet ﷺ was honored to experience.

When the Prophet Muhammad ﷺ had reached his fortieth year, he was sent with mercy for the whole world as a prophet and messenger of God to all people. He began to preach his message and invite people to faith. It was in the twelfth year of his calling, on the twenty-sixth day of the month of Rajab that the Prophet ﷺ went to the Baytullah (the Kaba) and sat by himself in front of one of the pillars. There he engaged in remembrance and meditation of the Lord Almighty.

Just then, Abu Jahl came in to meet with his helpers and henchmen. He saw Muhammad ﷺ sitting there all on his own, engaged in the worship of his

Lord. Seeing him thus, he thought to himself, "I will play him a prank," and going up close to him, he bent down and asked him, "Oh Muhammad ﷺ, are you a Prophet?" Muhammad ﷺ answered him directly, saying, "Yes, I am a Prophet." Abu Jahl went on to say, "How can you be a prophet whilst you sit here all alone? Where is your following, where are your helpers? Had there been any necessity for a new prophet, the call to prophethood certainly would have come to me. Look at my following, look at the number of my retainers!" And, striking an arrogant pose, he turned around and left. After Abu Jahl had gone, another one of his party came by with his group of followers.

He, too, approached the Holy Prophet ﷺ sitting there on his own, with the intention of doing something hurtful to Muhammad ﷺ. He spoke as Abu Jahl had spoken, then he turned and left. In this way, no less than seven of the notables of Quraysh came by with their accomplices and they all spoke the same words as Abu Jahl, as if they had previously devised a plan. As a result, the Holy Prophet ﷺ became very dejected and his spirits fell. He thought to himself, "It is now twelve years that I am calling them to Islam and to the belief in the Unity of Allah Almighty. However, far from accepting the Truth, they don't even understand the concept of the Messenger. A Prophet has no need of a following of servants and retainers. All that is needful to a prophet is Divine Revelation and the order to make known His Divine Command." Thus the Holy Prophet ﷺ grew sad.

That night was the twenty-seventh night of the month of Rajab, a Monday night. He proceeded to the house of Umm Hani who was the daughter of Abu Talib, the sister of Ali. She lived in her father's house, which was situated between Safa and Marwa. The Prophet ﷺ arrived at her house, and finding him downcast and dispirited, she asked him for the reason of this. The Prophet ﷺ explained to her what had happened and why he felt as he did. Now, Umm Hani was an intelligent and resourceful woman. She comforted the Holy Prophet ﷺ and said, "These men undoubtedly know that as a Prophet of Allah bringing the message of Truth you are not in need of servants and accomplices. But as they are a stubborn, envious and ill-tempered lot, they spoke these words with the sole purpose of insulting you and wounding your spirit." These words served to comfort the Prophet ❀ somewhat, but he still remained distraught. It is reported that soon after praying the night prayer (Salat-al-'Isha), he fell asleep in Umm Hani's house in a saddened state of mind.

Then the Lord of all Created Beings who had created Rasulullah ❀ before anything else, destining him to be a Messenger of many miracles and gifts of mercy to all the people in the world and endowing him with perfection and the ability to awaken love in the hearts of men; the Lord Almighty whose Glory reaches from end to boundless end, other than whom there is no God, in His aspect of Majesty and Might, addressed Himself to the angel Jibra'il ﷺ, saying, "My Beloved whom I have chosen from amongst all My Creation, the Best of them all, lies sleeping in the house of Umm Hani, aggrieved by the hurtful words of the unbelievers. Let your piety and obedience be an invitation to My Beloved. Go, adorn your dazzling wings with the gems of Paradise and enjoy the dignity of being at his service. Go and tell Mikha'il to leave off the weighing out of provisions this night, tell Israfil to abandon his trumpet for one hour, and tell Azra'il for this one night to refrain from taking any souls. Tell the angels of the lights and luminaries to festoon the heavens with lamps; tell Ridwan to embellish the gardens of Paradise, and admonish the angels to keep the gate to the pits of Hell firmly fastened and the demons of Hell not to move from their places.

"Tell the Huris to bedeck themselves and to set about scattering precious gems, preparing all the Paradise mansions. Say to the Throne-bearing angels: 'Wrap the sphere of the skies in its blessed robes and equip yourselves each with seventy thousand angels.' You, Jibra'il, repair to Paradise and there select a Buraq steed, then descend to the face of the earth. All the punishment in the graves shall be lifted for the duration of this night. Go to My Beloved who fell asleep of sad and dejected mind in Umm Hani's house, and be his companion. Awaken him gently and explain to him that this night he is to be shown his great destiny and the station of nearness (*qurb*) that excels all other stations of elevation and honor. Invite him to come along with you."

Buraq is Dispatched to His Noble Mount

Jibra'il ﷺ then went to the Paradise gardens where he beheld forty thousand Buraqs as they were grazing. Each one had the name of Muhammad ﷺ written across its forehead. Among them was one Buraq, which seemed sad and dejected; its head was bowed and tears were streaming from its eyes. Jibra'il ﷺ approached that Buraq without hesitation and asked him the reason for its distress. The Buraq then said, "As I was prancing about in Paradise Gardens, a voice suddenly came to my ear, which said, 'Oh Muhammad ﷺ!' No sooner had I heard this name spoken than I became enamored of the bearer of this name. For forty thousand years now I have been burning with the fire of separation and the hope of attaining union. Ever since I am weeping, in the sway of intense longing."

Jibra'il ﷺ had pity on the state of this Buraq and said to him, "Your beloved Muhammad ﷺ has this very night been invited to ascend to the Heavens. He needs to be transported from the Masjid-al-Haram (Mecca) to the Masjid-al-Aqsa (Jerusalem) by a Buraq steed. It is you I will select, so come now and attain fulfillment." Then he saddled the Buraq with a saddle of light and placed a bit in his mouth of green chrysolite. Next he went to the chamber, where the spiritual king of this world and the world to come, the Messenger to both mankind and Jinn, lay sleeping.

Prophet ﷺ Narrates His Mi'raj

Now, the compilers of Hadith have narrated in six collections of Hadith the story of the Prophet's ﷺ Mi'raj as it was told to them by no less than twenty of the venerable companions who heard it as the King of Prophets ﷺ told it to them himself. This then was his narrative:

"I had fallen asleep in Umm Hani's house, my eyes were closed, but my heart was wakeful. Suddenly, I heard the voice of Jibra'il ﷺ in my ear, and rising from my slumber, I sat up, finding myself face to face with the angel Jibra'il ﷺ. He spoke to me, saying, 'The Lord Almighty sends you His greetings of peace and invites you to come with me. I will carry you along, for the Lord wishes to shower upon you the diversity of His munificence. Of those that have gone before you, none has ever attained to such munificence, nor will any who are to come after you ever attain to it."

"I rose and wished to perform my ablutions. Water was ordered to be brought from the heavenly stream of Kawthar. Before I had even uncovered my hands and feet, preparing to take ablution, Ridwan had already brought two jugs full of water from the stream of Kawthar in pitchers of red ruby. He also brought a bowl of green emerald that had four corners to it. In each corner there was a gem that shone like the sun and lit up the night sky. I washed with this blessed water, and they clad me in a wrap of pure light and set upon my head a quilted turban of light.

"The story of this turban is this: eight thousand years before the creation of Adam, the angel Ridwan wound this turban in my name. Since that time up until now, forty thousand angels stand about this turban reciting praises and glorifying the Lord. After every single one of their glorifications, they recite blessings *(Salat-wa-Salam)* upon me. That turban has forty thousand folds, and in every one of these folds there are four lines of writing.

In the first line is written: Muhammad 🏵 is the Messenger of Allah.

In the second line is written: Muhammad 🏵 is the Prophet of Allah.

In the third line is written: Muhammad 🏵 is the Beloved of Allah.

In the fourth line is written: Muhammad 🏵 is the Friend of Allah.

"After this, Jibra'il 🏵 covered my back with a cape of light and fastened around my waist a belt of red rubies. He placed in my hand a whip made of green emeralds, which was embellished with four hundred pearls, each of which shone like the morning star. He clad my feet in a pair of slippers crafted from green emerald. Thereafter he took me by the hand and led me to the Haram."

In another narration, the Prophet 🏵 continues his account as follows:

"I made my ablution with the waters of the Zamzam well. Then I circled the Holy House seven times and prayed two Rak'ats at the Maqam Ibrahim. I came to the place called the Khatm and there sat down for a bit to rest. While I was sitting there, Jibra'il split my chest asunder and brought two large basins filled with knowledge and wisdom, respectively. Mikha'il brought three basins full of Zamzam water wherein they washed my entrails and my bosom. Then he opened up my heart and took from it the small black clump of clotted blood, while saying, 'This bit of clotted blood is the reason why men feel fear when they behold an awesome sight. I have taken it from you, for tonight you will behold the Heavens and the Lote Tree, the Divine Throne and Divine Court and the many strange and wonderful things they contain, and many great angelic creatures. Therefore I have cleansed you of this clot, so that you might gaze at whomever you will and speak what needs to be said without fear or constraint.' He then took from the basin the knowledge and wisdom contained in it and placed it within my heart. He tucked it in and closed my chest again, so that there remained no trace or scar.

"Jibra'il then took me by the hand and led me to a place outside of Mecca. I saw there the other great archangels, Mikha'il, Israfil and Azra'il, each surrounded by seventy thousand angels of their company. When they beheld me, they all stood to respectful attention and I gave them my greetings of peace. In answer to my greetings, they proclaimed the boundless graces of the Lord.

"Presently, Jibra'il said to me, 'Oh Prophet of Allah , I have brought you this Buraq from the Gardens of Paradise. Mount it now, for the Lord on High awaits your coming.' I turned and saw the Buraq, which was as bright as the sun and as swift as a flash of lightning. As soon as he lifted his foot to take a step he had already reached as far as the eye could see. In addition, this Buraq had two wings by his side, which he used whenever he wished to fly through the air."

The wise and learned have this to say about the Buraq: his body is smaller than that of a mule, but larger than that of a donkey. He speaks pure, intelligible Arabic. The Lord has created each of his limbs from a different set of precious materials. His hooves are made of corals; his feet are of gold. His chest is of red ruby stone, while his back is made pearls. The wings at his side are of ruby red. His tail resembles the tail of a camel. According to a different narration, his tail resembles that of a peacock and is of extreme comeliness. His mane was that of a horse while his feet resembled those of a camel. He was saddled with a saddle from Paradise, and his stirrups were of red ruby, beset with jewels.

Our Holy Prophet's ﷺ narration continues as follows:

"The angel Jibra'il ﷺ held the stirrups for me, saying, 'Mount!' As I made ready to mount him, the Buraq stirred restively. Jibra'il ﷺ addressed him, 'Oh Buraq, are you not ashamed of yourself? How dare you dare behave with such insolence? By the Grace of Allah Almighty whose Glory is vast and whose bounties are all-encompassing, beside whom there is no other Lord, never will you see a rider of greater merit and excellence!' At the angel's words, the Buraq blushed with shame and began to tremble all over. Large drops of sweat trickled from his brow and he said, 'Oh Jibra'il ﷺ, I have a request to make, and it was from this urgency that I behaved thus, not because I am reluctant to fulfill my duty. Now you have put me to shame.'"

The Holy Prophet ﷺ then turned to the Buraq and asked him what his request was and how it might be fulfilled. "Oh my Prophet ﷺ," replied the Buraq, "I have been stricken with love for you since before time began. For untold eons, I was immersed in yearning, submerged in an agony of love. Now, by the Grace of Allah, I have been granted the boon of beholding your light and perceived your blessed scent. My love now has blossomed forth and increased thousand fold. On the Day of Gathering, when you rise from your blessed resting-place, you will be brought to the place of gathering on a Buraq steed. The request of my love is this: that you will mount no other steed than me on that tremendous day, thereby completing my happiness and filling my heart with the light of joy." The Holy Prophet ﷺ answered and said, "I granted the Buraq his request and promised that I would mount no other than him on that day."

After hearing from the Buraq that he would be brought to the Site of Judgment on back of a Buraq, the Prophet 變, the Glory of all Creation, the Quintessence of all Being grew thoughtful as he pondered the fate and state of his nation on that day. The Lord Almighty who is aware of every hidden thing then made the angel Jibra'il 變 ask Muhammad 變 the reason for his sudden sadness. The Holy Prophet 變 replied:

"I have been informed by the Buraq of the honor that will be shown to me on that mighty day in that I will be fetched and mounted on a Buraq. It occurs to me to reflect on the state of my nation on that day: they are but weak, far from perfect, sinful mortals; how, on the Day of Judgment, will they go on foot to the place of assembly which is at a distance of fifty thousand years bearing the weight of all their sins? How will they manage to cross the bridge of Sirat, which is a stretch of three thousand years' wayfaring?

"I was then informed by Divine inspiration that Divine Grace would reach every single one on that day. Just as the Lord would send a Buraq to fetch me from my grave, so every single soul belonging to my nation would be sent a Buraq to bring him to the Site of Judgment. They would cross the Bridge of Sirat in a flash and they would traverse a road of fifty thousand years as if in a single moment. 'This is a Favor and Grant of Kindness to your nation, oh Muhammad 變,' I was told, 'therefore, let your mind be easy on this account.'

There is a verse in the Holy Quran relating to these events:

On that day that We shall muster the God-fearing to the All-Merciful with pomp.

(Mary, 85)

The Holy Prophet 變 then continued in his narrative:

"Learning of the promise of the Lord's Favor and Kindness, I mounted upon the Buraq filled with joy. Jibra'il 變 and a following of seventy thousand angels were at my right stirrup, Mikha'il 變 with seventy thousand angels was at my left stirrup, and every one of these angels held in his hand a candelabrum of light. Behind me went Israfil 變 with seventy thousand angels and on his shoulder he bore the saddlecloth of the Buraq. I begged his pardon for its great size and that he was made to carry it, since it nearly covered him entirely, but he answered me, 'Oh Rasulullah ﷺ, how many thousands of years have I been praying for the favor of being permitted to bear this weight of your Buraq's covering! At last the All-Gracious Lord has heard my pleas and granted me this favor!' 'Why did you pray for this?' I asked him. Israfil عليه السلام answered, 'For how many thousands of years did I worship the Divine Throne!'

"At last there came a voice addressing me, saying, 'What is it that you long for? Your prayer has been accepted.' I replied, 'Oh my Lord, when his time on earth has come, I pray that I might be granted one hour in the service of the intercessor for his sinful nation, whose name the King on the Day of Judgment has deigned to write on the base of the Divine Throne beside His own Blessed Name.' To this the Almighty Lord replied, 'I grant you your prayer. There will come one night during his lifetime in which I will grant him the experience of My Nearness. I will bring him from his lowly station on earth up to the highest Heaven. I will open for him the gates of My treasure houses with the Key of Witnessing. I will lead him from Mecca to the Bayt-al-Maqdis (Jerusalem), and until he arrives there, you will have the honor of carrying the saddle cloth of his mount.'"

The Holy Prophet ﷺ then continued:

"That night, the Buraq's feet did not touch the ground. All the way from Mecca to Jerusalem were spread the fine, flowered silks from Paradise, on which the Buraq trod. On my way, suddenly one Ifrit (demon) appeared before me and leaned towards me, with flames leaping from his mouth. Jibra'il عليه السلام then said to me, 'Oh Rasulullah ﷺ, let me teach you a few words to say, which will extinguish the fire of this Ifrit and undo his existence.' 'Do teach me, please!' I replied and he taught me these words:

A'udhu bi-wajhi-llahil-karim wa bi-kalimati-llahi-t-tammat-allati la yujawizuhunna barrun wa la fajir, min sharri ma yanzilu min-as-sama'i wa ma ya'ruju fiha wa min sharri ma yakhruju minha wa min fitan-il-layli wa-n-nahari wa min tawariq-il-layli wa-n-nahari illa tariqan yatruku bi-khayrin, ya Rahman!

(I seek refuge in the gracious nature of my Lord Allah, and in the perfection of the Divine Word which neither the righteous nor the transgressor is able to breach, from the evil which descends from the sky and that which rises up to it; and from the evil which comes forth from the sky; and from the tribulations of the night and the day, and from all the calamities of night and day, except for those that result in benefit, oh Lord of Mercy!)

"When this Du'a was recited, the fire of this Ifrit died down and the creature ceased to exist. A voice then came from my right side, saying, 'Oh *Muhammad* 🕌, stay for a moment and linger; for there is something I wish to ask you...' This voice called me three times, but I paid it no heed and went on. Then I heard a voice calling me from my left side, and it said, 'Oh *Muhammad* 🕌, wait awhile, I need to ask you something.' But again I listened not to it and passed on. Then I beheld a woman, magnificently bedecked in costly robes and lavishly bejeweled. When I passed close by her, I saw that she was a very old woman. Thrice she spoke to me, saying, 'Stop!' but I heeded not her call and passed on. "Ahead of me I saw an old man, bent over his staff and trembling in every limb. He, too, requested me thrice to stop and stay with him. 'Look at me and pity my condition,' he said, 'let me enjoy your beauty, for I have something I want to ask you.' But I passed him by, not heeding his pleas. After a while, I beheld a fresh youth of surpassing beauty whose face shone with light, 'Stay, oh *Muhammad* 🕌,' he addressed me, 'for I have things to ask of you.'

"At his words, the Buraq halted, and I gave him Salams. After responding to my greetings, he said, 'Good tidings to you! All good is in you alone and in your nation.' To this I rejoined, 'Alhamdulillah!' and Jibra'il 🕌 echoed my words. I then asked him who these people were whom I had just seen. He answered, 'The voice coming from the right was the voice of the unbelievers. Had you stopped there, your nation would have been overpowered by them, and reduced to contempt after your time. The voice coming from your left was that of the Christians; had you paused to stop there, your nation would have been overpowered by the Christian peoples after your time and subjugated by them. The woman you saw was this world, the *dunya*.

She appears finely decked out and attractive to those who wish to possess her. Her decorations and fine robes are meant to fool and deceive mankind.

'The fact that she appears to be an old woman indicates that the Last Day has drawn nigh. Had you been swayed by her appeal, your whole nation would have become obsessed with the goods of this world and would have worshipped them. The old man you saw was the accursed devil, Shaytan himself. He knows how kind and merciful you are by nature, so he tried to ensnare you by appearing pitiful to you. It was nothing but a guile to stay you. Had you been fooled by his words, your nation would never have been saved from his wiles, up to the very last drop of their blood, he would have gained the upper hand over very many of them. As for the young lad you saw, he is the religion of Islam. It was there that you stopped; therefore, after your time, your entire nation will be safe from the machinations of the enemy and the religion of Islam will endure.

'You had been concerned with a number of questions regarding your nation, such as, 'What will happen when they go out at night into the desert and run into a company of malevolent Jinn? What will be their state after I am gone?' Allah Almighty who knows all that is hidden and what is manifest then made that Ifrit appear to you and taught you the means of salvation. After your time, there will be no religion that will overcome this religion of Islam. The nation of *Muhammad* 🕌 will live according to the Divine Law of the Shari'a. Thus, in the final end, they will be saved from the wiles of Shaytan and reach to safety. Islam will remain on earth until the Day of Judgment. All that you have seen are signs from Allah who wishes to awaken you and relieve you of your fears and doubts.' And thus, Jibra'il 🕌 explained to me these visions.

"After some time we reached a place where date palms were plentiful. Jibra'il 🕌 told me to dismount there and to pray, so I did. When I had finished praying, Jibra'il asked me whether I knew this place where I had prayed and he told me that it was called Tayyiba (which is one of the names for Madinah al-Munawwara). And he told me that before

160

long I would migrate to this place. Next we came to a place, which was all white. Again Jibra'il told me to dismount and to pray there. Then he asked me if I knew the place, and when I did not he explained that this was the tree beneath which Musa had prayed when he came to the land of Madian.

"When Musa was fleeing from Pharaoh, he came to this land. Outside the city of Madian he saw some shepherds watering their flocks, and he saw two girls who were standing at a distance from the well, waiting for their turn. Musa felt sorry for the girls and went up to them to inquire why they waited. Learning their story, he said to himself, 'Herein lies great reward,' and disregarding his own fatigue, he went and watered their sheep for them. Then he withdrew to a tree and prayed beneath it. This very tree is the tree you have now prayed beneath, oh *Muhammad* .'

"Afterwards we came to yet another place, and Jibra'il said, 'Dismount, and pray here!' When I had done so and again did not know where it was that I had just prayed, he told me, 'This is Tur-i-Sina, Mount Sinai, where the Almighty Lord revealed Himself to His Prophet Musa and spoke to him, in answer to his supplication.'

"We continued apace and in time reached a grand mansion where again the angel bade me pray, explaining that this was the village where the Prophet 'Isa was born. When I had done praying, I beheld a group of people who were planting a field. No sooner had they planted a seed than it yielded seven hundredfold. I asked the angel who these people were, and he told me, 'These are the people who expend of their wealth in the way of Allah.'

"Then again, I beheld another group of persons, whose heads were being smashed with stones by the angels, but they grew back instantly, only to be crushed again. 'Who are these people?' I asked the angel Jibra'il . He said, 'They are those of your nation who abandoned the practice of prayer, and those who performed it negligently in that when rising from the position of Ruk'u or Sajda, they did not bother to straighten up completely, but fused the various postures and phases of the ritual prayer in heedless haste.'

"I then saw a certain group of people who were altogether hungry and naked. Around them grew weeds of fire and the angels were driving them to eat those fiery weeds just as animals are driven to pasture. I asked who they were and the angel said, 'They are those belonging to your nation who did not give the Zakat they were obliged to pay, and who had no compassion with the poor and destitute, the homeless widows and orphans.'

"Then I saw another people: to one side there was a spread of the choicest foods anyone could dream of, to the other there was some dreadfully smelling, rotten meat. These people never looked or turned to the delicious foods, but ate only of the carrion meat. 'Who are they?' I asked. 'They are men and women of your nation who engaged in all manner of unlawful sexual activities, while lawful spouses were available to them.'

"After these, I saw a group of men piling up wooden logs. They were trying to lift them up, but they failed at every attempt. Their strength was simply insufficient, yet they kept up their futile efforts. 'And who are they?' I asked. Jibra'il ﷽ told me, 'They are people of your nation who were engrossed in the affairs of this world (dunya). Whereas they had more than they could possibly use up, they were forever dissatisfied and tried to amass more and more. They are in love with the world and what it has to offer and they are constantly seeking to increase their share.'

"Then I saw a great stone, which had a little hole in it. Out of the hole came a snake and began to grow. Then it turned around and tried to go back through the little hole, but, having grown so large, it could not fit through it, and began to circle round and round the stone in confusion. I asked the Angel what this was, and Jibra'il ﷽ told me, 'This stone symbolizes the body of your nation, and the small hole within it signifies their mouths. As for the snake, it signifies all the lies, and bad, forbidden things, gossip and slander that issues from their mouths. Once these things have emerged from their mouths, it is impossible to swallow them again, and they will be punished for these things in this life and the life hereafter. They will hear worse than this and will be called to account. So exhort your nation to mind their words, and beware of speaking evil and hurtful things, so that they might find salvation.'

"Then I saw a person drawing water from a well. With great effort he drew the bucket up to the rim of the well, but he found no water in it, an empty bucket was all he got for his trouble. I asked about him and Jibra'il ﷺ told me, 'This is the condition of those who performed good works without a pure intention. Their aim was not Allah alone but the acclaim of men. Hence, though they put themselves through great trouble in their worldly lives, they reap no reward for it in the afterlife, but expose themselves only to greater troubles.'

"I saw another people bearing great loads upon their backs. Although they could hardly carry the weight, they said to their companions, 'Load me up with more!' 'Who are they?' I asked the angel Jibra'il ﷺ who answered me, 'These are the people who defrauded goods left in their safekeeping. Despite being weighed down with such great weight, they seek to increase their wealth by unrighteous methods.'

"Then I saw another group of people whose tongues and lips were distended and hung down loosely. Angels with shears of fire came and cut off these flapping appendages. But whenever they cut them, they would immediately grow back as they were before, and the angels would resume their cutting. 'Who are these?' I asked Jibra'il ﷺ and he replied, 'These are such persons as denounced their own people to their rulers and tyrants, the sycophants and toadies who upheld all their commanders' lies rather than trying to save their people from the injustice committed by their rulers.'

"Then I saw a people whose flesh was being cut by the angels and fed to them. 'Eat!' the angels ordered them. When they couldn't do this from the disgust they felt, the angels whipped them and ordered them again, 'Eat!' until they did so. 'Who are these?' I asked, and Jibra'il told me, 'These are people who spread calumnies about their fellowmen.'

"Next I beheld a people whose faces were black and whose eyes were blue. Their lower lips reached down to their feet, while their upper lip was affixed to their forehead. Blood and pus dripped from their mouths. In one hand they held a carafe full of fire, in the other hand a glass of fire. The blood and pus oozing from their mouths drips into the bottle and begins to boil. The angels order them to drink this, and force them to do so. But every time they try to fill their glasses and drink from them, the liquid boils so strongly and its stench is so disgusting that they cannot stand it and begin to bray like donkeys. The angels then beat them and make them drink it by force. 'Who are these people?' I asked Jibra'il. 'These are the wine-drinkers,' he replied.'

"Then I saw another group of people whose tongues stuck out from the backs of their necks and whose faces had become like the faces of pigs. From above and from below they were being whipped and beaten. 'Who are these people?' I asked, and Jibra'il 🌸 told me, 'These are people who bore false witness and gave false testimony, and in so doing wronged the servants of Allah.'

"Another group appeared whose stomachs were so bloated that they hung pendulously down and whose hands and feet were bound and fettered. They could not rise to their feet because of the weight of their stomachs, and fell rolling upon the ground. 'Who are these people?' I asked Jibra'il. 'These are people from your nation your practiced usury and misappropriated other people's property.'

"Next I passed some women whose faces were blackened and who were given robes of fire to wear. Angels were beating them with maces of fire so that they howled like dogs. I asked Jibra'il who they were and he said, 'These are the women who committed adultery and who caused their husbands pain and torment.'" "Next I came upon a group that was being slaughtered by angels with knives of fire. They came back to life, only to have their throats cut anew. 'Who are they?' I asked Jibra'il. 'Those are people belonging to your nation who killed a soul without justification.'

"Then I came by a group of people who were suspended in mid-air while fire issued from their ears and noses and mouths. Each one of them was attended by two terrible, vengeful angels, and each angel held in his hand a fiery stick of seventy knots. With these they were beating them continuously, without stopping, while they recited this very significant Tasbih:

Qadir, Muqtadir, Subhanallah.

Allah Almighty is the Mighty Avenger over His foes; Allah Almighty is the Most Powerful, Praised be He.

"I asked Jibra'il about these people and he told me, 'These are the people who outwardly confessed their faith, while in their hearts there was nothing but hypocrisy and disbelief.'

"Then I saw another group of people who were imprisoned in a valley of fire. They were being burnt to death, but they instantly came back to life, only to be burnt alive once more. Their punishment seemed very severe to me. 'Who are these people?' I asked the angel. 'These are people who failed to honor and obey their parents and who were rebellious and opposed them.'

"Next I came upon a people upon whose chests were placed bowls of fire, while the angels were beating them with big sticks. 'Who are these?' I asked, and Jibra'il said, 'These are the musicians who played the lute and sang songs to the people.'

"Then I heard a terrible noise and asked what it was. Jibra'il told me, 'A stone has fallen into the pit of Jahannam from its rim. It has been falling for three thousand years, and now it has hit the bottom. That was the noise you heard.'

About this stone there is the following narration: If a stone the size of a man's head is rolled down from the earthly skies, it will fall down to earth in twenty-four hours, even though it falls a distance of five hundred years. Consider this distance and then consider how far a stone of that size must fall if it falls for three thousand years! That is the depth of the pit of Hellfire; therefore, take refuge in Allah from its raging fires.

The Prophet continues:

"I then came to another valley from which issued the most noxious smells and dreadful sounds. 'What are these smells?' I asked, and Jibra'il answered me, 'That is the stench of Hell. Listen to what it has to say!' I listened and this is what I heard: 'Oh my Lord, send to me those servants whom you promised to me. My chains, my spikes, my fetters, my *Zakkum* trees and boiling waters and cauldrons of pus are ready for them, and other punishments as well. My snakes and scorpions have become many, and my depths unfathomable. Send me the servants You have promised to me, that I may begin to punish them..' This was the reply that the Lord Almighty gave in answer to this request of Jahannam: 'Oh Jahannam, I leave up to you these works! I will leave to you all those who attribute partners to My Holy Name, who disbelieve in Me and My Prophets, all those who are wicked and. villainous, be they male or female, and who disbelieve in the Day of Resurrection – all those I shall throw into your fires!' Jahannam was pleased with the Lord's promise and said, 'I am satisfied, oh my Lord!'

"After this we reached a valley in which blew a gentle breeze and sweet smells wafted all around. A pleasant and melodious air struck the ear. I asked, 'What is this most pleasing sound, where does it come from and what are these voices saying? What is this gentle wind and from where do these sweet smells come?' Jibra'il then explained to me, 'This is the smell and the breeze of Paradise. Just listen to what it says, and you will understand.'

"The breeze from Paradise spoke as follows, 'Oh my Lord, send to me Thy servants whom Thou hast promised to me. All the delights I have in store for them are ready: the pavilions, fine and heavy brocades and silks, carpets and wraps, the pearls, jewels, silver and gold; the amber and musk; the spreads and jugs and vessels; all the varied foods of Paradise, the rivers of milk, honey, wine and water; the Huris, Ghilman and Wildan and all the unspeakable delights of Paradise are stocked in abundance and overflowing plenty. Send Thou Thy promised servants to me so that I might present them with these untold pleasures and shower them with gifts of goodness.'

"The Lord replied to this lovely supplication of the Jannah: 'Oh Paradise, I shall send to you what you desire. I shall send you the men and women who believed in Me and worshipped Me alone, who recognized and honored My Messengers, engaged in beneficial actions and associated no partners to My Divinity. Whoever is in fear of Me and My Punishment, him I shall free and make safe from it. Whoever turns to Me in his need and invokes Me in extremis, to his need I shall hearken and his intent I shall see through.

Whoever grants Me a loan, I shall repay him manifold.[1] Whoever leaves all his cares up to Me, who entrusts all his affairs to Me, I shall take over for him all his labor. For I alone am Allah; there is no god beside Me. I fulfill all My vows; not do I turn back from My promises. All the believers have come to success. The Glory of the Creator outshines that of all His Creation.'

"To these words of Grace, Paradise replied, 'I am well satisfied, oh my Lord!'

Bayt-al-Maqdis

Now the Holy Prophet ﷺ saw a great many wondrous sights on the way to the Masjid-al-Aqsa, but these are the best known of them all, and we shall content ourselves with this much.

The Holy Prophet ﷺ continues his narrative:

"After this, we came to the Bayt-al-Maqdis. There I saw the angels descending down to earth. They came to meet me and give me the glad tidings of abundant blessings and boons that the Lord of Holiness and Grace was to send to me. They greeted me with these words: 'Salams to you, who are the first, Salams to you, who are the last, Salams to you, who are the assembler of men.' With this address they honored me greatly, still I asked Jibra'il, 'What kind of greeting is this - the First, the Last, the Assembler of Men is the Lord of the Worlds, Allah Almighty?' Jibra'il ﷺ then told me, 'Oh Rasulullah, on the Day of Judgment your tomb will be the first to open up, and then that of your nation. Therefore, they addressed you as the Gatherer. On that

---

[1] A loan here means the alms expended for Allah's sake on the destitute and impoverished and needy, and all the goods given away in the way of Allah - fi sabil-illah.

day, you will be the first to make intercession and yours will be the first intercession to be accepted. Therefore, they addressed you as the First. Of all the prophets in this world, you are the last to be sent, therefore they addressed you as the Last.'

"I then passed by them and came to the gates of the Masjid-al-Aqsa. I dismounted from the Buraq and Jibra'il tied him to a ring there. This was the ring to which the prophets and messengers always tied their mounts. The prophets and messengers came to greet me there and gave me much honor."

Now there are two accounts of the meeting of the prophets and messengers with our Holy Prophet ﷺ. One of them maintains that the Lord Almighty called the prophets back to life just for the sake of receiving the Holy Prophet Muhammad ﷺ with due formality; this implies that He resurrected them in their physical forms. The other, more commonly accepted version is this: that He Almighty called only their unblemished spirits to this meeting with the Prophet Muhammad ﷺ.

Let us continue with the Prophet Muhammad's ﷺ narrative:

"They appeared to me as exceedingly great, honorable and enlightened personalities. I ask Jibra'il who they were and he told me, 'They are your fathers and brothers, the prophets and messengers. Give them your Salams and salute them.' I greeted them accordingly and entered the Masjid-al-Aqsa together with them. The Iqama was called and I thought to myself, 'I wonder who will be the Imam of this gathering?' While I was yet pondering this point, Jibra'il took me by the hand and said, 'Go ahead up front, you are to be Imam, for you are the most excellent and the most highly esteemed.' So I stepped out in front of them all and led all the prophets and messengers in a prayer of two Rak'ats.'"

The scholars have proffered various views concerning this prayer, which was prayed here. If it were categorized as 'nafila' (supererogatory), this is contradicted by the fact that it was prayed in congregation, for it is not permissible for *nafil* prayers to be prayed in congregation. It also could not have been the 'Isha prayer, for this consists of four Rak'ats, while only two Rak'ats were here prayed. The most authoritative opinion on this is the following: the prayer, which Rasulullah led in the Masjid-al-Aqsa, is of the same kind as that which he led and prayed in each level of the heavens to which he ascended. And the one he prayed in the Bayt-al-Ma'mur and at the Sidratul Muntaha, in which he led the entire assembly of angels, and it partakes of its characteristics. It was performed upon the command of the Lord of the Worlds, Allah Almighty.

Meeting the Prophets

To continue in the words of the Holy Prophet ﷺ:

> "After completing the prayer, I turned my back to the Mihrab and my face to the assembly of prophets, on all of whom be peace, and I spoke to them. Every single prophet engaged in praise of the special gifts the Highest Lord had graced him with, and I also joined in the praise of Allah who equipped me with such outstanding gifts.

> "Ibrahim praised the Lord and said, 'Praise and glory to the Highest of the High who made me His intimate friend and gave me great possessions.'

> "Musa praised Him Almighty and said, 'Praise and glory be to Allah Almighty, the Highest of the High who spoke to me without intermediary, who caused Pharaoh and his henchmen to drown in the waters at my hand and who saved the Children of Israil. He made my nation a people guided to the Truth, judging by the Truth and striving for the good pleasure of Allah Almighty.'

> "Next the Prophet Da'ud came forth and praised the Lord, saying, 'Praise and Glory to the Divine Lord who made me king over such a great realm and who revealed to me the scripture of the Zabur. Who made iron to be as soft as beeswax in my hand, and who placed the birds and the mountains under my command, so that they all joined me in the praises of the Lord, who gave me knowledge of the law and the gift of sweet speech.'

"After him, his son Sulayman stepped forth and glorified the Lord thus: 'Praise and Glory be to the Lord, the Mighty, the Enduring, who gave me power over the winds, and made the Jinn and the demons subservient to me, so that they did whatever I wished. He taught me the languages of the birds and the beasts and gave me greater excellence than many of His servants. He gave me such an incomparably vast kingdom, which no other mortal can ever hope to attain.'

"Then 'Isa stepped forth and glorified his Lord, saying, 'Praise and Glory be to the Almighty Creator who, as He created Adam from clay, brought me into existence without the contribution of an earthly father. He created me solely through His Creative Word, 'Be!' He taught me the wisdom of the Torah and the Injil and the knowledge of the law. He granted healing to the sick, seeing to the blind through my supplication, and by means of me, He brought the dead back to life. He made me and my mother safe from the wiles of the accursed devil and he lifted me up into the heavens in my living, physical body.'

"After they had spoken, I said to them, 'You have now all voiced your glorification of the Lord; it is now my turn to glorify Him,' and I began by saying, 'Praise and Glory be to the Lord, the Forgiving, the Merciful the Abundant, Munificent, the Lord of Might and Honor who has sent me as a Mercy for the Worlds and as a Messenger of Joy to all humankind and as a Warner. He has sent a book to me that makes clear all things, and He has given my nation excellence over every previous nation. He has made my nation to be a people of the middle way. He split open my bosom and removed from it all sin. He has made my reputation to be blameless and He has given me victory over all created beings and made me the last and final of all prophets.'

"After I had completed my glorification, Ibrahim got up and said, 'You have been made more meritorious than all the other Prophets with regard to your being victorious and being the last and final of the Prophets.'"

Some authorities relate the meeting of the Prophets as follows:

When Rasulullah 🌸 came to the Bayt-al-Maqdis, all the Prophets and Messengers rushed up to greet him. They saluted and praised him in many ways and sprinkled upon him showers of light. They marched out ahead of the Buraq as far the Masjid-al-Aqsa. There, the Holy Prophet 🌸 dismounted from the Buraq, Jibra'il tied the halter of the Buraq and everybody halted. Then they addressed the Holy Prophet ﷺ and said, "Oh Habibullah ﷺ, it is for you to enter the Masjid ahead of us," and the Prophet Muhammad 🌸 answered, "You were sent before me as Prophets, you therefore have the right of precedence over me. Therefore, proceed into the sanctuary ahead of me." Then the Almighty Lord Himself addressed the assembly, "Oh My Beloved, you have attained a special station in this world by appearing with your message of Truth after all those present had gone before; but you are the one who has precedence over everything else that was in the hidden world before the Creation, for all was created from your light. Therefore, it is your right to proceed ahead of them all; enter now!"

At this command, the Holy Prophet 🌸 together with the angel Jibra'il عليه السلام entered and all the Prophets and Messengers followed them. Then Jibra'il called the Iqama, and the Prophet Muhammad 🌸 led the entire assembly of Prophets, Messengers and angels of the Muqarrabin in a prayer of two Rak'ats.

The Holy Prophet 🌸 resumes the narrative:

> "After we had prayed, I received an inspiration in my heart of hearts that it was now time to make supplication for my nation. I therefore raised my hands towards the heavens and began to plead for my weak and inadequate nation. I prayed for their salvation and safety, for grace and forgiveness, and for their release from Hell. All the assembled Prophets and Messenger and angels concluded my supplication by saying, 'Amin!'

> "At that very moment, I heard within me a voice which called to me, saying, 'Oh My Beloved, you are seated in the Masjid-al-Aqsa, it is the night of your Mi'raj. You who are praying here are the Beloved of Allah and a much-honored Prophet; those answering to your supplication are all Prophets and Messengers and angels of the

Muqarrabin, and He to whom you direct you supplication, He is the Most Merciful of the Merciful, the Most Bounteous of the Bountiful. He is Allah who leads all to the Light of His Guidance, the Sublime Lord of all Might and Glory. Beyond doubt, He will grant acceptance to your prayer, He will forgive the sins of your nation and grant them freedom from punishment. By My Might and Glory, I proclaim that I shall grant them of My Mercy. I shall clothe them with the honor of beholding the Sight of My Divine Beauty.'"

Oh Allah, grant us that our last breath might be one of faith, oh Lord of Mercy and Compassion! And grant us to behold Thy Divine Presence, for the sake and honor of Thy Prophet Muhammad ﷺ, Amin, ya Hannan, ya Mannan! (Oh Most Compassionate, Bounteous Lord!)

The Holy Prophet ﷺ continues:

"After this, Jibra'il came out, holding in his hand three cups. One of these contained milk, one wine and the third water. He told me to choose one of these and to drink it. I chose the one that held milk and drank from it, but there was a little left over in the cup. When I handed the cup back to Jibra'il, he said to me, 'You have chosen the natural disposition of Islam.' Then I heard a voice from the unseen, which spoke to me, saying, 'Oh Muhammad ﷺ, had you finished all the milk in the cup, not one of your nation would have had to go to Hell.'

"I then turned to Jibra'il and asked him to give the cup back to me so that I might empty it entirely. But Jibra'il said to me, 'All that has been written must come to pass; what has been decreed from before the beginning of time, must take place, oh Rasulullah ﷺ.'"

The scholars make this comment: There are seventeen benefits in the fact that the Holy Prophet ﷺ did not proceed directly to the heavens from the Kaba at Mecca in the night of his Mi'raj, but rather stopped at the Bayt-al-Maqdis and ascended from there.

If we were here to expound on all the seventeen benefits, it would take us a very long time; therefore, we shall content ourselves with the mention of only two points.

The first is this: Had our Holy Prophet ﷺ ascended to the heavens directly from Mecca on his Mi'raj and later told his people about it, it would have been very difficult for him to convince those among them whose minds were stubbornly set in opposition to him. However, the Holy Prophet ﷺ reported that he first went to the Bayt-al-Maqdis (the Temple site in Jerusalem) and that from there he ascended to the heavens. Even then, some of the most stubborn denied that this could have happened, and they challenged him, saying, "If it is true that you have been where you say you have, then tell us about the shape and structure of the Bayt-al-Maqdis. We have visited there before and so we know what it looks like, but we know that you have not been there before. If your description accords with what we know, then we will believe in what you tell us. We will then believe that in this night you have been to al-Quds, in full waking consciousness."

The Holy Prophet ﷺ then gave them the appropriate answers and described to them the shape and form of the buildings there, and thus he silenced them. In this way, the reality of the Mi'raj was proven.

But let me dwell on this subject a little longer: The day after the Mi'raj had taken place, the Prophet ﷺ told his people about it, but they called it lies, saying, "If you really went to the Masjid-al-Aqsa last night, then you must be able to describe it to us." Faced with this demand for proof, the Holy Prophet ﷺ experienced some confusion. He had been entirely engaged in holy converse with the assembled Prophets and Messengers that he had not so much as glanced at the building of the holy mosque there. But Jibra'il appeared to him just that moment and said, "The Lord Almighty sends His Salams upon you. He commands me to bring before you the Masjid-al-Aqsa for you to look at, so that you may give them the answers they desire." With that he revealed to the Prophet ﷺ the Masjid-al-Aqsa in its complete shape. Beholding the mosque in front of him, the Holy Prophet ﷺ was very glad and confidently told them to ask what they would of him. He answered them, giving precise names and descriptions of the building.

For instance, when they asked him how many columns the mosque had, the Prophet ❀ described to them each single pillar in detail, singling out whether it was made of marbled stone or of real marble. For each detail he gave exact descriptions. He even told them the distance between every single pillar. At last they said, "There is no doubt that he actually went there and saw what he says he saw there. Although we have been there countless times, we could never have given such a close description of all this." With this acknowledgment, they themselves silenced their own arguments and the reality of the Mi'raj was thus demonstrated.

Secondly, the site of the Bayt-al-Maqdis shall one day be the place of gathering. On the Day of Judgment all of Creation shall be assembled there. It was for this reason that the Lord Almighty brought His Beloved Muhammad ❀ whom He has honored above all the other Prophets and all other men to this place in his pure physical body. He imprinted his foot upon that place while he dwelt in the world, so that on the Day of Judgment when all creatures are resurrected and gathered in that place, the terror of it should be lessened and safety be found from its dread for the sake of the Prophet Muhammad ❀ who stepped in this place once before, during his life in this world. Thus it will be made easy for his nation to endure in that place and they will be protected from its awesomeness.

The Place of Gathering consists of fifty stations, and they will remain one thousand years in every station. Thus, that day will be as long as fifty thousand years. For the Holy Prophet's ❀ sake, the Lord Almighty makes the sojourn there easy for his nation and they will be protected from all the terror and fright of that tremendous day. Peace and Blessings from Almighty Allah be upon His Beloved and Chosen Prophet, Muhammad ❀, the Imam of the God-fearing, sallallahu 'alayhi wa sallam. Amin!

To return to the narrative of the Holy Prophet ❀:

"After this, Jibra'il took me by the hand and led me outside. No sooner had we stepped out than I beheld a flight of steps one end of which was placed upon the flat ground while the other end reached up and up and disappeared from view into the skies. One of its poles was made of red ruby while the other was of green emerald. The treads were of gold, silver and pearls, and each tread was made of a different precious stone. There were five hundred steps in all and each was embellished and embossed in a different and marvelous way. Never had I seen a thing of greater beauty.

"This stepladder was the angels' stairway, which they used to descend from Heaven down to the earth and to ascend up to the heavens again. The angel of death, Azra'il, uses this ladder when he comes to take home the souls of men. The spirits of men also climb up on that ladder when they leave this world. When a believer comes close to his death, the Lord shows him this stairway and he sees Azra'il descending upon it. He loses himself in the contemplation of that stairway and thus does not feel the agony of the throes of death. It is therefore that the eyes of the dead and dying are often found wide open and staring, gazing fixedly at the beauty of that staircase, which the souls must ascend. While he is yet gazing, his soul departs from him, and after the soul has gone, he can no longer close his eyes."

Oh Lord, we pray that the pangs of death be made light and easy for us and that we might draw our last breath with our faith intact, Amin!

The Holy Prophet # continued:

"The angel Jibra'il took me upon his wing. To the right and to the left the angels surrounded me and thus we ascended on that stairway straight towards the heavens."

There is the following account concerning this:

The Holy Prophet # stepped on a stone as he was attempting to affect his ascent. Under the pressure of the Holy Prophet's # blessed foot, this stone softened and became as soft as wax. Up to this very day, the imprint of the Prophet's # foot can be seen upon this stone. When the Holy Prophet # wished to raise his foot from the stone, by leave of the Almighty, this stone raised him aloft instead. At the same time, the steps of the heavenly ladder bent down and became one with the stone. The Holy Prophet ❀ then raised his foot off the stone and placing it upon the step of the stairs, said to it, "Stay, oh stone!" The step upon which the Holy Prophet ❀ trod then rose up and lifted the Prophet ❀ up. The next step then bent down and came to meet his foot, then it rose and carried him up with it. The next higher step then bent itself down to receive his foot, and raised it aloft when he him placed it upon it. In this manner the steps continued to bend and rise until they had carried the Prophet Muhammad ❀ all the way up to the heavens.

The stairs to the pavilions and palaces of the lofty gardens of Paradise behave in a manner similar to that of these steps. When this stone heard the Prophet's ❀ command telling it to stay, it obeyed that very instant and remained suspended in mid air, and even so it remains to this very day. From it many useful lessons may be drawn:

While it is only a stone, its unquestioning submission and obedience to the Prophet's ❀ command continues into our own time. Therefore, is it befitting of this noble nation to disobey and oppose the Holy Prophet ❀, having received the order from the Almighty to follow and obey his instructions, and having been cautioned and warned against all opposition to him? This is a point we must think about and take most seriously. To follow the Holy Prophet's ❀ enlightened commands and to emulate the actions of his right guidance, to obey him in perfect submission will save us from disgrace and punishment in this world and the world to come. We must always strive to reach for the happiness and bliss of both worlds. May Allah Almighty grant us His Divine Aid and Support and help us achieve Supreme Success, Amin.

There is another tradition that tells us the story as follows:

From this stone, the Prophet ❀ mounted the Buraq and the Buraq carried him up into the heavens.

Yet another report has the Holy Prophet ❀ relate as follows:

"At the foot of those stairs, I beheld a great angel. Had this angel spread out both its hands, all the seven layers of the earths and the seven layers of the heavens would have disappeared in them. This angel greeted me and showed me courtesy. Then he spoke to me and said, 'Oh Rasulullah ﷺ, I was created twenty-five thousand years before Adam. Since that time I have been waiting to receive you here, all the while reciting Salawat and blessings upon you in loving expectation of your advent. The Almighty be praised, for tonight I have attained my goal.'

"After I left that angel behind, I came to a sea, which had a depth of two hundred years' wayfaring. This sea remained suspended through the power of Allah Almighty and not one drop of its waters fell out from it. Whatever creatures there exist on land and in the waters, they all were present in that sea. It was also exceedingly stormy and full of waves."

It is said that the trembling of the air, which one sees when gazing into the sun is from the waves of that sea.

The Prophet ﷺ continues:

"After this we reached the home of the winds. The wind is bound tightly with seventy thousand strong chains and seventy thousand angels hold on to it firmly and keep it under control.

"After this, we reached the earthly skies, which Allah Almighty has created from green emerald."

According to a different narration, the Prophet ﷺ is to have said:

"It is created from water and steam."

The Prophet ﷺ called this Heaven 'Rafi'a', or according to another version, 'Raqi'a'. The keeper of this Heaven was Isma'il, for he is among the Prophets of the angels.

The Prophet ﷺ then proceeds to tell us of his journey through the heavens.

The Prophet's Visit to Heavens

About his journey to the First Heaven, the Master of All Humankind and Jinn 襲 narrated:

> "We then reached the first Heaven, Jibra'il ﷺ knocked upon its gate, crying, 'Open up!' The name of this gate is, 'Bab al-Hifz', the Gate of Protection, and it is made of red ruby stone, whereas its lock is made of pearls. From within the guardian of this gate, Isma'il, called out in a voice such as I have never heard before, 'Who is this demanding entry?'

> "Jibra'il thereupon answered, 'It is I, Jibra'il.' 'And who is that with you?' demanded the keeper of the gate. 'That is Muhammad 襲,' replied Jibra'il. The keeper of the gate then asked, 'Has he been given prophethood?' 'Yes,' replied Jibra'il, 'he has been given prophethood.' 'Has he been cited and invited to come here?' Isma'il demanded to know. 'Yes, he has been invited to come,' Jibra'il replied. Then Isma'il said, 'Welcome, welcome to you! What a delightful visitor!' With these words he opened the gate."

In another narration a differing version is related:

"Rasulullah 襲 rose up to the heavens using the rock in the Masjid-al- Aqsa as a stepping-stone to mount the Buraq. The distance from the earth to the Heaven is five hundred years' wayfaring. Each Heaven has a depth of five hundred years' traveling, and between two heavens there is a space of another five hundred years' travel.

Meeting Isma`il ﷺ

The Holy Prophet ﷺ resumes his narrative:

"When I entered this heavenly realm, I encountered Isma'il in his impressive aspect, seated upon a throne of light. One hundred thousand angels surrounded him, standing in front, in back, to his right and to his left. Each of these angels had another hundred thousand soldiers at his command."

Isma'il and all those with him engaged in this Tasbih:

Subhanal-malik-il-a'la.

Subhanal-'aliyy-il-azhim.

Subhana man laysa ka-mithlihi shay'in.

(Praise be to the Highest King; Glory to the High, the Mighty; Glory to Him who is unlike any other.)

I then saluted him and he returned my greetings and honored me. After this I beheld another group of angels, who stood in pious reverence in Qiyam, (the standing position of ritual prayer). They all were engaged in this Tasbih:

Subbuhun quddus Rabbuna wa Rabb-al-mala'ikati wa-r-ruh

(Praised be He with exalted praise, He who is holier than holy, our Lord and the Lord of the angels.)"

I enquired of Jibra'il about these angels' form of worship, and he answered, 'Since the day they were created they have been worshipping thus and so they will remain until the Day of Resurrection. Ask the Lord to grant this worship to your nation, too.' So I made supplication and the Lord granted this kind of worship to my nation. That is how the Qiyam came to be included in our prayer.

Apart from these, I beheld a number of angels created from wind and water. The angel appointed as their head and overseer was called Ra'ad (which means thunder). He is responsible for the clouds and the rains.

The Tasbih they were engaged in was this:

Subhana dhil-mulk wal-malakuti

(Praise be to Him in whose Hand lies the entire creation and its dominion.)

"From this angel's voice issued the sounds of thunder and lightning. In the heavenly sphere there remained not one empty space, angels were cramped even into the smallest corner, prostrating themselves and praising the Lord with manifold praises.

"Then I saw another angel who bore the shape of a man. Below his waist he was made of fire, while above the waist he was made of snow. The fire clung to the snow and although there was nothing separating these two elements, neither did the snow extinguish the fire, nor did the fire melt the snow. But tears were streaming down this angel's face, and as he wept, he recited this glorification (Tasbih):

Ya man allafa bayna-th-thalji wa-n-nar, allif bayna qulubi 'ibadikal-mu'minin.

(Oh Thou who hast joined the snow and the fire, unite Thou also the hearts of Thy believing servants.)

"I turned to Jibra'il and asked, 'Who is this angel and wherefore does he weep?' Jibra'il ﷺ explained, 'He is an angel, Habib by name. He weeps for the sins of thy nation and prays for mercy and forgiveness on them.'

"Then I saw Adam in the form in which he appeared in the world. He was draped in wraps of light and seated upon a throne of light. The Lord Almighty presented to him the souls of the departed, and whenever he perceived the soul of a believer, he rejoiced and said, 'A pure soul emerges from a pure body.' After this, he asked for forgiveness and pleaded for mercy upon that soul. Then the angels came and carried that soul up to a high and lofty place, as it is written in the Holy Quran:

No indeed; the book of the pious is in Illiyun; and what shall teach thee what is Illiyun? A book inscribed, witnessed by those brought nigh[2]. (The Stinters, 18-21)

"Whenever the souls of departed unbelievers and hypocrites are presented to him, he is vexed and curses them, 'An impure soul emerges from an impure body.' The angels then take that spirit and place it in a place called Sijjin, as it is written in the Holy Quran:

No indeed; the Book of the libertines is in Sijjin; and what shall teach thee what is Sijjin?
A book inscribed.   *(The Stinters, 7-9)*

"I then asked Jibra'il who was this person and he told me,' This is your first forefather Adam, go towards him and extend to him your greetings.' So I went to him and saluted him, and he replied to my salute, honoring me by saying, 'Welcome to you, oh my righteous son, oh righteous Prophet! Praise be to the Lord who has given me such a son as you.'"

"In this way he received me well, and I replied to his complimentary speech with these words: 'Praise be to the Lord who has given to me such a father as thou art one.' Then again, Adam spoke, glorified the Lord and said, 'Glory to the Almighty who has blessed you with such great wonders; who has brought you forth from my loins; may Allah always increase the blessings He showers upon you and make you steadfast and permanently grounded in them.' In reply to this supplication and well wishing, I said, 'Praise be to Allah, the Lord of Might and Bounty! He who created you from clay through His Divine Powers and who had you carried up to the heavens on the shoulders of angels. Who has made you the Qibla and commanded all the angels to bow down before you and who has made Paradise accessible for your sake.'

"To that Adam answered me as follows, 'For all the bounteous gifts granted to me that you have mentioned, you are still more blessed than I. For all the miracles and gifts that I was granted were only given to

---

[2] *Illiyun*: the uppermost Heaven, a word derived from the Arabic, meaning high, raised.

me for the sake of your light upon my forehead, I was favored with all these honors only for the sake of that radiant light.'

"He spoke many more things to me, and ended his speech by saying, 'From my time on until the time of your prophethood, only one in a thousand of my children were graced with entering Paradise, while nine hundred and ninety-nine were sent to Hell. When your time of prophethood came, only one in one thousand of your nation was sent to Hell and nine hundred and ninety-nine were admitted into Paradise. The Almighty placed your blessed name beside His very own Holy Name even before you appeared in this world and proclaimed your great worth to all of creation.'

Adam recited this Tasbih:

Subhanal-jalil-il-ajalli,

Subhanal-wasi'al-ghaniyyi,

Subhana-llahi wa bi-hamdihi,

Subhana-llahil-azhim. Istaghfirullah.

(Glory to the Mightiest of the Mighty, Glory to the All-Embracing, All-Abundant; Praised be Allah and glorified be He! Praised be Allah, the All-Glorious I seek forgiveness from Allah Almighty.)

"Then I saw a door to the right of Adam from which issued the sweetest of scents. Just to look in the direction of that door filled the heart with gladness and serenity. To his left there was another door; to look at it sufficed to make a man weep and the heart to become heavy. I asked Jibra'il about these doors, and he said, 'The door to the right opens upon Paradise. The souls of the blessed enter through that door, and whoever glances to the right, sees them and is gladdened. The door to the left leads to Hell, and the souls of the sinners must go through that door. Who looks to the left sees them on their way to Hell and is saddened by the sight.'

"Next I saw an angel who had the form of a cockerel. He was very large and his head touched up to the Divine Throne, while his feet were below the seven layers of the earth. He had two wings; when he spread these, they reached from the farthest east to the utmost west. The station of this angel is the Sidratul Muntaha, which shall be described in detail later on, inshaAllah. The angel's body is created of white pearl, while the comb on its head is of red ruby."

To rear a pure, white, unspeckled rooster in one's home is of great usefulness and has very special advantages. This is because of its resemblance to this angel, the Cockerel of the Divine Throne. It benefits not just the owner of the white rooster, but it also protects the neighbors and the environment from many disasters and bad things.

The Holy Prophet # is reported to have said about this:

"The white rooster is my sincere friend, and he is also the friend of my friend, the angel Jibra'il #. He is also the enemy of my enemy, Shaytan. The white rooster protects the house in which he is raised and its owner and entire household, as well as nine neighboring houses and their inhabitants."

There is only this condition attached to it: the rooster must be of a flawless white, without a speck. He is of even greater value if his crest is forked, as the Holy Prophet # says:

"The fork-crested white rooster is my dear and beloved friend. He protects four houses to the right, four to the left, four in front and four in back, altogether sixteen houses and their inhabitants from disaster and calamity." (Related by Abu ash-Shaykh from Anas.)

There is another Hadith related by Bayhaqi from 'Umar who claims that the Holy Prophet # said:

"This rooster makes known to Allah's servants the times for prayer. Whoever raises a white rooster in his house will be protected from three things: from the evil of Shaytan, the evil of the sorcerer, and the evil of the soothsayer."

However, he who raises a white rooster must on no account slaughter him, as those who know about these matters inform us in the *Fath-al-Qadir* will have us know: "Sorrow will not depart from the side of him who slaughters a white rooster."

Imam Tha'libi cites from the book entitled *Hayat al-Haywan* (The Life of the Animals) by Imam Dumayri:

"The Holy Prophet ✾ makes clear to us these pearls of spiritual wisdom when he says, 'There are three things that Allah Almighty loves and is pleased with: the voice of him who recites the Holy Quran; the sound of the rooster's call; the voice of him who prays for forgiveness in the time before the dawn.'"

To continue with the Holy Prophet's ✾ narrative:

"This angel who has the form of a rooster descends to the earthly skies when it is night, and this is his Tasbih:

Subhanal-malikil-quddus,

Subhanal-kabiril-muta'al,

La ilaha ill'Allah-al-hayy-al-qayyum.

(Glory to the All-Holy King,

Glory to the Great and Exalted God,

There is no God but Allah, the Ever-Living, Eternally Abiding.)

"I then asked Jibra'il, 'What is this?' and Jibra'il answered me, 'This is the reason he is called, 'the Rooster of the Divine Throne', for when it is night on earth, he descends to the worldly skies. After one third of the night has passed, he flaps his wings and says, 'Oh you who would be worshippers, arise and pray!' All of creation hears this call, all except mankind and Jinn. Therefore, when the roosters on earth hear the angels call, they too flap their wings and voice their call, saying, 'Oh you heedless ones! Arise and engage in remembrance of your Lord!' When half of the night has passed, this angel again flaps its wings and calls, 'Let those who would perform the supererogatory night prayer (Tahajjud); rise and pray!'

"When the roosters on earth hear this call, they too sound their call to pass on to men the message of the angel. When two thirds of the night have passed and only one third of it remains, the angel speaks up again and calls out, 'Where are they who would ask for forgiveness for their sins, whose sole hope and desire is the Lord of the Worlds? Let them rise and pray for forgiveness and present their invocations!' Again, the roosters on earth hear this call and pass it on to the people on the earth. When at last dawn begins to break, this angel flaps its wings once more and calls, 'Now let the heedless ones rise, though they be laden heavily with their sins.' After this, he again ascends to his station in the Heavens. Again, the roosters on earth hear his words and inform mankind of the angel's call. This same sequence is repeated every night, up till the Day of Judgment.'

"And Jibra'il continued, 'When the Day of Judgment is about to occur, this angel will want to call out his call as usual after the first third of the night has passed. But he is stopped by a call from on High, 'Oh My angel, do not awaken My servants!' In this way he is prevented from calling, and he and all the angels of the heavens with him realize that the Day of Resurrection is upon them. All at once they begin to weep."

That night will be the length of three days and three nights, and in that night neither the cocks will crow, nor will the dogs bark. Mankind will lie in a deep sleep of forgetfulness for three full days and nights. Only those who were accustomed to rise and pray the prayer of the night (Tahajjud) will awaken and rise to pray their Tahajjud as usual. But they will wonder and say, "Yet there is no sign of morning breaking, have we risen too early?" Then they will lie down to sleep a bit longer, and when again they awaken, still it will not be day. Then they will understand that it is the longest night before the Last Day, and that indeed it has finally begun.

They will then set about trying to wake up their companions, who were not used to rising for the night prayer, but whatever they do, they will not succeed in waking them, it is impossible. Then they betake themselves to the mosques, gathering there and repenting of their sins, praying for forgiveness. There they will remain for those whole three days and nights, weeping copious and incessant tears, imploring the Lord for mercy. When this period is over and the day dawns, the sun will be seen to rise in the west and the Gates of Repentance will be shut.

To continue with our Prophet's 🎴 narrative:

"I then came to a sea, which was whiter than milk and as viscous as the semen of men. Within it, I beheld things so exceedingly strange and unknown so as to defy all description. Their numbers were unaccountably great and beyond reckoning. I asked Jibra'il, 'What sort of sea is this?' and he answered me, 'This is the Sea of Life. On the Day of Resurrection, after every created thing has died its death, the Almighty will want to raise them all from their graves in order to mete out reward or punishment.

"He will then issue His Command and a rain will fall upon the earth from the waters of this sea. The rain waters will rise to a depth of forty yards upon the level earth and the ground will be drenched to its deeps. All the flesh and bones that have rotted in the earth will then be restored; all the skins and strands of hair and nerves will come together and appear once more. As soon as this water comes in touch with the earth, whatever is contained in it will instantly return to its former state. What has long been scattered will be assembled again, and all this will come to pass on account of the action of the waters of the Sea of Life.'

"After this, Jibra'il called the Adhan and Iqama, and I led all the angels and inhabitants in a prayer of two Rak'ats. Then I rose to the second level of the heavens."

The Second Heaven

Regarding his journey to the Second Heaven, the Best of all Creation 🎴 narrated:

"The Lord Almighty, praised be His Name, has created this Heaven from red coral and called it Qaydum. The name of its gatekeeper is Mikha'il. This Heaven appeared to me to be especially full of light and splendor, so much so that I was blinded and had to squint. The door of this Heaven is of pearls and its lock is of light. Jibra'il knocked upon this door and requested entry. The keeper of the gate, Mikha'il, called from inside, 'Who is it requesting the opening of this gate?' 'I am Jibra'il,' replied Jibra'il, and again the angel asked, 'And who is this with you?' 'This is Muhammad 🕌,' answered Jibra'il. Again the gatekeeper asked, 'Has he been given prophethood?' 'Yes.' Replied Jibra'il. 'Has he come here upon invitation and request?' asked Mikha'il. 'Yes,' said Jibra'il, 'invitation and request have gone before.' Then the gatekeeper said, 'Welcome to you, oh welcome guest! How agreeable a visitor!' With that, he opened the gate.

"I entered and beheld the guardian angel of this Heaven, Mikha'il. There were two hundred thousand angels at his service, each one of whom had another two hundred thousand helpers to assist him. I greeted him and he returned my greetings with reverence. He gave me the joyous news of the many honors and blessings the Almighty was to bestow on me.

"They were engaged in this Tasbih:

Subhana-llahi kullama sabbaha-llaha musabbihun,

wal-hamdu lillahi kullama hamid-allaha hamidun

wa la ilaha illAllahu kullama hallala-llaha muhallilun

wallahu akbaru kullama kabbara-llaha mukabbirun.

(Glory be to Allah whenever the glorifier glorifies Him;

And praised be He whenever the praiser praises Him;

There is no God but He each time this *Tahlil* is recited;

And Allah is Greatest each time this Takbir is affirmed.)

"I passed on and came upon another group of angels who stood in rows and were bowing in Ruk'u in perfect reverence and devotion. They remained always in this position and recited this Tasbih:

Subhanal-warithul-wasi'u-lladhi yudrikul-absar;

Subhana-lladhi la tudrikuhul-absar;

Subhanal-azhimul-'alim.

(Praised be He, the Heir Universal who sees, the All-Discerning;

Praised be He whom our eyes cannot perceive;

Praised be the Majestic, the All-Knowing.)

'Isa and Yahya (a)

"I asked Jibra'il, 'Since when have they been in this position of Ruk'u?' and he said, 'Since the day they were created they have always been bowing in Ruk'u, and thus they will remain until the Day of Resurrection, bowed in Ruk'u, reciting their Tasbih. Pray to your Lord that He granted to your nation this form of worship in their prayer.' I therefore prayed to Allah for this, and the Almighty granted it to my nation.

"After we passed on, I perceived two young men and I asked Jibra'il who they were. Jibra'il explained to me, 'These young men are the Prophets Yahya and 'Isa. They are related to each other, being cousins.' I saluted them and they received my Salams with reverence and greeted me, saying, 'Welcome to you, oh righteous Prophet, our righteous brother!' Then they gave me tidings of the many Gifts of Grace the Highest and Holiest Lord had in store for me.

"The Tasbih of 'Isa was this:

Subhanal-hannanil-mannan;

Subhanal-abadiyyul-abad;

Subhanal-mubdi-al-mu'id.

(Praised be to the All-Compassionate, the All-bounteous;

Praised be the Eternal, Never-Ending;

Praised be He who creates from nothing, then causes to die

and returns to its previous state.)

"After we had passed them, I saw a very great angel who had seventy thousand heads, and on every head there were seventy thousand faces. Every face had seventy thousand mouths and in every mouth there were seventy thousand tongues. Each tongue spoke a different language, which bore no resemblance to the next.

"Each tongue glorified the Lord as follows:

Subhanal-khaliqil-azhim;

Subhanal-azhimil-'alim;

Subhanallahi wa bi-hamdihi;

Subhanallahil-azhim wa bi-hamdihi,

Istaghfirullah.

(Praise be to the Creator, the Glorious;

Praise be to the All-Powerful, All-Knowing;

Praise be to Allah and glorified be He;

Praise be to Allah the Magnificent and glorified be He,

I beseech Allah for forgiveness.)

The Angel of Provision

"Who is this?" I asked Jibra'il ☆, who told me, 'This is the angel who is charged with the distribution of provisions, and his name is Qasim. He distributes to every single one his daily provision, no one receives more or less than his apportioned lot.'"

According to one narration, he is to have said, "If a person finds himself in straightened circumstances and in the morning prayer (Fajr) recites one-hundred times the last line of the Tasbih of this angel between the Sunna and the Fard Rak'ats, then Allah will supply him plentifully and make his provision bounteous." This is the line of this Tasbih:

Subhana-llahi wa bi-hamdihi,

Subhana-llahil-azhim wa bi-hamdihi

189

wa istaghfirullah.

(Praise be to Allah and glorified be He;

Praise be to Allah the Magnificent and glorified be He,

I beseech Allah for forgiveness.)

To continue with our Prophet's ❀ narration:

"After passing by this angel, I beheld an even greater, even more wondrous angel who was seated upon a throne of light. He was silent and of morose aspect. The throne he was seated upon had four corners and each corner was supported by seven hundred thousand pillars of gold and of silver. Around him were grouped such multitudes of angels, only the Omnipotent Owner of Might and Bounty, Allah Almighty alone knows their number. To his right angels were ranged row upon row, seventy thousand in all, dazzling in their light. All of them were clad in green and they gave off a lovely scent. Their words, too, were sweet, and their beauty was so great that it was impossible to gaze at them.

"To the left were another seventy thousand angels, ranged row upon row. Their aspect was of terrible and sinister portent, their faces were black as night and their speech was rude. Their clothing was ugly and the smells they emitted were noxious. When they began reciting their Tasbih, tongues of fire erupted from their mouths. They held before them fiery clubs and blades, and their eyes were so cruel, no one could stand to look at them for long.

"The angel seated upon the throne was covered with eyes from head to foot, which sparkled as Mars and Venus in the sky. He also had shimmering wings and in his hand he held sheet of paper, while before him there was a tablet. He gazed incessantly at that tablet and not once lifted his gaze from it. There was also before him a tree, and only Allah can know the number of its leaves. Upon each leaf was written the name of a certain person. Then there stood before him a type of vessel. At times he reached in it with his right hand and drew something out of it, handing it to the luminous and gentle angels to his right. At times he reached for something with his left hand and gave it to the pitch-black angels standing by his left side. As I looked at those dark angels, fear fell upon my heart and I began to tremble. I was seized by a weakness and prostration, and I asked Jibra'il, 'Who is this?' Jibra'il replied, 'This is the Angel of Death, his name is Azra'il. There is no one who can bear to look at him. It is he who ends all delights, and cuts off from all community.' He then went up to him and said, 'Oh Azra'il, this visitor here is the Prophet of the Last Times ﷺ, he is the Beloved of Allah, the Lord of Mercy. Speak thou to him!'

"Upon these words, Azra'il lifted his head and he smiled. Jibra'il approached him and saluted him. I also went up to him and proferred my Salams. He received my greetings and showed me great honor. Then he spoke, 'Welcome to you, oh Muhammad ﷺ! Allah has created no creature more honored than you, and to no nation has He given greater honor than to your nation. I am gentler and more compassionate towards your nation than to any nation that went before them.' In response to these words, I said to Azra'il, 'You have gladdened my heart, oh Azra'il, and cleared my mind of fear. Yet there remains one matter on my mind, for I have seen your state to be one of gloom and grief and I wonder wherefore.'

"Azra'il explained to me, 'Oh Rasulullah ﷺ, since the time the Lord Almighty has appointed me to my post, I have been living in fear of not being able to discharge my duty and of not being able to fulfill my responsibility. That is why I appear gloomy and depressed.' Then I asked him about the vessel he had before him, and he said, 'That is the entire world; everything from east to west, from one end of the world to the other is contained in this dish. I dispose of it at will.'

"Again I asked him, 'What is this tablet you are looking at?' and he said to me, 'This is the Lauh al-Mahfuzh, the Preserved Tablet, on which is inscribed the doom of those who are to die within the year. The angels write them down and hand the list to me. That is the Tablet.' 'And what is this page?' I asked. 'On this page is written the exact hour of time when these souls are to be taken away." And what is this tree?' I asked. He said, 'It is the tree of the lives of those living in the world. When a man is born, a leaf unfurls upon that tree upon which his name is written. When his time to die approaches, his leaf begins to yellow and wither and his name appears on the Tablet. I give this leaf to the angels, and they take it and mix it in his food so that he eats it. When he has eaten it, by the leave of Allah he falls ill, and when his time is up, his name is erased from the Tablet. I stretch out my hand and seize his soul, whether he be in the east or in the west of this world. If he is among the blessed, I hand him to the angels on my right, for they are the angels of Mercy. But if he is one of the sinners, I hand him to the angels to my left, for they are the angels of Wrath.' May Allah preserve us from the doom of the wretched sinners, Amin.

"Again I asked, 'How many of those angels are there?' and Azra'il replied, 'I do not know their number, but whenever I seize a person's soul, six hundred angels of Mercy and six hundred angels of Wrath are ready to do their duty. They wait expectantly to see to which group it will belong. These angels do their duty only once, the same angels never come twice, and so it will be until the Day of Judgment.' After this, I asked again, 'Oh Angel of Death, how do you take the soul of every single individual?' He replied, 'Since the time I was created, I have never moved from this spot. Seventy thousand angels are there to serve me, and each one of these has another seventy thousand helpers.

"Whenever I have to seize a person's soul, I give my order to them and they go out and bring the person's soul up into his throat. After that, I just stretch out my hand and grasp it from there.' I said to him, 'What I would wish for is that my nation, which is a weak nation, experience death in a mild and gentle manner.' He replied, 'By Allah, the Lord of Might and Majesty who has made you the Seal of the Prophets, He Almighty addresses me seventy times during one day and night, saying to me, 'Take the souls of those belonging to Muhammad's nation with lightness and ease, and judge their deeds kindly.' Therefore, I am given to more compassion towards your nation than to any of those who went before them.

"After this, Jibra'il called the Adhan and Iqama and I led the angels and all inhabitants of the second Heaven in a prayer of two Rak'ats. Then I continued my ascent to the Third Heaven."

The Third Heaven

The Mercy to all Humankind ﷺ continues in his narration, details of the Third Heaven:

"The Lord Almighty created this Heaven from copper and has named it Zaytun. The name of its guardian angel is Arina'il. Its gate is of white pearls and it has a lock of light. When Jibra'il knocked upon the gate, the guardian angel called from within, 'Who is it requesting entry?' Jibra'il answered, 'It is I, Jibra'il.' 'And who is this with you?' asked the keeper of the gate. 'It is Muhammad ﷺ,' replied Jibra'il. Again he asked, 'Has he been given prophethood?' 'Yes, he has,' answered Jibra'il. 'Has he received summons and invitation?' 'Yes, he has,' replied Jibra'il. Then Arina'il opened the gates, saying, 'Welcome to you, how pleasing a guest!' I entered this Heaven and I beheld Arina'il to be a great and majestic angel.

"He had at his command three hundred thousand angels who engaged in this Tasbih:

Subhanal-mutiyl-wahhab,

Subhanal-fattahil-'alim,

Subhanal-mujibi liman da'ahu.

(Praise be to the Giver of all things, the generous Bestower,

Praise to the Opener of All Ways, the All-Knowing,

Praise to Him who answers all prayers.)"

"I greeted this angel and he responded with full reverence and gave me news of many and varied blessings and gifts that were to come to me. After that, I went on and came upon a large group of angels ranged in rows and all in the position of Sajda. While bowing thus, they were engaged in this Tasbih:"

Subhanal-khaliqil-azhim,

Subhana-lladhi la mafarra wa la malja'a minhu illa ilayhi,

Subhanal-'aliyyil-a'la.

(Praised be the Almighty Creator,

Praise be to Him from whom there is no escape and no refuge but in Him; Praised be the Highest of All.)

"Jibra'il then said to me, 'They are perpetually engaged in this form of worship. Pray that the Lord grant that also to your nation.' Then I prayed to the Lord and He granted to my nation the Sajda in their prayer. This is the reason why the Sajda in our prayer is doubled: when I came and saluted them, they raised their heads from their Sajda to receive my salute, then they again bowed down. Therefore, my nation was obliged to perform the Sajda twice in their prayer."

Tasbih of Yusuf عليه السلام

"I then passed on, and I saw Yusuf in all his great beauty. Of all existing beauty, Yusuf was given one half. I gave him my Salams and he returned them with dignity and bade me welcome. He informed me of many miracles to come and he prayed for me.

"His Tasbih was this:

Subhanal-karimil-akram,

Subhanal-jalilil-ajall,

Subhanal-fardil-witr;

Subhana-abadiyyil-abad.

(Praised be the Most Bounteous of the Bountiful;

Praised be the Greatest of the Great;

Praised be the Peerless, Unique;

Praised be Eternal, Never-Ending.)

"After we had passed him, I saw Da'ud and his son Sulayman. I greeted them both and they returned my Salams with respect. They gave me great good tidings and said, 'Pray in this night that you might be given intercession for your nation and that the Lord grant them security.' In this way they counseled me."

"Da`ud's Tasbih was this:

Subhana khaliqi-n-nur;

Subhana-t-tawwabil-wahhab.

(Praised be the Creator of Light;

Praised be He who accepts Repentance

and the Bestower of All Good.).

"Sulayman's Tasbih was this:

Subhana malikil-mulk ,

Subhanal-qahiril-jabbar,

Subhana man ilayhi tasir-al-umur.

(Praise to the Lord of All Dominions,

Praise to the Compeller, the Imposing;

Praised be to whom all Things must return.)

Tasbih of the Tyrants

"After I left them, I came to an angel seated upon a throne. This angel had seventy heads and seventy pairs of wings, each pair spanning all the way from the east to the west. All around him I beheld enormous angels, each of which was extremely tall. These angels were punishing a certain group of sinners, beating them with sticks until they fell apart. Then they became whole again and the angels began beating them again. I asked whom this great angel was who I saw seated upon the throne. Jibra'il told me that he was the angel Soha'il and he told me that those I saw being punished were the unjust tyrants and cruel oppressors from among my nation. In this way they would be punished until the Day of Judgment.

"Their Tasbih was as follows:

Subhana man huwa fauqal-jabbarin;

Subhanal-musalliti fauqal-musallitin;

Subhanal-muntaqimi mim-man asahu.

(Glory to Him who is above all oppressors;

Glory to Him who attacks all attackers;

Glory to Him who takes revenge on whomever disobeys Him.)

"After this, I beheld a Sea of Fire surrounded on its shores by fierce and terrible angels. 'What is this?' I asked, and Jibra'il explained to me, 'This sea is the 'Sea of Sa'q' (Lighting), and these angels here throw down thundering bolts of fire and lightning from the heavens onto the earth.' As it written in this Holy Verse of the Quran:

He looses the thunderbolts, and smites with them whomsoever He will.

(Thunder, 13)

The Guardian Angel of Hell

"After this I beheld a door, which was made all of camphor wood. Its lower groundsill reached down to the lowest level of the earth, while its upper doorsill reached to just below the Divine Throne. This door was a double door, on which was mounted a lock as great as Heaven and earth together. I asked in amazement, 'What is this door?' and Jibra'il answered me, 'The name of this door is 'Bab al-Aman', the Door of Safety.' I asked why it was so called and Jibra'il told me, 'The Lord Almighty created Hell and filled it with various torments. There came a breath out of Hell, and all the creatures on earth and in the heavens appealed to the Lord for help and protection. Then, the Lord of All Majesty created this door between Hell and the rest of all creation, so that all the creatures of the seven heavens and earths will find safety from it. Therefore, the name of this door is the Door of Safety.'

"I then asked to see what was behind that door and asked for it to be opened, but Jibra'il 🕊 said, 'Behind this door you will find Hell, is that really what you want to see?' 'Yes, indeed, I wish to see it,' I said. Thereupon a Divine Command was heard, saying, 'Oh My Beloved, upon a sign of your finger, this door will open.'

"I then signaled with my hand and the door opened. I looked beyond it and this is what I saw: a great Minbar of iron, which had six hundred thousand pedestals. Upon it sat a great and terrible angel created from fire. He was busy twisting ropes of fire, making shackles and fetters of fire. His face was awesome and frightful to behold. His hand was powerful and his anger was plain to see.

"His head was bowed forward and he recited this Tasbih:

Subhana-lladhi la yajuru wa huwal-malik-al-jabbar;

Subhanal-muntaqimu min 'ada'ihi,

Subhanal-mu'ti li-man yasha'a,

Subhana man laysa ka-mithlihi shay'un.

(Praised be He who commits not injustice

and He is the Almighty, Omnipotent King;

Glory to Him who triumphs in revenge over His foes,

Praised be He who bestows on whomever He wilt;

Glory to Him who is unlike anything.)

"Flames leapt from his mouth as high as mountains, and from his nose darted flares of fire. This angel was exceedingly angry and full of rage, and his eyes, each one of which was as great as the whole world, blazed with fury. As I beheld this angel in all his awesome aspect, I felt afraid. Were it not for the grace and generous support from the Lord Almighty, I would have perished from fear. I asked Jibra'il, 'Who is this, the sight of whom makes me tremble?' Jibra'il told me, 'Be unafraid, for there is nothing there for you to fear. This is the Guardian of *Jahannam* (Hell) and his name is Malik. Allah Almighty has created him from His Wrath and since the day of his creation, he has never smiled yet. His fury increases with every passing moment. Go up to him now and salute him.' Thereupon, I went up and gave him my Salams, but he was so engrossed in what he was doing that he lifted not even his head. Jibra'il passed in front of him and spoke to him, 'Oh Malik, he who has just given you Salams is the Prophet of Allah, Muhammad ✿.'

"Jibra'il thus introduced me, and when he heard my name, this terrible angel rose to his feet and honored me with many compliments and respectful greetings, after which he spoke, saying to me, 'Oh Muhammad ✿, good tidings to you! For the Lord has vouchsafed to you many miraculous doings; and He is pleased with you: He has forbidden your body to the fires of Hell. From love and respect for you, He has also forbidden the fires to touch those who follow you. He has ordered me to treat the disobedient from among your nation with mildness and restraint. I shall wreak my revenge on those who refuse to believe in you.'

Beholding the Inhabitants of Jahannam

"I then said to Jibra'il, 'Ask him to show me Hell.' When Jibra'il told him of my request, he opened a hole the size of a needlepoint through which I could look into Hell. At first, a thread of black smoke came wafting through the hole. Had that smoke come from the hole for the period of one hour, all the heavens and the earth would have been filled with it. The light of the sun and the moon and all other luminaries would have been occluded, all would have been steeped in darkness and laid waste. But Malik stopped up that hole with his hand and the smoke ceased pouring forth. Then he said to me, 'Look through this hole and behold Hell.'

"I looked through the hole and I saw the seven layers of Hell stacked one upon another. The uppermost was the one reserved for the disobedient from among my nation and it is called 'Jahannam'. The punishments meted out here were less severe than in the deeper layers of Hell.

"I had not the strength to gaze at the extreme chastisements of those in the lower levels of Hell, so I only saw what went on in the first level in which were the unrepentant of my nation. I saw that in it there were seventy seas of fire along the shores of each of which was a city of fire. In each of these cities there were seventy thousand houses of fire and in each of the houses there were seventy thousand chests of fire. Each of these chests contained men and women, imprisoned therein, surrounded by snakes and scorpions. I asked the Guardian of Hell, 'Oh Malik, who are these people locked in these chests?' He told me, 'Some of them are people who oppressed their fellows and unfairly enriched themselves through their belongings. Others are those who became proud, and appointed themselves to be leaders and tyrants and ruled by cruel oppression. Greatness and Pride are attributes of Allah Almighty and befit Him alone.'

"Then I beheld a people whose lips were as the lips of dogs and camels. Their bellies were bloated and the *Zabaniya* (demons of Hell; myrmidons) beat them with mallets of fire until their entrails were ripped up and trailed out from their rear ends. Each time this happened, their entrails were recreated and the *Zabaniya* tormented them anew, and thus it continues. I asked who were these people, and Malik told me, 'These are the people who wrongfully took for themselves what belonged to orphans.'

"Then I saw another people whose bellies were swollen up like huge mountains. They were filled with snakes and scorpions that crawled about within and caused them great torment. Whenever they wished to rise to their feet, they could not do so for the greatness of their stomachs and the motion of the vermin in them, and they fell back down. I asked the angel, 'Who are they?' Malik replied, 'These are the people of your nation who committed usury.'

"Then I came upon a group of women who were suspended by their hair. I asked who they were and Malik said, 'These are the women who concealed not their hair and faces from unrelated menfolk and who revealed their beauty to men other than their husbands and caused their husbands pain and chagrin.'

"After them, I beheld a group of men and women who were suspended from their tongues by means of fiery hooks. Their fingernails were made of copper and with them they clawed and tore up their own faces. 'Who are these?' I asked, and Malik told me, 'These are people who swore by false testimony, and who were talebearers, spreading slander and gossip.'

"Then I beheld a group of women some of whom were suspended by their breasts while others were tied by their feet, head down. They were yelling and screaming incessantly. I asked about them, and Malik said, 'These are women who committed adultery, and such women who killed their children.'

"After these I saw a group of men who were tearing flesh from their own sides and placing it in their mouths. But they did not swallow it; they just hid it in their mouths. The *Zabaniya* were at them, forcing them to eat the flesh, and again, the same thing would take place: they tore of some flesh, placed it in their mouths and the demons of Hell would force them to eat it. This was their punishment. I asked who they were and I was told, 'They are those from among your nation who openly criticize and belittle people, and who talk behind their backs and spread malicious gossip about them as well. And those who wink and poke fun at people, making signs of derision with their hands, lips, brows or eyes.'

"Then I came upon another people whose bodies resembled the trunks of pigs, whose faces were like the faces of dogs, and who emitted fire from their rear ends. Snakes and scorpions were biting them, their flesh being eaten by them. 'Who are those?' I asked the Angel of Hell, and Malik answered me, 'They are those from among your nation who neglected to pray or perform their ritual ablutions, and who went about in a state of (ritual) impurity.'

"After that, I came to another group of people who were suffering from extreme thirst, and desperately crying for water. In response to their pleas, they were given goblets of fire filled to the brim with boiling water, and they were commanded to drink from these. Being forced to do so, as soon as the goblets came near to their lips, all the flesh of their faces began to bubble from the extreme heat of the water until it fell off and dropped into their goblets. When they had drunk the water, their intestines fell apart and emerged in tatters from their backsides. "Who are they?' I asked and Malik told me, 'These are people from your nation who used to drink wine and other intoxicants.'

"After this, I saw a group of women who were suspended from their feet, with their tongues protruding and hanging out. Angels with fiery shears clipped them off, but they grew back each time. All the while they were braying like asses and howling like dogs. 'Who are they?' I asked the angel, and he answered, 'These are the wailing women who used to loudly bemoan the dead.'

"Then I passed a group of men and women who were seated in copper ovens that were set upon a raging fire, whose flames licked their heads and enfolded their entire bodies. A vile stench arose from here. I asked the angel about them and he said, 'These are men and women who committed adultery.' 'And what is this terrible smell?' I asked. 'That smell comes from the discharge of their genitals.'

"Next I saw a group of women who were hung up while their hands were tightly bound to their necks. 'Who are these?' I asked. 'These are women who deceived their husbands and spent their husband's wealth without his knowledge,' answered Jibra'il.

"Next I saw a group of men and women who were being punished in the fire and the demons of Hell set upon them, beating them with fiery rods. The more they screamed, the harder they beat them. They drove blades of fire into their stomachs and whipped them with whips of fire. Their chastisement appeared very severe to me. I asked about them and Malik said to me, 'These are such as opposed and disobeyed their mothers and fathers.'

"Then I saw a people who wore great rings of fire around their necks. 'Who are these?' I asked the angel. 'These are the ones who defrauded goods left in their safekeeping.'

"Then I came to a group who were being slaughtered by the *Zabaniya* with knives of fire, but instantly they came to life, only to be slaughtered anew. 'Who are these?' I asked, and Malik told me, 'They are those who killed a soul without justification.'

"Then I saw people who were eating the most disgusting, stinking carcass. 'Who are these people?' I asked the angel. He told me, 'These are the people who spread slanderous gossip, and thereby ate the flesh of their brethren.'

"Next I saw a place in Hell which had two divisions, one for the men and one for the women, and both were being punished in a terrible fashion. I asked Malik who they were and he said, 'These are men who went out before their kings and rulers, beating with whips the weak and poor of the people, driving them away with cruelty. And these are women who seemingly dressed in a modest fashion, but in reality were naked and displayed themselves to strangers, for when they went about, they adorned themselves to make themselves appear attractive. Therefore, their heads have grown as big as a camel's hump, and they cannot enter the peace and safety of Paradise.'

"After this, I saw another group of men and women, all being punished in different ways, each distinct from the other. They were made to suffer the worst castigations of all those punished on this level of Hell. For example: they were impaled on poles of fire on which their flesh began to boil and drop off until only their bones remained. But Allah Almighty caused their flesh to grow back forthwith and their torment began anew. Some others were bound with shackles and fetters of fire, and that was their penalty. 'Who are these?' I asked again, and Malik answered and said, 'These are such people who whilst they were alive and well, neglected their prayers and abandoned worship.'

"Then I said to the Guardian Angel of Hell, 'Oh Malik, shut the Gates of Hell, for I have not the strength to regard any more of its sights.' Malik then said, 'Oh Rasulullah ﷺ, you have witnessed the terrors of Hell with your own blessed eyes so that you might pass on what you have seen to your nation as a warning. And may it serve to increase their fear of Allah and keep them from rebellion and disobedience, and make them steadfast in their worship and submission to Allah.

Jahannam has seven levels. What you have seen, is only its very first layer, and the punishments therein are light; they are as nothing compared to the deeper levels of Hell.'

Allah Grants the Prophet Intercession

The Holy Prophet ﷺ then began to weep from pity for his nation and for the terrors that lay in store for it, and as he wept, the great angels Jibra'il and Mikha'il and all the Muqarrabin wept with him and joined in his appeal for mercy. At last there came a call from the Lord Almighty, saying, "Oh my Beloved, for the esteem you hold in the Divine Presence, your prayer is answered and your intercession is granted; so be easy, for on the Day of Judgment, I will give you a special station of intercession and I will spare as many sinners as you ask for, until you say: it is enough! For We have chosen your nation above all other nations, and I have made you their intercessor, so intercede for whomever you wish, I will accept your supplication."

Other Guardians of Hell

Apart from Malik, there are eighteen other guardians of Hell, nineteen in all. Their eyes are like flashes of lightning and from their mouths issue tongues of flame and they never once feel mercy or pity, Their rage waxes continuously, for punishment and chastisement is their only task. They are of huge stature, so great that with one hand they pick up and throw seventy thousand sinners into the fires of Hell. Each of their teeth is big as Mount Uhud – so if one tooth alone is as great as a mountain, how great must their whole head, their entire body be! The breadth of the shoulders is a distance of nine days' traveling, and the thickness of their skin is a distance of three days' traveling! If he can grab seventy thousand sinners in the palm of one hand, how unimaginably immense must be the stature of this vengeful angel!

Each one of these angels of Hell commands a division of demons (*Zabaniya*) whose number is known to Allah alone. It is related that Allah described these angels to His Prophet ﷺ in the revelation of the verse:

I shall surely roast him in Saqar; and what will teach thee what is Saqar? It spares not, neither leaves alone scorching the flesh; over it are nineteen. We have appointed only angels to be masters of the Fire and their number We have appointed only as a trial for the unbelievers, that those who were given the Book may have certainty.

(Shrouded, 26-31)

When the Holy Prophet ❀ received this revelation, concerning the nineteen guardians of Hell, he became distressed on account of his nation, and pleaded for them to be spared. The Lord then addressed him, saying, "I have included in this Book (the Holy Quran) nineteen letters for your nation, oh Muhammad ❀; if your nation persists in constant recital and application of the words (comprising those letters), I will make them safe from the nineteen Guardians of Hell and their army of assistant demons." "What is this word of nineteen letters?" asked Muhammad ❀. "It is the phrase: *'Bismillahi-r-rahmani-r-rahim'*," spoke the Lord.

May the Lord Almighty spare us all and reprieve us on the Day of Judgment from the punishment of Hell for the sake of His Beloved Prophet Abul-Qasim Muhammad ❀! Amin.

The Holy Prophet ❀ continued:

> "The Guardian of Hell closed the hole to Hell and Jibra'il called the Adhan for prayer. I led the prayer as Imam and all the angels and inhabitants of the third Heaven prayed two Rak'ats behind me. After this we proceeded to the Fourth Heaven."

The Fourth Heaven

The Seal of Prophethood ❀ narrates, regarding his journey to the Fourth Heaven:

> "The Fourth Heaven is created of raw silver or, according to a different narration, from white pearl. The name of this Heaven is Zahir. Its gate was of Light and the lock to the gate was of Light and written upon it were the words, 'La ilaha illAllah, Muhammadan

Rasulullah.' The angel guarding the gate to this Heaven was the angel Salsa'il. After we had knocked on the gate and had answered the same questions as before, we were admitted and the gates were opened to us. I beheld the angel in charge, Salsa'il. He was responsible for all that happened here. Under his command were four hundred thousand angels, and each one of these angels commanded another four hundred thousand angelic lieutenants.

"These angels praised the Lord in the following words:

Subhana khaliq-iz-zulumati wa-n-nur,

Subhana khaliq-ish-shamsi wal-qamar-il-munir,

Subhana-r-rafi'-il-'ala.

(Praise be to the Creator of darkness and light,

Praise be to the Creator of the sun and the shining moon;

Praise be to the Highest of the High.)

"Among these angels I noticed a special group; some of them stood in Qiyam, some were prostrated in Sajda, their gaze unswerving from the place of their prostration, so rapt were they in devotion. Another party of those in Sajda were so entranced that they remained gazing at their noses.

The Tasbih of these three groups of angels was this:

Subbuhun quddus, Rabbun-ar-Rahman-ar-Rahim

illadhi la ilaha illa huwa.

(Glorified be our Lord, the All-Holy, the All-Compassionate,

The All-Merciful, besides whom there is no other god.)

"I then asked Jibra'il, "Is this their form of worship?' Jibra'il replied, 'Ever since they were created, they have remained in this pose of humility. Make supplication for your nation that they, too, might be given this form of worship.' I prayed and asked this for my nation, and my nation, too, was given this attitude of humility during their prayer.

"Then I met the Prophets Idris and Nuh. I gave them Salams and they replied reverentially, saying, 'Greetings to you, oh righteous brother, oh righteous Prophet of Allah ❀!' and they gave me glad tidings of many good things to come."

This was the Tasbih of Idris:

Subhanal-mujibi-s-sa'ilin,

Subhana qabzil-jabbarin,

Subhana-lladhi 'ala fa la yablughu 'uluwwahu ahad.

(Glorified be He who answers those who ask of Him,

Praised be He who constrains the tyrants,

Praised be He whose lofty height none can reach but He.)

The Tasbih of the Prophet Nuh was this:

Subhanal-Hayyil-Halim,

Subhanal-Haqqil-Karim,

Subhanal-Azizil-Hakim.

(Glory be to God, the Living and Gentle,

Glory to God, the True and Munificent,

Glory to God, the Powerful and Wise.)

Mansions of Maryam, Buhayyid and Asiya ﷺ

"Thereafter, I saw Maryam, the mother of 'Isa, and the mother of Musa, Buhayyid, and the wife of Fir' awn, Asiya – may Allah be well pleased with them. They all came to greet me. Maryam, the mother of 'Isa, had seventy thousand mansions, all made of white pearls. The mother of Musa had seventy thousand mansions all made of green emeralds. Finally, Asiya had seventy thousand mansions made of red corals.

"After this, I came to a great sea, the water of which was white with snow. 'What sea is this?' I asked. Jibra'il told me, 'This sea is called the 'Sea of Snow'.' After we had passed by there, we came to the sun."

According to one narration, the size of the sun was one hundred and sixty times the size of the earth. According to Ibn 'Abbas, the sun is as great as a distance of seventy years' wayfaring.

After Allah Almighty had created the Sun, He created a boat of pure gold in which He placed a throne of red ruby. This throne stands on three hundred and sixty legs and an angel holds on to each one of them. In this way they place the Sun in this boat and every day three hundred and sixty angels guide the sun-boat from east to west, and every night they guide it back from west to east. Then these angels engage in worship and the following day, another three hundred sixty angels come and perform this duty, and so it will go on until the Day of Resurrection. Every group of angels will only perform this duty once.

In the Holy Quran this verse refers to the movement of the sun:

> And the sun, it runs to a fixed resting-place; that is the ordaining of the All-Mighty, All-Knowing.   (Ya Sin, 38)

The learned commentators, may Allah have Mercy on them, have said that the sun comes to rest beneath the Divine Throne. The angels take the sun to its place beneath the Throne every night where it bows and prostrates itself before the Almighty Lord. Thus it will continue until the Day of Judgment is nigh. Then a Divine Command will be heard, "Let the Sun stop in the west, and let it rise from there!" (A detailed interpretation of this vision is given in the work entitled '*Ara'is-i-Salabi*'.)

The Prophet's narration continues:

"Thereafter, Jibra'il intoned the Adhan and Iqama, and I led all the angels and inhabitants of the fourth Heaven in a prayer of two Rak'ats. Then we proceeded to ascend to the Fifth Heaven."

The Fifth Heaven

The Beloved of Allah ﷺ narrates details of his visit to the Fifth Heaven:

"Allah Almighty created this Heaven from red gold and its name is
Safiya. The keeper of the gate is called Kalqa'il. As before, we
requested entry at its gates. After a set exchange of certain questions
and answers, the gates opened and we entered. Upon entering, I
beheld the guardian of this Heaven seated upon a throne of light. I
greeted him, and he returned my Salams with much respectfulness.
Five hundred thousand angels are at his service, and each one of these
has another five hundred thousand attendants at his disposal. They are
constantly engaged in glorification of the Lord, and their Tasbih is this:

Quddusun quddus Rabb-al-arbab,

Subhana Rabbinal-'alal-'azham,

Quddusun Rabb-al-malaikati wa-r-ruh

(Holy, Holy, the Lord of All Lords!

Glory to our Lord, the Lofty, the Majestic!

All-Holy the Lord of the angels and the spirit.)

"Having passed by these angels, I came upon another flock, and Allah
alone knows their number. These were seated in an attitude of perfect
devotion in the posture of Qa'da, never raising their gaze from their
knees as they recited this Tasbih:

Subhana Dhil-fadhlil-akbar

Subhanal-'adl illadhi la yajur.

(Praise be to the Possessor of Greatest Grace.

Praise be to the Perfectly Just One who wrongs none.)

"I turned to Jibra'il and asked, 'Is that their form of worship?' He
replied, 'Yes, since the day they were created, they have busied
themselves with their devotion. Entreat your Lord that He might grant

your nation this form of worship as well.' I prayed for this and the Qa'da (kneeling position) was thus included in our ritual prayer.

Prophets Isma'il, Ishaq, Ya'qub, Lut and Harun

"We passed on and met the Prophets Isma'il, Ishaq, Ya'qub, Lut and Harun. I gave them my greetings and they replied, 'Welcome to you, oh righteous son, our upright brother and truthful Prophet!' They greeted me with full honors and gave good tidings of great good things to be.

"Their glorification was the following:

Subhana man la yasiful-wasifuna 'azhmatahu wa muntahahu

Subhana man hada'at lahu-r-riqab wa dhallat lahu-s-sifaq.

(Glory to Him before the Extremity of whose Majesty all attempts

at description must pale,

Glory to Him before whom princes bow their heads and the

brazen are humbled).

"Having passed by, we came to a sea the expanse of which is known to Allah Almighty alone, none but He can say aught about it. I asked, 'What is this sea?' Jibra'il answered, 'This sea is called the *Bahru-n-Niqam*, the Sea of Vengeance. From here descended the waters of the flood of Nuh.'

"We passed on and Jibra'il called the Adhan and the Iqama, and I led all the inhabitants and angels of the fifth Heaven in a prayer of two Rak'ats. After this we ascended to the Sixth Heaven."

The Sixth Heaven

"Allah Almighty has created this Heaven from a yellow gem and has called it Khalisa. Its guardian is Samkha'il. We came to its gates and requested their opening; the customary question and answering took place and the gates opened for us. As we entered, I beheld the angel Samkha'il. He had six hundred thousand angels at his command, and each of these had another six hundred thousand helpers under him. All were engaged in glorification of the Lord, chanting these words:

Subhanal-Karim, subhana-n-Nur-al-mubin,

Subhana-lladhi huwa ilahu man fi-s-samawati wa ilahu man fil-ard.

(Glory be to the Munificent, Glory to the Unmistakable Light,

Glory to Him who is God of all that is in the heavens and on the earth.)

"I greeted the angel Samkha'il and he returned my greetings with full appreciation and ceremony. Then he made this supplication: 'May the Almighty bless your good works, your works of sanctity and the light within your heart!' to which I rejoined, 'Amin!'

"Then we passed on until we came upon a group of angels who are called the Cherubim (Karubiyun). Only Allah knows their number. Their chief is a great angel who is given seventy thousand angels in attendance. Each of these helpers had another seventy thousand angels to serve him. With loud voices, they are continuously chanting Tasbih and *Tahlil*. Passing by them, I met my brother, the Prophet Musa. I greeted him and he rose in response and kissed me between the eyes. Then he spoke and said, 'Praise be to Allah who has sent you and shown you to me. The Lord has given me tidings of the great miracles about to be performed. Tonight, you are to be honored by meeting and conversing with the Lord of the Universe. However, do not forget your weak nation. Whatever bliss you are granted, also seek it for your nation. Should anything be made obligatory on them, ask for it to be reduced to a minimum.'

"The glorification of Musa was this:

Subhanal-Hadi man yasha'u.

Subhanal-Mudillu man yasha'u;

Subhanal-Ghaffur-ur-Rahim.

(Glory be to Him who leads to righteousness whomsoever He will;

Glory to Him who leads astray whom He will;

Glory to the All-Forgiving, the All-Merciful.)

"Passing on, we reached the angel Mikha'il who was seated upon a tremendous throne. In front of him was a great set of scales. Each scale of the balance was so great that it might have contained all the heavens and earths. A great many scrolls of paper were stacked in front of him. I went up to him and gave him my Salams. He received my greetings and rose to greet me in return. Then he made this supplication on my behalf: 'May Allah increase your powers of sanctity and your bliss,' to which I replied, 'Amin!' He then gave me these joyous tidings, 'No nation has ever before received such goodness and munificence as the blessings with which your nation will be favored. Therefore their scales weigh heavier than those of all other nations. Happy is the man who follows you with love, and woe upon the man who turns against you and rebels.'

"There were so many angels surrounding Mikha'il that Allah alone can know their number. They all spoke to me and said, 'We are all subservient to your command, and we constantly recite Salawat upon you. From twenty-five thousand years before the creation of Adam until this very moment, there has been one particular angel responsible for the delivery of every single drop of rain or snow. For all the growing plants and fruits and crops, there is an angel assigned to every single one of them, and he performs his duty perfectly. Having performed his duty once, he does not repeat his chore again until the Day of Judgment. From this you can gauge the immense number of angels that are created.'

"The Tasbih of these angels is this:

Subhana Rabbi kulli mu'minin wa kafirin,

Subhana man tada'u min haybatihi ma fi butunihal-hawamil.

(Glory be to the Lord of every believer and every infidel;

Glory to Him, from awe of whom pregnant women bring forth what is in their wombs.)"

"The glorification of the angel Mikha'il is this:

Subhana-Rabbil-'ala

(Glory be to the Highest Lord.)"

According to one narration he ❀ is to have said: "If a person perseveres along his life in reciting this Tasbih, *'Subhana Rabbil-'Ala'*, when his time to die has come, the angel Mikha'il will send the Angel of Mercy to him with a gift. He who is visited in his grave by the Angel of Mercy is made safe from the punishment of the grave."

On account of this vision, the Holy Prophet ❀ included this Tasbih in his Sunna, since Muslims recite this phrase in every Sajda, so that they may ultimately reach to this felicity.

The Holy Prophet ❀ then continued:

"After this we reached a luminous green sea where there was a multitude of angels - Allah Almighty alone knows their number – and their Tasbih was this:

Subhanal-Qadiril-Muqtadir,

Subhanal-Karimil-Akram,

Subhanal-Jalilil-'Azhim.

(Glory be to the Mighty, the All-Powerful;

Glory to the Most Generous of the Generous,

Glory to the Glorious, the Illustrious.)

"I then asked, 'What sea is this?' and Jibra'il told me, 'The name of this sea is 'Bahr-al-Akhdar', the Green Sea.' Then Jibra'il recited the Adhan and Iqama, and I led the angels and inhabitants of the sixth Heaven in a prayer of two Rak'ats. Then we rose up to the Seventh Heaven."

The Seventh Heaven

Our beloved Prophet continued ❀ the narration of his visit to the Seventh Heaven:

> "Allah Almighty has it created from Light. Its name is Ghariba and the name of its guardian angel is Afra'il. Jibra'il requested entry at the keeper of the gates as he had done before, and after a succession of questions and answers, the gates swung open and we were admitted. I beheld Afra'il and the seven hundred thousand angels under his command. Each one of these had in turn seven hundred thousand helpers, and their glorification was this:
>
> *Subhana-lladhi sataha-s-samawati wa rafa'aha,*
>
> *Subhana-lladhi basatal-arda wa farashaha,*
>
> *Subhana-lladhi atla'al-kawakiba wa azharaha,*
>
> *Subhana-lladhi arsal-jibala wa haya'ha.*
>
> (Glory be to Him who has fashioned the skies as a roof and raised them aloft;
>
> Glory to Him who has flattened the earth and fitted it accordingly;
>
> Glory to Him who brought forth the stars and made them to be adornments;
>
> Glory to Him who has set up the mountains and fixed them in their places.)"

"I greeted Afra'il and he received my greetings with pleasure. He gave me glad tidings of many spiritual gifts of grace and much reward for accepted good works.

"Above the gate to this Heaven were written these words: *La ilaha ill-Allah, Muhammad-ur-Rasulullah, wa Abu Bakr as-Siddiq.* There I beheld an angel whose head was at a level with the Throne, while his feet were placed firmly on the earth. He was so great that he might have swallowed up all the seven layers of Heaven with one gulp, had Allah Almighty permitted him to do so. The Tasbih of this tremendous angel was this:

Subhanal-muhtajibi bi jalalihi,

Subhanal-musawwiri fil-arhami ma yasha'u.

(Glory be to Him who is veiled by His Majesty,

Glory be to Him who forms in the womb whatever He wills.)

"Then I saw an angel with seven hundred thousand heads, and each of these heads bore seven hundred thousand faces. On every single face there were seven hundred thousand mouths, and in every single mouth there were seven hundred thousand tongues and with each tongue he speaks seven hundred thousand different languages. This angel also has seven hundred thousand wings. Every day, this angel plunges seven hundred times into the Ocean of Light, which is in Paradise, and each time he comes up out of the water, he shakes himself. From every drop of light that flies off him, the Almighty creates an angel, which glorifies the Lord as follows:

Subhanaka ma 'azhama sha'nuka,

Subhanaka ma 'azhama makanuka,

Subhanaka sayyidi ma arhamaka bi khalqika.

(Be Thou glorified, how immense is Thy dignity!

Glory be to Thee, how high is Thy station!

Glory to Thee, my Lord, how great Thy Mercy on Thine creation!)

214

"After passing by this one, I beheld another angel, seated upon a throne. His head was beneath the Divine Throne, and his feet reached to the bottom of the earth. He was so great, that he could have swallowed up the world and what is within it in a single gulp. The tip of one of his wings touched the west, whereas the other touched to the east. Seven hundred thousand angels were at his service, and each one of these commanded another seven hundred thousand angels. 'Who is this?' I asked the angel Jibra'il. 'This is Israfil,' he told me. I went up to him and gave him Salams and he received them well and gave me great good tidings. His Tasbih was this:

Subhana-s-sami'-al-'alim,

Subhanal-muhtajibi 'an khalqihi,

Subhana Rabbina wa ta'ala.

(Glory be to Him, the All-Hearing, the All-Knowing,

Glory be to Him who is veiled from His Creation,

Glorified and exalted be He, our Lord Almighty.)

"After this, I came upon a person all drowned in Light. He was seated upon a throne in an attitude of awesome dignity, and before him was a multitude of little children. I asked Jibra'il who was this person of such light, majesty and awe, and who were all the children with him. The angel answered me, 'This is your great grandfather Ibrahim. He loves you and the entire nation that believes in you. He once prayed to the Lord of the Worlds that he might be of service to your nation, and the Lord heard his supplication. He gave him all these little children who are the little boys and girls from your nation who die before reaching adulthood. Allah Almighty has entrusted Ibrahim with their upbringing and education. Until the Day of Judgment, he will be instructing them in proper behavior and training their minds in the useful sciences. After having perfected their schooling, on the Day of Gathering he will lead them forth and bring them to the site of Resurrection. There, before the Lord's Holy Presence, he will entreat Him with these words: 'Oh my Lord, here are the youngsters of the nation of Your Beloved Muhammad ﷺ who died before reaching the age of maturity. According to Your order and command, I have taught and trained them in all useful branches of knowledge, and brought them before Thy Majestic Throne. Thine is all kindness, favor and grace.'

"At this invocation, the Almighty Lord will reply with the full glory of His Majesty, 'Oh children, go and enter the Gardens of Paradise.' Thereupon, these children will reply, 'Oh our Lord, by Thy Grace and Thy Munificence, let our parents go with us!' The Almighty Lord will again direct His Divine Speech at them, and say, 'You have nothing to answer for, go and enter into Paradise forthwith; as for your parents, they are accountable and there are things they have to answer for.' Again, these children entreat the Lord, 'During their lives in the material world, we caused them sorrow through our absence; now, by the vastness of Thine Mercy which floods the universal expanse, let us be the cause of happiness for them.' Upon this plea, the All-Merciful and Beneficent Lord accepts the children's supplications and addresses them, saying, 'Go then and take from the wine of the spring of Kawthar and give your parents to drink therefrom.'

"Thereafter, Jibra'il turned to me and said, 'Go ahead and give Salams to Ibrahim.' I stepped forth and greeted him, whereupon he honored me and received me well. Then he spoke to me, saying, 'Welcome to you, oh virtuous son and righteous Prophet! Tonight you are to be honored in that you will witness the splendor of the Lord of the Universe, and you will be admitted to behold all manner of sacred displays. As for your nation, it is the last of all nations and it will be a very weak nation, so do not neglect to intercede with your Lord on their behalf.'

"And he continued, 'Oh Muhammad ✿! Give Salams to your nation from me and convey to them my advice: the World (dunya) is of a passing nature and rapid in its decline. In the eyes of the Eternal Lord it is but base and contemptible matter. He attributes to it not even the value of a fly's wing. Tell them not to waste their lives in the pursuit of its vain beauties, its pomp and palaces; not to be deceived by its many and varied tastes, by promises of grandeur and large followings. For it is the world to come, which is lasting, and eternal. Therefore, let them busy themselves in following the pure ways of the Shari'a (Divine Law) by night and by day, and the guidance contained in your Sunna (practice of the Prophet ﷺ) and thereby gain the good pleasure of the Almighty Lord. The Gardens of Paradise are vast, so let them plant there many, many trees.'

"I asked him then, 'How does one plant a tree in the Jannah?' He replied, 'Through the recital of this Tasbih:

Subhanallahi wal-hamdu-lillahi

wa la ilaha ill-Allahu wallahu akbar,

wa la hawla wa la quwwata illa billahil-aliyyil-azhim.

(Glory be to Allah and Praise;

None is worthy of worship but Allah alone, and Allah is Most Great!

There is no Might and no Power save with Allah, the Exalted, Majestic.)

Tell them to recite this Du'a (prayer), for each time they recite it, a tree is planted in Paradise.'

"Then Jibra'il called the Adhan to prayer and made Iqama; I then led the angels and inhabitants of the seventh Heaven in a prayer of two Rak'ats, then we ascended to the Bayt-al-Ma'mur.

The Bayt-al-Ma'mur (The Heavenly House)

"This is a highly revered building in the Seventh Heaven. It is of the same size as the revered Kaba, which stands upon the earth and it is situated right above it. Were it to be let down from the Heavens, it would land right on top of the Kaba. Allah has created it from red ruby stone and given it two doors made from green emerald. Ten thousand lamps of pure gold illuminate it and it has a minaret of pure silver, which has a height of five hundred years' traveling. At the door of this building there is a Minbar (a pulpit), and every day since their creation up until the Last Day, seventy thousand angels come here to visit this house.

"In front of it there is a sea of light in which they first bathe, then take thereof a veil of light each and wrap it around themselves. This is their Ihram (ceremonial clothing of the pilgrimage). Then they begin to circumambulate the Heavenly House in Ihram, calling out *Labbayk* ('At Your service!'), as the pilgrims do on earth. Having once completed their Tawaf (circumambulation), these angels do not return a second time until the Day of Judgment, and it is only the angels of the seventh Heaven who go there at all. Jibra'il then took me by the hand and we went inside.

"He said to me, 'Oh Rasulullah ❁, do lead us here in prayer too!' Then he called the Adhan, and all the inhabitants of the seven heavens now followed as I led them in a prayer of two Rak'ats. When I beheld the immense multitude, it came to my mind, 'Oh if only my nation were granted such a communal prayer.' Thereupon, the Lord who knows all hidden thoughts, realized my secret wish in that He commanded, 'Oh Muhammad ❁! Your nation will be granted such a communal prayer: it will be on a Friday, and it will be obligatory.'"

It is written in some of the books of admonition:

"Every Friday the great angels assemble round the Holy House. Jibra'il calls the Adhan and Israfil delivers the Khutaba (sermon) while Mikha'il leads the prayer as Imam. All the angels of the seven heavens follow his lead. After the Jum'a[3] prayer is complete, Jibra'il addresses the gathering as follows, "Oh gathering of angels, bear

witness that I pass on the reward for this Adhan to the *Muadhdhins* [4] (callers to prayer) of the nation of Muhammad ❁!"

---

[3] Friday is called *jum'a*, which is derived from a word denoting gathering, uniting in communal activity.
[4] *Muadhdhin*, more commonly rendered as muezzin, the caller of the *Adhan*, who calls to prayer five times a day.

Then Israfil rises and says, "Oh ye angels! Bear witness that I donate the reward for this Khutba to all the Khatibs[5] of the nation of Muhammad ﷺ!" Then Mikha'il steps forth and says, "Oh angels, I too have made over the merit of leading this prayer to the Imam[6] of the nation of Muhammad ﷺ!" All the angels then present the merit for their prayer to those of the nation of Muhammad ﷺ who have prayed the Jum'a prayer.

Then there comes a call from the Highest Lord, saying, "Oh Angels of Mine! Do you seek to outdo Me in generosity, whereas I am He who created all Generosity and Munificence! Hear then My Decree: whoever honors the day of Jum'a from among the nation of Muhammad ﷺ, man or woman alike, I will forgive them their sins and free them from the torments of Hell!" Thus He Almighty grants us His Grace and Mercy. Oh Allah, make us also recipients of Your Munificence and ease our way to reach such a degree of merit, for the honor of the Trusted Prophet Muhammad ﷺ, oh Most Merciful of the Merciful, Amin!

"Then," continued the Holy Prophet ﷺ, "we ascended to *Sidratul Muntaha.*"

The Sidratul Muntaha

Concerning the 'Sidratul Muhtaha', the learned 'Ulama have proffered various differing opinions, particularly with regard to the statement: "It is called 'Sidratul Muntaha' (the lotus tree of the extreme limit) because it is the end of all that is knowable, and nobody can know what is beyond it." Some others have explained: "Whoever comes from above, arrives here and cannot pass on further down. Whoever comes from below, reaches this point and cannot ascend further. Therefore it is called by this name." Yet others try to explain it in this way: "The world of spirits ends at this point, therefore it is called the Lote tree of the extreme limit." Ibn 'Abbas tells us: "It is a tree which is made all of gold. Some of its boughs are made of emerald, some are of ruby. The tree measures a distance of one hundred

---

5 *Khatib,* the preacher of a khutba, sermon.
6 *Imam* is he who leads the congregation in prayer.

and fifty years journey from its foot to its top. Its leaves resemble the ears of the elephant, and they are very great: a single one of them would cover the entire world. Its fruits are shaped like water jugs. The whole tree is engulfed by light."

The Holy Prophet ❈ continues:

> "Upon this tree I saw such a number of angels that only Allah Almighty can know. They enfolded all the leaves of that tree and glittered like locusts, flashing like stars."

This holy verse was revealed concerning this vision:

> *Indeed, he saw him another time by the Lote-Tree of the Boundary nigh which is the Garden of the Refuge, when there covered the Lote-Tree that which covered; his eye swerved not, nor swept astray. Indeed he saw one of the greatest signs of his Lord.* (The Star, 13-18)

The commentators interpret this verse as meaning that the whole tree was surrounded and embraced by the multitude of angels upon it. It is related that there were as many angels upon the leaves of that tree as there are stars in the sky and grains of sand in the earth. Some angels took the form of golden butterflies. All of them came to greet the Prophet of Allah ❈, and when they beheld his saintly beauty, they all gave thanks to the Lord and gave to him the assurance of Allah's Mercy. They also made over all the merit of their devotional actions to the nation of Muhammad ❈.

Jibra'il, too, had his place upon the branches of this tree, and his was a branch made of green emerald. It was at a height of one hundred thousand years of journeying. There is a leaf there, the breadth of which is that of the seven layers of the heavens and the seven beds of the earth. Upon it there is a carpet spread of light, and on it there is a Mihrab made of red ruby. This Mihrab is the place of the Angel Jibra'il. Before it was placed a seat of honor reserved for the Holy Prophet ❈ upon which no one had sat since the day it was set in place.

Each of these was surrounded by forty thousand stools upon which angels sat reciting the Injil. To the left there were also ten thousand stools made of beryl, and the angels seated upon them were writing out the Zabur. Forty thousand other angels reciting the Zabur surrounded each seat. Behind us there were again ten thousand stools of red ruby. The angels seated on these were writing out the Holy Quran, and around each stool there were seated another forty thousand angels reciting the Holy Quran.

This has been explained as follows:

The wisdom of the Torah being placed before Muhammad ✿, the Injil to his right, and the Zabur to his left is this: before the Holy Prophet ✿, the Choice of all Humankind, had yet appeared in the world and begun fulfilling his mission, those Holy Scriptures had already been revealed. All of them contained descriptions of the Prophet to come and told of his characteristics and excellence, and of the preeminent position of his nation among all other, previous nations. The Holy Quran was placed behind him because its Judgment is to remain valid and unsurpassed until the Day of Judgment, and even the Day of Judgment would be conducted by its rulings. It is a sign of its remaining free and safe from abrogation, substitution, alteration or corruption.

The Holy Prophet ✿ continues:

> "Jibra'il then said to me, 'Oh Rasulullah ✿, I have a request to make of you: that you would deign to pray two Rak'ats here, so that my Maqam might gain blessings from it.' I therefore prayed a prayer of two Rak'ats there and all the angels of the Holy House and the Sidratul Muntaha followed suit." In this way the Holy Prophet ✿ was honored above the angels.

The Four Streams of Paradise

Rasulullah ✿ continues his account:

> "Below this tree there flowed four streams, two of which were evident and two of which were hidden. Jibra'il told me, 'The two hidden streams flow into the Gardens of Paradise, while the two visible ones flow down to the Earth. One of them is the Euphrates, the other is the Nile.' Then I beheld another stream, by the banks of which tents had

been set up that were of ruby, pearls and chrysolite. By their banks flew birds of emerald green whose necks resembled the necks of camels. Jibra'il then said to me, 'What you see here is the spring of Kawthar. Allah Almighty has made you a gift of it.'

As it is written in the Holy Quran,

Surely, We have given thee abundance (Kawthar); so pray unto thy Lord and sacrifice. Surely he that hates thee, he is the one cut off.   (Abundance)

"This stream flowed along over pebbles of rubies and emerald and its waters were whiter than milk. I took up a cup and drank from it. Its taste was sweeter than honey, and its scent more pleasing than musk. A spring gushed forth beneath that tree. Jibra'il told me its name: Salsabil. It was the source of two waters, one is Kawthar (Abundance); the other is Rahma (Mercy). Both streams flow before the gates of the Garden.

"Those entering into Paradise drink from the waters of Kawthar, and when they do so, all the calamities of the heart, base character and bad habits disappear and they become cleansed. Then they bathe in the spring of Rahma (Mercy). The men assume the dimensions of Adam, who measured sixty yards in height and seven yards in breadth. They will all be thirty-three years of age and will have green moustaches. As for the ladies, they will emerge as virgin girls of eighteen and their virginity will not be rent. Thus they will enter into Paradise, and never again will they age and become old. The spring of Salsabil is the source of these waters.

"Then I saw groups of angels passing in rows before the Sidra, and their rows were joined together. They formed such a long formation, that were a bird of swiftest flight to fly along it for a hundred years, he would not reach its other end. They moved faster than the wind, as swiftly as the arrow flies. I then asked Jibra'il, 'Whence comes this great multitude of angels, and whither are they going? And when did they begin their passage?' Jibra'il explained to me, saying, 'They have been passing by since the time they were created, ceaselessly in passage. I know not whence they come nor whither they are going.' I

222

marveled at their great number, remarking on it under my breath. Instantly this verse was revealed to me through Jibra'il:

...and none knows the hosts of thy Lord but He.   *(Shrouded, 31)*

"Then they brought before me three bowls; one containing wine, one containing honey and a third containing milk. I chose the one with milk and drank from it. Jibra'il then said to me, 'You have chosen the natural disposition of Islam and your nation will be firmly established in the religion of Islam. Had you chosen the cup of wine, your nation would have been a rebellious and fickle one.'

"I saw an angel at the Sidra greater than all the other angels I had seen. He measured a thousand times thousand years' wayfaring distance. This angel had seventy thousand heads. Every head had seventy thousand faces. On every face there were seventy thousand mouths. And each head was covered with seventy thousand cloths. Each one of these coverings was embellished with one thousand times thousand pearls. Each of these pearls was so great that there appeared a sea in its midst in which fish were swimming. Upon their backs was written the *Kalimat-ut-Tawhid*, the Declaration of Unity:

LA ILAHA ILL'ALLAH, MUHAMMADAN RASULULLAH.

"This angel engaged in exaltation of the Lord, placing one hand upon his head and one hand behind his back. The beauty of his voice was such that it caused a commotion at the Divine Throne itself. I asked Jibra'il to tell me who that angel was and he said, 'The Lord Almighty created this angel two thousand years before He created Adam.' I then asked where he had been all this time and where was his place of dwelling. Jibra'il replied, 'In Paradise there is a place to the right of the Divine Throne, that is the abode of this angel. From there he was brought here.'

Ramadan, the Blessed

"I went up to him and greeted him and he rose in answer to my Salams. Then he spread his wings, and all the heavens and the Earth were covered by their expanse. He then kissed my face and said,

'Good tidings to you, and to your nation! The Lord Almighty has decreed that your nation might have a singularly blessed month so that He might forgive them their sins. This holy month is the month of Ramadan and it is meant as a gift for you and your nation. For its sake your nation will find forgiveness. I have been sent here this very night to announce to you this great gladness.' Then I saw two boxes standing before him. On each of them there was a key of light. I asked that angel what was inside of those boxes. He told me, 'In one of these boxes there are the letters of release from Hellfire for those among your nation who fast the whole month of Ramadan until the new moon, up till the Day of Judgment.'

According to a different narration, the angel is to have said, "Every day of Ramadan, at the time of Iftar (the breaking of the fast), the Lord Almighty frees from Hellfire six hundred thousand of His servants who have fasted. When Jum'a (Friday) has come, He frees six hundred thousand prisoners every hour for twenty-four hours from Hellfire until the Night of Power has come. On that blessed night, that is to say, during the twenty-four hours making up that night and day, at the beginning of every hour the Lord frees from Hell as many of His servants as He has freed since the beginning of the holy month, including the Jum'a days. The last day of Ramadan, at the time of Iftar (the breaking of the fast), the Lord sets free as many of His servants as He has freed during the whole month, including the Jum'a days and the Night of Power."

The Holy Prophet ❀ continues:

"The angel told me that the other box contained this precious gift: 'On the Day of Judgment, seventy thousand persons of your nation will be granted entry into Paradise without questioning or reckoning. Their release certificates are contained in this box. In addition to these seventy thousand, each one of them will be granted the release of another seventy thousand from among his friends and relations and other disobedient Muslims. They, too, will be released without reckoning and granted accession to the heavenly gardens. This box contains the letters of release for all of them. Tuba, glad tidings to you and your nation, oh Rasulullah 🕸!'"

By the term "Tuba" he meant to say, "Oh Rasulullah 🕸, among all the countless and unbounded pleasures of the People of Paradise, the delights of the Tuba tree are reserved for you and your nation."

This expression is metaphorical; the part signifies the whole, and speaking about the Tuba tree, signifies the totality of delights in the entire heavenly realm. In the sense mentioned above, Tuba signifies a tree in Paradise. However, the word 'tuba' is also (grammatically) the feminine form of the word 'atyab', (which means better, more excellent). This can be interpreted as follows:

"I give tidings of gladness to you and your nation; those who pass their days in the world in a good way and spend their time in a commendable fashion, who perform good works all their lives, and when they reach the end of their days will return their trusts in the light of faith, uttering the words of unity; whose questioning in the grave by the angels Munkar and Nakir will be made easy and whose graves will resemble a Garden of Paradise in which they will be at ease; who on the Day of Gathering will be gathered under the Banner of Praise and who will receive many gratifications under the shadow of the Great Throne; who will be given their book of accounts into their right hand and whose reckoning will be light; who will cross the bridge of the Sirat along with those who are the first to cross it, and who will by the Grace of Allah be of those who enter Paradise freely, without questioning or Judgment; who will be granted the sweetest of all bliss in being privileged to gaze upon the Divine Beauty of the Lord and thus will have attained their ultimate desire – these are the tidings I give to you and your nation, oh Muhammad 🕸."

The Holy Prophet's 🕸 report continues:

"I then beheld another angel who had the shape and form of a rooster and was created from white pearls. This angel had seventy thousand wings to his left and seventy thousand wings to his right. On each wing there were seventy thousand feathers made of pearls, and seventy

225

thousand feathers made of rubies, and seventy thousand feathers of red gold, and seventy thousand feathers of silver, and seventy thousand feathers of pure musk, and seventy thousand feathers made of camphor, and seventy thousand feathers of ambergris, and seventy thousand feathers made of saffron. He reached in height from the Throne to the lowest of the seven layers of the earth. On each one of his wings were written these words:

Bismillahir-Rahmanir-Rahim, La ilaha ill'Allah, Muhammadan Rasulullah.

Kullu shay'in halikun illa wajhahu, al-Wahid ul-Qahhar.

(In the Name of Allah, the All-Merciful, the All-Compassionate. There is no God but Allah; Muhammad is Allah's Messenger. All must perish save His Divine Countenance, He who is One, the All-Vanquishing.)

"At every prayer time, this angel would raise his head and repeat the glorification:

Bismillahil-'azhim wa bi-hamdihi

(In the Name of Allah, the Mighty and in Praise of Him.)

"His Tasbih was thus:

Subhanaka, ma a'zhama sha'nuka.

(Praise be to Thee, how great is Thy Glory!)

"After this, he would flap his wings together, and as he did this, wondrous sounds issue forth from this flapping. When these tones reach the Paradise Gardens, the boughs of the trees of Paradise would bend and sway against each other, and it would carry on to the ruby and garnet domes of Paradise which resound with melodious echo. These tones rouse the Huris and Ghilman of Paradise, and they say to each other, 'Good news! The time for prayer has come to the nation of Muhammad ❈!' Then, this great angel begins to move and his movement makes the Throne tremble. The Lord then asks him, 'What makes you tremble?' and the angel answers Him, 'Oh my Lord, the nation of Muhammad ❈ has risen for prayer, and yet there are among them such a great number of sinners. Therefore I tremble.' The Lord thereupon says, 'Oh angel, be unperturbed! I am obliged to dispense of My Mercy upon those who pray. Witness that I train upon them the Gaze of Mercy and that I have forgiven them. I have freed them from Hellfire, for the honor of My Beloved, I have granted them dwelling in the Paradise of Mawa.' Thus the Lord proclaims His great Kindness and Munificence."

The Angel Jibra'il's Appearance

The Mercy to all the Worlds ﷺ continued his narration:

"Here, too, I beheld the angel Jibra'il in his very own shape and form. He had six hundred wings, which were made of various kinds of jewels and pearls. Whenever he would open up a pair of these wings. They filled all the space between east and west. The wings were embellished by all sorts of precious stones. It would have taken a swift-flying bird five hundred, or according to other sources, seven hundred years to measure the distance from one shoulder to the other.

Adhan

"Then we came to an open space from where we could hear the sounds of the writing of the Divine Pen. I said to Jibra'il, 'Go ahead', but Jibra'il answered, 'You go ahead, for in the eyes of Allah you are more honored than I and all the world.' I then passed on ahead of him and Jibra'il went behind me. We came unto a veil of gold. Jibra'il shook the veil and a voice was heard from behind it, saying, 'Who are you?' Jibra'il answered, 'I am Jibra'il, and Muhammad ﷺ is with me.' From within the veil this angel intoned: 'Allahu Akbar, Allahu Akbar.' From behind the curtain came a voice which said, 'My servant has spoken truly, I am indeed the Greatest, no Greatness is due to any but Me.'

"Then the angel called, 'Ash-hadu an la ilaha ill'Allah.' Again there was a call, 'My servant has spoken truly, Ana la ilaha illa ana, I am He beside whom there is no other God.' The angel repeated the words of the Shahada, 'Ash-hadu anna Muhammadan Rasulullah, I bear witness that Muhammad ﷺ is the Prophet of Allah.' Again there was a call, 'My servant has spoken truly, I have sent Muhammad 🏵 as My Messenger-Prophet. ' Then I heard the angel say, *'Hayy 'ala-s-sala, Hayy 'alal-falah.'* Another call was heard, 'My servant has spoken truly; he calls My servants to come to Me, worshipful. I have invited them to My gate, and whoever answers My invitation, will be saved and meet with success.' Thereafter I heard the angel say, *'Allahu Akbar, Allahu Akbar.'* Another call came, 'My servant has spoken the Truth: *Ana Akbar*, I am the Greatest.' The angel then said, *'La ilaha ill'Allah'*. A call came, saying, 'My servant has spoken truly, there is no God but I.'

"Then I heard another call, 'Oh Muhammad 🏵, Allah has honored you with perfect honor over all those who went before you and who are yet to come.' I then asked Jibra'il, 'Who is this angel?' Jibra'il told me, 'I swear by the Might and Glory of Allah who has sent you as His Messenger of Truth: I have never seen this angel, I do not know who he is or anything about him, but you are now about to find out.' I then asked, 'Are you not going any further then? Does a true friend leave his friend in midstream?' Jibra'il then said, 'Oh Rasulullah 🏵, every angel has his place and station beyond which he cannot go. If I advance even the breadth of a finger, the Wrath of Allah will burn me. My ultimate station is the Sidratul Muntaha. Up to this very moment, I have never gone as far as this point. For your sake and honor, however, I have been given permission, and I have brought you here. But I can proceed no further than this.'

"Then I asked, 'Is there anything you request of the Lord Almighty? If there is anything you desire, I will ask it of Him.' Jibra'il answered, 'My request of the Lord is that He permit me, when your nation is ordered to march across the Bridge of the Sirat, to spread my wing across that bridge and assist them in crossing it in safety in this way.'

"Then an angel stretched forth his hand from behind the veil, and in less time than the blinking of an eye, he pulled me through to the farther side. Then he said to me, 'Oh Rasulullah 🏵, proceed ahead of me.' In a short while, he had brought me before a curtain of pearls. When he stirred the curtain, an angel's voice was heard from behind it, asking, 'Who is this?' The angel accompanying me said, 'I am the angel of the golden curtain and with me is the most-honored Prophet of the Lord.' The angel behind the veil then said, *'Allahu Akbar'* and, stretching out his hand from behind the veil, he pulled me across. In as little time as it takes for the eye to blink, I had traversed the curtain and found myself standing before him, where he greeted me with every mark of honor and respect.

Rafraf

"In this way I passed through seventy thousand veils, each one of them made of a different kind of jewel. The distance between each of these curtains was one of five hundred years' wayfaring, and the thickness of each was that of another five hundred years. When I had passed through all of the veils, I remained all alone. Then Rafraf came to me and became visible in the shape of a green settee, which greeted me with greetings of peace. He spoke to me, saying, 'Seat yourself upon me, for I will be your transport.'"

During the night of his Mi'raj, the Holy Prophet ﷺ journeyed upon five different conveyances: the first was the Buraq, which took him up to al-Quds (Jerusalem). The second was the Mi'raj (the steps) on which he ascended up into the earthly skies. The third was the angel Jibra'il 's wing; on it he approached as far the veil. The fourth were the angels who pulled him from one veil to the next. The fifth was the Rafraf; with this he proceeded as far as Allah Almighty wished him to go.

Kursi

The Holy Prophet ﷺ continues:

"I mounted upon the Rafraf and it took me as far as the Kursi (Divine Courtyard). The Lord Almighty has created the Kursi from pearls, and it is very great, so great it is that it defies all description."

In the Holy Quran, Allah says about the Kursi:

His Throne (Kursi) comprises the heavens and the earth; the preserving of whom oppresses Him not. (The Cow, 255)

The most excellent of commentators, Ibn 'Abbas, says about this in his commentary:

"If the seven layers of the earth and the seven layers of the heavens were put together and spread out, next to the Kursi they would be as a tiny ring which has been lost in a desert." Between the Kursi (Divine Court) and the 'Arsh (Divine Throne) there are seventy veils. If not for these, the angels of the Kursi would be burnt from the Light of the Divine Throne ('Arsh).

The Holy Prophet 壐 continued his blessed narration:

> "I passed beyond those veils. Between each of the veils, I beheld various thrones that were bedecked with fine throws studded with many gems. All around the thrones curtains were drawn, as if these thrones were still waiting for their occupants. An air of expectancy surrounded these bejeweled seats of honor. I asked the guardians of these thrones, 'Who is to be seated upon them?' and they answered me, 'They will be occupied by the spirits.' I asked, 'The spirits of which prophets are they meant for?' and I was told, 'These are not for those ranking among the prophets; their ranks are far beyond that. These thrones are intended for the spirits of two groups from among your nation.' I asked again, 'Whose are these spirits?' And I was told, 'One group is made up of those who have learned by heart the words of the Holy Quran revealed to you, who understand its meaning and who act in accordance to its injections. The other group comprises those who rise at night to worship their Lord when all the world lies fast asleep.'"

> "Indeed, I beheld many wondrous marvels between the layers of these veils. I saw numberless strange seas and within them strange and wondrous creatures. I saw many angels of dreadful guise, but to comprehend them or describe or explain them exceeds all human means.

'Arsh

"After passing through all the veils, I reached the Divine Throne. Allah has created it of green emeralds and it has four legs of red ruby. The Divine Throne has as many tongues as there are created beings, and each of these glorifies the Lord unceasingly. An angel holds on to each one of the feet of the Divine Throne and holds it aloft until the Day of Judgment. On that day, there will be two angels holding each foot of the Throne, eight angels in all. The size of these angels is such that the distance between the heel and the ankles of each is that of five hundred years' wayfaring, and from their earlobe to their neck is another five hundred years' traveling distance.

"The Throne-bearing angels never once raise their heads to gaze upwards, for the dazzling gleam of the light of the Throne. One of these angels has the form of a man, and he is always praying, interceding on behalf of humankind, that they may be granted their sustenance and provisions and that their sins may be forgiven. The second one of these angels has the shape of an eagle and he is always praying for the provision of the birds and flying creatures. The third of these angels has the form of a lion, and he prays for the beasts of prey to be given their provisions. The fourth one is shaped like an ox and he prays constantly for the ruminant animals to be granted their provisions.

"Compared to the greatness of the Divine Throne, the entire Divine Court, the seven heavens and the seven layers of the earth are as a single lamp suspended beneath the sky. All around it are seventy thousand rows of angels circumambulating it at all times, reciting Takbir ('Allahu Akbar') and Tahlil ('La ilaha illAllah'). Behind them are again seventy thousand rows of angels standing upright and reciting Takbir and *Tahlil*. Behind them are one hundred thousand rows of angels who hold their right hands clasped over their left hands and each one of them recites a different Tasbih. Seventy thousand veils separate these angels from the Divine Throne.

"Then I beheld a single pearl of emerald green upon which was written this line of writing:

LA ILAHA ILLALLAH, MUHAMMAD-UR-RASULULLAH, ABU BAKR AS-SIDDIQ WA 'UMAR AL-FARUQ

**THERE IS NO GOD BUT THE ONE TRUE GOD (AL-LAH);
MUHAMMAD IS THE MESSENGER OF ALLAH.
ABU BAKR - THE TRUTHFUL, AND 'UMAR - THE ONE WHO
DISTINGUISHES TRUTH FROM FALSEHOOD.**

"The Declaration of Unity (Kalimat-at-Tawhid) is written on the base that supports the Divine Throne, and upon the legs of the Throne itself, and it is written over the gates of the Seven Heavens. Sometimes, this phrase was added: 'I have strengthened him through Ali.'

"When I reached the Divine Throne, I witnessed great events. One drop fell from the Throne into my mouth and the sweetness of it surpassed everything I have ever tasted. When I had swallowed it, the Lord of the Universe enlightened my heart with the knowledge and wisdom of all that had gone before and was yet to come. The light from the Throne surrounded me and I was engulfed by it. I was aware of nothing but that light. When faced with this light, I perceived everything through my heart's eye as clearly as though I were looking through my eyes. I perceived what was behind me as clearly as that, which was before me, at a level with my chest.

"After all this occurred, I came into a state when I heard absolutely nothing, not the voices of the angels, nor the sound of any other thing. This state caused me to experience great terror. Then I suddenly heard a voice that seemed to be the voice of Abu Bakr saying to me, *'Qif, ya* Muhammad, *inna rabbuka yusalli.* (Stay your step, oh Muhammad ﷺ, for your Lord is praying blessing.') When I heard this voice, all the terror departed from me completely, and I began to wonder, 'What is Abu Bakr doing here? Has he surpassed me, I wonder? And what does this mean, the Lord is praying, the Lord Who is free from all exigence! What could be the meaning of all this?'"

This is a very important subject which needs to be well understood: the reason for the Holy Prophet ﷺ proceeding to the Divine Throne was not to see the Lord Almighty, for Almighty God is exempt from any particular place. The Holy Prophet ﷺ was taken to these stations in order to witness

the entirety of creation, and to see the manifestation of the Divine Lord's
Supreme Majesty and Power, as He says in these verses of the Holy Quran:

Indeed, he saw one of the greatest signs of his Lord. *(The Star, 18)*

...that We might show him some of Our signs. *(The Night Journey, 1)*

Apart from this, there is another matter that it is crucial to understand: Let
it not be imagined that the greatness of the things described in this account
are exaggerated, as the Lord has described in the aforementioned verses.

Indeed, he saw one of the greatest signs of his Lord. *(The Star, 18)*

As the Lord of the Worlds Himself here describes a thing as being 'great';
how great then must it be! For perhaps the Holy Prophet ﷺ has given us
only a summary report of what he saw in accordance with our minds'
capacity; most of what he saw he did not reveal to us, for it is not possible
to give a description of the greatest things that he witnessed, as the mind of
man is not equipped to comprehend such things. Therefore, he did not
mention those matters; this must be understood.

The Vision of the Divine Beauty

The Holy Prophet ﷺ continues his account:

"When I reached to the Divine Throne, I wished to remove my
sandals, but the Throne spoke to me and said, 'Oh Beloved of Allah
ﷺ, step upon me with your blessed sandal, so that I might rub the dust
from it on my face, and take pride in the fact that the dust from the
sandal of the Beloved of Allah ﷺ has fallen upon me.'

"Again I tried to remove my sandals, but this time a call came to me
from the Divine Person, saying, 'Oh My Beloved, do not remove your
sandals so that My Throne might be honored and blessed with the
dust from the soles of your sandals.' I then entreated my Lord, saying,
'When You called the Prophet Musa to come to the mountain of Tur
(Sina'i), You ordered him to remove his sandals.' Again this word
came to me from the Divine Person, saying, 'In My view, you are more
cherished and honored than he; Musa was My Word (Kalimullah),

whereas you are My Beloved (Habibullah). Look ahead and see what you will see!'

"I looked and I saw a great sea, so great that there was no end to it, and no shore in sight. On its near side there was a tree, and upon that tree, there was a bird the size of a dove. In its beak this bird bore a piece of clay as big as a lentil. 'Do you know what this is?' I was asked. I answered, 'My Lord knows best.' And He Almighty told me, 'You are forever entreating Me to forgive your nation their sins. This sea is the likeness of the Sea of Mercy. That tree signifies the world, the dove-like bird is the likeness of your nation and that bit of clay is the likeness of their sins. Now you have seen the relation of your nation's sins to the vastness of My Mercy, so let your heart be at rest.'"

When the secret of that, which the mind is incapable of grasping, was revealed to the Holy Prophet ❀ in this Holy Verse of the Quran:

He stood poised, being on the higher horizon, then drew near and suspended hung, two bows'-length away, or nearer, then revealed to His servant that He revealed. His heart lies not of what he saw; what, will you dispute with him what he sees?

(The Star, 6-12)

He, the Almighty, addressed him in the following words:

"Draw nearer to Me, oh you Best of all Mankind! Draw nigh, oh Ahmad, oh Muhammad, so that The Friend may be in intimate association with His friend!"

In this way, the Holy Prophet ❀ was granted the unmediated vision of the Sublime Beauty of He who is beyond all space and time, free from all conditions or qualities, the Unmitigated Principal of all things.

This is the avowed preference of the Ahl as-Sunna wal-Jama'ah (People of the Sunnah of Prophet ❀ and the Majority).

The Tahiyyat Prayer

To continue with the Holy Prophet's ❀ account:

"When faced with the unparalleled honor of a glimpse of the Lord's Divine Beauty, it came to me to express myself in the following words:

At-tahiyyatu li-llahi was-salawatu wat-tayyibatu.

(Salutations be to Allah, all praise and glory to Him; all worship and good works are due to Him Almighty) which is to say, 'All praise, exaltation and worship in speech, all worship through actions and property is due to the Almighty alone, the only One to whom worship is due.'

After I had pronounced these words, the Lord of Might and Glory answered me, saying:

As-salamu 'alayka ayyuha-n-nabiyyu wa rahmatullahi wa barakatuhu;

(And salutations to you, oh Prophet, and the Mercy of Allah and His Blessings) which is to say, 'Peace be upon you, oh Prophet; may you be safe from the trouble and difficulties of this world and the next, oh My glorious Prophet! May the Mercy and Blessings of Allah be upon you.'

"In this way, He proffered very special greetings upon me. In response, I said:

As-Salamu 'alayna wa 'ala 'ibadillahi-s-salihin;

(And peace be upon us and upon the righteous servants of the Lord), that is to say, 'May the peace of this world and the next be upon us, for our answering and acceptance of these greetings, upon all us Prophets of the Lord, and upon His righteous servants, which is the name given to the nation of Muhammad.'

"Jibra'il was informed of this secret, and from his post he concluded:

Ash-hadu an la ilaha ill'Allah, wa ash-hadu anna Muhammadan 'abduhu wa rasuluh.

(I bear witness that there is no god but Allah and I bear witness that Muhammad is His Servant and His Prophet.)

After this, Allah Almighty, the Possessor of Majesty and Glory, asked me, 'Do you know, oh Muhammad, which actions the inhabitants of

235

the heavens approve of and what they desire to be done?' I replied, 'Oh my Lord, I know nothing, and You know everything; moreover all that is hidden and secret.' Again the Lord spoke to me and said, 'Oh Muhammad, do you know what actions the heavenly hosts love and approve of?' Again I replied, 'Oh my Lord, I know it not, for You know all things, and you know all that is hidden.' After this, He in His Grace and Infinite Kindness and Benevolence taught me all the knowledge I was in need of.

"Then again He asked me the same question, 'Do you know what actions the heavenly hosts rejoice in and are happy to see performed?' This time I answered, 'They are happy with works that are performed in compensation for sins committed and with works that lead to raised stations in Paradise - those are the works the heavenly folk rejoice in.' The Lord of Hosts continued to ask me, 'And what are these works that are compensation for sins committed?' I answered, 'On a cold day, to perform one's ablutions with cold water and in such a way that one's limbs are wetted entirely; to walk the distance required to join the prayer in congregation; after having prayed one prayer, to wait for the next (that is to say, to make ready as the time approaches, and to wait in readiness); these are actions that are compensation for sins. Whoever performs such works, he will live his life in goodness and righteousness and only good will be his lot. He will be as pure as on the day his mother brought him into the world.'"

The meaning of these last two statements can be understood as referring to good works in general, but it can also be understood as supplication and incentive, in which case it would be read as follows:

"Whoever persists in these three actions, I pray and plead that his may be a goodly life. May he always be surrounded by goodness and remain as pure as on the day he was born."

To pursue the Holy Prophet's account:

"Then my Lord resumed His questioning and said, 'Which are those actions that lead to high stations in Paradise?' And I answered, 'To share food with people and to show hospitality, to give Salams to a

Muslim whom one encounters on the road, to rise for prayer at night when everyone is asleep - these three actions lead to high stations in Paradise.'

"After this the Lord Almighty said to me, 'Speak, oh Muhammad!' 'What shall I say, oh my Lord?' I answered. He said, 'Recite this Du'a:'

Allahumma inni as'aluka 'amalan bil-hasanati wa tarkan lil-munkirati, wa idha aradta bi-qawmin fitnatan wa ana fi-him, fa-qbidni ilayka ghayra maftun.

(Oh my Lord, I ask of You to be granted good works and to be released from bad actions, and should You have decreed disaster for a people and I should be among them, then take me from their midst before calamity takes its toll.)"

The Leader of the World, the Foremost and Elect of all the Sons of Adam, the Messenger of Allah, Muhammad 🏵 thus reached the Station of Nearness and was granted the vision of Divine Beauty. From the Station of the Knowledge of Certainty ('ilm al-yaqin), he passed to the Station of the Witnessing of Certainty ('ayn al-yaqin) through holding direct converse with the Lord of Majesty and Might. His blind faith in the unseen was turned into faith supported by direct witnessing. The Exalted Lord Almighty informs of this in the revelation of this verse of the Holy Quran:

The Messenger believes in what was sent down to him from his Lord.

(The Cow, 285)

Here the word 'messenger' (rasul) indicates Rasulullah, Muhammad our Prophet 🏵.

The Holy Prophet 🏵 recounts:

"Concerning the above mentioned verse, I said, 'Yes my Lord, I believe in all that has been revealed aforetime.' The Lord then asked, 'And who else believed in it?' I said, *'And the believers; each one believes in God.'* (The Cow, 285) The Lord then asked again, 'And what else do they believe in?' I replied, *"And His angels, and His Books and His Messengers. We make no division between any of His Messengers* (The Cow, 285); we accept and confirm them all.' The Lord then asked, 'What did

237

the believers say when the revelation came to them with the laws and injunctions from their Lord?' I answered, 'They said, *We hear, and obey* (The Cow, 285) oh my Lord!' The Lord then said, 'You have spoken truly, oh Muhammad, for they have received My Word and pledged obedience to My Commands. Now ask of Me what you wish, it will be granted.'

"To this I said, '*Oh Lord, grant us Thy Forgiveness; unto Thee is the homecoming.* (The Cow, 285) Admit us to Your Divine Presence having granted us Your Mercy and Forgiveness.' Thereupon the Almighty replied, 'I have forgiven you and your nation.' And after this, the Lord of Majesty and Might spoke:

God charges no soul save to its capacity, standing to its account is what it has earned, and against it what it has merited. (The Cow, 286)

"And after this, He said, 'Oh Muhammad, this night is the night of gifts, ask therefore for whatever you wish, it will be granted.' I then said,

Our Lord, take us not to task if we forget or make mistake. (The Cow, 286)

"The Lord then said, 'I have forgiven you and your nation for whatever sins they have committed from heedlessness and forgetfulness. And I have forgiven them the sins that they were forced to commit. So ask again, it will be granted.' I said,

'*Our Lord, charge us not with a load such as Thou didst lay upon those before us.*'" (The Cow, 286)

The Holy Prophet ❀ wished to express this: "Do not charge us with as heavy a load as that which You laid upon previous nations." This alludes to previous injunctions, which required the giving away of one fourth of one's possessions in Zakat, the cutting off of a defiled piece of clothing; swift punishment for crimes committed, and similar punishments. For instance, something that was permitted to them before was forbidden to them as a punishment for their crimes; if they committed a sin during the night, it would be written upon their foreheads or above their doors, in express letters, stating the crime and the punishment due to the perpetrator: "This man has committed a crime during the night and as a punishment, he must kill himself (for instance, by burning or by cutting off certain limbs)." Thus the sins they committed were out in the open and on that account they suffered public disgrace.

The obligation to always pray in their churches was also imposed on them; it was not lawful for them to pray in any other place. On a day of fasting, it was forbidden to them to take any food or drink after the onset of the night, or to approach their women after that hour.

To continue with the Holy Prophet's 🏵 narration:

> "I made supplication for my nation that they might not be burdened with all the weight that previous nations had to bear. My Lord then said to me, 'I have granted ease to your nation and made their burdens light. So ask of Me what you want, it will be granted.' Then I said, (in reference to disasters and calamities):

> *Our Lord, do Thou not burden us beyond what we have the strength to bear.*

> *(The Cow, 286)*

> "The Lord answered, 'I will not place upon you and your nation burdens which exceed their strength to carry them. But ask more of Me, I will grant it.' 'I replied, *'Pardon us!'* (The Cow, 286); ' and He replied, 'I have pardoned you and your nation.' *'Forgive us!'* (The Cow, 286).' 'I have forgiven you and your nation.'"

According to another version, the Holy Prophet 🏵 here explicitly asked for pardon for each and every act of disobedience, to each of which the Lord Almighty replied, "I have forgiven them."

The Prophet 🏵 continues,

> "At last I said, *'Have mercy on us'*, (The Cow, 286), and the Lord answered, 'I have mercy on you.' Then I said, *'Thou art our Protector;'* (The Cow, 286) and the Lord said, 'The Friend and Protector of all believers is Allah Almighty, Lord of Might and Glory; the unbelievers have no Protecting Friend.' Then I said, *'And help us against the people of*

239

the unbelievers'. (The Cow, 286) And the Lord replied, 'Up to the Day of Judgment, I have made you and your nation to be victorious over the unbelievers.' The Lord then asked again, saying, 'Oh My Beloved, other than this, if there is anything you should wish for, ask it of Me, for I will grant it to you.' Thereupon I said, 'Oh my Lord, you have chosen Ibrahim to be Your intimate friend, and have spoken to Musa without intermediary. To Da'ud You granted great possessions, and made iron to be soft as wax in his hand; You have made the mountains and its stones and the birds of the air to be subservient to his command, so that they joined him in singing Your praises. Idris You have transferred to a high place. To Sulayman You gave a kingdom and such possession as no one after him will ever come to possess and enjoy. And You made subservient to him mankind and Jinn, the demons and wild beasts, the birds and the winds. And You also taught him the tongues of the birds and the beasts. To 'Isa You gave knowledge of the Torah and the Injil, and by his prayer, You made the blind see, the afflicted whole, and the ailing to regain their health; You made him revive the dead, and You made him and his mother safe from the wiles of the devil and gave them protection. What will be the equivalent gift You will make to me?'

"The Lord Almighty replied to this in all His Grandeur and Majesty, saying, 'Oh Muhammad, I have chosen you as My Beloved, just as I chose Ibrahim as My faithful friend. To be the Beloved of Allah is even more excellent than being His bosom friend. I have also privileged you with the vision of My Divine Beauty, and I have spoken to you without intermediary, even as I spoke to Musa.'

"'Beyond this, I have given you the chapters of the Quran, 'al-Fatiha' (The Opening) and the end of 'al-Baqara' (The Cow), which are both from the treasure troves of My Divine Throne. These were not given to any Prophet before you, but reserved for you and your nation.'

"'Also, I have sent you as My Messenger to all the peoples of the world, to mankind and to Jinn, be they black or white or of any other description; never before have I sent a Prophet with so universal a mission.'

"'I have made the whole earth a means of cleansing for your nation. When you find water and are sound enough to perform your ablutions, make *Wudu* and take your *Ghusl*. But when you do not find water or you have not the strength to wash, you may perform *tayammum* and cleanse yourself by means of the dust of the earth.'

"'I have made the whole Earth to be as a *Masjid*, a place for prayer, so that wherever you may find yourselves, you may pray and perform your worship.'

"'I have made lawful to you and your nation the spoils of war, so that you may profit from them. To previous nations these were not lawful.'

"'And I have strengthened you in that I have cast fear into the heart of your enemy, even if there is a distance of one month's journey between you and them.'

"'I have granted you the right of intercession for whomever you desire. I have sent down to you the greatest and most august of all revealed scriptures, the Glorious Quran. And I have split your breast and removed from you all sinfulness.'

"I have elevated your name, for wherever My Name is mentioned, there your name is pronounced as well.'

Did He not find thee an orphan, and shelter thee? Did He not find thee erring, and guide thee? Did He not find thee needy, and suffice thee? (The Forenoon, 6-8)

"When the Lord Almighty had spoken to me thus, all I could answer was, 'Yes, my Lord, all these great favors You have bestowed upon me and honored me beyond all measure.'

"Then the Lord spoke again and said, 'Among all the people belonging to your nation, I have made one group in whose hearts resides the Holy Quran. (The Holy Quran is easy to memorize, to be learned by heart and recited from memory.) This was not given to other nations before yours; they did not commit to memory the books their prophets brought to them. This privilege I have reserved for your nation alone. I have made your nation more excellent than all previous nations; your nation is a nation of the middle way, and a nation of justice.'

"'You I have created before anything else, and I have sent you on your prophetic mission as the last of all the Prophets. I have given you to drink from the waters of *Kawthar* (abundance), and I have given you eight shares; these are: *Islam*, the *Hijra* (migration), war against ignorance, *Salat* (ritual prayer), *Zakat* (obligatory donations to the poor), the fast of Ramadan, enjoining good and discouraging evil *(amr-bil-ma'ruf wa nahiy-'an-il-munkar)*."

"After the Lord stopped speaking, I asked Him, 'Oh my Lord, after I had passed and seen all of creation, I experienced a moment of extreme terror. At that moment, I heard a voice that sounded to me exactly like the voice and inflection of Abu Bakr, and it said to me, 'Oh Muhammad ❀, stay your step! For Allah is praying (raining His blessings).' When I heard this, two questions arose in my mind. One was this: Has Abu Bakr overtaken me and come here before I have? The second question on my mind was this: My Lord has no need to pray, and yet I am told He is praying, what can that mean?'

"The Lord then answered me, 'Indeed, I have no need to turn to any in prayer, but recite the verse which I have revealed unto you:

It is He who blesses you, and His angels, to bring you forth from the shadows into the light. He is All Compassionate to the believers. (*The Confederates, 43*)

This verse will teach you that the meaning of My prayer is nothing but Mercy for you and for your nation.'

'As for Abu Bakr, oh Muhammad, it is as with the staff of the Prophet Musa, your brother among the Prophets. Musa always had his staff with him and it was for him something familiar and friendly. Therefore, when on the mountain of Tur (Sina'i) he was nearly overcome with awe as the Divine Call came to him, We addressed him, saying, 'What is that in your hand, oh Musa?' and Musa answered Me and said, 'It is my staff.' When he remembered the name of this familiar object, the excessive dread and awe he felt at the Divine Call departed from him. In this instance you are like Musa, oh Muhammad. The most familiar being in this world and the closest to you is your friend Abu Bakr. When you were in the grip of awesome terror, We created an angel for you in the shape and form of your familiar friend Abu Bakr and gave him his voice and tone with which to speak to you, so that you might feel the comfort of that familiarity when you heard him speak. Then the awesomeness and terror left you entirely, and so that you were not totally overcome by the majesty of this revelation and were able to ask what you wish from the Divine Essence. By means of this familiarity you were able to speak normally and without dread. I have in My Divine Majesty made Myself free from all defect and weakness, and My Mercy outstrips My Wrath. Therefore, state your wishes, and ask of Me whatever you need and desire.'

"After these words, the Lord added, 'What of the Angel Jibra'il's request, which he asked you to make?' I replied, 'Oh my Lord, You are the All-Knowing; there is no need to speak of it, as You know already, all Bounty and Munificence being Thine.' The Lord replied to this, 'I do grant his request and fulfill his wish. On the Day of Judgment when your nation prepares to cross the Bridge of Sirat, let them take a hold of his wing and cross with ease. Only the ones who loved you and your companions will cross with ease; I grant My Divine Sanction.'

"To this I rejoined, 'Oh Lord, you have sent punishment upon the nations that went before mine in many and varied forms. There were some upon whom You sent a rain of stones to destroy them; while others you drowned in the waters. Some were destroyed by Jibra'il's shout, and some You caused the Earth to swallow. Some perished when You sent against them a rain of fire, and others died in a harsh, bitter wind. Oh Lord, what will become of my nation after I have gone?'

"The Lord of Mercy and Munificence, the Lord of the Universe then intoned in all His Majesty and Splendor, 'My Wrath has been spent on those nations before thine; upon your nation I will shower only Mercy. I will transform their badness into good actions. To the corrupt among them I will grant the gift of repentance, and bring them into a good state of being. I will deliver them from their bad traits and help them acquire good characteristics. I will rid them of their ignorance and change their minds to understanding and perfect knowledge. Whoever calls upon Me, saying, 'Oh My Lord!' and turns to Me with true humility in his heart, to him I will answer, 'I am at your service, oh My servant; tell Me what it is that you desire, and I will create it.

'To you I give the right of intercession for your nation, oh Muhammad, you may be the advocate on their behalf, and I pledge to accept all your intercession.'

"And then He Almighty said, 'Oh Muhammad, I have not made your nation excessively wealthy, so that their accounts will not be overly long. And I have not made their bodies very great, so that they might not require much of worldly food and drink and dress. I have not made their lives to be exceedingly long, so that their hearts might not be blackened by pride in reliance upon a long lifespan and that they might always be aware of death and make their preparations for the afterlife that follows. I have not made death to come to them suddenly, but I have made illness precede it and provide a cause, so that they might not meet with a sudden death when they have plunged and sunk in the sea of heedlessness. When they fall ill, they repent of their sins, they pay their debts, they try to make up for past mistakes and shortcomings, and they make their last will and testament. I have brought them into the world after every other nation, so that their time in the grave might be of short duration; they will remain trapped in their tombs only until all the people of their nation have come and gone. When that is done, their time is up and they will attain to their blissful stations in Paradise, enjoying its undying delights.'

"Then the Lord said to me, 'Oh Muhammad, sometimes your nation will be obedient to Me, at other times they will be rebellious. Their obedience to Me meets with My Pleasure, and to Me are acceptable all their works, which accord to My Good Pleasure; I forgive them their minor misdoings and accord to them generous recompense. For I am the All-Bountiful, and I show Myself to them in My aspect of Bounty. The disobedient among them are subject to My Judgment; but because it is the Judgment of past eternity, I forgive them their disobedience, for I am the All-Merciful, and I show them My Mercy.'

"And then He said, 'Oh Muhammad, say to your nation: 'The Lord Almighty says to you: just as you love a person for that he shows you loving kindness and generosity, I am much more deserving of your love and affection than any other in this world. For I have created you when you were naught and I have given you a pleasing form and fine limbs and I continue to ceaselessly shower you with innumerable blessings. Not a moment passes in which I do not bestow upon you a new form of goodness. Therefore you ought to love Me more than any other, obeying My Commands and submitting to My Law.'

"And again, He Almighty says to you, 'If you are going to fear anything that dwells between Heaven and earth, it is I whom you ought to fear more than any, for My Power pervades all and everything. My chastisement is violent and swift, no one can flee or hide from it, or run to another master in order to save himself from Me, for no one has such powers. As this is the reality, you must beware of acting contrary to My wishes and commands.'

"And the Lord said, 'If you are going to ask of any, I am most worthy of being asked, for it is I alone who accepts all prayers of need and fulfills all wants.' And He says: 'You feel shame and regret when you have ill-treated someone or been unkind, whereas I am the most deserving of your shame and remorse, for I have brought you into being when you were naught and to this very moment I have heaped upon you endless gifts and blessings. I have made you safe from all manner of affliction, and yet you disregard My injunctions and do what I have forbidden to you. Therefore, contrition is your due and restraint from actions that I have prohibited. Obey Me and My Commands!'

"And the Lord addresses Himself to you, saying, 'If you choose for reasons of personal and covetous choice, I am the most deserving of your preference, for I am your Creator, and your Provider, and the only object of your worship. Therefore, turn to Me, worshipful, in your actions and with meritorious conduct.' All this He Almighty commanded me to expound to you.'

Allah Complains About the Ummah

"Then Allah Almighty complained to me about my nation. One of His objections was this: 'I do not ask of them to perform anything ahead of time, all I ask is for them to do what they should in its own time. But, by contrast, they ask of Me to provide them ahead of time. While I have provided them perfectly for so many years, they are not satisfied, even though they do not know whether their lives will last long enough to use up what they have been given. Even so, their greed for the things of this world is ever increasing, and they complain of not having the wherewithal of a livelihood, always asking for more. Do they not regard the birds in the skyways? Every morning the birds of the fields leave their nests with empty crops to return in the evenings having eaten their fill, though the whole world be covered in snow. Does not your nation take a lesson from this? While the whole world is covered in snow and not a speck of earth is to be seen, He who provides the birds with their shares, will He not provide them also with their own portions? Why does your nation not place their reliance on Him who has forever guaranteed their subsistence?

"'The second complaint is this: 'I do not give their provisions to any other than them; in spite of this, they perform actions for the sake of other than Me (that is to say, they behave hypocritically and occasion false appearances).

"'My third complaint is this: While they are consuming the portions that I have provided for them, their gratitude goes out to someone else. They will say, for instance, 'In my vineyard I had a harvest such an amount and from my fields such an amount, from my trade so much.' But was it not I who caused the vines to grow in his vineyard and the crops in his field, and who gave him success in his commerce? Why do they remember Me not and mention not My Name when they speak of the yields of their vineyards and fields, and the profits of their trade? Wherefrom is this heedlessness; do they feel no shame?'

"'And My fourth complaint is this: Mine is all Might and Glory; it is I who grants Honor in this world, in the grave and in the world to come. Even so, they still look to honors coming from other sources.

They will say, for instance, 'Were I only to occupy high office, I would surely grow very rich.' Thus they expect honor to come to them through riches and high office, whereas all these are only of a passing nature. When death comes to them, all connection ceases. Does that signal true honor? It is My Command, by which they must abide, it is I who gives them Honor and Dignity in this world and the next.'

"'My fifth complaint against them is this: I have created Hell for the unbelievers. Why is it that they persist in performing actions that will land them in Hellfire?'

"To these charges against my nation, I replied, 'Oh my Lord, Your Word is true, my nation is guilty of all that You have laid against it. But You are He who covers all shame and forgives all sins; You are the Supremely Rich and Generous, the Clement and All-Forgiving Lord (ar-ra'uf wa-r-rahim). In Your Infinite Grace and Kindness, forgive them their failings, conceal their disgrace, and in Your Endless Benevolence, pardon their great and small sins! Let them be overtaken by Your Boundless Mercy and with Your All-Gracious Compassion lead them into the Paradise, oh My Lord!'

"In answer to this supplication, the Lord Almighty said to me, 'Had your nation not been so sinful, I would have created a nation of sinners, so that I might make Myself known as the Forgiver of Sins in that I granted them forgiveness. Oh Muhammad, You are My Beloved, as you are My servant. All Creation I have brought into being for your sake alone. Because of your nation's sins, I have created My Mercy Oceans. Oh Muhammad, regard the high station of honor and dignity you have been granted, in that you are honored by an encounter with My Divine Beauty. I have granted you direct intercourse with My Divine Person, without interpreter or intermediary. Whoever is acceptable to you is also acceptable to Me, and he who refuses you, is refused by Me, too.'

"Then He said, 'Indeed, you will be the first of all the Prophets to enter Paradise, and no Prophet can enter it before you. Your nation will be the first nation to enter Paradise and no other nation will be admitted before they have gone in.'

"After this He said, 'Oh Muhammad, set not your hopes on any nation of mankind, for they have nothing at all. Let your hopes always be pinned on Me and let your converse be with Me, for to Me is your return. Do not become attached to this world in your heart, for I have not created you for this world.'

"Then He Almighty said, 'Oh Muhammad, of your nation I have forgiven one third for your sake; another third I will forgive on the Day of Judgment, so that the high regard and station you occupy in My Regard may become clear to all creation on the Day of Gathering, oh Muhammad.'

"After this, the Almighty informed me of a great many weighty and important matters, but He denied me permission to divulge this knowledge to you.

"It was made obligatory upon my nation to pray fifty times during one day and one night and to make ablutions for major impurity seven times, and to wash a defiled piece of clothing seven times. He commanded me to make these conditions known to my nation in His Name. I then replied, 'Everyone who comes home from a journey, brings presents for those who remained at home; therefore, give me something to take back to my nation as a present.' The Lord Almighty then said, 'One of the gifts to your nation is this: as long as they reside in the world, I will be their Helper; I will protect them from disaster and calamity and I will grant success to their good actions. I will grant them various favors. When they pray to Me, I will accept their prayers, I will protect them from what they fear and I will grant them what they desire.

"'Another gift to your nation is this: When their lives come to an end, I will be their Helper. I will protect them from the wiles of Shaytan and I will give them tidings of Paradise and show them their stations within it. I will make it easy for them to draw their last breath and I will help them pass over into the Hereafter in safety.

"'Another gift to your nation is this: When they are placed within their graves, I shall be their only Helper. I will release them from the darkness and oppression of the grave; I will lighten their tombs and make them spacious and wide. I will assist them in answering the questions of the angels Munkar and Nakir and I will make their tombs to be as a Garden of Paradise.

"'Another gift to your nation is this: When they arise from their graves, I will be their sole Helper. I will raise them from their tombs and make them light of face and clothe them in garments from Paradise. I will help them mount upon their steeds and lead them to the site of the Gathering with an entourage of angels in a display of splendor and grace. I will spare them the terror of that Dire Day. I will lead them underneath your banner and give them to drink of the waters of the Pool of *Kawthar*. I will make them to be close associates and companions of the prophets, messengers, saints and martyrs and the righteous whom I have favored with a place beneath the shadow of My Divine Throne. After having been given many special favors from Paradise, their books of reckoning will be placed in their right hands, and their accounts will be made light and their scales of the balance made heavy for them. I will help them cross the Bridge of Sirat with lightness and ease and lead them into the highest gardens of Paradise in the Boundlessness of My Grace.'"

May Allah Almighty gladden our hearts with these gifts, which He granted us all for the sake of His Holy Prophet Muhammad 🕌, Amin! Oh Most Merciful of those who show Mercy!

The Holy Prophet 🕌 continues:

"The Lord then said to me, 'Oh Muhammad, of all created beings, you are the one who has reached the highest honors. On the Day of Resurrection I will give you such great honors as will stupefy the whole world with wonderment. Oh Muhammad, do you wish to behold what I have prepared for your nation?' I replied, 'Oh Lord, I wish to see it, yes.' He then said, 'My trusted servant, the angel Jibra'il will show it to you.'

"As soon as I returned from there, Rafraf came into view. I seated myself upon him and he carried me down. I descended as far as the

249

Sidrat-al-Muntaha where I met with Jibra'il who said to me, 'Good tidings to you, oh Muhammad ❀, for you have been chosen as the best of all Creation and the foremost of all Prophets and Messengers. The Lord Almighty has greeted and honored you as He has not honored any other created being, neither from among His Prophets or His Messengers, nor from among His Angels brought Nigh.'

"Then Jibra'il said to me, 'Come with me, for I am to show you Paradise.'"

Paradise

The Seal of Prophethood ❀ continued:

"So Jibra'il brought me to Paradise. On its gates I saw written these words:

For one gift of Sadaqa, ten rewards are granted.

To one who gives on loan, eighteen rewards are granted.

"I asked Jibra'il, 'What is the secret wisdom of these lines, that one gift of Sadaqa carries ten merits, while a loan given carries eighteen merits after it?' Jibra'il told me, 'Oh Rasulullah ❀, sometimes Sadaqa is given to one who is in need, sometimes to one who is not. Not so, however with a loan: a loan is given only to him who is in need of it.'

"Upon the highest rim of the gates of Paradise I read these three lines. In the first line was written:

LA ILAHA ILLALLAH, MUHAMMADUN RASULULLAH

In the second line was written:

MA QADDAMNA, WAJADNA; WA MA AKALNA, RABAHNA; WA MA TARAKNA, KHASIRNA.

(What we have sent before us, here we have found; what we have eaten has remained with us as gain; and what we have left behind, is our loss.)

"In the language of the People of Paradise, this means to say: 'Of what we owned, that which we spent in the way of goodness, what we gave to the poor and the needy as Sadaqa, today we have found it here waiting for us. As for that part of our property which we used up and expended, we have already had the good use of it; as for that, which we have left behind us when we died, we were misled and now count it as our loss.'

"In the third line was written:

'THE NATION OF MUHAMMAD ﷺ IS A NATION OF GREAT AND ABOUNDING SINFULNESS. THEREFORE THEY ARE SO PLACED AS TO BE THE NATION OF MUHAMMAD ﷺ, SO THAT THEY MIGHT FIND THE LIGHT OF GUIDANCE AND BECOME ENLIGHTENED. HEREWITH THE LORD WHO IS THE ALL-FORGIVING MANIFESTS THE BLISS OF LIGHT UPON LIGHT. HE FORGIVES ALL THEIR SINS AND TRANSGRESSIONS, GREAT AND SMALL, SECRET AND OBVIOUS, COMMITTED KNOWINGLY OR UNKNOWINGLY, ALL VICE AND DISGRACE. THROUGH HIS FAVOR AND GRACE AND BOUNTY, HE AIDS THEM IN ATTAINING HIS ALL-ENCOMPASSING MERCY, GRATUITOUSLY, AND HE BRINGS THEM INTO THE HIGHEST OF THE GARDENS OF PARADISE. HE MAKES THEM TASTE THE GREATEST DELIGHTS AND THE HIGHEST JOYS OF ALL, AND HE MAKES THEM ENDLESSLY SATISFIED. THIS IS WHAT DISTINGUISHES THE NATION OF MUHAMMAD ﷺ AND ENDOWS THEM MORE HIGHLY THAN ANY OTHER NATION.'

As it is written in these verses of the Holy Book of the Quran:

Say: 'Oh my people who have been prodigal against yourselves, do not despair of God's mercy; surely God forgives sins altogether; surely, He is the All-Forgiving, the All-Compassionate. *(The Companies, 53)*

You are the best nation ever brought forth to men, bidding to honor, and forbidding dishonor, and believing in God. Had the People of the Book believed, it was better for them; some of them are believers, but the most of them are ungodly.

(The House of Imran, 105)

To continue in the words of Prophet Muhammad ﷺ:

"The gate of Paradise was made of red gold, and the thick-ness of the doors was five hundred years' of traveling. The gate had four hundred columns, which were of pearl, of topaz, of ruby and of emerald. In the middle of each of these pegs there was a great ring of red ruby stone of immense dimensions. In it were contained forty thousand cities, and each city had forty thousand domes. Within each of these domes dwelt forty thousand angels holding two platters each in their hands. One was filled with celestial raiment; the other was filled with light. I asked Jibra'il about them and he told me, 'Oh Rasulullah, these angels were created eighty thousand years before Adam, and since that time they are waiting in this very place, bearing platters of light. Their sole purpose is to plead for you and for your nation. On the Day of Resurrection, when you appear before your nation in honor and bliss, the moment your foot touches the threshold, these angels will welcome you and your nation and bestrew them with the contents of their platters as they pass through the gates of Grace and Bounty.'

"Then Jibra'il knocked on the gates of Paradise. The guardian angel of the Garden, Ridwan called out asking, 'Who is it?' Jibra'il answered, 'It is I, Jibra'il.' 'And who is it with you?' asked the Keeper. 'He is Muhammad ﷺ,' answered Jibra'il. 'Has his time of prophethood arrived then?' asked the angel from within. 'Yes, it has come,' replied Jibra'il. 'Alhamdulillah!' said Ridwan and opened the gates. I then saw that the hinges of the door were of silver, its threshold was of pearl and its casings were of precious jewels.

"We stepped inside and I beheld Ridwan, seated upon a carved throne, surrounded by a host of angels who stood in attendance. They gave me honor and saluted me with respect. I greeted them and gave my Salams. Ridwan answered me and welcomed me with joy, giving me these good tidings, 'Most of the People of Paradise are from your nation.' I asked him, 'Tell me about my nation.' He said, The Lord Almighty has divided the Jannah into three parts, two of which are appointed for your nation, while one is for all other nations.' In front of Ridwan there were a great number of keys, and I asked him, 'What are these keys?' He told me, 'When a person of your nation pronounces the words, *La ilaha ill'Alla*h, the Lord Almighty creates for him a mansion in Paradise, and He gives the keys to this mansion into my safekeeping. On the Day of Resurrection, when that person rises from his tomb, I give him the keys to his mansion and he takes up residence therein.'

"Then I noticed the helpers and assistant angels of Ridwan. One stood guarding the gate to the Garden and each one had seven hundred thousand other angels to serve him. But Ridwan had seventy thousand commanders, and each of these commanded a troop of seventy thousand angel soldiers.

"The Tasbih I heard Ridwan utter was this:

Subhanal-khallaqil-alim,

Subhanal-karimil-akram,

Subhanal-musibu man a'tahu jannata-n-na'im.

(Praised be the All-Knowing Creator,

Praise be to the Most Bounteous of the Bountiful,

Praised be He who leads into Paradise Bliss whosoever obeys Him.)

"Then I was shown the bliss of Paradise. In a word, I beheld such a wealth of manifold delights that, even were I to spend the rest of my lifetime trying to describe them, it would not suffice to complete the task.

"The walls of the Jannah were thus: one brick was of gold, the next of silver. Then followed one of red ruby, and next one of green chrysolite, then a brick of pearl. In place of mortar, musk and camphor had been used. The thickness of the wall was a distance of five hundred years' traveling. At the same time it was so clear as to be transparent from inside out and outside in, as a window of glass. From there, all seven layers of the heavens and of the earth were visible, including the Divine Throne and the Divine Court. The soil of Paradise is made up of musk, amber and camphor; its grasses were of saffron-yellow and purple hues. The pebbles there consisted of emeralds, rubies and pearls. Then I beheld the habitations of Paradise; some where made of rubies, and their domes were of pearl. Some were of gems and their domes were of emeralds, while others were all of gold. In every mansion there were seventy thousand palaces and to every palace there were seventy thousand suites. Every suite consisted of seventy thousand rooms. In every room there was a throne, either made of silver or of gold. Upon each throne was a tent of beryl, in every tent there were seventy thousand beds of embroidered silk. Each of these differed from the other, and they were filled with amber and musk.

"The Huris in them wore robes so transparent that their skin and flesh and bones, nay, even the marrow of their bones were visible. Each one of the Huris wore upon her head a crown embellished with jewels, and each had forty thousand locks of sweetly scented hair curling down. Each lock was adorned with seventy thousand adornments, and each one of these trinkets separately emits the sweetest of notes, a delight to the ear. In front of each of the Huris seventy thousand servants stand in attendance. Around each of the thrones are set up stools made of silver, pearls, emeralds and camphor, each differing from the other.

"Then I beheld the rivers of Paradise, of milk, of water, of wine and of honey. A branch of these four rivers flows to each one of the Paradise homes and the water is whiter than camphor, sweeter than honey and its scent more fragrant than musk.

"I also beheld there the springs of Rahiq, Salsabil and Tasnim. The banks of these rivers and the brim of these springs are of gold and pearls, of silver and rubies. The pebbles in the riverbeds and at the mouth of the springs are various precious gems and pearls of many colors. The foam upon the waters is of musk and amber, and around the fountainheads grow hyacinths and saffron crocus. The trees I saw there were so great that if a man on the back of a swift horse were to ride at full speed for seventy thousand years, he would not emerge from under its shade. The roots of these trees are of gold, their branches of ruby, pearls and chrysolite. Its leaves are of silk, brocade and velvet. Each one of its leaves reaches from one end of the world to the other. Each fruit of this tree is as great as a great water jug, and each one has seventy different flavors. Each of these fruits offers itself to the People of Paradise. Whenever they desire to eat of it, it falls from its branch and upon a platter of gold comes floating up to their mouths, without effort or a moment's delay. Even were this tree to be at a distance of a thousand years' wayfaring, as soon as one of the blessed wished for its fruit, it would be right there at his disposal, close to his lips. He would then eat from it as much as he wished, and after he had eaten, a new fruit would immediately take the place of the one consumed.

"I also beheld birds in these trees of Paradise, alike unto camels. They were colored in all the hues of Paradise. They flew about before the divans, singing hundreds of different tunes and melodies. The People of Paradise ask one of these birds, 'Which is more beautiful, your voice or your form?' and they receive this answer, 'My flesh is the best of all.' After saying this, he instantly turns himself into a roasted fowl and presents himself to the dweller of Paradise, should he have expressed an appetite. He is just as he wants him to be, and after he has eaten, he instantly comes back to life and sings anew in the boughs of the tree. All these birds sing the praises of the people of Paradise.

About the Paradise Gardens

"I was shown eight different Paradise gardens, and four of these were actual gardens and orchards. Their names were Firdaws, Ma'wa, 'Adn and Na'im. The four others contained palaces and pavilions amidst gardens and orchards. These were Dar-us-Salam, Dar-al-Jalal, Dar-al-Qarar, and Dar-al-Khuld.

256

"In each of these four last-mentioned gardens there were gardens and flowering meadows as numerous as the stars in the night sky and grains of sand in the desert.

"The sky of the highest Paradise is the base of the Divine Throne. I was shown only the mansions in the Paradise of 'Adn (Eden), and they were as the starry skies at night. A great many of them were destined for my companions and for people of my nation. Each of these mansions was as great as the distance between Heaven and earth. Jibra'il showed me these mansions and told me the names of those who were destined to inhabit them. I espied one which was higher and larger than the others and I asked whose was this great mansion. Jibra'il told me, 'It is the mansion of Abu Bakr as-Siddiq.' Then he showed me those belonging to 'Umar, 'Uthman and Ali.

Here, the Holy Prophet ﷺ paused to turn to Abu Bakr and he said to him:

"Oh Abu Bakr, I have seen your palace in Paradise, it is made all of red gold. And I have seen all the immense favors and rewards, which lie in store for you there." To this Abu Bakr replied, "May the owner of that Paradise pavilion be sacrificed for you, oh Prophet of Allah ﷺ!" The Holy Prophet ﷺ then went and told 'Umar that he had seen the palace destined for him in Paradise and that it was made of ruby. "A great many Huris were there, and as I entered inside it, I remembered your jealousy." After this he said to 'Uthman, "I saw you in each of the heavens, and I have seen and regarded your house in Paradise."

After this He said to Ali:

"Oh Ali, I saw your shape in the fourth Heaven. I asked Jibra'il about it and he told me, 'Oh Rasulullah ﷺ, the angels yearned to see Ali, therefore the Lord Almighty created an angel in the form of Ali and placed him in the fourth Heaven where the angels can go to visit him. Then I went inside your designated palace. I picked a fruit of one of the trees and sniffed at it. A *Huri* came out from it, drawing her veil across her face. I asked her, 'Who are you?' She answered, 'I was created for your brother and cousin Ali, oh Rasulullah ﷺ.'"

Then the Holy Prophet ﷺ, the Messenger to both mankind and Jinn, the Imam of both Sanctuaries continued:

"Before me I heard footsteps and I asked Jibra'il, 'Whose footfall is this?' He answered me, 'It is the tread of your Muadhdhin Bilal, oh Messenger of Allah!'"

According to one tradition, the Holy Prophet ﷺ asked Bilal:

"On the night of my Mi'raj, I heard the sound of your step in the gardens of Paradise. What have you done to achieve such high rank?" Bilal answered the Prophet ﷺ, "There is nothing very special in my works. Only, as often as I break my Wudu', I perform ablution anew, and after repeating my Wudu' I pray a prayer of two Rak'ats." The Prophet ﷺ then said, "These then are the actions which have allowed you to run ahead of me."

The Holy Prophet ﷺ continued:

"Again I heard the sound of a footfall ahead of me and I asked Jibra'il who told me, 'It is the step of Ghamsa bint Milhan, a daughter of one of the Ansar renowned for her patience in poverty.' I also saw two great mansions belonging to Zayd bin 'Amr bin Nufayl, and I asked wherefore he was so honored. One reason was this: that he lived according to the law of 'Isa, and another was that he accepted the new law when I was given prophethood and the law of 'Isa was superseded, and he lived by it for the rest of his days. Therefore he was given double reward.

"Then I came upon domes built all of pearls and their mortar was of musk. I asked Jibra'il who they were meant for and he told me they were for the *Imam*s and Muadhdhins of my nation.

"And I saw this, too: Ja'far ibn Abi Talib flying along with the angels. And I saw my uncle Hamza reclining on a divan in the Gardens of Bliss. I saw also my wife Khadija of blessed memory in a pavilion of pearls built over one of the rivers of Paradise."

The Tuba Tree

Allah's Messenger continued:

"I came upon a tree in Paradise of such beauty as nothing I had seen before this could equal. When I came up to its trunk and looked aloft, I realized how tremendous a tree it was. Its boughs spread out in all directions so that nothing else was to be seen but this tree. It gave of such a fine scent that in all Paradise I had not smelled anything finer. I examined the whole tree. Its leaves were white and red and green and yellow and each had a special coating and covering in the distinctive colors of Paradise. The fruits of this tree were like long poles. Each one of them contained the pleasures and delights, all of the good tastes and smells that are found in Heaven and on earth - all were assembled in a single fruit of this tree.

"I remained spell-bound before the wondrous beauty of this tree and the loveliness of its form, and I asked Jibra'il, 'What tree is this?' Jibra'il told me, 'Its name is 'Tuba', it is the Tuba Tree.'

The Waters of Kawthar

"In the middle of the Jannah, I saw a river that sprang from somewhere by the pillars on which rests the Divine Throne. Its flow was made up of water, milk, wine and honey, and yet these four did not mix. The banks of this river were of chrysolite and the pebbles of the riverbed were precious gems. Its mud was amber and its weeds were saffron crocuses. All along its banks were innumerable drinking cups of silver, as many as there are stars in the sky. Birds whose necks were as the necks of camels flew alongside. Aah, for to eat of their flesh and to drink of the waters of that river - a sign of the Lord's manifest Favor!

"I asked Jibra'il about this river and he told me, 'This is the water of Kawthar. Inform your nation of this. In every grove and garden of Paradise there flows a stream the waters of which rise from the spring of Kawthar.' Along the banks of this stream, I saw tents of pearl and red ruby. I asked Jibra'il and he said, 'Those are the dwellings of your wives.' Within the tents I espied moon-faced Huris whose features shone with the radiance of the sun. All at once, they broke out into song, and this is what they sang:

We always sing our tune, never do we tire;

We are always pleased, and we know no sadness;

We are always clothed, we are never bare.

We are forever young, and never shall grow old;

We are contented anytime, never are we cross.

We shall always be, never we shall die.

We belong to them, and they to us forever; ah, everlasting bliss!'

"The Huris' voices reached to all the far corners of Paradise. They reached every pavilion and every tree, and all resounded with such profound bliss that, were only the slightest part of it to reach the Earth, no trouble would remain upon it, nor death.

"Jibra'il then asked me, 'Do you wish to behold their beauty?' 'Indeed, I do,' I replied. Thereupon, one tent flap was lifted and I glimpsed a face of such beauty, that even were I to spend the rest of my life my life trying to describe it, I would not accomplish even a fraction of its description. Their faces were whiter than milk, their lips redder than red ruby, and more radiant than the sun. Their complexions were softer than the velvety petals of the red rose or the softest silken cloth. More luminous were they than the moon at its fullest, and their scent was more pleasing than musk. Their tresses were of the darkest shade of ebony. Some wore them plaited, while others wore their hair loose, and some bound it with ties. Those who wore their hair loosened were covered by it as by a tent when they were seated, their hair reaching down to their feet. Each had in front of her a servant. Jibra'il explained to me, 'These are intended for your nation.'

"One of the most amazing things I saw in the Jannah was the four rivers that flowed through it.

As Allah Almighty describes in His Holy Book:

This is the similitude of Paradise, which the God-fearing have been promised: therein are rivers of water unspoiling, rivers of milk unchanging in flavor and rivers of wine — a delight to the drinkers, rivers, too, of honey purified; and therein for them is every fruit and forgiveness from their Lord. (Muhammad, 15)

To continue in the Prophet's ❀ words:

"I asked Jibra'il, 'Whence do these waters come and whither do they flow?' He told me, 'All I know is that they flow out of the pool of Kawthar, but their actual source I cannot tell. You are most highly esteemed in the Divine Presence; perhaps if you ask, you will be told.' While yet thinking about this matter, my eye fell upon an angel so great, Allah alone knows his true size. He had a great number of wings and he spoke to me, saying, 'Place your blessed feet upon one of my wings and shut your eyes!' I did as he bade me, and he flew off. After a while he told me to open my eyes again, and when I did so, I beheld a tree. Beneath this tree, I saw a dome, which was so great that were you to place the whole world upon it, it would resemble a bird that has alighted upon a huge mountain. There was a golden key to this dome and it had a door made of beryl. I then perceived that the four rivers issued from beneath that dome.

"After I had seen that much, I wished to return, but the angel said to me, 'Don't you wish to enter that dome and find out the actual source of these waters?' 'The door is locked,' I answered. The angel replied, 'But you have the key.' 'What is that key?' I asked, marveling. The angel said, 'The key is this:

BISMILLAH-IR-RAHMAN-IR-RAHIM

Speak these words, and the door will open.'

"So I stepped forward and spoke these words: 'BISMILLAH-IR-RAHMAN-IR-RAHIM;' and lo, the door sprang open. I then saw that the four rivers flowed from the four walls of the building. The angel said to me, 'Look carefully!' and as I did so, I saw that on one wall were written the words; Bi-ISMi (In the Name of), on another wall: ALLAH (Allah), on the third wall: AR-RAHMAN (the All-Merciful), and on the fourth: AR-RAHIM (the All-Compassionate).

From the mouth of the letter 'mim' in the word Bi-ISMi flowed the river of water; from the eye of the letter 'ha' in the word ALLAH flowed the river of milk; from the mouth of the 'mim' in the word AR-RAHMAN flowed the river of wine; from the mouth of the 'mim' in the word AR-RAHIM flowed the river of honey. Thus I saw that the sources of the four rivers were these four holy words.

"When I wished to depart from this place, a Divine Address came to me, saying:

Inni man dhakarani bi-hadhihil-kalimat wa qala bi-qalbin salihin 'Bismillah ir-Rahman ir-Rahim' saqaitahu min hadhihil-anharul-arba'a.

(Whoever remembers Me by speaking these words BISMILLAH-IR-RAHMAN-IR-RAHIM with a pure heart and sincere intent, him I will give to drink from these four rivers of Paradise.)

All Praise is due to the Lord of the Worlds, Amin.

"I saw some palaces and pavilions of the Jannah, which were of pearls and rubies. Between each of them lay a distance as great as east is removed from west. I asked Jibra'il, 'For whom are these pavilions?' and he told me, 'They are for such people as took a blind man by the hand and led him for seven paces.' I asked, 'Shall I give news of this to my nation?' and he answered, 'Yes, give them the good news, but know that there is even better cheer yet ahead, and tell them of that as well. If a Muslim rises in the morning, saying 'Bismillahir-rahmani-r-rahim', then makes his ablution and prays his morning prayer, Allah Almighty will prepare for him a place in Paradise which is twenty times as large as the Earth from east to west.'

"After this, I came to see Idris, the Prophet, and I saluted him. He returned my Salams ceremoniously and bade me welcome. I then said to him, 'What a beautiful place you have come to dwell in!' He said to me in response, 'What is it to me; if only I could have been in the world now to be reckoned as one of your nation!' I then said, 'You have been spared the pangs of death and have reached this high station; what do you want of the world?' He answered me, 'And if I had to suffer the death throes of the entire world since the day of its

262

creation, if only I had been honored to be alive in your time, thus to be counted as one of your nation...' I then asked him, 'Oh my brother Idris, what is the reason for this desire of yours?' He replied, 'Whichever Paradise mansion I go to, however many Huris I turn towards, all of them are saying, 'We belong to the nation of Muhammad 🕌.'

"One day I came to a mountain, which they call the 'Jabal-ur-Rahma', the Mount of Mercy. Its peak reaches up to the Divine Throne and it is made of musk and amber. There are two entrances set upon this mountain, both made of pure white silver. The distance between these two doors is so great that a rider galloping in haste upon a swift steed for five hundred years would not be able to cross it. Inside it were such a great number of palaces and mansions that would be impossible to enumerate. To attempt to describe their beauty and splendor is likewise beyond all human means. I asked, These mansions belong to which one of the Prophets?' The Lord Almighty then addressed me, saying, 'This is not a place belonging to any Prophet, but for any one of the nation of Muhammad who prays two Rak'ats, to him I will give a mansion here.' For these reasons I wish to belong to your nation.'

"In a word, I there witnessed Divine Gifts of Grace such as no eye has seen, no ear has heard and no man's heart has ever imagined. After all was done, I left the Jannah together with the Angel Jibra'il and we descended once more to the seventh Heaven. I spoke to the Prophet Ibrahim. We saluted each other and he congratulated me on my Mi'raj. He did not put any questions to me.

"Then we descended to the sixth Heaven and I met the Prophet Musa who also congratulated me on the Mi'raj. We greeted one another, then he asked me, 'Oh Rasulullah 🕌, what has been imposed upon your nation?' I began to tell him, 'The Lord has commanded them to pray fifty times during one night and one day, to fast six months of the year, to wash seven times when having incurred a state of major impurity, and to wash a contaminated garment seven times to purify it.' When Musa had heard all this, he replied, 'Your nation has not the strength to keep all these commands. By Allah, before your time, I have experienced the nature of man, I employed various and sundry means to persuade my nation, the Bani Isra'il, by oath and by injunction. Still, they could not fulfill this obligation. Go back, implore the Lord that He lessen the burden for your nation.'

"Thereupon I turned back until I reached the Sidrat-al-Muntaha where I threw myself down in prostration before the Lord, pleading with Him, 'Oh my Lord, my nation is a weak nation; fifty prayer times a day, six months of fasting, seven purification baths, they and I will not be able to keep, and we will fall short of our requirements. By Thine Grace and Loving kindness, lighten our load!'

"After this plea, ten prayer times, one month of fasting and one bath were lifted. Again I met the Prophet Musa and told him what I had been given. He said, 'Your nation will still not be able to carry forty periods of prayer, five months of fasting and six purification baths, they will fall short of their requirement. Have pity on your nation and plead for their load to be lightened. ' So again I went back to the Sidra and begged Allah to lighten my nation's burden. Again ten prayer times, one month of fasting and one bath were lifted from them. I came back to the Prophet Musa and told him what I had received. He said, 'Your nation is a weak nation, thirty times of prayer, four months of fasting and five baths are still too much for them. Go back and ask for their load to be lightened.' Again I returned to the Sidra and threw myself down before the Almighty, praying that He might lift some more of the load off my nation, and again my prayer was granted. I came back and spoke once more to the Prophet Musa; again he sent me back, and I went yet again to plead with the Lord and to ask for more lightening of the task. In this way it went on, until I had received the command for my nation to keep five prayer times during one night and one day, to fast one month a year, to bathe once for purification and to wash their polluted garment once only. When I came back and told Musa what the Lord had commanded, he said, 'Go back again and ask to be given less.' But I replied, 'I have now gone many times and asked for the load to be lightened for my nation, and each time the Lord granted it to me. I am ashamed to go back again, this much I am willing to accept.'

"After I had left Musa, I received a Divine Call, 'I have lightened the load of worship for My servants, I accept that they pray five prayers daily. Oh Muhammad, let them pray five times a day and I will grant them the reward of fifty prayers. Anyone belonging to your nation who intends an act of goodness and later fails to carry it out, I will grant him one reward him in accordance with his intention. If he performs the action as he intended, I will grant him a tenfold reward, and increase it up to seven hundred fold, layer upon layer of recompense. Even if he intends to perform a sinful action and in the end he does not do so after all, I will write a reward for him for not having committed a sin. And should he commit it, I will write for him a single sin.'

"After this, I climbed upon the wing of the Angel Jibra'il and we came to the Bayt al-Maqdis (Jerusalem). I saw the Buraq tied to the ring where I had left him. I entered the mosque and prayed there two Rak'ats of thanks to Allah Almighty for His Infinite Grace and Favor, Mercy and Munificence upon me, all praises be to Him Almighty! Then I mounted again upon the Buraq and in less time than it takes to bat an eyelid, I arrived back in Mecca. By the Infinite Power of Allah, I found that during my absence my bed had not even grown cold yet."

The Duration of the Mi'raj

'Ammar told us, "The Mi'raj of our Holy Prophet 🕸 took place in three hours." Abdullah bin Munabbih however tells us, "Rasulullah's 🕸 Mi'raj was accomplished within four hours."

The truth of the matter is that Allah alone knows how long it really took. It is one of the articles of our faith to fully believe in the reality of this Mi'raj. Whoever refuses to believe that the Holy Prophet 🕸 went as far as Jerusalem is reckoned an unbeliever. For there are hard proofs for this fact, as declared in the Holy Book of the Quran:

> *Glory be to Him who carried His servant by night from the Holy Mosque to the Further Mosque the precincts of which We have blessed, that We might show him some of Our signs. He is the All-Hearing, the All-Seeing. (The Night Journey, 1)*

Whoever denies that the Prophet ❀ actually ascended from the *Masjid-al-Aqsa* (Jerusalem) to the heavens is a heretic (literally, an inventor of harmful innovations) and has gone astray. For it has been determined by way of Hadiths of many different paths of extraction that the Prophet ❀ did actually ascend to the heavens. We declare our belief and confirm them all.

Therefore, because the honor of ascension was granted to him, the Holy Prophet ❀ bears the epithet of *Sahib-al*-Mi'raj, 'He who was granted ascension to the heavens'. May Allah's Blessing and Benediction be upon him, Amin.

The Prophet's ❀ Return From Mi'raj

Another one of the Holy Prophet's ❀ names is *al-Muayyad*, 'he who is strengthened, corroborated', for Allah Almighty confirmed all that he brought home from his Mi'raj.

When Muhammad ❀ returned from his Mi'raj, he asked the angel Jibra'il, "Who will believe me when I tell them that I have performed a Mi'raj?" Jibra'il then answered him, "Abu Bakr will confirm whatever you say, for he is *Siddi*q, Truthful."

When it was morning, the Holy Prophet ❀ stepped forth into the *Haram-ash-Sharif* in an exalted state of bliss and enlightenment. When he sat down, Abu Jahl, the enemy of Allah went up to him and, seeing the Prophet ❀ in an aura of light and majesty, he thought to himself, "There is something strange about this; let me go and find out and see whether I can't manage to annoy him a bit." So he sat down beside the Holy Prophet ❀ in order to vex him in some way and said to him in mockery, "Oh Muhammad ❀, you look so happy. I guess you must have come across something useful?" "Yes indeed," replied the Holy Prophet ❀. Abu Jahl then went on, "And what was that?"

"Last night the Angel Jibra'il came to me and took me along with him while I was wide awake." Abu Jahl asked, "Where did he take you to?" The Holy Prophet ❀ answered, "He led me from the Kaba al-Mukarrama to the Bayt-al-Maqdis (Masjid-al-Aqsa). Abu Jahl then asked, "You are telling me, that this very night you were at the Masjid-al-Aqsa (in Jerusalem), and that you came back to Mecca and are right here among us this morning?" "Yes," replied the Holy Prophet ﷺ, the Rightly-Guided Messenger, the Intercessor on the Day of Reckoning. Abu Jahl then had this suggestion to make, "If I called together the people, would you repeat to them what you have just told me?" "Yes," said the Holy Prophet ﷺ. Thereupon, Abu Jahl called out in a loud voice so all could hear, "Come here, all you sons of Ka'b, oh people of Quraysh!"

When they had all assembled and were seated around him, Abu Jahl turned to the Prophet Muhammad ﷺ and asked him to repeat before the assembled Quraysh what he had told him privately. The Holy Prophet ﷺ then said, "Last night Jibra'il came to me and took me along with him." "Where did he take you to?" everyone wanted to know. "He took me to the Bayt al-Maqdis, to Jerusalem," said the Prophet ﷺ. They said, "Last night you went all the way to Jerusalem and yet you are here among us this morning?" To this the Holy Prophet ﷺ, the Prince of the Prophets, the Light of the Eyes of the Saints replied, "Yes, indeed."

But they would not believe him and said he lied.

Aisha as-Siddiqa (the Truthful) relates the following concerning this controversy:

> "When the story of the Mi'raj became known, some of those who had declared their faith earlier, apostatized and fell away from their new faith. Some of the idolaters went to Abu Bakr and told him about this. His response was to ask them, 'Is that really what he says?' 'Yes, that is what he claims.' 'If he says so, then it must be true. If he says that he went and came back in one night, then he truly did do so.' Again they asked him, 'Do you then confirm the claims he makes?' Abu Bakr replied, 'And were he to claim to have gone even farther than that and to have returned in that same night, I would believe him and confirm the truth of it.' From that day on, Abu Bakr was given the by-name 'as-Siddiq', a title meaning 'the eminently Truthful'."

The assembled idolaters challenged the Holy Prophet 🕌, saying:

> "We know what the Holy Mosque, the Bayt-al-Maqdis in Jerusalem
> looks like; if you have truly been there, you will be able to answer our
> questions when we ask you concerning its shape and aspect? There are
> many among us who have been there on repeated occasions. If you
> can give the answers corresponding to reality, it will be known that
> you have really been there."

Then they began to ask him questions concerning the appearance of the
Bayt-al-Maqdis. The Lord of Absolute Power, Allah Almighty then revealed
to the Holy Prophet 🕌 a vision of the Bayt-al-Maqdis at Jerusalem, so that
he saw it before his very eyes. Whatever they asked him about it, he was
able to describe to them all the details of the holy site. The men listening to
him were forced to admit, "By God, everything he tells us about it is true.
Even those among us who have been there many times could not describe
it in such accurate detail." Then they said, "We are not satisfied to hear that
you went there and came back. Tell us about our caravans." The Holy
Prophet 🕌 then said, "I chanced upon such-and-such a caravan belonging
to a certain tribe at a place named Rawha. They had lost one of their camels
and were searching for it. I was very thirsty, and there happened to be a cup
of water there. I took it and drank from it, then I placed it back where it
had been. When the men of the caravan return to you, ask them about this
cup of water: did they find it full of water, or not?"

Later this caravan arrived. People questioned them as the Prophet 🕌 had
told them. They confirmed all he had said and recounted, "At Rawaha we
had lost our camel and we went in search of it. When we returned, we
found that someone had drunk the water we left in the cup, it was empty."

They asked the Prophet 🕌, "Tell us about our caravan, which was
journeying in the other direction." The Prophet 🕌 agreed and said to them,
"I met them in a place called Tan'im." Then they asked him to relate in
greater detail their numbers and burdens and beasts, and when their return
to Mecca could be expected. The Holy Prophet 🕌 replied to every one of
their questions, giving even the names of the men in the caravan. He said,

"On such and such a day at sunrise, this caravan will arrive, and at its head will go a white camel, tinged with black."

On the day he had indicated, all those assembled went out into the desert to watch for the caravan's arrival, though there was still no sign of it. Some said, "It arrived at the time he said it would." Others said, "As soon as the sun rose, the caravan appeared." Others again said, "The caravan was seen with a white camel leading it." They confirmed everything the Prophet ❊ had said about the caravan and all turned out to be true. They all witnessed these events, but despite that there could be no doubt as to the Prophet's ❊ journey to Jerusalem and his return in one night, not one of them believed in him, all called him a liar.

One day after his Mi'raj, the Angel Jibra'il came again to the Holy Prophet ❊ who was in a state of vexation because of his nation. The angel said to him:

"Oh Prophet of Allah ❊, do not grieve all that much over your nation, for today I have come to you with great good tidings." The good tidings he brought were these:

In the fourth Heaven there is an angel who commands twelve thousand angels. During your Mi'raj, when all the other angels rose from their places to greet you, this angel did not rise to his feet along with the others. Today when I passed by the gate of that Heaven, I heard the sound of moaning, and when I turned to look, I saw that the sad sound came from that particular angel whom I was used to seeing. I saw that his wings had been plucked, and his light had been taken from him, he lay bundled in a corner, sighing pitifully. When he saw me, he began to weep. I said to him, 'Why do you weep, you who are such a great and honored angel?' He said, 'I am that angel, but I have committed a grave error. For my Lord has reproached me, saying, 'Why, when My Beloved Prophet ❊ came to the heavens to visit you, did you not rise to welcome him?' I answered, 'Oh my Lord, at that time I was so absorbed in my worship and adoration of Your Almighty Holiness, that I did not think of deflecting my attention to anything else. I saw Muhammad ﷺ coming, but I did not think it so important an event.'

"'The Lord then loosened His Wrath against me, and brought me into this condition in which you behold me now, my light withdrawn, my feathers plucked, and myself demoted from my angelic station. Oh Jibra'il, pray, intercede for me with my Lord!' I therefore prayed to the Lord and begged Him to pardon His angel's failing, who pledged never to commit another act of negligence. The Lord Almighty then replied, 'Let him recite *Salat-wa-Salam* on My Holy Prophet ﷺ, and I will forgive him.'

"I went and told this to the angel, who immediately started reciting peace and blessings upon the Prophet ﷺ, and when he had recited them ten times, all his wing feathers had grown back, and he flew off joyfully.'"

"This is the good news I have come to tell you, oh Rasulullah ﷺ. For the Lord will forgive and pardon all those from your nation who recite peace and blessings to you with a loving heart and He will grant them access to Paradise."

When the Holy Prophet ﷺ came out to his companions after this, his face was as radiant as the moon at its fullest, and he smiled so broadly that his back teeth showed. He then informed his companions of the good tidings the angel had brought him, of how the Lord would forgive all those who recited Salat-wa-Salam upon him, and all his blessed Companions rejoiced with him.

Allahumma salli wa sallam wa barik 'ala

Sayyidina Muhammadan wa 'ala alihi wa sahbihi wa sallam tasliman,

wal-hamdu-lillahi-rabbil-'alamin.

The Early Muslims in Madinah

Two of the main tribes of Madinah were the 'Aus and the Khazraj. They were deeply divided against each other, sporadically engaging in enmity and civil war, then again concluding fragile peace agreements. The Khazraj were often allied with the unbelievers of Madinah, with whom they lived side by side.

The Jews were *Ahl al-Kitabi* (People of the Book), and possessors of knowledge, while the Khazraj still worshipped idols. Whenever they happened to be on bad terms with the Jews, the latter would say to them, "Soon a prophet will be sent, his day is at hand. When he appears, we shall follow him and you will perish; we will destroy you entirely." However, when Muhammad 🕌 had come to Madinah, they said, "This man is no prophet!" As it is written in the holy verses of the Quran:

When there came to them a Book from God, confirming what was with them and they aforetimes prayed for victory over the unbelievers — when there came to them that which they recognized, they disbelieved in it. (The Cow, 89)

When some of the Khazraj heard the talk of the Holy Prophet 🕌 at one of the fairs, they said to one another, "This must be the Prophet the Jews were warning us of. Let us go to him before they do!" So they went to Muhammad 🕌, and he recited to them the Sura Ibrahim from the Quran. They were very impressed by it and became Muslims at his hand. They said, "We have accepted Islam as our religion and Muhammad 🕌 as our Prophet. Now we will return to our city and tell our people what we have seen and heard. Perhaps Allah will unite them through you, for we are a people torn apart by hatred and strife. God-willing, we shall meet again next year at al-'Aqaba."

The six men of Khazraj who became Muslims at this time were Abu Umama of the Bani Najjar; 'Auf bin Harith; Rafi' bin Malik; Qutba bin Amir; 'Uqba bin Amir; and Jabir bin Abdullah bin Ri'ab.

When they returned to Madinah they began to speak to their families and relations about the new teaching they had embraced, and in this way, the Light of Islam began to spread in the city.

In the following year twelve of their number set out to meet the Holy Prophet ﷺ at the place named al-'Aqaba, and all twelve gave their pledge to the Holy Prophet ﷺ. These twelve men were As'ad bin Zurara; 'Auf bin Harith and his brother Mu'adh bin Harith; Rafi' bin Malik; Dhakwan ibn 'Abdu Qays; 'Ubada ibn al-Samit; Yazid bin Tha'laba; 'Abbas bin 'Ubada; 'Uqba bin Amir; Qutba bin Amir; Abul-Haytham ibn al-Tayyihan and 'Uwaym bin Sa'ida. The pledge they gave the Prophet ﷺ consisted of the following undertaking: they vowed to associate nothing with Allah; not to steal; not to commit unchaste acts; not to kill their children; not to slander anyone; not to disobey the Prophet ﷺ in any matter that was right.

The Holy Prophet ﷺ then asked his uncle 'Abbas: "Last year six men came to me from Madinah and accepted Islam; this year twelve people came, inviting me to come with them to Madinah. What do you say to that?" 'Abbas answered, "There are not twelve, but more than twelve thousand people living in Madinah. If you ask me, I would advise you to send your representative there first. If all goes well and if they duly honor him, then it may be alright for you to go there." The Holy Prophet ﷺ agreed with this, and sent with them Mus'ab bin 'Umayr who was also a man of Quraysh. He was instructed to teach the new religion and the reciting of the Holy Quran, and he stayed in the house of As'ad bin Zurara. As'ad's house thus became the first gathering place for the Muslims of Madinah, and their number rapidly increased.

Now Sa'd bin Mu'adh and 'Usayd bin Hudayr were leaders of their clan, and they had not yet become Muslim. One day Sa'd came by the place where Mus'ab was sitting reading Quran, Suratul Inshirah, "the Expanding". Sa'd heard it and was intensely moved by the sound of these words, so that he asked Mus'ab to read it again. Sa'd became Muslim then and there, as did his friend 'Usayd. With them all the men and women of their clan joined Islam, for they were the chiefs of their clans. All the clans of 'Aus and Khazraj now had Muslims among them, except for the Bani Umayya bin Zayd.

The Second Tryst at 'Aqaba

Again it was the time of the pilgrimage, and Mus'ab returned to Mecca. The Muslim Ansar (the Helpers from Madinah) came to the annual fair together with the pagan pilgrims. Seventy men of the nobles of Madinah came to the Holy Prophet ﷺ to invite him to Madinah. They came to him as he was sitting beside his uncle 'Abbas and they made him a great show of their respect. They took their oath of allegiance to the Holy Prophet ﷺ whom many of them had never seen before, and this time the oath included a pledge of war against the unbelievers.

The Prophet's uncle 'Abbas had not yet accepted Islam, and he now said, "I am not a follower of his religion, but he is the son of my brother, and therefore he is of my flesh and blood. In Mecca, he has a large and influential family, whereas in Madinah he has no blood-ties. He has seen a lot of suffering here. However, if you are taking him away to Madinah and are unable to be faithful to what you have promised him and unable to protect him, then it is better he stays here where he is." Then they took the solemn pledge to defend and protect the Prophet ﷺ at all costs, and the Holy Prophet ﷺ also pledged himself to them.

The Meccans heard the news of this tryst, and they were disturbed at the prospect of Muhammad ﷺ being taken away to Madinah by his followers. The Prophet ﷺ told his followers, "Begin now to leave for Madinah," and they left in small groups of two or three at a time, to settle in Madinah. The

Holy Prophet ﷺ himself remained in Mecca until the month of Rabi' al-Awwal.

Gradually, Quraysh began to notice the absence of various people from among their number. Abu Jahl said before a gathering of Quraysh, "If Muhammad goes off to Madinah, he will grow strong there and return to destroy us." The next day they called a gathering, which the accursed Shaytan himself attended, having adopted a human form. He came to them in the guise of a venerable old man, and spoke up, saying, "This man seduces everyone with his sweet words and pleasing countenance; people see him, they hear him speak and they fall for him. There is only one thing for us to do: he must be killed." The gathering applauded his speech and agreed. It was decided to send a man from each of the tribes to lie in wait for Muhammad ﷺ every night from now on, so that his blood would not fall on any one tribe, thereby triggering a blood feud.

At this moment, the angel Jibra'il appeared to the Holy Prophet ﷺ, revealing the following verse and ordering him to leave Mecca that same night.

> *And when the unbelievers were devising against thee, to confine thee, or slay thee, or to expel thee, and were devising, and God was devising; and God is the best of devisers.*

(The Spoils, 30)

The Hijra

When the Holy Prophet ﷺ knew that he had to leave the city of his birth, he called Ali to him and said to him, "I have a number of items in safe-keeping. As I am departing tonight, I leave these with you to return to their owners within three days. Tonight you sleep in my bed in my stead, and fear not, but cover yourself with my mantle. No harm will befall you. Afterwards come and follow me."

He then went to the house of Abu Bakr, and it was already late at night. Abu Bakr had prepared two Hijin camels for the eventuality of their departure from Mecca. Now the Prophet ﷺ came to give him the signal. They planned to meet after midnight at a cave some distance from Mecca. Abu Bakr then called his daughter Asma to him and said to her, "Muhammad ﷺ and I are headed for the cave on Jabel Thaur where we intend to be for three days. Come and bring us food every evening, and tell us news of the movements of Quraysh." Then he called for his man who looked after the camels and told him to make them ready by the following Monday.

Abu Jahl and his men surrounded the house of Muhammad ﷺ that night. As they sat waiting for him to emerge, they were overtaken by sleep, and the Holy Prophet ﷺ passed by them without their noticing him. As he left the house, he recited the beginning of *Sura YaSin*, up to the verse:

And We have put before them a barrier and behind them a barrier; and We have covered them, so they do not see.   *(YaSin, 7)*

Reciting these verses, he strewed dust upon their heads. In this way he passed unnoticed from the house and came to the meeting place with Abu Bakr. Together they proceeded towards the cave. Abu Bakr wished to carry the Holy Prophet ﷺ on his back, but the Prophet ﷺ would not accept this. So, in order to obscure their footprints, Abu Bakr would step backwards and forwards and sideways to cover all traces of the Holy Prophet ﷺ.

Back at the house, Iblis who was among those who lay in wait for Muhammad ﷺ suddenly cried, "Muhammad has escaped!" They checked on him and found his bed occupied, and they believed it to be Muhammad sleeping wrapped up in his mantle. In reality it was his cousin Ali sleeping in his cloak. When Ali lay down to sleep, the Lord of the Heavens had said to His angels Mikhail and Israfil, "If I made you to be as brothers in this world, would either of you agree to meet death in place of him whom his enemies mean to kill? Would either of you go and lie in his bed?" But neither of the angels wished for death, they would have chosen life.

That being the case, the Lord said, "I have therefore made Muhammad and Ali to be as brothers; Ali has taken Muhammad's ﷺ place in his bed in his stead, knowing of their intention to kill him. Go now and stand guard by his head and foot." In the morning, when the idolaters saw Ali emerging from the Prophet Muhammad's ﷺ house, they were dumbstruck with amazement. Immediately they went to the house of Abu Bakr, knocked on the door and demanded of his daughter Asma where her father was. Asma replied, "I don't know," whereupon Abu Jahl slapped her face so violently that her earring flew off. Then they offered a reward of two hundred curly-haired camels to the man who would find Muhammad and Abu Bakr and bring him back to Quraysh. Asma went to the cave for three days and brought the fugitives food and news from the city.

Once a search party of idolaters passed close by the cave, so that their voices were heard in the cave. Abu Bakr grew restive, but the Holy Prophet ﷺ motioned for him to be calm. "Be at rest," he said, "for Allah is with us. If two people are together and Allah is the third, do you really think we will be captured?"

As it is written in the Holy Quran:

> *If you do not help him yet God has helped him already, when the unbelievers drove him forth the second of two, when the two were in the Cave, when he said to his companion, 'Sorrow not, surely God is with us.' Then God sent down on him His Sakina (inner peace) and confirmed him with legions you did not see; and He made the word of the unbelievers the lowest; and God's word is the uppermost; God is All-Mighty, All-Wise.*

> *(Repentance, 40)*

According to one narration, Shaytan led the search parties up to the cave, following their traces. Shaytan even peered inside the cave, but could see nothing, and said, "There is nothing within."

The Snake Bites Abu Bakr ◌

Meanwhile Abu Bakr as-Siddiq was reciting and the Holy Prophet ﷺ had laid his head upon his knee. At that moment a snake stuck its head out of its hole up high in the wall, and Abu Bakr was frightened, so that he closed up the hole with a piece of his garment. Every time the snake showed itself in a different hole, he stuffed up the hole with a piece of cloth. At last, when the snake came out of a hole very close to him, he obstructed it with the heel of his foot. The snake bit him and from the pain, tears rolled down his cheeks, onto the face of the Prophet ﷺ who was lying in his lap.

The Holy Prophet ﷺ awoke and asked him what had happened. Abu Bakr told him that a snake had bitten his foot. The Prophet ﷺ then spoke to the snake and said to him, "Are you not ashamed of yourself for biting the foot of my beloved friend and causing him such pain?" The snake was given speech and it replied, "Oh Prophet of Allah ﷺ, one day long ago I heard a word of the Prophet 'Isa who said, 'After my time there will come a Prophet and his name will be Ahmad. This Prophet will endure great tribulations at the hands of his own people. He will flee from them and hide from them in a cave for three days. This is written in the Holy Book of the Injil.' Since I first heard these words, 450 years have passed by, and for all that time I have been living in this cave and waiting. Since I first heard this Prophet's name, I became enamored with him. I have spent my time opening holes like windows in this rock so that I might catch a glimpse of this Prophet ﷺ when his time has come. Now it has come, and this good friend of yours has nothing better to do than close up all my carefully excavated windows. That is why I had to bite him, oh Muhammad ﷺ."

The snake had bitten a piece the size of a pigeon's egg out of the foot of as-Siddiq, but the Holy Prophet ﷺ put his lips to it and sucked out the poison. He spit it out in front of the entrance of the cave and there grew up a bush with green leaves and white flowers, with red fruits that grew from the blood of as-Siddiq and furry seeds, which grew from the poison of the snake. A wild rose it was, with bright red hips, a plant of many beneficial properties.

Then the Holy Prophet ﷺ stroked the snake that had bitten Abu Bakr's foot. The snake was the color of saffron and gave off a beautiful scent. The Prophet ﷺ said to it, "Promise me that you will not bite anyone belonging to my nation from now on." The snake gave its word, and the Prophet ﷺ prayed for its progeny to become numerous and for its scent to remain with it until the Day of Judgment. To this very day this snake is found frequently in Mecca and its body gives off a lovely scent. No one hurts it, and it harms no one.

At the entrance to the cave a rock dove had made her nest, and a spider had woven its web across the entrance. A wind arose and spread dust over everything, giving it the appearance of having been undisturbed for a thousand years.

The Lord Almighty ordered the angels Jibra'il and Mikha'il to go look after His Prophet 🕌. When they got there they met the spider that was weaving its web. "What are you doing?" they asked it. "I am concealing the Holy Prophet 🕌," answered the spider. "How do you think you can hide him," the angels laughed, "your web is not even able to keep out the wind, one gust and it is blown away."

The spider replied, "Oh Jibra'il, this web is not like any of my own webs, this web I am spinning upon the command of the Almighty; try it out if you like." So the mighty angel Jibra'il whose single scream makes cities crumble tried with all his force to tear the web of the little spider, but try as he might, he could not snap a single thread of its silk.

The pursuing search parties following the footprints came very close to the cave, but seeing the nesting dove and the spider's web, they said to the guide who had led them there, "We took you to be a clever person, but now you seem to be the most silly of us all. Had anybody entered this cave, do you really think this bush would be covering the entrance, and this spider's web remain unbroken? And what about the nesting dove sitting on its eggs? Would it not have flown away and abandoned its nest?"

They had come so close that Abu Bakr could see their feet. He began to weep. "They have come for us," he said. The Holy Prophet 🕌 recited:

...When the unbelievers drove him forth, the second of two, when the two were in the Cave, when he said to his companion, "Sorrow not, surely God is with us."

(Repentance, 40)

But Abu Bakr continued to tremble, and he said, "Oh Messenger of Allah ❄, if I had one thousand souls at my disposal, they should all be your ransom. But what if they were to kill you? What should then be left in this world of any worth? The Muslims will be forsaken and destitute." The Holy Prophet ❄ then answered him, pointing at the wall of the cave, "Oh Abu Bakr, look here." When he looked, he saw a door there, and it was open. Through the open door he could see an ocean so vast its farther shore was not in sight. But on the shore near them lay a boat. The Prophet ❄ then said, "If they come to get us, we will simply board that ship and sail away. Allah Almighty will shut that door, and they will never reach us, in all eternity." With these words, the Holy Prophet ❄ made Abu Bakr feel at ease.

The Holy Prophet ❄ and Abu Bakr remained in this cave for three days and nights. On the morning of the fourth day which was Thursday, the first day of Rabi' al-Awwal, they mounted the camels that their servant Amir had brought, along with the Bedouin guide who was to lead them to Madinah. They set out on the journey.

Muhammad ❄ was very much affected by the solemnity of this moment of departure. When they had reached a certain point, the Prophet ❄ halted his camel and turned towards Mecca, giving expression to his grief. The angel Jibra'il then came to him and said, "Oh Muhammad ❄, your heart is sore at leaving the city of your birth and upbringing, but your Lord would have me reveal to you these tidings:

He who imposed the Recitation (Quran) upon thee shall surely restore thee to a place of homing. Say, 'My Lord knows very well who comes with guidance, and who is in manifest error.' (The Story, 85)

This verse was the announcement of the Conquest of Mecca, and with these good tidings Allah Almighty consoled His Prophet ❄. Muhammad ❄ and Abu Bakr; their servant and their guide then continued on their journey to Madinah. They rode for twenty-four hours without halt after leaving the cave of al-Thaur. Quraysh were out all over looking for them, and many a man was out bounty hunting for the two hundred camels that had been promised as reward.

After twenty-four hours a rider showed himself and cried out to them, "Oh Muhammad, who will deliver you from my hand this day?" The rider was one Suraqa bin Malik, a brave warrior and bounty hunter. The Holy Prophet ❀ answered him, calling back, "The Mighty and All-Vanquishing Lord Allah Almighty will deliver me from your hands!" At that moment the angel Jibra'il appeared to the Prophet, giving him Salams from his Lord and saying, "The Lord Almighty has made the earth subservient to you, it is at your command!"

As Suraqa came riding towards them, the Holy Prophet ❀ ordered the earth to swallow him, and the earth swallowed the four legs of the horse up to its knees. When Suraqa saw what was happening, he cried out, saying, "Mercy! Mercy! I will never again raise my hand against you, I will be your helper from now on!" Then the Prophet ❀ commanded the earth to let him go, and he went free again. Three times he broke his word, and three times Muhammad ❀ commanded the earth to swallow him, until his stubborn will was broken.

He took from the Holy Prophet ❀ as a token of their agreement a sign or word written on a stone or pottery shard. However, he later kept quiet about this event, and when he met the pursuers, he told them Muhammad ❀ had gone by a different route. When he came back to Abu Jahl, he told him he had not seen Muhammad ❀. In the eighth year of the Hijra when the Prophet ❀ was returning from the Battle of Hunayn, Suraqa went out to meet the Holy Prophet ❀, presenting his token and accepted Islam at his hand.

The First Hijri Mosque at Quba

The people of Madinah had news of the Prophet's ❀ departure from Mecca, and they expected him with great eagerness. Every morning at dawn some of the men of the Bani 'Amr in the oasis of Quba would go out to look for him. One morning, on a Monday, the twelfth day of Rabi' al-Awwal, one of the Jews of Quba detected the white of their garments against the black volcanic rock, and as he knew that the people of Quba were expecting a visitor, he called out to them, "He has come! Your expected visitor has come!" All at once an atmosphere of festiveness engulfed Madinah, all the people came streaming out into the streets to meet the travelers whose light outshone even the fierce brilliance of the midday sun. They met the Holy Prophet ﷺ and Abu Bakr as-Siddiq in the shade of a palm-tree. They remained for a while in joyful contemplation of the Prophet's light-filled countenance which most of them had not seen before. Then it was decided to house the Holy Prophet ﷺ at Quba for a while, in the house of an old man of the 'Aws, Kulthum bin Hidm of the Bani 'Amr. Abu Bakr stayed in another village closer to Madinah, al-Sunh, at the house of a man of the Khazraj. The people of Madinah came in groups to greet the Prophet ﷺ every day and he stayed for a fortnight at Quba. During this time the foundations of a mosque were laid at Quba.

A mosque that was founded upon godfearing (Taqwa) from the first day is worthier for thee to stand in; therein are men who love to cleanse themselves; and God loves those who cleanse themselves. (Repentance, 108-109)

Ali arrived at Quba a few days later, finding the Holy Prophet ﷺ and his company there. From riding so hard and fast his legs were hurt, but the touch of the Holy Prophet's ﷺ hands restored them to health on the spot. The building of the mosque at Quba was completed on a Friday, and it was named *Masjid-al-Taqwa*. The Holy Prophet ﷺ prayed Jum'a there together with one hundred Muslims, and it was the first *Khutba* and the first Jum'a prayer of Islam.

After the Jum'a prayer the whole Muslim population of Madinah accompanied the Holy Prophet ﷺ and Abu Bakr as-Siddiq into the city. On foot they went as well as on camel and horseback, glad of heart and reciting Takbir (Allahu Akbar) as they went along, so that Heaven and earth resounded with their joy. The women and children accompanied the procession, singing the song of welcome, which is sung around the world to this very day.

The Song of Welcome

> *Tala'al-badru-'alayna*

(The full moon has risen over us)

> *min thaniyat-al-wida'*

(From the moment of departure)

> *wajaba-ash-shukru 'alayna*

(Gratitude is our duty)

> *ma da'a lillahi da'.*

(For that a caller summons us to Allah).

> *ayyuhal-mab'uthu fiha*

(Oh you who are sent to her, i.e. the city of Madinah)

> *ji'ta bil-amril-muta'*

(You have come with a command to be obeyed)

> *ji'ta sharraftal-madina*

(You have come and honored the city)

> *marhaban ya khaira da'.*

(Welcome to you, oh best of Callers!)

The entire population of the oasis lined the road to greet the Prophet ﷺ as he rode into town. From the rooftops came shouts of welcome, and men stood before their houses, catching hold of the halter of the Prophet's ﷺ camel as he passed by, inviting him to alight and honor their abode. The Holy Prophet ﷺ however blessed them each with a smile and rode on, saying, "Let my camel pass, for she knows her way. I will descend where she decides to kneel."

A King of Yemen is Granted Shahada

There was one man, Khalid bin Zayd, whose wife said to him, "Go and place food and water for the camel in front of our door, perhaps the Prophet's ﷺ camel will stop and he will stay with us." Now Khalid bin Zayd who was called Abu Ayyub said to himself sadly, "There are so many houses vying for the honor of housing the Holy Prophet ﷺ, how should this honor fall to us?"

This man, Abu Ayyub al-Ansari, was a descendant of the ancient kings of Yemen who were called Tuba in their time. His ancestor was a king, Abu Qarib, who had lived four hundred years before the time of the Prophet ﷺ. He was an idol-worshipper, but he heard from his Christian advisors about the Prophet who was to come. They spoke to him of the description given in the Torah and the Injil, and of the Divine Guidance he was to bring. The king Abu Qarib was then impassioned by love for the Prophet ﷺ and began to yearn for him. He asked his wisemen whether he could see this Prophet, and he learned that this could not be, for another four hundred years were to pass before he was to arrive. They foretold that he was to be born at Mecca where his people would badly mistreat and abuse him, and that he would migrate to Madinah on Divine Command where he was later to die and be laid to rest. This king therefore set out for Mecca with many precious gifts, and presented the *Kaba* with its very first *Kiswa* (covering). Then he proceeded on to Madinah.

Once in Madinah, he acquired a house for his descendants. Along with the house, he voiced his request, in that he wished to offer his services to the Prophet to come ﷺ. He said, "Oh Prophet of Allah ﷺ, I have heard of your qualities, and your excellence and power, and I have heard that your nation is to be the best of all nations of the People of the Scriptures, and the most highly honored in the sight of Allah. Without having seen you, I have fallen in love with you. I confirm your prophethood and your mission; I desire to be of your religion and to be accepted as one of your nation. However it is not possible for me to share your blessed lifetime, therefore I wish to dedicate my life to you and hope that my petition may be acceptable to you. I humbly ask that on the Day of Judgment I might find shelter under the Banner of Praise together with those belonging to your nation." This petition he sealed in several places with seals of amber, wrapped it in layers of silk and placed it within a small box and said, "Oh my son, I have brought you and your family here from the Yemen. Remain here and make your home here, and take care of this box for as long as you live. When your end has come, pass it on to your son, and enjoin him to pass it on to his, and he to his, until the honored Arabian Prophet, the Hashimi Qurayshi Muhammad ﷺ appears. After he has announced his prophethood, suffered from the injustice of his people and migrated from his home Mecca to this city of Madinah, then the time will come, for this box to be handed to him. This is my behest."

Now Abu Ayyub ul-Ansari was the seventh generation since the time of this ancestor. He had kept the box, but everything else he owned had been lost in the course of time, and he had become a poor man. Being totally absorbed with his daily affairs, he had all but forgotten about the box that had been passed down to him. When the Holy Prophet ﷺ had entered Madinah, people wanted to entice the camel to come to rest before their houses by offering it food and by making noises to attract the animal, but the camel graced none of them with its attentions. In reality, the angel Jibra'il had descended and was leading it by its halter. When they reached the door of the house of Khalid bin Zayd (Abu Ayyub), the angel forced the camel to kneel, even though there was nothing special about the house. Khalid then spoke to his wife, saying, "The Holy Prophet's camel has knelt down before you, you have attained this bliss." From happiness both of them began to weep. With a show of great reverence he led the Holy Prophet ﷺ into his house.

The Holy Prophet ﷺ moved into the ground floor, saying, "This ground floor is suitable for all those who will come to visit us. Now go and bring us what you have held in safe-keeping for us." Khalid thereupon asked, "What have we got in safe-keeping, oh Messenger of Allah ✿?" The Holy Prophet ✿ answered, "Go and bring the piece of paper contained in the box that has come to you from your forefather of the kings of Yemen." Witnessing this manifest miracle of the Holy Prophet's ✿, Khalid remembered the box that he had inherited, and reciting *Salat-wa-Salam* he went to fetch it. Before the Holy Prophet ✿ even looked at the piece of paper, he said, "He wishes to enter my religion, and wishes to be of my nation. The Lord Almighty has accepted his ardent wish, and I too accept him into my nation." In this way another miracle was manifested.

After they had eaten their meal in the lower room, the Holy Prophet ✿ wished to retire to rest. Khalid and his wife stood in front of the door to the upper room and said, "The Holy Prophet ✿ lies in the room below us, how can we step on top of him in the upper room?" From shyness and awe they remained in front of the door to the upper apartment, holding hands and not sleeping. In the morning they entreated the Holy Prophet ✿ to occupy the top floor, explaining to him that they had not slept all night for fear of failing him in reverence. The Prophet ✿ was very pleased with them, and prayed for him: "Oh Khalid," he said, "may the Lord make you honored, blest and esteemed in this world and the next. "

As a result of this supplication, the honor and blessings conferred on Abu Ayyub are manifested unchanged to this day. Known throughout Turkey as "Sultan Eyyop", he lies buried at the walls of Istanbul where he breathed his last during a campaign against the city in the time of Yazid. His tomb has become a place of pilgrimage and visitation for many pious travelers ever since. May Allah grant us his intercession, and that of the many noble companions who lie buried in Asia Minor and neighboring lands. Amin.

The Holy Prophet ✿ remained in Abu Ayyub's house for one month, or according to a different source, for seven months, until his mosque and the adjacent living quarters were completed. During this time, he sent one of his men back to Mecca with Zubayr bin Harith with two camels and five hundred dirhems in order to fetch his two daughters Fatima and Umm

Kulthum, as well as his venerable wife Sauda. Abu Bakr sent for his son Abdullah, his young daughters Aisha and Asma, and their mother Umm Ruman. After the Holy Prophet ﷺ had left Mecca, Hijra (migration) became incumbent on his companions who had stayed behind. These emigrants were named *Muhajir*, those who had left behind their homes and their families and fortunes for the sake of Allah. The Muslims of Madinah, the Ansar or Helpers welcomed them and took them into their houses. Whoever had more than one room in his house, housed one of the Muhajirin in the other room. If a person had only one room, he would set up a curtain dividing it in two, and take a Muhajir into his house, and share all his food and household goods with him. Because of the help they gave the Muhajirin, these Muslims of Madinah were named al-Ansar, the Helpers. On account of the help that the Ansar extended to the Muhajirin, they were rewarded with much mercy and forgiveness.

In the Holy Quran Allah Almighty says of those who will come after and who wonder as to the reward they will receive:

And as for those who came after them, they say, "Oh our Lord, forgive us and our brothers who preceded us in belief, and put Thou not into our hearts any rancor towards those who believe. Our Lord, surely Thou art the All-Gentle, the All-Compassionate."

(The Mustering, 10)

In this holy verse lies the proof that he who prays for the noble companions of the Prophet ﷺ and holds no envy or enmity against them in his heart, will receive of the recompense that they themselves have received. It is also proof that the Holy Prophet ﷺ holds a higher station than all the other prophets because of the quality of his companions who pray for their deceased ancestors, forebears, teachers and brothers in faith. For this is expressed in the saying of the Holy Prophet ﷺ, "You are the best of nations", and he is the most highly honored of all Prophets of Allah.

Events of the First Year of the Hijra

In the first year of the Hijra the Holy Prophet's daughter Ruqiyya died. Also the faithful companion As'ad bin Zurara passed away. During this first year he also took Aisha, the daughter of Abu Bakr to wife. Two years after the death of his wife Khadija he had asked for her hand in marriage, while still in Mecca. She was at the time a child of seven years of age. When the Holy Prophet ﷺ moved to Madinah, she was nine. The Holy Prophet ﷺ said to Abu Bakr, "Have your family come to Madinah," and Abu Bakr sent for his wife, his son Abdullah and his young sisters to come.

The unbelievers of Madinah started a rumor, saying, "We have made a magic charm that will make anyone who believes in Muhammad ﷺ childless." When the unbelievers among the Arabs heard of this, they felt glad. The Prophet ﷺ however told his followers not to worry, there was nothing to worry about, for Allah Almighty had promised His Prophet ﷺ that his nation would survive until the Day of Judgment. That very year Abdullah bin Zubayr of the Muhajirin and Nu'man bin Bushr of the Ansar were born. These births made the Muslims glad and they greeted them with Takbirs of gratitude, and the unbelievers were seen to have been lying. Also Dihya ibn Abi 'Ubayda bin Mas'ud as-Saqafi was born that same year.

Referring to her marriage to the Holy Prophet ﷺ, Aisha later said, "I have a higher standing than any of the other wives of the Holy Prophet ﷺ because of these events: I came to his house a virgin; when the angel Jibra'il came with a revelation, I was listening; when the hypocrites told a lie about me, a holy verse was revealed on my behalf; I saw the angel Jibra'il; and, when the Holy Prophet ﷺ fell ill and died, his grave was made in my house."

During that first year of the Hijra the prayer was changed to four Rak'ats while it had hitherto consisted of two Rak'ats.

The Beginning of the Islamic Calendar

When the Holy Prophet ❀ came to Madinah, he ordered the counting of a new calendar beginning with the date of the Hijra. Thereafter the year of the Hijra was taken as the beginning of the Islamic calendar. Before this time there had been no regular count of the years. The years were only remembered by certain important events that had taken place in them, such as a great famine, or a flood, or by the ascension to the throne of a certain king or ruler, or by his death.

In the time of the Prophet Ibrahim a new calendar was begun with the building of the Kaba. In the time of Qusa bin Kilab a great war between the Bani Nadir and Bani Ma'bed was fought, which was called by the Arabs *"Ayyam-al-Qatl"*, and the years were counted from that event onwards. Then the Kaba was destroyed and re-erected, and again the years were numbered after that event. The Prophet Muhammad ❀ ordered the years to be counted from the Hijra onwards. Some factions later counted the years from the killing of Hussayn bin Ali, while others counted from the death of Mu'awiya who was the enemy of Ali. Some even take the death of Yazid as the starting point of their calendar. It is reported that the Holy Prophet ❀ said, "Every nation must have a way of counting its years in order to relate and know its own history."

The Command to Fight the Idolators

When the Holy Prophet ❀ moved to Madinah, the people of Mecca said, "Now at last we are rid of him." Allah Almighty then revealed the following verses:

> *Leave is given to those who fight because they were wronged – surely God is able to help them – who were expelled from their habitations without right, except that they say, "Our Lord is God."* (The Pilgrimage: 39, 40)

With the revelation of this verse, all the verses enjoining patience and tolerance were repealed, and the Holy Prophet ﷺ began sending out his men on various raids. They began to attack the caravans of the unbelievers and confiscating their goods. When they began raiding in the vicinity of Mecca, the Meccans were unable to leave their city, and the caravan routes were interrupted. This interfered with their trade and after a time they began to feel the squeeze.

The first year of the Hijra was filled with such raids. At times the Holy Prophet ﷺ would go out himself, at other times he would send out his men. All of these smaller raids led up to the Battle of Badr.

When this verse was revealed, the Holy Prophet ﷺ sent his uncle Hamza bin Abdul Muttalib out with thirty riders of the Muhajirin towards the seashore on the seventh day of Ramadan in the seventh month of the Hijra. This was the first raid the Muslims undertook. The Holy Prophet ﷺ on this occasion gave Hamza a white piece of cloth to be their flag and himself gave it to Hamza. He commanded Hamza to go to the seashore and to intercept the Quraysh caravan coming from Sham (Damascus) which was laden with goods. He commanded him to take possession of the caravan and to confiscate their goods. Hamza set out for the seashore and arrived there before the caravan did. But Abu Jahl had also come to the shore with three hundred men, ahead of the caravan. Majdi bin 'Amr al-Juhani was one the chiefs of that area and he was at peace with both parties. He intervened between the two sides, and implored Hamza to turn back for the sake of their friendship, and saying to his men, "Safety is better than spoils of war", he turned back. Abu Jahl returned to Mecca with the caravan.

The Expedition of 'Ubayda bin al-Harith

During the month of Shawwal the Holy Prophet ﷺ received news of a troupe of armed men were leaving Mecca headed for Madinah. He sent against them Abu 'Ubayda ibn al-Harith with sixty or eighty riders from the Muhajirin.

That same day the caravan of Abu Jahl arrived at Mecca, and he told the people there that Muhammad 🌸 was making preparations for war against them. The Meccan chiefs therefore gathered and decided to send a fighting force towards Madinah, intending to take prisoner any Muslims they should encounter.

At the well of Ahya the two parties met. No fighting took place that day, except for one arrow shot by Sa'd ibn Abi Waqqas. A few persons left the company of the unbelievers and joined up with the Muslims. That had been their intention from the outset, to link up with the Muslim army when they encountered them. In this way the Muslims emerged strengthened, without having engaged in battle.

The Raid of Kharrar

In the same month, the Holy Prophet 🌸 sent a party of eight men of the Muhajirin out with Sa'd ibn Abi Waqqas after a caravan from Mecca. They went as far as Kharrar in the Hijaz, but again they found the caravan had already passed.

The Raid of Abwa

In the month of Safar, the Holy Prophet 🌸 set out with a company of men of the Muhajirin and Ansar. He appointed one of the companions to be in charge of the city of Madinah in his absence, and on this occasion he appointed Sa'd bin 'Ubada, and he gave his uncle Hamza the white banner mounted on a lance. Abwa was a place situated between Mecca and Madinah. The chief of the Bani Damra, Nahis bin 'Amr, rode out to meet the Holy Prophet 🌸 and reached an agreement of peace with him. It was here that the Holy Prophet's 🌸 mother was buried, so he visited her grave and after remaining there until the end of the month of Safar, he returned to Madinah.

The Raid on Buwat

In the month of Rabi' al-Awwal the Prophet 🏵 had news of the return of
the Meccan caravan from Sham. He gathered a company of two hundred
men and led them out of Madinah, leaving Sa'd bin Mu'adh in charge of the
city. The flag was carried by Sa'd ibn Abi Waqqas. They rode as far as
Buwat, which was near a mountain, named Radwa. The information about
the caravan proved to be imprecise, and they had already missed it. They
returned to Madinah without an encounter.

The Raid on al-'Ushayra

Three months later there was news of another rich caravan coming from
Sham. The Holy Prophet 🏵 set out with a group of riders, Hamza being
given the white flag. They rode as far as 'Ushayra in the valley of Yanbu',
which opens out on to the Red Sea southwest of Madinah. There the
caravan was expected to pass, but it so happened that again they had missed
it, and it had already passed.

On the way the Holy Prophet 🏵 stopped to pray beneath a tree at a place
called Dhatul-Saq. Later a mosque was built in this place and it is a place of
pilgrimage. He also drank from a well called "al-Mushayrib".

It was on this raid that the Holy Prophet 🏵 gave Ali his nickname Abu
Turab, father of dust. The Prophet 🏵 was looking for Ali and could not
find him. He looked all around for him, and finally came upon him, fallen
fast asleep amidst some young palm trees; his face embedded in the fine
dust. The Prophet 🏵 stirred him with his foot, saying, "Wake up, ya Aba
Turab, (oh Father of Dust)."

According to a different narration, Ali was praying at the foot of a tree, and
rubbing his face in the dust in supplication. He waited until he had
concluded his prayer, then the Holy Prophet 🏵 is supposed to have said to
him, "Oh Father of Dust, your worship is very good, for you are of the
lineage of the Pride of Both Worlds, Muhammad." Ali was proud of this
epithet.

'Ammar bin Yasir relates: We were sleeping at the foot of a palm tree. The Holy Prophet ﷺ came to awaken Ali, and he touched his face lightly with his blessed cloak and said, "Oh Ali, there are no more wretched creatures on earth than these two: Uhaymir of Thamud who slaughtered the camel of Allah, and he who shall strike your blessed face and make your blood flow down your beard."

This happened before Ali's marriage to Fatima. They were married in the second year of the Hijra during the month of Safar. There is another tradition that claims that the real reason why the Holy Prophet ﷺ called Ali "Abu Turab" was that whenever Ali was angry at his wife Fatima he would not speak to her. He would not argue with her, but he used to sprinkle dust on his head. Whenever the Holy Prophet ﷺ saw that Ali's head was dusted, he knew that he was angry at Fatima, and he would ask him, "What is your trouble, oh Abu Turab?" But Allah Almighty knows the truth of the matter.

The Raid on Safawan, the First Expedition to Badr

The Holy Prophet ﷺ stayed in Madinah only a few nights after he returned from the Raid on 'Ushayra. News was brought to him that Kurz bin Jabir al-Fihri had raided pasturing camels belonging to Madinah at a distance of three days' journey. The Holy Prophet ﷺ set out to pursue him at once, and rode till he reached the valley of Safawan, in the neighborhood of a well-named Badr. But Kurz had escaped and he could not catch up with him. He remained there for three days, then he returned to the city, and stayed there for the remaining months Ramadan.

The Expedition of Abdullah bin Jahsh (The Raid on Nakhla)

It was toward the end of the month of Rajab when the Holy Prophet ﷺ called Abdullah bin Jahsh and gave him ten men each of the Muhajirin and the Ansar. He gave him a letter, ordering him to open it only after having traveled a distance of three days, and to tell his companions about it. If any of them wished to turn back then, he should not pressure them to stay.

When they had been on the road for three days, Abdullah opened the letter and read it. It instructed him to go on to the valley of Nakhla, which lies, between Mecca and Ta'if, and to find out what the Quraysh were up to. He told his companions about the message and said, "I will stay here at all costs, and whoever wishes for martyrdom, let him proceed, but whoever wishes to turn back, he is free to do so." None of his companions backed out. They reached Nakhla and waited there. Before long a caravan of Quraysh came by, carrying loads of dried grapes and leather and other merchandise. They deliberated amongst themselves, "If we attack the caravan, we will have disobeyed the Prophet ﷺ, for he gave us no orders to fight. If, however, we don't attack them, they will reach Quraysh and give news of us." Further they reflected that this was one of the holy months in which fighting is forbidden, this being the very last day of Rajab. If they waited until nightfall, it would be the beginning of Sha'ban, but by then the caravan would have entered the protection of the sacred precincts. So they were hesitant and undecided. In the end they decided to make the attack, and one of their number shot a man of Kindah. The others surrendered, so they made two prisoners, and returned to Madinah.

News of this spread far and wide. In Mecca people were horrified that the Prophet's men fought in the sacred months. The Holy Prophet ﷺ himself was also aggrieved at the incident, saying, "I did not order you to fight in the sacred month." He held the two prisoners and the goods of the caravan, and waited for Divine Guidance as to what to do in this matter. The remaining Muslims in Mecca wrote a letter, saying that Quraysh made them feel shame for that their Prophet ﷺ had violated the holy months, and asking for the prisoners to be sent back. The Holy Prophet ﷺ was very disturbed by this, until a verse was revealed to him:

> *They will question thee concerning the holy month and fighting in it. Say: "Fighting in it is a heinous thing, but to bar from God's way and disbelief in Him, and the Holy Mosque, and to expel its people from it – that is more heinous in God's sight; and persecution is more heinous than slaying."*   (The Cow, 217)

With the revelation of this verse, the Prophet's heart was relieved and he gave orders for the booty to be distributed and the prisoners to be ransomed.

The Changing of the Qibla

Up until this time, the Jews, the Christians and now the Muslims had all turned in prayer toward the Holy House in Jerusalem, which was now destroyed, but still served as the Qibla, the direction of prayer. In the same month of Sha'ban a revelation came changing this direction of prayer for the Muslims. From now on they would turn towards the Kaba in Mecca, and this was to be the new Qibla for all times.

> *We have seen thee turning thy face about in the heavens; now We shall surely turn thee to a direction that will satisfy thee. Turn thy face towards the Holy Mosque; and wherever you are, turn thy face towards it.*   *(The Cow, 144)*

The Fasting of Ramadan

When the Holy Prophet ❀ came to Madinah, he saw that the Jews fasted on the tenth day of Muharram. Asked why they fasted on that day, they explained that it was the day on which Fir'aun had been drowned and the Prophet Musa with the Children of Israel had been saved. Therefore their Prophet had enjoined fasting in them on that day.

The Prophet Muhammad ❀ then called his Companions and ordered them to fast on that day as well. Later the Holy Prophet ❀ wished for the Muslims to also have fasting days of their own, and before long this verse was revealed to the Prophet, making fasting obligatory on them:

> *O believers, prescribed for you is the Fast, even as it was prescribed for those that were before you – haply you will be godfearing.*   *(The Cow, 183)*

After the revelation of this verse, the Prophet ❀ prayed for the time of fasting to be made more specific, and he received a revelation concerning the month of Ramadan.

...the month of Ramadan, wherein the Quran was sent down to be a guidance to the people, and as clear signs of the Guidance and the Salvation... (The Cow, 185)

When the moon of Ramadan was seen, the Muslims were to fast, and when the moon of Shawwal appeared they are to break their fast and give their Sadaqat-al-Fitr. The fast on the tenth of Muharram is also recommended. Some of the Muslims fasted on this day, and attained divine reward, but whoever did not fast incurred no blame.

The Great Battle of Badr

In the second year of the Hijra, on the first day of Ramadan, news came that Abu Sufyan was approaching with a great and richly laden caravan, accompanied by 'Amr ibn 'As. The angel Jibra'il brought this message to the Holy Prophet ❀: "Go out and fight them, the victory will be yours." The Prophet ❀ thereupon informed his Companions, saying, "Make ready and know that Allah has promised you victory." The Companions made their preparations. Sa'd bin Khaysana and his father made ready to go, but the Prophet ❀ said to them, "Let one of you go and one of you stay." They threw lots and Sa'd drew his lot. "Oh Sa'd," pleaded his father, "will you not cede your lot to me, and let me go in your stead?" Sa'd replied, "Father, had you not brought me up to seek the honor of fighting for Truth, I would leave it to you." He was martyred in this battle, and his father was later martyred at Uhud.

The Holy Prophet ❀ left Abdullah ibn Umm Maktum to lead the prayers in his absence and himself set out with three-hundred and ten men towards Badr. Two riders were on horseback, seventy on camels, the remaining men were on foot. The Prophet ❀ went on his own camel, Qaswa. After a two days' journey they heard that Abu Sufyan's caravan had not yet arrived and the Prophet ❀ looked out for it. The angel Jibra'il came to the Prophet ❀ and informed him that Allah Almighty would make the Muslims victorious over the unbelievers. The Prophet ❀ was very happy for that.

Basbas bin 'Amr al-Juhani and 'Adiy bin Abi Zaghba al-Juhani were sent to scout out the area and bring news of the approach of the caravan. They came to a well and met two men there who had come to sell food and drink to the passing caravan, as was the custom of the time. One of them said to the other, "Tomorrow the caravan will pass by here, and I will sell them something, so I will be able to repay my debt to you." When they heard these words, they asked no further questions, drank water from the well, and returned with the news. Not long after this, Abu Sufyan came to that same well with 'Amr ibn al-'As, asking them whether they had any news of Muhammad and the men of Madinah. "No," they replied. "Has nobody passed by here then?" asked Abu Sufyan. "Only two men who came and watered their camels and rode on," replied the Arabs. Hearing this, Abu Sufyan quickly turned around and followed the tracks of the two riders. They picked up some camel droppings and discovered in it pieces of date stones. From this they concluded that the riders must have come from Madinah, for, "No camel eats dates except the camels of Madinah," they said. "Muhammad is on our trail." They speedily turned the caravan back in its tracks.

Abu Sufyan sent a hired scout, Damdam bin 'Amr al-Ghifari by name, to ride to Mecca at top speed and to call out from the mountaintop that anybody interested in his property should grab even an old broomstick and come forth to its defense. There was not a person in Mecca who had not invested in that caravan. Abu Jahl said to 'Ubada, "You are related to Muhammad; should we win this battle, we will expel the Bani Hashim from the city." They picked up the Prophet's 🏵 uncle 'Abbas and forced him to accompany the army. Abu Jahl stood at the gates of the city and watched the thousand armed men pass by, and was very proud and happy. "All the nobles of Mecca have taken to arms," he said, "let Muhammad and his men not think that this caravan is like the caravan of Ibn Hadrami! Soon they will know that it is not so!"

Abu Sufyan and 'Amr ibn al-'As turned around to the well of Dhat-al-Qarn and led the caravan to the road by the seashore. They rode back five halts and came to Jiddah by way of the coastal road. From there they reached Mecca. The armed men had already left the city, headed for Badr. The angel

Jibra'il informed the Holy Prophet that the caravan had changed its route and was headed for Mecca via Badr. The Holy Prophet had been informed of victory, but he had hoped that this would mean taking possession of the rich caravan, rather than fighting a pitched battle:

> And when God promised you one of the two parties should be yours, and you were wishing that the one not accoutered should be yours; but God was desiring to verify the truth by His words, and to cut off the unbelievers to the last remnant, and that He might verify the truth and prove untrue the untrue, though the sinners were averse to it. (The Spoils, 7)

When Abu Sufyan reached Mecca, he felt himself in safety. But two of his sons had gone out with the Meccan army. He sent a message back to the army, saying, "God has saved your property and delivered us; now there is no point in going to war without profit, so turn back." This message was delivered to the army at Wadi Rauha. Opinions were divided, as to whether they should advance or retreat. Abu Jahl however said, "By Allah, we will not turn back until we have been to Badr and spend three days there and feast and drink wine, and listen to the girls play for us." But two hundred armed riders of the Bani Zuhra turned back, and there were nine-hundred and fifty men who continued on with Abu Jahl.

The Holy Prophet wanted to hold a council, for he had not brought out his men to make war, but rather to take hold of the caravan and its goods. The first to speak was Abu Bakr, "Oh Messenger of Allah," he said, "Those who are coming to fight us are our relatives. Nevertheless we will do whatever you command us to do, we will sacrifice our souls in your way." Then 'Umar spoke up and said, "Oh Prophet of Allah, may our souls be your ransom, we will not deviate from this way, as long as even one of us is left."

The Holy Prophet then said, "Be seated; of you I am certain," and from his words it became clear that he wished to hear how the Ansar felt about joining in the fight. Sa'd ibn Mu'adh got up and said, "Oh Prophet of Allah, is it us whom you are calling?" The Prophet answered, "Yes, it is you whom I wish to hear from, for I have migrated from my home and come to live with you." Sa'd answered, "Oh Prophet of Allah ﷺ, may our lives and souls and all our possessions be ransom in your way." The Prophet ﷺ was happy to hear these words, and calling Sa'd to himself he kissed his face and said to him, "Oh Sa'd, may Allah reward you well."

Then the army began to move towards Badr. At a certain distance they began scouting out for movements of the Qurayshi troops. The next day, the Holy Prophet ﷺ mounted his camel and went to the well. There he came upon an old man whom he asked for news of the caravan of Quraysh. The old man told him that the caravan had reached Mecca in safety, but that an army of Quraysh was headed towards Badr to fight Muhammad. The Holy Prophet ﷺ asked, "Do you know where Muhammad is?" "I heard on a certain day that the army was at a certain spot, and if this is true, then today they must be at such-and-such a place. Tomorrow they will be here." Then the Prophet ﷺ prayed and sent Ali, Sa'd ibn Abi Waqqas and Zubayr bin Awwam to guard the outpost.

They brought news to the Holy Prophet ﷺ that Quraysh were at a distance of one hour's journey from the well at Badr. At nightfall they apprehended some of the watermen of the Quraysh who had come to fill their waterskins. They pressured them into telling them where Quraysh were camped, and how many of them there were. The water bearer said, "I can't say how many there are, but every day they slaughter nine or ten beasts for food." From this the Holy Prophet ﷺ understood that there must be between nine hundred and a thousand men. Then he asked the man how many nobles of Quraysh were among them, and he enumerated their names: "'Utba, Shayba, Umayya, Abu Jahl, Nabih, Naufal, al-Harith bin 'Amir, Munabbih, Suhayl..." and others he mentioned. Thereupon the Prophet ﷺ turned to his companions and said, "Mecca has thrown to you choice pieces of its liver!"

The companions said, "Oh Prophet of Allah ﷺ, they have not reached the wells of Badr yet, it is best we get there first." The Prophet ﷺ agreed and they stopped up the wells and built a cistern so that they would have plenty of water, and the enemy would have none. The next day the two armies

298

came face to face. Abu Jahl saw that the Muslims were much fewer than they and he spoke derisively in their face: "If it is true what Muhammad says, then we are out to fight the God of the heavens. But only he who fights against me, is then fighting the God of the heavens!"

One man from the tribe of the Bani Makhzum who was allied with Abu Jahl stepped forth and said, "I swear to God that I will drink from their cistern or destroy it or die beside it!" With these words he made for the cistern. Hamza drew his sword to prevent him, and he cut off his foot and half his leg as he was near the cistern. The man fell onto the ground, but continued crawling towards the cistern and threw himself in it, with the purpose of fulfilling his oath. Hamza followed him and smote him in the cistern so that he died there. After this, the unbelievers asked for water to drink from the cistern, which was now contaminated with blood, and the Muslims were disinclined to give it to them. But the Holy Prophet 🕌 said to them, "Let them drink, do not prevent them."

They drank, and every man who drank of it on that day was killed in battle, but for one. The next day the troops were arrayed and stood facing each other. Abu Jahl prayed, "Oh Lord," he said, "Thy help be with him whom You love best." Immediately this verse was revealed:

If victory you are seeking, victory has already come upon you; and if you give over, it is better for you. But if you return, We shall return, and your host will avail you nothing though it be numerous; and that God is with the believers. (The Spoils, 19)

At that time the Muslim army had no tents. Sa'd bin Mu'adh made a shelter for the Holy Prophet from palm fronds, saying, "Oh Prophet of Allah 🕌, remain here in the shadow of these branches while we go out and meet the enemy." The Holy Prophet 🕌 entered the shelter they had made for him and prostrated himself in the dust, praying, "Oh Lord, grant us Thy Help which Thou hast promised to us!" Then he stepped outside the shelter and took a branch or an arrow and with it dressed the ranks of the Muslim soldiery.

From the pagan army 'Utba bin Rabi'a, Shayba bin Rabi'a and his son Walid stood up and challenged the Muslims to battle. Abdullah bin Rawaha,

'Auf bin Harith and Mu'adh of the Ansar went out to meet them. Seeing them, 'Utba said to them, "We have no business with you. We wish for an encounter with our equals." Thereupon the Prophet ﷺ sent out Ali ibn Abi Talib, 'Ubayda bin Harith and Hamza ibn Abdul Muttalib to fight them. They attacked each other, and Hamza slew Shayba, while Ali slew Walid in the first onslaught. Only 'Utba struck 'Ubayda such a blow that his leg was cut off and the marrow was oozing out. Ali and Hamza came to his aid and struck 'Utba to his death. Then they brought 'Ubayda into the Presence of the Prophet ﷺ. He looked at his leg, and said to him, "Good fortune to you, 'Ubayda, for you are presently to enter Paradise. 'Ubayda replied, "In me is realized the word of Abu Talib which he spoke when he said, 'We will not give him up till we lie dead around him, and be unmindful of our women and children.'"

Then the battle began in earnest with an arrow from Quraysh mortally wounding Mihja', a freedman of 'Umar. Harith bin Suraqa was pierced in the throat by another arrow while he was drinking and fell a martyr. The Holy Prophet ﷺ entered the shelter of the hut they had built for him and placing his face in the dust prayed fervently to Allah, "Oh my Lord, we have relied on Thy promise, do send us Thy support!" The angel Jibra'il then descended with one thousand angels and announced to the Holy Prophet ﷺ, "Oh Muhammad ﷺ, Allah Almighty has sent you peace and victory," and he recited to him the following verse:

When you were calling upon your Lord for succor, and He answered you, 'I shall reinforce you with a thousand angels riding behind you.'   (The Spoils, 9)

The angels stood arranged in rows, and each one of them held in his hand a spear with which they smote the heads and necks of the unbelievers. The following verse tells of this:

When thy Lord was revealing to the angels, I am with you; so confirm the believers. I shall cast into the unbelievers' hearts terror; so smite above the necks, and smite every finger of them!'   (The Spoils, 12)

Then the Holy Prophet ﷺ took up a handful of dust and hurled it at the faces of the unbelievers. Allah made a wind spring up at that moment that carried the dust into the eyes of the idolaters, so that they were momentarily blinded and could not see. They perished instantly when struck by the angelic swords. When the Muslims saw the enemy fall under unseen blows, they realized that there was another force at work here besides their own efforts at war. As it is written in the Holy Quran:

You did not slay them, but God slew them; and when thou threwest, it was not thyself that threw, but God threw, and that He might confer on the believers a fair benefit; surely God is All-Hearing, All-Knowing. (The Spoils, 17)

In this way the unbelievers were routed. Among them were some men of the Bani Hashim who had been forced to join in this campaign, such as 'Abbas bin Abdul Muttalib, 'Aqil ibn Abi Talib, Abul-Bakhtari and others. The Holy Prophet ﷺ had given orders not to kill them, but to give no quarter to Abu Jahl if they encountered him. The Prophet ﷺ retreated into the shade of the shelter and began to pray and give his thanks. The Muslims went after the fleeing enemy. A Muslim by the name of Abu Yasir recognized 'Abbas and called out to him, "Muhammad ﷺ told us not to kill you," and tied his hands. 'Abbas had twenty dinars in his belt, these he gave to Abu Yasir. Together they went to the presence of the Holy Prophet ﷺ. Mujadhdhar bin Ziyad came across Abul-Bakhtari and called to him, "The Holy Prophet ﷺ wishes for you not to be killed." Abul-Bakhtari pointed to the friend at his side and said, "Then refrain also from killing my friend." This Mujadhdhar could not accept, and so a fight between them began in which Mujadhdhar slew them both. The Holy Prophet ﷺ was very grieved when he learned of the death of Abul-Bakhtari, and Mujadhdhar fell down and begged his forgiveness, kissing his hands and feet.

Mu'adh bin 'Amr of the Ansar had sworn he would kill Abu Jahl. He looked out for him and espied him astride his horse. With one sweep of his sword he cut off his leg so that he fell underneath his horse. Abu Jahl's son Ikrima then came and wounded Mu'adh on his hand and arm, so that his arm was swinging loosely at his side, held only by a piece of skin. He continued to fight in this condition until the pain became intolerable, and he cut it off by standing on it with his foot. Then he continued to fight.

Searching among the dead, Abdullah bin Mas'ud saw Abu Jahl. He recognized him and went and sat upon his chest. Abu Jahl opened his eyes once more and recognized him, saying, "You have climbed high, you little shepherd." Abdullah bin Mas'ud replied, "Praise be to that King who has put you to shame," and with that he cut off his head and the Holy Prophet ﷺ gave thanks to Allah Almighty. According to one narration, Abdullah bin Mas'ud invited him to Islam before he killed him. Abu Jahl's answer was only, "Go and tell your prophet that as much rancor as I have held against him thus far, I shall hold against him even more from now on." When these words were reported to the Holy Prophet ﷺ he commented, "The Pharaoh I have had to deal with was much worse than the Pharaoh of Musa; for when Musa's Pharoah was on the verge of drowning, he accepted the God of Musa and the Bani Isra'il, whereas this one increased a thousand fold in his disbelief."

At nightfall all the soldiers returned to camp. There was a dried-up well at the entrance to Badr, and the Holy Prophet ﷺ had the corpses of the unbelievers piled into this well. As they threw them into the pit, the Holy Prophet ﷺ stood beside it and said, "Oh people of the pit! You were an evil kinsfolk to your Prophet. You called me a liar and expelled me from your city. Have you found that what Allah promised you is true? I have found that what my Lord promised me is true." The Muslims said, "Oh Prophet of Allah ﷺ, are you calling to the dead bodies?" The Holy Prophet ﷺ answered them, "They hear as well as you do, but they cannot answer me."

There is a disagreement as to how many died at Badr. Some narrations say there were forty-five dead and some say there were seventy-two dead. There is no doubt about the number of dead among the Muslims: six of the Muhajirin and eight from among the Ansar: fourteen in all.

After the battle was over, disputes arose as to the division of the spoils. One group said, "Whatever we find is ours," while another group was of the opinion that everything should be brought before the Holy Prophet ﷺ and they would wait to see what was his command. Promptly a verse was revealed concerning this:

> *They will question you concerning the spoils. Say: 'The spoils belong to God and the Messenger; so fear you God, and set things right between you, and obey you God and His Messenger, if you are believers.* (The Spoils, 1)

The spoils were then all collected in one place and Abdullah bin Ka'b was set to guard over them.

The next day the Holy Prophet ﷺ sent Zayd bin Harith back to Madinah to give the news of the victory and the slaying of Abu Jahl. He met 'Uthman bin 'Affan coming back from the cemetery. His wife, the Prophet's own daughter Ruqiyya, had been very ill when they went out to Badr, and 'Uthman had been ordered to stay at her side. She had died that day and they had buried her. Zayd gave him the news of Abu Jahl's defeat, and 'Uthman's heart was gladdened in spite of his grief, as were the hearts of the townspeople of Madinah.

Some of the defeated Meccan soldiers made their way back to Mecca. The first to get there was al-Haysuman bin Abdullah. When he was asked for news, he told of all the nobles who had been killed in the battle. Safwan bin Umayya was sitting in a corner, and when he heard the names of the Qurayshi chiefs, he spoke up and said, "This fellow must be mad! Ask him about me!" They said to Haysuman: "What about Safwan bin Umayya?" "Are you jesting with me?" he said, "He is sitting here in the corner of the temple, but I saw his father and brother as they were being killed." Speaking these words he began to weep, and they realized that he was indeed telling the truth. Abu Lahab was ill that day, and when he received this bad news, his state worsened and the next day he was dead. No one could approach his blackened and swollen corpse. When his son 'Utba came and saw his father's condition, he pulled down the whole house and buried his father within it.

The Holy Prophet ﷺ gathered all the companions and asked them their opinions about the distribution of the spoils. 'Umar said, "The prisoners should be killed and their possessions burnt, for they are filth and evil." But the Holy Prophet 🕸 was not pleased with these words. Abu Bakr said, "These prisoners are our relatives. Allah Almighty gave us victory over them. Let the prisoners pay ransom for themselves, and let their belongings be distributed among the companions." The Holy Prophet 🕸 agreed with this opinion, and said, "Be patient and let us see what Allah Almighty commands us to do."

According to the law of previous nations, the spoils of war were not lawful and had to be burnt or buried. Before the time of our Prophet 🕸 none of the spoils taken from an enemy were lawful to the victor. But in the time of our Prophet 🕸 the spoils of war were made lawful to the Muslims.

Before long this holy verse of the Quran was revealed:

It is not fitting for any Prophet to take prisoners of war until he has subdued the (uprising in the) land. You desire the chance goods in the present world, and God desires the world to come; and God is All-Mighty, All-Wise. Had it not been for a prior prescription from God, there had afflicted you for what you took, a mighty chastisement. Eat of what you have taken as booty, such as is lawful and good, and fear you God; surely God is All-Forgiving and All-Compassionate.

(The Spoils, 67-69)

The next day the Prophet 🕸 together with the bulk of soldiers departed for Madinah. The stopped and halted at a certain distance from the city. There the captives were presented to the Holy Prophet 🕸. ʿUqba bin Abi Muʾayt was among those Meccans who had spat in the Prophet's face. The Prophet 🕸 said to Asim ibn Thabit, "Go and make true my pledge." ʿUqba said, "Oh Muhammad, if I am to die, who will look after my children?" The Prophet 🕸 answered, "Hell!" Then he was put to death.

After that he ordered Ali to strike the neck of al-Nadr bin Harith, for he was that person of whom Allah says in the Holy Book:

And when they say, "Oh God, if this be indeed the truth from Thee, then rain down upon us stones out of Heaven, or bring us a painful chastisement."

(The Spoils, 32)

When they came to Madinah the captives entered with their hands shackled. Sauda, the Prophet's wife saw them and exclaimed, "Why did they not fight like their forebears and die a noble death?" The Holy Prophet ✿ happened to hear these words and was unsettled by them. He said by manner of reproof, "Oh Sauda, are you trying to raise trouble against Allah and His Messenger?" Sauda immediately repented of her words and quickly went over to Aisha, just as the Holy Prophet ✿ was entering her room. She said, "I am an old woman, but I do wish to remain in the Prophet's wedlock until the Last Day. Please help me in this matter." The Holy Prophet ✿ then forgave her.

The Holy Prophet ✿ did not ransom the captives but waited for their Meccan relatives to come and pay their ransom. Abu Sufyan meanwhile advised his fellow Meccans, "Wait before you ransom the prisoners, for Muhammad is asking a very high price. I had two sons, one of them, Hanzala, became Muslim and was slain; the other, 'Amr, is their prisoner. Still I am waiting, and I counsel you to wait as well." But nobody listened to him. The son of Abu Wada' could not wait and he went to ransom his father and returned with him to Mecca. Then the other Meccans began to pay the ransom for their near and dear ones. The Holy Prophet's ✿ uncle 'Abbas was also taken prisoner in the battle.

'Abbas Enters Islam

The Holy Prophet ✿ said to him, "Oh 'Abbas, you are the richest of all the captives; three of them, 'Aqil, Naufal and 'Utba are the sons of your brother. But they are poor, so do you pay their ransom?" 'Abbas answered, "Oh Messenger of Allah, I am inclined towards Islam, and they forced me to come along from Mecca against my will." The Prophet ✿ replied, "But outwardly you resemble one of the unbelievers." "The person who took me captive took from me my belt containing a certain sum of dinars, let that be my ransom," replied 'Abbas. "That money belongs to the Muslims, that

305

cannot be your ransom," answered the Prophet ﷺ. 'Abbas said, "There is nothing else I possess with which I might ransom myself."

The Prophet ﷺ then said, "If I tell you about what you are hiding, will you use it to pay your ransom?" "Yes, I will," answered his uncle. Thereupon the Holy Prophet ﷺ said, "Do you remember one night when you put a number of coins in a bag, placed them in the hand of your wife Umm al-Fadl, saying, 'Go and bury this in such a place in the house, should anything happen to me, use this money and divide it among my four sons.' This is what you said, isn't it?" 'Abbas was astonished, "Who told you about this?" he asked. The Prophet ﷺ answered, "The angel Jibra'il tells me these things." Then 'Abbas made his Shahada and said, "That night there was no one in the house but Umm al-Fadl and myself, therefore you must be telling the truth."

That is how the Prophet's ﷺ uncle 'Abbas came to accept Islam, and this verse was revealed on this occasion:

Oh Prophet, say to the prisoners in your hands: If God knows of any good in your hearts He will give you better than what has been taken from you, and He will forgive you; surely God is All-Forgiving, All-Compassionate. (The Spoils, 70)

The Holy Prophet ﷺ said to 'Abbas, "Oh uncle, Allah Almighty has sent down this verse on your account."

'Abbas grew very rich when he entered Islam and he used to say, "Allah Almighty has promised two things to me: one of them that I would become rich in this world, and the other that I would find forgiveness in the other world. Now He has fulfilled His promise to me in this world, and I am hopeful that He will fulfill His promise to me in the other world as well."

The angel Jibra'il came and said, "'Abbas possesses four virtues," whereupon the Holy Prophet ﷺ said to him, "Oh uncle, Allah has praised you for the possession of four virtues: tell me which ones they may be." 'Abbas answered, "Even before I became a believer I never worshipped the idols; I never cast my eye on another man's wife; I never told lies; and I never ate of what was *haram* (forbidden)."

When the Holy Prophet ﷺ had migrated to Madinah, he left two of his daughters behind in Mecca, for they were married to unbelievers. The Prophet ﷺ was worried about them. One of them was Ruqiyya who was married to ʿUtba bin Abi Lahab, the other was Zaynab, married to Abul-ʿAs. When the unbelievers forced the Prophet ﷺ to leave Mecca, they said to his sons-in-law, "Leave Muhammad's daughters, divorce yourselves from them and let him look after his own daughters." But Abul-ʿAs loved his wife Zaynab and would not dismiss her. Now Abul-ʿAs had become the prisoner of the Holy Prophet ﷺ, and he told him to send word to Mecca that they might ransom him.

He sent a message to Zaynab, but Zaynab possessed nothing but a necklace, which she had inherited from her mother Khadija. This she sent as ransom for her husband. When the Holy Prophet ﷺ saw and recognized the necklace, he became sorrowful and wept. The Companions then said, "We ask for nothing, we forego our part of his ransom." The Holy Prophet ﷺ handed the necklace to Abul-ʿAs and said to him, "Oh Abul-ʿAs, my daughter is not lawful to you, since you are yet an unbeliever. If you accept Islam, I will give her to you." Abul-ʿAs said, "No, I will not become Muslim." The Holy Prophet ﷺ then said, "In that case, when you have reached Mecca, send my daughter back to me." Abul-ʿAs said, "So be it, I will send her." The Holy Prophet ﷺ then sent Zayd bin Harith to Mecca with Abul-ʿAs, and he brought back Zaynab with him. Some time after this, Abul-ʿAs migrated to Madinah and became Muslim. The Holy Prophet ﷺ then married him anew to his daughter Zaynab, and returned to him all the possessions which the companions had taken from him aforetime.

The Story of Wahab bin ʿUmayr

There lived a man in Mecca by name of Wahab bin ʿUmayr. He had one son who was captured in the Battle of Badr. He went to Safwan and said, "I want to retrieve my son, and at the same time I want to kill Muhammad.

Meanwhile you take charge of my family and look after them." Safwan accepted this, and said, "I will take care of them."

Wahab prepared himself, girded his sword and set out for Madinah. In the mean time the angel Jibra'il came to the Holy Prophet 🕮 and informed him of Wahab's coming. When he arrived at Madinah, he went straight to the Holy Prophet 🕮. "Why have you come, oh Wahab?" the Holy Prophet 🕮 asked him. Wahab was going to say, "I have come to ransom my son, but I have nothing with which to pay the ransom, so just give him to me!" But his tongue became tied and he could not utter a single word. The Prophet 🕮 then said to him, "If I tell you what you came for, will you then accept Islam?" Wahab agreed to this. Then the Prophet 🕮 explained to him the whole story and said, "You went to Safwan and told him that you were going to kill Muhammad, and you asked him to care for your family. Safwan accepted and told you to go ahead with your intention."

When he heard these words, Wahab became convinced that Muhammad 🕮 was indeed the Prophet of Allah and he uttered the words of the Shahada and became Muslim. The Prophet then said, "Now that you have become Muslim, I will return to you your son. Go back to Mecca and hold on to your Islam. Explain your way to whomever asks about it, but take care, and call to Islam only in a concealed way." Wahab returned to Mecca, and said to his people, "Oh people, Muhammad 🕮 is a true Prophet of Allah! He told me every word of the private conversation I had with Safwan." Then he stayed there summoning people to Islam. Through him many became Muslims.

In ten months the Holy Prophet 🕮 had gone out on seven raids. He participated in four of these himself, while in three others he sent his companions and did not go himself.

The Raid on the Bani Sulaym in al-Kudr

After returning to Madinah and staying there for merely a week, the Holy Prophet 🕮 himself set out on a raid against the Bani Sulaym.

The unbelievers of Madinah inhabited fortified strongholds which surrounded the city at a distance on all four sides, such as Khaybar, Bani Nadir and Fadak. When the Holy Prophet ﷺ came to Madinah, he called them to Islam, but not one of them accepted his call, they ignored and disregarded him. When the Battle of Badr was successfully fought, these unbelievers began to worry and said, "Now that he's dealt with the Quraysh, he's going to turn against us." From jealousy they sought to unite with Quraysh and turn against the Prophet ﷺ with joint forces. They gathered their confederates from the Bani Sulaym and Bani Ghatafan to fight against Muhammad ﷺ.

There was a watering place three days' journey from Madinah, by the name of Qarqara-tul-Kudr. To this they now proceeded. The Holy Prophet ﷺ received this information and he gave Ali ibn Abi Talib the banner of the Muslims. They reached the place in only two days. Hearing of this, the Arabs were frightened, and leaving everything behind, they fled. The Prophet's ﷺ men led away their herds and cattle and returned to Madinah where they rested for two days.

The Raid of Sawiq

In the month of Dhul-Qa'da the Raid of Sawiq occurred, and it came about in the following way:

Abu Sufyan had a son by the name of 'Amr who had been taken prisoner. Abu Sufyan was constantly saying, "If only I had been along at the Battle of Badr, then I would have acted in such a way and dealt with them in such a way..." The people of Mecca grew tired of hearing this and said to him, "So, go now and do it!" One man called Hamid came to Abu Sufyan said, "By God, I will go and kill Muhammad and, if it is made easy, I will destroy his whole house and family." So Abu Sufyan quickly made ready two-hundred riders and they set out for Madinah. When they approached the town, they stopped and stayed with the Bani Nadir who sent fifty more men with them.

They came to a field where there were two Muslims of the Ansar working, and they killed them. Then they set fire to a place outside of the city. News of all this reached the Holy Prophet ﷺ, and he speedily rose to pursue Abu Sufyan. Abu Sufyan fled at great speed, taking three stages in one day. The Holy Prophet ﷺ could not catch up with him. Abu Sufyan's flight was such that whoever had provisions in his traveling pack threw them all by the wayside in his haste. Therefore, this raid was called the Raid of Sawiq and it took place in the month of Dhul-Qa'da, because it was followed by the month of Dhul-Hijja. The Holy Prophet ﷺ sacrificed two sheep and called the Muslims to the sacrifice, ordering them to sacrifice as well. This was the first 'Id-al-Adha in Islam. The Prophet ﷺ slaughtered the sheep by his own hand, one for himself, and one for those of his nation who were unable to slaughter.

In the month of Dhul-Hijja the Prophet ﷺ accepted the ransom for those taken prisoner during the Battle of Badr. In the month of Rabi' al-Awwal the Holy Prophet ﷺ wed his daughter Umm Kulthum to 'Uthman. 'Uthman had formerly been married to the Prophet's ﷺ daughter Ruqiyya, but she, sadly, had died.

The Raid of Dhu Amarr

Again it was in the 25th month of the Hijra in the month of Rabi' al-Awwal that the raid of Dhu Amarr took place. This raid is also called the Raid of Ghatafan. Dhu Amarr is the name of a place in the Najd. The tribes of the Bani Tha'laba and Bani Muharib were renowned as extremely fierce, war-like men, and they were now engaged in setting their forces on a war footing against the Muslims. No sooner had the Holy Prophet ﷺ heard about this that he left 'Uthman ibn 'Affan in charge of things in Madinah, and set out with an army of 450 men. When the pagan Arabs heard of the strength of the force the Prophet ﷺ was leading against them, they all fled into the mountains. Only one person from the tribe of the Bani Tha'laba was taken prisoner, and when he was brought into the presence of the Holy Prophet ﷺ, he met his fate ordained from pre-eternity, and beholding the

Prophet's pure and holy countenance, he begged for pardon and submitted to Islam. Rasulullah ﷺ left this man in the care of Bilal, so that he might teach him what he needed to know.

The day of the battle had been a rainy one, and the Holy Prophet ﷺ had been thoroughly drenched. He retreated to a quiet place, took off his clothes and hung them upon a tree to dry. Then he lay down to rest and fell asleep. The unbelievers watched every movement closely from their hiding places in the mountains. When they saw the Prophet ﷺ lie down to sleep they immediately went to their chief to inform him of this. His name was Du'thur. They said to him, "Their Prophet is lying all alone and is asleep; if you trust yourself at all, don't let this opportunity slip by." Indeed, the Prophet ﷺ lay there all by himself, but Du'thur could not see the invisible armor that clothed him through Divine Providence, nor could he perceive the sudden inspirations he was equipped with, so he instantly grabbed the hilt of his sword, and ran to where the Prophet ﷺ lay. He stopped by his blessed head, drew his sword, and cried, "Who will now rescue you from my might?"

Now this source of guidance, this example of living faith, the pride of all creation, without a trace of anxiety and from the full love of his heart answered: "Allah." The power of the Divine Name spoken through the blessed mouth of the Holy Prophet ﷺ made the sword tumble from the hand of the idolater, so that it landed in the hands of the Holy Prophet ﷺ himself. He then turned the phrase around and said to the man, "And who will rescue you from me now?" At this very moment the pagan Arab grew aware of the power of Prophethood, and Du'thur melted before the mighty light of this holy person. He pleaded, "Is it at all possible for me to reach forgiveness?" he asked, "Not in order to save my skin, or to have it my way, but after all my insolence to become a slave at your doorstep and to attain to my eternal destination?" The source of mercy, Rasulullah ﷺ answered him, "What are you waiting for, come out of the blackness of your ignorance and the obscurity of your unbelief; demolish it at once and gather around our holy scripture of the Quran, where everyone stands side by side and learns his lesson." "Yes, but how can I cleanse myself of the filth of my idolatry, what do you recommend that I do?" "Speak the words of the Kalimatu-Shahada," answered Rasulullah ﷺ.

Meanwhile, Du'thur's men were watching this scene from afar, wondering what was going on. They found it hard to understand how an unarmed man lying supine who found himself suddenly under attack, would utter nothing but the holy word 'Allah' with such perfect love and confidence that it knocked the sword out of the hand of the strongest man - what a strange thing it was that they were witnessing! And not only that: now they also heard Du'thur yelling at the top of his voice:

ASH-HADU AN LA ILAHA ILL'ALLAH, WA ASH-HADU ANNA MUHAMMADAR-RASULULLAH.

For indeed, the man upon whom Divine Grace falls, cannot be veiled from it by human upheaval. When the sun rises, the veil of darkness cannot prevent it from shining. This condition serves us as a good example of how all things existent are but a plaything before the merciful and wrathful aspects of the Lord Almighty. How he who only a moment ago was the most vicious of the heathens can testify less than a minute later that Muhammad ﷺ is the Prophet of Allah.

He returns to his people in a state of bliss. They receive him with great amazement, and ask him what on earth has happened to put him in such a state. Du'thur tells them that up to this moment they have been living on the level of base animals deprived of higher feelings, but that at last the mercy of Allah has manifested. With the appearance of true faith he has felt the coming of ease and joy, and he exhorted his people to join him in the faith of Islam. A great number of his people came to Islam then through Du'thur, in consequence of which this verse was revealed:

O believers, remember God's blessing upon you, when a certain people purposed to stretch against you their hands, and He restrained their hands from you; and fear God; and in God let the believers put all their trust. (The Table, 11)

In other narrations there are given a variety of reasons for the revelation of this verse, but this is the correct one. For the duration of these events the Holy Prophet ﷺ stayed away from Madinah for eleven nights.

The Raid of Bahran

After the Raid of Dhu Amarr, the Raid of Bahran took place against the Bani Sulaym. The reason was this: news was received that in the area of al-Furu' a number of unbelievers of the Bani Sulaym were assembling against the Muslims and getting ready to launch an attack. Thereupon Muhammad set out with three hundred men to forestall the attackers. As soon as the tribes heard of the advance of the Holy Prophet's ﷺ forces, they dispersed and fled into the hills. Muhammad ﷺ returned to Madinah, having remained for twelve nights outside of the city.

The Bani Qaynuqa

After this, in the month of Shawwal, the raid on the Bani Qaynuqa took place. This tribe had broken their covenant with Muhammad ﷺ and joined the other tribes against him. When he had assembled them in their market and addressed them, the unbelievers of the Bani Qaynuqa said, "Oh Muhammad, do you think us to be just as the Quraysh?! If it is war you desire, that is fine by us! That is our occupation; we destroy all that comes in our way."

On the eleventh day of the month of Shawwal he set out from Madinah. He handed the standard to Hamza and sent him to the Bani Qaynuqa. Hamza fought them for several days, and then he placed them under siege. The Holy Prophet ﷺ came up to the gate of the fortress. Those within asked for quarter and the Holy Prophet ﷺ said, "Your quarter shall be to be killed and to have your property taken from you." Then Abdullah bin Ubayy ibn Sulur came and pleaded on their behalf, and the Holy Prophet ﷺ granted them their lives, condemning them to exile. So they all left their homes and departed. The people of Madinah were troubled at their departure, for they were wealthy people and their business was essential to them. Thereupon the Prophet ✾ broke into their strongholds and confiscated their goods, concerning which this verse was revealed:

> *Know that, whatever booty you take, the fifth of it is God's and the Messenger's, and the near kinsman's, and the orphan's, and for the needy, and the traveler, if you believe in God.* (The Spoils, 41)

Therefore, with this revelation, the spoils of war were made lawful and the Holy Prophet ✾ received one fifth of the booty and took whatever he pleased thereof; the remainder was distributed among the Companions of the Prophet ✾, one fifth went into the Bayt-al-Mal, the Public Treasury. Then the Holy Prophet ✾ returned to Madinah.

The Raid on al-Qarada

In this same year the foray of Zayd bin Harith took place. Zayd bin Harith set out by command from the Holy Prophet ✾ and with one hundred men proceeded to a watering place in Najd called al-Qarada. They meant to intercept the caravan of Quraysh. The reason for this was, after the defeat of Badr the idolaters were consumed ever more by feelings of revenge. Abu Sufyan was encouraging everybody to participate in the caravan trade, so that the profits could be invested in the outfitting of an army to take their revenge for the defeat at Badr. The Quraysh now abandoned the caravan route leading to Sham (Damascus), instead preferring the route through Iraq. Abu Sufyan's caravan set out from Sham, and the Holy Prophet ✾ learned of this. With Zayd bin Harith at its head, he sent out a band of his men to intercept the caravan. The Quraysh all fled, and the caravan with its goods was brought back to Madinah.

In this same year Hafsa, the daughter of 'Umar had the great gratification of entering into wedlock with the Holy Prophet ✾. In this way 'Umar had the good fortune of becoming the privileged father-in-law of the Holy Prophet ✾.

In the month of Sha'ban in the fourth year after the Hijra. In the same month the Holy Prophet ✾ married Hafsa, the daughter of 'Umar.

The Marriage of Fatima to Ali

The marriage of the Holy Prophet's ❀ daughter Fatima to Ali took in the second year after the Hijra. In writing about this subject we will not neglect to dwell a bit on this illustrious personality.

Fatima az-Zahra was the youngest of the Holy Prophet's ❀ daughters. She is given a certain rank in the Divine Presence, having been created pure and undefiled; moreover, it is disclosed that she is signified as the specific meaning of this holy verse, assuming its outward meaning has been well understood:

> *Wealth and sons are the adornment of the present world; but the abiding things, the deeds of righteousness, are better with God in reward, and better in hope.*

> *(The Cave, 47)*

Fatima is referred to in the saying of the Holy Prophet ❀: "She is my soul."

When the sons of the Holy Prophet ❀ were honored to enter the World of Beauty (the afterlife), and the unbelievers said about the Holy Prophet ❀ that he had remained childless and unblessed, and his pure heart was disturbed thereby, this holy Sura was revealed, in reference to his daughter Fatima:

> *Surely We have given thee abundance; so pray unto thy Lord and sacrifice. Surely he that hates thee, he is the one cut off.* *(Abundance)*

This is the reason she came to be called "Zahra" as well as Fatima. She was innocent, pure and undefiled; she was one of those who attract the love of people, and who are made safe from the fires of Hell. Whenever Fatima came into the presence of her blessed father, the Holy Prophet ❀, he would rise from his seat at the table, greet her by holding her by her arms and seat her by his right side. Therefore, she reached to the taste of true faith and became one of the friends of God.

The People of Truth have said: If the Holy Prophet ❀ or members of his family are mentioned in a Dhikr gathering, it becomes obligatory for that gathering to stand up out of respect for those persons.

315

When Aisha one day asked the Holy Prophet 🌸 about these special gifts of Fatima, he answered, "Fatima is my mirror, in which I am shown myself."

The Sahaba and the Ahl as-Safa knew about the stations granted to Fatima in the Divine Presence. Abu Bakr as-Siddiq had asked for her hand in marriage. The Holy Prophet 🌸 replied, "Oh Abu Bakr, so far no revelation has come to me concerning the question whom my daughter Fatima is to marry." After this 'Umar proposed and he gave him the same answer. Then the Companions of the Holy Prophet 🌸 said to Ali, "What if you asked and proposed marriage to her?" And Ali answered, "The Lord Almighty has made her a present for me. I have seen our marriage performed in the world of the Divine Throne."

In truth Ali had seen a dream which had been interpreted as signifying his marriage to Fatima. His dream had been concerned with figs and olives. In the end this was confirmed by the revelation of the verses:

By the fig and the olive and the Mount Sinai and this land secure! We indeed created Man in the fairest stature Then We restored him the lowest of the low.

(The Fig)

The external interpretation and specific meaning of this glorious verse being is:

For the sake of the essence of the two beautiful beings (i.e. Hasan and Hussayn), and for the sake of the heart of Muhammad 🌸 which is the 'land secure', the human soul attached to Fatima and Ali was manifested in the fairest stature, thereafter sent down to the lowest of all low levels, which is the world we live in.

The angel Jibra'il transmitted the Divine Revelation in the following way: "The union between Fatima and Ali has been concluded in the Divine Presence beyond all space by the Almighty Himself, so let it be performed by My Beloved in this visible world."

The Holy Prophet 🌸 called Ali and Fatima to himself and informed them of this circumstance. Ali was deeply grateful for this tremendous grant from the Almighty. The noble companions of the Prophet 🕌 were invited and the marriage ceremony was performed according to revealed ritual. The Holy Prophet 🕌 delivered the following speech on the occasion: "I give you my daughter Fatima as your maid servant, provided that you will be her slave."

From these words of the Prophet 🕌 the great value Islam places on the institution of marriage becomes apparent, inasmuch as the wedding couple wishes to become one spirit through the union of their two bodies.

When the marriage ceremony was concluded, the Holy Prophet 🕌 asked for two cups of water to be brought, and he took water from one of them in his blessed hand and sprinkled it upon the blessed chest of his daughter Fatima, praying, *"Inni a'udhuha bika wa dhurriyataha min ash-shaytan-ir-rajim,* I seek refuge for her and her offspring from the accursed Satan." Then he took water from the other cup in his blessed hand, and sprinkled some of it on. Ali's back and shoulders, praying also on his behalf for the Almighty to bless him and grant him abundance.

Fatima's dowry consisted of six things: a rug, a waterskin, a pillow filled with date palm fibers, one flat wicker basket, and two bowls.

When the angel Jibra'il was commanded by the Lord to make the Holy Prophet 🕌 ask his daughter what she wished for her dowry, Fatima az-Zahra, this pure and holy part of the Prophet 🕌 replied, "Endless thanks to my Lord for the special gifts I have been given. All I wish for as my dowry is that on the Day of Judgment, when the records are unclosed I am granted intercession on behalf of those believers who are deprived."

Fatima was asked what she wished for her dowry, for the Lord would have given to her whatever she desired. Fatima answered, "Oh Prophet of Allah 🕌, if I asked for money and gold, how would I, the Prophet's 🕌 daughter differ from the girls of the rest of your nation? All I want is to be granted intercession on the Day of Judgment for your sinful nation. Such a promise I wish to receive, oh my father, who thou art 'a Mercy for the Worlds.' I want to enrich and comfort all those girls who are poor and destitute. For when a poor girl marries and goes to her new home, she may be received with lack of tact and asked, 'What have you brought from your father's house as your dowry?' Then her heart is smitten by these harsh words, and she says, 'What can I do? This is all that the Lord has apportioned to my family of lawful means; surely, my father was no servant of a tyrant, committed no injustice, inclined not toward any hypocrite, did not run after unlawful gains, nor did he acquire riches by inflicting harm on others; he has not mistreated his maidservants, he did not sell his honor, nor did he seek his gain by degrading himself in front of mean men. All he did was to equip me with virtues such as chastity, honor, goodness and contentment and marry me off with them as my dowry.' And may she be able to say, 'The founder of my religion married off his own daughter with a dowry of a handful of things.' That is my wish: that she might refer to me."

May this great lady of Islam, this most delicate and shy manifestation of our Lord, not exclude us from her intercession. Amin.

Upon her marriage to Ali, a letter of Light was sent by the Lord Almighty, saying that the right of intercession was given to Fatima for the Day of Judgment, to be the bridal gift for the Nation of Muhammad ❀, and to be a helper to her father who is the 'Mercy for the Worlds'. This right of intercession is the most *halal* (lawful) of all things. This paper was brought and stored in a bottle, all the Sahaba saw it, and the marriage contract was signed by the angel Jibra'il and by the bride's father. When she was at the point of death, she asked Ali to lay this upon her chest, under her burial shroud, so that she might have her claim ready to show when she entered the presence of the Lord Almighty.

Other Marriages

As mentioned earlier, the daughter of the Holy Prophet ❀, the wife of 'Uthman, Sayyida Ruqiyya died during the Battle of Badr. In the same year Khunays ibn Khudhafah, Umar's son-in-law also died, and his daughter Hafsa was widowed. 'Umar wished to marry his daughter to his friend 'Uthman, and originally 'Uthman had agreed, but later he changed his mind and declined. This refusal hit 'Umar very hard. When the Holy Prophet asked for Hafsa's hand, 'Umar's joy knew no end, and he felt unspeakably honored at becoming the Prophet's ﷺ father-in-law. The Prophet's ﷺ other daughter, Umm Kulthum, he ﷺ gave to 'Uthman in marriage. 'Uthman therefore acceded the honor of having married two daughters of the Holy Prophet ﷺ, therefore he is called Dhi Nurayn, or "possessor of two lights".

That same year the Holy Prophet ﷺ married Zaynab, the daughter of Khuzayma. On the 15th of the month of Ramadan, the Prophet's ﷺ blessed grandson Hasan was born into this world.

The Battle of Uhud

The Quraysh could not forget the heavy losses they had suffered in the Battle of Badr, and their reliance on their powers was shaken. They had lost seventy people in one encounter, and most of them had been the foremost and eminent men of Quraysh. In short, all of Mecca was in mourning. Abu Sufyan stood up and yelled at people, saying, "When will Badr be avenged?" Ikrimah, the son of Abu Jahl, said, "What has happened to us? At one time the murder of a single person would spark off lengthy bloodletting in revenge. The losers would kill in revenge attacks for as long as it took for them to be victorious. Now Muhammad's troop has condemned us to disgrace. We have lost so many of our noblest sons, yet we make no move to avenge them.

"Surely, this can only mean that we are totally destroyed. Why does no one avenge the death of my father? We have made great profits from the caravan trade, but nobody can deny the superiority of the Muslims in strength of mind; this we must try to destroy by our means. For instance, we should compose poetry of propaganda to incite all the tribes of Arabia with their songs and dirges to join their forces to ours. It won't do to waste any time, for those followers of Muhammad grow stronger with every passing day. Also, we should give all the women in Mecca who have lost their husbands, brothers or sons the task of encouraging the fighters."

Thus in Mecca, people spoke as if the city were to remain theirs for ever. Abu Sufyan donated fifty thousand pieces of gold in order to encourage the fighting men. Allah Almighty instantly informed His beloved Prophet ﷺ of this development in the revelation of this verse:

The unbelievers expend their wealth to bar from God's way; and still they will expend it, till it is an anguish for them, then be overthrown.... (The Spoils, 36)

As for the women, they mingled among the men, saying, "We swear that we want to drink the blood of the murderers of our sons, husbands and brothers." At the head of them all was Hind, the wife of Abu Sufyan, the mother of Mu'awiya, the grandmother of Yazid; Umm Hakim, the daughter-in-law of Abu Jahl; Rayta, the wife of Amr ibn al-'As; Balza , the wife of Safwan ibn Umayyah; and, Hamnah, the wife of Mus'ad ibn 'Umayr. Hind promised the slave Zubayr - who was called Wahshi - his freedom and a handsome reward besides, if he succeeded in killing Hamza, the uncle of Muhammad ﷺ.

The Quraysh were thirsting for blood and prepared their move. There were fifteen women who accompanied the army, playing on their drums and singing lewd songs: "We don't want men in our beds who lie asleep all day in their houses, we want men who exact revenge for Badr."

They went to Abbas, the Prophet's ﷺ uncle and asked him, "What shall we do?" Though Abbas had already embraced Islam in his heart, he did not yet show it openly. He objected that he had been very much worn out in the Battle of Badr, and defeated on all accounts and could therefore not come along this time. He then sought to inform the Holy Prophet ﷺ immediately, so he wrote a letter and hired a man to deliver it to the Holy Prophet ﷺ as quickly as possible. The messenger found the Holy Prophet ﷺ at Kuba and gave him the letter. The Holy Prophet ﷺ gave 'Umayya the letter to read, but ordered him to keep the matter to himself. He then went to the house of one of the notables of Kuba, Sa'd ibn Rabi', and there explained to him in a confidential manner the contents of the letter he had received concerning the war preparations of the Quraysh. After lengthy deliberations he ordered the return to Madinah. This occurred in the third year of the Hijra in the month of Shawwal. The Holy Prophet ﷺ sent out two reliable men as scouts who brought him news of the approaching army of Quraysh, and that their riders had passed the fields of Madinah. The Holy Prophet ﷺ sent out Hubab ibn al-Mundhir who had been the commanding officer at the Battle of Badr to learn about the strength of the enemy forces. In this way they took all necessary precautions to forestall a sudden, unexpected attack, setting up watches at all the important points. Sa'd ibn Mu'adh and Sa'd ibn 'Ubayda held the night watch before the Prophet's mosque. The women and children of the town, and the old and feeble were ordered to withdraw to safe quarters.

One morning the Holy Prophet ﷺ called together the leaders of the Sahaba and Ansar and convened a war council. He said to them, "If it is reasonable, we should close the gates of the city and defend our area from inside, without leaving the city. Only in case the enemy enters the city, we would engage in battle with them." The Holy Prophet ﷺ had sent out Hubab ibn al-Mundhir to scout out the positions of the Quraysh. He now returned and reported that they were encamped at a place called 'Uray, one day's journey from Madinah. The army of Quraysh had arrived at the foot of the mountain of Uhud on a Wednesday and remained there till Friday. This was also confirmed in the letter sent by Abbas, the Prophet's ﷺ uncle. The Holy Prophet ﷺ is reported to have seen this dream on Thursday night: "I saw in my dream a herd of cattle being slaughtered and I saw a gash open upon the blade of my sword; upon my back I wore a suit of mail, and my hand I stuck into the collar of a suit of mail." And this is the interpretation he gave to it: "The slaughtered cattle are those of companions who will be martyred; the blade of my sword being broken means that one of my family will be killed; and that firm coat of armor signifies Madinah."

We have already mentioned that it was the Holy Prophet's ﷺ wish only to engage in battle with defensive intent, and to leave the city of Madinah only in case of enemy attack. Moreover, the enemy was in a consolidated position, and he thought that the Bedouin tribesmen gathered in the environs of the city of Madinah could not stay there for long. On the other hand there were some enthusiastic young men who had not participated in the Battle of Badr who said to the Prophet ﷺ, "Oh Prophet of Allah! You would be depriving us! Already we were not able to go to Badr, and our hearts are swelled with faith and wish to fight for it!" The much-beloved uncle of the Holy Prophet 鸞 Hamza said, "Oh Prophet of Allah! I find it very difficult to stay locked up within the city."

Thereupon the Holy Prophet 鸞 said, "Very well, so make ready for battle!" Preparations then were made. At that time he spoke these words of profound meaning: "If you are patient, you will again encounter help from Allah." That same day in the Khutba of the Jum'a prayer the Holy Prophet 鸞 spoke of the virtue and merit of a battle waged for the sake of Allah and for the defense of one's homeland, which is the mantle of religion. After the prayer of 'Asr he took Abu Bakr and 'Umar with him into his own blessed apartment and they donned their battle dress. They wound the turbans that they wore on such campaigns, put on their coats of mail and girded their swords.

Outside all the Companions were waiting for the Prophet 鸞 in a state of readiness and excitement. The population of the whole town had gathered, and everyone was waiting for the Holy Prophet 鸞 to come forth. Sa'd ibn 'Ubada and 'Usaybin ibn Harith who were among the elders of the Sahaba grew aware of what was going on and they spoke to the Sahaba, "You have said, 'Let us go out to meet the enemy', but you have committed a grave mistake. You ought not to place your opinion against that of Rasulullah 鸞 You should defend Madinah from within because that was his enlightened opinion."

These words impressed themselves strongly on those who had been in favor of leaving the city to fight the foe, and they regretted having spoken out against the wishes of the Holy Prophet. Just then the Prophet Muhammad 鸞 emerged from his room. The Sahaba said, "Oh Rasulullah, if our opinion was contrary to your view, we beg your pardon, we will do whatever you say. If you think it better not to leave the city, we will stay within and defend Madinah when it is attacked." Thus they expressed their remorse. However, the Holy Prophet 鸞 spoke to them and said, "Nay, for when a prophet of Allah has girded himself for battle to combat the enemy of God, he will never lay down his arms, unless the Command of the Lord comes to him."

With these words he sprang upon his steed, and sounded the battle cry. He left Ibn Ummu Maftun in charge of the city of Madinah and set out through the gates. The hypocrite Abdullah bin 'Ubayd ibn Salul had before joined the army of Muhammad 🕌 along with his three hundred men. However, when the ideas he had brought up for discussion were not found acceptable, the hypocrisy he concealed in his inner thoughts became manifest, and he used this as an excuse to turn back with his three hundred men.

Sa'd ibn 'Ubada and Sa'd ibn Mu'adh were in armor and rode ahead in front of the Holy Prophet 🕌, in direction of the mountain of Uhud. They spent the night at a place called Shaykhayn, halfway between Madinah and Uhud. The Holy Prophet 🕌 warmly greeted the younger boys who had come with them to this place, namely 'Usamah ibn Zayd, Abdullah ibn 'Umar, Thabit ibn Zayd, Abu Said ibn 'Utbi. He said to them, "We are facing a great battle and it is not the place for children. You will have to turn back from here and go home."

Rafi' bin Hajid was one of these children. When he now saw the Holy Prophet 🕌 turn back the young boys, he tried to make himself look bigger by standing on tiptoe. In this way he managed to stay with the soldiers.

His friend Samurah saw what he had done and said, "Oh Rasulullah, please don't leave me out! I always throw Rafi' when I am wrestling with him, so please let me be in your army, too." The Holy Prophet 🕌 smiled at the faith and earnestness of these youngsters and said, "Alright, show us: wrestle with your friend Rafi', let us see." In the wrestling match that followed Samurah demonstrated his wrestling ability, and made plain how much he wished to fight for the noble cause of Islam and be martyred in the way of Allah, so he too was accepted into the Prophet's 🕌 army.

There were seven hundred fighters in the army of the Prophet 🕌. That night the officer of the watch was Muhammad ibn Maslama-t-al-Ansari. He patrolled the outer fringes of the army's camp with a troop of fifty men. The army marched to a place one mile north of Madinah behind a red mountain called Uhud. There the headquarters were set up facing Madinah. The standard was given to Mus'ab bin Amir, and Zubayr ibn al-'Awwam was appointed the commanding officer. The Holy Prophet ﷺ set his uncle Hamza at the head of the soldiery as their commander.

He selected fifty strong and good marksmen and set at their head Abdullah ibn Jubayri. These were positioned to defend the pass, in order to prevent a likely attack from behind the lines. They were placed under very stringent orders. They were told, "Whatever happens to us may happen, whether we lose or win, unless you receive orders from me, do not under any circumstances leave your position. Even if all the unbelievers are slaughtered and nobody at all is left, if you have no word from me, do not leave your place."

Because the army of Quraysh had suffered grievous losses in the Battle of Badr, this time they had prepared themselves with great care, and their soldiery was well equipped with double coats of mail, whereas only three men of the Muslims had any coat of armor. The enemy army had a cavalry regiment, but on the Muslim side only the Holy Prophet ﷺ and Abu Bakr were mounted on horses. All the other fighters were infantrymen. The commander of the right wing of the enemy's army was the famous Khalid bin Walid; commanding the left wing was Ikrimah, the son of Abu Jahl. The commander of the cavalry was Safwan ibn Umayya, and at the head of the archers stood Abdullah bin Rabi'. Abu Sufyan had the general command, and there was a special subsidiary commander, 'Amr ibn Asta.

As for the Muslim army, the commanding officer of the right wing was 'Ukasha bin Muhsin, and the left wing was commanded by Abu Maslama bin Abd-ul Asad. The Holy Prophet ﷺ took his place in the very middle of the army. Abu 'Ubayda was the vanguard; he had occupied the high rank of Marshal of the Muslim army at Badr as the *'amin-al-umma'*, safeguard of the nation.

Though it was the custom of the Quraysh to sound the drum when they went to war, now the women were now beating the tambourines and singing their songs, saying that no man should approach his wife before the fallen at Badr were avenged. "We are the daughters of the morning star; only if you wipe out the Muhammadan army will you be entitled to consort with us." In this way they encouraged the soldiers.

As for the Muslims, the Holy Prophet 🕌, the pride of humanity astride his steed, called out *Takbir* in the Muhammadan mode. The spiritual emanation of this voice magnified the sound of the Sahaba's chanting of 'Allah, Allah'. The earth itself participated in this call. All attention was focused on the Holy Prophet 🕌 and the words that were to issue from his blessed mouth. All hearts were burning with the desire to attain martyrdom. Finally, the Holy Prophet 🕌 spoke, "There is no escape from fate, fear cannot deter destiny; to fear the enemy of God is shameful, to confront him is honor and glory." He drew his engraved sword in front of them all and called out, "Who will take this sword and give it its right?" A few of the companions called out, "Oh Rasulullah 🕌, we will give it its right." But the Holy Prophet 🕌 did not answer them, but repeated his question once more. Now there was among them Abu Dujanah who was deeply moved in spirit and always wept, saying time and again that he was prepared to die for the Prophet 🕌 at any given moment. He now spoke up and asked, "Oh Prophet of Allah 🕌, what is its right?" The Holy Prophet 🕌 answered, "The right of this sword is to strike the foe until its blade be bent." "If it be your command, I am the man for that," said Abu Dujanah, and the Holy Prophet 🕌 relinquished his sword to him, patted him on the back and in advance gave Abu Dujanah the rank of one of the great martyrs of Islam. These words filled Abu Dujanah with such passion, that he instantly threw himself into the fray of battle. He strode out in full assurance of his power, casting about him proud and confident glances.

Pointing to this type of gait and demeanor that Abu Dujanah exhibited, the Holy Prophet 🕌 said, "That is a gait which is hateful to Allah; however in such a place as this it is the most acceptable of bearings, for it is the way to move in front of the enemy of Islam. In the face of an infidel who challenges Allah and His Prophet ﷺ, insisting on his unbelief, and in violation of the rights of all creatures, if a believer does not see himself as stronger and more steadfast than a whole army, his faith has not yet attained perfection."

Abu Dujanah's gait and bearing came not from his own reckoning: his prancing and strutting about was in the Name of Allah, his severe looks were cast for the love of Rasulullah ﷺ. Abu Dujanah was immersed in the quality of al-Kibriya, the Divine Greatness. The Holy Prophet ﷺ himself was also emptied of his own self, and the manifestations of the Divine Majesty were upon his person. This drawing of Divine Power into one's own actions elicits even the envy of the heavenly angels. But of this matter we shall speak only this much. There is another type of gait which is similar to the one mentioned. When a person relies on his own counterfeit existence and engages in a contest of greatness with the Power of the Divine.

Such haughty ones the Lord Almighty brings down low and leaves destitute, inasmuch as it is written in the Holy Book:

And walk not on the earth exultantly; certainly thou wilt never tear the earth open, nor attain the mountains in height. (The Night Journey, 37)

This is how the fighting began:

There was a renegade from the tribe of the Aws by the name of Abu Amir. Although he had read in the holy books about the coming of a prophet before the Prophet Muhammad's advent, he apostatized from envy after Muhammad ﷺ had manifested his Prophethood. Abu Amir took fifty men with him and went to join the Meccans. He became very friendly with the pagans of Mecca, Muhammad's ﷺ enemies, boasting of himself, "My people love me very much; if they see me on the battlefield, they will desert Muhammad ﷺ and come to me." This man joined Quraysh and went out to battle with them. He stepped forth, and cried out to the troops: "Oh men of the Ansar!" he said, "I am sure you know me, I am Abu Amir."

327

The Ansar replied, "Oh yes, we know you very well for the impious, corrupt person that you are, but make sure you know this well: the Lord Almighty Allah will not fulfill your desires." Abu Amir was very surprised when he heard them speak to him thus and he cried. "What has happened to my people, it is not so very long since I left them." Not only his people, even his own son would not know him whom the Holy Prophet ﷺ had formerly called a depraved person. The Aws engaged in battle and were put to flight. Seeing this, the clansmen of the Hawazin were also frightened, and withdrew as well.

There was a man by the name of Quzman who fought fiercely in the Muslim army. In spite of the fact that he fought on the Muslim side we call this man a *munafiq,* a hypocrite, for in the noble religion of Islam the most important thing is the intention. What separates mere custom from worship is the intention. Though this Quzman displayed a great deal of bravery in the wars of Islam, on account of his intentions he was plunged into the abyss of eternal failure and deprived of reward. This is how it happened: when the Holy Prophet ﷺ rode out from Madinah with his felicitous army, this hypocrite stayed behind with some excuse. When the women began to make fun of him, he ran after the army, caught up with them and began to fight at the head of them all. But his aim was worldly gain and reputation and fame, what a shame. He was, however, an excellent fighter, a fact that did not escape the attention of the Sahaba. They said to the Holy Prophet ﷺ, "Is he not a gallant fighter?" but the Prophet ﷺ answered, "What use is it to him to be deprived in the world to come, for he will fail to achieve it. And so Allah strengthens His religion through a man of no worth." Certainly the outcome was as the truthful Messenger ﷺ foretold.

Meanwhile the battle gained force. The standard-bearer of the unbelievers, Talha, stepped into the fray and challenged the Muslims to a duel, crying, "Let that man step forth who wishes to send me to Hell, or wants to be sent to Paradise by my hand!" This mockery of his religion offended Sayyidina Ali badly, and he stepped forth instantly and said, "I am the man you seek," and with that the Lion of Islam attacked and struck Talha a fierce blow.

The standard then passed from his hand into the hand of his brother. Against him stepped forth Hamza, the Prophet's ﷺ uncle, a lion of Allah on whom the Holy Prophet ﷺ himself had conferred rank when he said of him, "My right hand is my uncle." He slew him as well, and the standard then was passed into the hand of Abu Talha. Sa'ad bin Abu Waqqas, the chief archer of the Muslims, hit him with an arrow. In order not to let the flag drop to the ground, it was taken up by Musafi bin Talha, and he was struck down by an arrow from Asim bin Thabit bin Abul-Aqlah. Thereupon, his brother al-Julas ibn Talha picked up the flag, and Talha ibn 'Ubaydullah slew him. In brief, no less than seven men of the sons of 'Abd ad-Dar lay slain beneath the standard, fathers and sons together. After this the flag was passed on to Artal ibn Shubayda of the house of Abdullah. Again it was Hamza who paid him his due. Then it was held for a while by Shuray ibn Qarir, but he too was soon killed. Now there was none of the sons of 'Abd ad-Dar left to hold the flag aloft. One of their slaves stepped forth, a man by the name of Su'ab. He was killed by Quzman. In this way Quzman continued to inflict heavy loss upon the enemy. On one occasion he killed seven of them in one single attack.

When the Holy Prophet ﷺ was told about this, again he said, "So what, and even so, of what use is it to him? In spite of all his merit, he shall go to Hell." The Prophet's ﷺ blessed companions (Ashab-us-Safa) were greatly surprised at this, "How can this be," they wondered among themselves, "that he is of the people of Hell-fire?" but they refrained from asking out of respect for the Prophet ﷺ. Whatever questions they may have had in their mind, the time for their answer was rapidly approaching. For somewhat later Quzman was suddenly heavily wounded in battle, and he fell upon the battlefield, blood gushing from several wounds on his body.

Qatada bin Nu'man seeing him in this condition, immediately ran to his side and said to him, "I congratulate you, oh Quzman, you are tasting blessed martyrdom, you are drawing nigh to the Divine Presence, relinquishing your soul in His Name." Quzman however gave this answer, "I have nothing to do with these things you speak of, I don't understand your Shahada and all that; besides, I did not come here to fight in the name of any religion. As for your aim to proclaim the Word of Allah, that never even crossed my mind. All I wanted was to prevent the Quraysh from appropriating the date palms of Madinah, and to make a great name for myself, that is why I came."

Having spoken these words, he took his sword and split his gut with his own hand, dying a renegade and falling into the pit of eternal damnation. Only then did the Sahaba understand the wisdom of the enlightened Prophet ﷺ who by the light of his Prophethood was able to hear and see and know all things, and who had said about Quzman every time his name was mentioned, "He belongs to the dwellers of the fire."

As the battle was growing ever more pitched, the pagan womenfolk kept beating on their tambourines to embolden their men. The Muslim fighters carried out another assault. First Abu Jabir ibn 'Amr ibn Haram fell as a martyr, after him his brother-in-law 'Amr ibn Jamir was thrown onto the field, crying, "My God, I too wish to be martyred in Your cause! Together with my son I came here in Your Name, do not turn us away without granting us the taste of martyrdom!" With these words he threw himself into the fray and struck the enemy. Allah heard their prayer and both he and his son Hal'at bin 'Amr achieved martyrdom together.

After these martyrs, the famous Hanzala stepped out into the battlefield. His father's name was mentioned here just a short while ago, he was the depraved renegade Abu 'Amir. Hanzala had called out to him on the battleground, "Don't you dare slander the Holy Prophet ﷺ! Anyone who opposes the blessed Prophet ﷺ cannot be my father! Islam relies on the right of the blood bond (family), but the family tie not founded on right is abolished!" With this he turned on him to attack him, occasioning his flight.

This blessed champion was the brother-in-law of the hypocrite Abdullah bin 'Ubayy ibn Salul. The night he was to marry Abdullah's sister, he heard the news that the Holy Prophet ﷺ was going to war. Instantly he sprang out of the bed of his bride, and ran out to the battlefield, crying, "May my soul be ransom for the Prophet ﷺ," and began to forge ahead into the enemy lines. He came up to the headquarters of the commander of the Quraysh, Abu Sufyan. Just as he was about to bring down his sword upon the head of Abu Sufyan, the aide-de-camp of Abu Sufyan, Shahada ibn Aws came running from behind and felled this young Muslim fighter in his tracks. Still, this was a blow to the morale of the enemy.

On the other side, Abu Dujanah who had taken the famous sword of the Prophet ﷺ to battle under the condition of defending the Islamic Law without batting an eyelid in the face of death, had wound his red turban which meant to say, 'I take my life into my hands', and was thrashing at the unbelievers who stood in front of him. At one point he broke through the ranks of the unbelievers and reached the place where the women were singing courage to their menfolk with songs and tambourines. There stood Hind, the wife of Abu Sufyan, the commander of the unbelievers, and he rushed to attack her. Nobody could withstand the fury of his attack, so there was none who could approach in order to defend her.

Just as he was about to bring down his sword upon her head, he suddenly withdrew it, saying, "I will not pollute the sword of Muhammad ﷺ with the blood of a vile creature such as you." The Holy Prophet ﷺ was watching Abu Dujanah and conferred on him by his gaze the rank of marshal in the Divine Government. Above all, the companions intensely admired such bravery. However, the time had come for Abu Dujanah to encounter his appointed position in the Divine Palace beyond time and space. Several of the unbelievers banded together and suddenly sprang out of their concealment and wounded Abu Dujanah so gravely that he fell to the ground. Ali came running up and smote the unbelievers but even so, Abu Dujanah closed his eyes and turned his head towards the place where Rasulullah ﷺ was standing.

The Holy Prophet ﷺ commanded, "Bring Abu Dujanah to me, at whatever cost, and if you have to give your life to do it." All the Sahaba rushed to carry Abu Dujanah to the presence of the Holy Prophet ﷺ. Abu Dujanah embraced the Prophet's ﷺ feet, saying, "Endless thanks to Allah for giving me all I had asked for. Oh Rasulullah ﷺ, are you satisfied with me?" The Holy Prophet ﷺ replied with tears in his eyes, "How should I not be pleased with you? I am satisfied, and Allah is well pleased with you. Go now to your Lord and give Him my Salams." Thus Abu Dujanah entered the world of Divine Beauty while gazing at the beauty of Muhammad ﷺ. Moreover, when Abu Dujanah was mortally wounded, he had cried in his heart, "Oh my Lord, take me to die by the feet of Thy Beloved." This supplication was transmitted to the pure and shining heart of Ahmad, the Chosen One (Prophet Muhammad) ﷺ, and made him promptly give the order, "Quickly bring Abu Dujanah here to me." This is what is called the 'Faith of Love', may Allah vouchsafe us his blessed intercession.

Ali fought in such a way that not a pagan house remained in Mecca that had not been touched by his sword. If Hamza's two hands were the equivalent of a whole army, the sword of Ali which he held with both hands smote the unbelievers in front of him and stretched them to the ground. The army of the Quraysh began to retreat. First of all the women who were singing exciting tunes to the soldiers began to flee into the hills, even though Hind was at the head of them. The enemy threw off all their baggage and fled. Ali routed the battlefield. When the commander of the regiment of archers, Abdullah ibn 'Uways saw the state of confusion of the enemy, he said, despite the command of the Holy Prophet ﷺ, "There is now no more need to guard this pass. Ahead of us all is clear, let us go out onto the battlefield."

Even though Abdullah bin Jubayr insisted, "But Rasulullah ﷺ told us not to leave this place under any circumstances, unless he gave the command," he said, "Don't listen to him, the foe is defeated, no danger remains, why should we stay here and guard this place?" And so it happened that only seven or eight men remained with Abdullah ibn Jubayr, all the others left. The commander of the right wing of the enemy army, Khalid ibn Walid who was an expert in battle stratagem, realized what was happening. By conducting a turning maneuver on the Muslim lines, he launched a sudden attack.

Abdullah bin Jubayr and his seven or eight archers were hopelessly overpowered, and although they defended their position valiantly to their last breath, they all fell as blessed martyrs. The fortunes of battle that had at first been favorable for the Muslims suddenly reversed and turned against them.

In fact, since the beginning of the battle, Khalid ibn al-Walid had been observing the left wing of the Muhammadan army, but he was prevented from attacking them because of the archers stationed there. Now he found the opportunity. After gaining control of this position, it became an easy task to strike the Muslim army from behind. The Muslim warriors who just a moment ago had been victorious were surprised by this sudden turn of events.

The Martyrdom of Hamza

The time drew nigh for the Prophet's ﷺ favorite uncle, Hamza to suffer holy martyrdom. Hamza killed one of the most entrenched enemies of Islam, Sabah Gawshani. This lion of Islam fought so fiercely, it was impossible to come near to him. The pagans considered how they might do away with this tireless warrior, and as no one could come close to him, they pondered on ways of destroying him from a distance. The deed was done by Hind's Abyssinian slave Wahshi, who was skilled in the art of spear throwing. This unfortunate miscreant, blinded by desire for worldly gain, hurled his spear from cowardly concealment, and Hamza was seriously wounded. Just as Hamza was about to reciprocate, his soul was taken from him.

Wahshi cut out the liver from the corpse of the Holy Prophet's ﷺ most beloved uncle, and he cut off his ears and brought them to Hind, the wife of Abu Sufyan, the mother of Mu'awiya, the grandmother of Yazid. Hind began to chew on his liver, but she could not swallow it. That is why she was called 'the eater of the liver' (akalat-al-kabad). She took the ears of this blessed person, strung them on a string and hung them around her neck, and presented her own necklace to his slayer, Wahshi. She promised to pay him the remainder of his reward upon her return to Mecca and to never be remiss in her feelings of gratitude towards him until the day she died.

When the Muslims witnessed Hamza being killed, they were totally perplexed. Thus Ibn Qam'iah killed the Muslim standard-bearer Mus'ab bin Amir, making him a martyr. Mus'ab bore a strong resemblance to the Holy Prophet ﷺ, and suddenly word went round that the Holy Prophet ﷺ had fallen. This false rumor completely confounded the Muslim warriors, and even the most steadfast and valiant among them were as if their backbone had been broken.

The valued companion Yaman was thus martyred by Muslim hands, although his son Hudhayfa cried out, "Don't strike him, he is my father." In the face of this, Hudhayfa cried out loudly, "Oh Lord, they did it unknowingly, forgive the Muslims for it!" and he carried away his father's corpse. Both Yaman and Thabit ibn Waq'ash were old men, and the Holy Prophet ﷺ had not wanted them to go out to battle, but both had insisted, so the Holy Prophet ﷺ had accepted their pleas and they attained their goal.

In this way, the whole Muslim army was thrown into disarray. Only twelve fighters remained around the Holy Prophet ﷺ and they formed a protective ring around him. The Prophet ﷺ himself entered the protection of Faith and was sheltered beneath the shield of Divine Love. From time to time, he prostrated himself in sajda, saying, "Oh my Lord, do You not wish for Your Unity to be made known?"

Umm Ummara Joins the Battle

As already mentioned, the rumor that the Holy Prophet ﷺ had been slain left even the most determined of men in a witless state of mind. Umm 'Umarra, hearing that the Holy Prophet ﷺ was dead, threw herself into the fray of the battle, yelling, "Ya Rasulullah!" Zayd bin Asim's wife Nusayba, of the family of Ma'zin bin Najash, the daughter of Ka'b al-Ansar - one of the great mothers of Islam - had taken the oath of allegiance to the Holy Prophet ﷺ at Aqaba. Together with her husband and son, she had invited the Prophet ﷺ to come to Madinah. Now she threw herself upon the enemy and attacked them furiously, striking out at whomever she could reach, while at the same time searching tearfully for the Holy Prophet ﷺ.

Meanwhile, the Holy Prophet's ﷺ general, Ali, was fighting the pagans with such fury and speed that his striking sword resembled a flash of lightning as it rose and fell on the battlefield. He, too, was looking for the Mirror of Truth, Muhammad's ﷺ blessed countenance, which was nowhere to be seen. 'Umar ibn al-Khattab threw his sword aside and remained motionless in a desolate mood. The uncle of Anas bin Malik, Anas Abu Nadir saw 'Umar sitting there disconsolately as he was passing to the other side while trying to break through the enemy lines. He asked him, "Oh 'Umar, what is it with you that you are sitting here, your weapons thrown aside?" 'Umar answered, "Whom should I fight for now that the Prophet is killed?" Abu Nadir then said to him, "Oh 'Umar, come to your senses and rise from your seat! Know that the presence of Muhammad ﷺ who is a manifestation of the Divine Unity cannot ever disappear! The time to really fight has now come!"

These words of Abu Nadir infused 'Umar with new life, he reached for his sword and took up fighting the enemy with renewed vigor. Abu Nadir was wounded in eighty places. He was so disfigured by the many lance thrusts that none could recognize him except his sister. When she heard that there was an unknown martyr, she went to the field and identified him by the tips of his fingers.

Now the Muslims began to stir anew and their battle spirit was rekindled. Everybody was out looking for the Holy Prophet ﷺ, but the first person to espy him was Ka'b bin Malik. As he was wearing his helmet, all that was seen of him were his blessed eyes. Those blessed eyes which were a window to the Truth, met the eyes of Ka'b bin Malik who cried out, "Oh Muslims, here is the Prophet ﷺ, he is here!" In his great joy, he showed them to the place. All the Sahaba came running to where he stood and ringed around him. But the unbelievers had also heard Ka'b's cry of joy, and they drew near the spot as well. Ali and his comrades scattered the pagans closest to the Prophet ﷺ.

The unbelievers joined forces and they launched a second attack on the Holy Prophet ﷺ. This time they came very close. The Sahaba lay on top of the Holy Prophet ﷺ protecting him with their bodies as a shield, and taking the rain of arrows upon themselves. Some were wounded and some died as martyrs. Talha's arm was wounded in defense of the Prophet ﷺ and he was disabled.

The noble lady warrior Umm Ummara already mentioned passed between Ibn Qami'ah and the Holy Prophet ﷺ just as he attacked the Prophet ﷺ with a fierce blow of his sword. Umm Ummara struck him with her own sword, but the accursed Ibn Qami'ah was wearing double armor and the sword cut through only one layer of armor. Ibn Qami'ah dealt Umm Ummara a blow that hit her armpit, but the Holy Prophet ﷺ held out his blessed hands and stroked her shoulder, and she was miraculously healed in an instant. Thereupon this noble lady said, "Oh Rasulullah, I wished to become a martyr from the bottom of my heart, but you have kept me from it." That noble mother of Islam later struck yet another one of the most vicious enemy warriors who attacked the Holy Prophet ﷺ, and cut his leg in two so that he fell from his mount.

According to one narration the son and husband of this lady were seriously injured and at the point of martyrdom, when they heard the voice of Umm Ummara, they called out, "Oh mother, let me just see you one more time," and her husband called, "Come, my sweet wife, sit by my side for a bit," but Umm Ummara answered, "They are attacking the Holy Prophet ﷺ, I must rush to defend him from their attack. Tell the Lord Almighty I am waiting to die by the side of the Holy Prophet ﷺ. May the Lord grant me, too, the rank of martyrdom! Go before me and give my Lord this message." That was her answer.

However, this great lady had already been promised a tremendously high rank in the life of eternity: One day the Holy Prophet # had held up his hands in prayer and prayed, "Oh my Lord, do not separate me from Umm Ummara and her family!" All the Sahaba had wept as she was given her rank. How great a distinction for Umm Ummara to be singled out by him who is honored with perfect favor in the Divine Presence!

The unbelievers attacked with increasing fury. Sa'd ibn Abi Waqqas shot the arrows given to him by the Holy Prophet # one by one and they each hit their goal without fail. Every time he handed him an arrow, he said to Sa'd: "Oh Sa'd, may my father and mother be your ransom, may Allah accept everything you say!" With these words, he conferred upon him the very highest rank. Therefore Allah Almighty granted every one of Sa'd ibn Abi Waqqas' wishes.

This fact was well known among the Sahaba, wherefore they said, "If we offend him we will necessarily receive a curse in return." They paid meticulous attention to be respectful of all his rights and wishes. In his old age, Sa'd lost the outward signs of his high rank, and the Sahaba said to him, "Oh Sa'd, you who are the beloved companion of the Holy Prophet #, why do you not pray for your eyesight to be restored, for whatever you wish for comes to pass." Sa'd ibn Abi Waqqas answered them, "I love the Divine Decree more than mine eyes; if I had one thousand eyes and all thousand of them became blind, I would not trade the opening of even one eye for His Decree."

Among the archers there was one youth in particular who attracted the Holy Prophet's # blessed attention. His expert marksmanship and skill pleased him greatly. He went up close to this youth. As he was shooting an arrow at the enemies of Islam, he heard him say, "Take this, my Qurayshi friend" to which the Holy Prophet # replied, while patting him on the shoulder, "My son, how much more you would have achieved had you shot your arrow in the name of Islam."

The Prophet 🕌 is Wounded

The pagans launched another fierce attack from another quarter, and this time they came very close to where the Holy Prophet 🕌 was standing. He was wounded in this onslaught and the destiny of Islam seemed to be endangered. There were four accursed persons of Quraysh who had sworn a pact to annihilate the Holy Prophet 🕌: `Utba ibn Abi Waqqas, Ibn Qami'ah, Ubbay bin Khalaf and Abdullah bin Shahab. The accursed `Utba ibn Abi Waqqas injured the Holy Prophet's 🕌 blessed lips. One of his teeth was broken, thereby martyred. The enemy of Allah Ibn Qami'ah struck the upper half of the Holy Prophet's 🕌 blessed countenance, the Mirror of Truth, and two of his helmet rings became embedded in his cheek.

As Abu 'Ubaydah was attempting to remove these rings from the Prophet's 🕌 blessed face, he pulled them out together with two of his own teeth. He was later asked by his companions, "While you were working at removing the rings from the Prophet's 🕌 blessed face, did you not feel the pain of your teeth being drawn out?" To this Abu 'Ubaydah r-plied, "What pain? When I drew near to the face of the Beloved of Allah, such was the flow of mercy that I received that nothing remained in me of myself." However, none can understand these words who has not reached to the station of 'ishq (Love), and is yet engrossed in the density of this material world. For those, our words have no meaning. Only this much let us say: generally when a man falls in love with a girl, at the sight of her he feels no desire for food or sleep, nor does he feel any pain. This state may be likened to that of intoxication with the Divine; it is a spiritual opiate to which Abu 'Ubaydah had access. May Allah endow our words with beneficence.

The Glory of all the World, the Prophet Muhammad 🕌 was bleeding heavily from his face, and he wiped his hand over the wound in order to still the flow of blood. He said, "Oh Lord, what good can come to a people who have blooded their Prophet's 🕌 face? No good can come of them, but they did it because they do not know, so forgive them." For the Lord had made plain His Divine Will: "If only one drop of My Beloved's blood falls to the ground, I will manifest My overwhelming power." The Holy Prophet interceded with the Lord, pleading, "Oh Lord, my people are ignorant, if only Thou wouldst guide them." He thereby forestalled the Anger of the Divine.

Ali was trying to staunch the flow of blood. When the Holy Prophet's daughter Fatima heard in Madinah that her father, the Mercy to the Worlds, had fallen in battle, she ran to the battlefield. Seeing her father's pure face all covered in blood and her husband Ali soiled from trying to wash it off with water, she cried out in tears, "Oh beloved father of mine, they have cut your face because of your calling them to Allah!?" Having assessed the situation, she instantly began to wash his holy face with her own hands, but the blood would not cease to flow. She said to Ali, "Burn a piece of cloth, so we can staunch the wound with the ashes." So they burned a piece of cloth, Fatima laid it upon the wound with her own hands, and the flow of blood was stopped.

Then the Holy Prophet said, "Who will sell his life for me?" 'Umara bin Ziyad bin Saq'an said, "Oh Prophet of Allah, I am ready to do so," and he and the fourteen fighters he had brought along with him joined forces and threw themselves against the enemy, fighting until they all blissfully fell as martyrs. The Holy Prophet wished for Ziyad to be brought to his side, and they brought him to the Prophet's side before his soul had quite left his body. For Ziyad had wished to die gazing at the Prophet's holy face. Ziyad opened his eyes once more to gaze with love upon the pure countenance of Muhammad; he pronounced the words of the Shahada and was reunited with the Divine Presence. How blessed was he to surrender his soul while resting in the Holy Prophet's lap! Could there be any station higher than this? Was Ziyad the only holder of this station, to die in the favor of the Prophet's embrace? Certainly not, for most of the fighters in the cause Islam achieved this lofty station.

Allah Offers Martyrdom

A Muslim was eating some dates when the Holy Prophet announced that the Lord Almighty Himself had offered the cup of martyrdom, and called for those wishing to attain that rank to come forth. The man thought to himself, "Perhaps by the time I finish eating these dates I will be too late to obey my Lord's command," and he threw the dates away. On account of one word from the blessed mouth of the Holy Prophet 🌸 he threw himself into the fray without delay and fought until he was cut down and martyred. Then again, there was Wahab bin Kabus who holds one of the foremost ranks in the Divine Order of things. Of him as great a personality as 'Umar was to say, "Oh, if only I could be like Kabus, if only I could pass into the afterlife as the son of Kabus did."

Wahab bin Kabus together with his cousin Qaris bin 'Aqad was on his way from Jabal Muzayana to Madinah to visit the Holy Prophet 🌸, ignorant of the battle that was being waged. No sooner had he reached Madinah where he heard the news of the Prophet's 🌸 engagement in battle against the unbelievers, then he immediately set out for Uhud to join in the fray. He reached the army of the Prophet 🌸 at a most critical moment. Because of the archers' mistake and disobedience to the Holy Prophet's 🌸 advice, the Muslim army was surrounded and forced to withdraw. The enemy made use their momentary strength in attacking the Prophet's 🌸 position with full force. Wahab – may Allah be well pleased with him – fought against the unbelievers with such force that he seemed to be a whole army of men, as though he had been granted extraordinary spiritual powers. The enemy was dispersed, but another group launched a second attack. The Holy Prophet 🌸 asked, "Who will go out against this new wave of attackers?" Wahab bin Kabus was worn out from fighting and had withdrawn into a corner to rest. Despite this, he instantly rose and said, "By your leave, oh Prophet of Allah 🌸, I will go out and fight them anew." This answer of Wahab's, colored with the colors of Divine Love and Faith pleased the Holy Prophet 🌸 greatly. "Rise, Wahab," he said; "I give you the good news of Allah."

These words promising him the highest of all ranks issuing from the blessed mouth of the Prophet 🌸 were the strongest weapon Wahab possessed. Again he fought the enemy forces to his utmost power, and again he dispersed them, but now his force was spent, and according to the tidings of the Prophet ﷺ he was blissfully admitted into the Presence of the Divine. The Holy Prophet ﷺ went up to Wahab's dead body and stroked and kissed him. "Oh Wahab," he said, "I have come to visit you and I give Salams to your spirit, for I am pleased with you, and may Allah be pleased with you as well." Thereby he showed him the very highest station.

Now there was a certain Jew living in Madinah by the name of Mukhayriq who lived by the law of the prophet Musa and who was known for his great learning and virtue. This man had become Muslim, but out of consideration for his circumstances he had so far kept his Islam secret. However, when the battle of Uhud began, he felt a great yearning and desire to be of service to the Holy Prophet ﷺ. When he could not sit still any longer, he went to the heads of his clan and said to them, "Do you have any doubt that I am the most learned among you in the knowledge of the heavenly scripture?" They answered him at once, "No, we haven't a grain of doubt that you are the most knowledgeable amongst us all."

"Know then that the Prophet of the Last Times who has been foretold in all the Holy Books, is Muhammad ﷺ who this very day is fighting the pagan Quraysh at Uhud. For us it is the very best way to success if we joined him and lent him our support." "But today is the Sabbath, it is forbidden to us to do any work," they replied. Mukhayriq replied, "Muhammad ﷺ who is the first and the last of all the prophets, has come to change the Shari'a, the holy law. Let us cut a long matter short, you have just con-firmed that I know more about the laws of religion than all of you, so come along, let us sacrifice our souls for the sake of the Holy Prophet ﷺ this very day."

But though he tried his best, he could not persuade them to leave their error behind and to accept Islam as the true choice of Allah. Mukhayriq therefore proclaimed his faith in the new religion all alone, and came into the presence of the Holy Prophet ﷺ at Uhud. "Oh Prophet of Allah, will you accept me, I have come to give my life and soul for you, and I make over all my possessions and belongings to you. I ask you to dispense of my property in the cause of this noble religion and for the love of Muhammad

🌸, and for this battle fought for the sake of the Word of Allah." After that, he went out to fight. He fought with bravery and valor, and was at last slain, dying a martyr. The Holy Prophet 🌸 praised him when he said of him, "Mukhayriq is the best of his people.

Still the enemy cavalry pressed in on the Prophet 🌸. One of the enemy horsemen was 'Uthman bin Mughira of the Bani Makhzum – may his name be cursed. He attacked the Prophet Muhammad 🌸 and fell into the trench that Abu Amir had dug for the Holy Prophet 🌸. He was slain by the sword of Harith and plunged into the pit of everlasting despair.

Umm Ayman is Injured

At this point in the battle, Umm Ayman was injured. She was one woman whom the Holy Prophet 🌸 loved exceedingly much; she had been his wet-nurse and he honored her by saying about her, "(She is) my mother after my mother." This highly honored lady of Islam was one of the women who looked after the wounded in battle and distributed water. She was wounded by the treacherous Khayyam.

The Holy Prophet 🌸 said to Sa'd ibn Abi Waqqas, "Here, take this arrow and shoot the man who wounded my nurse," and he prayed after that to the Lord, "Oh Allah, make his arrow hit its mark!" The arrow Sa'd shot upon the Prophet's 🌸 command did not miss its mark and felled Khayyam to the ground. After this again Sa'd shot the arrow that the Prophet 🌸 gave him and killed one of the unbelievers, Malik bin Zuhayr who had hidden behind a rock and who had caused the Muslims great losses.

Though the enemy army had at one point very nearly routed the Muslims who were dispersed by attacking fighters, the Muslim army pulled itself together and the enemy was pushed back. Then there was a lull in the fighting.

The Holy Prophet 🌸 found it unsuitable to stay any longer on the open ground that he and his companions were occupying, and they withdrew to a more protected position behind the mountain of Uhud. When Abu Sufyan saw the Muslims gathering on the plain of Mt. Uhud, he contemplated attacking them again with another band of soldiers. But the Holy Prophet ﷺ prayed to Allah Almighty, saying, "Oh my Lord, do not permit these unbelievers to climb these heights, so that they might not defeat this handful of true believers; prevent them from achieving this!" In answer to the Holy Prophet's ﷺ supplication the pagans were not able to scale the heights of Mt. Uhud.

The Meccans finally decided to withdraw, but before they went, Abu Sufyan wished to have certain news of the Holy Prophet's ﷺ condition. "Is Muhammad with you?" The Holy Prophet ﷺ commanded his companions to give no answer. This time Abu Sufyan asked, "Is Abu Bakr with you?" and he yelled three times, but again the Prophet ﷺ would let no one answer for him. After this Abu Sufyan asked about Ali and 'Umar, but no one answered.

Thereupon Abu Sufyan turned and said to his men, "This means to say that they are dead, the backbone of Islam is therefore broken. We have attained our goal; this new religion is extinguished." Hearing these vile words from the commander of the pagan army, 'Umar the general of the new Shari'a could stand no more. He turned and yelled back at him, "Oh no, you vile and treacherous one, who has declared war on Allah and His Holy Prophet ﷺ, go tell your men that Allah has withered the lips of him who tries to extinguish this religion! All those about whom you ask are among the living, and they are soldiers of Allah's army. They will come to exact their revenge on you yet."

When Abu Sufyan heard 'Umar speak these intrepid words, he was greatly astonished, and all he could say was, "The fortunes of war are variable. Today we have had our revenge for the Battle of Badr." But 'Umar yelled back at him again, answering, "Nay, it is not at all like that, in this too, you are in error. For our victory is from the bounty of Allah, while your victory is from the world of the fire which is the place of purification for the unbelievers." Abu Sufyan then called upon the idols that he worshipped, and honored them, saying, "Oh great Hubal!" The Holy Prophet ﷺ, a confirmed servant of the Lord, commanded 'Umar to reply in such a way as to affirm the Unity of Allah. 'Umar raised his voice and called out:

ALLAHU LA ILAHA ILLALLAH, ALLAH IS THE MOST HIGH AND ETERNAL.

Abu Sufyan, when he heard these words spoken in reverence, was confounded once more and could think of nothing to say but, "And we have 'Uzza as well." To this 'Umar replied once more, "And Allah is our Lord." Abu Sufyan then said, "Oh 'Umar, your word is more to me than the word of Ibn Qami'ah, tell me truthfully: is Muhammad still alive?" 'Umar replied, "I swear by Allah the Almighty that he is listening to all our prattle, that is the truth. Next year we will be back to measure ourselves against you, then we will see how it shall be."

The Death of Ubayy bin Khalaf

The Holy Prophet ❀ commanded 'Umar to speak these words, and 'Umar obeyed his order. Then he advised his companions to let him know immediately should they run into Ubayy bin Khalaf, and for no one to touch him. For before this time, while in Mecca, this man had said to the Prophet ❀ whenever he ran into him, "Oh Muhammad, I am feeding a horse named 'Awd, and it is from the back of this horse that I am going to kill you." The Holy Prophet ❀ had answered him, "Not so, for Allah Almighty will deal you death at my hands, while you are yet astride that horse."

This treacherous man had been taken prisoner at Badr, had been ransomed and saved, and yet had not changed his ways. He returned to fight the Prophet ❀ at Uhud. Suddenly he approached Muhammad, yelling at the top of his voice, "It's you or I, Muhammad!" The Prophet's ❀ companions closed round him and prepared to assail him, but the Holy Prophet ❀ had forbidden them to touch him, and ordered them to let him know when he came. Speaking the name of Allah upon his lance, he stepped out in front of them all, and hurled his lance at the accursed man, so that it broke his rib. The stricken man turned his horse and fled, crying out, "Muhammad has killed me!" Abu Sufyan met him and held him, saying, "What has happened to you, there is no injury to be seen, no blood, and you are a strong man, what is it with you?" But the man insisted, "I don't know what it is, or how I am wounded, but I know that this is going to kill me! I cannot stand this," and he rode on to the Meccan camp where indeed he died and went into the everlasting fire, which is the place of cleansing for those who disbelieved.

Later the Holy Prophet 🕸 was asked about these events, and he explained that when he had thrown his lance, the angel Jibra'il had lifted up the rib so that the weapon struck his liver and destroyed it. Then the angel had lowered the rib again so that there was no visible trace. Yet, the man was mortally wounded.

The pagans were finally convinced that they would not succeed in defeating the Muslims completely that day, so eventually they turned away from them, and rode back to camp.

The Holy Prophet 🕸 ordered Muhammad ibn Maslama to find Sa'd bin Rabi', and he added, "I have seen Sa'd with twelve spears stuck in him, and I love Sa'd as I love my own eyes. Go and find him for me!" Muhammad ibn Maslama went out to the battlefield to find Sa'd. He went about calling, "Sa'd bin Rabi', where are you?" but he received no answer. At last, he called, "Oh Sa'd, I have been sent by the Holy Prophet 🕸 to find you, it is my blessed duty to find you, he wishes to know what happened to you." Hearing the Holy Prophet's 🕸 name mentioned, Sa'd then answered, "I am among the slain, and at this moment I am contemplating the Presence of Allah; I am submerged in the fragrance of Paradise, gazing at the Beauty of the Divine, drunk with the Love of Muhammad 🕸; come to me, here I am." These words led him to where he lay.

Muhammad ibn Maslama ran to the place the voice came from, and he found Sa'd in a pool of blood. He took him in his arms and once more Sa'd opened his eyes. "You have been sent by Muhammad 🕸, oh Muhammad bin Maslama?" he asked him. When Muhammad bin Maslama answered him that this was so, he said to him, "Tell our revered Prophet ﷺ that I am sending him my Salams, and tell him that I have attained the Presence of the Beloved. Go give my Salams also to my people and say to them that if they wish to attain supreme success they should serve and support the Holy Prophet ﷺ, and seek to increase their love for him. Tell them that as long as they possess the strength to flutter an eyelid they should not fail in his service." Then saying, "Oh Rasulullah, may you be satisfied with me!" he closed his eyes and surrendered his soul, entering the abode beyond all space.

The Holy Prophet ﷺ wandered across the battlefield and stopped in front of each of the martyrs, gazing at each one separately. His eyes filled with tears that Allah alone could dry and they fell upon each one of the martyrs. He prayed for each of them each and informed of their various stations. When he came upon his blessed uncle Hamza, the great lion of Islam and champion of mankind, the most valiant hero among all the other martyrs, he saw what had been done to him, how his blessed corpse had been mutilated, his ears cut off, his liver torn out. He threw himself upon his dear uncle's holy body.

Never had the Holy Prophet ﷺ been seen to be so affected by anything as by these barbarous acts perpetrated on his beloved uncle, they were most hurtful to the Prophet ﷺ. As the Lord saw that His beloved Prophet ﷺ would not be able to bear the pain, He sent the angel Jibra'il to show him the high station Hamza now occupied in the Divine Presence. Then he was ordered to pray the prayer of the dead for the martyrs, and he prayed for every single one of them. When he came to pray over his uncle Hamza, he was so overcome that he could not pray. After he was composed, he prayed not less than seven times.

The Funeral Prayer in Islam

Oh Traveler on the road to Truth! You who are seeking the light of real knowledge! Even if it is an aside from our main topic here, I cannot pass without at least a brief mention of how immensely important the funeral prayer is in Islam.

In the illustrious religion of Islam, the funeral prayer tells of the spiritual station which material man occupies in the Divine Presence, and Islam is the only religion to possess such form of worship. It is a station reserved for the Holy Prophet 🕸 that is hereby open to all mankind, as a Divine grant for his nation. It is a form of prayer that combines similarity with exception, for in that it consists of Qiyam (standing in prayer) it shows its similitude, and in that it contains no ruku' (bowing low) or sajda (prostration), it shows its exception. This is how the funeral prayer is prayed: The dead body of the Muslim is placed before the congregation praying the funeral prayer. The imam leading the funeral prayer stands at the height of the dead man's chest, making his inner reality to be his Qibla. But lest any take this for a sign of idolatry, I hasten to elucidate as follows:

The chest is the location of *iman* (faith); the heart located at its center is the site of the call to Allah. On this site the Divine Gaze is trained, and it is the center of the organization of the human being. Therefore, when a true believer leaves this world and reaches his Lord, Allah Almighty orders the Muslims: "The heart of this servant of Mine was full of faith, and it was the established resting place of love, for Myself and My Beloved. This servant lived with Me, he walked with Me and rested in Me, he hurt no one, and he never inclined towards idolatry, disbelief, or hypocrisy. He was never slave to any tyrant. He always preserved his inner secret in the fairest of forms. In brief, he did not damage his distinction of *"laqad karramna bani adama"* (We have honored the Children of Adam – The Night Journey 70). He was not separated from Me for a single moment. Now he has passed into the other world and come to Me. Rise now and make him to be your Qibla! I graciously deign to descend upon his inner reality, so pray the funeral prayer over him, for in truth the Qibla is ever Mine," speaks the Lord. This is the significance of the funeral prayer.

Therefore, when the Holy Prophet 🕸 was about to pray the funeral prayer over his beloved uncle Hamza, he plainly perceived the Descent of Divine

Grace and could not get his fill of it. For that, he stood again and again, intoning the prayer anew.

More Examples of Pious Women

The sister of Hamza, Safiya, had come running out from Madinah to the field of Uhud as soon as she heard the news of her brother Hamza. The Holy Prophet ﷺ gave orders to the Companions to keep her away from the body of her dead brother, lest she see the state he was in. While the Companions tried to deter her from searching for the body of Hamza among the fallen, this blessed lady spoke, "Don't try to hide my brother from me, I know he has fallen as a martyr. It is not such a terrible thing to die for the sake of Allah, in exchange for his soul my brother has received great reward and immeasurable gain. That is to say, Allah Almighty Himself has ransomed him which is why I wish to see his holy body."

When he heard this answer from Safiya which bespoke of her deep faith and a heart filled with love and closeness to the Almighty, the Prophet ﷺ changed his mind and told his Companions to show her the body, saying, "She has earned the right to see him," while at the same time he prayed, "Oh my Lord, just as You have shown me the special rank my uncle Hamza holds in your Divine Presence, show it also to his sister who is the embodiment of love and faith." So they told her what had happened to the blessed body of Hamza and showed him to her. Safiya beheld the body of Hamza in the shape it is preserved in the Divine Presence, fully aware and in a wakeful state, sentient perception of his station, and she asked of him his intercession, while to people in general he appeared as a mutilated corpse. She touched him with fondness, reciting the holy words:

inna llillahi wa inna ilayhi radhi`un.

Surely we belong to God and to Him we return. (The Cow, 156)

This lady was not the only example of perfect love of faith that the Holy Prophet ﷺ implanted in the hearts of those blessed martyrs in a brief period of time. Countless other examples could be cited, and assuming the reader's consent, we shall mention here yet another blessed lady.

There was a woman of the Ansar who had one son who was a paragon of beauty and a brother and a husband, who both excelled in bravery. When she was informed of the death as martyrs of her dearest ones, successively, this respectable lady cried out repeatedly, "I want you to give me news of the Holy Prophet 🌸!" In the end she learned where the Holy Prophet 🌸 was and she went to him and gazed at his blessed countenance, which mirrors the aspect of the Divine, and she called out, "Oh Rasulullah, now that I am seeing your blessed face all my troubles and woes are as nothing to me."

What a wealth of religious sensitivity, what ardent love of faith! Thereafter the Holy Prophet 🌸 had all the martyrs gathered. The spiritual beings of these warriors having departed for the Presence of the Divine, their pure and blessed remains, which are likened to the soul's bride, were wrapped in their winding sheets, covered as they were in their martyr's blood. Without being washed they were reposed with awe and veneration in the earth who is their original mother, while the Holy Prophet 🌸 addressed the congregation as follows: "I bear witness that these friends of mine placed their own self-interest last and that they surrendered their lives and souls in Allah's cause. Yes, in the eternal world to come, on that second Day of Gathering, those who were wounded for the sake of Allah will rise from their graves, blood flowing afresh from their wounds. No man nor angel will at that instance not feel passionate love for the color of that martyr's blood, and indeed will become intoxicated on the scent issuing from it."

How fortunate that man for whom none other than the Holy Prophet 🌸 bears witness! As much as he has said to Jabir, "Oh Jabir, when your father was dying the death of the martyr, Allah Almighty spoke to him without intermediary, and without veils and said to him, 'Oh My servant, you who are giving up your life and soul for My sake! Whatever it is you wish for, tell Me, let Me know your every desire!' Thereupon your father answered, 'Oh My Lord, I have attained the goal of my faith in that I have come to You.

What more is there left to wish for? Only for those whom I left behind in this world do I wish that they should know of my condition and of what You have granted to us.' For the sake of your martyred father's request, the Lord Almighty has commanded me through the revelation of these verses to make known the fate of the martyrs:

Count not those who were slain in God's way as dead, but rather living with their Lord, by Him provided, rejoicing in the bounty that God has given them, and joyful in those who remain behind and have not joined them, because no fear shall be on them, neither shall they sorrow, joyful in blessing and bounty from God, and that God leaves not to waste the wage of the believers. And those who answered God and the Messenger after the wound had smitten them -to all those of them who did good and feared God, shall be a mighty wage; those to whom the people said, 'The people have gathered against you, therefore fear them'; but it increased them in faith, and they said, 'God is sufficient for us; an excellent Guardian is He.'"

(The House of Imran, 169-173)

In this battle, the Muslims lost over seventy men who fell as martyrs, mostly from the Ansar. Their pure remains were delivered two by two to their original element, Mother Earth. For many of them no winding sheet could be found, such as Mus'ab bin 'Umayr, the great standard-bearer of Islam, whose garment was not long enough to cover his feet. They covered them instead with branches from the rue-bush. Those who were close to one another and good friends in life were laid together in their graves in death. Hamza' s nephew (the son of his sister) was buried together with Abdullah bin Jahsh; Abu Jabir, his brother-in-law 'Amr bin Jamul and Khazraj bin Zayd were all laid in a grave together. There were also many wounded among the Muslims who needed to be looked after and attended.

The losses of the enemy did not exceed thirty men. The Muslims were full of deep remorse for not having heeded the advice of the Holy Prophet 🕉 at the outset of the battle. The Prophet 🕉 therefore gathered them all and addressed them: "Be not overly distraught, for you have been forgiven. The conquest of Mecca is near. However, be wary now, for the band of hypocrites is about to split off. We return to Madinah, and you will see clearly on their faces who is a true believer in Islam and who is not. The hypocrites will be weeded out."

The Holy Prophet ﷺ turned once more towards the martyrs buried in the field, gave them his tender Salams and bade them farewell. Then he turned back towards Madinah with his Companions, although his blessed face was wounded. When the seriously injured were taken aside to be cared for, he spoke to the Companions of the condition of the enemy. "Now Abu Sufyan is thinking, 'Why didn't we complete what we had set out to do, to eliminate the Muslim threat?' and he will be planning a new attack. Ikrimah, the son of Abu Jahl is lamenting, 'The revenge for my father's death is not yet complete, although we have dealt a painful blow to the Muslims, we are yet returning without having settled with them once and for all, we have not entirely eradicated them.' Is there not one person among you who will show them that Islam is here to stay, that the cause of 'La ilaha illAllah' will remain until the Last Day? We ought to follow them and make sure that their taste for launching a new attack is thoroughly spoilt, so that they understand that the essential reality of Islam has not been weakened."

Upon this Abu Bakr and Zubayr together with seventy men made ready on the spot, presenting themselves before the Holy Prophet ﷺ, saying, "Your wish is our command, oh Rasulullah!" After the Holy Prophet ﷺ had prayed the morning prayer with them in the Prophet's Mosque in Madinah, he called for Bilal al-Habashi, and commanded him to call out: "Let all the fighters of the Battle of Uhud assemble here, let them prepare to pursue the enemy." Bilal called out this command of the Holy Prophet ﷺ with his strong voice, and the valiant warriors came running. Those who were only lightly wounded tied up their wounds and came along.

On the other side, Abu Sufyan had gone as far as Rawha when he decided to return to Madinah and launch a second attack on Islam. The Holy Prophet ﷺ left the city of Madinah under the aegis of Ibn Ummi Maktum and gave the Muslim standard into Ali's hands. Although he himself had been injured, he mounted his steed and counting the seventy men Abu Bakr had assembled round him, there were six-hundred warriors setting out from Madinah that day.

They reached a place called Hamru-al-Asad at a distance of eight miles from the city, there the Holy Prophet ❀ decided to set up camp. Abu Ma'bad, the chief of the Khuza'a, gave them his condolences for the losses they had suffered at Uhud. Ma'bad told them he was intending to travel to Mecca on some business and bid them farewell. Although the Khuza'a were not yet declared Muslims, their hearts already inclined towards Islam. When Abu Ma'bad passed the place of Rawha he made sure to call on Abu Sufyan. In the course of their conversation, Abu Sufyan asked him for news, as Ma'bad had expected him to. Ma'bad answered, "Wallahi, by God, I don't know, but Muhammad is moving against you with an army the likes of which I have not seen before, composed in particular of those who were not able to come to Uhud with him." "How is that possible," exclaimed Abu Sufyan, "we had all but eliminated their main power and thrust!" "That I can't say, all I know is that I have never seen such an army. They came to Hamra-al-Asad. Before you leave this place here, I think you will be seeing the hooves of their horses." As soon as Safwan bin Umayya - may his name be cursed – heard this, he said to Abu Sufyan, "Come, now that we have emerged victorious, let us not return to be beaten and defeated." Abu Sufyan's heart then filled with fear, and abandoning his plans, he returned to Mecca.

The Holy Prophet ❀ meanwhile returned to Madinah. The city was filled with grief, there were tears shed in every house except in the houses of the hypocrites whose faces were glad. When the Holy Prophet ❀ heard the shrill wails of the women coming from every house, he said, "Only for my uncle there is none who would weep," and he added with tears brimming in his blessed eyes, "My dearest uncle, is there no one left at all to cry for you?" When the Ansar heard these words of the Holy Prophet ❀ they came running with their wives to the presence of the Prophet ❀ to give their condolences. From then on it became customary for each house to mention foremost the name of Hamza when bemoaning the dead and fallen. They sought to please of the Holy Prophet ﷺ by adopting this practice. The Holy Prophet ﷺ only forbade loud manifestations of grief like weeping and wailing, loud screaming and beating oneself, as was the custom in those times. He did say, however, that the tears flowing from grief are a rain of mercy in their own right.

Nowadays some people have abandoned these prophetic injunctions and the spiritual dimensions of this religion. The Holy Prophet ﷺ has taught a valuable lesson to those cold-hearted people who fail to understand these issues. Some people claim that in Islam there is no such thing as mourning; nay, they go even further. If a Muslim who loves his Prophet ﷺ more than he loves his own soul, happens to look a bit sad on the day that those lofty persons who were a living particle of the King of Prophets ﷺ passed away, they will say to him, "Oh my brother, how is it that you are out of sorts today? You do not belong to the people of error, do you? For you must know, surely, that there is no mourning in Islam."

This we do not understand very well: if there is no mourning in Islam, that is to say, if there is no compassion – may God forbid this ever be so - is our whole religion then swindle and fraud? Oh no, on the contrary, Islam is a religion of decency and decorum, kindness and compassion, and above all, mercy. When, for example, our neighbor dies, you will never express yourself lightly and pleasurably on that day. How much more must this be the case when one of the great personages of Islam is engulfed by sorrow! How can it be counted among the precepts of our religion to remain as unmoved as a piece of wood by such events? It must be understood that the compassion felt in the face of any disaster is a mercy resulting from familiarity with the venerated Prophet ﷺ; on that account, how could this coldness of feeling towards him be evidence of anything but the lack of connectedness to the Holy Prophet ﷺ, the Glory of the Worlds?

The Military Defeat at Uhud

Oh you who wish to taste of the sweetness of faith! We now ask ourselves this question: what wisdom lay in the defeat of the blessed Sahaba at the

Battle of Uhud? We shall try to give an answer. There were those who would readily give their whole heart for this noble religion of Islam and follow the Holy Prophet ﷺ perfectly and there were those of doubtful adherence to the faith, that is to say, the hypocrites. Of the second group, there were some who were to enter Islam in the future, for example Khalid ibn al-Walid, who was a genius of warfare. For the sake of the good deeds to be performed in the future, Allah Almighty in His Divine Wisdom and Subtlety permitted him this show of outward success, as a pre-empted reward, so that all his might and glory might not be broken.

For Khalid's most glorious and honor-filled future was yet to come when the Light of the Quran - which is the backbone of all Islam - would blot out his stubbornness and zealotry. Moreover, at the armistice of Hudaybiyah, they were defeated by the sword of the Quran. In submission to the power residing at Madinah they bowed their heads and accepted Islam. Khalid ibn al-Walid became a great and mighty commander and was raised to the rank of "Sayfullah," the "Sword of Allah." He came to be one of the mightiest swords in the conquests of Islam and is counted amongst the most eminent of the Sahaba.

It is related that when the Holy Prophet ﷺ was in great distress and separated from all of the Sahaba during the Battle of Uhud, the Lord of the Worlds sent to him five angels. The angels said to him, "Oh Rasulullah, we have come to your aid, whatever you wish, we will do it." One of the angels said, "I am the angel in charge of the wind; if it is your wish, I will blow your enemies to pieces as happened to the people of 'Ad." The Holy Prophet ﷺ said to him, "Go away and tend to your own business." The second angel came and said, "Oh Prophet of Allah! I am the angel in charge of fire; if you command me, I will rain fire upon them and burn them up, for the Lord has sent us to thee!" But the Holy Prophet ﷺ wished to accept no help from this angel either.

Then the third angel came up to him and said, "As I caused the earth to open in order to swallow Qarun, thus I will cause the earth to open and close over all of them, if you will only permit me." The fourth angel came and said, "I am the angel in charge of the waters; if you permit, I will drown them in a flood like the flood of Nuh, though this be a waterless country." And the fifth angel spoke and said, "I am the angel of thunder and lightning. Allow me, and I will strike them with bolts of lightning and destroy them utterly."

The Holy Prophet ﷺ then wept, "Oh my Lord, have mercy on my people, for they do not know me. If they knew they would not act as they do." He refrained from asking the Lord to destroy his enemies, he prayed for His mercy upon them. He said then, "Maybe there are some among them who are Muslims, or some whose children will become Muslim – how should I curse them?" and he did not do so. Despite the fact that they did him such harm and caused him so much hurt, he would not curse them, for all prophets' curses instantly take effect, but they also decrease the rank and station of that prophet. Therefore the Prophet Muhammad ﷺ became a Mercy for the Worlds.

Events that Shaped
the Growing Muslim Community

Events of Bir Ma'una

In the fourth year of the Hijra in the month of Safar, Abu Bara' `Amir bin Malik bin Ja'far, the chief of the tribe of Bani `Amir of the Najd came to Madinah to visit the Holy Prophet ﷺ. The Prophet ﷺ invited him to enter Islam, and he was not averse to it, but he said, "Send some Muslims to my tribe to instruct them in this new teaching." The Holy Prophet ﷺ said, "I do not trust the people of the Najd. They may do harm to my friends, and my companions are a trust given to me by Allah. I am responsible for their lives. Your nephew `Amir bin Tufayl has spoken such a word against me: 'Let the deserts be yours, and the cities be ours'. In these words is hidden treachery."

Abu Bara assured the Holy Prophet ﷺ repeatedly that he would guarantee the Muslims' safety and that he would give them a letter of safe passage. Finally the Prophet ﷺ ordered that a letter be written to `Amir bin Tufayl bin Malik, the nephew of the chief of the Bani `Amir, Abu Bara. It was not known in Madinah that within the tribe there was a dispute about the leadership, and that Abu Bara's nephew aspired to become the chief in his place. So, a deputation of Muslims was sent forth under Mundhir bin 'Amr, comprising seventy God-fearing, abstemious men, of the most exemplary among the Muslims in piety and knowledge, who made a living by gathering wood by day and selling it in the evening. Seventy men whose lives were firmly established in the faith were sent out to the Najd.

These noble personages went as far as the watering place called Bir Ma'una where they halted. The Prophet's ﷺ letter was given to Haram bin Milhan to deliver to 'Amir bin Tufayl, may his name be cursed. Before even looking at the letter he had been handed, this unbeliever rushed to kill the Prophet's ﷺ precious friend. Then he tried to incite the rest of the tribe to go out and kill the whole delegation of Muslims, but mostly they refused to violate the promise of security, which Abu Bara had given these men. Therefore, this accursed unbeliever appealed to the tribes of the Bani Sulaym of 'Usayya and Dhakwan who had recently had hostilities with Madinah, and gathering a force of men, they rushed on that group of pious men at Bir Ma'una who had come to instruct them in the Unity of Allah and to teach them about resurrection of death. All of them were massacred, but for one man who was left for dead, Ka'b bin Zayd of the Bani Najjar. This man was picked up from among the slain and eventually made his way back to Madinah.

Two men were out pasturing the camels at the time of this massacre, 'Amr bin Umayya al-Damri and Mundhir bin Muhammad bin 'Uqba, and thus they survived the slaughter. When they came to the scene of the disaster and saw what had happened, Mundhir ibn Muhammad asked his companion 'Amr for his opinion on what they should do. 'Amr said, "We ought to return to Madinah and inform the Holy Prophet ﷺ of this state of affairs." But Mundhir bin Muhammad said, "I wish to remain here with my martyred brothers, I too wish to die a martyr and return to Allah forthwith!" With these words he threw himself upon the enemies of God and His Holy Prophet ﷺ and fought until he fell a martyr. 'Amr was taken prisoner, but 'Amir bin Tufayl set him free after learning his name and lineage, for he said, "My mother has vowed to free a slave. On this account I set you free." This noble person returned safely to Madinah. When the Beloved of Allah ﷺ learned of what had befallen at Bir Ma'una, he was greatly aggrieved and distressed, in fact it may be said that no other event affected him as strongly as this. For one whole month, he invoked against the treachery of these unbelievers at the end of each prayer. It was not long before each and every one of them came to grief and was plunged into the pit of eternal damnation.

The Day of Raji'

The same year some men from the lesser tribes of 'Adal and al-Qara came to the Holy Prophet ﷺ saying, "We have accepted Islam and are therefore in need of some instruction. Please send us some people who can teach us what we need to know of Islam." The Holy Prophet ﷺ sent Asim bin Thabit of Aws back with them, together with fourteen companions. When they had reached a watering place called Raji' between 'Asfan and Mecca, the hypocrites of the tribe of Hudhail made plain the treacherous villainy within their hearts, and betrayed them by summoning the other branches of Hudhail for support against them. When the Bani Lihyana of Hudhail received this call, they sent one-hundred archers and two-hundred warriors to lie in wait for the Muslims. The Muslims realized the situation and immediately sought refuge behind a mountain. The unbelievers surrounded the mountain and called out, "If you give yourselves up, you may get away with your lives, otherwise we shall kill you all!" The Muslims answered, "We are Muslims and we are disciples of Muhammad, the Prophet ﷺ. We will never accept quarter from an unbeliever!"

Asim raised his hands and prayed to the Lord, his heart burning within him, "Oh Allah, I have only one request, and that is that You should make known to Your Beloved Muhammad ﷺ the plight of this handful of believers, that is all I would pray for at this moment." For these great Sahaba it was of the utmost importance that the Beloved of Allah, the Holy Prophet ﷺ be satisfied and pleased with them, more so even than attaining the everlasting peace and bliss of Paradise. The station of these Sahaba was that of soldiers of Love, and Love means giving pleasure to the Beloved; the Lover desiring the pleasure of his Beloved strives neither for glory nor for abasement. Therefore, Asim prayed to the Lord to make known to the Holy Prophet ﷺ that they went gladly to receive martyrdom for the cause of Islam. "Through the means of Your Power make it known to him," he prayed, and his prayer was accepted. As he was dying a martyr, Allah showed to His Holy Prophet ﷺ through spiritual communication that he had gone to the Presence of the Lord along with his Companions. Also, he learned that two of the Muslims had been captured, Khubayb of Aws and Zayd of Khazraj. The Prophet ﷺ informed his Companions of this without having left Madinah.

The unbelievers sent out some men to bring a part of Asim's dead body, (his skull, as at Uhud he had killed two of the standard-bearers of Quraysh whereupon their mother had sworn she would drink wine from his skull), but as he was dying, Asim had made yet another supplication to his Lord: "Oh Lord, do not let the enemy touch my dead body." The word of this great Lover of the Divine caused a great swarm of bees to appear on the material plane and set about his body so that the men sent by the idolaters could not approach from the density of that insect army and had to turn back.

As for the two captives, they were bound and brought back to Mecca and sold there. Khubayb was bought by the sons of Harith bin 'Amr whom he had killed in the Battle of Uhud, who sought to avenge their father's death. At one point during his imprisonment Khubayb called for a razor with which to clean himself before he was to die. The wife of Harith bin 'Amr saw him. Then she noticed that the three-year old grandson of Harith bin 'Amir was playing close by. The woman began to scream with fright, saying, "Now he will kill that child, he knows you intend to kill him, he will avenge himself on that child." But Khubayb answered her, "Don't worry, have no fear, for we are of those who have sat with Muhammad ﷺ and taken our lessons from the Holy Quran. We are the followers of him who is a mercy for the worlds. Feelings of revenge have no place with us, nor are we of those who act on the impulse of their egotistic drives, we will raise the sword against a man only in the name of Allah."

Some days later they took Khubayb outside of the precincts of the Haram to kill him. He asked only for enough time to pray two Rak'ats. The idolaters deliberated whether to grant him his wish or not, and after a long discussion they agreed to let him pray. For they said, "That moment will be more bitter for him than death, he will suffer the greatest suspense then." Khubayb stood before his Lord to pray, and he prayed his two Rak'ats with the greatest reverence and peace of mind and made supplication to his Lord Almighty. After the accursed unbelievers had discussed among themselves in what way they should kill him, he delivered himself of these verses, just in order to refute their wrong thoughts about him:

"As a Muslim I die; on account of Islam, my noble religion, my life is put to an end. It matters not how I surrender the boon of my soul; I yield it exultantly. Think you that I attach to it any importance? Whatever death I am to suffer, it is for the sake of the Almighty Allah. Even were I to be torn limb from limb, He will restore me, if He likes, to a perfect body in eternal gardens, and to a grant of most bounteous gifts."

Having recited these verses with dignity and composure, and after thus expressing his love, he added, "Oh my Prophet ﷺ, be my witness! I die a martyr to the God you have taught me!" and with these words on his lips, he surrendered his soul.

It is said that after the martyrdom of this lofty personality it became the custom for a condemned man to pray two Rak'ats before he is put to death.

The other captive, Zayd bin-al Dathinna of Khazraj was bought by Safwan bin 'Umayya to avenge on him the death of his father 'Umayya bin Khalaf. When they were about to put him to death, they invited all the chiefs of Quraysh to the execution. Abu Sufyan came at the head of them all and put the following question to Zayd: "Oh Zayd, now answer me truly, and know that if you give me the answer I wish to hear of you, you can be sure to have saved your life. This then is my question: if Muhammad were in your place and he were the one to be killed, would you not be happier for it?" This great lover of Allah replied, "What are you saying, accursed one, even were I to be cut to pieces and left to die bit by bit, I would not have a single thorn pierce the blessed body of our Holy Prophet ﷺ!" Then Zayd was put

to death by Safwan's slave Nistas and entered the Presence of the Lord
Almighty.

In the fourth year of the Hijra, drinking alcohol was forbidden. The Jews
came to the Holy Prophet ﷺ concerning litigation among themselves; the
Holy Prophet ﷺ proceeded according to the Shari'a of their prophet Moses,
which prescribed stoning to death. In this year in the month of Sha'ban the
blessed daughter of the Holy Prophet ﷺ Fatima az-Zahra gave birth to
Hussayn. Also in this year the daughter of 'Umayya bin Mughira, Umm
Salama who had been widowed and who was forty-four years of age
married the Holy Prophet ﷺ and became one of the 'Mothers of the
Faithful'. Zaynab the daughter of Khuzayma died that year. Zayd bin
Thabit learned Hebrew in that year in a fortnight.

The Expulsion of the Bani Nadir

The unbelievers could not stand the Light of Islam, for when it began to
spread its blessings in the city of Madinah, their influence was diminished.
Therefore, they resorted to vicious propaganda against the Muslims and
hatched the most wicked of plots. They produced as much provocation as
they possibly could. They would make a problem of the association with the
hypocrites and break the agreements that had been concluded with them.
They sought whatever means were necessary to weaken Islam and resort to
any base measure. At the same time, they understood very well that the
revelation of the noble religion of Islam, which proclaimed the Unity of
Allah and the resurrection after death, was a danger to their influence, and
that their arbitrary prevalence had finally come to an end. The Ansar tried
more and more to break the economic power and preponderance of the
unbelievers through the spoils of the wars they had fought. In this way,
people who were deeply addicted to usury became ever more restless and
uncertain, and the whole ugliness of character that they kept hidden under
their wealth was gradually beginning to show. In the Holy Quran their ugly
traits are shown up one by one, in these verses:

...and the unbelievers who listen to falsehood, listen to other folk, who have not come to thee, perverting words from their meanings... their hearts God desired not to purify. For them is degradation in this world, and in the world to come awaits them a mighty chastisement; who listen to falsehood and consume the unlawful.

(The Table, 41)

Hearing these verses, the unbelievers grew ever more averse to the Muslims, attempting to hurt the Holy Prophet ❀ in every way. At last, the Lord Almighty informed His Beloved that the end of tolerance had come. The Holy Prophet ❀ had shown them every possible forbearance, and put up with them for a long time with patience and gentleness. He had permitted them to maintain their religious institutions and had not interfered in their religious customs; he had even respected their dead in that he would instantly rise to his feet when he saw one of their funeral processions, and order his companions to stand in honor of the deceased. For the heart of the Holy Prophet ❀ beat with compassion for all living creatures, his was the complete manifestation of mercy. In those days, the Holy Prophet ❀ warned the People of the Book in these words:

Say: 'People of the Book! Come now to word common between us and you, that we serve none but God, and that we associate not aught with Him, and do not some of us take others as Lords, apart from God.' *(The House of Imran, 64)*

Allah speaks: "Oh My Beloved, make known: Oh People of the Book, come and let us unite in one indisputable word, let us not worship each other or any helpless human being, let us adore no God other than Allah; and should they turn away from your invitation, bear witness and say to them, 'We are Muslims'." However it was of no use; the unbelievers did not understand this generous forbearance, but continued to use all manner of fraud and trickery, not shunning the worst sort of deceitful stratagem.

For example, in order to lead people astray, they would accept Islam only to revoke it the following day. The chiefs of Quraysh appealed to the unbelievers to help them find a way to eliminate Muhammad ❀. The great companion of the Holy Prophet ❀, Talha bin Bara, made the following

362

bequest when he was on his deathbed: "Should I die during the night, I beg you not to tell Muhammad ﷺ of it, for it might be that he wishes to attend my funeral. I am afraid that this might be an occasion for attack by the unbelievers, and it is my wish that the blessed foot of the Holy Prophet ﷺ be untouched, even by dust."

Why the Bani Nadir Were Expelled

When 'Amr bin Tufayl let 'Amr bin Umayya free after just cutting off his forelock, and refrained from killing him because of his mother's oath to set free a slave, 'Amr bin Umayya returned to Madinah. On his way he met two unbelievers of the Bani `Amir, the tribe which had massacred his fellow Muslims at Bir Ma'una. When they had laid themselves down to rest, he killed them, believing this to be just revenge. Then he returned to Madinah and informed the Holy Prophet ﷺ of what he had done. The Holy Prophet ﷺ said, "What you have done is an ugly deed, for I had given these men guarantees of safety." But 'Amr bin Umayya had known nothing of this. "Oh Rasulullah," he said, "the Bani `Amir have slaughtered all my companions, and now they are waiting full of rage for the slightest occasion to wreak their revenge on you. They say that at the first opportunity they will put you and your faithful to the sword. Thinking these men also belonged to that tribe, I killed them." "Let them speak as they like," replied Muhammad ﷺ. "Our Protector and Mighty Support is Allah, He is all we could wish for; He suffices us. On us it is now incumbent to pay the blood wit for these two souls unjustly killed."

The Holy Prophet ﷺ then went to the Bani Nadir who lived two miles outside the city of Madinah in their well-stocked and fortified houses. He took with him Ali, Abu Bakr and 'Umar, as well as Zubayr and Talha, Sa'd bin Mu'adh, Sa'd bin 'Ubayd and 'Usayd bin Khadri. They went to ask help of the Bani Nadir in paying the blood money for the slain men, on the force of the mutual agreement existing between the Bani Nadir and Bani `Amir. The Holy Prophet ﷺ explained the matter to them. They answered, "Oh Abu Qasim, whatever you wish, we are at your command, we will do as you request. But do stay awhile with us so that we may prepare for you a meal and regale you thereby. Also we will consult with our religious leaders, and if they agree to accept Islam then the whole of the tribe will convert to the new religion." Then they withdrew for a while among themselves.

There they began to plan an assassination, deliberating on various ways of performing the deed. One of them, Sallam bin Nishkam counseled against this, saying, "Don't even try to do anything like that, for Muhammad 🏵 is under Divine supervision and he will be informed by heavenly means. Then our fate will be a grim one, for we will be counted as breakers of the treaty." But his warnings went unheeded. They decided to roll a great rock off the roof of the house where the Holy Prophet 🏵 was seated. Allah Almighty informed His Prophet 🏵 of their intentions and he instantly rose and returned to Madinah forthwith. From there he then sent Muhammad bin Maslama back to the Bani Nadir, telling him the exact words he was to say: "For that you were intending to slay Muhammad the Prophet 🏵, you shall be expelled from your homes and houses after a period of ten days."

The Bani Nadir then renewed their treaty with the unbelievers of the Bani Qurayzah. As they were preparing to leave their houses, the head of the hypocrites, Ibn Ubayy sent word to them, urging them to stay where they were, but to show the Muslims strong opposition. He promised to secure the support of the Bani Qurayzah for them, and also to send two thousand soldiers to their aid. "You need not move from your fortresses at all," he told them. "This is a unique opportunity; if you stand firm and we combine our forces, and it will be an easy thing for us to do away with Muhammad and his party." Allah Almighty tells His Holy Prophet 🏵 of this situation in these verses of the Holy Quran:

> *Hast thou not regarded the hypocrites, saying to their brothers of the People of the Book who disbelieve, 'If you are expelled, we will go forth with you, and we will never obey anyone in regard to you. If you are fought against, we will help you.' And God bears witness that they are truly liars.* (The Mustering, 11)

Relying on the words of the hypocrite, the Bani Nadir sent word to the Prophet 🏵 that they would not leave their dwellings, saying, "Do whatever you wish." Thereupon in the fourth year of the Hijra in the month of Rabi' al-Awwal, the Holy Prophet 🕸 mustered an army of his companions, and leaving Ibn Ummi Maktum in charge of the city of Madinah, he placed the banner in Ali's hands and set out for the settlements of the Bani Nadir to the south of the city. But the help of the Bani Qurayzah and Ghatafan did not come to the Bani Nadir, and when the hypocrite Ibn Ubayy saw that none was forthcoming, he saw himself powerless to do anything for them.

As the Holy Quran recounts:

> *If those are expelled, they will not go forth with them and if they are fought against, they will not help them. Even if they helped them, they would surely turn their backs, then they would not be helped. Why, you arouse greater fear in their hearts than God; that is because they are a people who understand not.*

(The Mustering: 12, 13)

The Holy Prophet 🕸 besieged the Bani Nadir for fifteen days. At the end of that time, the Bani Nadir asked for safe passage for themselves and their transportable belongings, other than their arms and armor. The Holy Prophet 🕸 granted them permission, and so they left Madinah. Among their chiefs who went to Khaybar were Sallam bin Abul-Huqayq, Kinana bin Rabi' and Huyay bin Akhtab. Another group of them emigrated to Sham. Among the confiscated goods were fifty coats of armor and fifty helmets, as well as three hundred and forty swords. Muhammad 🕸 wished to distribute these spoils of war exclusively among the Muhajirin, the emigrants from Mecca, because the Muhajirin shared their possessions with the Ansar.

The Holy Prophet 🕸 wished thereby to lighten the burden the Muhajirin imposed on the Ansar. He therefore addressed the Ansar, "If you wish I will distribute their property among you as was done before. Then you again will have joint possessions with the Muhajirin. But if you agree, I will only distribute it among the Muhajirin this time, and you will have your own property to yourselves."

The Ansar replied with tenderness, "Oh Rasulullah 🏵, all we possess is yours; distribute this property among our brothers of the Muhajirin, and should it please you to give them our property as well, we are satisfied with that. We only ask you not to separate them from us. Our brothers who have left all their houses and possessions behind for the love of Allah Almighty and set out on the Hijra, let them stay in our houses and share with us what we have, our hearts find gladness with them and our houses are filled with the blessings they bring." Everyone present was filled with emotion. Abu Bakr rose and publicly thanked the Ansar for their generosity. Allah Almighty sent the angel Jibra'il to inform the Ansar of their station. Though the Ansar were also needy, they placed the need of the Muhajirin above their own. By Divine Command the famous sword of the leader of the Bani Nadir Ibn Ukayf was given to Sa'd bin Mu'adh of the Ansar as a gift.

Thereafter news came that the Bani Ghatafan of Najd were preparing a campaign against the Holy Prophet 🏵. He put his son-in-law 'Uthman in charge of the city, mustered an army and set out towards the Najd. They reached a place called Shekh at a distance of two stops from Madinah in the lands of the Ghatafan, but the people all fled into the mountains and no one stood against them, so they returned to their houses without a fight.

Every year at Badr there was a fair, and people came from all over to buy and to sell their wares. Now the Holy Prophet 🏵 said to his Companions, "We have a tryst with Abu Sufyan to meet again at Badr the following year. The time has now come to go to the meeting place. I will leave the city in charge of Abdullah bin Rawahay, and Ali shall carry the banner of Islam." They set out from Madinah, five hundred fighting men in all, and eventually arrived at Badr. Abu Sufyan had also set out with a band of pagans. When he heard of the size of the Muslim army, he decided to turn back, thereby losing a lot of the esteem the other tribes held for the Quraysh. The Muslims returned to Madinah after profitable trading and with good gains.

The Story of Zaynab bint Jahsh

When the Holy Prophet ﷺ married the Crown of all virtuous women, the lady Khadija, she made him the gift of a slave she owned, Zayd by name. Now the Holy Prophet ﷺ soon grew very fond of Zayd, so much so that he formally adopted him into his family as a foster son. Zayd was not of Meccan origin; he had been brought there as a captive and sold into slavery. Zayd was a man whose everlasting future was to be very bright, and whose eternal bliss was sheer light.

The merchants who came to Mecca and saw Zayd there returned to their country and reported to Zayd's father that his son was well and living as a slave in the household of a highly esteemed person in Mecca. As his father and uncle had not the money to pay his ransom, they set to thinking how they could possibly free him. But the merchants who had brought the news said, "Zayd lives in the proximity of a person who is so full of compassion that when he sees how you feel about your son, he will probably let you have him."

His father and uncle then went to Mecca and came into the presence of the Holy Prophet ﷺ. "We have come to ask you for something," they said. "We ask you for our son!" The Holy Prophet ﷺ asked them, "Who is your son?" The father of Zayd then said, "Our child is Zayd, and he is my only son. He lives in your household as a slave. However, we possess nothing with which we might pay for his manumission. However, if you will be so generous and grant us respite, we will pay our debt to you in time. If you will only let our son go with us now."

The Holy Prophet ﷺ replied, "I am in no way interested in your material debt, and I ask nothing of you. I will call for Zayd to come, so that you may speak to him. If he wishes to leave with you, he is free to do so."

He called for Zayd to come and said to him, "Zayd! These two men have come, saying they are your father and uncle. They have come to take you home with them. The choice is yours, if you so wish, you may go with them." Zayd then replied, "I have no one in this world but you, oh Rasulullah! You are to me as father and mother; you are all and everything to me. I beg you not to send me away from your presence, or is it that I am burdensome to you?" With these words he began to weep, and his father, his uncle and the Holy Prophet 🏵 himself wept with him. Finally, the father of Zayd said, "He is your son," and withdrew from the Prophet's 🏵 presence in an attitude of humility and pious reverence.

In return for this display of devotedness to him, the Glory of the Worlds 🏵 adopted Zayd as his son. It was the custom in those days that an adopted son was considered in all respects just as a natural son.

Oh Traveler on the Way to Truth! Zayd, whom the Prophet 🏵 loved so much, was one of the first persons to join Islam. As we have already mentioned, he was destined later to reach such an elevated station that he kept the company of Abu Bakr, 'Umar and 'Uthman, having been made Commander-in-Chief by the Prophet 🏵 himself. Aisha reports: "Whenever the Holy Prophet 🏵 sent Zayd out on any military mission, he was sure to be sent as the commander of the company."

The criteria of Islam being the purity of intent and strength of faith, this shows the degree of freedom granted to this slave whose love and devotion were so extraordinary.

Zayd was martyred in the Raid of Mut'a when he was fifty-five years old. He is honored by the plain mention of his name in the Holy Quran. His station was so elevated that the Prophet 🏵 - one day when he was sitting with his Noble Companions, in order to make known Zayd's high degree in the Divine Presence - began asking him these questions, "Kayfa asbahta, ya Zayd? How have you woken this morning, oh Zayd?" Zayd replied to this, "Oh my Prophet 🏵, I have awakened as a believer." "To everything there is a deeper truth; what then is the deeper reality of your faith, oh Zayd?" Zayd began to explain the reality of his faith: he said that he had clearly beheld the reality of the spiritual world and become aware of the secrets of the Divine Dominion. He even went as far as asking the Holy Prophet 🏵, "Shall I set forth who of the forebears of the here-assembled Noble Companions shall dwell in Heaven and who shall reside in the fire?" But the Holy Prophet who was sent as a Mercy to the Worlds motioned him to be quiet.

Then he spoke to him, saying, "Oh Zayd, do not put into words whatever knowledge you have that goes beyond what has been said, and do not risk losing these gifts which are the result of your piety and obedience. Know that these are special grants with which you have been favored by the Lord of all created beings!" Thereby he informed all the companions of Zayd's lofty station in the Divine Presence.

The son of 'Umar relates: "My father 'Umar apportioned a greater allowance to Usama the son of Zayd than to me, his own son. When I enquired after the reason for this, he answered me, "The Holy Prophet ﷺ loved him more than he loved you, and he loved his father more than he loved your father."

The Prophet ﷺ married this much-treasured man to his very own cousin, the daughter of his paternal aunt, Zaynab.

Oh Traveler on the Road to Truth! Unfortunately, despite the millions of minarets that point heavenwards and resound, five times every day with the blessed name of Muhammad ﷺ, carrying the echo as far as the Throne itself, despite the mention of this name through many centuries and its firm hold over the hearts of hundreds of millions, there are people who are loath to admit the perfection of a moral ideal as incorporated by the Prophet Muhammad ﷺ, and who therefore have construed out of a marriage that took place in the fifth year of the Hijra a fallacy with which they try to launch an attack on those whose hearts are sincerely devoted to the Holy Prophet ﷺ. Therefore I wish to set forth this incident in full detail and I beg you to read and consider carefully what we relate.

Zayd, the freed slave and adopted son of the Holy Prophet ﷺ, asked for the hand of the Prophet's ﷺ cousin Zaynab bint Jahsh in marriage. She was of noble parentage; on her father's side she was descended from the Asadi tribe, on her mother's side she was Hashimi, being the daughter of Umayma, who was Abdul-Muttalib's daughter, the Holy Prophet's ﷺ aunt. The Prophet ﷺ had always preached that not a grain of sand existed

369

without the Will of Allah, and that he who excelled in pious reverence of the Lord and exhibited the most Compassion for His Creation was preferable to the Divine Presence. He now could not refuse Zayd's request, although in the community, Zayd was nevertheless regarded as nothing but a freed slave, whereas he occupied a high station at the court of the Heavenly King. Knowing this very well for a fact, the Holy Prophet ❁ did not refuse Zayd's request. Making Zaynab accept him as her social equal, he let Zaynab's family know that it was his wish to marry her to Zayd, requesting them to make known to her this circumstance.

Zaynab was told of the Prophet's wishes. Of course, she could not refuse his express wish, but there was something, of which she had not uttered a word to any soul. This concerned the love that she bore in her heart for the Holy Prophet ❁. Zaynab confided this to no one except to Allah Almighty, who is Lord over the hearts of men.[7]

Zaynab, who knew that love means ensuring the pleasure of the beloved, for fear of denying the Holy Messenger's ❁ directive accepted the Prophet's ❁ dispensation when he made known to her that he was giving her to Zayd. But Zaynab and her husband Zayd only managed to live peacefully with each other for one year.

Nevertheless, contrary to what is related in quite a number of books, Zaynab never once said to Zayd, "You were nothing but a slave, whereas I am the daughter of a noble family." Only when Zaynab was by herself, she addressed herself to the Lord Almighty who hears the sighing of every anguished heart, and to him she confided her burning tears: "Oh Allah, the whole created universe turns between two of your fingers, that of Mercy and that of Wrath! Make it possible for me to attain my beloved, let me be wed to him, oh my Lord!"

---

[7] The excellence of this is expressed in the following Hadith: "If someone is in love and he hides his passion and keeps it to himself, and he dies in this condition, he will have died a martyr."

Finally, Allah Almighty accepted the prayer of her burning heart, and the voice of her fiery passion. Divine Agency decreed that Zayd was to divorce Zaynab and this decree was made known to the heart of Zayd, her husband. He came to the Holy Prophet ﷺ and said, "Oh Rasulullah ﷺ! Zaynab has hardened against me and her words are harsh. Permit me to divorce her." To this the Holy Prophet ﷺ replied, "Hold your wife firmly!"

Then the Prophet ﷺ received this revelation:

> *When thou saidst to him whom God had blessed and thou hadst favored, 'Keep thy wife to thyself and fear God,' and thou wast concealing within thyself what God should reveal, fearing other men; and God has better right for thee to fear Him. So when Zayd has accomplished what he would of her, then We give her in marriage to thee, so that there should not be any fault in the believers, touching the wives of their adopted sons, when they have accomplished what they would of them; and God's commandment must be performed.* (The Confederates, 37)

This Divine Command needs some further elucidation. "You have kept secret a matter, which I (the Divine Person) would disclose, for the sake of your people, lest they might reproach you for marrying the divorced wife of your adopted son. You thought they might criticize you for that and thereby risk loss of their faith. When Zayd came to you complaining of Zaynab, you said to him, "Keep your wife to yourself and fear God!" Whereas there was nothing in this matter that was to be feared before God, it was only your feeling for your people that they might not be led to reproach you for this action and from there fall into doubts and disbelief. But God has greater right to be feared than mankind. When the time had come for Zayd to sever his connection with his wife Zaynab, while you were shy of the talk of the people, We charged you with openly making known the state of the affair and to inform that there is no blame on the believers in marrying the divorced wives of their adopted sons, once they have dismissed them charitably."

Oh Seeker after Truth! This incident was one of the greatest trials for the Holy Prophet ﷺ, for which he suffered benevolent reproach from his Lord, which turned into great mercy for his people.

In the end, Zaynab's prayer found acceptance with the Almighty Lord, and the divorce from Zayd took place. Zaynab returned to her parents' house. Her people were very hurt by this and only when the Holy Prophet ﷺ took Zaynab into wedlock was their grief dispelled. Actually, Zaynab had only accepted to marry Zayd so as not to spurn the Prophet's bidding. Now the time had come when her fervent prayers to Allah Almighty were to be answered and she was to attain her utmost delight. As has been set forth in the holy verses mentioned above, Zaynab was duly married to the Holy Prophet ﷺ and became one of the Mothers of the Faithful.

The Battle of the Trench

As mentioned before, the unbelievers were trying to raise a united force of all the important Arabian tribes against the Prophet Muhammad ﷺ. In particular, the tribes of the Bani Nadir and Bani Qaynuqa who had been exiled from Madinah on account of their assassination attempt on the Holy Prophet ﷺ did not cease working against Islam and trying to harm the Pride of the Worlds ﷺ.

These dangerous enemies met at Khaybar, which became a nest of intrigue and mischief making. The heads of the unbelievers, such as Sallam ibn Abi-l-Huqayq, Huyayy ibn Akhtab, and Kinana bin Abi-l-Huqayq went to Mecca and conspired with the chiefs of Quraysh. They came with a suggestion, which was more than welcome to the Quraysh and which met with enthusiastic approval.

They said, "There is only one means left to us in order to eliminate Muhammad ﷺ, and that is to march on Madinah with combined forces. What do you say to that?" The chiefs of the Quraysh replied, "Whatever is necessary and required, we are ready to do it."

The chiefs of Bani Nadir then went to Ghatafan and told them of their plan to strike out against Muhammad ﷺ, and elicited their support, promising them half of the revenues of Khaybar, should they agree to be their accomplices in the struggle against Muhammad ﷺ. They also made the Bani

Asad who were allies of the Ghatafan participate in this campaign. The Bani Sulaym were related to the Quraysh by blood-ties, hence they too were obliged to join.

The leaders of the Quraysh gathered at Dar-un-Nadwa. They decided to oppose the Prophet of Allah ✿, who preached the religion of Allah and proclaimed the unlawfulness of idol worship and the principles of justice and honor. They declared war against Muhammad ✿ whose pure heart beat with compassion for all of creation. The fortunes of Islam were to be assailed by grave danger. A force of thirty thousand men now stood assembled against the band of believers.

It was in the fifth year of the Hijra in the month of Dhul-Qa'da that the enemies of God marched against the Muslims. The Quraysh army comprised four thousand men and fifteen hundred camels. The standard-bearer was 'Uthman, the son of Abu Talha. At a place named Marr-al-Zahran the army coming from Mecca joined forces with the contingent of Ghatafan coming from the Najd under the command of the chief of the Bani Fazara, Uyayna bin Hisn. The leader of the Bani Murra, Harith ibn 'Awf joined them there as well. The army of the Bani Asad under the command of Talha, and that of the Bani Sulaym and the tribes of Ashja' had united their forces and came to meet the army. The army of the Arabs thus consisted of three divisions: firstly, the division of Ghatafan fighters under the command of the famous leader Uyayna ibn Hisn; secondly, the Bani Asad under command of Talha; thirdly, a troop of tribesmen allied to the Quraysh. The army's supreme commander was Abu Sufyan.

When Muhammad ✿ heard of these war preparations, he gathered all his Companions to discuss how they should meet such a tremendous force. Salman al-Farsi was familiar with tactics of war from his country of origin. He spoke up at the gathering, saying, "Oh Prophet of Allah ✿, if you permit, I will set forth how we ought to proceed in this battle. This time we are the defenders of our city, and in defensive warfare trenches have been used with great success. Therefore, we should dig trenches all around the city of Madinah." Salman's suggestion met with approval and he was made general commander in the Battle of the Trench.

Oh Traveler on the Road to Truth! Since the name of Salman al-Farsi has been mentioned, I cannot pass on without adding a few words about this noble personage. Salman was of Persian origin and had set out on the search for Truth at a tender age, when hardly more than a boy. In this cause he left his homeland and searched far and wide for a teacher to lead him to his goal. He came in contact with a number of Christian ascetics and holy men, and he learned from them about the anticipated coming of a new prophet. By the time Islam was revealed, Salman had fallen into slavery and was working for his master at Madinah. It was there that he found what he had been seeking. He met the Holy Prophet ﷺ and was drowned in the love of him. Later he experienced the rare distinction of being granted this special privilege by the Holy Prophet ﷺ; he reached a rank and a station higher than we can imagine, in that he was singled out in the Holy Prophet's utterance:

"Salman is of my household."

How lofty a station, how elevated a delight, to be raised to the station of a member of the Prophet's ﷺ household, a truly majestic gift! May the Almighty grant him his intercession, Amin.

The following event served as occasion for this utterance of the Prophet Muhammad ﷺ:

A verbal controversy had arisen between Salman al-Farsi and one of the noble companions of the Prophet ﷺ, on account of which the companion was somewhat hurt and offended. Some time later, this companion challenged Salman before a gathering of the companions with the intention of shaming him before them. He began asking all those present about their family tree and lineage. For it was one of the characteristics of the Arabs of the Jahiliyya (the Age of Ignorance, the time before the revelation of Islam) to take great pride in their lineage and they competed with each other in noble descent. After the revelation of Islam, however, this custom was renounced, and preference and rank was attributed to him who excelled not through noble descent, but through piety. As set forth in this holy verse,

Surely the noblest among you in the sight of God is the most godfearing of you. God is All-Knowing, All-Aware. (The Apartments, 13)

That is to say, Allah Almighty gives preference to him who excels in pious veneration and awe of the Lord and who shows the most mercy and compassion towards Allah's creatures.

As they were all recounting their lines of descent and the greatness and importance of their fathers and forefathers, they would ask, "How do they call you, what is your patronymic?" The question was put to 'Umar who answered:

"I am 'Umar, the son of al-Khattab!"

Salman al-Farsi sat there, his head bowed, his eyes damp with tears, his heart filled with tenderness. "They call me 'Child of Islam'," he answered, thereby demonstrating how faith had taken possession of all aspects of his life. When those present heard these words, it was as if fire fell into their hearts and they repented of their talk and their tactless questioning, and the questioner began to weep.

The Guardian of the Holy Law, 'Umar, then said, "Let none of us ever ask such unsuitable questions again. Should Salman ever have to repeat his answer to this question, we shall all of us burn." The other companion turned to Salman and pleaded with him to forgive the questioner.

When word of this reached the Holy Prophet ﷺ, he called his companions and said to them, "Salman is of the people of my household," and Salman was henceforth known as belonging to the company of Muhammad ﷺ.

Oh you who travel the Road to Truth! As we delve into the source of Islam, we find that among all the noble companions who traveled on the high road of Islamic teaching and under the shadow of Heavenly Ascent, the group traveling at the greatest speed were always the slaves. This is because their worldly fortunes were so discouraging, they were forlorn strangers in this world of semblance, and they were of the broken-hearted.

Allah Almighty has proclaimed:

"Verily, I dwell in the hearts of the broken-hearted."

Now, among the noble Companions of the Prophet 🌸 who were with Salman al-Farsi there was one named Hilal. This companion was the slave and the groom of a rich man, who was also a companion of the Prophet 🌸. One day this honored companion fell ill and was laid low with a raging fever. The angel Jibra'il came to the Prophet Muhammad 🌸 with a message from Allah Almighty, saying, "Oh Prophet of God, arise, the Lord sends you His Salams. 'One of My servants is ill', He will have you know. 'Let My Beloved go and visit My servant for My sake, as for his own, and let him enquire about his well-being.'"

Immediately the Holy Prophet 🌸 arose that his faithful companions wished to learn his intended destination. Muhammad 🌸 mentioned the name of the house he was instructed to visit, and the companions rushed ahead to alert the people of that house of the blissful advent of the Holy Prophet 🌸, as was their habit and custom. When they gave the good tidings to the head of the household, he at once began to prepare to receive the Holy Prophet 🌸. He rose to meet him at his gate, saying, "Welcome to you, oh Prophet of Allah 🌸, what great honor and blessing you bring to my house!" The Holy Prophet 🌸 however answered, saying, "No, it is not to you I have come. Where is Hilal?" His owner thereupon said, "I don't know, oh Prophet of Allah. If you will permit, I will send someone to fetch him." The Prophet said, "It is because of this, because you do not know where he is, that I will not enter your house. I have come here upon Divine Command. I know where Hilal is, open the door of the stable, there you will find him lying ill, and it is there that I will visit him!" The slave's owner then said, "Oh Muhammad 🌸, by your leave, I will have him brought out of there so that you may visit him." "No," said the Prophet 🌸, "when it was time you should have concerned yourself with him and have had him brought out of there. Now it is too late for that, for I have been ordered to go and visit him where he is. So, open the gates of the stable for me, quickly!"

The gate was opened. From his excessively high fever Hilal was quite beside himself. As soon the Holy Prophet 🏵 entered the stable, Hilal came to and exclaimed, "Oh my Lord, where am I? I perceive the fragrance of Thy Beloved, it is the scent of Mercy that envelopes me!" and he sat upright and looked about.

The Holy Prophet 🏵 said to him, "Oh Hilal, do not tire yourself, I have come to see you." "Oh, Rasulullah 🏵," cried Hilal, "how could you come here, to this lowly place. By your leave, let me crawl outside the stable, and let me take your orders there." "No, Hilal," answered the Prophet 🏵, "do not move from your place. My Lord has commanded me, in the Name of the Lord of all Beings, and in my own name, to visit you right here, in this place where you stay."

Then the Holy Prophet 🏵 bent down and embraced Hilal and kissed him, and they both wept.

Now, back to the scene of the war council: Salman's suggestion was accepted, and the Muslims began to make preparations for the defense of the city. The Holy Prophet 🏵 together with Salman went to the site of the prospective trenches, and personally drew the demarcations of the ditches that were to be dug. Madinah was perilously exposed on the side facing Syria; all the other sides were made up of walled houses, which more or less formed one continuous city wall.

The Prophet 🏵 ordered men to begin the digging of trenches in groups of ten at the exposed front, which meant that each man had to dig about one yard of ground. The women, children and the infirm were sent to the fortified areas of the city. The Holy Prophet 🏵 himself participated in clearing away the earth, while he recited verses of poetry. Thereby he encouraged his companions to work with greater vigor and enthusiasm. The noble companions answered to this by saying, "Until our last breath we will continue to fight for your cause, oh Prophet of Allah 🏵!"

The Holy Prophet ﷺ then made this supplication, "Oh Lord! Had You not guided us in Your Grace and Mercy, how sorry would have been our state! We would not have known about worship, nor would we have followed the path of guidance!"

Being experienced in the digging of such trenches, Salman ul-Farsi was able to do the work of ten men. There was, however, one trench in which a big boulder obstructed the digging, and no one could split it. Neither the strength of Salman, nor the utensils the Sahaba employed made the slightest dent on this rock. It would neither budge from its place, nor could they split it at all. This incident was reported to Muhammad ﷺ who smiled and went over to the site himself. "Give the pickaxe to me," he said. Then he began invoking the Divine Name, repeating the words, "Bismillahir-rahmanir-rahim," the Bismillah, which is the key to resolving all difficulties, and the fundamental tool of the Muslims. As soon as his pickaxe touched the unmovable stone, it slid from its place and broke up into pieces.

The words of the Bismillah were the tool wherewith the Holy Prophet ﷺ performed the miracle of splitting the moon asunder, and whereby the fire of Nimrod was transformed into light. With them, Musa's shepherds' staff was invested with power, so that it could overthrow and obliterate Pharaoh's claims to lordship.

Sparks flew under the blows of the Prophet ﷺ as he wielded the pickaxe, and the rock broke up into three pieces. It was shown to Muhammad ﷺ in a vision that Sham would soon fall under the domination of the Muslims, and he exclaimed, "Allahu Akbar! By Allah, at this moment I behold the red roofs of Damascus!" In this miracle he announced to the Sahaba that Sham would be given into Muslim hands before long.

A second blow of the axe, and in the flying sparks the Holy Prophet ﷺ perceived that Yemen would be given to him. He announced to his Companions, "Now I see the gates of the city of Sanaa..."

At the third blow of the axe in the Name of Allah, the rock turned into salt and ice. The Holy Prophet ﷺ again proclaimed Allah's Greatness, "Allahu

Akbar!" and said, "By Allah, I now behold the white houses of Mada'in belonging to the Khosroes. The arm-rings of Khosroes will be slipped onto Saraqa's wrist." He herewith manifested a plain visionary miracle.

Nowadays, fourteen centuries after the lifetime of this holy man, there are disrespectful people who - from spiritual poverty - claim that his revelations were due to what they assuredly refer to as "epileptic fits", although they have never met the Prophet ﷺ face to face. Let us then ask them a simple question: what kind of invalid is he, before whose strength even the hardiest of men showed deference, and before whose judgment all respectfully deferred their own opinions? As for those ill-fated miscreants who refuse to confirm him, they are unwittingly proven false by the tidings he brought. The Book, the Glorious Quran which is Muhammad's ﷺ teacher and which confirms that his judgments will never be invalidated through the passage of time. More and more it is now being read in Western countries.

For centuries, millions of people have followed in his footsteps, not from pressure of power or money, or on account of organized propaganda campaigns. They remember his name five times a day, at the very least. How many historical celebrities were affected by the love of the blessed Prophet ﷺ! What manner of epileptic is he, who is honored and revered by so many mighty rulers, men of valorous exploits, as well as men of reason and excelling in intellect?

While digging the trenches, the Holy Prophet ﷺ made this supplication for his Companions, the Noble Sahaba:

"Oh Lord, make them flourish in their eternal destinations!"

The trenches were completed within a period of two weeks. The enemy army was seen to be approaching. The Holy Prophet ﷺ assembled and mustered the army of the believers in the Unity of Allah, and led them outside of the city, behind the hill of Sal'. There they stood arrayed, waiting to face the enemy. Although the tribesmen of the Bani Qurayza were still guarding their neutrality, the Holy Prophet ﷺ knew very well that they were waiting for the first good opportunity, and in order to forestall any possible attack from their side, he sent Maslama bin Aslam to speak to them.

Prior to this, Huyayy bin Akhtab had made this request of the chief of the Bani Qurayza, Ka'b bin Asad: "We have here come together with Muhammad's own clans people in order to shed his blood; do not let this good opportunity for erasing the notion of 'Islam' slip by!" To this Ka'b bin Asad replied, "I am fearful, for Muhammad ❀ is true to his word, and mindful of the treaty we have with him." However, he was only looking for ways to break out of this agreement. In the end, Ka'b bin Asad was snared into breaking the treaty with Muhammad ❀. The Muslims were informed of this development.

The Bani Qurayza had a guarantee of safety from the Bani 'Aws. Therefore, Sa'd ibn Mu'adh, Sa'd bin 'Ubada, Abdullah bin Rawaha and Khawwat bin Jubayr now went to the Bani Qurayza to warn them of the evil consequences of their breach of contract. But however much they tried to talk sense to them, they trusted more in the words of the idolaters, and refused to listen to these high-minded Sahaba. "We have no contract with this man Muhammad ❀ whom you call Rasulullah, the Messenger of God. We do not recognize any existing agreement with him," they rejoined.

This made things even more critical for the Muslims, for the Bani Qurayza, being of Madinah, would be able to show the unbelievers beleaguering the city where lay the weak points of its defense. As for the hypocrites within, they too were increasingly active and gaining strength. The Holy Prophet ❀ said, "Let no mention be made of this the breach of contract by the Bani Qurayza in a way that might frighten the Muslims. Faith, Iman, makes all things crumble before it, and purity of intention, Ikhlas, obliterates all wickedness. Allah is the best of Protectors. He will suffice us, and the future belongs to the believers."

In the Holy Quran this is referred to in these verses:

When they came against you from above you and from below you, and when your eyes swerved and your hearts reached your throats, while you thought thoughts about

God; there it was that the believers were tried, and shaken most mightily.

(The Confederates, 10)

The enemy then proceeded to attack, launching with full force a startling, all out assault. Again the destiny of Islam seemed to be endangered, and many eyes stared wildly in shock, many hearts throbbed in terror. Many thoughts crossed the minds of the Muslim soldiers, concerning Allah and what He had in store for them. This was a moment of great trial for the believers, in which they were severely shaken.

Beware, oh True Believer! Take full account of the meaning of this sacred verse, and remember that in this world of tribulation you are subject to trials at every moment!

The hypocrites were not able to stand the menace of this war in the way the true Muslim fighters did. One by one they came to the Holy Prophet ❈ with some form of excuse and requested permission to leave the battlefield, professing concern for their families and children. Allah Almighty informed His Holy Prophet ❈ of their true motivations for fleeing the battleground.

As they came face to face with the powerful army which had come to destroy the religion of Islam and its noble Prophet ❈, the true believers - whose love belonged to Allah Almighty and whose sincere devotion was with their Prophet Muhammad ❈ - stood unwavering in their faith and their complete reliance on the wisdom of the Divine Decree, as transmitted to them by the Prophet of Allah ❈, and attested to their surrender in a way that stupefied those who had not yet tasted the sweetness of true faith. "This is what Allah and the Holy Prophet ❈ have promised us, and assuredly Allah and His Prophet ❈ are true to their word," they firmly spoke, thereby passing this very harsh test of faith.

The siege lasted a full twenty days. The Prophet's companions frequently went without food for days. As the siege wore on, it increased in severity. The enemy made every attempt to cross the trenches, but did not succeed. The enemy troops tried to breach the trenches and enter the quarter of the women and children, the infirm and aged.

The Prophet 🕊 himself appointed his commanders, and he himself undertook to defend the most dangerous parts of the front, thinking that perhaps the Ansar would be anxious about this development. Sa'd ibn 'Ubada and Sa'd ibn Mu'adh of the Ansar heard of this, and they went to the Prophet Muhammad 🕊 in order to reassure his noble concern, saying to him, "Oh Rasulullah, Beloved of the Lord! You have propounded to us Allah's Will and have given us the benefaction of Islam! You are ever the pinnacle of our joy! The Ansar have no life of their own, all their lives belong to you - so have no worry for us!"

These words brought tears to the eyes of the Holy Prophet 🕊 which were as windows to the Truth. He bowed down in prostration and prayed, "Oh Lord! Send Your Divine Support upon this small band of Muslims who believe in Your Unity! If it be Your Will, send against their foes an angelic army, or turn the elements of nature that follow Your Divine Command against the enemy. Fulfill Your Promise to me, however You choose to do it!" When he raised his head from his Sajda, he turned to his friends and said, "The enemy may do whatever he likes, the Lord Almighty is on our side!"

But the hypocrites realized the peril of the situation, and when they met a man whose faith was yet new and tender, they would say, "Muhammad 🕊 has promised us the treasure troves of Khosroes, the gardens and pavilions of San'a, the mansions of Caesarea, did he not? Now we have for days endured this siege behind these trenches, as we have hitherto not experienced. Yet we have not taken even a single step toward the promised goal." With words such as these they sowed poison seeds into the hearts of the newcomers.

The unbelievers changed the commander of their forces every day. Finally, with winter setting in, they grew tired of waiting and they were running out of fodder for their animals. Therefore, they decided on one final concerted effort, staging an all-out offensive in which different divisions attacked together in one general assault.

The first to break through the trenches on horseback was the famous Arab warrior 'Amr ibn 'Abdu Wudd, before whose strength everyone trembled. He was an old man of ninety who had been injured at Badr and who had sworn not to comb his hair until he had taken his revenge. Behind him came the brother of 'Umar, Dirar ibn-al-Khattab, Hubayra bin Abi Wahb, and Ikrima ibn Abi Jahl, each one of whom was the equivalent of an army. Beating their horses to exert the utmost effort, they suddenly dashed through the trenches at their narrowest part. Abu Sufyan and Khalid ibn-ul Walid came to the edge of the trench to assist, but as they could not cross it, they contented themselves with being onlookers.

But 'Amr ibn 'Abdu Wudd dashed ahead of his companions on horseback, looking for the Holy Prophet ✸ and yelling all the while, "Where are you, who started all this business of 'La ilaha illAllah'? Who wishes to destroy all inherited tradition by this claim of One God only, and resurrection after death? I have come and I am ready! I challenge you to send me a man who will fight me, send out one your fighters!"

The Holy Prophet ✸ looked at his men and asked, "Who will step forward and fight him?" Even though all the great Sahaba were assembled there, no one wanted to go out and meet this challenge, for this ruffian was known as a fierce warrior who was capable of single-handedly throwing a whole company in disarray. Therefore, all were hesitant to volunteer and none stepped forth.

But let it not be assumed that the Noble Sahaba hesitated because they were loath to give up their lives - never! Each one of the Noble Companions would gladly have been the first to surrender his soul for the sake of Muhammad ✸, all of them fully aware of the merit of a martyr's death. With the greatest pleasure they would have performed this duel in his blessed presence, until their cloaks fell off their backs. No, the reason for their reservation was this: if any one of them rose to meet the challenge and was martyred without having killed 'Amr, this would greatly strengthen the morale of the infidel army, while weakening the resolve of such ditherers as were under the influence of the hypocrites, increasing the fear in their hearts. Some of the Sahaba even went out to battle without their armor, and when asked why they answered, "Those who love their Lord Creator fear not death!"

The Prophet's ﷺ general, Ali who was still quite young at that time, stepped out in answer to the Prophet's ﷺ question and said, "Oh Rasulullah ﷺ, I will go forth and fight this fellow." But the Prophet ﷺ answered, "No, Ali, this fellow is 'Amr! Sit down!" Again 'Amr yelled, taunting them even louder this time, "I thought you were all hungry for Paradise? So there is none of you wishing for its joys now?" The Inheritor of the Prophet ﷺ, Ali again spoke up, saying, "Oh Holy Prophet ﷺ! And even if he is 'Amr, give me permission to go and fight him!" But the Prophet ﷺ declined and insisted that he remain seated. Then the infelicitous challenger attacked the Prophet ﷺ with sordid speech. Now the Lion of Islam, Ali the Victor, the son of Abu Talib could restrain himself no longer. "Oh my Noble Prophet ﷺ! I beg your permission! At least let me prove that I am his equal!"

Everyone's eyes filled with tears and hearts beat in alarm, when the husband of Batul (Fatima) rose with such firm determination. Even the Holy Prophet ﷺ could no longer restrain him, but he did strip off his own coat of mail and invested Ali with it. With his own hands he girt him with the sword called "Dhul-Fiqar". Both Heaven and earth stood silent as they watched Muhammad ﷺ, the interpreter of the Lord of Unity, perform this ceremony on Ali. Then the Holy Prophet ﷺ prayed over him, kissed him on the forehead and sent him out against 'Amr.

Ali stepped out onto the battleground on foot, whereas 'Amr was mounted. In great suspense, the whole of creation stood watching the scene that was about to unfold, the contest between these two armies: between the hero who confirmed the Unity of Allah and him who denied it, between the Friend of God, the human lion, and the enemy of God, the uncouth champion of idolatry and spiritual darkness.

It was 'Amr's custom to say to his opponent at the outset of a contest, "I grant you three wishes!" When he saw Ali coming to meet him, true to his

384

habit he said, "You who are coming out against me! Three wishes I grant you, ask of me whatever you wish!" Ali replied, "Alright, my first wish is that you might come to reason and surrender (i.e. accept Islam). Think of your future in the everlasting abode." "What," roared 'Amr, "you still persist in this solicitation!" "What else have I to persist in?" replied Ali. "How can you suggest such a thing to me? Do I look like one who surrenders (i.e. a Muslim)?" "If that is so, then leave the battleground." "What! To become the mockery of the Arab women!" "Right then, come on and fight!" said Ali.

Upon this, 'Amr let out long and loud peals of laughter, mocking Ali and saying, "Such bravery and daring, I have never heard the likes of it in all my living memory! But tell me, do you know who I am?" Ali answered, "Only too well. You are 'Amr, the enemy of God." "And who are you?" "I am a servant of Allah, Ali the son of Abu Talib." "Ah, woe is thee, oh Ali! I was a good friend of your father for many long years. I am therefore loath to shed your blood. Is there none among your uncles who is my peer, which they might have sent him out against me? I find it hard to raise my hand against thee!"

To this Ali replied, "The Holy Prophet ﷺ, the Beloved of Allah, has set his hopes on me, just as Abu Sufyan and the chiefs of the idolaters have pinned their hopes upon you. For me it will be a pleasure to shed your blood in the name of Allah Almighty!" These words of Ali pierced his misbelieving heart as if a pointed lance. "I will not condescend to fight you from atop my mount," he said. "As you wish; we have exchanged words enough," replied Ali, "let us not waste our breath, but fight if we must." These words from Ali again painfully pricked 'Amr's false pride. He instantly dismounted and smote the leg of his own horse with a stroke of his sword, filling all the onlookers with terror. Then he fiercely came towards Ali. As Ali began to parry his strokes, the Muslims looked on with tearful eyes, for 'Amr's onslaught had cloven Ali's shield in two and wounded his blessed head. Witnessing this, the Holy Prophet ﷺ began to pray, "Oh my Lord! My uncle 'Ubayda fell a martyr at Badr, my other uncle Hamza fell at Uhud.

385

There is no one left to me of my family but Ali, my father's brother's son. If he too is now taken from me... I beseech Thee not to leave me all alone."

The Sahaba who heard the Prophet's ❈ supplication were moved to tears and shaken by sobbing. But now came Ali's turn to reciprocate. He drew the sword that Rasulullah ❈ had girded him with from its sheath, saying, "Oh my Lord! Make true what Thou hast promised to Thy Prophet ❈! I pray Thee to invest Thy Prophet's ❈ sword with Thy Power, so that my arm might manifest Thy Divine Might!" With a mighty cry of "Allahu Akbar!" he charged towards 'Amr, and with a single sweep of his sword Dhul-Fiqar he dispatched him into the pit of eternal damnation.

Regarding this great event, the Holy Prophet ❈ is to have said, "There is no more accomplished person between the Earth and the Throne than Ali. He is the leader of him who takes me to be his leader. Ali alone can acquit my debt."

After this, Munabbih of the sons of Abdul-Dar rode out onto the scene of battle. He was met by Zubayr who smote him a stroke of his sword that clove this stubborn disbeliever in two. Whenever people said to Zubayr, "What a powerful sword you possess!" Zubayr would reply, "It is not a question of the sword, it is a question of the arm that wields it!"

Then 'Umar's brother, Dirar ibn al-Khattab, Abu Jahl's son Ikrima and Khubayr ibn Wahab strode out onto the field one after the other. When 'Umar came out to meet Dirar, the latter fled the field. Ali and Zubayr went out to meet the other two, who lost their courage and fled also. As Ikrima was fleeing, he lost his helmet. The poet Hasan bin Thabit pursued him, declaiming derisive verses. Nawfal fell into a trench and cried out when they were pelting him with stones, "Kill me at least in a soldierly way!" Ali then leapt into the ditch and severed from his body the head filled with delusions of disbelief.

This was the most important day of the Battle of the Confederates. Even though the Muslims were content to have slain their most vicious enemies, and the unbelievers were distressed at having lost some of their strongest fighters, yet the Muslims were subjected to the rain of arrows and hail of stones hurled at them. So much so that the Pride of the Worlds had to pass up four times of prayer (later making up for them as Qada), as he could not absent himself from the fighting.

The next day the Confederates, i.e. the pagans and the unbelievers drew an even closer ring around the Muslims. The Bani Qurayza drew close to the place where the Muslim women were staying. They decided to attack from this front. One of the unbelievers managed to make his way up to the gates of the fort. Safiya bint Abdul-Muttalib noticed him and grabbed a tent pole and brought it down upon the unbeliever's head. He fell senseless to the ground. When the unbelievers who were preparing to attack on this front learned of his death, they desisted from their offensive, deeming the place well defended.

The Muslims sorely felt their lack of numbers in those days. The Bani Qurayza united with the Quraysh and their arrows rained incessantly upon the outnumbered Muslims. However, it was the Will of Allah that the Muslims should prevail over the unbelieving foe. Upon the Command of the Almighty, the elements of nature began to strike back at the besieging army. Suddenly a great whirlwind arose and flattened the enemy's headquarters, scattering their stores of grain. Allah's invisible army had come and brought relief and comfort to the Muslims.

This event is mentioned in the Hoy Quran in these verses:

> O believers, remember God's blessing upon you when hosts came against you and We loosed against them a wind, and hosts you saw not; and God sees the things you do.
> (The Confederates, 9)

Before long, the enemy army's beasts began to die and great dissent broke out between the Confederates consisting of the pagans, unbelievers and hypocrites. The conversion of Nu'aym ibn Mas'ud al-Ghatafani to Islam was cause for the greatest discord among them.

In Nu'aym's heart a spark of faith had long been kindled, and when the campaign against Muhammad # began, he took counsel with himself, thinking, "Why should I stubbornly persist in my error? Should I deny myself the boon of following in the steps of Muhammad 🕌, who defends the rights of the weak, who demonstrates high moral character in utter disregard of any benefit to his own person, and who tells of the life to come when the oppressor will cry from woe, and the oppressed will shout from joy. But," thought he to himself, "to this day I have not been received within the noble religion of Islam. What can I do for Islam, to make up for this loss and to gain acceptance?"

Nu'aym belonged to the notables of the tribes of the Ashja', and he was the leader of a very numerous group of men. He decided that he must come to the aid of the Muslims with the forces he commanded. First he went to the head of the Bani Qurayza, Ka'b ibn Asad. He was sitting together with the chiefs of the tribes when Nu'aym entered. They received him with honor and began to speak of the war situation. After listening to them for a while, Nu'aym spoke up, saying, "I don't know what you think of me, but I believe you know that I have feelings of closeness and regard for you, is it not so?" "No doubt this is the case," replied the chief. "Is their anything you wish to say to us, oh Nu'aym?" "Indeed there is," replied Nu'aym, "I am thinking of the outcome of this affair and I see your position as being dismal." "How is that, what news have you heard?"

"No, I have no news to bring, it is just to say that this matter displeases me. Both the tribes of the Ghatafan and the Quraysh have come here and besieged the Muslims for days on end, but they are holding out and successfully pursuing their defensive tactics. The animals of the assaulting army are beginning to perish, storms and rain have brought down their tents, their grain stores are giving out and various rumors are coursing throughout the camp. Dissent is breaking out among the rank and file of this discordant mingling. This dissension needs be, will lead the troops to split up, as they grow weary of the siege. Eventually you will be left to your own devices. These are my thoughts. You will in that case fall straight into the hands of the Muslims which is bound to have dire results." "These thoughts of yours indeed describe what is no remote probability, quite possibly the outcome will be such. However what can we do at this point, oh Nu'aym?" Nu'aym replied, "You must take some persons of Quraysh and Ghatafan as hostages. They will then of necessity remain steadfast until the end." Ka'b ibn Asad answered to this, "You have spoken very truly, oh Nu'aym, you are right, this is what we ought to do."

Nu'aym left them at that and proceeded straightway to the gathering of Abu Sufyan. There, too, Nu'aym was well received and greeted with familiarity. Nu'aym broached the subject without delay. "Have you heard already?" he said. Abu Sufyan, surprised, said, "Good news, we hope!" Nu'aym said, "The Bani Qurayza regret having broken their treaty with Muhammad ﷺ and have concluded a new secret treaty with him. They have found a way of gaining his pardon, and this is their ruse: they have promised to take hostages some of the nobles of Quraysh and Ghatafan and deliver them to the Muslims. That is what they have promised them. Bear this in mind: if there is any such suggestion by the Bani Qurayza, don't be deceived into delivering hostages to them. It would be a great pity."

Abu Sufyan was much worried by these words. In order to learn whether the Bani Qurayza were really considering such an action, he sent a man over to their camp to find out. He was to deliver the following message to them, "We have come to this juncture at the instigation of the Bani Qurayza and of your chiefs. You have led us into this pinch, and now you act coolly towards us. You desist from commanding a heightened offensive, and the siege might last long in this manner. Our losses are great; our beasts are suffering badly. Therefore, we ought to strike out tomorrow in a joint effort to end this whole affair as soon as possible. That is what appears to us to be the right course."

To this the response was, "Tomorrow being the Sabbath, all work is forbidden to us. The day after we will be willing to do battle. But under one condition: that you send seventy of your foremost men to us as hostages, so that we might be certain that you would not desert us." When the Quraysh and Ghatafan heard this reply, they said, "Nu'aym has indeed spoken truly," and they answered the Bani Qurayza, "We will neither submit to you any hostages, nor will we ask any support from you. We shall return to our country and leave you in the hands of the Muslims. They will mete out your punishment to you."

The Bani Qurayza on the other hand thought, "Indeed, what Nu'aym has told us is coming true, but it is too late to do anything about it." They regretted having broken their contract with Muhammad ❀, and leaving the battleground, they withdrew into their fortified dwellings. This caused a serious rift in the relation between the unbelievers and the Arab tribes. Even if the siege still lasted, it had lost a lot of its weight. Later, when it became known to the Holy Prophet ❀ that Nu'aym had been the cause for this rift, he prayed for him. Therefore, oh true Believer! The word has a spirit of its own. At times it can bring life, at other times it can destroy. Do you not see how one command issuing from the Divine Throne can set thousands of men marching? Therefore, man must look not to the causes of a thing but to the Causer of causes. For the Divine Will is not in need of a cause, it is rather the causes that are in need of the Divine Will.

The siege wore on, and the Muslims were growing weary of it. One day at the 'Asr prayer, the Mercy to the Worlds, Muhammad ❀ entreated the Almighty, "Oh my Lord! Do not try this band of Muslims who assert Your Oneness with overly hard trials! They will never turn away from You, so expose not their faces to the enemy's arrows for much longer!" No sooner had he completed his supplication than the signs of good cheer appeared on his blessed countenance. For the Highest Envoy of the Divine Dominion, the archangel Jibra'il had come to him to announce glad tidings: by Divine Command the wind, joined by forces of the Divine Regiment, was to turn against the unbelievers, rendering ineffectual all their rage and fury.

Indeed, before long, a wind of such force arose that it seemed to rip the earth apart. Not a thing could be seen, the whole world was plunged into the darkness of night and a great fear and loathing befell all men. In view of this situation, Abu Sufyan lost all hope of victory. Half of his army had deserted, and he said to himself, "There is no use in further persisting in this matter. Anyway, there is dissension between us and the Bani Qurayza. I'm leaving, and everybody else should also go home." So speaking he turned and departed. In this way the storm clouds on Madinah's horizons were scattered.

The Holy Prophet # rose and told his companions of this loss of morale in the enemy camp, and as soon as dawn broke, he sent Hudhayfa to spy out the enemy camp and bring word of their movements. Hudhayfa bin Yaman went and spied into the enemy encampment, observing their disarray. As he was returning he encountered six horsemen who said to him, "Oh Hudhayfa, go and tell your friend that Allah has turned against his enemies to destroy them!" Hudhayfa said to them, "But who are you? I know you not!" The horsemen replied, "Just move along! Your friend knows who we are, he is informed by Divine Agency, your task is only to deliver this message to him." When Hudhayfa presented all this to the Holy Prophet #, he smiled so broadly that his teeth showed, and announced that these horsemen had been angels in the guise of human beings.

The army of the Meccan Arabs left behind them much of their bulk and dross, and plenty of grain that they had kept in store for fodder. All of this now fell to the Muslims. Even the twenty camel-loads of grain that Abu Sufyan had been sent by Huyayy, the head of the unbelievers, were confiscated by Muhammad's # men.

In this war, there were five martyrs on the Muslim side: two of these were from the clan of 'Aws, and three were from that of the Khazraj. One of these was Sa'd ibn Mu'adh, one of the most important of the Ansar whom the Holy Prophet # loved dearly. Sa'd had been seriously injured during the fighting. When the warring was over, the Prophet # had a tent erected in the courtyard of the mosque, especially for nursing his beloved companion. The Prophet # himself came and tended to him. The lady Rufayda who was a skilled nurse dressed his wounds under the Holy Prophet's # supervision. However, this much beloved companion was beloved also by Allah, and his wounds would not heal. Thus he drank the cup of death and died a martyr's death.

What bliss came to that lofty person whose wounds were nursed and tended by the blessed hand of the Holy Prophet ❀ himself. May Allah Almighty grant him his intercession, Amin.

Aisha relates: The mother of Sa'd was with us in the fort where we were staying. I was strolling outside of the walls of the fort when I heard footsteps. I looked and I saw it was Sa'd ibn Mu'adh who was running out to the battlefield, his spear in his hand. When she saw her son, his mother said, "Sa'd, my son, you are late, go hurry! Give your life and soul for the sake of this religion! Do not forsake the Prophet ❀, all that you have, offer it up for him!" Thus she saw him off. Sa'd's armor was too small for him, so that his arms remained uncovered. An arrow shot by Ibn il-'Arqa hit him on the arm and wounded him deeply. It was this wound that he died from.

The Treachery of the Bani Qurayza

The Holy Prophet returned from the Battle of the Trench to his home in the first week of the month of Dhul-Hijjah. No sooner had he laid off his armor and weapons than the messenger-angel Jibra'il appeared to him and announced to him his Lord's Salams and the Command: "My Beloved! It is My Divine Wish that the Muslims instantly go after the Bani Qurayza who are bent on general destruction!"

The Bani Qurayza did not appreciate the kindness shown to them by Muhammad ❀, though they had seen the Bani Nadir evicted from their homes. They knew not the value of being permitted to stay, nor the freedom afforded to them regarding the management of their own affairs, their economic and religious concerns. Their only response to all this kindness had been treachery and deceit.

As mentioned before, after the treachery of the Bani Nadir, the pact with the Bani Qurayza had been renewed under the same conditions. However, they still nurtured rancor in their hearts and were ever on the lookout to initiate intrigue and mischief. Invariably, they worked against Islam, finally allying themselves with the fiercest enemy of Islam, Huyayy ibn Akhtab, thus breaking their treaty with Muhammad ﷺ. In this way they betrayed the Muslims at the most critical moment, when they were in greatest need of support. For this reason, it was necessary to punish the Bani Qurayza, for the victory of Islam at the Battle of the Trenches to be complete.

It was now very unlikely that the Muslims would be attacked again by the pagan Quraysh, or for that matter, other Arab tribes. For they had expended their final war effort in the Battle of the Trenches, and their drive and energy was exhausted. In particular, the slaying by Ali of 'Amr ibn Abdu Wudd, who was commonly known as the "equivalent of a thousand men", had struck terror into the hearts of the Quraysh warriors, so that there was little likelihood of danger coming from the side of the pagan Quraysh.

However, the grudge against Islam held by the unbelievers and their arrangement with the hypocrites now posed the greatest danger to the Muslims. It was therefore essential that they should be made to feel the consequences of their dishonest dealings and harmful intentions towards Islam. Therefore the Holy Prophet ﷺ was commanded by Divine Command to return to warring forthwith and to pursue the Bani Qurayza, before he had even stripped his battledress.

Once more the Holy Prophet ﷺ took up his weapons and called for Bilal. "Oh Bilal!" he said, "call upon all those who uphold the Lord's Law not to lay down their weapons, and to remove their battledress not just yet. Call them to assemble for the 'Asr prayer in the quarter of the Bani Qurayza!" The Noble Companions assembled. The Holy Prophet ﷺ placed the banner into Ali's hand and sent him on ahead, while he himself went on behind.

As they marched along, the Mercy to the Worlds, the Foremost of the Prophets ﷺ spoke to his Companions, "Should the Bani Qurayza show us no enmity and greet us with friendliness, then I will pray to the Lord for them to be pardoned." Again he said to Ali who was marching at the front of the company, "Oh Ali! Proceed only as far as the entrance of their fort. If you see them manifesting any sign of regret for what they have done, come and inform me of it."

Ali rode on ahead of the army. Coming up to the fort of the Bani Qurayza, he heard such disparaging words spoken against the Holy Prophet ﷺ that far from denoting contrition or remorse should have made even the tongue that spoke them weep.

The Holy Prophet ﷺ came to a well and waited there for news from Ali. But when he heard of the slanderous language they had used against him and of their resolve to resist, he decided to besiege them. The leaders of the Bani Qurayza then grew stubborn. Instead of begging for pardon for their treachery, they set their minds on defense.

The siege lasted for twenty days. Finally, the head of the tribe, Ka'b, gathered together all the dignitaries of the unbelievers one Friday and said to them, "There remains to my mind no more doubt or hesitation that this man Muhammad ﷺ is the prophet foretold in all our Holy Books, the Prophet of the Last Times ﷺ. In my opinion we all ought to accept him and his message and become Muslims. That will be our way out of the plight we are in. What do you say?"

The unbelievers however answered, "That is impossible!" "In that case, let us all put our own families, wives and children to death, so that they do not remain a worry on our mind; then let us go out and fight in the open!" They answered, "After having lost our wives and children, what value will remaining alive have for us?" and they rejected Ka'b's proposal. Then Ka'b said to them, "In that case, this is what we should do: Tomorrow is Saturday, the Sabbath. Muhammad ﷺ is assured that on that day we will not engage in any hostile actions. Let us therefore suddenly strike forth unexpectedly, and make a sudden sortie!"

This jarred with the religious feelings of the unbelievers, and they rejoined, "Impossible, we would be defaming our Holy Sabbath! That we will never do!" Ka'b then said, "Alright, what then do you say that we should do? We are now under siege for over twenty days, and hunger is no longer far from us. We will not be able to hold out much longer. Moreover, it is our own fault. We had a treaty with Muhammad ﷺ which guaranteed us the control over our lives, our possessions and our religious practices. He respected the conditions of this contract, while we, in return, allied ourselves with his mortal foes that were bent on his destruction. We became a threat to them, instead of being partners to a binding agreement."

The unbelievers then replied, "Let us send word to Muhammad 🕌 that we will accept a judgment by Sa'd ibn Mu'adh of the tribe of 'Aws. For there is a pact between the 'Aws and the Bani Qurayza. Therefore, let us ask for Sa'd ibn Mu'adh to preside in judgment over this affair!" This decision was accepted unanimously by the heads of the tribe, and the Holy Prophet 🕌 did not refuse their request.

Sa'd ibn Mu'adh had been badly injured in the Battle of the Trench and was being nursed in a special tent erected for him in the courtyard of the Prophet's 🕌 mosque in Madinah. He was close to his death when this message was brought to him. This was Sa'd's judgment: the rebellious, weapon-bearing men among them and the traitors who had opposed Muhammad should be executed, while women, children and the infirm should fall into Muslim hands as captives. Their possessions were to be regarded as spoils of war. That was the judgment passed on the Bani Qurayza.

Oh Traveler on the Road to Truth! There are some who attempt to denigrate Islam by maintaining that this was a very harsh judgment on the part of Sa'd ibn Mu'adh. Considering the murderous intentions of the Bani Qurayza against the Muslims, and their betrayal of the besieged community (of Madinah), which amounted to treason, even though they were obliged to them by terms of contract, surely no other punishment would have been just. For the mercy shown to the wrongdoer is a betrayal of the wronged.

If, God forbid, the unbelievers had won in this conflict, they would doubtlessly have put to death all the Muslims, including the women and children, with no consideration of their defenselessness. In fact, when asked to do so, the Holy Prophet 🕌 often ruled in accordance with the previously revealed Holy Scripture, if he received no specific revelation. The ruling which Sa'd ibn Mu'adh gave was in accordance with the Torah. The unbelievers consented to this verdict; they found it to be appropriate. When the Prophet 🕸 heard of the verdict which Sa'd had given, he said, "This is the judgment of Allah!"

Some Western writers have said, "Sa'd bin Mu'adh gave such a strict verdict because he had been injured by the Bani Qurayza and he was motivated by a need for retaliation." But this is a mistaken judgment, for it was not the Qurayza but the Quraysh who had inflicted on Sa'd the wound from which he died. The man whose arrow had struck him was Ibn il-'Arqa and he was a man of the Quraysh.

We must take careful note of the following:

The Holy Prophet 🕸 who is our leader in the spiritual domain, always forgave any hurt that was inflicted upon his own person, and he applied his merciful qualities to those who attacked him. However, in his position as guardian of his people's life and freedom, when justice needed to be carried out, he would unquestioningly impart to criminals their just deserts.

In the holy text of the Quran, Allah Almighty declares the extent of His Prophet's mercy and compassion, and the events of Muhammad's 🕸 life display this to all of creation. Yes, the Holy Prophet's mercy was so great that it confounds the mind. There are countless instances; mention of just a few examples may suffice:

A dignitary of the Bani Hanifa, Thumama ibn Athal, was taken prisoner and brought to Madinah into the presence of the Prophet 🕸. This man was one of the most rebellious and was transformed into one of the foremost Muslims by the compassion flowing from the gaze of Muhammad 🕸. All his coarseness turned into delicacy, and his defiance into favorable inclination. As soon as he returned to his tribe, he ordered that the grain transports which hitherto had passed from Yamama through Mecca should no longer stop by there.

This put the Meccans under great pressure and the pagan Quraysh felt it as well. The Prophet's 🕸 enemies at last wearied of the situation and they pleaded with Thumama that they would do anything he asked for, accept any condition he imposed on them, if he would only exert his influence to keep them from starvation.

Thumama answered them, "You are the enemy of Muhammad 🎖, the great and noble Prophet of Islam. You were the reason he migrated from his hometown, you went out to war against him, and you sorely mistreated his followers, the Muslims. Therefore, I am unable to accept your request, I will not let one single mouthful pass by your way."

Hearing this, the Meccans felt helpless and were distressed. One thing they still felt sure of was the Holy Prophet's 🎖 mercy and compassion towards all of God's creation.

The Meccan chiefs conferred with one another, saying, "Let us make a petition to Muhammad 🎖. We'll say that Thumama is obstructing the delivery of grain to us, and ask him to intercede for us in this matter." So they made a petition to the Holy Prophet 🎖 concerning their situation of need. This noble personality, who was not sent "but as a mercy to the worlds" extended his open-handed compassion even to the most hardened unbelievers, for he replied to them, "Alright, I will ask Thumama to comply with your request."

Those who had just recently entered the fold of Islam were greatly astonished by his reply. The Holy Prophet 🎖 then turned to them and answered the unvoiced questions in their hearts, "There exists not a single particle without Allah," he told them, "and they too are a manifestation of the Divine Name. It is because they do not know me that they have become my enemies. It befits the station of man to help those who bear him enmity and not to exact revenge. You, through the Lord's preferential treatment, have attained to guidance, while they are touched by the emanation of the Divine Name 'al-Mudill', He who leads astray."

Another example of the Holy Prophet's 🎖 generous compassion was his forgiveness towards the slayer of his beloved uncle Hamza, the lion of Islam. There was also the instance of the woman who tried to assassinate the Prophet 🎖 himself through poison. Muhammad 🎖 forgave her, too, even as he lay on his deathbed, on the verge of his transition into the World of Divine Splendor when he spoke, "At this very moment I feel the pangs of the poisoned food given to me by that woman." She also was forgiven.

Then again, when Abu Jahl's son Ikrima who had performed indescribable acts of brutality towards Islam, came to his senses and became Muslim, he came before the Holy Prophet ﷺ. All the Sahaba saw the misdeeds of both, father and son, pass before their mind's eye and they went pale and tense, trembling with suppressed rage. "Look at this fellow," they began to mutter among themselves, "after all that he has done, he has the nerve to present himself to the Presence of the Holy Prophet ﷺ." The Holy Prophet ﷺ was aware of their words, and assuming they would sooner or later say hurtful words to Ikrima, he in his unselfish benevolence exhorted them, "Whoever has any love for me, let him refrain from saying one word to Ikrima about his father!" In this manner he forestalled any comment.

When the Holy Prophet ﷺ sent his commanders out on a campaign, he would give them the following orders: "While you are punishing those who have wronged you, do not touch those who stayed in their houses and performed no hostile actions against you; respect the defenseless state of the women, take particular care with those of them who are nursing young children; do not touch the ailing, take away none of their food or drink; do no damage to their buildings and do not touch their trees."

In view of this, every person of culture and conscience, whether he be Muslim or not, should respectfully acknowledge the sweeping generosity of the Best of Mankind, Muhammad ﷺ. Then they will not find the punishment dealt to the Bani Qurayza excessively harsh. For they had not only fought against the Holy Prophet ﷺ, but they had endangered the very destiny of Islam itself, in that they collated their forces with those of the enemy of God, attacked the safe shelter where the pure wives of the Prophet ﷺ were guarded and did all they could to endanger their safety. As if that wasn't enough, they took to themselves Huyayy bin Akhtab who had been one of the instigators of the War of the Confederates and one of the intriguing villains banished by the Muslims. Him they had befriended, aided and abetted, and inciting all the tribes of Arabia to rise up against Islam. Likewise, they supported the Arabs attachment to idolatry.

Therefore, the Eternal Lord sent the Holy Prophet 🕸 to punish the Bani Qurayza. There is no other way; when the Divine Will comes to pass, the wrongdoer can do aught but cry, "Woe!"

Let us now ask of those who would rally against the Prophet Muhammad's 🕸 actions, while concealing the reality of this issue: In our own day and age, what consequences would a group of people suffer who engaged in such disruptive activities leading to similarly widespread social unrest? How would they be restrained and dealt with nowadays?

Also it must be understood that this punishment was the punishment of Allah. For when Huyayy ibn Akhtab was being brought to Khaybar, he had pledged not to stand against the Prophet 🕸, and Allah was his witness. Now he suffered the consequences of this pledge. Therefore, the Holy Prophet 🕸 said, "Oh people, there can be no objection to the Command of Allah. It is a Divine Judgment, a Conclusion of Heavenly Authority. It is a penalty from the Almighty."

In all, two hundred and fifty people of the Bani Qurayza were executed. Among them was only a single woman, the one who had killed Haddash of the Ansar.

The Reconciliation at al-Hudaybiyah: How the Swords were Returned to their Sheaths and Minds were Conquered Instead

Al-Hudaybiyah was the name of a well that lay one mile's distance from Mecca, and the settlement near the well bore the same name. A most important treaty between the Muslims and the Quraysh was signed here, which is known as the Reconciliation of Hudaybiyah. Outwardly, it might have looked like defeat and surrender for the Muslims, but in reality this reconciliation was a clear triumph, which won over hearts and minds, a remarkable success, and far-reaching victory for the Muslims.

The Muslims were emigrants from their original hometown of Mecca and they were always homesick and longing for the place of their earlier years. Moreover, the Kaba was not the property of the Quraysh, but belonged to the whole Arab nation; the Quraysh were only the guardians and caretakers. Even an enemy, who came to town with the intention of performing a pilgrimage to this holy site, was permitted entry. The Muslims were now eager to perform the pilgrimage to the site where Prophet Ibrahim had erected a temple on command of the Lord. The Prophet Muhammad's ❀ mission involved bringing back to life the religious faith and practices of his ancestor and prophetic predecessor Khalil Ibrahim. The Kaba was the Qibla, that is to say the Lodging of the Divine. Allah Almighty, who is beyond all direction of time and space, commanded the entire Creation of dependent Beings to turn towards this Qibla and to make supplication to Him Almighty.

Although the Holy Prophet ❀ was a great exception in that he, on account of his spiritual nobility, had never veered from the revealed religion of Ibrahim, most of the Arabs had turned into pagans. Despite this, the Arabs all held the Kaba in great esteem, and during the designated months came streaming towards Mecca to perform their pilgrimage. All warfare was prohibited, during the holy months (Ashhur-al-Haram). The same tribesmen, who thirsted for each other's blood, then refrained from fighting and united around the Kaba. This was well known to the Muslims, who were in their rights to say, "Although the visit to the House of the Lord is our ancient right, we have never yet performed the pilgrimage. For six long years we have been deprived."

The Hajj being one of the five pillars of Islam, the Holy Prophet ❀ at last decided to go to Mecca to visit the Holy House. He informed his Companions and they prepared and donned the Ihram, the pilgrims' garb, in order to perform 'Umra, (the lesser pilgrimage), and selected the camels for the sacrifice. The Prophet told his Sahaba not to go outfitted for war, so that the Quraysh might know they were coming with peaceful intentions and only to take with them their swords to protect them on the journey.

Some of the Ansar also begged for permission to come along and the Prophet # granted it to them. Altogether with Muhajirin and Ansar, 1500 Muslims set out for Mecca.

When they had reached Dhul-Hulayfa, the Prophet # told them to separate the camels intended for the sacrifice. He also sent a man of the Khuza'a ahead to the Quraysh who was not known to them as a Muslim to learn of their reaction to the approaching Muslims. This man of Khuza'a whose name was Khirash bin Umayya came as far as Asfal (a quarter of Mecca). He went around among the people, listening to their conversations and opinions on the Muslims' approach, seeking to learn whether they would agree to their entering the town, or not. He found that they were unanimously against the Muslims and intent on going against them by force. They would not permit them to come near the Kaba. He also learned that an armed band of Quraysh had encamped at Dhu Tuwa, and that one of their foremost commanders, Khalid ibn-al-Walid was with them. He, along with Abu Jahl's son Ikrima had each come with an armed battalion and advanced as far as Kura'ul- Ghamim which lies between Rabi' and Hajfar, about eight miles from where the Muslims had halted.

Khirash bin Umayya of the Bani Khuza'a had barely escaped from the hands of the Quraysh. Had it not been for Hulays bin 'Alqama, who was the chief of the Ahabish, and had a reputation for being a fierce warrior, he would not have escaped alive. He brought to the Holy Prophet # all he had learned of the movements of the Arabs in that area. The Prophet # then said to his Companions, "Since Khalid ibn al-Walid has already reached Kura'ul Ghamim, we shall change our course and pass on further to the right."

When the commander of the Quraysh cavalry, Khalid ibn al-Walid saw the dust arising from the Muslims' horses, he instantly spurred his horse and sprinted back to Mecca to inform the Quraysh. "The Muslims have reached Ghamim by way of the pass of al-Murar," he told them.

The Holy Prophet # was riding his camel Qaswa. When he had reached the pass, the camel knelt and nothing would move her to continue on her way.

The Companions thought the animal had tired of the journey, but the Holy Prophet ﷺ said, "No, it is not because she is tired that Qaswa has stopped in her tracks. That is not her nature. The One who restrained the elephant from entering Mecca has kept Qaswa back as well."

The Prophet ﷺ considered it inappropriate to enter the holy city of Mecca in a martial manner. All the more so, as by virtue of his prophetic vision he foresaw many Quraysh soon entering the fold of Islam. The news Khirash had brought them forced the Muslims to gird their swords, but the Prophet Muhammad ﷺ said, "Leave your swords in their sheaths, I will win over their hearts and minds." And he turned to 'Umar, saying to him, "Will you go to them and explain that we haven't come with the intention to make war but for the purpose of peace?"

To this 'Umar replied, "Oh my Prophet ﷺ! My life and soul belong to you, there is nothing I wish for myself, but that my soul would continue in your service a while longer. My hope is not to depart from this life before having completed my service to you. The leaders of the Quraysh know of my violent anger against them. Therefore, they will very probably seek to avail themselves of this opportunity to murder me. Moreover, I have no close clansmen in Mecca whose protection I could claim. Perhaps you might send 'Uthman ibn 'Affan instead? His tribe is strongly represented in Mecca, and many of his relatives live there. However, if you command me to go, so be it. I will set out this very instant."

The Prophet ﷺ replied, "Yes, what you say is more suitable," and turning to 'Uthman bin 'Affan, he said, "Rise, 'Uthman, and go to the Quraysh. Tell them in engaging words that we have not come for war. Go also and find our brothers in Mecca who are forced to conceal their Islam. Give them our Salams and comfort to their hearts."

When 'Uthman approached Mecca, the chiefs of the Quraysh were pleased and received him well. They offered him to go round the Holy House and to make Tawaf. But he declined, saying, "As long as the Imam of the

Prophets 襚 cannot perform Tawaf, I too will not perform it." Hearing this, they detained 'Uthman.

The Muslims meanwhile had reached the well of al-Hudaybiyah, and the Prophet 襚 ordered them to encamp at this place. They drew water from the well once only, then it went dry. Here the Prophet 襚 manifested another miracle and made the water of the place well up again, so that no one suffered any thirst. The tribe of Khuza'a, which lived in this area had not yet accepted Islam, but the tribesmen inclined towards Muhammad 襚 and were allies of the Muslims. They informed the Muslims of the situation in Mecca and the movements of the Quraysh. When Budayl ibn Waraqa heard of the Blessed Prophet's 襚 presence at Hudaybiyah, he came with a deputation of his people to visit him.

He too told of the Quraysh's intention to block the Prophet's progress into Mecca. The Holy Prophet 襚 sent Budayl into Mecca to tell the Quraysh that the Muslims had only come to perform a pilgrimage, and to venerate the Holy House, intending to return to Madinah as soon as they had completed their 'Umra. But when Ikrima and his band of ruffians heard his request, they rejected it straightaway, saying, "Don't speak to us of Muhammad!" 'Urwa bin Mas'ud al-Thaqafi however said, "This one time, let us hear what he has to say. If it suits us we can agree, if it doesn't, we can always turn him down." Harith ibn Hisham and Safwan ibn Umayya agreed and said, "Speak then, if you must." Budayl told them all the words the Holy Prophet 襚 had spoken, and they listened attentively. At last 'Urwa rose and addressed the Quraysh, asking them, "What do you think of me? Do you trust in me? Am I not as your father, and are you not as my children?" The Quraysh answered, "We trust you in every respect." "In that case," he said, "I see it fit to accept Muhammad's 襚 offer. I find his suggestion agreeable. Therefore I will go to him at once and speak to him about this matter between you."

The Quraysh agreed to 'Urwa's going to speak to Muhammad 襚. When he came into the presence of the Messenger of Allah 襚, he explained that he had come on behalf of the Quraysh and began to speak, "Oh Muhammad

❀! Know that the Quraysh are fully prepared and expecting you. All the Bedouin tribes here are under the sway of the Quraysh. You will understand that your hastily put together troop here is as nothing compared to the strength of the fully equipped force awaiting you. Apart from that, let us assume for a moment that you would vanquish the Quraysh: you would have then destroyed your own people – a wrong unheard of in the history of mankind! Similarly, if the force gathered around the Quraysh were to be set in motion, it would crush you and those with you like specks of dust."

Thus 'Urwa spoke biting words to the gathering of Sahaba whose hearts were bound to the Holy Prophet ❀ in utter sincerity. At long last, Abu Bakr could stand no more and spoke to 'Urwa in a hostile manner, saying, "Be careful, 'Urwa, these men here belong to the Messenger of Allah ❀, none of us has any self-interest left within. As you have failed to grasp this, you cannot see that the power of faith follows the pursuit of truth."

'Urwa was dumbfounded by these words. Who was the speaker, he wondered, and looking around, he recognized Abu Bakr. He then said to him, "I would reply to this, oh Abu Bakr, but as I remember the good I have seen from you in the past, I will desist." With that he turned once more and addressed the Holy Prophet ❀. When he paused in his speech, he reached over in the manner of the Arabs to stroke the Prophet's ❀ beard, in an overly familiar fashion. Aware that this act signified a lack of respectful remove, Mughira bin Shu'ba al-Thaqafi who attended to the Holy Prophet ❀ cried out in an state of eagerness inspired by love, "Beware, oh 'Urwa! Take your hand away from the face of the Messenger of Allah ❀ before you lose it!" Mughira spoke these harsh words even though 'Urwa was his maternal uncle.

'Urwa looked about to see who was insulting him in this way, and when he recognized his brother's child, he was dumbfounded and thought to himself, "So the love this Messenger of Allah ❀ inspires in his followers knows not the ties of blood nor does it bow before force." This was indeed the case; these souls fluttered about the Holy Prophet ❀, fitted with the wings of the attestation of Eternal Unity and the Divine Sending of the

Holy Prophet ﷺ, like moths around the lamp. If as much as a single hair fell from the head of the Beloved of Allah ﷺ, they would dive to pick up this hair and it was more precious to them than all the riches of the world. 'Urwa realized this very clearly now, and he also understood, that there was no way to extinguish the blaze that had been ignited on Mount Hira when Muhammad ﷺ had taken up the cause of "La ilaha illAllah" single-handedly.

Then the Heavenly Prophet ﷺ began to speak, "Know that we have come only to perform the rites of our pilgrimage. We are willing to conclude a ceasefire with the Quraysh. But if they insist on making trouble, we will be forced to use our arms and we shall fight to the very end."

'Urwa returned to Mecca and explained all he had seen and heard to the Quraysh. He said, "I have seen the palaces of Khosroes, I have been at the court of the Emperor of Byzantium and at the royal residence of the Negus. I have seen and spoken to a great many high and mighty kings in my time. But, by God, never have I seen a king among his people like Muhammad ﷺ among his companions. When Muhammad ﷺ prepares to speak, a silence settles on the assembly, a hush befalls both Heaven and earth as if they were straining to hear his words. Not one of them even lifts his gaze from the ground. It will not be easy to do away with this band, for they will never abandon him for any reason. Therefore, we must tread the path of concession and reconciliation."

The chief of the Ahabish, Hulays who had followed this discussion from its outset was very intrigued by all this. He decided to go and see for himself, so he hastened to the Muslim camp. There he beheld a great many camels being prepared for the sacrifice, decorated in festive ribbons and colorful ornaments. The Sahaba were reciting "Labbayk" in loud, ringing voices, which means "Command us, oh Lord, we are at your beck and call." (*Labbayk Allahumma labbayk, la sharika laka labbayk.*)

The leader of the Ahabish was astounded by this display of pious reverence and sincere devotion by the Prophet's followers. He immediately went to the Quraysh and told them, "If you are counting on us to support you against the Muslims of Muhammad ﷺ, forget it. How can you think of preventing a group of pilgrims from visiting the House of Allah? Indeed, you are our allies, but in this matter, count us out. Surely the Arab tribes will not approve of your blocking these pilgrims from their visit to the Holy House."

The Quraysh thought about what he had said and in the end they were forced to admit that they had to agree to a truce. They sent Suhayl bin 'Amr who was a well-spoken and eloquent man as a go-between to the Messenger of Allah ﷺ. Suhayl was one of the fiery orators of the Quraysh. When he met with the Permanent Pride of All Mankind, he said to him, "Oh Muhammad ﷺ! If you would accept what the Quraysh are suggesting, we will make peace with you. Our first stipulation is this: you may enter Mecca this year, but not to make Tawaf. You will return to Madinah without having made Tawaf for this reason: if you were to complete your visit of the Holy House this year, we would have forfeited all honor and dignity. The Arab tribesmen would assume that Muhammad ﷺ and his companions entered Mecca by force and defeated the mighty Quraysh. You may return next year to make your Tawaf."

After they had discussed all these points in detail, the Holy Prophet ﷺ accepted the postponement of their pilgrimage until the following year. He then ordered Ali to write down the treaty. Then Ali - who was ever close to the Prophet ﷺ, who enjoyed his complete confidence - made to write down the contract. He began by writing the momentous words, which are pronounced at the outset of every undertaking to ensure its success: Bismillahir-Rahmanir-Rahim. Suhayl, however objected to this formula, and insisted that he should write the words *'Bismika Allahumma'* (In Thy Name, oh God), deeming the treaty to be deficient if this phrase were not employed. Though some of the companions demurred, the Holy Prophet ﷺ ordered Ali to write *"Bismika Allahumma."*

After these words, he continued to write: "Muhammad, the Prophet of Allah ﷺ agrees to the terms of the truce" but Suhayl raised objections. "If we had accepted you as 'Rasulullah'," he said, "there would have been no fighting, nor would it this truce have been necessary. There would be no cause for contention between us, nor would we have barred you from visiting the Holy House." Thereupon, the Holy Prophet ﷺ changed the wording of the text and ordered Ali to write 'Muhammad ibn Abdullah'. At this, the Companions were very distressed and trembled with rage. But Muhammad ﷺ himself never lost his solemnity and composure and said, "Oh Ali, cross out what you have written and write instead 'Muhammad ibn Abdullah'. For their denial of my prophethood changes nothing at all, I am indeed Rasulullah, the Messenger of Allah Almighty. His confirmation is all that matters; His acceptance suffices me."

For Allah declares in His Glorious Quran, which will remain fresh and alive until the end of time and contains all that is needful for the whole Muslim community:

It is He who has sent His Messenger with the guidance and the religion of truth, that He may uplift it above every religion, though the unbelievers may be averse.

(Repentance, 33)

With this Divine Appellation 'Muhammad ar-Rasulullah,' He Almighty affirmed His Beloved Prophet ﷺ, saying to him, "My Beloved, I have equipped you with Divine inspiration."

Therefore, the Prophet ﷺ in whom were manifested the qualities of this verse of glory said to Ali, "No harm, oh Ali! Cross it out and write 'ibn Abdullah'." Ali who up to this time had not once opposed the wish or will of the Holy Prophet ﷺ, and who had not once hesitated to fulfill the slightest indication of any wish he expressed, this great Imam now paused. His hand refused to erase the words he had written, "Muhammad ar-Rasulullah." Tears burning in his eyes, he said, "Oh my Prophet ﷺ, I cannot erase these words." Upon this the Holy Prophet ﷺ said to him, "Know, oh Ali, that one day a similar thing will happen to you." This referred to an event in the future.

Through miraculous vision, the Holy Prophet ﷺ informed of Ali's actions after the Battle of Siffin: When Ali was signing an agreement of truce with the governor of Sham, Mu'awiya, the latter in his rebelliousness objected to the use of the term 'Amir-al-Mu'minin', the Commander of the Faithful, saying, "Were I to accept you as Commander of the Faithful, I would be your follower and this fighting would not have taken place. Therefore, cross out this title 'Amir-al-Mu'minin', and simply write 'Ali ibn Abi Talib'."

Of this event the Holy Prophet ❀ informed Ali many years before it took place by means of prophetic vision. When the time came and Ali saw confirmed the Prophet's ❀ vision and his words to him at Hudaybiyah, he said, "You have spoken truly, oh Rasulullah," and he crossed out the term 'Commander of the Faithful' and simply wrote, 'Ali ibn Abi Talib'.

Oh Seeker of the Truth! The mention of this great Imam who never once hesitated or wavered at any request the Holy Prophet ❀ made of him, brings to mind another story, precisely illustrating this point, which we commend to the worthy reader's regard.

One day in Ramadan, the Holy Prophet ❀ pointed to a melon atop a high shelf and asked the Companions assembled in his blessed presence to kindly cut it up for him, as he was much in the mood of eating a melon. Each one he asked replied, "Oh Rasulullah ❀, perhaps you have forgotten that we are fasting today." At last Ali chanced to stop by and the Prophet ❀ said to him, "Oh Ali, I have an appetite for this melon, won't you cut it up for us so we may eat it?" Ali immediately rose to get the melon from the shelf and began to cut it up. The Companions present at the time said to him, "Oh Ali, you must have forgotten that it is Ramadan." Ali, the mirror of the Holy Prophet ❀, the gate to the citadel of wisdom replied, "It is from his Holiness that I learned about the fast of Ramadan; if he says, 'Eat!' I eat, and if he says, 'Fast!' I fast. That is all."

The Holy Prophet ❀, Imam of all Prophets, then smiled and said to the Companions, "We shall all eat of it, for just now the angel Jibra'il has come to tell me that today is the 'Id of Ramadan. But take heed, all of you, and try to be a bit like Ali."

Only once did Ali oppose the Holy Prophet ❀, saying, "I will not cross out the words I have written, Muhammad Rasulullah." Therefore the Holy

Prophet ﷺ said, "Give it to me, I will write it myself." With his own blessed hand, he crossed out these words in the contract and wrote in their stead, 'Muhammad ibn Abdullah'. Later this incident gave rise to some dispute. Some people asked, "How could the Prophet who was purportedly unlettered, and unversed in the art of reading or writing, how could he have written his name with his own hand?" This is a very crude and base way of thinking. It is true that the Holy Prophet ﷺ did not read or write books as we do, but if he wished to do so, he was able to read or write whatever he wished. Nothing is more inappropriate than to look for the Prophet's ﷺ 'school teacher' for the Prophet ﷺ was called 'unlettered' (ummi) because in reality he is the mother (umm) of all knowledge. Otherwise, how could he have left behind such an ocean of knowledge, since he had no formal schooling?

It is actually more than futile to speak of his miraculous deeds to a person who does not regard the mere existence of the Prophet Muhammad ﷺ as a miracle. Allah is the teacher of all prophets. The Holy Prophet Muhammad ﷺ was taught by Allah Almighty. The first Scripture He created were the Preserved Tablets; the last was the book containing Eternal Knowledge, the Ultimate Word that took the shape of Mercy. The Holy Prophet ﷺ, the Canon of Truth, should he need to read or write in the sense that you understand? But even for those who cannot comprehend the real inner meaning of the Prophet's existence, those who only view his outward form, there is no need to engage in dispute concerning the ability of the Holy Prophet ﷺ to write his name and patronymic. For even an ignorant simpleton can learn to write his own name by imitation. To proceed in our story: The ceasefire was designed to last for ten years, thus it was written down. The conditions of this treaty were very hard, and outwardly, it looked as if the Muslims were at a disadvantage.

These were the articles of the treaty:

1. For the afore-mentioned reasons the followers of Muhammad shall this year turn back without having made Tawaf of the Kaba.

2.   They may return to Mecca in the following year to make their visit, but they may stay no longer than three days and the Quraysh will leave the town for the duration of their visit.

3.   The Muslims will not enter the town with their weapons and war gear at the ready, but will leave their swords in their scabbards.

4.   Whoever comes to the Muslims from the Quraysh without leave will be returned to the Quraysh. However, any Muslims coming to the Quraysh will be surrendered to Quraysh. Should a Muslim come to Mecca, he will not be returned to the Muslims. The followers of Muhammad ❀ are not to have any contact with any believers who might be living in Mecca. However, if any of the emigrants to Madinah wish to remain in Mecca, there will be no interference, they will be left in peace.

5.   All tribes other than Quraysh will be left to choose for themselves. If they wish, they may enter into a pact of safety with Muhammad ❀, or if they wish, they may conclude such an agreement with the Quraysh.

The Companions of the Holy Prophet ❀ thought all the conditions of this treaty were exceedingly harsh. In particular, they found it very hard to accept that anyone coming to the Quraysh from Muhammad's ❀ side was not to be returned, whereas anyone coming from the Quraysh to Muhammad ❀, and be he a Muslim, must be returned to the Quraysh. With ʿUmar as their spokesman, they asked the Holy Prophet ❀ how he could possibly accept such a treaty, how he could consider delivering a Muslim into the hands of the idolaters? They maintained that he ought to reject this one condition at the very least, and if necessary cancel the whole agreement. But Suhayl vehemently insisted on this clause, saying that their refusal to accept it would invalidate the whole contract.

In the end, the Holy Prophet ❀ smiled and said, "Oh ʿUmar, assuming one of them came to us as a Muslim, and we returned him to them; in that case the blood wit for the injustice and mistreatment he suffered at their hands would be paid by the Almighty. No greater blessing can be imagined for that person. As for those who would desert us and join the unbelievers, all connection with them would be severed in any case."

All these points were written down. Just as they were about to sign and witness the contract in the presence of elders from both sides, the son of the Qurayshi delegate Suhayl came running up, having escaped his captors. His name was Abu Jandal and he was a dedicated believer, imprisoned by his own father. The fetters on his feet clanked in rhythm with his loud shouts of "Allahu Akbar" as he ran up to them. He threw himself at the Prophet's blessed feet, utterly exhausted, kissing them and pleading, "Oh my Prophet ﷺ, save me! For the love of you I have fled from the torment these heathens are inflicting on me. Just look at me!" With these words he exposed to view the wounds and injuries all over his body, such as no man should be made to suffer. In reality, the Lord Almighty was showing them an example of a believer who, though entangled in the drama of this worldly life, was replete with religious passion.

The Sahaba were overcome with emotions of pity and compassion. But the Qurayshi delegate Suhayl was only further enraged by the deep feelings his son Abu Jandal exhibited towards the Holy Prophet ﷺ and the noble religion of Islam. "This incident will immediately prove whether you intend to honor the treaty we are about to sign, or not," he declared. "You will instantly surrender to me my son, Abu Jandal!"

The Prophet ﷺ answered, "We have decided to sign the contract, but we will make an exception for Abu Jandal. Whoever comes after this, him we will return to you." Suhayl replied, "In that case the treaty is pointless." The Prophet ﷺ then said, "Alright, we will leave Abu Jandal at Hudaybiyah." But Suhayl insisted obstinately and refused to accept this. Outwardly this treaty was very harsh indeed, but seen with the eye of Muhammad ﷺ, it contained great good. Therefore, the Holy Prophet ﷺ finally consented to return Abu Jandal to his father's hands. This decision completely unsettled the Companions and they became quite agitated. Abu Jandal pleaded with Muhammad ﷺ, saying, "I throw myself upon your mercy! Will you really deliver me into the hands of the unbelievers although I am a Muslim, oh Rasulullah ﷺ? Can you permit them to torment me even worse than before, oh my Prophet ﷺ?"

The Holy Prophet 🕉 then made Abu Jandal sit by his side and asked him, "Oh Abu Jandal, is there any love that you feel for me?" "Of course, my Prophet 🕉," answered the man. "And what of your love for this religion of Islam?" "For it I would sacrifice everything," replied Abu Jandal. "It is therefore that I am surrendering you to them, Abu Jandal," replied the Prophet 🕉, "for you will be made to suffer just a little more in the name of Allah for my sake and for the love of Islam, but your Lord has heard your supplication and your soul will no longer feel any of their mistreatment, only your heart will feel some pain. You must know that Allah Almighty has given you great merit for that your tribulation is great.

"The reward for your patience will be vast stations in the Divine Realm. For the Lord Almighty has linked with your destiny the coming to Islam of hundreds of thousands of non-believers. In a very short time, you will come to understand the underlying wisdom. This treaty will enable us to freely contact a great many people. The sun of Islam will rise and become visible. Whoever sees this sun will become enamored of Islam. At this time, the enemy does not permit us any contacts and we cannot approach the Arab tribesmen because of the false propaganda they have spread about us, but you will be the means for reversing this evil." Thereupon Abu Jandal answered, "Oh Rasulullah 🕉, for your sake, for the sake of this way I am content, even were they to cut me to pieces, bit by bit. As you wish, so let it be," he said. He was then returned to his father Suhayl, the delegate of Quraysh, and the contract was signed.

Of course, the Companions did not perceive the situation as their Prophet 🕉 did. 'Umar, in particular, who was of a very violent nature, could not come to terms with this contract. When Abu Jandal was delivered back into the hands of his enemies, 'Umar could not keep his composure any longer. He approached the Holy Prophet 🕉 in a state of blunt rage and asked him these questions, "Are you not the true Prophet of Allah?" "Yes," Muhammad 🕉 replied, "I am in truth the Prophet of Allah." "Is our religion not based on the Truth? Is the path we follow not a true path?" "Yes, it is the Truth," answered the Prophet 🕉. "If that is the case, why then do we acquiesce to so much abasement and humiliation?" The Holy Prophet 🕌 then said, "Be careful, oh 'Umar! For I am the Prophet of Allah 🕌, and I cannot disobey my Lord!" With these words the Holy Prophet 🕌 uttered a warning to 'Umar, though he expressed this with the characteristic delicacy that was his mark.

He indicated to him indirectly that he was just short of rebelling against the Lord Almighty, thereby preserving him. Had he simply said, "'Umar, you are on the verge of rebellion", 'Umar would have been devastated. 'Umar went on to say, "Oh my Prophet 🕌, did you not say we would reach the Kaba and make Tawaf there, and did you not tell us that Allah would support us?" Rasulullah 🕌 replied to this, "Yes, indeed, I did say we would make Tawaf, but I did not say that it would be in this year. We will come again." 'Umar then left the presence of the Holy Prophet 🕌, went to Abu Bakr and said to him, "Oh Abu Bakr, what kind of a treaty is this, which imposes such rigid conditions on us!" Abu Bakr thereupon said, "Oh 'Umar, there is no need to be upset, for Muhammad 🕌 is an exalted Prophet. He does aught but what Allah Almighty commands him to do. There is doubtless wisdom in everything he does; only we cannot yet understand it. Be patient."

The Holy Prophet 🕌 ordered the Sahaba to begin the sacrifice of the camels they had brought with them. But although the Pride of the Worlds repeated his order thrice, not a single man moved to act on his command, except Abu Bakr as-Siddiq and Ali. All the noble Companions were thinking to themselves, "Perhaps the Holy Prophet 🕌 will take pity on us and make changes to this treaty."

These thoughts disturbed the Holy Prophet 🕌 greatly. In a vexed frame of mind, he proceeded to the camp of his retinue where his estimable wife Umm Salama was staying. When she perceived his state, Umm Salama was quite upset and said to him, "Oh Prophet of Allah 🕌! Never before have I seen you in such a condition! What has happened?" The Holy Prophet answered her, "Oh Umm Salama, the companions who yesterday were ready to die for me, today will not heed my words!"

413

Umm-al-Mu'minin, the Mother of the Believers Umm Salama then said, with the intention of defending the Sahaba, "Oh no, Rasulullah ﷺ, it is not because of their unwillingness, it is only because of their inability to understand the true wisdom of this treaty. In particular, that they act as they do because of their sincerity towards you. They are thinking, 'Now the enemy has prevailed over our noble Prophet ﷺ and imposed their will on him'. This thought makes them deaf and dumb with anger. They are thinking that perhaps the Prophet ﷺ will take into account their disapproval and make changes to the treaty. But then, your actions and doings speak louder than your words. Go out to them now and begin to sacrifice the camels, and shave your head. You will see them following suit."

The Holy Prophet ﷺ was very pleased with these words of Umm Salama and said, "Do you really think so, Umm Salama?" "Yes, oh my Prophet ﷺ," she said, and the Holy Prophet ﷺ thereupon arose and went out to the camels. Umm Salama then prayed fervently, "Oh my Lord, do not embarrass me now!" And truly, when the Holy Prophet ﷺ began to slaughter his camels, all the Companions followed his example and slaughtered their sacrifices as well, thereby emerging from their state of Ihram.

The Pledge of Allegiance, Baiyat-i-Ridwan

Oh Seeker of the Truth! On the occasion of the Truce of Hudaybiyah a very important and deeply meaningful event took place, which became known as the *Bi'at-i-Ridwan*, the Pledge of Allegiance.

It has already been told how the Holy Prophet ﷺ had sent 'Uthman into Mecca to inform the Muslims living there in concealment of their faith of the negotiations which the Holy Prophet ﷺ was conducting with the Quraysh in the name of Islam. He was to tell them that before long Islam would openly shine forth in Mecca, giving them glad tidings of the Conquest of Mecca. The reasons for the delay have also been related. Now that the contract was signed, everyone waited for 'Uthman's return. A rumor began coursing the camp that 'Uthman had been martyred. The Holy

Prophet ﷺ was sitting beneath a mastic tree (Pistacia lentiscus) when this rumor reached his ears. He said, "If this is true, I cannot turn back without punishing Quraysh, we will then be obliged to fight them." He sent a crier to call for all the Muslims to hear: "The Holy Prophet ﷺ wants all those to come forth who are willing to pledge their lives for the sake of Islam!"

The Sahaba who heard this call all came running to the presence of the Prophet ﷺ, saying, "Oh Rasulullah ﷺ! We have accepted the God you taught us, we have placed you on our heads as the crown of joy, we are enamored of the religion you have brought us, we are ready to sacrifice our whole existence for Islam! Are you yet in doubt about us?" "No," replied the Prophet ﷺ, "it is for another reason: on account of this particular pledge, very special blessings will manifest. I have called on all that will remain steadfast and faithful to come to me now. So, who will stand by me till this affair is ended, who is prepared to give his very life and soul?"

Men and women then gathered in the presence of the Holy Prophet ﷺ in a spirit of utter love and devotion, and placing their hands beneath the blessed hand of the King of Prophets ﷺ, they pledged themselves to him: "Oh Rasulullah, we solemnly pledge to die for you and not to turn back. Our whole being belongs to you." There was only one man among them, the hypocrite Jadd ibn Qays who hid behind his camel in order not to commit himself by this pledge. The Holy Prophet ﷺ who knew how hugely important this pledge was in the Divine Presence, wished that 'Uthman might not be deprived of the unfathomable blessings because of his absence. Therefore, he called to his Companions to be his witnesses and said, "Oh my Lord! My left hand shall stand for that of 'Uthman," placing his left hand below his right hand. In this way, he let 'Uthman partake of this pledge of allegiance and of its inherent blessings.

The Eternal Lord speaks of this event, which took place on the worldly stage between His Beloved and his Companions in the revelation of the Holy Quran:

Those who swear fealty to thee swear fealty in truth to God; God's hand is over their hands. Then whosoever breaks his oath breaks it but to his own hurt; and whoso fulfils his covenant made with God, God will give him a mighty wage.

(Victory, 10)

If one reads attentively, it will appear that the Lord here indicates to His servants that there will remain no trace of deficient existence in His Beloved, but rather that he will become completely immersed in the Lord and established in permanence. However, this interpretation relates to those who have tasted of real faith; as for believers who are yet on the level of imitative faith, they may glean this meaning from this verse: Allah's Might is above and beyond their powers.

Allah indicates the great good tidings of Divine Pleasure contained in this pledge of Hudaybiyah in this verse:

God was well pleased with the believers when they were swearing fealty to thee under the tree, and He knew what was in their hearts, so He sent down the Sakina (inner peace) upon them, and rewarded them with a nigh victory and many spoils to take; and God is ever All-Mighty, all-Wise. (Victory, 18)

There is yet another subtle lesson to be learnt by the Nation of Muhammad from the Truce of Hudaybiyah. First of all, this treaty teaches us composure in the face of adversity; next, it counsels us to look ahead to the consequences of an action, and finally it indicates that mental power will certainly overcome physical force. As an example, let us say we see something bad. If we go and try to crush it right away it, that may not be very efficient, but if we contain our impulse and are patient, and wait for the right time to deal with the matter, it will be much more effective. All these lessons are contained in the events at Hudaybiyah.

The outcome was as follows:

Gradually, results began to appear from this treaty which outwardly seemed to be a defeat for the Muslims, but which in reality was a victory. For the radiance of the Holy Prophet's ﷺ inspired countenance, his prophetic refinement, the compassion and support he dispensed upon all, the unbeliever not excepted, the mercy he showed to his foes, the freedom Islam preached, the abhorrence and banning of idol worship – most of the pagans who witnessed these signs began to direct their hearts towards Islam, and even the ones who were not honored with the destiny of becoming Muslims, became less hopelessly entrenched in their enmity.

In a short while, this peace treaty became a major cause for the spread of Islam, as the unbelievers were now free to mingle with the Muslims. This social intercourse won over people's minds, so that people came in great numbers and melted down their coarseness in the crucible of the Prophet Muhammad's ❀ gentle radiance, so that it was turned into subtlety and delicacy. The leaders of the idolaters found themselves increasingly isolated.

This verse was then revealed:

> *Surely, We have given thee a manifest victory....*   *(Victory, 1)*

The unbelievers who came to visit their relatives who had become followers of the Prophet ❀ saw that their condition was excellent and that they did not wish to return. In a very short time, the Muslim ranks swelled and many more accepted Islam than in the year before the treaty of Hudaybiyah.

Khalid ibn-al Walid, the staff general and cavalry commander of the pagan Arab army then turned to Islam. The man who was to become the future conqueror of Syria and to gain the title of "Sayfullah," the Sword of Allah, became Muslim, and he was a great boon for the Muslims. The leaders of the unbelievers were plunged into despair. Only then did 'Umar begin to understand the wisdom of the Truce of Hudaybiyah.

One day the Prophet ❀ had 'Umar called and said to him, "'Umar, once you wished to speak to me in private. Now I wish to see you privately." 'Umar then realized his mistake. "Yes, oh my Prophet," he said, "I have opposed you in many matters, but I always rely on your magnanimity, for you have always answered my roughness with gentle pardon. You wish to remind me of the Truce of Hudaybiyah, is it not so? On that day I railed against you and was insolent, but it was because of my strong faith in you.

Yes, I complained to you of you – to whom else could I have taken my complaint? Please forgive my failings, we are people whom you saved but yesterday from the age of ignorance." The Holy Prophet 🕮 smiled at 'Umar's words and answered him in courteous terms and treated him kindly.

The clause in the treaty of Hudaybiyah concerning the return of those who fled to Madinah applied only to the men, not to the women. On their account the following verse was revealed:

> *Oh believers! when believing women come to you as emigrants, test them, God knows very well their belief. Then, if you know them to be believers, return them not to the unbelievers. They are not permitted to the unbelievers, nor are the unbelievers permitted to them. Give the unbelievers what they have expended; and there is no fault in you to marry them when you have given them their wages. Do not hold fast to the ties of unbelieving women, and ask what you have expended, and let them ask what they have expended. That is God's judgment; He judges between you; and God is All-Knowing, All-Wise.(The Woman Tested, 10)*

During this period 'Utba bin Asid became Muslim in Mecca, and when the mistreatment he suffered from the unbelievers exceeded all limits, he decided to flee from Mecca to Madinah. The Quraysh sent after him two men with the mission of bringing 'Utba back to Mecca. 'Utba cried out and pleaded, "Oh Rasulullah 🕮! Do not deliver me into their hands, for I cannot I bear to be among the unbelievers again!" But the Holy Prophet 🕮 replied, "We cannot break our pact with the Quraysh. You will return for the sake of Islam. Be patient. Allah will surely open a path for you and those like you. For this noble religion you must endure a bit of hardship." And he prayed to the Lord Almighty, "Oh my Lord God! Make it easy for them and show them a path for salvation!" Then he returned 'Utba to the envoys of the Quraysh.

On the road, 'Utba said to the men who were taking him back, "Why is it that you want to inflict cruelty on me? Why don't you just let me go?" They answered, "You are one of the Muslims. It is a pleasure for us to torment you and cause you to suffer." They traveled up to the place called Dhul-Hulayfa. 'Utba thought of ways to free himself from the hands of his merciless captors. He was a very strong man. At a certain point he managed to wrest the sword from the hand of the man who was guarding him, and with a single stroke he severed his head from his trunk, shouting, "Just deserts for him who intended to torment one who only desires to follow the Path of Truth and who bows before no one but Allah!"

The unbeliever's head rolled in the sand and his friend took to flight. He barely managed to escape from 'Utba. Somewhat later, 'Utba came again into the presence of the Holy Prophet #, defending himself thus, "Oh my Prophet #! You accorded to the letter of the articles in the treaty you have concluded. I fled to Madinah, they sent men after me to bring me back; they demanded me from you, you delivered me in to their hands, they took me away. Therefore, you are blameless; you have not broken the truce. As for me, after I was handed over, I defended myself and with Divine Help and Succor, I was spared. This has no more to do with the treaty of Hudaybiyah. Will you now not grant me permission to stay in Madinah?"

The Holy Prophet # replied, "The treaty stipulates as a necessary requirement that you be returned whenever they demand it. Therefore, I cannot keep you here in Madinah. Go wherever you wish, as long as you leave the city of Madinah."

'Utba immediately left the city when the Prophet # ordered him to do so, and settled near the coast at a place called al-'Is. The Muslims remaining in Mecca heard of this, and one by one they began to move north toward al-'Is. In a short while quite a number of Muslims were gathered at al-'Is. Even Abu Jandal managed once more to escape from the prison his father kept him in, and he, too, joined 'Utba at al-'Is. Before Abu Jandal's arrival, 'Utba had been the leader and Imam of the group, but when Abu Jandal arrived, he took over as Imam.

One day they decided that they had sufficient numbers to find a way of joining the Holy Prophet #. For in the treaty, the unbelievers had demanded that all fugitives to Madinah must be returned to Mecca. "Now

Allah has given us the means for doing away with this clause. We are now a group of some strength, comprising seventy men. Let us therefore resort to harassing the passing caravans of the Quraysh. They will then go to Muhammad ﷺ of their own accord and beg for this condition to be annulled." They put their decision into action and began to waylay the Quraysh caravans. It was not long before a delegation of Quraysh came to the Holy Prophet ﷺ, asking him to cancel the condition concerning the return of the fugitives to the Quraysh. After this, the Prophet ﷺ wrote ʿUtba a letter, inviting him and his companions to come and stay with him at Madinah.

When this letter arrived, ʿUtba was already very ill, nearly at the point of death. When they told him that the Prophet ﷺ had sent him a letter, he seemed to come back to life in spite of his grave condition. "Read it to me!" he demanded. The Prophet's ﷺ letter was read to him: "The Quraysh have requested that the clause for the return of the fugitives from Mecca to Madinah be annulled. We now invite you and your companions to come and stay with us at Madinah." ʿUtba thanked Allah and pronounced blessings upon the Holy Prophet ﷺ, then he said, "Allah has made me the instrument for relieving the Muslims of the worst and heaviest demand of the treaty of Hudaybiyah. Thanks to Him and unending Praise and Glory." Then, turning to his friends, he said, "Go to the Prophet ﷺ and give him my Salams, with the expression of my veneration. You have heard for yourselves that he is pleased with me, so be my witnesses in the Presence of Allah Almighty and hurry to Madinah at once." With that he pressed the letter to his eyes and forehead and passed from this world of woe to the Eternal Abode. Abu Jandal prayed the funeral prayer over him, and after they had buried him at al-ʿIs, they departed for Madinah.

After this, the caravan routes of the Quraysh were opened again and caravans traveled along them unmolested.

As mentioned before, this term of the agreement did not apply to the women. There was nothing in the treaty that demanded their return to the unbelievers. In these days Umm Kulthum, the daughter of ʿUqba, one of the leading Quraysh, became Muslim. Her brothers al-Walid and 'Umara came and demanded her extradition. The Holy Prophet ﷺ refused to comply with their demand. Thereafter, the Sahaba who had unbelieving wives who had remained in Mecca divorced themselves from them.

In this way, they evaded the treaty of Hudaybiyah. Some time after this, the Holy Prophet ﷺ said, "The time has come for the disclosure and spreading of Islam." For the religion of Islam was never meant to be restricted to one people, one community, or one continent. It was meant as a universal religion, to be spread from one end of the world to the other, and the Imam of Prophets ﷺ was sent as a messenger of glad tidings and as a Warner, to teach and to make known his message far and wide.

For indeed Islam is a religion of Unity, its monotheism balancing the excesses of idolatrous similitude with Allah's absolute incomparability. It proclaims the Oneness of Divinity. It values the mind's reason. Judged by a sound mind, every revealed law proves to have a rational basis. Islam disapproves of idolatry, injustice, hypocrisy, and unbelief, and whoever is inclined towards these things is considered an unbeliever. It forbids the worship of any feeble human creature and discourages men from becoming a tyrant's knaves. It prevents people from trampling under foot the natural morality of mankind. The observance of the rights of all sentient beings is the most eminent of all God-pleasing acts.

The most preferential status in the community is due to the most reverent towards the Lord Almighty and the most compassionate towards His Creation.

He shall not be questioned as to what He does, but they shall be questioned.

(The Prophets, 23)

This signifies that everyone but Allah Almighty is to be held responsible, whether he is the president or a sheikh, a religious teacher, a scholar or a man of virtue. Everyone will be called to account, according to the teaching of Islam.

Islam rules that the ruler be judged by the same criteria as the slave. All worldly activity is to be hallowed by the intention to strive for the world as if one was never to die, and to work for the afterlife as if one were to die tomorrow. Islam values all knowledge; it prefers the corrupt man of learning to the ignorantly devout worshipper.

Islam demands the Remembrance of Allah (Dhikrullah) to be pronounced not only in words, but demands that the Dhikr be contained in all deeds and states of mind, and its application to all circumstances.

Wealth is acceptable as long as it does no harm to another man. Islam has made the poor man to be the brother of the rich man. Islam teaches us that if a person is amenable to a tyrant, his name will be erased from the slate of Islam. This religion being the religion of love, his name will be written in the book of those who busied themselves with the love of other than Islam, and who were ruled by the opinions of their lower soul. The foundation of disbelief is the exaltation of the base, and the abasement of the high and noble.

Messages to Various Rulers

After the treaty of Hudaybiyah, all these issues were brought out into the open and publicly proclaimed. The Holy Prophet ﷺ gathered all his Sahaba around him and related to them what had been revealed to him concerning his own noble person:

And We have not sent thee, save as a mercy unto all beings. (The Prophets, 107)

He went on to say, "Now the time has come to proclaim the truth. I am about to send you each with a written message to the kings and lords of the great civilizations of this day and age. But beware from falling into disagreement with one another as did the disciples of Isa." Then he sent various Sahaba to these kings: Dihya bin Khalifa was sent to the Byzantine Emperor Heraclius; Abdullah bin Hudhafa as-Sahmi to the Khosroes of Iran, Parviz; Hatib ibn Abi Balta'a to the Aziz Muqawqis of Egypt, and 'Amr ibn Umayya was sent to the Negus of Abyssinia. Salit bin 'Amr al-Amiri he sent to the ruler of Yamama; and Shuja' bin Wahb to al-Mundhir al-Ghassani, the lord of Damascus as his messengers and envoys.

At this time the holy verse was revealed:

Alif. Lam. Mim. The Romans have been vanquished in the nearer part of the land; and, after their vanquishing, they shall be the victors in a few years. To God belongs the Command before and after; and on that day the believers shall rejoice in God's help; God helps whomsoever He will; and He is the All-Mighty, the All-Compassionate. (The Romans, 1-5)

423

The Byzantine Emperor Heraclius

According to this Divine statement and indication, in the year that the Holy Prophet 🌼 indicated, the Byzantine Emperor Heraclius moved out with a great army against Iran and vanquished them. On the occasion of his victory he came to Jerusalem and was greeted there enthusiastically by the people of the city. All the streets were laid out with carpets and strewn with flowers. The Prophet's 🌼 letter happened to reach him just at that time, while he was in Jerusalem. In these days, the Ghassani were under the protectorate of Byzantium. Their chief, al-Mundhir al-Harith of the tribe of Hauran resided at Busra. The Muslim envoy Dihya handed the epistle over to al-Mundhir al-Harith of the Hauran who brought the letter to the Emperor.

The Emperor read the letter, then turned to his retainers and said, "Bring to me some of the Arabs who live in these parts." For the Emperor wished to gather reliable information concerning the character of Muhammad 🌼 before he left Syria. So people were sent out to find such persons who had information about Muhammad 🌼. It so happened that Abu Sufyan was traveling in business to Ghaza. He and his entourage were invited to an audience before the imperial presence. That day the Emperor ordered his state pavilion to be lavishly adorned and decorated with luxurious trimmings. He seated himself upon the throne, his crown upon his head. The dignitaries of Byzantium, the spiritual heads of the Empire, his bishops and abbots were all assembled round him.

When the Arab merchants entered, the Emperor asked them the following questions: "Is there any one among you who is personally acquainted with the Prophet who has sent me this letter?" Abu Sufyan stepped forward and said, "It is I who am closest to him," even though he himself had pronounced upon the death of Abu Jahl, "Not to worry, I will put an end to this affair which Muhammad 🌼 has begun; I will cause his name to be forgotten." The Emperor then asked him, "I wish to put some questions to you. What kind of a family does this Prophet of yours hale from?" "His family is one of the noble families of Arabia." "Have there been others in his family who claimed to be a Prophet?" "No!" "From what level of society are the people converting to his religion?" "They are from the lower social classes." "Are the followers of this religion on the increase?" "Yes, they are increasing." "Have you ever known this man to tell a lie?" "No, never!" "Have there been any who turned their backs on him and their pledge to him?" "No! However, it is not very long since we have concluded a treaty with him. We shall see whether he sticks to the terms of this treaty or not."

"Who was victorious and who was defeated in the wars you fought against him?" "Sometimes he won, sometimes we did." "What does this Prophet ﷺ teach you?" "He says: the only entity worthy of worship is Allah, who is the master of the creative Word 'Be' and it came to be!', who with His knowledge guides and directs all of Creation and dispenses His wisdom. Him you must worship, and you must know that all of creation exists only through Him and through His Love alone gains perpetuity. You shall not ascribe to Him any partners, confronting His Divine Person with the claims of your own selfishness. You are to perform ritual prayers, and as a visible sign and proof that you attribute no partners to Allah, you are to bow low and place your forehead upon the ground in prayer, thereby acknowledging your own weakness and haplessness. You must preserve and value your honor, guard your chastity, maintain the honor of mankind, as you would watch over the honor of your family and children. You are not to spread lies and you are to be observant of the bonds of kinship. In addition, Muhammad ﷺ is greatly opposed to the worship of idols. He insults our gods, and of your religion he says that it has been altered and corrupted."

The Emperor Heraclius listened to Abu Sufyan's words attentively and with great interest. The notables and spiritual leaders surrounding him waited with barely concealed excitement for the Emperor's reaction to all this. Finally, he spoke: "There is no doubt in my mind that the person giving you this counsel is indeed a prophet," he said. Abu Sufyan was dumbfounded and the bishops and abbots began to stir uneasily. "Yes," he went on, "this great man is a prophet. For you yourselves say that he is descended from an eminent family and all prophets are scions of noble houses. You have also said that no one else in his family has ever laid claim to prophethood. This indicates that he has not professed this calling motivated by family considerations. You have also said that his family does not partake of the affairs of state, which in turn informs me that this person is clearly not after the accession to worldly power.

"Furthermore, you have never known this man to tell a lie. He, who tells no lie to his fellow men, does not lie about God. You say that his friends and followers are mainly recruited from the materially less endowed of the community. It has always been this way: the very first followers of all prophets have been the weak and indigent. When I asked you whether his following is increasing, you told me that it was. This is always the case with true religions. Then I asked whether he has ever been known to practice deceit. This you denied. That too is a characteristic of a true Prophet. You say he preaches that Allah alone is to be worshipped by His servants; therefore it is beyond doubt that this man is a real prophet. And I inform you that in a short while he will become lord of the place I now occupy. Indeed, I knew of the impending appearance of this prophet, but it was beyond my ability to know that he would appear in Arabia. Ah, if only it were given to me to travel to Arabia and greet this Holy Prophet 🏵, so that I might wash his blessed feet with my own hands..."

When he had concluded his speech, he pressed the Prophet's 🏵 letter to his eyes and lips and said, "I order this letter to be read aloud and heard by all those present here with me." This was the text of the letter the Holy Prophet wrote:

Bismillahir-Rahmanir-Rahim

From Muhammad, the servant and prophet of Allah to Heraclius, Emperor of Byzantium:

Peace be to him who follows Guidance, who treads the Path of Truth. I invite you to come to Islam and to become Muslim. You live in peace and safety. And if you embrace Islam, Allah will reward you twofold. For if you were to accept Islam, all those with you would needs be follow suit, and you would become the means for their treading the straight path.

Therefore, your reward would be doubled. If however you reject my call, the responsibility for your whole people plunging into error rests upon you.

Oh People of the Book! Come and let us come together in one word: let each and everyone among us accept it in equal parts: let us be servants of the one and only God worthy of worship, Allah, and let us worship none other but Him Almighty. We should ascribe no partners to Him, nor adopt any other as our Lord."

As the letter was read out loud, the sparks of faith in the heart of the Byzantine Emperor were kindled and fanned into flames, whereas the shadow in the hearts of the priests increased in darkness and density. The principles set forth in the Prophet's ﷺ letter caused the whole organization of the priesthood to collapse. This document proclaimed that the keys to the gate to the Divine Presence were no longer held by the heads of a religious hierarchy, such as priests, hojas or sheikhs, but were to be accessible to anyone, in correspondence with the level of sincerity in his heart. The weakest wrist and feeblest arm could grasp this key to the Divine Presence; it all depended on the degree of faith and sincerity of intention, for any soul could reach to the source through the striving of love. In brief, the whole organization wanting to monopolize religious establishment was dealt a heavy blow, and its fanatic zeal was sharply clipped.

A profound silence fell upon the whole assembly. When the reading of the letter was over, the Emperor turned to the Arabs in his company and dismissed them. "You are free," he said, "you may now go." And they departed from his Imperial Presence.

A pitched battle now raged within the heart of the Emperor, between the yearnings of his soul (ruh) and the desires of his lower self (nafs). His imperial rank and station poured water onto the flame of enthusiasm for Islam. He lacked not respect for the prophetic envoy, but the desire for worldly rank and honors threw a veil over the light of faith awakening in his heart.

The Khosroes of Iran, King Parviz

Abdullah bin Hudhafa was sent to Iran as the Prophet's ﷺ ambassador with a letter addressed to the Khosroes of Iran, King Parviz. He was a king who competed with Allah for majestic greatness, who thought he could shield himself against His Divine Anger, not knowing that Allah abases every atheist and brings him low at last. When this king saw his name written in one line with the name of Rasulullah ﷺ at the letter's heading, all his blood flowed into his face from fury, and his hairs stood on end, and he was like a rabid dog who sees his reflection in a body of water.

This man was attached to his throne with so much pride and conceit, that he could only assume that Muhammad's ﷺ letter had come from a mighty sovereign and lord over a worldly realm. He did not know that Muhammad ﷺ was a man who all alone had begun the campaign of "La ilaha illAllah" in a cave on Mount Hira, and who still patched the rents in his clothes himself and darned the holes in the cap that covered his blessed head. He could not know that the original copy of this document was written in the Divine Kingdom. He only saw that the name of Muhammad ﷺ was written before his own name. This sufficed to trigger off an uncontrollable fit of rage. "Who is this insolent wretch?" he cried, "How dare he approach me thus? Who is this man who would place his name before mine?" With these words, he began to tear up the prophetic letter.

The unfortunate man failed to realize that along with the Prophet's ﷺ name he also tore up his own. For that is precisely what happened. The Byzantine Emperor had pressed the Holy Prophet's ﷺ letter, which was written with Love and Eternal Wisdom, to his face. This reverence gained his kingdom continuity and duration. The Khosroes by contrast tore up the Prophet's letter in contempt. He himself, his kingdom, and power were subsequently torn up as well.

This happened in the following way: When Parviz, king of Persia received the Prophet's ﷺ missive, he sent orders to the Governor of Yemen, Badhan by name, instructing him that "In the Hijaz a man has arisen who claims to be a prophet. He has had the gall to address a letter to our Imperial Presence, announcing his mission as he would to those ragged desert Arabs. I direct you to apprehend this man forthwith, sending him to me as soon as possible." Having received this forceful order from Khosroes, Badhan sent two men to the Prophet ﷺ with a letter containing these words, "You are herewith obliged to present yourself before his Imperial Majesty at the earliest possible opportunity. If you listen to me and set out at once with the messengers who deliver to you this letter, I will personally intercede on your behalf with the Shahinshah and write a letter of this intent. If, on the other hand, you do not comply, the Persian army will set out against you, destroying the Hijaz and striking you down completely."

When the Holy Prophet ﷺ had read the letter, he said to the envoys who had come to fetch him, "I will answer you tomorrow; now you may go and rest!" When the agents of the Persian king had gone, the Sahaba said to their Prophet ﷺ, "What do you command us to do? Should we prepare to set out against the army of Persia?" "That will not be necessary, "answered the Holy Prophet ﷺ, "for I anticipate a disclosure from the Lord of the Worlds concerning the fate of Parviz." The Prophet's ﷺ friends and companions waited with him in a state of great excitement. That very night the Holy Prophet ﷺ received a revelation, which was an example of Divine Power acting directly on the worldly plane. Allah Almighty informed him, "Oh My Beloved! This very night I have permitted that Parviz be destroyed by his own son Shirawayh, for that he tore up your letter and intended to remove you from the face of the earth. In the morning, you will inform the envoys of this Divine dispatch."

The Holy Prophet ﷺ called the envoys and said to them, "Go back now to where you have come from. For this very night the Lord has wreaked His revenge on your Shah who vied with the Lord Almighty for Imperial Glory. He was slain by his son. Before long, Islam will come also to his capital city. Therefore, may he also find his way into the noble religion of Islam and gain safety. Go now and tell this to Badhan."

The envoys were startled and amazed, but they could do nothing but return to Badhan and relate to him what had transpired. They asked him about what the Holy Prophet ﷺ had said about the Shah Parviz. Badhan replied, "Indeed, it has happened just so. The night you went to deliver your message to Muhammad ﷺ, Khosroes Parviz was slain by his son. I have now received an order to stay all attacks against that man. Moreover, in the face of this manifest miracle, I too embrace the faith of Islam. I shall send him a letter begging the Messenger of Allah ﷺ for forgiveness on my behalf." All the Persians in his company then turned to Islam and surrendered.

The Holy Prophet ﷺ answered Badhan in another letter, appointing him to be the Governor of Yemen. He was the first governor to be appointed by Muhammad ﷺ in the period of his spiritual leadership.

This was the content of the letter the Prophet ﷺ had sent to Khosroes by the hand of Abdullah bin Hudhafa:

Bismillahir-Rahmanir-Rahim

Peace be upon those who follow the Guidance and the Way of Truth, and who believe in Allah and His Prophet.

I testify that there is no God but Allah and that I am sent as His Prophet, in order to lead mankind from darkness into light, and to gather them from error to right guidance, and as a Warner.

Come to Islam and find safety therein. If you reject it, the sins of all the fire worshippers are upon your collar.

The Negus of Abyssinia

'Amr ibn Umayya al-Damri brought Muhammad's letter to the Negus of Abyssinia and delivered it to him. After the ruler of Abyssinia had read the letter, he called the Prophet's ﷺ cousin Ja'far who was living in this country into his presence and said, "Be my witness that I have accepted Islam!" He hosted the emissary of the Holy Prophet ﷺ with courtesy and grace.

Then he sent sixty men, among them his own son, to the Prophet ﷺ in order to take Bi'at, the pledge of allegiance, but the ship went astray and sank with all its passengers.

The Negus passed away in the ninth year of the Hijra. His name was Ashamet bin Bahir. But he was not the Negus for whom the Holy Prophet ﷺ had prayed the funeral prayer in his absence, that was a different king, (according to Sahih Muslim).

The Prophet's ﷺ envoy had another mission to fulfill as well. He was to bring the emigrants who had settled in Abyssinia back to the Hijaz and tell them that they could now come to Madinah. Also, he was to perform the Nikah ceremony for the daughter of Abu Sufyan, Umm Habiba who was to be wed to the Holy Prophet ﷺ. The Prophet ﷺ had sent Khalid ibn Sa'id to be his Wakil (his proxy) when the ceremony was performed. Umm Habiba had become Muslim in Mecca in spite of her father's obstinate perseverance in his unbelief. She had migrated together with her husband 'Ubaydullah ibn Jahsh to Abyssinia, but after some time there he had forsaken Islam and become a Christian. She had then been divorced from him.

This great lady was equipped with such a love of Islam that she did not wish to return to her father's house as he was one of the leaders of the misbelievers. In Abyssinia, she was left quite alone and destitute. Therefore, Allah Almighty decreed that her broken heart be mended and her love for Islam rewarded. So that she might again acquire kith and kin of her own, she was granted acceptance among the company of the pure wives of the Holy Prophet ﷺ.

Umm Habiba was a lady of great distinction. One day her father came to the blessed abode of the Holy Prophet ﷺ and was about to sit down upon a certain cushion, when she immediately raised her objection, saying that it was the cushion belonging to the Prophet ﷺ. "But am I not your father?" Abu Sufyan then said. "Faith and unbelief cannot abide side by side!" she retorted.

The Negus then performed the Nikah ceremony for Umm Habiba with the Holy Prophet ﷺ in the presence of Ja'far, and he presented her personally with a gift of four hundred gold dirhams as a bridal gift. Then he gave Ja'far and the other Muslim Muhajirin permission to depart for Madinah. These eagerly awaited travelers met Allah's Messenger 🏵 at Khaybar, wherefore he was greatly gladdened, and said, "How then shall I thank my Lord? Shall I rejoice for the victory of Khaybar, or for the arrival of Ja'far's company?"

The Muqawqis of Egypt

Egypt's ruler was the Muqawqis. The Prophet's 🏵 missive was handed to him by Hatib bin Balta'a. The Muqawqis read the Prophet's 🏵 letter, and wrote him his reply in Arabic. This was the content of his reply:

To the son of Allah, Muhammad 🏵, from the leader of the Copts, Muqawqis: I extend to you my greetings of Peace. I have read your letter and understand that you are calling me to Islam. I knew there was yet a prophet to come to the world, but I thought he was to arise in Damascus. I have entertained your messenger with honor and respect. I send you now as a gift from me two (slave) girls who occupy a special place among the Copts, along with a robe of honor and a saddle beast for a mount. I wish you peace.

In his letter, the Muqawqis does not make clear whether he accepts Islam or not. As for the girls he sent, although in most sources they are referred to as slave girls, the fact that the Muqawqis says that they "occupy a special place among the Copts" indicates that they were high-born women of Coptic society. The term "slave-girl" occurring in the letter simply denotes "a girl" according to the Coptic usage of the language in those days. The Holy Prophet 🏵 took one of these sisters for his own wife. Her name was Marya, and in time, she was blessed with the birth of a son, Ibrahim. The other sister, Shirin by name, was given to Sha'ir Hasan. Both girls radiated everlasting bliss, and before they even reached Madinah, they had, through the instruction of the Prophet's 🏵 envoy Hatib ibn Balta'a, been enflamed with ardor for Islam, and both became Muslims. The mule the Muqawqis had sent him was named Duldul. The Prophet 🏵 mostly rode upon this mule, up until the events of Hunayn.

In the hearts of these non-Muslim rulers, the power of Islam and the promise of bliss of eternal happiness rose as a never-setting sun, so that they inclined towards the new faith. They confirmed Muhammad ﷺ as a Prophet of Allah, but they did not openly proclaim their belief, since they could not renounce the worldly power over their dominions – such power as would weaken even one who has reached to the station of trustworthiness in the Sight of the Divine.

The Chief of Yamama

The chief of Yamama, Hawdha bin Ali, replied thus to the Prophet's ﷺ letter:

"Oh Muhammad! Everything you say is correct. Can you, however, assure me that were I to embrace Islam, you would assign to me such a place of power as I now hold? If you will give me such a position and such powers, I will immediately come and join you."

The miserable beggar! He could not know that in the whole world there was no kingdom comparable to the spiritual nation of Muhammad ﷺ! It was entirely unlike the government of cruel and unjust leaders. The Holy Prophet ﷺ answered him with these lines:

"I was not sent to impart power and influence to people, nor with such things as would flatter and satisfy their whims."

Yes, the Holy Prophet ﷺ was sent to the world in order that the weak might easily obtain their rightful dues from the strong, that the servant might know his place and believe in the Unity of Allah, resurrection after death, and that he might escape from being smothered by the denseness of his lower soul, so that he might encounter the refinement of spiritual delights, find his true origins and learn to decipher the Divine signature imparted to him (i.e. realize his divinely ordained destiny).

The Chief of the Syrian Arabs

The chief of the Syrian Arabs, al-Mundhir al-Harith Ghassani, tore up the Prophet's ﷺ letter when he received it. When the Holy Prophet ﷺ heard of this news, he inveighed against him, and before long he found his place in the pit of eternal damnation. Al-Mundhir al-Harith was a governor under the rule of the Emperor Heraclius. Enraged by Muhammad's ❀ letter, he sought permission from the Emperor to muster an army and to march against Rasulullah ❀, but the Emperor refused him his Imperial consent.

Challenges and Achievements of the New Muslim Nation

Preparing for the Conquest of Khaybar

After the Truce of Hudaybiyah, the Conquest of Khaybar was one of the most important issues for the peace and security of Islam, and it was also the wish of Muhammad 🕌. Khaybar was a city situated three days' journey to the north of Madinah, and fortified with many strongholds of the unbelievers. The strongest of all these forts was named Al-Amuse, situated atop a very steep and inaccessible hill. This assemblage of forts was called "Khaybar" which means "a fortified location". It was a very fertile region, a wide spread of fields and palm groves. It had for a long time been the center for unbelievers living in Arabia, and a place of refuge for them, whenever they suffered a defeat.

To here the heads of the Bani Nadir had retreated, and after Huyay bin Akhtab of the Bani Qurayza had fallen, Sallam ibn Abi-l-Huqayq took his place. Sallam ibn Abi-l-Huqayq had inherited a vast fortune, and he was a very influential merchant. He and many unbelievers like him wished to see Muhammad 🕌 and his band of Muslims undone, so they poured great sums of their money into this scheme. With all their might they tried to motivate the other tribes to ally with them against the Muslims.

Sallam ibn Abi-l-Huqayq personally went to the Bani Ghatafan. He convinced them and other related tribes to agree to an alliance against Muhammad 🕌. The Prophet Muhammad 🕌 was informed of all their schemes and preparations for war against him. Hardly twenty days had passed since he returned to Madinah from Hudaybiyah. Now he sent Abdullah ibn 'Atiq of the Khazraj clan to relieve them of Sallam ibn Abi-l-Huqayq who was behind all the intriguing. Abdullah was successful in his enterprise and killed Sallam ibn Abi-l-Huqayq. Asir bin Zaram now took his place.

Asir went round all the tribes, attempting to persuade them with words and bribes. The ranks of their army were thus swelled considerably, and rumor had it that they were ready to strike out against the Muslims at any moment. The head of the hypocrites, Abdullah bin Ubayy bin Salul, then sent word to them, "You are much stronger and more numerous than the Muslims. They don't even have proper weapons. All you have to do now is launch an attack on Madinah, everybody will assist you in that."

Diplomatic Solutions Failed

The Holy Prophet ❀ therefore sent Abdullah bin Rawaha and a few men with him to Khaybar to scout out the situation and investigate it in detail. He returned, bringing news from Khaybar that indeed the enemies of Islam had carried through their preparations to a most dangerous level. Hearing this, the Prophet ❀ sent Abdullah right back to Khaybar to invite Asir bin Zaram to come to Madinah. If he came, Muhammad ❀ would confirm him in his recognition of their sovereignty over Khaybar. Asir bin Zaram at first accepted this invitation and set out for Madinah with thirty men. However, in the middle of the road, he turned back on his word, saying, "I will not respond to this invitation of Muhammad ❀". Abdullah bin Rawaha then said to him, "Oh enemy of Allah! Are you falling back on your word?" Swords were drawn on both sides, and in the fighting which ensued only a single delegate escaped.

The unbelievers continued to poison the atmosphere with their money and provocations. Finally the Holy Prophet ❀ said, "There will be no peace before they are chastened, for they are always plotting against the cause of Islam. There is no way to reach an agreement with them by way of

436

compromise or friendly accord, since they do not keep their word. They will continue to pose a danger to Islam, and defensive strategy will not serve as a deterrent in this case."

Meanwhile, the unbelievers had been stirring up the tribe of Ghatafan. They had attacked the herd of the Prophet's ﷺ camels, which were pasturing on the meadows of Zikard, and captured twenty of his camels. They killed the camel herder, the son of Abu Dharr al-Ghifari, and took his wife captive. The first of the Muslims to hear this news was the marksman Aslama. He and some of his friends went after the camel robbers and showered them with a heavy rain of arrows. In this way they took the Prophet's ﷺ camels from their hands, but most of the thieves got away and fled to the valley where their commander Uyayna waited for them. Aslama returned to Madinah and said to the Prophet ﷺ, "Oh Rasulullah! If you give me one hundred men, I will round up all the bandits and bring them here." The Holy Prophet ﷺ replied, "If the enemy asks for quarter, treat them with kindness!" Again we see how perfect is the way of Islam.

Three days after this incident, the events of Khaybar took place. Islam was determined to replace oppression with justice, ignorance with knowledge, disbelief with the light of faith. It was in the seventh year of the Hijra at the beginning of the month of Muharram that one thousand four hundred Muslims rode out of Madinah in order to forestall an imminent attack on the city by the unbelievers and their allies of the Ghatafan. Two hundred of the Muslims were mounted on horses. This time the Muslim army flew three banners, one of which was made from the headscarf of Aisha. This one was given to Ali. As they marched along, the Muslim army sang this marching song:

Allahumma lau la anta ma-htadayna

Oh Lord, hadst Thou not guided us, we never would have found the straight path;

Wa la tasaddaqna wa la sallayna

Nor would we have known aught of the giving of alms or of the performing of prayer.

Faghfir fida'an laka ma abqayna

Thou art the only one who can forgive us, and may we be sacrificed for the love of Thee,

Wa-l-qina sakinatan 'alayna

And send upon us Thy calm and grace,

Inna idha siha bina 'atayna

so that if we are called, we might come running;

Wa thabbit-il aqdama in laqina

And steady our step and make us steadfast in the battle fray,

Idha aradu fitnatan 'abayna

And if the enemy wishes to cause harm and hurt, we do renounce it,

wa nahnu min fadlika ma-staghnayna.

For we are never aloof from Thy Grace and Mercy.

The Muslim army set out, first chanting Takbir, then sounding this marching song. The Mothers of the Believers also came along on this campaign, saying, "Oh Rasulullah, grant us permission to come along, at least we can hand the fighters their arrows, look after the wounded and pass out water. That way we will at least have served the noble cause of Islam in some measure."

The chief of the tribe of Daws, Tufayl bin 'Amr ad-Dawsi had come to Mecca to see the Holy Prophet ❀ before he had made the Hijra from Mecca to Madinah. After having met with Muhammad ❀, the sun of Truth shone forth in his heart, and he became a Muslim. Although at the time he had wished to remain in the vicinity of the Holy Prophet ❀, Muhammad ❀ had said to him, "You are now under my command. Go back to your tribe and tell your people of the Islam you have found. Make it sweet for them, so that they might know its taste." With these words he sent him back to his people, and this esteemed tribal chieftain had been furthering the cause of Islam ever since. On account of his dedicated efforts, four hundred persons became Muslim.

It so happened around this time that this distinguished servant of Allah and some of his Muslim companions had set out for Madinah to visit the Holy Prophet ﷺ. As soon as they arrived, they heard of the decision to take that stronghold of mischief and intrigue, Khaybar. Tufayl bin 'Amr hastened into the presence of the Holy Prophet ﷺ, saying, "I have come to your aid, oh my Prophet ﷺ!" These words pleased the Holy Prophet ﷺ greatly.

Abu Hurayra was from this tribe as well. He was granted special honors by the Holy Prophet ﷺ on account of this incident:

One day Abu Hurayra, who hardly ever left the Prophet's ﷺ side, said to him, "Oh Rasulullah ﷺ, if only I would never, ever forget anything you said!" The Holy Prophet ﷺ smiled at these words and extended his hands, which were manifestly quite empty, but in reality brimming with spiritual content, and made as if to fill Abu Hurayra's lap by the handful. Then he said, "Oh Abu Hurayra, from now on you will forget nothing you have ever heard me say!" With this he was admitted into the inner circle of those devout followers known as the 'Ashab-as-Safa'.

When the Holy Prophet ﷺ learned that the tribesmen of the Ghatafan had allied themselves with the opposing forces, he turned his army first to Raji'a, which is a place between Khaybar and Ghatafan. There they left the bulk of their baggage and equipment, then proceeded onwards to Khaybar.

Approaching the Battle

The Bani Ghatafan had armed and prepared themselves to aid the unbelievers in battle, but when they realized how much they were thereby endangering themselves, they withdrew and returned to their camps. Twenty thousand enemy soldiers assembled at Khaybar, with the battle-famed Marhab as their commander. When they approached Khaybar, the Holy Prophet ﷺ commanded a halt. They stopped to eat. Their food consisted of fried flour. When they had prayed the noon prayer and rested for a while, the Prophet ﷺ commanded the army to resume its march. They reached Khaybar just at nightfall. The Prophet ﷺ then called for them to halt, and he made the supplication that he always made before stopping at a place:

Inna nas'aluka khayra hadhihi qaryati wa khayra ahliha wa khayra mafiha, wa na'udhu bika min sharriha a sharri ahliha wa sharri ma fiha.

"Oh Lord! We ask of Thee whatever is good of this place, and of its people and of what is in it, and we take refuge with Thee from its evil, and from the evil of its people and from what is within it."

Then night fell. The Companions asked the Prophet ﷺ, "Are we to take Khaybar now, oh Rasulullah ﷺ?" "It is not my custom to attack a place by night," he replied. So the army of the Prophet ﷺ waited for the dawn. In the morning they entered the city sounding the Takbir (Allahu Akbar). At the same time the Prophet ﷺ ordered that no one be harmed before it was clear whether Khaybar had decided to fight the Muslims. The Holy Prophet ﷺ wanted them to behold the forces of Islam and the powers of faith before they went to war against them. He hoped that they might understand that faith or conscience would not be violated and therefore desist from intrigue and mischief making. He would then have left Khaybar after concluding a compromise agreement with them. However, the unbelievers had irrevocably decided on war. They had sent their women and children ahead, along with their supplies to the fort of Na'im only the soldiers remained to man their various fortifications.

Sallam bin Mishkam of the Bani Nadir joined the unbelievers even though he himself was sick unto death, and yelled, "War!" When the Holy Prophet ﷺ learned of their firm resolve to go to war, he exhorted his companions once again and reminded them of the great merits of struggling against unbelief and oppression. Truth was going to war against falsehood, and the first act of war was an assault on the fortress of Na'im. The commander of the assault troops was Muhammad bin Maslama. The battle began and proceeded with ferocity.

Muhammad bin Maslama decided that the soldiers needed a break and gave orders to this effect, while he himself withdrew to rest at the foot of the fortress walls. But Kinana, the commander of the unbelievers' forces, had noticed Muhammad bin Maslama resting by the ramparts. So, taking advantage of the situation, he rolled a huge millstone down from the top of the castle walls, and thus this valiant Muslim commander was martyred. When the Muslims beheld their commander crushed beneath the stone, they roused themselves to renew their attacks with vigor and ferocity, and the fortress finally fell to them.

After this decisive conquest, the forts of the unbelievers fell until only one remained. This was the castle of Qamus, which had walls that were thought impossible to scale, and therefore it held out against the Muslims. Its commander was Marhab. The Holy Prophet ❀ appointed Abu Bakr to lead the troops in the assault, but try as he might, he could not bring about a decisive victory.

The next day the Prophet ❀ sent out 'Umar in command of the troops. But again they returned without success. Then the Prophet ❀ spoke, "Tomorrow I will give my banner to whom Allah has vouchsafed success and victory, one who loves Allah and His Prophet ❀ exceedingly, and who is also beloved of Allah and His Prophet ❀. Allah has given the power of conquest and victory into his hand."

The person thus honored was of course none other than Sayyidina Ali. But the Companions wondered at these words and waited impatiently for the morning to come. Nobody had thought of Ali, as he was suffering from an eye complaint just then. When dawn broke, the Prophet ❀ called for Ali to come to him. He had very bad pain in his eyes, which he was later to describe in these words: "I thought the stars were falling from the skies into my sleeve, and in such a state I went to the Holy Prophet's ❀ Presence."

Ali Leads the Fight by High Example

The Holy Prophet ❀ then addressed Ali, saying, "Oh son of my uncle, oh Ali! I am well aware of the pain in your eyes. However, if I were to kiss your eyes, which behold the truth, all your pain would vanish, by the leave of Allah. For today there is an important task before us." And so it was. As soon as the Prophet ﷺ touched his blessed lips to Ali's eyes, which were sighted with vision of the Truth, all pain instantly left them. Then the Prophet ﷺ prayed for him and clothed him in his own armor and girded him with his sword. He handed him the banner of Islam, saying, "Ali! Our Lord has decreed that the conquest of this fortress will be achieved by thy hand!" Then he kissed him upon his forehead and prayed for him, saying these words, *Udkhul 'ala barakati-llah!* (Enter with the blessings of Allah!) Thus Ali was appointed commander of the troops and sent to take the fortress of Qamus. He proceeded to its gates forthwith.

Meanwhile the unbelievers, in order to show that their morale was unbroken despite the Muslim onslaught, prepared to wed the daughter of one of their chiefs to the son of another dignitary. The bridegroom approached his bride as was their custom, bearing a tray of jewels in one hand and a tray of sheer gold in the other, in order that she permit him to lift her veil. However, this girl vehemently rejected her groom, saying, "My face will not be revealed to you on account of some rocks or nuggets of gold! He who wishes to see my face must bring before me that ragged Arab who is marching up and down in front of our gates!"

These words from his beloved incited fiery ambition in the young man. He stood, girding his weapons and ran to challenge the man outside the gates. It was the custom in those times that two opponents would first engage in lengthy verbal exchanges before the clash of arms. Thus the young man began extolling his own virtues and his position among the notables of Khaybar. Ali gave the requisite replies, then he said, "Let us not waste our time with words. Your bride and your people await you, as the Holy Prophet ﷺ and my companions are waiting for me! Let us begin to measure our prowess in battle!" The young man instantly sprang from his horse. The spectators from atop the castle walls were bursting with excitement. Those who heard Ali speak and recognized him cried, "Khaybar is lost!" while the Muslims cheered and uttered loud cries of Takbir.

Ali then said to his foe, "I will grant you another favor. Because you have only just been separated from your beloved, I leave to you the right of the first strike." For with the vision of sainthood, Ali glimpsed the outcome of the contest. So the son of the chief of Khaybar struck the first strike against Ali, but he succeeded only in opening a breach at the edge of Ali's shield, which did not even touch the Prophet's ﷺ cousin. Now it was Ali's turn to strike. In one fell sweep he wrestled his enemy to the ground, pressing his shoulders down with his knees. He was about to sever his head from his body with the Prophet's ﷺ sword, when his enemy who had not yet lost his fighting spirit, as a last measure of defense hurled his spittle into Ali's face. Instantly, Ali withdrew his sword from the young man's neck and said, "Get to your feet!" His rival rose, stupefied. He failed to understand what was happening to him. He said to Ali, "What is the meaning of this? You spare my life just when you have the best opportunity to end it, you withdraw your sword just as you are about to cut my head from my trunk?"

Ali then explained in the special way given to him:

> "We fight our foes in the name of Allah and Rasulullah, His Holy
> Prophet ﷺ. We do not even touch a hair on the head of our enemy at
> the behest of our own lower nature. When you spit into my face at the
> moment I was about to sever your head, my *nafs* (lower nature) welled
> up within me. Then I thought, this will never do, this is not befitting
> of my honor that I should slay a man partly for the sake of Allah and
> partly for the sake of my own *nafs*, so I staid my hand. I am one who
> was brought up by the hand of Muhammad ﷺ, who has come to lead
> mankind out of darkness into the light. He extends the hand of mercy
> even to his enemy. On our way, it will not do to follow the dictate of
> our lower nature *(nafs)*, it is forbidden to us. Therefore, let us do battle
> once again."

The chieftain's son was confounded by these words and deeply awed at this enemy, who shrank not even in the face of death. He began to consider his words seriously. Ali had spoken directly to his inner being and the full impact of his words began to take hold. These words reined in his *nafs*, which commanded him to cut his adversary's neck instead of receiving his munificence. He thought to himself that such virtue and strength of character must outweigh a hundred brides, a thousand castles and uncounted coffers of jewels.

The leavening of creation takes place between the fingers of Wrath and Mercy. This is another example of how an obstinate enemy is saved from the manifestation of His Wrath and attains to His Mercy instead.

The young man then said to Ali, "After you have shown me the way to this high level of virtue to which you are privy, I ask you to mete out the punishment for my impudence. Accept me into the fold of Islam, let me testify to my faith in Islam in the Presence of the Prophet Muhammad ﷺ, then put me to death. The reason I wish for death is that I fear it might be said among you that I accepted Islam for fear of a second battle contest."

In answer to this, Ali broke out into loud cries of Takbir. He said, "Every man will meet his Maker in the end; Allah knows and regards the inner faith and conscience of every single one of us, his secrets and his innermost hidden thoughts. We do not interfere with Him. As you state your wish to become Muslim, we are now brothers and take our sustenance from the holy words of the Quran." The young man then wept and accompanied Sayyidina Ali, loudly proclaiming his faith in the words of the Shahada: *Ash-hadu an la ilaha illAllah, wa ash-hadu anna Muhammad-ar-Rasulullah.*

The Lion Kills His Prey

The unbeliever warriors observing these developments from above seethed with the rage of their disbelief and hastily prepared for battle. All at once, the warrior Marhab who was known for his ferocity in battle stepped out and challenged Ali. With the first stroke of his sword he clove Ali's shield in two, but Ali himself was unhurt. Now the turn came to Ali to return the strike, and for Marhab's dream to become true. For that very night Marhab had seen a dream in which a lion tore him to pieces. He lived to see his dream fulfilled, for he was dispatched to eternal damnation by the claws of the Lion of Islam, Ali.

Following the death of Marhab, the unbelievers' forces made a general sortie, but their morale was broken by the fall of their hero, and their fighting soon grew listless. Before long, Ali and his company entered the stronghold, all the fortresses now being in Muslim hands. Khaybar had fallen. There were fifteen martyrs among the Muslims, whereas ninety-three fighters of the unbelievers met their fate in this battle. In this way this entire region, famed for its dates and lavish produce, fell into the hands of the Muslims.

The Results of War

The unbelievers now fell to entreating the Holy Prophet ﷺ, the teacher and exponent of the religion of Islam, which has made mercy to be the foundation of its faith, "Leave us our fields, we will give you half of our yields as tribute." The Holy Prophet ﷺ was ready to accept this and asked, "Whom shall I send to oversee the dividing of the harvest?" The unbelievers suggested Abdullah bin Rawaha, for that he was so well known for the justness of his dealings that even the unbelievers said of him, "Allah upholds Heaven and earth simply because of this man's righteousness."

Of the part due to the Muslims, one-fifth belonged to the Prophet ﷺ, the remainder was placed in the Bayt-al-Mal (public treasury). The prisoners of war were all gathered in one place. Among them was Rabi' bin Ubayy and Safiya, the daughter of Huyay bin Akhtab, one of the chiefs of Khaybar, and the widow of Kinana bin Sallam ibn Abi Huqayq. Safiya, who held a place of high esteem among her people, was a newlywed bride, and the Holy Prophet ﷺ gave her to Dihya. Dihya was famed among all the companions for his good looks, and for his complete devotion to the Holy Prophet ﷺ and he was also the tutor of Hasan and Hussayn, the Prophet's ﷺ grandsons. Because of the angels' love and longing for humankind, the angel Jibra'il would mostly assume the pleasing form of this man, Dihya, when he brought a revelation to the Prophet ﷺ.

One day when Hasan and Hussayn were little children, they hopped onto the lap of the figure they took to be their tutor Dihya, and began rummaging through his pockets. In reality it was the angel Jibra'il who turned to Muhammad ﷺ and asked, "What are they looking for, oh Rasulullah ﷺ?" "They believe you to be their tutor, Dihya," answered the Prophet ﷺ. "Dihya generally brings some grapes with him in order to please them." Jibra'il then prayed, "Oh my Lord, do not shame me before these children of the Prophet 's ﷺ family, and create Thou some grapes in my pockets now!" Instantly grapes appeared in his pockets and the children rejoiced in their find.

But these words are addressed to those who have sensed the taste of real faith. Whoever is still shrouded in the coarse cloth of material density and has not known the influence of the transcendental in his life, will fail to understand any of this.

The Story of Safiya bint Huyay bin Akhtab

This is how Safiya was given to Dihya. Dihya, however deemed himself unworthy of her and went to see the Holy Prophet ﷺ about it. "Oh my Prophet ﷺ," he began, "Safiya is the daughter of a chieftain, and her husband was of the chiefs of the Bani Nadir. I beg you not to settle her upon me, for this would be extremely humiliating for the unbelievers. For the honor and high regard you have shown me by this gracious gift, I give abundant thanks and praise to the Lord of the Worlds, and I pray for endless blessings and benedictions upon you. Yet I would ask that you take the lady Safiya for yourself!"

The Holy Prophet ﷺ found Dihya's proposal acceptable, and called for Safiya. After he had enquired about her condition and state of well being, he put before her the choice of becoming a Muslim and being accepted among his wives, or to refuse Islam and remain in the condition of a captive bondmaid. As there is no compulsion in matters of faith, the choice was hers entirely. But the sun of Truth had not yet risen in Safiya's heart, so she replied roughly, "I will never enter into your religion!" The Holy Prophet ﷺ replied thereto, "You are free to act according to your conscience, we will not interfere. The choice is up to you."

446

But Safiya was able to insist only for a day or so on her own religion, before the light of the Prophet's ❈ disposition and demeanor began to flood her whole being.

The leniency which the Great Teacher ❈ showed to his enemies, the nobility towards those who had pushed only for his destruction, called to life that spark of faith which had been placed in her heart in the World of Spirits. The love she now felt turned her feelings of hurt over the loss of her father and husband, who both had died in stubborn defense of their disbelief, into revulsion. Her real love appeared and focused on the Truth of the Worlds, Muhammad ❈. Whereas before Safiya had perceived only Muhammad the man, she now began to see the prophet in him, as well.

Finally she could no longer contain herself, and came into his presence, weeping, "Oh Rasulullah ❈", she said, "will you forgive me?" The Holy Prophet ❈ answered her, "Good news, I hope! What has happened that you address me now as Rasulullah, whereas hitherto I was to you only Muhammad?" Safiya went on to say, "Will I be forgiven in the life to come, oh my Prophet ❈, will you accept me into the faith?" The Prophet ❈ then began reciting Takbir, and told her that the Lord of the Worlds accepted anyone who yearned for Him. "Do not weep, oh Safiya, for I testify to your faith in the Divine Presence."

Safiya recited the attestation of the creed of Islam and the Holy Prophet ❈ was moved by this demonstration of her sincerity. It was foreordained for her to become one of his honorable wives, and this was now being affirmed. The Prophet ❈ said to her, "The time has come for me to grant you your freedom. The choice is yours: if you so wish, I will take you into Nikah and you shall be my wife; if you do not wish for that, I will marry you to whomever you wish from among my friends and companions." Safiya answered, "Oh Rasulullah! Know that from now on I have no more will of my own, everything pertaining to myself is thine. I have no wish outside of what is your will, which is all that remains. If you see me worthy of thyself, then it is for you to accept me."

447

The Holy Prophet ﷺ then married Safiya to himself and she became one of the Mothers of the Believers. She received from him a special distinction in that he said to her, "Heedlessness is a fundamental quality of mankind. Therefore, should at any time anyone from our community regard you in an untoward way, then tell that person that you are not only the wife of Habibullah, but also the daughter of a prophet, Harun."

How the Holy Prophet ﷺ Dealt With His Enemies

The Battle of Khaybar was won, the unbelievers were pardoned and a general sense of peace and relief spread far and wide. Still there were some among the unbelievers who were not content to leave things as they were. For instance, the widow of Sallam bin Mishkam, Zaynab by name, sought means for avenging the death of her husband and ending the Prophet's ﷺ life.

She resolved to invite the Holy Prophet ﷺ for a meal; when he accepted, she asked around to find out which part of the animal he preferred. She learnt that it was the sheep's shoulder. So she went about to prepare a meal. She roasted a lamb, and invited the Prophet ﷺ and a few of his chosen friends to dine at her house. But she had concentrated a deadly poison in the shoulder of the lamb that was intended for the Holy Prophet's ﷺ meal.

The Holy Prophet ﷺ accepted her invitation graciously, and sat down at the table to eat. The meat was distributed among the invitees, and the Prophet ﷺ tore off a piece of the lamb's shoulder, placed it in his mouth and began to chew on it. But almost immediately he spat it out and cried to his companions, "Do not eat of this! It this poisoned! The lamb cries out to me, 'Don't eat me, Rasulullah, for I have been poisoned.'"

This one morsel which the Prophet ﷺ chewed without even swallowing it sufficed for the poison to take effect on his blessed body. Instantly they administered certain medicines and performed cupping on him. That way the worst was averted, but Bishr bin Bara' had followed his Prophet ﷺ and placed the meat in his mouth when he had. He had however swallowed a mouthful of the meat, and all medicine and administrations proved to be useless. He went into convulsions and struggled for his life. The Holy Prophet ﷺ asked who had poisoned the lamb. Zaynab, the widow of Sallam bin Mishkam admitted that it was she who had cooked the meal and added the poison. Asked how she could conceive of committing such a crime, she answered, "I wished only to test you, for if you were a true prophet, the poison would do you no harm. If, however, you were not a true prophet, the poison would kill you and we would be well rid of an impostor. That was my intention."

The Holy Prophet ﷺ then said, "I forgive the attacks that are made upon my person, therefore I forgive you for this attempt on my life. But my friend and companion Bishr is very ill indeed from your poison. Should he die from the effects of this poison, know that I will have you executed in retaliation, according to the Divine Law revealed to me." Zaynab thereupon said, "I now know and believe in the truth of your prophethood. If your friend should die, I will gladly accept the verdict of retribution. But dare I ask for your intercession, oh Rasulullah ﷺ, that the Lord Almighty might not censure me for my deed in the world to come!" With these words she withdrew from the Prophet's presence.

Before long, Bishr passed away, and Zaynab was executed in retaliation. At the very end of his life, with his very last breaths, the Holy Prophet ﷺ is reported to have said, "I am now feeling that terrible poison with which Zaynab at Khaybar poisoned that lamb!"

Thus the unbelievers performed one treacherous act after the other. The Holy Prophet ﷺ was ready and willing to forgive the assault on his blessed person, but he had to punish the harm done to his friend according to the judgment of the revealed Divine Law. He was the leader of the spiritual empire, sent to deliver men from darkness into the light, and truly, he was a savior of mankind.

Oh Traveler on the Way of Truth! While this is the historic truth, there are some historians who, though they have no knowledge of the real course of events, nonetheless assert that in the lifetime of the Prophet ﷺ a certain

Kinana (the husband of Safiya) had hidden a great treasure. (This had belonged to the Bani Nadir who had fled to Khaybar after the Battle of the Trench.) They claim that in order to procure this wealth for themselves, the Muslims tormented Kinana and put his whole family to death. However, this is a fabrication. For one thing, Kinana was the murderer of Muhammad bin Maslama, and he was put to death in retaliation. It is simply not true that his whole family was punished by death, for his own brother was still alive in the time of 'Umar's Khalifate. The Holy Prophet 🌸 never permitted any person to be tortured for the purpose of procuring information.

'Umar in his time grew tired of these people who refused to give up their wickedness and who knew not how to yield. As if that were not enough, they had beguiled his own son Abdullah bin 'Umar so that he fell from a wall, and broke both arm and leg. Thereupon 'Umar exiled them to Syria. They came before him and bitterly complained, "Oh Commander of the Faithful! Muhammad the Prophet 🌸 never did to us what you have done! He partook even of our business dealings, while you do drive us from our very homes!" Again it was the sons of Abu-l-Huqayq of whom this incident is related.

In brief, if an unbeliever was executed, it was definitely in retribution for a murder he had committed, or because he had gone too far in his mockery of the Muslims, and broken all accepted rules of conduct. For the stronger Islam grows the greater its allowance for mercy and pardon. Wherever it sees oppression, it will replace it with justice, and it will set knowledge in the place of ignorance. Knowledge is described as a Ray of Light from the Lord; it is regarded as the greatest gift that is granted by the Divine Lord and incorporated into the hearts of His chosen and beloved servants. It bespeaks of the rightful placement and expenditure of these blessings and bounties, when the fruits of knowledge become manifest. These entail being observant of the rights of all created beings, knowing the aim of Creation, feeling the urge to return to one's original (spiritual) homeland, and having a sense of honor and shame. If, however, knowledge is taken to mean only studying, its real meaning is not grasped; the result of study is only an amassing of information.

Therefore, just as Islamic warfare was essentially defensive, so the punishments prescribed by Islam are not based on personal or emotional judgment. The wars were fought either to forestall an enemy attack, or because the enemy suddenly appeared before the Muslims and needed to be stopped.

The conquest of Khaybar therefore represented a great gain for the Muslim objectives, and opened a whole new avenue for its spread. The hidden wisdom of the treaty concluded at Hudaybiyah gradually came to light. Had it not been for that treaty, the victory at Khaybar would have been difficult, and one of the foremost enemies of the Muslims, the unbelievers, would not have been so swiftly punished for their wicked mischief. The victory at Khaybar took the unbelievers by great surprise. In this way one of the chief enemies of Islam was crushed, whereas the other, i.e. the heathen idolaters, were kept at a safe distance.

The income from the gardens of Khaybar was split into two equal parts. One half was distributed among sixteen hundred of the warriors, whereby the two hundred horsemen among them received a double share. The other half of the income was set aside for the costs of entertaining guests and for the travel expenses of the envoys. Of the eighteen hundred parts to be divided among the warriors, one part fell to the Holy Prophet ﷺ.

After the Prophet ﷺ left Khaybar, he departed for the place where of old the 'Ad and Thamood had dwelled, called Fadak. A tribe of unbelievers who tilled the soil and planted the land had settled in this valley. The Prophet ﷺ invited them to come to Islam, but they refused and threatened the Muslims with arms, challenging them to send forth their champion for a duel. They were met by Zubayr, who dispatched his opponents to the pit of eternal damnation forthwith. But the unbelievers had set their minds on hostilities, and stepped forth to measure themselves against Ali's sword. One by one these stubborn, misguided individuals fell to their punishment, until the fallen numbered no less than eleven. The Muslims meanwhile had entered a place called Wadi-al-Qura. At long last the unbelievers gave up their armed efforts, and were willing to accept the same conditions of peace as had been imposed on the unbelievers of Khaybar. This meant that their belongings were divided up among the Muslim warriors, and they had to leave behind the fields they had hitherto tilled. The people of Tayma were obliged to make tax payments.

Many people now began streaming into the Islamic fold. For instance many members of the Ash'ari tribe from Yemen came into the presence of the Holy Prophet ❀ with Abu Musa al-Ash'ari. Islam grew stronger and stronger. The lone call of the Prophet ❀, 'La ilaha illAllah', which had rung out from the mountain cave of Hira, drew mankind out of darkness into light. It was something the mind initially could not accept; it took faith to do that, for it was a matter, which the eye of reason could not perceive. But the eye of faith saw, and believed in it, so that in the end even reason had to accept this call that is destined to resound in the created universe until the end of time.

From all sides people came streaming to listen to the words of the Prophet ❀, and they came to consult his blessed presence in all matters that concerned them. This great Prophet ❀ abandoned all self-interest, striving tirelessly to draw men out of darkness into light. He lent his ear to everyone, listened to people's ideas, drew up plans for work to be done, personally led the prayers, preached sermons of admonition, and gave enlightened guidance. In one person, he was teacher, leader, judge, supreme worldly and religious authority, helper and assistant to all. He looked after all the material and spiritual needs of the Ashab us-Safa'. He listened to everyone, solved everyone's problems according to their level, justly distributed his graces and kindnesses, hurt no one and never infringed on the rights of brotherhood. All these qualities were combined in the person of this great and noble Prophet ❀.

To illustrate this point, just one small example: One day the Holy Prophet ❀ was sitting with Abu Bakr as-Siddiq and 'Umar Faruq and a Bedouin Arab. The Holy Prophet ❀ asked for some water, and he drank from the

452

cup, leaving a bit in it when he was done. 'Umar asked the Holy Prophet 🕮 for permission to give this water to Abu Bakr as-Siddiq. Thereupon the Holy Prophet 🕮 pointed to the Bedouin sitting to his right and said, "'Umar! Al-ayman f-al-ayman! The right, the right!" thereby ordering him to pass the cup to the Arab sitting to his right. Even though there was doubtlessly no companion of greater merit than Abu Bakr, the Prophet's 🕮 action leaves no doubt as to the subtlety of his feelings and the delicacy of his behavior.

The Prophet's 🕮 'Umra

A year had passed since the treaty of Hudaybiyah, and according to the conditions of the treaty, the Muslims were now entitled to enter Mecca and perform the rites of 'Umra, provided they left their weapons outside of town. It was in the eighth year of the Hijra, at the beginning of the month of Dhul-Qa'da that the Holy Prophet 🕮 gave orders to all the companions who had been with him at Hudaybiyah to prepare to travel to Mecca to perform the visit to the Holy House of the Lord.

Everyone made ready to go with great joy and excitement. The chiefs of the unbelievers were to leave the town of Mecca for the duration of the Muslims' stay. What a joyous day that was to be, when the Muslim community which at Badr had numbered no more than three hundred and some men, now set out in full force, soon to embrace not only the Arabian peninsula, but the whole world.

They set out and left their weapons at a place called Batn Bajih at a distance of eight miles from the city. A guard of two hundred riders was left to guard their belongings.

When they had drawn close to Mecca, the Holy Prophet 🕮 began intoning 'Labbayk', and the voices of the Muslims rose up to the Divine Throne. Abdullah bin Rawaha held the bridle of his camel Qaswa. He fell into a swoon and began to recite these (translated) verses:

Get out of his way, you unbelievers; make way.

Every good thing goes with His Apostle.

Oh Lord! I believe in his word,

I know God's truth in accepting it.

We will fight you about its interpretation,

As we have fought you about its revelation

With strokes that will remove heads from shoulders

And make friend unmindful of friend.

When 'Umar heard him, he said to Abdullah, "Oh Abdullah bin Rawaha! You are sitting here in the presence of the Holy Prophet ✿, in Allah Almighty's holy shrine, and reciting poetry, singing folksongs?" The Holy Prophet ✿ heard their interchange and intervened on Abdullah's behalf, saying, "Oh 'Umar, do not bother Abdullah bin Rawaha, for his poetry and songs are more penetrating than the most piercing arrow; his words will strike straight at the hearts of the chiefs of the unbelievers." Abdullah bin Rawaha at that moment became the spokesman of the Holy Prophet ✿. All the Prophet's companions gathered in a knot around the Prophet's ✿ camel, as the unbelievers looked on in amazement from the hills. It was a heavy and painful blow to their pride and disbelief. Finally, the Muslims approached with loud cries of Takbir and entered the holy city of Mecca, the home of Islam in a state of intense excitement. The Holy Prophet ✿ immediately began to perform the Tawaf, the visit of the Kaba, and the Sa'i between Safa and Marwa. The Companions all followed suit. They performed three circumambulations of the Kaba running swiftly, in order to give the lie to the malicious claim of the Meccans that the air of Madinah had debilitated the emigrants. In this way, the Holy Prophet's dream, which he had seen before the events of Hudaybiyah, was fulfilled.

In the eighth year of the Hijra, in the month of Safar, the great general and Cavalry Commander Khalid ibn al-Walid together with 'Uthman bin Talha of the Bani ad-Dar had gone to Madinah and embraced the light of Islam. Even before this, 'Amr bin 'As who was known to be very clever and astute had presented himself to the Prophet # and become a Muslim. Each of these men had their own special distinction, and the Quraysh were adversely affected by their defection.

The Battle of Mu'ta

There was a town in Syria called Mu'ta in the district of the Balqa' which was renowned for its swords. The very best pieces were forged there. In the eighth year of the Hijra, in the month of Jamada-l-Awwal a big battle took place here. The reason for fighting was this:

The Holy Prophet # had invited all the great kings and rulers of the time to join Islam and sent to each an envoy bearing a letter. Harith bin 'Umayr had been sent to Busra which was under the protectorate of Byzantium, but directly ruled by the tribal chieftain Shurahbil bin 'Amir al-Ghassani. This chief and his whole family had become Christian, although they were Bedouin Arabs. They murdered the Prophet's # envoy when he came to them and he died a martyr. The Holy Prophet # received the news of Harith's murder with great sorrow and told his companions that this matter should not be dismissed and passed over lightly, even if the enemy were very powerful. He told them that revenge would need to be exacted for the murder of this precious companion, and he sent them to the place where he fell, so that they might read Fatiha for his soul.

The Prophet # put Zayd bin Harith in charge of a force of three-thousand and one hundred fighting men, and accompanied them up to the place called Thaniyat-al-Wada, the Valley of Farewell.

As mentioned before, Zayd was the Holy Prophet's # freedman who had become one of his trusted companions. He was a member of the community just as Ali's brother, Ja'far ibn Abi Talib, or one of the eminent of the Ansar, Abdullah bin Rawaha. For Islam brought equality to all men and there is no discrimination.

The Holy Prophet # appointed Zayd as the commander of the Muslim army, and gave the banner into his hand. "Should Zayd fall in battle," he said, "let Ja'far ibn Abi Talib take his place. If he should fall, then Abdullah bin Rawaha will succeed him. After him you may select any one from among your number." He also exhorted them and said, "Do not forget that you are going to battle in honor of Harith's blessed memory, not for the sake of victory! Therefore, before doing battle, try to call the enemy warriors to Islam. If they accept your call, forego the battle; Harith would be most pleased with such an outcome."

When Shurahbil's spies brought him news of the Muslims' movements, he prepared to equip an army of one hundred thousand men to face them. The Byzantine Emperor thereby expressed his approval of a murder committed by one of his tribal chieftains, rather than his censure, thus bringing war upon his whole realm. He even proceeded personally as far as the town of Ma'ab in the district of Balqa'. Su'ud bin Amir had before this time gone forth against the Muslim army at Wadi-l-Qura and fought them, but the band of soldiers was dispersed and he himself was slain.

When the Muslim army arrived at Ma'an, they heard that they were going to face an army of one hundred thousand Byzantine soldiers. The army's commanders met for a war council. Zayd bin Harith, the commander-in-chief, said, "Let us send word of this to the Holy Prophet ﷺ, and wait for his answer for two days, then act according to his command." However, Abdullah bin Rawaha opposed this view and said, "Actually, we have not set out for to gain a victory, we have come only for to honor the blessed memory of Harith bin Umayr. Just as we might accomplish this visit in physical reality, so it might be done also in the spiritual realm. That is to say, it will be of even greater value if it is accomplished through martyrdom. Remember, our aim is not to gain victory, but to gain martyrdom. The Holy Prophet ﷺ himself gave us indications of this even as we were setting out. Therefore, let us not stall, but proceed forthwith!"

The Prophet's friends accepted Abdullah bin Rawaha's words with a stout heart. When they reached the place called Mu'ta, they were met by an army of one-hundred thousand fully equipped soldiers and mercenaries, while they were a force of a mere three-thousand Muslims. Zayd bin Harith rode out onto the battlefield with the banner in his hand. He attacked the enemy with great enthusiasm and vigor. At last he fell, mortally wounded by multiple spear-wounds and passed the banner on to the hand of Ja'far ibn Abi Talib. Ja'far parried many a fierce attack, until his right hand was severed. He then held the banner aloft in his left hand, until he lost that hand as well. He then wrapped the Muslim standard around his own person, until at last he was martyred after having received no less than ninety injuries. Instantly Abdullah bin Rawaha took up the flag and threw himself into the thick of the battle, until he too received the cup of martyrdom that his soul so eagerly awaited and he regained his eternal homeland.

Ten Muslim warriors were thus martyred, and the Muslim army was badly shaken, being left without real leadership. The banner, however, never touched the ground, it was upheld by Abu Yusru'-l-Ansari. He passed it on to the next in line, handing it to Thabit bin Arqam al-Ajlani. He wished to hand the banner to Khalid ibn al-Walid, who initially refused, saying, "You are both my senior in years, and you belong to the veterans of Badr. Your rank is therefore higher than mine." Thabit bin Aqram replied, "You are an eminent general, and I took up the banner only in order to give it to you." With these words he handed Khalid the banner of Islam, and turning to the Muslim warriors, he asked them, "Do you accept Khalid's leadership?" A great cheer of acclaim rose from the Muslim multitude. Thus Khalid took up the flag and set about ordering the troops.

He engaged in battle with such skill and bravery that he broke to pieces eight or nine swords in the fury of his onslaught. The battle gained momentum, and with it Khalid's competence and courage soared to new heights. The enemy forces outnumbered the Muslim army by such a large margin that it was inconceivable how three thousand Muslims should prevail over one-hundred thousand well-organized soldiers! The enemy troops were astonished to find a small army willing to face such an overwhelming force. At nightfall both sides withdrew to rest.

In the morning, to their great surprise, the enemy army found itself face to face with a different lot of soldiers and took them to be reinforcements for the Muslim troops that had arrived during the night. (Khalid had reorganized the troops in such a way that none of the enemy soldiers was faced with a man he had seen the day before). Then he launched an even fiercer assault than on the day before, and in the face of this sudden attack the enemy forces faltered and were forced to withdraw, leaving behind much of their heavy gear and baggage. But of course they were backed by another large taskforce.

Khalid regrouped his forces right away and said, "This victory will suffice us. It is a great boon for us that they have been forced into this retreat; at the same time it is an important opportunity. I have no doubt that you all wish to become martyrs right here and now, but such easy martyrdom is not to be your lot. You will achieve martyrdom only after you have slain and dispatched to eternal perdition a larger number of truth-deniers! Today we have not the chance for that. Let us now return to Madinah safely, with dignity and firm footing in our faith. This will be a great victory and a sweet boon from our Lord."

Thus the Prophet's ﷺ army returned to Madinah, safe and sound. But the Holy Prophet ﷺ had been following the events on the battlefield by means of the prophetic vision given to him, describing what he saw to the companions grouped about him in the holy mosque. At one point he said, "Just now my beloved friend Zayd has been martyred," and his eyes, which served as windows to the Truth of the Lord, filled with tears. After a short silence, he continued, "Now the flag has been passed to the hand of Ja'far ibn Abi Talib, he smites the enemy with all his might. Ah, now his right hand is cut off, he takes the flag with his left, and continues to beset the enemy."

The Prophet's ﷺ companions listened in suspense to the visions he was relating and sobbed with emotion and grief. "Now his left arm also is severed," continued the Holy Prophet ﷺ, and raising both his hands, he prayed, "Oh my Lord, do Thou give my beloved cousin two wings in the stead of both his arms!" Somewhat later he informed them that his prayer had been granted and that Ja'far had attained his ultimate aim and fallen as a martyr. It was then that Ja'far was given the name 'Ja'far at-Tayyar', Ja'far, the Flying.

After this, the Holy Prophet # related how the flag was given to Abdullah bin Rawaha and how this venerable companion of the Ansar was martyred. Then he told of Khalid ibn al-Walid taking up the banner of Islam and of his ferocious onslaught against the overpowering enemy, and of the many swords that broke in his hand. Then he said, "Now the enemy has withdrawn in dread and Islam has come out of it in good cheer. Khalid has now received the rank of 'Sayfullah' (Sword of Allah)." It was for his achievement in this battle that the Holy Prophet # gave Khalid ibn al-Walid the rank of field marshal.

The Story of 'Amr ibn al-'As

In that same year, the eighth year of the Hijra, in the month of Jamadi-al-Awwal, the Holy Prophet # received the news that the tribesmen of the Bali and Quda'a were rounding up the herds belonging to the people of Madinah in the Wadi-al-Qura, intending to drive them off. He therefore designated 'Amr ibn al-'As, whose mother was of the tribe of the Bali and who was known for his cunning, to command a punitive force of three hundred fighters. When 'Amr ibn 'As approached the enemy lines, he learned that the enemy was more numerous than anticipated, and he sent Rafi' back to Madinah to inform the Prophet # of this and to request reinforcements. The Holy Prophet # then immediately sent out Abu 'Ubayda with two hundred men to his aid. Among them were his close friends Abu Bakr as-Siddiq and 'Umar al-Faruq. As the Prophet # was sending them out on this campaign, he said to them, "I am sending you out as support troops in order to fend off the enemy attack and to punish these brigands, under the one condition that you do not break the unity of your ranks, and do not fall into dissension."

With this advice, the Holy Prophet #, the Guide of Men's Hearts, manifested another miracle concerning the behavior of 'Amr ibn 'As towards those who had come to support him. He warned the companions in advance of division and disunity among the ranks, for after all, their aim was to join forces in order to chastise the enemy. When the support column joined up with the troops of 'Amr ibn 'As, their commander Abu 'Ubayda wished to perform the duty of the Imam for the soldiers by right of seniority. However, 'Amr ibn al-'As reacted vehemently to this, saying, "No! The command of this force is mine, you have command only of an auxiliary troop; therefore, it is for me to be the Imam!"

Abu Bakr, 'Umar and Abu 'Ubayda exchanged glances and remembered what the Holy Prophet 🕷 had said to them in parting, "Do not fall into dissent!" They therefore quickly consented to 'Amr ibn al-'As' views, bearing in mind the Prophet's admonition and the aim of their mission. The following morning they launched a fierce attack on the enemy and returned to Madinah victoriously.

Upon his return to Madinah, 'Amr ibn al-'As, who remained unaware of the feigned approval of his leadership by the Great Sahaba, deemed himself to be as close to the Holy Prophet 🕷 as for instance, Zayd bin Harith. He ventured to put this question to Prophet 🕷: "Whom do you love the best?" In answer to this the Holy Prophet 🕷 made mention of his honorable wives, (thereby giving a subtle interpretation of the secrets of the holy verse:

(Your wives) are a vestment for you, and you are a vestment for them.

(The Cow: 187)

This indicates that nothing comes before the love of one's family; it is foremost in a man's life. But 'Amr ibn al-'As pursued the matter, saying, "I do not ask about the women, I am asking about the men." "The father of my wife Aisha, Abu Bakr as-Siddiq," the Prophet 🕷 replied. "And after him?" "Umar al-Faruq", said the Prophet 🕷. In the hope of hearing his own name mentioned yet, 'Amr ibn al-'As persisted in his questioning. "And after these, who is it that you love the best?"

The Holy Prophet ﷺ then began to list all those blessed companions who had confronted a hostile world with the call of 'La ilaha illAllah' that had proceeded from a cave on Mount Hira. He named those valiant souls who had made enemies of even their closest relatives, who had left behind all they owned and disregarded all concern for their own advantage, driven solely by the love for the call to Allah. Then 'Amr ibn al-'As realized that his name would not be listed among those whom the Holy Prophet ﷺ loved best and he fell silent.

'Amr ibn al-'As himself relates how he entered Islam:

> "After the War of the Confederates, we all returned to Mecca and were close to despair. For although we were in every material aspect superior to Muhammad ﷺ and his band of followers, they had begun to gain over us in many ways. Whereas before the Muslims had only claimed the eternal life as their own, they were now able to say that this world also was at their feet. I then thought, 'It is best that I go to the Negus of Abyssinia. For in any case, one day Muhammad ﷺ and his friends will return to their native place, Mecca. If my people gain the upper hand over Muhammad ﷺ, I can come back and resume residence there in peace. If Muhammad ﷺ is victorious over my people, at least I will not have had to witness that defeat with my own eyes.' Some of my friends agreed and accompanied me, and taking with us many and precious gifts, we presented ourselves before the Negus."

> "Then one day, Muhammad ﷺ sent 'Amr bin Umayya to the Negus as his envoy. Intending to take advantage of this situation, I went to the Negus, since I assumed that he would be displeased by Muhammad's ﷺ agent. I thought he would hand him over to me for me to deal with, in which case he would incur no blame, as the man would have been murdered by one of his own people. When I put these ideas to the Negus, he flew into a rage and drove me from his presence. I then said, 'Had I known that I would occasion such anger, I would not have been so bold.'

> "The Negus grew even angrier at that and said, 'You wish me to deliver into your hands the envoy of such a luminary who is visited by

the messenger angel himself when he comes to deliver Divine Messages!' I then asked the Negus, 'Is that truly what you believe?' He replied in a stern manner, 'Don't waste your words! Muhammad ﷺ is a true Prophet. If you are a real man, confess Islam and know that one day he will vanquish all his opponents. Just as Musa was Kalimullah and beat Fir'aun with the staff in his hand, so Muhammad ﷺ is the Proof of Allah and will persuade those who argue against him.'

"I left the presence of the Negus feeling utterly dejected. I now was sure that there was no other way to get ahead in the world than by becoming Muslim. I made up my mind to it and secretly set out for Madinah. Then I grew aware that Khalid ibn al-Walid was following me. 'Where are you going?' I asked him. Khalid was an open-minded, outspoken person. He did not yet know of my decision. He replied, 'No need remains for stubborn persistence on the way of disbelief that our fathers and forefathers have shown us. There is not a grain of doubt that Muhammad ﷺ whom we used to know as 'al-Amin' is a true Prophet. I am on my way to Madinah into his presence to surrender all that I am and own that he may teach me the worship of the God that he preaches. I will entreat him to forgive me for all the outrage and insolence I have worked against him before this day. If I can achieve his pardon, there is no man happier than I.'

"In this way we proceeded to Madinah together and met with a gracious reception by Muhammad ﷺ. Thus we entered Islam."

The Battle of Murays

The Quraysh tribe was held in great esteem by all other Arab tribes and regarded as especially privileged, on account of their descent from the family of Ibrahim and their pureblooded Arab lineage.

The tribe of the Bani Khuza'a were allied with the Quraysh. Incited by the Quraysh, Harith bin Dirar, the chief of the clan of Bani Mustaliq, which belonged to the tribe of Khuza'a, decided to launch an attack on Madinah. The Holy Prophet ﷺ asked Zayd bin Husayb about the situation and conditions. Zayd replied by messenger, informing that preparations for an

462

attack were under way. The Holy Prophet ﷺ received this news and taking along his wives Aisha and Umm Salama in his retinue, he set out with one thousand of his trusted friends and veteran fighters.

When this became known among the Bani Khuza'a, fear spread among them and the tribesmen dispersed, among them their chieftain, Harith bin Dirar. Only the men of Murays were left to face the Muslim army, and in the skirmish that followed, they lost ten of their number, while six hundred were taken prisoner. The Muslims also took from them two thousand camels and five thousand sheep.

Among the prisoners of war was Harith bin Dirar's daughter, Juwayriya. She was part of the share of the spoils that fell to Thabit bin Qays. Thabit presented her to the Holy Prophet ﷺ as a gift. Her father, Harith, was one of the chiefs of the Arab tribes and he sent word to the Prophet ﷺ that he wished to pay his daughter's ransom so that she be returned to him. He wished not for a chieftain's daughter to be reduced to the status of a captive slave girl. The Holy Prophet ﷺ then said, "I leave the decision up to your daughter. You may come and ask her yourself. We will see what she will choose for herself." Harith was given free passage and he came to see his daughter Juwayriya. He said to her, "My daughter, don't shame me before my enemies. Muhammad ﷺ has left the decision up to you; if you wish, you may come home with me, if you wish, you may remain here."

Juwayriya replied, "Oh father, you have misunderstood Muhammad ﷺ. How can anyone ever wish to be separated from him, after having entered the ocean of his munificence and perceived the heavenly scent of Allah's Mercy? Even were he to drive me away, I would not depart from the gate of the Beloved of Allah!"

Juwayriya's reply was related to the Holy Prophet ﷺ whose heart beat with compassion for the entire creation. He said, "I will set her heart at ease by admitting her among my wives." Juwayriya was thus granted a great favor and became one of the Mothers of the Believers. The Muslims then set free all the other prisoners of war they had taken at Murays, saying, "It is against the rules of good conduct for us to keep as slaves any person who belongs

to a tribe which is connected to our Holy Prophet ❀ through family ties."
Juwayriya acquired the unique distinction of being permitted access to the
presence of the Light of Prophethood ❀ while at the same time serving her
people, for she became the means for their liberation from bondage.

Slander of Aisha

In the course of these events, what became known as 'the Calumny'
concerning the Prophet's ❀ youngest wife Aisha took place. Aisha had
accompanied the Holy Prophet ❀ on his campaign against the Khuza'a. On
the return journey, Aisha was suddenly found to be missing from her
camel's howdah, and everyone grew worried about her. The fact of the
matter was that she had dropped her necklace and had gone to look for it
during a rest stop, and had been left behind in this way. She had been found
by Safwan who mounted her on his camel and led her to rejoined the
caravan.

There were some among the community who were jealous of Abu Bakr's
close attachment to the Prophet ❀ and who secretly welcomed this
opportunity to harm him. They began to gossip about his daughter Aisha,
the Prophet's ❀ wife, regarding what had happened between her and
Safwan bin Mu'attal. One of the most vicious slanderers was the hypocrite
Abdullah bin Ubayy bin Salul who went as far as claiming openly that Aisha
had known Safwan from childhood, implying that she had a long-standing
motivation for an illicit relationship. They claimed that Aisha's excuse for
her absence was unacceptable, for there was just as much probability for
her truthfulness as there was for her lying. These words affected the Holy
Prophet ❀ very much, but he refrained from passing his verdict on Aisha
immediately. Aisha, on their return to Madinah, developed a fever and went
to stay at her father's house. The Prophet ❀ asked 'Uthman's opinion in
this matter. 'Uthman said, "God forbid! I do not believe Aisha capable of
such an execrable act."

In this connection, an incorrect narration is sometimes quoted, according to
which the Holy Prophet ❀ is to have asked Ali for his views on the matter,

and Ali is to have replied, "Oh my Prophet ❋, are there no girls in the whole town of Madinah other than Aisha?" Thereupon the Holy Prophet ❋ is to have said, "Oh Ali, the divorce of my wives is in your hands!" On account of these words which 'Uthman is said to have witnessed, Aisha is supposed to have borne a grudge against Ali. However, this is an entirely faulty, unreliable narration.

For one thing, the words that are here attributed to Ali were not spoken on this occasion, but rather during the apportioning of booty, as we will have occasion to relate further on. For Ali had not a grain of doubt in his heart that the allegations proffered against Aisha were lies and slanderous fabrications. However, he is reported to have said, "Investigate this matter thoroughly, so that the calumny fathered by the hypocrites will be entirely cleared up. Aisha will stand out as a shining example of chaste and virtuous womanhood."

Everyone knew Aisha to be in complete possession of her mental abilities. If she had indeed – God forbid! – stooped so low as to commit so heinous an act, would she have gone about it in such a crude and vulgar way? For her naïveté and imprudence alone are proof of her innocence. Let us regard this matter from a spiritual standpoint: assuming our faith had risen to the station of Love, we might grow aware of a voice speaking to us in our heart, telling us that the Companion on High, the Ever-Watchful Lord is also a Jealous Lord. Finding His Beloved to be excessively occupied with the love for his wife Aisha, the Divine Lover therefore made His Beloved feel some pain, thereby calling his heart back to the One True Love. More than this need not be said.

The remainder of the story is told in Aisha's own words:

"When the Holy Prophet ❋ intended to go on a journey, he would cast lots among his wives. On the raid preceding the raid against the Bani Mustaliq, the lot had fallen to me, so that I accompanied him in his illustrious entourage. As the verses concerning the veiling of the Prophet's ❋ wives had already been revealed, I was placed in a Howdah (a kind of covered cabin) upon a camel. On the return journey, the Prophet ❋ halted at a stop one day's journey from

465

Madinah. There I got out of my Howdah, and following the call of nature, I went to a place outside the camp to relieve myself. When I came back, I felt my chest, and noticed that I had lost the string of beads I had been wearing. I turned back to look for them, but that delayed me so, that the army had already decamped and gone by the time I returned.

"The porters had loaded my Howdah upon the camel, thinking I was inside it, for I was still a very young thing and brought little weight to bear. Therefore, they had lifted the contraption onto the camel without second thoughts. Having found my necklace, I returned, just to find that everyone had departed. I thought to myself that surely they would notice my absence and turn back to look for me, so I sat down on the spot and fell asleep. While I slept, the man rode up whose job it was to ride after the army and see that they had left nothing of importance behind. He would catch up with the troops at the next rest stop. This man was Safwan bin Mu'attal. He recognized me, and I awoke with the words he pronounced:

Inna lillahi wa inna ilaihi ra'ji'un. (Surely we belong to God and to Him we return.)

(The Cow, 156)

"I instantly covered myself with my mantle. Safwan dismounted from his camel, and turned away until I had mounted upon it. After I had mounted, he led the camel on. We caught up with the army in the noonday heat.

"In the meanwhile, my absence had been noticed and there was a great commotion. Everyone was talking about me; the whole caravan was in an uproar. 'She is done for,' they said, and the worst calumny was invented and spread about by the chief of the hypocrites, Abdullah bin Ubayy bin Salul.

"At last, the Prophet's 🏵 party arrived at Madinah. After our return, I fell ill and my illness lasted for a month. But this time I missed the kindness and favor with which the Holy Prophet 🏵 used to treat me when I was ill. He would only come into my room and ask, 'How is she?' This made me very sad, all the more so as I knew of nothing. Finally, my illness abated, and I began to convalesce. One night, I went outside with the mother of Mistah. As soon as we were finished, I returned to my chamber with the mother of Mistah.

"There she happened to trip over her gown, and I heard her say under her breath, 'May Mistah stumble'. I said, 'Mind your words, what are you saying? Would you reproach one of the veterans of the Ansar who fought at Badr?' 'My dear,' she said, 'do you not know what they are saying about you?' 'What are they saying then?' Thereupon she exclaimed, 'Verily I witness that you are a pure believing woman,' and she related to me in full detail all the calumnies and slander that were being spread about me. In reaction to this, I fell ill again and was quite beside myself. I went home, weeping. The Holy Prophet 🕸 again came in, and again he enquired, 'How is she?' I could no longer contain myself and I cried, 'Oh Rasulullah! With your permission, I will go to my parents' house!' He consented, and I went there, weeping all along.

"It was my purpose to learn the whole truth from them. I asked my mother, 'What are they saying about me?' 'My daughter,' she replied, 'don't worry about it. If a woman is the wife of such a great man, and if in addition to this she is beautiful and he loves her, and if there are other wives as well, then such words are of no great import. Have you not heard of this up till now?' 'Praise be to Allah! Do you mean to say that everybody is speaking such things about me?'

"That night I wept and cried the whole night through till it was morning. As the sun rose and I was still crying, my father entered the room and pointing at me asked my mother, 'Why is Aisha crying?' My mother answered, 'Have you not heard what people are saying?' My father then said, 'Be quiet, daughter,' and he himself began to weep. But I was unable to stop crying. Both my parents came and sat by me, and both were very unhappy.

"Meanwhile Rasulullah 🕸 had called Ali and Usama, to take counsel with them about the matter of divorcing me. When he asked Ali for his opinion, he said, 'There is no need to doubt Aisha's virtue. You may call in her maid to verify this. I do not believe Allah Almighty will leave the matter as it stands. Perhaps you ought to wait until the truth is revealed to you' The Prophet ﷺ then called my maid Burayra and asked her, 'Oh Burayra! You know how severe is the punishment for lying to the Prophet ﷺ? Answer my question truly then, for it may be that the truth will be revealed and you will be shamed. Have you ever seen anything in Aisha that would make you suspect her?' Burayra answered, 'I swear by the Lord who sent you with the Truth, the only time I ever got angry at Aisha was when she fell asleep on account of her youth and the sheep ate the dough. I had prepared the dough one day, and had told her to watch it while I lit the fire. While she watched, she fell asleep and her pet lamb came and ate it up. Other than this incident, I know of no fault in her.'

"Then Usama was asked for his opinion and he said, 'Oh Rasulullah! I believe that Allah Almighty keeps the family of the Prophet ﷺ pure and exempt from major sins.'

"The Prophet ﷺ then went to the mosque and ascended the Minbar (the pulpit). Casting fierce looks at Abdullah bin Ubayy bin Salul, he began to speak, 'Who will defend me against a man who even goes so far as to dispute the honor and chastity of my family? I only know of goodness, honor and virtue on the part of my household. As for the man they speak of him, too, I know nothing but goodness; he never entered my house but I am with him.' Sa'd bin Mu'adh of the Ansar then rose to his feet and said, 'Oh my Prophet ﷺ! If those who offend you should be of the Aws, I will knock off their heads to set things right for you! Even if they are of the Khazraj, I will do whatever you order me to do!'

"The chief of the Khazraj, Sa'd bin 'Ubada then rose, and unaware of the wrongfulness of placing tribal honor above the honor of Islam, and of opposing the Model of Mankind in judging according to the standards of the days of Jahiliyya. In this way the Aws and Khazraj almost came to blows. The Holy Prophet ﷺ spoke from the Minbar, saying, 'It is an ugly thing to behave like this in my presence!' He calmed them down and finally silenced them.

"I had to tell myself that all this was happening because of me, and this thought caused me to weep all day long and robbed me of my sleep at night. I wept until the break of day. My parents began to worry about me, and were inclined to think that so much crying would damage my health. My mother and father sat by my side. One of the Ansar women came in, wishing to visit me, and I asked her in. While we were sitting together, the Holy Prophet ﷺ came, gave Salams and sat down. Since the beginning of this slander attack, the Prophet ﷺ had not once sat down by my side.

"A whole month had passed and the Prophet ﷺ had received no heavenly revelation on my behalf. After he had seated himself, the Holy Prophet ﷺ began to speak, intoning the words of the Shahada. Then he continued with grave dignity, 'Oh Aisha, as is well known, many things are being said about you and have been brought to my attention. If you are innocent of these sins, Allah will surely clear you of these allegations; Allah will provide proof of your innocence. If however, contrary to your custom, you are guilty of what they say, turn to Allah and repent of your sin. For Allah accepts the repentance of the sinner when he repents.'

"When the Holy Prophet ﷺ had finished speaking, my tears suddenly dried up. I turned to my father who was sitting beside me and said to him, 'Do reply to the Prophet ﷺ on my behalf.' My father said, 'By Allah, I do not know what to say. What answer can I give the Holy Prophet ﷺ?' Then I turned to my mother and begged her to speak for me, 'Do you answer him,' I said. She gave me the same reply as my father had. Since I was still so very young, I did not yet know very much of the Quran, only this much I could say, 'By Allah, you have heard all this and you believe in your heart that it has taken place as you have been told. If I were to say to you that I am innocent, you would not believe me, while the Almighty knows that I am free of blame in this matter. Were I to confess my guilt in spite of being innocent, you would be ready to believe me. By God, I find no way to explain this to you. What else can I say but the words of that righteous servant of the Lord, the father of Yusuf when he said:

But come, sweet patience! And God's succor is ever there to seek against that
you describe! (Joseph, 18)

"After this I again took to my bed in a state of indescribable dejection.
I hoped that Allah would clear me of all their allegations. But I never
thought it would happen through such a long verse of revelation. I
thought perhaps the Holy Prophet ﷺ would be shown a dream in
which he was told of my innocence. For I regarded myself as too
unworthy and lowly to be spoken of in the Holy Quran. However,
Allah knows best. The Holy Prophet ﷺ had not yet left our company,
nor had any of us yet gone outside, when he began to exhibit the signs
of revelation descending on him. Drops of sweat as large as hailstones
appeared on his skin as the truth was revealed to him, although it was
a cool winter's day.

"They covered him up and placed a pillow beneath his blessed head. I
felt great relief, knowing that I was innocent. But until the Prophet ﷺ
returned to his normal state, I was afraid that my mother and father
would die from fear of a revelation confirming all that people said
about me. When the Holy Prophet ﷺ returned to us, he laughed and
these were his first words, 'Good news to you, oh Aisha, and know
that Allah Almighty has cleared you of all allegations!'

"My mother said with tears in her eyes, 'Go to your husband, my dear!'
But being coy, I said, 'No, I will not go to him. I will praise none but
Allah Almighty and to Him give my thanks!' (Aisha affected this
attitude as she was engulfed in rapture over the divine revelation
concerning her.)

"Somewhat later the Prophet ﷺ ascended the Minbar and announced
the verse that had been revealed on my account. After he had
descended again, Abdullah bin Ubayy bin Salul, Mistah and Hassan bin
Thabit were punished by flogging."

The Divine Verse revealed on Aisha's behalf was this:

Those who came with a slander are a band of you; do not reckon it evil for you;
rather it is good for you. Every man of them shall have the sin that he has earned

470

charged to him; and whosoever of them took upon himself the greater part of it, him there awaits a mighty chastisement. Why, when you heard it, did the believing men and women not of their own account think good thoughts, and say, 'This is a manifest calumny'? Why did they not bring four witnesses against it? But since they did not bring the witnesses, in God's sight they are the liars. But for God's bounty to you and His mercy in the present world and the world to come there would have visited you for your mutterings a mighty chastisement. When you received it on your tongues, and were speaking with your mouths that whereof you had no knowledge, and reckoned it a light thing, and with God it was a mighty thing.

And why, when you heard it, did you not say, 'It is not for us to speak about this; glory be to Thee! This is a mighty calumny'? God admonishes you, that you shall never repeat the like of it again, if you are believers. God makes clear to you the signs, and God is All-Knowing, All-Wise.   (Light, 11-18)

In her time, Maryam, the mother of 'Isa, was also the victim of this sort of slander. Her name, too, was cleared by the revelation of the Quran. Allah declares the innocence of the cherished Mother of the Believers, Aisha, stating clearly that the allegations against her were nothing but vicious slander and insubstantial gossip.

But a great lesson is to be learnt from this holy verse: it indicates how every believing man or woman should behave. When one hears a bad word concerning anyone, one ought to think well of this person and assume the best. Just as no one would have a doubt about his own person and would like to be thought of as blameless, even if appearances seem to contradict the truth. One should refrain from baseless, unproven gossip and say instead, 'This is plainly slanderous defamation.'

Alas, how far we are from such good manners! Even today there are such enemies of Islam, who try to use this story of the calumny against Aisha for their own means. They make a big fuss over this story and never once mention the Quranic verse that was revealed in this context. At the same time these people appear to be profoundly devout. What can we say about them, except to leave them to Allah.

There is a Hadith which says: "Anybody who spins intrigues against a believer behind his back and slanders him, will be imprisoned in the afterlife in a morass of pus and purulence, until what he has alleged is proven. As there is no substance to it but the words he has spoken, there will be no means to prove his claim. Therefore he will to remain in it forever!"

The Conquest of Mecca

The time had come for the cleansing of idols of that hallowed place which is called 'Bayt-ullah', the House of Allah, which was erected by the venerated ancestor of the Holy Prophet ﷺ, Ibrahim. For even though the Noble Companions of the Prophet ﷺ had a glimpse of their hometown when they performed 'Umra, their yearning was not stilled.

It was just at this time that the unbelievers of the Quraysh broke the terms of the agreement of Hudaybiyah. According to the terms of the agreement, the Arab tribes were free to choose their allegiance; they were free to choose to ally themselves either with the idolaters or with Muhammad, the Prophet ﷺ.

One of these tribes was that of the Khuza'a. According to the agreement of Hudaybiyah, they were under the Prophet's ﷺ protection and had become allies of the Muslims. Their rival tribe, the Bani Bakr had formed an alliance with the Quraysh. These tribes were rivals from way back, and their enmity had been somewhat muted by the arrival of Islam. But now, relying on their powerful ally, the Bani Bakr attacked the Bani Khuza'a afresh. Abu Jahl's son Ikrima, Safwan bin Umayya, Suhayl bin 'Amr joined the Bani Bakr in disguise by night and attacked the Khuza'a. The Khuza'a were forced to seek refuge in the precincts of the Haram. Against the opposition of his own tribe, the chief of the Bani Bakr pursued them into the boundaries of the sacred area, saying, "We don't recognize any forbidden zone or sanctuary," and they killed several of their number, driving the rest to flight.

This incident directly contravened the agreement of Hudaybiyah. The Holy Prophet ﷺ was sitting in the mosque when he heard excitement and commotion going on outside. Asking about the noise, he was told, "Forty men of the Bani Khuza'a have come with 'Amr bin Salih, asking for support!"

The Holy Prophet ✤ admitted them into his presence and asked them for the details of their story. Hearing their tale, the Holy Prophet ✤ showed much concern and told them to expect more support than they had hoped for. He sent a delegation to the Quraysh, specifying these three conditions: the Quraysh were to pay the blood-wit for those killed of the Bani Khuza'a; the alliance between the unbelievers, Bani Bakr and Quraysh was to be cancelled and the Quraysh were to forego their protection; and, should they act to the contrary, the agreement of Hudaybiyah would be declared null and void.

The Quraysh then sent Kurtad bin 'Amr as envoy to Madinah to announce that they considered the treaty of Hudaybiyah to be invalid, but they immediately regretted this step. Harith bin Hisham, Abdullah ibn Abi Rabi' and Safwan began to argue and quarrel with their companions and finally they sent Abu Sufyan to Madinah to renew the contract.

Abu Sufyan's daughter, Umm Habiba had become one of the wives of the Holy Prophet ✤. She had been among the first Muslim emigrants to Abyssinia. Her husband had there become a Christian, but her own faith in Islam remained unshaken, even though she was left destitute. She said, "Even were I to die completely alone and forsaken, I shall never return to the house of my idolatrous father."

The Holy Prophet ✤ heard of this venerable lady's steadfast piety and her deplorable situation, and had offered her the protection of marriage. She now lived in Madinah, and it was to her that her father first turned upon entering the town. When he wished to seat himself upon the cushion the Holy Prophet ✤ was accustomed to use, Umm Habiba quickly removed it, saying, "This is Habibullah's place! You are an impure idolater, and it is not right for you to sit in the place of him who is living Proof of the Divine!" Her father, Abu Sufyan then said, "But I am after all your father, am I not?" She replied, "In Islam, Allah is the reference for all kinship. I have no place with those who associate partners with Him." She made it very clear that it was not a question of natural relationships. How significant a religious sensibility is the love of Islam!

Umm Habiba nonetheless enquired wherefore he had come to see her. Abu Sufyan answered that he had come to renew the treaty of Hudaybiyah, and he asked her to be the intermediary in this matter. She told him that she was not in the habit of interfering in the affairs of the Holy Prophet 🕸 and that he would have to see him for himself. She showed him little interest, barely being polite. But Abu Sufyan, poor soul, was still barred from perceiving the light of prophethood in him who was the Pride of all the World. He did not realize that in the view of one who was cognizant of the Perfume of Divine Mercy, he was of less account than a mosquito's wing in the whole sublunary region.

As his daughter gave him such unhelpful replies, he decided to address the Holy Prophet 🕸 himself. Receiving no admission to his presence, he turned to Abu Bakr and the leaders of the Muhajirin and Ansar. They told him, "We can give no personal guarantees of safety. We have entirely surrendered ourselves to Muhammad 🕸, so we have no more individual opinion or will. We only consider it binding upon us to protect a person to whom he has extended his protection."

Then Abu Sufyan turned to 'Umar, who was known for his violent nature. 'Umar responded in a characteristically harsh manner, "You miserable ingrate! How you dare come to me, asking for intercession! You who at Uhud caused injury to the Prophet's 🕸 noble countenance, which is the mirror of Allah's Truth, you who let your vicious wife Hind eat of the liver of our beloved companion Hamza? I should be your intercessor? If all the world were fallen to ruin, and nothing remained but an ant with a broken leg, I would ally myself with it to fight against you! Be gone and speak to me no more!" he said.

Abu Sufyan next went to see the Prophet's 🕸 daughter Fatima, the Crown of Womanly Virtue, and spoke to her, saying, "Oh you who are

Muhammad's ﷺ most beloved daughter! I entreat you to grant me protection!" Fatima however replied, "It is not for me to grant it to you, I have neither right nor authority for that." Abu Sufyan then pointed to Hasan who was yet only a child of five, running about the yard. "Ask this child then to get up in front of the people and announce to them that he grants me quarter; that will satisfy me." But Fatima replied that it was not their custom to mix up children in the affairs of adults.

Finding all doors firmly shut against him, in his extremity Abu Sufyan finally turned to Ali, and entreated him with great urgency, so that at last Ali suggested to him this gesture, "Go to the Prophet's mosque and make a public announcement that you are renewing the treaty of Hudaybiyah, then turn and leave forthwith." Abu Sufyan then said, "But will the matter be achieved simply by my making such an announcement?" Ali replied, "That I cannot say, however I see no other way open to you." Having no other recourse, Abu Sufyan accepted Ali's prompting, went to the Prophet's ﷺ mosque and said for all to hear, "I am herewith reinstating the agreement of Hudaybiyah!" Then he mounted his camel and turned to leave. The Muslims looked at each other in bemusement, asking, "What does he mean to say by that?"

Abu Sufyan's return to Mecca was delayed. The leaders of the misbelievers grew restless and began to mutter among themselves their worst fears. "He is very long in returning from Madinah. Could it be that he has inclined towards Islam?" As Abu Sufyan returned without positive results to his mission, he entered the city by night and went straight to his house. He was met by his savage wife Hind. "Where have you been so long?" she berated him. "Everyone has grown suspicious of you already. It seems you have achieved no good results either, have you?" Abu Sufyan said to her, "The followers of Muhammad ﷺ are not as you think. They are more devoted to him than ever any son was to his father. Never has there been a ruler on the face of the earth who commanded such respect and obedience in his followers. Let this serve you as an example: When I went to see your daughter and wished to sit down, she prevented me, saying, 'You may not sit here, for it is Muhammad's ﷺ place, and you are morally and ritually impure.' When I said to her, 'But I am your father!' she answered me, 'I am a Muslim and you are an idolater, I am not related to you, for kinship in Islam is reckoned according to the Truth of Allah.' She wouldn't even look at me. So judge for yourself, with such a people, can there be any dealings? I was treated with disrespect by every person I went to see."

He also told her what Ali had advised him to do. Hind then flew into a rage and beat him a blow on the chest, yelling at him, "You have been taken advantage of by them and have returned without accomplishing anything." This left Abu Sufyan in a very difficult position. His wife insulted him, his people were suspicious of him, accusing him of collaboration with the Muslims. When it was morning, he went to the temple, and brought a sacrifice before the idols Assal and Naila, which were between Safa and Marwa, resolving in his heart to remain steadfast in his adoration of them until his dying day.

Meanwhile people began gathering round him, asking what message he had brought from Muhammad ﷺ. They wished to know whether he had brokered a new agreement, on the terms of the truce of Hudaybiyah. Abu Sufyan told them what had transpired, explaining the event. His people were angered against him just as his wife had been, saying, "You have returned in a most helpless condition; neither have you been able to renew the truce, nor have you given a declaration of war. Now what are we to do? Neither can we continue to live our lives in peace and freedom, nor can we prepare for warfare."

Abu Sufyan replied to their attacks and accusations, "If any one of you were to go there, he would return with no other result. Muhammad's ﷺ mind is made up, his resolution is fixed, and his companions submit to him entirely. Whoever goes there and experiences this atmosphere of total surrender cannot fail to be astonished." But his people continued to press him for information. "Did Muhammad ﷺ not answer you when you came to his mosque and made your announcement about renewing the truce of Hudaybiyah?" "No, he did not," said Abu Sufyan. "In that case," they said, "let us prepare for war."

The Holy Prophet ﷺ also engaged in preparations for war. The time had come to put an end to the injustice ruling in Mecca for twenty-one years, the moment was drawing nigh for the rays of the sun of faith to melt down the ice of obstinate disbelief.

One day, when the Holy Prophet ﷺ was sitting by the door of his dwelling, he called for Abu Bakr to come to him. Abu Bakr came, and upon a sign of the Prophet ﷺ he knelt before him. They conversed with each other secretly, a fact which set the companions wondering. Then the Holy Prophet ﷺ called for 'Umar to come into his presence. He spoke to him about the conquest of Mecca in a confidential manner. Suddenly 'Umar called out, "Are they not the ones who call you a sorcerer? Are they not the people who proclaimed a three years' boycott on you and your followers? Who would not employ or engage in any business with any of us unless he renounced his affiliation with Muhammad ﷺ? Who refused him even a piece of bread? Are they not the leaders of the disbelievers who invented all manner of slander and evil talk against Islam and seek to harm it in every way?"

'Umar lost control over himself and gave vent to his feelings of anger and rage. The noble companions who were watching from afar this private consultation of the Prophet ﷺ with his two trusted friends, wondered what could be the subject of this conversation that caused 'Umar to lose his temper so vehemently. But they were bound by the rules of good manners and did not approach the Prophet ﷺ before he called them into his presence.

Finally he did summon them and they drew near, wondering what orders the Imam of all Prophets would impart to them. The Holy Prophet ﷺ said, "You are wondering what I have been talking about to these two friends, and what it is that put 'Umar into such a state, is it not so? I will give you a likeness of each of these friends." And, looking Abu Bakr in the face, he continued, "Abu Bakr resembles my ancestor Ibrahim Khalilullah in that he is softer even than oil." Then he turned his blessed face towards 'Umar, smiled and said, "This friend of ours resembles the great prophet Nuh,

Najiullah, the Intimate Friend of the Lord. He is harder even than stone. But in this matter it seems, his word will prevail. There is no other way to eradicate unbelief and draw a line for injustice, so let preparations for battle be made forthwith."

The noble companions did not know what the subject of the conversation had been, they were ignorant of the Holy Prophet's ✼ decision. But they went their way without asking a single question. As 'Umar was of such an angry nature, no one dared to approach him. But they assembled around Abu Bakr, and put their question to him, saying, "Rasulullah ✼ has spoken to you; what did his decision refer to?" Abu Bakr answered them, "The Holy Prophet ✼ said that we ought to put an end to the iniquity that dwells in Mecca, where man-made idols are worshipped. He said it will take a long time to bring the tribes round to the true path, if we do not first teach the leading clan of Quraysh a lesson. He was therefore in favor of a campaign against the Quraysh and asked for my opinion. I replied, 'Oh Rasulullah ✼, you know well that in the end they will become your followers.' The Holy Prophet ✼ then called in 'Umar and asked him for his opinion in this matter. 'Umar replied, 'To show them mercy would amount to betrayal of those they wronged. Unbelief and injustice must be eradicated. Therefore it is needful to prepare for battle against those idolaters who have driven you out of your homeland, pelted you with stones, attempted your assassination, and who would extinguish the light of faith at the slightest prompting, were they given the means to do so.' Those were 'Umar's thoughts."

When the companions understood what was at stake, they immediately undertook preparations for a campaign against the idolaters of Mecca. Word was sent to all the allied tribes to make ready for war. But the nature of the plan was kept secret, and only the senior ranking Muslims who had taken part in the battle of Badr had any knowledge of the reasons behind these preparations. One of these was Hatib bin Balta'a. He wrote a letter to the Quraysh and intended to send it through the hand of a woman. This letter informed them of the Prophet's preparations and of his intention of waging war against them. However, the Holy Prophet 🌸 received news of this by Divine Messenger and it was revealed to him to confiscate this letter.

He called his beloved son-in-law Ali and said to him, "There is a woman in a certain place who is about to depart with a message to the Quraysh, informing of our intentions. She bears on her person a written missive. Go immediately to intercept her, and take with you Zubayr and Miqdad." Ali immediately did as Muhammad 🌸 ordered, found the woman and said to her, "You are bearing a letter and I am ordered to take it from you; please hand it over." The woman was startled and began by denying the allegation, but Ali said to her, "Beware! I have come by order of the Holy Prophet 🌸 who is the recipient of heavenly revelations. There can be no mistake in the news he gives us. You are a woman, so we do not wish to lay hands on you: do not force us to do so. There is no need to deny the truth, we know you have hidden the letter on your person, so come along and bring it out, lest we strip you."

The woman did not understand what she had got involved in. At last she produced the letter, which she had hidden beneath her hair. It was taken to the Holy Prophet 🌸. The writer of the letter, Hatib bin Balta'a, was summoned, the noble companions assembled and everyone was taken aback. 'Umar, the stern upholder of the Shari'a, trembled from rage in every limb. The Holy Prophet 🌸 then addressed them, "Hatib, is it you who wrote this letter?" Hatib replied, "Yes, my Prophet 🌸! But let it not be misunderstood, let no one doubt my faith, it is unbroken and there is not a grain of uncertainty in me, nor the slightest reservation as to your holy person. My love for you falters not a single moment, but all this is known to your prophetic personality.

"My intention was this: you know that there is no one more friendless among the Quraysh than I, having no kinship to clan or tribe among them. I therefore have no one in Mecca to whom to entrust my family and loved ones. I wrote this letter to the Quraysh so that I might have some claim over them, so that they might protect my family there. I now know it was from ignorance, and that unwittingly I have committed a great sin. I beseech you by your mercy and compassion to forgive me!"

The content of the letter was this: "Oh assembly of Quraysh! Let it be known to you that the Holy Prophet 🕌 has sent word to the tribes allied with us to send their warriors, and that he is engaged in preparations for war against you. Soon this army will rush on you and break over you like a tidal wave. Even were he to come all alone, Allah is with him. Your situation is therefore very grave. I recommend that you mobilize your own resources."

When the letter had been read, 'Umar spoke, "Oh Rasulullah!" he said, "This man has tampered with the fate of Islam, for can there be any greater crime than informing the enemy of all the plans and preparations which you have seen fit to keep secret? That there are such hypocrites among us! Just give me leave to sever his head from his trunk!" With these words he reached for the hilt of his sword. But the Mercy of the Worlds, the Holy Prophet 🕌 only smiled and said, "Withdraw your hand from your sword, oh 'Umar! For neither you nor I can do anything to Hatib, nor will even Allah Almighty punish him. He has the distinction of having fought in the Battle of Badr, and about those valliant men Allah Himself has said, 'Whatever you do, I have already forgiven you.' He Almighty has given this decree into their hands." When they heard the compassion of this prophetic decision, the Companions were so moved that their eyes filled with tears and even the Prophet 🕌 wept.

Oh Traveler on the Road to Truth! Why has Allah Almighty granted such an enormous reward to those who fought at Badr? Although the story has been told in greater detail above, let us just recall the essential points in a few words. The two great battles in early Islamic history were the Battle of Badr and the Battle of Uhud. Whenever the unbelievers undertook to extinguish the Light of Islam, they were confounded and their hand remained powerless against the Muslims. As they had failed to draw a veil over the light of Muhammad 🕌, they finally decided to face him in battle, and thus the Battle of Badr was fought. On that day all the worldly forces conspired against the Prophet #, including his own clan and family.

Reason could not grasp how the handful of Muslims took upon themselves every kind of exigence and dearth, following the call to success *('Hayy 'ala-l-falah')*. But it is because of their perseverance that for fourteen centuries five times a day the inspired suggestion of eternal monotheism, 'La ilaha illAllah', rises heavenwards from millions of minarets; it is because of the insistence against all odds of these few companions who gathered around the Prophet # in order to preserve the purity of their intention.

Therefore, what reason could not grasp, faith was able to perceive. Those gathered around the Noble Prophet # on the day of Badr, renouncing all they had and were for the sake of this faith, were given special distinction by the Lord Almighty in that He proclaimed, "Whatever you do, I have forgiven you in advance." Hatib bin Balta'a was one of those granted this privilege. Thus the Battle of Badr is held in the highest esteem by Islam. But as this battle nonetheless took place in this worldly abode of imperfection, there may indeed have been some instances of misconduct, enacted by some on account of their lapses. Since, however, they were of the Companions of Badr, they are not judged harshly for their failings, whereas those who did not participate in Badr are called to account for every minute deed and action.

To continue in our narrative: At the beginning of the month of Ramadan of the eighth year of the Hijra, the Holy Prophet # had completed his preparations for the campaign. His army was equipped and the hearts of all the warriors beat with the desire for victory, infused by Divine Support. Some of the tribes that had allied themselves with the Muslims following the truce of Hudaybiyah now sent their soldiers to join the troops at Madinah. On the tenth of the month of Ramadan the Prophet # set out from Madinah with ten thousand men. He rested at a place one way station's distance from Mecca, called Marr al-Zahran. Along the road two thousand more warriors joined the Prophet's # army.

This is an interesting point: whereas in the year of Hudaybiyah the Prophet ﷺ had commanded only fifteen hundred men, his army now consisted of no less than two thousand. Those who had then opposed the truce of Hudaybiyah, now clearly saw the Prophet's wisdom. He had sheathed his sword at the time and striven instead to win over the hearts and minds of men, and they were shamed before him.

The Holy Prophet ﷺ commanded his men to break the fast at nightfall, and to light a great bonfire after the Iftar. When the bonfire burned, the desert was lit as if it were the holy Valley of Tuwa (Wadil-Ayman Tuwa, where Allah revealed Himself to Musa). The Quraysh saw this great conflagration and wondered what it portended. They surmised that it was the Muslim camp, but they wondered at their great number, judging by the extent of the blaze.

At this point the Prophet's ﷺ uncle 'Abbas announced his Islam, and taking his family and household with him, he proceeded towards Madinah, and met the army of the Prophet ﷺ on the road. The Prophet ﷺ was very happy to see him and embraced him, saying, "Oh my dear uncle, my heart is glad that you have completed your Hijra before the order to emigrate is revoked!" Abbas sent his family and retainers ahead to Madinah and joined the Prophet's ﷺ army.

At a spot called Aywa the Prophet ﷺ was met by his cousin Abu Sufyan bin Harith bin Abdul-Muttalib, his son Ja'far bin Sufyan and his aunt 'Atiqa bint Abdul-Muttalib and her son Abdullah who wished to excuse themselves and ask the Prophet's ﷺ pardon. But the Holy Prophet ﷺ was not minded to accept their plea at this time, for they had been the cause of much harm.

The Mother of the Believers, Umm Salama then said, "Oh my Prophet ﷺ! You have been known to pardon even the most hardened of the disbelievers, showing them kindness and mercy. Here have come to you the sons of your aunt and your uncle, will you not extend your mercy and forgiveness to them as well, so that they may not be singled out as the worst offenders?" thus interceding for them. Abu Sufyan bin Harith himself turned to Ali and implored him, saying, "The Prophet ﷺ refuses even to look at me! What will become of me now?" The soul-mate of the Holy Prophet ﷺ, Ali then told Abu Sufyan bin Harith, "Go now to the presence of the Prophet ﷺ and recite to him this verse, which is the speech of the brothers of Yusuf when they came before his throne:

"By God," they said, "God has indeed preferred thee above us, and certainly we have been sinful."
(Joseph, 91)

This they did, following Ali's advice. The Holy Prophet ﷺ then replied,

No reproach this day shall be on you; God will forgive you; He is the most Merciful of the merciful.
(Joseph, 92)

All of them then shed the bittersweet tears of sin forgiven. The blazing fire the Muslim army had lit at Marr al-Zahran struck great fear into the hearts of the Quraysh, for they believed it to be a huge force of invaders. The whole town of Mecca was in uproar and the leaders of the unbelievers collectively attacked Abu Sufyan, saying, "Now what is to become of us?" Abu Sufyan bin Harb took with him two of his men, Hakim bin Hizam and Budayl bin Warqa and climbed to the top of the hillock overlooking Marr al-Zahran to reconnoiter the situation. There they were apprehended by the watch guarding the Prophet's camp and taken prisoner.

That night, the Prophet's ﷺ uncle 'Abbas mounted the Holy Prophet's ﷺ mule and rode about the outskirts of the camp, thinking that much harm would befall the city of Mecca if the Muslim army were to invade it of a sudden and the Quraysh were to respond with all the force they were capable of. He wished he could find a person to talk to, to try to dissuade them from action of arms, and to convince them to seek quarter instead. All of a sudden, he recognized Abu Sufyan's voice from afar. "Is it you, Abu Sufyan?" he called. "Yes, it is I, 'Abbas! What will become of me now?" was his answer. 'Abbas then said, "Follow me!" and taking Abu Sufyan from the hands of the guards, he led him to the Presence of the Holy Prophet ﷺ. The resting soldiers looked up here and there to see who was moving about the camp by night, but recognizing Abbas riding the

Holy Prophet's ❁ mule, they called to each other, "It's only Muhammad's ❁ uncle 'Abbas," and they went back to sleep.

They had to pass by Sayyidina 'Umar. He recognized Abu Sufyan the moment he set eyes on him, jumped up and grabbed him by the collar. "Here is the enemy of Allah, of the Prophet ❁ and of our religion. At last the time of your death has come, thank God that you have fallen into my hands!" When 'Abbas pleaded for him, 'Umar rejoined, "Pardon for this man?! He has no faith, he shall have no forgiveness! Leave him to me that I may punish him!" At last 'Umar went to the Prophet ❁ and said to him, "We have caught Abu Sufyan and he is brought here before you! With your leave, let him be punished, for Islam has had much harm from his hand and mouth. Let it be me who strikes his head off his neck!" 'Abbas quickly entered the tent of the Prophet ❁ and pleaded for Abu Sufyan's life. One of them grabbed the hilt of his sword, while the other pleaded for mercy. The Holy Prophet ❁ then turned to his uncle 'Abbas and said to him, "You take charge of him and hold watch over him tonight."

Early the next morning 'Abbas took Abu Sufyan to the Prophet ❁. The Prophet ❁ said to Abu Sufyan, "Oh Abu Sufyan! Has the time not come for you to confirm that there is no God but Allah? Do you not believe at last that there is nothing worthy of worship but Allah?" Abu Sufyan thought about this. How could he forsake the idols? Or rather, he had made himself into an idol, so how could he smash it? Islam had forbidden the worship of a mere mortal, and the Quran was revealed to all men as equals. Before God, the master and his slave were on the same level. How could he abide by this? But he was now in a very delicate position, indeed. Finally, after much thought, he answered, "La ilaha illAllah."

The Holy Prophet ❁ then continued his questioning. "Has the time not come for you to confirm the prophethood and mission of Muhammad ❁?" he said. Abu Sufyan answered, "I still have some reservations as to that, give me a little more time."

Now 'Umar was pacing up and down outside the Prophet's ❀ tent. Hearing Abu Sufyan speaking these words, he was unable to contain his feeling of outrage and began muttering aloud to himself, "Ah, if only you were now outside here with me, you would not be uttering such rot. You can be thankful that you are in the Prophet's ❀ blessed presence, if not for that I would hack you in two." 'Abbas thereupon said to Abu Sufyan, "Oh Abu Sufyan, be reasonable! 'Umar is waiting outside and you can hear for yourself what he thinks about you. He is reviewing in his mind all the heinous misdeeds you have visited on the Muslims. He says you have committed countless murders, you are the villain who incited all the Arab tribes to warfare against the Muslims; it is you who planned the attempts on the Holy Prophet's ❀ life. You are the miscreant who repeatedly attacked the city of the Prophet ❀, Madinah. Any single one of these crimes would justify the penalty of death, what of the sum total of these deeds? Were it not for the Holy Prophet's ❀ mercy and forbearance. Yes, this is what 'Umar is saying as he prowls outside this tent." Taking 'Abbas' advice, Abu Sufyan pronounced the words, 'Muhammedun-Rasulullah ❀' without further hesitation.

Oh Traveler on the Road to Truth! This was how Abu Sufyan declared his allegiance to Islam, at least in words. Abu Sufyan had worked great harm against Islam, that is true. He had equipped whole armies to fight the cause of Islam, he plotted to assassinate the Prophet ❀, he tried to extinguish the light of Islam with might and with main. But to no avail, all his efforts failed and his undertakings floundered. Now, when he had fallen into evil straights and was left to face the enemy all on his own, without the backing of friends, arms or riches, yet the Holy Prophet ❀ showed him such nobility of character that Abu Sufyan was compelled to profoundly reconsider.

The Holy Prophet ❀ wished that Abu Sufyan might see for himself that when a thing has been decreed by Divine Providence, no power on earth is able to change it. The party of Allah is bound to win at all events. Therefore, he signaled to his uncle 'Abbas to take Abu Sufyan to the pass by which the Muslim army was bound to traverse. Later, he countered all the evil Abu Sufyan had wrought against Islam with the loftiness of his spiritual station by decreeing that all those who sought refuge in the house of Abu Sufyan would be safe. He thus seemingly granted him a privilege that was to instill love and pride in him. In reality, however, the Prophet's ﷺ order contained a message that ought to have shamed him utterly, for it meant to say, 'Look here, this generous privilege is Islam's answer to all your misdeeds.'

'Abbas took Abu Sufyan to where he could watch the army pass and would be able to tell the commanders of the companies. The Prophet's ﷺ troops passed, one company following the other, leaving Abu Sufyan immensely impressed. He asked 'Abbas to identify for him the formations as they passed by. First of all came the company of the Bani Sulaym, a thousand men under the valiant command of the hero Khalid ibn al-Walid who had gained the rank and title of 'Sayfullah', the Sword of Allah. When they had drawn up level with Abu Sufyan, they all called out with one single shout, "Allahu Akbar!" and the heavens echoed with their call.

These words meant to say: the hapless idol man has made of himself shall be demolished, and this meaning had come to life in the Takbir Abu Sufyan witnessed, passing right in front of his eyes. He was dumbfounded and reeled from the impact of this momentous Takbir uttered in perfect faith and devotion by the Muslims passing before his eyes. He enquired of 'Abbas who they were, and 'Abbas' answers only increased his wonderment.

Next came the company of Zubayr ibn al-'Awwam who marched by with four hundred men, holding aloft the banner of the Muhajirin. When they had come abreast with Abu Sufyan, their cry of "Allahu Akbar" rose and mingled with the angelic commotion in the heavens above. Abu Sufyan was completely stunned by these sounds. Again he asked 'Abbas who these people were. When he told him that it was the company of Zubayr ibn al-'Awwam, he only managed to stammer, "What, your sister's son?"

These troops were followed by the three hundred troops under the command of the great Abu Dharr al-Ghifari. They, too, called out "Allahu Akbar" in an ear-shattering wave of sound. Abu Sufyan asked who they were and was told that these were the Bani Ghifar. Thereupon he said, muttering to himself, "How amazing! In such a short time, such a short time!"

After these a battalion of the tribe of the Khuza'a came into view: five hundred riders of the Bani Ka'b, and eight hundred infantrymen, followed by the archers of the tribe of Muzayna, and four-hundred foot soldiers of the Bani Lab.

As the tribe of Ashja' marched by, a joyous air of victory in their bearing, Abu Sufyan asked 'Abbas, "Which tribe is this?" Being told that it was the tribe of Ashja', he again muttered under his breath, "How strange! They were Muhammad's ﷺ most embittered enemies! Now they are so closely allied to him! How perfect is their compliance!"

Next eight hundred men of the tribe of Juhayna and several other tribes marched by. Abu Sufyan's mind boggled as he beheld these forces, and, he repeated to himself, askance, "Such an increase in so short a time!" While Abu Sufyan was yet lost in his thoughts, the Holy Prophet ﷺ, girded with Divine Protection that was fitted on him by the Divine Agent, mounted his blessed red camel Qaswa, and rode out chanting Takbir, while lights sparkled all around him. Before him went Ibn 'Ubada with the banner of the Ansar; to his right was Abu Bakr as-Siddiq, the Friend of the Cave, and to his left rode Usayd, with a company of five thousand men, all calling out loudly, "Allahu Akbar!" As the army of the Ansar with Sa'd bin 'Ubada at its head, came up level with Abu Sufyan, Sa'd reminded everyone of the words Abu Sufyan had spoken at Uhud, when he had asked, "Is Muhammad ﷺ dead?" He cried out, "This is the day when all shall receive their just deserts, today we shall seize the Holy Kaba!"

Hearing these words, Abu Sufyan grew pale and ashen-faced, but there was nothing he could say to these Muslim warriors. The Holy Prophet ﷺ himself rode by, and Abu Sufyan asked him, "Did you hear the threat uttered by Sa'd bin ʿUbada?" The Holy Prophet ﷺ replied, "Today the Kaba shall be dressed in glory!"

When Abu Sufyan observed this display of power, he turned to ʿAbbas and said, "The property and authority of your brother's son has increased considerably!" These words indicate that although Abu Sufyan had declared his Islam when faced with the choice of death, he had not really come to terms with it. ʿAbbas answered him firmly, "Hold your tongue, Abu Sufyan! This is not a question of worldly power, but of prophethood!

"Had Muhammad ﷺ been looking for power and worldly dominion, would he have taken upon himself so much suffering and mistreatment, utterly disregarding his own well-being? Would he have let them stone him at Ta'if, from where he left with bloodied feet, would he have had his blessed face wounded at Uhud where one of his teeth was martyred? Would he have migrated from his native land, if it was worldly dominion that he was seeking? You must remember very well when Muhammad ﷺ began to preach Islam and you had all assembled at Dar un-Nadwa. It was decided then to go to Muhammad ﷺ or to call him to come there and ask him what he was after.

"If he wished to found a state of his own and be the ruler of us all, you immediately would have pledged your allegiance to him, you would have unconditionally given the entire Arabian Peninsula into his hands. Had it been beautiful women and girls that he sought, you would have found him the loveliest of all Arabia and presented them to him, on the one condition that he stop preaching 'La ilaha illAllah'. And do you remember his reply to you at that time? Did he not say to you, 'You misunderstand me. It is the Unity of the Divine that I preach, and the resurrection after death!' Therefore, if it were as you seem to think, and Muhammad ﷺ was only after wordly gain and power, he would have accepted what was offered to him at Dar un-Nadwa. What you see and witness here is not a display of worldly force, it is the power of prophethood, the strength of revelation!"

Oh Traveler on the Road to Truth! On the subject of the strength of revelation, let me add a few words to what already has been said. The power of revelation is a strange power, unlike anything else. Millions of people will follow that power, and millions of hearts beat for the recipient of revelation, millions of eyes shed tears for him, and give their hearts to the message he brings, even willingly lay down their lives when called upon to do so.

Truly, this must be the case. For nowadays, who has seen the Holy Prophet ﷺ, who has heard the harmonious sound of his voice issuing from his blessed lips? And yet, there are untold millions of people following the way he has shown, and thousands of minarets intone his beloved name, as they resound with the words of the Shahada. Every year, millions of people travel to the holy place where he lies buried, to kiss the resting place of his relics.

Has Muhammad ﷺ left any material benefits to make people perform all these acts of love? There is no need to go any further. If it could be ascertained beyond doubt that there existed a tiny bit of cloth which Muhammad ﷺ used only once to wipe the sweat off his face, there are people living today who would be willing to give millions for the possession of this scrap of cloth. What is this power that instills such love in people's hearts, although they never saw the man, and never heard his voice? It is the power of revelation.

Here is an example of what I mean. The famous Ibn Sina, whose blessed memory has for centuries been highly honored, had a very talented non-Muslim student whom he taught day and night for nine years. One day Ibn Sina fell ill and it was well after midnight when he woke up his student, saying, "I am burning. It would seem to me that were you to bring me water from the well across the way for me to drink, I would recover." His student replied, "Oh my master, the weather is very bad, moreover I am covered in sweat. If I were to get up and go out just now, surely I would fall ill as well. Please be patient."

There is a Hadith of the Prophet ﷺ in which he says, "The cure to some illnesses is hidden in the strong desire for certain things." The great physician Ibn Sina can be expected to have known and relied on this Hadith. However, the required precondition for being able to act on this Hadith is that a person be qualified to do so. It is not intended that any reckless individual may apply this to himself.

After a little while, people began to gather at this fountain to make their ablutions, despite the severe cold that made their breath steam. Ibn Sina called his apprentice and said to him, "Take a look at this!" The apprentice failed to understand and asked, "What is it about?" "Never mind, just get yourself up and observe this scene. Explanations will follow later," said his teacher. The apprentice then rose, and after he had regarded the spectacle of the people making their ablutions, Ibn Sina began, "The issue at stake is this: many times in the course of our lessons you were amazed at my deliberations, and there were times when you told me, even if I were to claim to be a prophet, I would indeed be credible. I laughed at that, of course. Now pay attention and try to follow my reasoning.

"I have been teaching you now for years, throughout many days and nights, until you are now nearly my equal in knowledge. In this respect, you do owe me quite a bit. Yet, for all your indebtedness to me, I am unable to induce you to get up in the middle of the night to fetch me a glass of water from across the street, even though I am burning with feverish thirst. Your excuse may be acceptable, but there ought to have been enough love in you for you to have overcome your objection, and my word ought to have sufficed to move you into action. Now let us consider what we have seen here: these people have taken to heart the message delivered by one who lived many centuries ago, whose face they have never seen, whose voice has never spoken to them.

"They have risen from their soft, warm beds, have left the sweet embrace of their wives, in order to perform their ablutions with this ice-cold water. The power which causes them to do this willingly and gladly is called the power of revelation, none but the authority of a prophet can achieve such a thing."

Oh Seeker of Truth! In the course of history, there has been many a tyrant desirous of such power over men. Many a dictator has envied the prophets of the desert this power, saying, "Ah, if only I had the power of 'Isa or Musa!" Whatever systems of oppression they invented and applied, at their demise their systems perished along with them. Perhaps even during a tyrant's lifetime, the sycophants who lived off him and obligingly stood before his throne in a show of false respect, would have turned against him and risen in rebellion, had he suddenly chosen to dismiss them.

All this goes to show that the power of revelation is unlike any other power on earth. It does not compare with any power of the material dominion.

To return to our narrative: After the Holy Prophet's 🕸 entire army had marched by the pass where Abu Sufyan stood watching, 'Abbas set him free and told him to go his way. Abu Sufyan immediately went down to Mecca along with Hakim bin Hizam. He proceeded to the Haram and addressed his people on these words: "There is nothing to be done, Muhammad 🕸 is coming. He approaches with a mighty army, against which we have no means of resistance. Do not even toy with the idea of opposition for a single minute. There is nothing left to do but give in and say, 'I have become a Muslim.'" The Quraysh then asked him, "What did Muhammad 🕸 say?" "He has said, 'Whoever enters the mosque will be safe; whoever lays down his arms will be safe; whoever remains in his house and shuts the door, and whoever is within the house of Abu Sufyan will be in safety.'"

Hearing these words, the infamous liver-eater Hind threw herself at her husband, grabbed him by his beard and yelled, "Oh ye men of victory! Slay this useless old man who has lost his mind! What a miserable protector for your people!" But Abu Sufyan just said to her, "Let go of my beard, for I tell you, if you do not do as I have done, you will not be able to save yourself. Go now go back to your house; there is no need to waste many words over this. Go into your house and shut the door."

When this woman with a heart of stone who had eaten the liver of the Prophet's 🌸 cherished uncle Hamza, and who incited the pagan army to warfare, being herself the equivalent of hundreds of unbelievers, when Hind heard her husband's conclusive and despairing words, she realized that the situation indeed was hopeless.

She fell silent and went into her house. The Meccans fell into confusion and there was great commotion. Some people sought refuge in the Haram, some betook themselves to the house of the leader of the clan, Abu Sufyan. Others locked themselves in their own houses, some took up arms, others laid them down. Of all the brave warriors of the Quraysh, only Ikrima, the son of Abu Jahl, Suhayl, the son of 'Amr, and Safwan, the son of Umayya gathered around themselves some fighting men and got ready for battle, determined to resist.

The Holy Prophet 🌸 had given orders to his commanders to fight only if the Quraysh attacked them. They were divided up into different wings. He himself entered Mecca by way of the pass of Adhakir.

The armed band of the Quraysh launched an attack on the wing commanded by Khalid ibn al-Walid at Khandama, in order to prevent their passage into the town. In the skirmish, Kurz bin Jabir and Khunays bin Khalid bin Asram were killed. Although Khalid admonished the attackers time and again, they would not listen, so that in the end Khalid "Sayfullah" was forced to inflict punishment on them. Those who insisted on resistance were punished, the remainder fled.

When the Holy Prophet 🌸 beheld the Kaba, he began to recite Takbir, and of course all the Sahaba followed suit, so that the whole town reverberated with the calls of "Allahu Akbar", and even the tiniest pebbles echoed the sound. The Holy Prophet 🌸 had wound about his head his black turban, which symbolized the attribute of Majesty. It was a Friday. After he had ordered the banner of the Prophet 🌸 to be placed at al-Hajun, he proceeded straight towards the Haram and stood before the doors of the Holy House. Everyone waited with great excitement for him to speak. At last he said, "Let everyone expect goodness from me, and know that I was sent as a mercy to the worlds. Islam covers up all the badness which went before, therefore you all are free." Thus he pronounced his judgment and decree.

The Arabs of those times had set up three-hundred and sixty idols in the house erected by the noble ancestor of the Prophet Muhammad ❀, Ibrahim Khalilullah. The Holy Prophet ❀ entered the Kaba together with his trusted general, Ali. As soon as they set foot in it, the Prophet ❀ recited this holy verse from the Quran:

> *"The truth has come, and falsehood has vanished away; surely falsehood is ever*
> *certain to vanish."* (The Night Journey, 81)

They proceeded to topple the idols one by one, and they threw them down from their pedestals. A few idols were hung from a very high place. The Prophet ❀ said to Ali, "Come, Ali, step on my shoulder, and fetch down those on top." But Ali replied, "Oh my Prophet ❀, I would rather that you step upon my shoulders and bring them down." At this, the Holy Prophet ❀ smiled and said, "The whole of creation rests upon my shoulders; how will you be able to withstand that weight? It is therefore better that you step upon my shoulder and climb up." He repeated his command and Ali obeyed him. He stepped upon the Prophet's ❀ shoulders in order to throw down the top row of idols. But when he lifted his head and looked about, he experienced a wondrous state and saw what he had never before beheld: he found himself to be gazing at the world of the Divine Throne. He saw that the head of the Prophet ❀ covered the Throne. As he bent forward full of awe, he beheld the heavenly regions, which were covered by Muhammad's ❀ chest. When he looked down at the regions below him, he beheld the Earth, which was covered by Muhammad's ❀ blessed feet.

(This part of the story relates to those who have tasted of real faith; who remains trapped in the density of materialistic thought cannot know anything of that taste.)

The Prophet ❀ circled the Kaba seven times and the Sahaba and his friends followed in his footsteps. Abu Sufyan was standing by one side. As he watched the Tawaf of the Prophet ﷺ and the Sahaba, he thought to himself, "Ah, if only I had an army and could fight against this man once more, if only I could destroy him with my newly gained knowledge, if only I had another chance to measure myself against him." As he was thinking these thoughts, the Holy Prophet ﷺ passed by close to him. He said, "This man will disgrace you again, he will bring you down low and then desert you." Abu Sufyan stared straight ahead and in order to conceal the matter from the Sahaba who were near, while he said aloud, "Now my faith is stronger than before."

The Holy Prophet ﷺ continued his circumambulation of the Kaba. At a certain point Fudala approached him with the intention of slaying him. The Prophet ﷺ observed Fudala as he slowly drew up to him, and finally addressed him, "Are you Fudala?" "Yes," said the man, greatly surprised. "What were you thinking just now?" the Prophet ﷺ continued to ask. The man replied, "I was not thinking of anything, I was busying myself with worship," and he assumed a posture as of pious humility. The Holy Prophet ﷺ laughed at this and said, "Repent of what you had planned in your mind, for I am girded with the armor of Divine Protection. I will not leave this world before I have perfected the religion of Allah."

Oh Traveler on the Way to Truth! The story of the conquest of Mecca and the Holy House contains some subtle points, which I will try to elucidate:

Firstly, it signaled the beginning of a period in which the heart of every God-seeking person would be turned towards Islam; and, secondly, it points to the fact that this noble religion brought by the Holy Prophet ﷺ was never meant to remain the privilege of the Arab people alone, but was destined soon to spread all over the world. The Holy Prophet ﷺ made these issues abundantly clear. For instance, Bilal was a black Abyssinian slave. He attained the status of a freedman, and in reality he was one of the great Friends of Allah about whom the Holy Prophet ﷺ said, "Look here at the first fruit of Abyssinia." Likewise he said about Salman al-Farsi, "He is the first fruit of Iran." And about Suhayb ar-Rumi he said, "He is the first fruit of Byzantium." By his describing these companions by these names, he indicated in advance the extent of the conquests of Islam.

After he had recaptured his native city, the Prophet ﷺ pronounced, "This was destined to be and it came to pass."

The noble companions whose hearts beat with the love for their Prophet ﷺ asked him where he intended to lodge. The Pride of All Prophets ﷺ replied, "I will stay at just the place where the Quraysh assembled to pledge themselves to the destruction of Islam." This refers to the following events: When the Holy Prophet ﷺ single-handedly began to preach the Unity of Allah on Mt. Hira, the leaders of the Quraysh had assembled at Mahsab, and sworn this solemn oath: "Until Muhammad ﷺ foregoes his claims and surrenders himself, there will be no intermarriage between the clans of the Bani Hashim and the Bani Abdul-Muttalib, nor will there be any business dealings or other gainful transactions." Regarding these events, this verse of the Holy Quran was revealed by Allah to His Prophet ﷺ:

Those are they that say, "Do not expend on them that are with God's Messenger until they scatter off."   (The Hypocrites, 7)

However, the devoted followers of the Holy Prophet ﷺ had borne all the cruelty and mistreatment visited on them by the dark-spirited, evil-minded idolaters. They lived off the love they held for their Prophet ﷺ, and their spiritual strength grew in the same proportion as their trials and tribulations increased.

Therefore, the place the Holy Prophet ﷺ chose to make his headquarters in Mecca is highly significant. By doing so, he struck the unbelievers a very heavy blow, as is revealed in the Holy Quran:

Yet unto God belong the treasuries of the heavens and of the earth, but the hypocrites do not understand.   (The Hypocrites, 7)

Now at last they understood, for Allah was very plainly saying to them:

"The Lord has willed to house His Beloved ﷺ at the very place where previously you gathered and took an oath to extinguish the light of the religion I have sent to you."

495

****

The Haram ash-Sharif was cleansed of all the idols and their greatest one, the famous Hubal, was smashed to pieces. As he was smashing the idol, Zubayr called out to Abu Sufyan, "Oh Abu Sufyan! Look at the state of your idol now, upon whom you placed so much hope in the Battle of Uhud!" Actually, whenever the Muslims remembered Abu Sufyan's misdeeds and actions against Islam, their eyes filled with tears and their expressions darkened.

One day this incident occurred: Bilal, whose calling of the Adhan the Divine Throne listened for, was giving Abu Sufyan a piece of his mind when Abu Bakr as-Siddiq happened to pass by. He overheard Bilal's words and admonished him not to speak to Abu Sufyan in such a manner. Later Abu Bakr as-Siddiq told the Holy Prophet ﷺ about this, and the King of Prophets ﷺ said, "Oh Abu Bakr! If you have offended Bilal by your manner, know that you have offended Allah Almighty as well. Therefore, go quickly and make it up with him!"

I leave it for everyone to glean the subtle meaning of this matter.

****

After the Holy Prophet ﷺ had finished his prayer at the Kaba, he gave a Khutba (sermon) in which he addressed not only the gathering of the Arabs present, but the dwellers of the whole world. This is the meaning of what he said:

"La ilaha illAllah, there is no God other than Allah, no one is worthy of worship other than He who is without partners. Idolatry is now abolished, no one is to worship any other man, or what is made of stone, wood or clay. Allah has made true His promise, He has given support to His servant and has routed those who gathered against Him, wishing to extinguish the light of Islam. All the blood feuds and litigations of the Age of Ignorance (Jahiliyya) are now superseded and abolished. The only appointment to be upheld is the custodianship of the holy Kaba and the distribution of water to the Hujjaj (pilgrims)."

"Oh people of Quraysh! Allah has lifted from you all the self-conceit of the Age of Ignorance, the vainglory of your predecessors and your pride in the rotting bones of your ancestors. All of mankind is descended from Adam, and Adam was created from clay. The Lord Almighty has made you male and female, and divided you up into many peoples and tribes so that you might understand each other and live together as one spirit in a multitude of bodies."

Oh Traveler on the Road to Truth! This is the moment to pause in reverence before the Holy Prophet's ﷺ enlightened speech. Notably, he begins his sermon with the affirmation of the Unity of Allah, which is the foundation of all religions.

The aim of creation is to regain connection with one's origins. The purpose of life is to find one's way back to the Lord of all being, driven by the urge of love. Attachment, ardent desire, realization, i.e., knowing, finding, being. This was the first point the Holy Prophet ﷺ made in his sermon.

Secondly, he spoke on the issue of blood feuds. This was one of the customs of the Arabs of old. If a man was killed, his family and clan would exact revenge on the murderer. If they failed to seize him, or if they could not kill him, revenge would be carried out on another member of his family, thus setting in motion a chain reaction. In his sermon, the Holy Prophet ﷺ who was sent with mercy for all the worlds, addressed himself to this dreadful custom and announced its abolition.

As anywhere else in the world, so also the society of Arabia was divided up into classes. A person's status was determined by his wealth, rank and descent. One class was wont to dominate, and was given preference and privilege over another class. This is a breach of the principle of spiritual equality of mankind.

Among the Hindus of India there are four castes. The lowest of these castes, the Shudra, are regarded as hardly distinct from the animals. The

Brahmins, the highest caste, regard them as polluted and are vehemently opposed to their advancement. The principle foundation of Islam however is to assure all men of their equality before God.

To further illustrate this point: There happened to be a slight cooling of relations between Salman al-Farsi and a certain Sahaba, such as it occasionally happens among men. Once, at a gathering of Sahaba, this man, in order to shame Salman, broached the subject of descent. He began asking all those present about their ancestry and lineage, with the aim of boosting his pride and abasing Salman. 'Umar was also among those assembled there. At last the turn came to Salman, and when asked about his parentage, he replied, "You ask me who was my father? Let me say that I am the child of Islam."

This reply was related to the Holy Prophet 🕊 who immediately said, "Because Salman regards himself as descended only from Islam itself, I hereby declare that Salman shall belong to my own household; Salman is one of the Ahl al-Bayt. In this way, Salman was granted the highest rank and standing, and it signaled that those in a like situation should be treated with the same respect as Salman and honored likewise.

The Hadith, "Verily your Lord is one and your father is also one," indicates how the order of preference in society should be established. The Hadith continues: "Therefore, neither does the Arab have preference over the non-Arab, nor the non-Arab over the Arab; nor does the black have preference over the white, nor the white over the black, or the black over the red-skinned nor the red over the black-skinned. The right of preference belongs to him whose heart beats with the most compassion for Allah's creation. Whoever is most zealous in fulfilling Allah's commands, his is the right of preference."

After ending his sermon, the Holy Prophet 🕊 gazed at the crowd listening to him. The gathering consisted of the heads of the proud Quraysh who had been at the forefront of every attempt to destroy the noble religion by all the means at their disposal. They had insulted the Holy Prophet 🕊 in the worst way with their words. They had taken up arms against him. They had strewn thorns in his path, pelted him with stones, bloodied his blessed feet. They had left nothing undone to make miserable the life of this special guest from the Divine Abode of Unity. They had tortured the Muslims by burying them in the burning hot sands of the desert. They had intended to smother Islam at Madinah. Had their siege of Madinah met with success, they would no doubt have burned all the Muslims alive.

Now they stood in the presence of the Prophet ❀, listening to the rivers of Divine Wisdom pouring from his blessed lips. When the Prophet ❀ had finished speaking, all were plunged into profound thoughts. The Prophet ❀ then said, "You are now wondering how I will deal with you." Everyone waited tensely for him to pronounce judgment. "There will be no censure, you are all free." Thereupon those whose fate it was to gain eternal bliss began to weep, while the hardened rebels saw their swords drop from their grip and stood completely bewildered.

The idolaters had confiscated the houses belonging to the Muslims. The time for this injustice to be punished had now come, but the Holy Prophet ❀ said to his friends and to the Muhajirin, "Whoso loves me will forego his claims (on property and possession)." Without blinking, the friends and fellow-fighters accepted this order of the Holy Prophet ❀ and did not object. Thus the incomparable civilization of Islam began to show itself to the world.

The time for prayer had passed. Bilal was ordered to climb to the roof of the Kaba and to call the Adhan. Yet there had been a time not long ago when he had been forced to lie on a bed of burning hot bricks for calling out the attestation of Muslim faith. Even then he had continued to cry out, "Ahad, Ahmad", thus giving an example of what religious fervor really means. Now his voice rose above the rooftops of Mecca, ringing out with the Muhammadan Adhan. It sets forth the conditions for the elevation of man: to recognize the Eternal Oneness of Allah and to verify that Ahmad (i.e. Muhammad) is His Prophet ❀. When he turned to the right he remembered the world of the souls, and he called the blessed souls to

MUHAMMAD

prayer; when he turned to the left, he called to the multitude of the rebellious to come to success and to make their declaration of unity. The idolaters stood rigidly frozen to their places. When they heard the sound of the Adhan, those whose lives and possessions had just been spared, could not stand the attack of rebellion from within. 'Utba bin Usayd cried out, "Thank God that my father has died and is spared from listening to this voice!" Some others took to muttering, "What pleasure is now left for us in life?"

Abu Bakr as-Siddiq took his own aged parent by the hand and brought him into the presence of the Prophet ﷺ. Although his mother Salma had been one of the first to embrace Islam, his father still had not done so. When the Prophet ﷺ saw his Friend of the Cave leading the old man by the hand, he said to him kindly, "Why do you thus accommodate the old man? We would have gone to him to visit him." Abu Bakr replied, "Oh my Prophet ﷺ, it is needful that he come to you, may your favors be abundant." Thereupon the Prophet ﷺ said, "His son has a great claim on me, so great that I cannot ever repay him," thus expressing his very particular favor.

The heads of the Arab clans who had been most opposed to Islam and done it the most harm had fled during the conquest of Mecca. One of these was Safwan bin Umayya who fled to Jeddah. The Holy Prophet ﷺ extended his pardon to them all, even sending to Jeddah his turban as a token of his pardon. Safwan came into the blessed presence of the Holy Prophet ﷺ, and asked the Prophet ﷺ to give him a period of two months' time to deliberate whether he could accept Islam or not. But this gifted tutor of minds said to him, "Safwan, I grant you four months for this. Look around, examine it closely, think on it, ponder over it, and if you should meet with guidance, what a great good thing!"

That is the high road of Islam; those who say that Islam was spread by fire and sword ought to reconsider and judge more fairly.

Ikrima, the son of Abu Jahl fled to Yemen. His wife, Umm Hakim, pleaded with the Holy Prophet ﷺ for him also to be pardoned. She then wrote her

500

husband a letter, saying, "Come quickly, for Muhammad ﷺ has granted everyone his pardon, so don't prolong this life in misery unnecessarily."

Ikrima thereupon came home to his wife, and wanted to approach her in the marital manner. But Umm Hakim said to him, "You may not now approach me, as you are an unbeliever, and I have become Muslim." She refused him, and took him to see the Prophet ﷺ first. Seeing them coming, the Holy Prophet ﷺ said to his companions, "Let no one who has any love for me say a word to Ikrima about his father's misdeeds, for the mention of this might vex him." Again Muhammad ﷺ demonstrated the delicacy and finesse so characteristic in that he forbade all mention of Abu Jahl's injurious actions, even though he had been one of the worst offenders.

In the face of this fact, let all those hang their heads who would write in their books that the Holy Prophet's ﷺ mother, father and beloved uncle, Abu Talib left this world in a state of unbelief. The parents of the Prophet ﷺ were the channel through which he passed into this world. How can they imagine that the Light of Prophethood passes through a channel containing disbelief? What a horrific error that is! It is conclusive proof that they who claim these things have not yet smelt the sweet perfume of Muhammad's ﷺ blessed scent!

Ikrima came up to the Prophet's ﷺ tent accompanied by his wife Umm Hakim. Although she was wearing a veil, she asked for permission before entering, saying, "Oh Rasulullah! I have brought Ikrima with me!" The Holy Prophet ﷺ called to her, "That is good, let him enter." Ikrima entered the presence of the Prophet ﷺ who said to him, "Welcome to you!" Ikrima replied in a very modest fashion, saying, "My wife has told me that you have granted me pardon and safe treatment." The Holy Prophet ﷺ answered, "Yes Ikrima, I have assured you of safety, I am your guarantor."

Praised be Allah, who causes the entire created universe to revolve between the two fingers of His Mercy and His Majesty! Abu Jahl's son had been as hard-hearted as his father, and now he had somehow changed! He was too shy to look up and face the Prophet's gaze, but he did deliver the words of the Shahada in a lively tone. After he had voiced this attestation of his faith, he made this supplication, "I hereby seek refuge with you, oh my Prophet 🕮! Whatever I have done in the past, whatever enmity I have perpetrated against you, whatever my words and deeds, it was from my ignorance and lowliness of spirit. For the love of the God whom you have taught me, forgive me. I vow to spend in the cause of Allah many times the sums of money, which I spent in the time of my ignorance on the exploits of disbelief. I will fight for Islam as long as I live, until I fall slain as a martyr, inshaAllah."

The Prophet 🕮, the Mercy of the Worlds, then prayed for Ikrima's supplication to be accepted, and it was.

Oh Traveler on the Road to Truth! Lest this point be misunderstood: after the Holy Prophet 🕮 had delivered his khutba at the conquest of Mecca, he said, "Go now, all of you, you are free!" However, the declaration of a general amnesty entailed no compulsion to accept the new religion in exchange for freedom.

The Prophet 🕮 Forgave the Crimes of Jahiliyya

Muhammad's 🕮 erstwhile enemies came up to him one by one and expressed their remorse. Even Wahshi, who had murdered the Holy Prophet's 🕮 beloved uncle Hamza whom once he had referred to as his right hand, stepped forth. Wahshi was no ordinary killer. His murderous deed would have put even the wild beasts to shame. Hind, the mother of the famous Mu'awiya had commissioned him with the promise of reward. "If you kill Hamza," she had said, "and bring to me his liver, his ears and his nose, I will give to you not only a handsome sum of money, but this precious necklace as well."

He had promised not to disappoint her, being keen on the reward. So he had hidden himself behind a boulder, slain Hamza in a cowardly and treacherous ambush and mutilated his corpse. He had slashed him up so savagely that the Muslims looking for the dead and wounded on the battlefield failed to recognize him. They reported to the Holy Prophet 🕮,

"We could not find his blessed remains." The Prophet ﷺ answered, "I will know my uncle by his scent," and he began searching for him until he found him, albeit in an unrecognizable state. He embraced him tearfully and, although loud wailing and keening is forbidden in Islam, he asked the women of Madinah to weep for his beloved uncle and to sing eulogies, as no other family members were left to do so. According to one tradition, the Holy Prophet ﷺ prayed the funeral prayer over him seven times, according to another narration seventy times.

Oh Seeker of the Truth! Wahshi was a hired killer. He killed for Hind's money and to win favor with Abu Sufyan. Now the same man presented himself before the Holy Prophet ﷺ and pleaded, "Accept my declaration of faith." The Holy Prophet ﷺ accepted his faith and Wahshi became a Muslim. He came again the next day and sat among the Sahaba. The Prophet's eyes filled with tears at the sight of him and he said to him, "When I see you, I see before me the terrible state of my uncle when last I set eyes upon him, and it affects me strongly. But you, too, are now a believer and are implied by the verse,

Say: 'Oh my people who have been prodigal against yourselves, do not despair of God's mercy.' (The Companies, 53)

The Holy Prophet ﷺ had seated himself on a high place upon the rocks of Safa. There he accepted the pledge of those who now entered Islam. First the men came to him, then the women. As he would not take the hand of any woman he was not lawfully entitled to touch, the Prophet ﷺ had a bowl of water set before him. Into this he dipped his hand, then the women dipped their hands into it after him, taking the pledge in this manner. The women were bound by an oath, in which they pledged to abide by the rules of good conduct and decency as defined by the religion of Islam. Some of the most highborn women of Arabia were among those who took this pledge, for instance Hind, 'Utba's daughter, wife of Abu Sufyan and mother of Mu'awiya, and Arwa, the daughter of 'As bin Umayya and 'Atiqa.

Hind came to the Prophet ﷺ wearing a veil, for this was the custom among the Arabian noblewomen. Hind's motive, however, was not her hauteur, but rather that for the moment she preferred to conceal herself from the Holy Prophet ﷺ. When she made her pledge, she asked, "What do you wish us to pledge ourselves to?" The Glory of all the World, Muhammad ﷺ replied, "You shall swear to worship no deity but Allah." "But," she said, "Is that not the pledge you already took of our men? We accepted this alongside them." "You are not to steal," continued the Prophet ﷺ. "From time to time I take a few coins out of Abu Sufyan's pocket; is that going to be forbidden as well?" Abu Sufyan was present at this occasion, and he said, "As for what is past, may it be lawful; we will now consider what lies ahead of us."

"You shall not slay your own children," continued the Holy Prophet ﷺ. She replied, "When our children were young, we cared for them well; when they were grown, it was you who slew them."

****

The Holy Prophet ﷺ spent about two weeks in Mecca then prepared for the return journey to Madinah. He left Mu'adh bin Jabal behind in Mecca to teach the Quraysh the ways of Islam.

Oh Seeker of the Truth! Mu'adh bin Jabal came to greet the Prophet ﷺ at the Battle of Tabuk. When he shook his hand, the Holy Prophet ﷺ remarked, *"Kabadat yadaka, ya Mu'adh?* Your hands have become calloused, oh Mu'adh!" Mu'adh replied, "Yes, my Prophet, for I try to follow the way you have shown, and in order to gain a living for my wife and family, I hire myself out for daily wages. Therefore my hands have grown rough and calloused." The Holy Prophet ﷺ then lovingly kissed his hands and turning to the Companions said, "Here you have a pair of hands that Allah Almighty is loath to burn in the fires of Hell," thereby making known to all his Companions the rank conferred upon Mu'adh.

Mu'adh stayed in Mecca in obedience to the Holy Prophet's ﷺ command and endeavored to teach Islam to the Meccans. He had also ordered him to guard a few of the precious objects housed in the Kaba, for in bygone days, the followers of the religion of Ibrahim had brought many rare and costly gifts to the Holy House of God, which had been salvaged while the idols were being destroyed.

Among the heathen idols were the graven images of the Shaykh of Prophets, Ibrahim and his son Isma'il, all of them most sumptuously adorned. There was also a portrait of the prophet 'Isa. This signifies that Christianity had indeed made its way to Mecca and was represented in the Holy House.

The Incident of the Bani Jadhima

Oh Traveler on the Road to Truth! Nothing distressed the Prophet ﷺ so much as this incident. He had sent envoys to all the tribes in order to call them to Islam. Khalid ibn al-Walid had come from Nakhla and he sent him to the Bani Jadhima who lived about one way-station's distance from Mecca. They chose to come out and meet him as an armed force. Some of them were then taken prisoner and forced to disarm. The prisoners were divided up among the Ansar and the Muhajirin and those of the Bani Sulaym who had gone out with them. "We have become Muslims," they said, but Khalid ibn al-Walid was suspicious of them and accused them of just playing with empty words while concealing their hypocrisy, and he feared they would commit treachery against Islam. He therefore ordered the prisoners to be executed. The Muhajirin and Ansar, however, did not accept this order and set the prisoners belonging to them free.

Khalid then said, "I am the Amir here, I am in command! You are required to obey me!" But the Muhajirin and Ansar answered, "We have heard from Muhammad ﷺ: *La ta'ata li-makhluqin 'inda ma'siyatil-khaliq;* that is to say, there is no obedience due to the creature when he disobeys his Creator. In plain speech: if you obliged to obedience, and it turns out that you are ordered to do what is in contradiction to the Divine Law, then you ought to refuse compliance with that order. Therefore, whoever you may be, we refuse to obey you."

The Bani Sulaym, however, executed some of the prisoners they had taken. When the Holy Prophet ﷺ heard of this event, he was very much aggrieved.

Nothing had ever affected him so much before. His eyes were filled with tears of compassion and pity and he exclaimed, "Oh my Lord, I am innocent before Thee of what Khalid has done!" He kept repeating these words over and over, then he called for Ali and said to him, "Go and represent me in this case. Take with you enough money and merchandise to pay the blood wit of those killed and to pay indemnity for the damage that was done."

Ali set out and spoke to the tribesmen in such a way that their hearts were satisfied. He paid the blood wit of those murdered and even gave them somewhat more than was due to them, saying, "Perhaps there has been some damage that we have not taken into account; let this be in ransom for it." The Holy Prophet ❀ began to interrogate Khalid, saying, "Does this noble religion not forbid us to strike after a man has surrendered? Is a Muslim not such a person from whose hand and tongue everyone is secure? We are not ordered to annihilate humanity but to give it new life! We are here to replace oppression and injustice with justice, and to bring faith wherever we encounter unbelief! Khalid, oh Khalid! For this you will be brought to account before the Lord Almighty! Oh my Lord, I am innocent before Thee of the deed that Khalid has done!"

Khalid was greatly surprised when he encountered such anger from his Prophet ❀, and he said, "Oh my Prophet ❀, their words came not from their hearts!" The Qibla of all Prophets ❀ again replied sternly in a harsh manner, "Did you cut open their hearts and look inside?" Thus he reprimanded him most severely and remained angry with him for several days, for in Islam it is considered wrong to shame a person by exposing him to disgrace.

The Battle of Hunayn

Oh Traveler on the Road to Truth! Following the conquest of Mecca, the tribes of Arabia entered Islam in great numbers.

When comes the help of God and victory, and thou seest men entering God's religion in throngs.

(Help: 1, 2)

The Companions of the Prophet ﷺ were overjoyed at the rapid development of Islam, as described in the above-mentioned holy verse. Only Abu Bakr was beset by sadness and took to weeping. When asked the reason for his grief, he answered, "A time will come when the very opposite of this verse will be manifested. Just as people are now streaming into the fold of Islam, a day will come that will see men running away from the religion of Islam in masses."

The Holy Prophet ﷺ himself said in a Hadith: "A time will come when a man will live as a Muslim from morning to evening, and from evening to morning he will live as an infidel."

Oh Lord! As You have brought us into this world as Muslims, grant us to leave this world again as Muslims.

After the conquest of Mecca, the clans and tribes that had sided with the Quraysh now inclined towards Islam and the number of Muslims greatly increased. Only the tribe of the Hawazin persisted in enmity and decided to make war against the Prophet ﷺ. They allied themselves in this endeavor with the Bani Thaqif. It was very disagreeable for these two warlike tribes to witness the daily increase of the Muslim numbers, and their jealousy robbed them of rest. For over a year the Hawazin had been trying to incite the Arabs to rise up and fight against the Muslims. In the end, all the tribes allied with the Hawazin and the Bani Thaqif agreed to unite in the valley of Hunayn, which lies between Ta'if and Mecca. The only tribesmen not to participate in this alliance were the clans of the Bani Ka'b and the Bani Kilab.

Malik bin 'Awf was appointed as the supreme commander of the Hawazin. He took all the women and children of the tribe along to the army's encampment. They also took along a very old man named Durayd bin al-Simma, who was experienced in all aspects of warfare and exceedingly clever. Some say he was over one hundred and twenty years old, while others claim that he was as old as one hundred and sixty years of age. Allah knows best. In order to profit from his skill and wisdom, they carried him along to the battlefield in a sort of howdah.

When they came to the spot, which is named Awtas, Durayd said, "This is a very suitable place for a battle, as the ground is neither too hard nor too soft." When he heard the sounds of women and children, he asked, "What have you brought them along for?" Malik, the chief commander, answered, "We brought them along so that the soldiers would have no reason to look back, nothing to distract them, and that under no circumstances would they think of running back home." To this Durayd replied, "Take heed! If a soldier is driven to flight, there is absolutely nothing that will stop him. Should retreat indeed become expedient, their dishonor will be even greater because of the presence of their women. Apart from that, have the clans of the Bani Ka'b and the Bani Kilab joined in the alliance?" Hearing that they had not, he continued, "Had this day been a day of honor, they would have participated in this battle."

These words displeased the commander-in-chief, Malik, so that he said to the ancient sage, "Your words are the result of your great age and infirmity." "Mark my words all the same, for I speak from my vast stores of experience. If all goes well, nothing will help you but men who are able to use the lance and the sword. But if defeat and misfortune are to be your lot, you would only be further disgraced and publicly scorned with your wives and families at your side."

The army of the Hawazin comprised twenty thousand fighters. Hearing of such a great force assembled against him, the Holy Prophet ﷺ instantly made preparations for war. He sent out Abdullah al-Aslami in disguise as a spy to the enemy camp in order to achieve full reconnaissance of the situation and the strength of the enemy. He scouted out what was needful to know and the Prophet ﷺ ordered preparations to proceed accordingly.

A defensive strategy against the enemy needed to be devised, and money had to be borrowed. Thirty thousand dirhams were borrowed from Abu Jahl's foster-brother Abdullah bin Rabi'. Arms were to be procured, and

Safwan bin Umayya was asked to supply them from his armory. However, he had still not become a Muslim, so he asked, "Do you wish to take them from me by force?" "No," replied the Holy Prophet ﷺ, "I ask them from you on loan and they shall be returned. In case of damage they shall be replaced." Safwan then agreed to the deal and loaned the Holy Prophet ﷺ three hundred suits of armor and sufficient arms to go with them. Nawfal bin Harith bin Abd ul-Muttalib donated three hundred lances and spears. So the Prophet ﷺ completed his preparations. He left 'Attab bin Asid and Mu'adh bin Jabal in charge of Mecca; Mu'adh was responsible for religious affairs, whereas 'Attab took over the governing of the town, although he was only twenty years old at the time.

On the seventh day of the month of Shawwal in the eighth year of the Hijra, the Holy Prophet ﷺ set out from Mecca towards Hunayn with an army of over twelve thousand soldiers, astride his mule Duldul. The army consisted of one thousand men of the Muhajirin, four thousand of the Ansar, five thousand of the tribes of Juhayna, Muzayna, the Bani Sabur, Aslam, Ghifar and Ashja', and two thousand men from the people of Mecca. Among these there were some non-Muslim idolaters, such as Safwan bin Umayya.

On the eleventh of Shawwal, the Prophet ﷺ and his resplendent army reached the valley of Hunayn. So great and magnificent seemed their force that the commanders began to boast that surely such an army would never see defeat. But the Holy Prophet ﷺ warned them and said, "These words smack of unbelief." As events were to show, the Muslims were at first faced with defeat, in spite of their sure expectations of victory. This is referred to in the Sura named 'Repentance':

God has already helped you on many fields, and on the day of Hunayn, when your multitude was pleasing to you, but it availed you naught, and the land for all its breadth was strait for you, and you turned about, retreating. Then God sent His Sakina down upon His Messenger and upon the believers, and He sent down legions you did not see, and He chastised the unbelievers and that is the recompense of the unbelievers. (Repentance: 25)

The Muslims were overly sure of their victory and fell into the error of over-reliance on their own devices. Therefore the Holy Prophet 🕮 warned them that all power and might to change things lies in the hands of Allah Almighty alone.

The front lines of the Muslim army were made up of young men from Mecca under the command of Khalid ibn al-Walid. Trusting in the pride and strength of their youth, they had declined to gird themselves with the armor provided for them. This was one of the reasons for the rout, the other being the two thousand non-Muslims who marched with the Muslim army.

The enemy army had availed themselves of the stronger positions, and the Muslim army could not advance for the hail of arrows. It was the hour before the break of dawn. The Imam of Prophets 🕮, set forth the battle strategy to the Muslim soldiers and distributed the banners. One was given to Ali ibn Abi Talib, one to 'Umar ibn al-Khattab and one to Hubab ibn al-Mundhir. The fighting began and Hawazin lay in wait. The company of Khalid ibn al-Walid encountered a rain of arrows and fell into disarray. Line upon line, the Muslim fighters began to waver, and twelve thousand fighters were forced to retreat.

No more than a handful of his closest companions remained to surround the Holy Prophet 🕮. A disaster was in the making. Those who had only recently entered Islam were shaken in their faith. Abu Sufyan, the father of the famous Mu'awiya said, "Their flight will not be halted before they get to the sea." Jabala ibn al-Hanbal who was a brother of Safwan cried out, "Today the sorcery of Muhammad 🕮 has been foiled," and he rejoiced in this. Safwan had not yet become Muslim, but all the same he scolded his mother's son, saying, "Shut up! May Allah cause your tongue to falter! For it is better to be ruled by a man of the Quraysh, whoever he may be, than by a man of Hawazin!"

Everyone was in a state of great perturbation except the Holy Prophet 🕮. There came a moment when he wished to remain all alone on the scene of battle with the forces evoked through the powers of his faith. He expressed his wish to Ali, 'Abbas, 'Umar, Abu Bakr and Usama, and told them to leave off guarding him and to go and fight against the enemy. The Holy Prophet ﷺ was now left all alone to face the attacking warriors of the unbelievers' armies.

Heaven and earth remained speechless and the Throne trembled at this spectacle.

Oh Seeker of the Way to Truth! Just try to fathom the depth of this matter: the Eternal Pride of all Humankind, the Holy Prophet Muhammad ﷺ now faced not only one tribe, or one nation, not even a single world, but the whole universe, the entire creation. In facing his foe and addressing him with the whole Majesty of his Prophethood, his steadfast courage, his close communication with the Lord Almighty, and his perfect reliance on Allah became apparent. These were his words, "Here I am, Servant and Prophet of the Lord Allah. I am the Prophet from the lineage of Abdul-Muttalib. Why do you hesitate, go ahead and charge! Empty your quivers, hurl your spears! Aim all that you have at me - I challenge you now!"

Then he called for 'Abbas. 'Abbas had a strong voice, so that everyone present heard him answer, "At your service, oh my Prophet ﷺ!" The Prophet ﷺ commanded him to call together the Muhajirin and Ansar immediately. So 'Abbas called out with a loud and ringing voice, "Oh you Ansar and People of the Tree, come and gather here!" No sooner had he voiced this command than they all rallied round their leader, crying, "Labbayk," as if with one great voice. Those who could not ride up on their horses dismounted and came running swiftly on foot. The followers of Muhammad ﷺ were assured of victory.

The Prophet ﷺ then prayed, "Oh my Lord, make true Your promise to me!" Thereupon, an invisible army manifested itself, though none could perceive it. Before the Holy Prophet ﷺ gave the command for the assault, he took up a handful of dirt in his hand and threw it in the direction of the unbelievers' army, saying, "May their faces be blackened!" Then the Muslims proceeded to the attack and they fiercely drove into the enemy ranks. The soldiers of the Hawazin responded in kind and a pitched battle took place. Ali countered these onslaughts with his customary bravery and slew the standard-bearer of the Hawazin. The Prophet ﷺ commented, "Now the oven is hot."

The unbelievers were badly routed and began to retreat in chaos. They managed to regroup their forces at Ta'if and Awtas. At Awtas, Durayd had gathered together a few thousand fighters, intending to engage in battle with the Muslims once more. The Holy Prophet ﷺ sent out Abu Amir al-Ash'ari against him. Abu Amir was slain by the son of Durayd ibn al-Simma and the Muslim banner was taken from his hands. At this point Abu Musa al-Ash'ari, Abu Amir's cousin, joined the fray and rescued the standard. Rabi' bin Rufay' then charged against Durayd and killed him. As he lay dying, he said to his killer, "Tell your mother that it was you who killed me." When Rabi' later told this to his mother, she said, "By Allah, Durayd set free three women related to you."

A great number of prisoners fell into Muslim hands. Among them was the Holy Prophet's ﷺ foster-sister Shayma. As she was taken prisoner, she said to her captors, "Take me to my brother." Asked whom she meant by this, she replied, "Muhammad ﷺ is my milk-brother." Immediately they brought her into the Prophet's ﷺ presence. When he saw and recognized his foster-sister, his eyes filled with tears. He rose from his seat, took off his cloak and laid it on the ground for his sister to sit on. They remained seated together in conversation for a long time. Then he made her a present of many camels and other gifts and honored her with hospitality. The Prophet ﷺ loved his foster-sister Shayma very much. Their wet-nurse Halima as-Sa'adia used to say, "When Muhammad ﷺ was a small child, he never used to suck from my left breast. Whenever I wanted to give him the left breast, he would point to his foster-sister Shayma and make signs as if to say, "That one is rightfully hers to drink." Oh Lord, grant us his intercession. Amin.

Those who had escaped rallied their forces and tried their luck one more time at Ta'if, which was a well-fortified city. The people of Ta'if joined forces with the remnants of the army that had suffered defeat at Hunayn. They reinforced the city's defenses and laid up stores that would last them through a long siege.

The Holy Prophet ﷺ ordered that the prisoners taken at Hunayn and their property be brought to al-Ji'rana and kept there while he proceeded towards Ta'if. Khalid ibn al-Walid had preceded him and laid siege to the city. Four days into the siege they brought and installed an engine of war with which to hurl rocks to break through the fortress walls, if all else were to fail. The siege lasted for another twenty days. Then the Prophet ﷺ took counsel with his companions and asked them for their opinions on what should be done. Nawfal answered, "Oh Prophet of Allah! The fox is hunted down in his den. We need not follow them into it, for eventually they will be compelled to emerge. If we just leave it as it is, no harm will come from it, but the ultimate decision is yours." The Prophet ﷺ however, whose only aim was the defense of the Muslims, did not wish to pursue any aggressive action and therefore discontinued the siege.

Some of the Prophet's ﷺ friends and companions wished that he might curse them, but the Holy Prophet ﷺ, the Mercy to all the World, said, "I have been sent to bring guidance to mankind; therefore, I will pray on their behalf, that guidance may reach them as well." And he raised his hands in supplication.

The Division of the Spoils

The Prophet ﷺ returned to al-Ji'rana where all the prisoners of war were kept. There was also an enormous pile of booty. In all, there were six-thousand prisoners, four-thousand okes of gold and silver, twenty-four thousand camels, and forty thousand goats and sheep.

The Holy Prophet ﷺ, the Mercy for all the World, waited for a long while for the relatives of the prisoners to come and ransom them, but not a single person came. The spoils were divided into five parts, four of which were given to the deserving warriors. One fifth was placed in the Bayt-al-Mal (public treasury) which provided for the poor and destitute.

Many of the chiefs of Mecca made a show of having accepted Islam, but they were in reality very uncertain of their new faith. When they saw the scales of destiny tipping in the direction of Islam, most of them had declared their faith in order to secure their positions of worldly power. But still they could not rid themselves of their doubts and remained of two minds about the new arrangement. In the language of the Holy Quran they are referred to as the 'mu'allaf al-qulub', that is to say, those whose hearts were reconciled with Islam by means of material advantages. "Islam will make us rich," they said to themselves, and therefore did not oppose Islam.

This custom continued up until the time of 'Umar. During his Khalifate, he decreed, "The light of Islam has now flooded the four corners of the earth; and there is no believer left who will renounce his faith at the suggestion of any two-faced person," therewith abolishing this procedure.

The *'mu'allaf al-qulub'* comprised twenty-nine people. At their head was the principle commander of the unbelievers, the famous Abu Sufyan and his no less famous son Mu'awiya, who bore the nickname of being one of the *'duhat al-arba'a'*, i.e. one of the four exceedingly clever men. The Lord's Beloved ﷺ gave the most valuable items from among the spoils to these men, which became known as *'muallaf al-qulub'*. Abu Sufyan and his family were given three hundred camels, and one hundred and twenty okes of silver. Hakim bin Hizam received two hundred camels; Madr ibn al-Harith ibn Kalada al-Thaqafi received one hundred camels; Qays bin 'Adiyya received a hundred camels; Safwan bin Umayya got one hundred camels; Huwaytib bin Abd ul-'Uzza, al-Aqra bin Habis, 'Uyayna bin Hisin, Malik bin 'Awf received one hundred camels each. Apart from these, numerous people received fifty camels each.

The soldiers were each given four camels and forty sheep; the horsemen among them were given twelve camels each, as well as one hundred and twenty goats each.

Oh Traveler on the Road to Truth! This you must know: as long as man has not sampled the taste of true faith, and not reached the station of Love, he cannot easily be freed of his material bonds. He attains to full abandonment only after he has been cleansed in the fires of Love. Moreover, the desire for high rank and dignity does not easily depart from a man.

Those who benefited most from the distribution of booty were the Meccans and those who had recently entered Islam.

Because of this there was some talk and grumbling among the Ansar. Some of them spoke, "Our blood has not yet dried on the swords of the Quraysh who fought against us, thirsting for our lifeblood and eager to destroy the religion of Islam. And although it was us who were stalwart in facing the worst dangers during the most difficult days, others are to reap the rewards of our efforts now that the days of leisure have come."

The Holy Prophet ﷺ, the most enlightened soul in the entire universe, sensed their bitter complaints with his fine sense of mercy and compassion. He called to him one of the leaders of the Ansar, Sa'd bin 'Ubada and asked him if it was true that such words were being bandied about among his companions. Sa'd answered, "Allah and His Prophet ﷺ know best; none of the senior companions have said anything of what is reported. But I too have heard that among the younger folk some have fallen to the influence of the hypocrites, who indeed have voiced such feelings. I appeal to your clemency and intercession on their behalf, and would ask pardon for them." The Prophet ﷺ then ordered Sa'd bin 'Ubada to call a meeting of the Ansar. When they had all assembled, the Holy Prophet ﷺ gave a khutba of great eloquence in which he said, "Oh People of the Ansar! Is it not true that you were on the road of error before this time and that Allah made you reach to right guidance through my mediation? While you were engulfed in discord and strife and killing each other in lawless brigandry, did Allah Almighty not unite your hearts through my mediation? Did Allah in His Grace and Goodness not show you a road out of your hapless poverty, and lead you on the road I was honored to show you, into a life of prosperity and comfort? Have you not found contentment and felicity?"

Oh Traveler on the Road to Truth! As the Holy Prophet ﷺ delivered this speech, the Ansar fain would have swooned under its impact, and the tears

515

flowed freely from their eyes. They replied, "Yea, oh our Prophet ☙, it is from the Almighty's eternal favor and thanks to the Holy Prophet's ☙ intercession that all goodness has come to us." The Holy Prophet ☙ then continued, "This is not the answer I expected from you. You ought to have said instead: 'Oh Muhammad ☙, we believed in you at a time when everyone else rejected you and called you a liar; we opened our arms for you and our hearts. When you were an outcast, and destitute, we gave you protection. You came to us as a poor man, and we looked after you and gave you our support.' If that had been your speech, then you would have spoken truly and I would confirm all your words."

This address fell upon the hearts of the Ansar like fire, and each one of them sobbed aloud and shed many tears. The Holy. Prophet ☙ was moved with compassion and his eyes also brimmed with tears. A great silence fell upon the assembly. After a pause, the Prophet ☙ continued to address the gathering of Ansar. "Oh you people of the Ansar!" he began, "Other than you will carry off the sheep and goats and camels that we have given them. As for you, you will take back with you Muhammad ☙, the Prophet of Allah to his home. Now I ask you, do you want me or is it sheep and goats that you wish for? What is better for you: to return to your hometown with me, or to return enriched in worldly goods and gain?"

None of those assembled had the strength even to breathe when he had finished his speech. The young people who had been complaining shed tears of remorse, whereas those who burned with love for the Prophet ☙ wept for having caused pain to their beloved Prophet ☙. When at last they spoke, their voices trembled, "Oh Rasulullah ☙! Forgive us, for it is only yesterday that you saved us from the Days of Ignorance we were caught up in; forgive us, do not tax us for our failings. It is you we want, and all we desire."

The Holy Prophet ☙ then said, "Oh you of the Ansar! Know that if I were given the choice among the people, I would always choose the Ansar. For the Ansar are as the inner layer of my clothing, whereas all other folk are as my outer clothing. After my time is done, you will be overtaken by strife and discord, and exposed to the hurt of the sword. Until we meet again, be patient, don't give up, and do not abandon the cause of Allah. For the sake of Allah and His Truth, you must be prepared to face all manner of hardship."

The Holy Prophet ﷺ hereby indicated that among those referred to as the *'mu'allif al-qulub'* there were such that would use religion as a means for pursuing their own political goals; who would, in the name and under the cover of religion perform every sort of cruelty.

All of the Ansar called out with one voice, "We are well content with our Prophet ﷺ!" and they wept copiously. They were very moved by the gracious words this great Prophet of the Lord ﷺ spoke to them. The Holy Prophet ﷺ then lifted his hands and made supplication for the Ansar and their families and descendants, and such was his du'a that it would have made even angels weep.

The chiefs of the Hawazin then came to al-Ji'rana and made their declaration of faith in the unity of Allah. The Holy Prophet's ﷺ wet-nurse Halima as-Sa'adia was of the Bani Sa'd who were related to Hawazin. The leader of this delegation, Zuhayr Abu Surad then addressed himself to the Holy Prophet, saying, "We ask for the return of the captives. Among the women are the sisters and relatives of your wet-nurse Halima. It is therefore that we are so bold as to speak to you about the return of our families and children." The Holy Prophet ﷺ gave them this reply, "I leave to you all the prisoners given to the clan of Abd ul-Muttalib, that is to say, all those belonging to the house of Hashim. I set them free. As for the others, you must come again at the time of prayer and make your request of the Muslim Jama'at. Hopefully, they too will agree to set free their prisoners."

The time for prayer came, and the delegates put forth their petition to the assembly of Muslims, just as they had done to the Holy Prophet ﷺ. The Holy Prophet ﷺ assisted them in their plea, saying, "I have set free all the prisoners belonging to my own family, and I recommend that you too set free the prisoners belonging to you." All the Sahaba of the Ansar and Muhajirin and other tribes then followed the example of the Prophet ﷺ and freed the prisoners that were in their hands. In that way, six thousand people were set free all at once.

In consequence, Malik bin 'Awf of the Hawazin tribe, who had for a whole year been doing his utmost to damage the Muslims, accepted right guidance and entered into the fold of Islam.

In the course of this year, the eighth year of the Hijra, Marya, the Coptic bondmaid of the Holy Prophet ❀ gave birth to a son who was named Ibrahim. He remained in this world for only eighteen months, before he was taken to the next world. His father, the Holy Prophet ❀, placed him in his grave with his own hands while the tears were streaming down his face. "The Holy Prophet ❀ is weeping," his friends thought, and in answer to their unspoken thoughts, the Holy Prophet ❀ replied, "These tears are a rain of mercy."

That same day, the sun was eclipsed. The Arabs saw the eclipse as bearing relation to the death of the Prophet's son Ibrahim, and they said, "Even the sun shares in the grief of our Prophet ❀." Hearing of their words, the Prophet ❀ called for all the Muslims to gather and addressed them, saying, "The sun and the moon are both signs of Allah, as it is written:

> and of His signs are the night and the day, the sun and the moon. Bow not
> yourselves to the sun and moon...   (Distinguished, 36)

"They do not move in accordance to the birth or death of any individual, but only to the will of Allah who created them." Then he led the congregation in the prayer of the eclipse (Salat al-Kusuf).

Some people have a wrong understanding of this prayer, thinking that it is the purpose of this prayer to remove the eclipse of the sun or moon. Some even say, "Scientific discovery has advanced so much since those days that we are now able to predict the occurrence of an eclipse long in advance of the event; what need is there for prayer in this case?" Just as every prayer has its time, the time for the prayer of the eclipse is just that, the event of an eclipse. Therefore, these prayers are to be prayed at exactly those moments.

The Ninth Year of the Hijra

Repudiation and Choice

This is the story of the Repudiation and Choice. In the ninth year of the Hijra, the Holy Prophet 🕮 was angered at his wives for a whole month. This event is called *'Ila wa Tahyir*, which means "Repudiation and Choice." Certain traditionalists claim that it took place in the fifth year of the Hijra, but there is stronger evidence for it having been in the ninth.

The Holy Prophet 🕮 lived a very simple lifestyle, far removed from any pomp or extravagance. A European scholar who studied this matter closely wrote about it: "Muhammad 🕮 began preaching the unity of Allah single-handedly; but when he returned from the Farewell Pilgrimage with one hundred and forty thousand people he did not set about building himself a palace. He took up his normal activities again; there was no difference in his devout and humble lifestyle. He could easily have built himself a place and begun to live a life of wasteful indulgence, but nothing could have been further from his mind than that. Such qualities are found only in men who bear the marks of prophethood."

One of the customary actions of the Holy Prophet 🕮 (Sunna) was to distribute all dispensable leftovers from his household after nightfall, including any money.

Some of the wives of the Prophet 🕮 came from the noblest families of Arabia. Aisha, for instance, was the daughter of Abu Bakr. Hafsa was the daughter of 'Umar. Juwayriya was the daughter of the tribal chief of the Bani Mustaliq. Safiya was the daughter of the chief of Khaybar.

In reality, just to be the wife of the Prophet 🕸 conveyed a very high rank upon a woman. But as is the wont of women and of all humankind, the wives of the Prophet 🕸 wished to partake of the comforts and amenities that other, more ordinary women enjoyed. The Muslims now had all the means at their disposal, and through the acquisition of the spoils of war, their former indigence was relieved and they had all they needed to lead a comfortable and profitable life. Despite this general improvement of living conditions, in the house of the Prophet 🕸 himself no changes took place, he persisted in the old style of life. On some nights there was even no fuel to light a fire. In all his lifetime, the Prophet 🕸 never ate more than one meal a day.

One day Aisha and her companions gathered and talked among themselves. "We lived through the toughest times, we know Islam in its very beginnings and we put up with every hardship along the way. There were days when we had no cooked food to eat, and when there was nothing wherewith to light our houses at night. We lived through all these troubles and took them upon ourselves gladly. But now, by the Grace of God, times have changed. All houses are filled with provisions and the gains of war. Everybody lives well and enjoys their life. But in our house, the Holy Prophet 🕸 still insists on giving away everything at nightfall; he leaves no leftovers in his own house. Why don't we all get together and when the Prophet 🕸 again distributes the spoils, leaving nothing for his own household, we will insist all together that he leave some of it for our own purposes."

They were all agreed on this. One day, when the Holy Prophet 🕸 was again dividing up the shares of booty and apportioning them to various members of the community, Aisha and Hafsa came up to him and said, "Oh Rasulullah 🕸! Every time you give all away and leave nothing for the house. We lived through times of want and dearth during the first days of Islam. Now Allah Almighty has blessed the community with great gain, and although everyone else is enjoying it freely, for us there is no change at all and no improvement."

These words intensely distressed the Holy Prophet 鸞. "Are you criticizing me for what I do, do you wish for other than what I wish?" he asked of them, and he was much aggrieved by this incident. His peace of mind was rent and when Ali chanced to come by, he perceived the Holy Prophet's 鸞 distress. He was much troubled by it and asked him about his grievance. The Holy Prophet 鸞 answered, "Aisha has incited her co-wives so that they complained to me about the provisions they receive." Ali, whose sole aim was the Holy Prophet's 鸞 happiness, then said to him, "Oh Rasulullah 鸞! Are there no other girls left in all of Madinah but Aisha?"

(Some people attribute this saying of Ali's to the occasion of the calumny of Aisha, but this is completely wrong. When the Prophet 鸞 asked for Ali's advice on that occasion, there was no one who was willing to defend her to the extent that he did. He said to the Prophet Muhammad 鸞, "Oh Rasulullah, Aisha is innocent, she is a model of virtue and chastity. Until you receive a revelation concerning her innocence, I hold it is better to wait.")

Thereupon the Holy Prophet 鸞 replied, "I leave their divorce in your hands, oh Ali. Divorce whichever one of them that you would." Ali immediately departed from the presence of the Prophet 鸞.

The Prophet 鸞 was angered at all his wives. During these days he also happened to injure his leg and withdrew into his room. He called for his daughter Fatima to come and look after him. She came and took care of him.

'Umar reports:

> "I had a neighbor from among the Ansar and we were very close. We used to see each other frequently. One night there was an urgent knocking upon my door, and I rose in haste to see who it was and what was the matter. It was my neighbor, who said, "Umar, a terrible thing has happened.' 'What is it? Have the Ghassani decided to invade

Madinah as they were planning to do? Have they begun to attack us?' 'No,' he replied, 'it is much, much worse..' 'No doubt, but what then can it be? Quickly, tell me!' 'The Prophet ﷺ is divorcing the lot of his wives!'

"I barely could wait for the morning to come. I proceeded to the Holy Mosque, prayed the morning prayer with the Prophet ﷺ, and when the prayer was done, he withdrew into his private apartments without speaking a word to any of us. I too rose and went to see my daughter Hafsa whom I found in tears. I began to scold her, 'Have I not told you before that you must do nothing at all to upset the Holy Prophet ﷺ?' Then I left her and returned to the Holy Mosque, and found the Sahaba standing there by the Minbar, weeping. I went up to them and sat down.

"All were terribly sad; nobody wanted to talk. I myself was in a tormented state, unable to sit quietly. I rose and approached the apartment of the Holy Prophet ﷺ and asked the personal attendant of the Prophet ﷺ, Rabbah by name, to do me the favor and tell the Holy Prophet ﷺ that I wished to speak to him, but I received no admission. I returned to the mosque, racked by anxiety. I was in a state of great dejection and knew not what to do about it. I just could not hold myself still, so again I went up to the Holy Prophet's rooms and implored the servant Rabbah to ask permission for me to enter, and again I received no reply.

"This time I called out loudly, 'Rabbah! Please request permission of the Prophet ﷺ for me to enter, it is not that I have come to plead on behalf of my daughter Hafsa. Should the Holy Prophet ﷺ order it, I am ready to strike off her head.'

"At last the Prophet ﷺ could no longer stand the noise I was making, and he gave me permission to enter into his presence. When I entered, I found the Prophet ﷺ on a bed of woven reeds, the imprint of which was visible on his blessed body. I looked around the room; in one corner there was a handful of oats, and a sheepskin was hung on the wall; that was all. My eyes overflowed at the sight of this poverty. The Prophet ﷺ then asked me why I wept and I replied, 'Oh Rasulullah ﷺ,

how should I not weep? Whereas the Khosroes and the Caesars live their lives immersed in oceans of pleasures, I find you in these circumstances of lowliness and need - what should I make of this?'

"The Prophet ﷺ replied, 'The pleasures of Muhammad ﷺ do not resemble the worldly pleasures of a Khosroe or a Caesar.' Full of apprehension I then asked, 'Oh Rasulullah ﷺ, have you divorced your wives?' 'No,' he rejoined, 'I have not.' I was filled with such happiness and relief at this reply that I broke out into loud exclamations of Takbir, then I said to him, 'Oh Rasulullah ﷺ, all the Sahaba are weeping, let me go to them and assuage their fears.' And I departed from his presence."

The Prophet's ﷺ anger against his wives lasted for one month. When the period of Repudiation *(Ila)* ended, the verses of Choice *(Takhyir)* were revealed. These are the verses:

O Prophet, say to thy wives: 'If you desire the present life and its adornment, come now, I will make you provision, and set you free with kindliness. But if you desire God and His Messenger and the Last Abode, surely God has prepared for those amongst you such as do good a mighty wage.' (The Confederates: 28, 29)

In these verses, the Lord Almighty instructed His Prophet ﷺ to set before his wives an alternative, so that they might choose what they desired most. But the Prophet's wives ﷺ by now were eaten by remorse. They had not expected the desire they had voiced, which was after all nothing but a whim, to produce such serious consequences. Of course, they all gratefully and gladly chose to remain in the Holy Prophet's ﷺ wedlock, and to continue as the "Mothers of the Faithful", may Allah assure us of their intercession.

Developing Diplomatic Ties and Accommodating Leaders of the Previous Era

The proud Quraysh were accustomed to wielding power in the city of Mecca. It was therefore unbearable for them to submit to the leadership of the man the Prophet ﷺ had delegated to this post, 'Attab bin Asid, a man of the Abdu Shams, who was very young in years. Some of them came to Madinah to complain about this. Abu Sufyan found it impossible to accept the rule of this young man over himself, and therefore moved to Madinah. He was instated as governor over the province of Najran. His son Mu'awiya became an official of the treasury, and apart from being extremely clever, he was thus kept under close observation so that he might not busy himself in stirring up mischief. That is the reason why he was admitted into the immediate company of the Holy Prophet 🕸. Claims that he was engaged in the writing down of the revelation are baseless.

When the Holy Prophet 🕸 returned from al-Jirana, he wrote a letter to the ruler of Bahrayn, al-Mundhir bin Sawa, which was delivered by the hand of al-'Ala ibn al-Hadhrami. Al-'Ala traveled to Bahrayn and delivered the Prophet's 🕸 letter to al-Mundhir. He read it thrice, then he declared the Shahada, and with him all the Arabs of Bahrayn became Muslim. Only the unbelievers and fire worshippers living there did not accept Islam and refused to forego their ancient rites. Al-Mundhir bin Sawa sent a message to the Prophet 🕸 asking for advice on how to deal with them. The Prophet 🕸 replied, "Faith is a matter of conscience, there can be no compulsion in religion. Leave them free to worship as they would and impose a tax upon them."

After this, the Prophet 🕸 sent a letter to the Asdis, the rulers of 'Uman, Jayfar bin Julanda and his brother 'Abbad. 'Amr ibn al-'As was entrusted with the letter and both Jayfar and his brother 'Abbad accepted Islam after some initial hesitation.

'Amr ibn-al-'As was employed in the treasury. He collected the zakat from the wealthy of that region and gathered the jizya (poll tax, tribute) from the fire worshippers of the area.

Oh Traveler on the Way to Truth! Let it not be assumed that the jizya is intended as a punishment for those who decline to enter Islam. No! The jizya was instituted to provide the government with the means of upkeep for the country and a relief fund for the poor. Just as zakat is collected from every Muslim, so the jizya is imposed on every non-Muslim under Muslim rule, and it is not to exceed an amount that a man can gladly give without feeling pinched. Most of what has been collected from people is then expended on public works in their own community and on general humanitarian projects.

Here is a vivid example of this: in the time of 'Umar, the Muslims conquered the lands of Syria for Islam. An epidemic broke out in one province, and 'Umar said to his commander-in-chief Abu 'Ubayda, "Return all the jizya you have collected from the people within two days and move the army out of that area." Abu 'Ubayda complied with this order and was met with consternation by a people who had never before witnessed such an action on the part of their rulers and overlords. They asked him why he was returning their money to them after having collected it. The Muslims replied, "We did not collect this money from you as a tax, for the Muslims are not violent usurpers. We collected this money from you in order to improve conditions for you in your own land. Now an epidemic has broken out in your country and we are leaving. Why should we therefore take your money with us?"

On that day a hitherto unheard of thing happened: the Christians with their priests all gathered in their churches and prayed, "Oh Lord! Do not take away from us the armies of Islam, make not the Muslims depart from our lands!" Such is the greatness of Islamic civilization, and the character of the great leaders of Islam and followers of Muhammad's 🕮 teachings.

The Holy Prophet 🕮 sent a letter to Jabala bin Ayham, who was representative at Balqa' of the ruler of the Ghassan tribe, inviting him to Islam. Jabala immediately accepted Islam and submitted to the Prophet 🕮. He sent many gifts to the Prophet 🕮 along with his letter of acceptance.

The Prophet 🕮 also sent a letter to the chief of the tribe of Judham who were settled around Sham. This chief was Farwa bin 'Amr, the same man who had previously been dispatched to the post of governor at Ma'an by the Byzantine Emperor. He, too, accepted Islam and submitted to the Prophet 🕮. When his tribe found out about it they flogged him to death.

That year there was a famine at Madinah and food was scarce and costly. The people went to the Holy Prophet ﷺ and asked him to consider fixing food prices. He replied with the wisdom of the supreme teacher of minds, "Whatever you do, not this! It is very bad for the people. The only one to fix prices is Allah. After a few days, things will again take their accustomed course."

Various Envoys Visit the Prophet ﷺ

In this year, some of the leaders of the Bani Tamim came to Madinah and brought with them some of the best and eloquent poets and singers of their people. Their purpose was to free their prisoners.

The poets challenged the Holy Prophet ﷺ to a contest of poetry recital and came to the gate of his house. They addressed him, saying, "Oh Muhammad ﷺ, come out and engage in a song contest with us, let us recite our poets of praise." The Prophet ﷺ came out and said to them, "I have been sent by the Lord of the Heavens to perfect the moral qualities; Allah is my witness and I am His witness, I have come to bring good tidings, to warn and to be His deputy. I am charged neither with bringing poetry, nor with composing laudatory verses. However, since you have come all this way, speak up and recite your verses. Surely there will be a Muslim among us who is able to reciprocate in your art."

Thereupon the famous poet and reciter, 'Utarid bin Hajib of the Bani Tamim who was known for his eloquence and word-power, stepped forth and began to sing the praises of his tribe in well-set and impressive verse. When he had finished, the Holy Prophet ﷺ gave Thabit bin Qays of the Ansar permission to reply to the challenger. Thabit immediately rose and began to recite a piece that filled all souls with a sense of awe, concerning Allah's Majesty and the Mission of His Holy Prophet ﷺ.

Next, al-Zibriqan, one the most famous poets of the Bani Tamim rose and recited a laudatory poem. The Prophet ﷺ requested Hasan bin Thabit (the Prophet's ﷺ most favored poet) to answer him. Hasan bin Thabit rose and began to intone a beautiful and deeply meaningful ode about the honor and dignity of faith in Islam. Hearing him sing these words, al- Aqra bin Habis who from pre-eternity was destined to embark on this way, ceased to conceal the truth and openly exclaimed, "The poetry of this noble person is incomparably superior to our own sort of poetry, and there is a special kind of sweetness in its tone. My friends, I declare my faith in Muhammad ﷺ and his revelation," and together with him his companions also entered the fold of Islam.

This shows that nobody could measure himself with the eloquence of the Quran. Had they been able to do it, they would not have resorted to arms. As it is clearly stated in the Divine Scripture:

Say, 'Then bring you ten suras the like of it.' (Hood, 13)

Say: 'If men and Jinn banded together to produce the like of this Quran, they would never produce its like, not though they backed one another.'

(The Night Journey, 88)

But this they could not do, and the contest became an issue of honor and shame. Since they could not bring verses like unto the divinely revealed scripture, they resorted to force of arms. But they could not resist the Muslim forces, so again they tried to challenge through their speeches and poetry. The followers of Muhammad ﷺ, however, showed themselves to be just as superior in this respect as they were on the battlefield.

Envoys came to Madinah from the Himyarite kings of Yemen to meet the Holy Prophet ﷺ. These envoys were much more polite and sophisticated in their manner than the envoys that had come from the Bani Tamim. Because they were such distinguished personalities, they sang eulogies about the Prophet's ﷺ honor and glory. They learned the main principles of Islam and its foundation and returned to their country.

Twelve people from the tribe of 'Uzra arrived, bringing the zakat that was due from their clansmen. They joyously joined the fold of Islam, saying, "Oh Rasulullah ﷺ! We are accustomed to doing trade with the Damascenes who are under the rule of the Byzantine Emperor Heraclius. Has anything come to you concerning him?" The Imam of Prophets 🕸 replied, "I give you good tidings: Sham (Damascus) will be conquered for Islam in a short while, and Heraclius will hand it over and leave."

Qasida-i-Burda: The Ode of the Mantle

The circumstances of the composition of this ode were as follows: Among the famous masters of eloquence of the Arabs there was a man named Zuhayr who composed many poems. Zuhayr had two sons, Bujayr and Ka'b who were also renowned as poets. Ka'b in particular was the rightful successor of his father, being just as fiery a poet as he. When the Holy Prophet 🕸 had returned from Mecca to Madinah, Ka'b's brother Bujayr came to Madinah and met the Prophet 🕸. He became totally enamored by this meeting and accepted Islam at his blessed hands.

His brother Ka'b, however, was less enthusiastic and reproached his brother for what he had done. "How could you abandon our father's religion?" he reprimanded Bujayr, and set to writing a poem insulting the Holy Prophet 🕸 in his person, and insulting even more the religion he had brought.

The Holy Prophet 🕸 always forgave attacks on his own person, but he had no tolerance for attacks on Islam itself. Ka'b bin Zuhayr in writing this insulting piece against the noble religion of Islam, angered the Prophet 🕸 so that he ordered him to be punished. His brother Bujayr sent him a composition in verse full of advice and admonition. These verses stirred Ka'b and a spark was ignited in his chest. He could not remain in his place, he set out at once and proceeded to Madinah.

There he went straight to Abu Bakr as-Siddiq and entreated him to take him into the presence of the Prophet 🕸. Abu Bakr led him to the Prophet's 🕸 mosque and said, "Oh Rasulullah 🕸, here is a man who wants to give his oath of fealty to you!" Ka'b then kissed the hand of the Prophet 🕸 and swore his oath of allegiance. He knelt down before the Holy Prophet 🕸 in perfect poise and suggested the following, "Oh Rasulullah 🕸! Do you accept that Ka'b bin Zuhayr repents of his past sins and rubs his face in the dust at the feet of your enlightened person?" The Holy Prophet 🌸 answered, "So be it!" Ka'b then added, "Oh great and noble Prophet 🌸! Oh you who are the Mercy of the Worlds! This Ka'b bin Zuhayr is none other than I myself!"

When the Ansar heard these words, they rose to their feet in alarm. "Permit us, oh Rasulullah 🌸, to mete out his punishment!" they said. But the Prophet 🌸 replied, "Let it be. For he has repented, and Islam blots out the sins that went before it. Ka'b has now become a Muslim." When Ka'b perceived the degree of compassion with which the Holy Prophet 🌸 was endowed, he could not keep himself from composing some verses in praise of him. This ode is known as the Banat Suad. When the Prophet 🌸 heard these verses recited, he grew exceedingly glad and began to whirl around. During his whirling, his cloak fell from his blessed shoulders. When the poem had been read and the recitation was over, the Holy Prophet 🌸 draped this same cloak around the shoulders of Ka'b. Ka'b kept this cloak as long as he lived, and he cherished it more than anything else he possessed.

After Mu'awiya had become governor of Damascus, he knew very well how to exploit such things, and he offered Ka'b ten thousand dirhams for the cloak. But Ka'b declined and answered him, "The scent of the Holy Prophet 🌸 wafts at me from this cloak. I prefer that no one should wear it but I." He turned down Mu'awiya's request. After Ka'b had died, Mu'awiya offered his heirs twenty thousand dirhams and thus bought the cloak off them. This is the cloak that was passed down from hand to hand, from predecessor to successor, along the long line of kings and sultans.

'Adi bin Hatim had also become Muslim this year. The Prophet 🌸 was much inclined towards him on account of his extraordinary munificence and generosity. He was one of the great Sahaba. 'Adi bin Hatim was the son of the famous Hatim al-Tayy.

After Ali had cleansed his father's temple of idols, 'Adi had fled to Damascus. Ali had returned to Madinah, and after sorting out affairs there, had returned with 'Adi's sister Safana as his prisoner. The Holy Prophet ﷺ set Safana free and sent her to her brother. Safana's heart had been touched by the light of prophethood and she felt attracted to Islam. When she came to her brother's side, she spoke to him of right guidance and suggested to him that were he to behold Muhammad's ﷺ blessed face, all his sorrows and worries would fall away from him.

With a deep sigh she said, "Ah, that our dearest father had to leave this world before having seen this outstanding man, without beholding this great gift to mankind!" Something then awoke in 'Adi's heart, and taking his sister with him, he went to Madinah and came into the presence of the Holy Prophet ﷺ. The Prophet ﷺ welcomed him, saying, "Welcome to you, oh son of proverbial munificence!" And, turning to the Sahaba, he pronounced, "Because the open-handed, generous man shows such strong reliance on Allah Almighty, he will receive special gifts in the life to come." At these words, the Sahaba became very joyful.

Oh Seeker after Truth! Let me relate to you something about Hatim al-Tayy, although it has no direct bearing on our story. Hatim al-Tayy was known for his extreme largesse, which was so great that whenever a man of his circle found himself in dire straits, he would refer to Hatim al-Tayy as the proverbial solver of all problems. "I will go to Hatim and ask him to give me what I need to bail me out," he would say to himself.

Once a man who lived rather a great distance from Hatim's dwelling place was sorely pressed from want of funds. For days he fretted and worried about this, while his situation steadily worsened, until one day his wife said to him, "Whatever we try to do to pull ourselves out of this trouble, it just gets worse. How long is this to go on? Why don't you go now and speak to Hatim al-Tayy and ask him to help you for once."

The poor man saddled his beast and, placing his entire hope on Hatim al-Tayy set out to find him. But when he came to the area where Hatim wielded his influence, he found that another man had taken over from him. Hatim himself had changed his robes and gone off to unknown parts. The needy man's last hopes were dashed and he fell into despair. He had no choice but to turn back without having accomplished anything, and so he did, in a state of utter dejection.

On his way back he had to stop somewhere for the night. He there encountered a vagrant of strange and wild appearance. They became acquainted, and the nomad's attentive gaze observed the man's oppressed state of mind and asked him, "Why are you in such a state of despair, what is your trouble?" The needy man began relating to him of his troubles, telling him that he had set his last hopes on Hatim al-Tayy, relying on the generosity and compassion he was known for. "But fate has shattered this my last hope, for I found not him, but in his place a brutal tyrant who has usurped his lands. I am now returning from there, a broken man with no recourse."

Thereupon the dervish, who was in reality Hatim al-Tayy himself, rejoined, "Do not worry, for Allah will make all everything difficult easy and will right every wrong. Believe in your heart that from now on all your material worries have been taken from you." The man was taken aback and said, "Are you jesting with me?" "Far from it," replied the other, "know for certain that from this moment on all the worries weighing on your mind have been taken from you." "But how?" "You will now take me and lead me to the tyrant who has usurped the lands of Hatim al-Tayy and he will remunerate you with much more than you ever expected." "How strange! Who are you, and what will come of handing you over to that tyrant?" "He is searching for me and has promised a large reward to him who delivers me into his hands." "But who are you?" asked the man in amazement. "I am he on whom you placed your hopes, whom you came to see in your extremity and of whom you expected support. I am Hatim al-Tayy."

"Oh, oh," said the man in need, "how can I do this deed? How can I endanger your life? For were I to deliver you to the tyrant who sits in your place, he would surely kill you." "Let him do as he wills. Since you have placed your hopes on me, this is what I am able to do for you at this moment, even if the price of it should be my own head. Still this has to be, I insist on it. Let us not delay any longer."

And so they both traveled back the road he had come. He handed Hatim al-Tayy over to the usurper who sat in his place, and he received in exchange the promised reward that was much greater than he had ever imagined.

Then the tyrant looked at the man who had brought him Hatim as his prisoner and said to him, "I have paid you the sum of the reward that I promised him who would bring Hatim to me, and I will not take it away from you; do not fear. But there is something I wish to learn from you. Please explain this to me: You do not strike me as a man who has the strength or power to track down and capture the likes of Hatim al-Tayy. For I have sent out many able and skilled trackers to get a hold of him, and they all returned without him. Tell me how you did it, how you were able to catch such a man."

Now the man spoke up and said, "Ah, the story was quite a different one, for in reality I did not apprehend him. I have fallen on very hard times and in the extremity of my need I could think of no other way to save myself but to turn to Hatim al-Tayy, who is known for his generosity from east to west. Thus, to plead for his intervention, I set out on my journey. But when I arrived here, I heard that you now occupied his place, and all my hopes were suddenly dashed. Hopeless and wretched, I journeyed homewards, when I encountered this person and told him of my woes. When he had heard of all my troubles, he sacrificed his own life in order to solve my problems, and this is the way we came before you."

These words had such an effect upon the tyrant who had usurped Hatim's throne that all the cruelty and hardness departed from his heart and was instead transformed into good and pure intention. The usurper repented and immediately reinstated Hatim al-Tayy in his original place.

The Battle of Tabuk

Tabuk was a well fourteen way stations' distance from Madinah. The settlement, which lay between Madinah and Damascus, took its name from this watering place. The Battle of Tabuk took place in the ninth year of the Hijra and it was to be the last raid in the Holy Prophet's ✿ lifetime.

After the Battle at Mu'ta, the Emperor of Byzantium, Heraclius, considered plans for an invasion of Arabia, and to this end he convened with Ghassani tribesmen who were Arabs converted to Christianity. Two other tribes joined their alliance, the Judham and Lakhm, and together with the Byzantine army, they constituted a mighty army.

Merchants bringing olive oil to Madinah brought news of these developments. It was even known that the Emperor had promised the soldiers in his army one year's pay in advance if they joined in this campaign. The Christian Arabs appealed to Heraclius and convinced him that Muhammad ﷺ had died and that the Muslims were suffering badly from famine and drought. These kinds of rumors were spread throughout the land.

The Holy Prophet ﷺ for his part began to equip a large armed force and engage in preparations for a new campaign. He sent out special agents to all quarters to mobilize fighters from Mecca and all the tribes. Those who were not so badly hit by the general famine were ordered to give all possible support to the army, and they contributed much in aid to the war effort. The wives of the Holy Prophet ﷺ gave all their jewelry and Abu Bakr donated his entire fortune. 'Uthman gave three hundred camel-loads of provisions and an abundant amount of gold. The Holy Prophet ﷺ made special supplications for each of them.

Oh Traveler for the sake of Truth! Whenever the Holy Prophet ﷺ embarked on the warpath, he made as if to go off in another direction. This was his honorable custom. But on this occasion, as it was extremely hot and there was a terrible drought all over the land and because the enemy was exceedingly powerful and the journey a long one, he informed the troops of his destination so that everyone could prepare himself accordingly.

The hypocrites who were not taking part in the campaign thought to dissuade those who were going along by cunning words and warnings. They would say, "How can you go out in this terrible heat, don't go to join this campaign." But the true friends of the Holy Prophet ❀, the Noble Companions would say, "The heat of Hell (Jahannam) is worse than this."

The head of the hypocrites, Abdullah bin Ubayy as-Salul said, "Does Muhammad ❀ think that the Byzantine Empire is a plaything? I know for sure, as if I had seen it with my own eyes, that he and all his associates together with him will be surrounded and taken prisoner." Thus he tried to raise doubts in people's minds. But those who were true in their attachment to the Holy Prophet ❀ and his cause, who were steadfast in their love and who suffered not from split allegiances, said, "All our will and decisive power belongs to Muhammad, our Prophet ❀." They were ready and determined to do battle and quickly completed their preparations.

There were some among the people whose situation did not allow them to accompany the Holy Prophet ❀ on this campaign, either because they were physically unfit, or because they had not the means. They came into his presence and wept for this. The Glory of the Worlds was very moved by their show of feeling, and the Lord Almighty did not delay to send down a verse to His Beloved, referring to this particular situation and informing of the special favor they had found:

> There is no fault in the weak and the sick and those who find nothing to expend, if they are true to God and His Messenger. There is no way against the good-doers – God is All-Forgiving, All-Compassionate – neither against those who, when they came to thee, for thee to mount them, thou saidst to them, 'I find not whereon to mount you'; they turned away, their eyes overflowing with tears of sorrow, because they found nothing to expend. (Repentance: 91, 92)

Muhammad's ❀ army was now mustered and a deputy had to be appointed to watch over Madinah while the Holy Prophet ❀ was away. The Companions all wondered who it would be this time. The Sultan of Prophets ❀ finally announced, "My representative this time shall be Ali." Ali began to entreat the Prophet ❀ not to leave him behind in Madinah with the women and children. The Prophet ❀ answered him, indicating the high honor which was bestowed on him, saying, "Do you not want to occupy the same place in relation to me that Harun took in relation to

Musa?" Ali then submitted to the Holy Prophet's ❀ will and accepted to stay behind in the city.

On a Thursday in the month of Rajab in the ninth year of the Hijra, the Prophet ❀ set out from Madinah with an army of thirty thousand men. Among them were ten thousand riders.

On their way they passed by the place where of old the people of Thamood lived in houses they had hewn out of the sheer rock. The Holy Prophet ❀ counseled his army, "This is a place which saw the Wrath of the Lord. Let no one go near the dwellings of these people who were thereby destroyed, nor let anyone drink from their wells."

At one point, the Prophet's ❀ camel got lost. The hypocrites instantly used this opportunity, and Zayd al-Lusayt al-Qaynuqa'i said, "Muhammad ❀ says he is a prophet and gives us tidings allegedly from heavenly sources. How strange then, that he cannot tell us where his camel has gone to..." To this the Holy Prophet ❀ replied, "I have heard one of you say such a thing about me. Up until now, it has never been my way to claim for myself as my own achievement what I have done or what I know. I have always said, 'My Lord informs me, my Lord commands me.' I have ever said that I am commanded to make known what He lets me know. Never have I claimed anything for myself, I have only told you what He gives me to know. Therefore, He has now made known to me where my camel has strayed. It is in a certain valley in a certain place. Its halter has become entangled in the branches of a tree; that is why it is held up. Go there and find her for me and bring her back." They set out at once and found the camel in exactly the spot he had described to them and brought her back.

The Prophet's ❀ army halted at the watering place of Tabuk. There was only very little water in the wells. As soon as the Prophet ❀ had performed his ablutions, a miracle was manifested in that the waters suddenly rose to such an extent that the whole army drank their fill and had more than enough. They advanced up to the border of the lands of Sham. Not a trace was to be seen of the Byzantine troops, nor of the Arab tribesmen who had sided with them. But the challenge, which the Prophet's army presented to the Byzantines struck fear into the hearts of all that saw them pass.

The Prophet ﷺ saw by the Light of his Prophethood. Had he foreseen a fierce battle, he surely would not have left Ali behind in Madinah. In this instance, the Prophet ﷺ stayed at Tabuk for twenty days. During these weeks, he received visits from the tribes living in the region of the Gulf of Aqaba and the chief of the Ayla, Yohanna, who came to deliver the jizya. He also made the Holy Prophet ﷺ the present of a white mule. The Christian tribes of Jerba and Azruh also came to meet the Prophet ﷺ and to deliver their jizya. In return, the Holy Prophet ﷺ gave them a guarantee of protection by the Islamic state.

The Prophet ﷺ then sent Khalid ibn al-Walid with four hundred and fifty riders to the ruler of Dumat ul-Jandal, Ukaydir. Khalid, 'Sayfullah', managed to apprehend Ukaydir as he was out hunting with a small company of retainers outside the walls of the fort. He was taken to the Prophet ﷺ and later, when the conditions of the truce had been negotiated and agreed, he was set free.

At Tabuk, the Holy Prophet ﷺ consulted with his companions, as to whether they should further advance or stop there. 'Umar's answer was, "If it is the Divine Command, let us proceed." To this the Holy Prophet ﷺ replied, "Had I received a Divine Command regarding this matter, I surely would not have asked your opinion, would I?"

The Prophet ﷺ said, "In Sham there is a plague and it is not good to travel into a country where a plague is raging." Therefore, he ordered them to turn back and return to Madinah.

Ammar bin Yasir led the Prophet's ﷺ camel by the halter and Hudhayfa ibn al-Yamani drove it from behind. There were twelve men among the hypocrites who had previously conspired among themselves to assassinate the Prophet ﷺ. Now as they passed by Aqaba during the night, they were waiting for the right moment to attack. But the Prophet ﷺ received a revelation, informing him of their intentions. He said aloud, "Do you see that dense blackness there ahead of us?" "Yes, we do, oh Rasulullah ﷺ!"

replied his Blessed Companions. "There are twelve of the hypocrites there engaged in evil intention."

When Usayd found out about this affair, he wanted to have the hypocrites put to death. But the Prophet ﷺ would not agree to this, though he did inform his beloved friend Hudhayfa of their identities, every single one of them. "There are three hundred men and seventy women belonging to the hypocrites who are always frequenting me. Outwardly they appear to be Muslims, but inside they are unbelievers. Their punishment can only come from Allah, it is so heavy that only He can mete it out..."

Oh Traveler to the Truth! The following exchange took place between 'Umar and Hudhayfa during the time of 'Umar's Khalifate. One day 'Umar asked Hudhayfa about something that had intrigued him for a long time. "Oh Hudhayfa!" he said, "The Prophet ﷺ was extremely fond of you and he told you many of his secrets. He informed you also of the identities of the hypocrites. I ask you to please tell me: are there hypocrites among the governors whom I have delegated to their posts?" To this Hudhayfa answered, "Yes, there are." "Who are they?" 'Umar wished to know, and he insisted very forcefully in his questioning. Hudhayfa however remained steadfast, saying, "Do not insist, oh 'Umar: I am not authorized to tell you," and 'Umar had to leave it at that.

Masjid al-Dirar

The hypocrites endeavored to avail themselves of every opportunity to create discord, and when they failed in sowing strife within the family, they tried to turn the Muslims against one another. To this aim, they decided to erect a new mosque opposite the Prophet's ﷺ mosque at Quba. Their pretence was that the sick and elderly should find therein a place for prayer and refuge, but in reality they built it to split the Muslim community of Quba. Behind this plan was the infamous villain Abu Amir who urged his men on, saying, "Go ahead, start building the mosque and see to it that as much weaponry as possible is hidden and stored in it. Meanwhile I shall go to the Byzantine Emperor and ask him to send an army to drive Muhammad and his companions out of Madinah."

He set out towards Damascus while his friends built the mosque and waited for his return. When the Holy Prophet 🕸 was on his way to Tabuk, these hypocrites asked him to come to visit their mosque and pray for them there. The Prophet 🕸 told them he was on the point of traveling and thus occupied with other affairs. On his return from Tabuk, he received a revelation concerning this mosque:

> *And those who have taken a mosque in opposition and unbelief, and to divide the believers, and as a place of ambush for those who fought God and His Messenger aforetime – they will swear, 'We desired nothing but good'; and God testifies they are truly liars. Stand there never. A mosque that was founded upon godfearing from the first day is worthier for thee to stand in; therein are men who love to cleanse themselves; and God loves those who cleanse themselves.*

> *(Repentance: 107, 108)*

Thus the Almighty commanded the destruction of this edifice built by traitors who only intended to use the mosque as a facade to disguise their lair. The Holy Prophet 🕸 sent out his companions Malik bin Dukhshum and Ma'n bin 'Adiy to go and burn down the mosque of opposition, as it came to be known.

It was the month of Ramadan when the Holy Prophet 🕸 returned safely from Tabuk to Madinah. Upon his return, he was extremely displeased with those Muslims who had stayed behind from this expedition unexcused. Among them was Abu Lubaba who thereupon solemnly swore an oath that he would tie himself to a pillar in the mosque and not leave that spot until the Prophet 🕸 had forgiven him. Whenever he had to answer a call of nature (break his wudu), his daughter undid his bonds, and afterwards, tied him up again to the pillar. He spent his days and nights there weeping about himself, saying, "What a vile and despicable character I am, for to have presumed to set my opinion against that of the Holy Prophet 🕸!"

At last a verse was revealed, which announced his pardon, and a messenger came announcing the good news to him. When this man wished to untie his bonds, Abu Lubaba stopped him, saying, "Endless praise be to my Lord for this gracious pardon, and for His honoring me thus. However, by my oath I have sworn that I will not move from this place until the Beloved of Allah ❀ himself comes to me and unties these ropes." And he wept copiously as he spoke.

The Prophet ❀ was told of Abu Lubaba's oath, so he went to him and unbound his ties.

Also among those who had stayed behind unexcused were Ka'b bin Malik, Murara bin al-Rabi' and Hilal bin Umayya. They now went to the Prophet ❀ asking for forgiveness. The Holy Prophet ❀ commanded all people to shun them for fifty nights and not to keep their company, nor speak any word to them. After that time had passed, they were pardoned.

There was a man named 'Urwa bin Mas'ud of the tribe of Thaqif who was held in high esteem among the Arabs. He caught up with the Prophet ❀ on his return journey from Tabuk and was graced with the acceptance into Islam. He returned to his tribe, wishing to speak to them about the Islam he had found, but they were hostile and shot arrows at him from all sides, so that he fell a martyr.

Later that year, the leaders of that same tribe came to Madinah and offered to submit to the Prophet ❀ and to accept Islam, but they asked to be exempted from praying. The Prophet ❀ answered them, "No good can come of a religion which has no prayers." Then their chief asked the Holy Prophet ❀ for permission to retain their idol al-Lat for a period of three years. The Prophet ❀ answered, "Idol worship and the worship of Allah do not go together." In the end, he agreed to let them continue for one more month, and they accepted Islam and attained to true guidance.

That same year the Bani Sa'd bin Bakr sent a representative to the Holy Prophet ❀ whose name was Dimam bin Tha'laba. He questioned the Prophet ❀ about the revelation he received from Allah and when he had asked all his questions and satisfied his need for knowledge, he accepted Islam and returned to his tribe to teach them the ways of the new religion. He explained what Allah has commanded us to do and what He has forbidden, and before the night was over, there was not a man or woman in the tribe who had not become Muslim.

In that year also the Negus of Abyssinia, al-Asham bin Abjar passed away. When the news of his passing reached Madinah, the Holy Prophet ﷺ with all the Sahaba prayed the funeral prayer for him. This is the basis of the custom of praying the funeral prayer for those who are not present. (*Salat-al-Janaza 'ala-l-Gha'ibin*).

Oh Seeker for the Way to Truth! Here it made clear to all that it is of the Sunna of the Holy Prophet ﷺ to conduct the funeral rites for a person *in absentia*, that is to say for one who has died at a distant place.

That same year in the month of Sha'ban, the Holy Prophet's ﷺ beloved daughter and the respected wife of 'Uthman Dhi-Nurayn, Umm Kulthum, passed away from this fleeting world of appearances to the eternal abode of lasting peace.

In the month of Shawwal, the infamous leader of the hypocrites, Abdullah bin Ubayy bin Salul died.

Oh you who you seek nothing but the Light of Truth! This man's death contains a great lesson for the Muslim nation. Abdullah bin Ubayy was a hypocrite who frequented the assembly of the Holy Prophet ﷺ. He used to hear the precious words that issued from the Prophet's ﷺ mouth and to listen to his Divine Inspirations, and yet he persevered in his friendship with the enemies of the Prophet ﷺ, casting aside his association with the Holy Prophet ﷺ for the sake of paltry material advantage. He took part in some of the schemes they plotted against Islam and he was a thorn in the side of the Muslims. When they went to the Holy Prophet ﷺ to complain about him, all the Holy Prophet ﷺ would say was, "What can we do? Outwardly he confesses to being a Muslim. There is nothing we can do, but Allah's punishment of the hypocrite is heavier than that of the unbeliever. This matter is best left in the hands of Allah Almighty."

When death approached this man, he called to his side his son Abdullah, and knowing that the Prophet 🎔 was well disposed towards him, he said to him, "Oh my son, I know that the Prophet 🎔 will not turn down your request. For I myself have lived my life according to the dictates of my ego, and I don't dare approach the Prophet 🎔 now that death is knocking at my door. I have only one request: that the Holy Prophet 🎔 might grant me the shirt that covers his blessed body as a shroud for me when I am dead. That is all I want, and I implore you to ask him for me, for his compassion is great."

Abdullah went to the assembly of Muhammad 🎔 and informed him of the condition of his father. He said, "If you fulfill his last wish, he will be assured of Divine Grace and Forgiveness, therefore he has sent me to you. But yours is the command, oh my Prophet 🎔!" Abu Bakr was present at this meeting and he cast agitated looks at the Prophet 🎔, wondering what he would do next. Even more upset was 'Umar, the strict keeper of the Shari'a who never was able to tolerate this sort of thing; he stared at the Prophet 🎔 in great suspense.

The Mercy to the Worlds 🎔 thereupon made ready to remove his shirt to give it to the dying man, when he saw 'Umar's face turn dark with suppressed rage. He turned to him and said, "Oh 'Umar! I am the sole reason for man's creation, I cannot refuse anything that is requested of me. Even to my enemy I stretch out the hand of mercy. Why then do you show annoyance? Be patient and wait for the Judgment of the Lord." With that he took off his shirt and sent it to the leader of the hypocrites.

Some time later, the news of the death of Abdullah bin Ubayy bin Salul was brought. Everybody was wondering whether the Prophet 🎔 would pray the funeral prayer over him or not. The Holy Prophet 🎔 was making ready to pray over him when a Divine Command reached him in form of a revelation forbidding him to pray over the dead man, thus:

And pray thou never over any one of them when he is dead, nor stand over his grave; they disbelieved in God and His Messenger, and died while they were ungodly. *(Repentance, 84)*

Oh Traveler on the Way to Truth! Man trembles in awe when faced with this holy verse, which refers to those who in the life to come will not be brought before the Holy Presence of the Almighty Lord. They form a group apart, upon whom a curtain will fall after they have confessed their sins and they will be taken away to be punished as they deserve. The nature of what lies in store for them remains concealed.

This Divine Command makes it plain to every Muslim for whom the funeral prayer is not to be prayed. Certainly, there are people who harbored evil intentions towards Islam, but with their last breath embraced the faith and repented, full of remorse. Therefore, his friends may think, "We ought to think good of him, wash his body and pray the funeral prayer for him."

However, take the case of Abdullah bin Ubayy: he had no real faith, he believed not in the greatness of the Holy Prophet ✸, but when he was about to die, he begged to be given the Prophet's ✸ shirt, so that his last clothing on earth might be the very cloth this holy man wore next to his blessed skin. But of what benefit was this to him? While there was still time, he had joined forces with the enemies of the Prophet ✸, he had been a hypocrite with regard to his religion and his relationship to Allah and His Prophet ✸.

He had preferred the mean gains of worldly benefits to the superior excellence of spiritual merit; but now, when all was said and done, he would have directed his attention to the Holy Prophet ✸. That kind of faith is not acceptable to Allah Almighty. He forbids the Muslims to pray over such a man, for, "We do not acknowledge his claim to humanity," says the Lord.

The Pilgrimage of Islam

In the ninth year of the Hijra, the Kaba was cleansed of all traces of idolatry and preparations were made for the Hajj to be performed according to the rites of Ibrahim. The Holy Prophet ✸, having returned from Tabuk, sent his faithful companion Abu Bakr to lead the Hajj with a caravan of three hundred pilgrims. Sa'd bin Waqqas, Jabir and Abu Hurayra were sent along with the pilgrims as their guides and instructors. Twenty camels were also taken along as sacrificial animals. Not long after the Hajj caravan had set out, a revelation came to the Holy Prophet ❀, which had important implications for all the pilgrims to Mecca. He therefore sent 'Ali after them, entrusting to him this special task, to impart and expound the revelation of the Sura Bara'at (Repentance).

When they arrived at Mecca, Abu Bakr gave a Khutba before all the assembled pilgrims and taught them the rites and rituals of the Hajj. The Muslims then performed the Hajj according to what they had learnt, and the unbelievers performed it as they were wont to do. 'Ali then arrived and recited the Sura named 'Repentance' and said to them, "It follows from the revelation of these holy verses that in the coming year no unbeliever shall perform the Hajj, nor should any ever perform Tawaf completely naked, and none of the pagans may enter the Kaba."

However, those unbelievers who had concluded a special treaty with the Holy Prophet ❀ and had abided by its terms, had nothing to fear, it would be honored. The other idolaters under contract with the Muslims who failed to observe the conditions stated were given four months of respite, after which the Muslims were free from any obligations towards them. 'Ali's address made a great impression on all those present. Afterwards, Abu Hurayra went around, repeating the words of this proclamation of Bara'at (freedom from obligation) over and over again.

The pagans then all entered into Islam, and the love of Islam spread far and wide. The Muslims began to reap the fruits of their nine years of work for the cause of Islam. Everywhere the spread of faith and security was to be observed. Never before in history had there been, nor could there ever have been such a state, for the spiritual emanations of Muhammad the Prophet ❀ had begun to pervade the hearts and minds of men. The once lonesome call of 'La ilaha illAllah', like a never-setting sun, had climbed to its zenith and shone forth strongly now. Deputations and envoys began to arrive

544

from all over the world, and as the command for zakat collection was revealed, living conditions for the Muslims began to improve. A poll tax (jizya) was also exacted from the non-Muslim peoples living within the state of Islam.

The Holy Prophet ﷺ who was very polite and of refined manners, received the envoys well and treated them attentively. He greeted them according to the customs of their respective countries of origin, and presented them with the best robes and cloaks of honor.

Events of the Tenth Year of the Hijra

Many Thousands Enter Islam

Most of the deputations who came to Madinah in this year came to see his Blessed Face and hear the Divine Wisdom that he uttered, and many were honored with the acceptance of Islam. From Bahrain there came sixteen people from the tribe of Abdu-l-Qays, and with them came a very famous Christian holy man named Jarut. They all became Muslims at the hand of the Prophet ﷺ.

A deputation also came from the Bani Muntafiq, who was stunned when they entered the presence of the Prophet ﷺ. They wished to become Muslim, and the Blessed Prophet ﷺ stretched out his hand. With tears in their eyes, they received the ineffable blessings of Islam. Then they returned to their tribe.

Envoys even came all the way from China. Their ruler asked to have a picture of the Holy Prophet ﷺ, if one existed. Now the Prophet ﷺ had forbidden all manners of images, but he had them bring a piece of parched deerskin and he carefully focused his attention upon it so that his blessed features were reflected thereon. Then he folded it up and ordered them not to unfold it until they had given it to their ruler. The deputation left and did as he told them. When their king opened up the piece of deerskin, he beheld the blessed features of the Holy Prophet ﷺ, and as he gazed upon this blessed reflection on the deerskin, it began to dissolve. He entered Islam, together with his envoys.

Now there remained not a tribe or clan in all Arabia that could stand against the Islamic state founded by the spiritual power of the Prophet Muhammad ﷺ. From far and wide people came trooping towards Madinah and joined the faith. It was at this time that this Sura was revealed:

> *Bismillah-ir-rahman-ir-rahim. When comes the help of God, and victory, and thou seest men entering God's religion in throngs, then proclaim the praise of thy Lord, and seek His forgiveness, for He turns again unto men.* (Help)

Those who understood the subtle meaning of these verses gleaned from them an indication that the Prophet's ﷺ time on earth was nearing its completion, and their eyes filled with tears. For in truth, his sacred task was nearly completed. The wisdom behind the mission of this noble soul was that he might lay the foundation of Islam, and this had been accomplished. Abu Bakr as-Siddiq was one of those who grasped the hidden meaning of this divinely revealed text, and he wept. "Yes," he said, "it is obvious that, after having delivered the message and inculcated the articles of faith, the Holy Prophet ﷺ will not remain in this world much longer. " When 'Abbas enquired of the Prophet ﷺ personally about this, he only confirmed it. For the Holy Prophet ﷺ had delivered everything that was revealed to him in word and deed and application, nothing was missing or left in doubt.

Islam was no longer confined to the Arabian Peninsula and the Arabian tribes. In the seventh year of the Hijra, letters of invitation to Islam had been sent out to all corners of the world, signed, sealed and authorized by Muhammad the Prophet of Allah ﷺ. Even the enemies of Islam were now inclined to believe that this religion was not to be shaken or removed.

The Farewell Pilgrimage

In this year, the tenth year of the Hijra, the Holy Prophet ﷺ intended to perform the Pilgrimage, and since it was to be his last pilgrimage on earth, it is called the *Hajj al-Widaa*, or the Farewell Pilgrimage.

During this Hajj the following verse was revealed, which expresses the Divine Intention even more clearly:

Today I have perfected your religion for you, and I have completed My blessing upon you, and I have approved Islam for your religion. (The Table, 3)

In the tenth year of the Hijra, the Holy Prophet ❁ announced to his companions his intention to travel to Mecca for the purpose of performing Hajj. People from outlying regions began streaming towards Madinah in great numbers when they heard of the Prophet's ❁ intention, in order to accompany him on this pilgrimage. The Prophet ❁ and his family and companions left the city of Madinah after praying the noon prayer when only five days remained till the month of Dhul-Hijjah. They proceed up to Dhul-Hulayfa, and stayed there the night.

In the morning, they donned their Ihram (pilgrim's garb), prayed the noon prayer, then a company of forty thousand pilgrims set forth for the holy city of Mecca. This tremendous caravan of Hujjaj (pilgrims) reached Mecca on the morning of the fourth Sunday of the month of Dhul-Hijjah, entering the Haram-ash-Sharif by the door of the Bani Shayba. The Holy Prophet ❁ invoked this supplication, "Oh my Lord! Increase this Holy House in honor and reverence!" Then they began to perform their Tawaf, after which they ascended the hill of Safa praising and glorifying the Lord, then descending from the hill of Marwa and performing the Sa'i (the swift passage between the two hills).

Just at that moment, Ali arrived with a great Hajj caravan coming from Yemen. Muslims began coming from all over the land, gathering at Mecca. The Hajj season happened to fall in the month of March, around the time of the spring equinox. The day of 'Arafat was a Friday, and the Holy Prophet ❁ performed this Hajj al-Akbar with a multitude of forty thousand pilgrims. Therefore, this Hajj was at once very sacred and solemn, and at the same time filled with sadness, for the Leader of all Prophets ❁ in his Khutba said,

"For it may be that you will not see me among you in this place after this year."

The Prophet ❁ in his Khutba on this occasion spoke very moving words, primarily concerning the rights of women and orphans. He said:

"Every forbidden action must be carefully avoided, but none more so than these two things: the rights of women and orphans must not be infringed, for on the Day of Reckoning, there will be no intercession for these two sins before the Divine Presence."

He also expounded in great detail on the grievousness of all usury, and impressed upon all the tribes that all blood feuds were hence abolished, that the believers were to live with each other as brothers, and that any property not given voluntarily was not lawful. After that he said,

"I leave you two things, which, if you hold fast to them shall preserve you from all error: the Book of Allah, and my Sunna. Your downfall begins with your departure from these two."

Thus he concluded his Khutba. That day, the noon (Zuhr) and the afternoon ('Asr) prayers were joined and prayed with one Adhan and two Iqamas, just as the evening (Maghrib) and night ('Isha) prayers were joined and prayed with one Adhan and two Iqamas.

A woman from the tribe of the Khaz'am came to the Holy Prophet ﷺ and asked, "Oh Rasulullah ﷺ! My father is a very old man and has not the strength to perform the Hajj himself. Is it lawful for me to perform it in his stead?" The Qibla of the Prophets, Muhammad ﷺ replied, "Yes, it is lawful."

Just at that moment, Fadl bin 'Abbas happened to steal a glance over to the women's side. The Holy Prophet ﷺ stretched out his blessed hand and turned Fadl's face away from the women's side of the tent.

Oh Traveler on the Way to Truth! Stoning the devil is indeed a significant act of devotion, just as fasting expresses a state of godliness, and prayer means to engage in a dialogue with the Almighty Lord, and the Hajj is a visit to the House of God. The person performing Hajj announces his intention to renounce the claims of his lower soul (nafs) by stoning Shaytan at Mina, thus signaling that henceforth he will struggle against the ego, which holds him in its grip.

The Holy Prophet ﷺ gave a Khutba in Mina, in which he set forth at length the abolishment of blood feuds and the inviolability of every man's life and possessions. He exhorted them, saying, "As long as your rulers hold on to the Book of Allah, as long as nothing comes between them and Allah's Word, obey them in every way. A time will come when there will be conflict between the Quran and your chiefs; at that time you should engage in the faction of the Quran." And he went on to describe the appearance and characteristics of Dajjal. He explained in detail on what depends the advancement, eminence and perfection of man in his temporal and eternal future.

Then he counseled the congregation, "Oh people! Have I delivered my message? Have I made clear my mission?" and from thousands of hearts shouts of assent rose to the heavens, as the crowd called out, "Yes, you have, oh Rasulullah ﷺ!" The Holy Prophet ﷺ raised his hands to Heaven and called Allah to witness, saying, "Oh my Lord, bear witness!"

Then he continued, *"Man kuntu mawlahu, fa-Aliyyun mawlahu"* which is to say, "Whose close friend I am, his close friend is also Ali. Oh Allah, be the friend of him who is his friend, and the foe of him who is his foe, and aid him who gives his aid to him."

Then he bade farewell to his nation, saying, "Let those who are present here inform those who are absent." The Hajj company then entered Mecca, performed the Tawaf al-Widaa (the parting circumambulation), drank of the water of the Zamzam well from the hand of Ibn 'Abbas and thus completed the rites of the Hajj. Then the Holy Prophet ﷺ returned to Madinah. When the city of Madinah came into view, the Prophet ﷺ felt such joy and elation at its sight that he cried out with a loud shout:

**LA ILAHA ILLALLAH, WAHDAHU LA SHARIKA LAH, LAHUL MULK
WA LAHUL HAMD, WA HUWA 'ALA KULLI SHAY'IN QADIR.**

(There is no god but Allah, the One and Only, who has no partners; in His possession is all there is, and to Him is due all praise; and it is He who has power over all things.)

False Prophets Appear

In the tenth year of the Hijra there arose in Yemen the false prophet Musaylima-tul-Kadhdhab (that is: Musaylima the Liar), and Abhala bin Ka'b who is called Aswad ul-Anas. Abhala had gained control over San'a and the representatives of Islam there had a hard time of it. The Holy Prophet ﷺ was stirred by these events to take action and he sent a special envoy to the Muslims of the Yemen, instructing them to punish Abhala the impostor.

He also sent a message to the Muslims of the Najd concerning Musaylima the Liar, ordering them to take revenge on him. "Allah has informed me in my dream that very soon two enemies of Allah will meet with their demise," thus informing his Noble Companions.

Around this time, another false prophet arose of the tribe of the Bani Asad. He was a chief of his tribe, named Tulayha bin Khuwaylid. A band of soldiers was sent against him and in the eleventh year of the Hijra he was defeated. It was important to take seriously these uprisings in the Najd and in the Yemen, even though the bulk of Muslim trade was with Sham (Damascus). On the twenty-sixth day of Safar the Holy Prophet ﷺ ordered preparations to be made for a campaign against the tribes of the north and sent an army out to the region of Balqa, in the precincts of Damascus, under the leadership of Usama bin Zayd bin Harith.

As mentioned above, Zayd was a freedman who was very dear to the Holy Prophet ﷺ, and he was as fond of his son Usama as he was of one of his own children. Usama was still very young when he was made commander of a whole army, according to some reports he was no older than eighteen years of age. The Holy Prophet ﷺ called Usama into his presence and said to him, "Direct your men towards Sham and avenge the defeat of Mut'a. Go to where your father was martyred and let the horses trample down the enemy of Allah."

The day after this, the Prophet ﷺ was taken ill. The companions began to wonder whether the campaign would be cancelled, but the Holy Prophet ﷺ said to them, "The command will under no circumstances be recalled," and though he was already succumbing to his illness, he personally placed the banner in Usama's hand. Usama handed it to Burayda bin Husayb al-Aslami and the troops left the city of Madinah. The army assembled at Juruf, and all the great Sahaba, Abu Bakr, 'Umar, Sa'd and Said made preparations to accompany Usama's retinue.

An Unprecedented Legacy

The foundation of Islam had been laid, and it would not be long before shafts of light from that never-sinking sun were to penetrate into every dark corner. All was set and prepared. Had it not been for such tragedies as the assassination of 'Uthman, and the disastrous emergence of Mu'awiya's covetousness that split up the nation; had it been possible to preserve the tremendous dynamic force with which the Holy Prophet ﷺ infused early Islam, and had it been feasible for Siddiq-al-Akbar (Abu Bakr) and Faruq al-A'dl ('Umar) to sustain and protract this force, then Islam would be the only system ruling the world today and no other religion would be left to rival it. For never in history has there been any leader who, in so short a period as ten years, achieved such tremendous and lasting results.

It was not the work of an ordinary human being to institute an administration based on justice that taught people the meaning of freedom and that operated on the basis of a formal code of law. It is no minor achievement to have changed a people whose previous custom was to bury their female infants alive, who were morally lax and indifferent into a nation of followers of a religion inspired by Divine Wisdom, high moral motivation and striving for virtue, even when it worked against their own personal advantage. This was achieved within a mere decade, for before the call to Islam there had been nothing at all like this. It was a force capable of teaching wisdom and virtue to those great men who were trained at the Holy Prophet's ﷺ knee during twenty-three years; and not only to their contemporaries, but to their successors and descendants up to the Last Day.

The army of Islam had consisted of three hundred and thirteen men at the Battle of Badr. By the time of the conquest of Mecca, the number of Muslim fighters had increased to ten thousand. In 'Umar's Khalifate, the ranks had swollen to hundreds of thousands of men. But those first ten thousand, who preached faith where they encountered unbelief, justice where they saw oppression and knowledge where there was ignorance, were the forerunners of that formidable, later army. They established the foundations of Islam, for the Quran is not preserved in lines of writing but within the hearts of men.

The Holy Prophet ﷺ had gained Divine Approval for having accomplished his mission in the revelation of the following verse:

> *Today I have perfected your religion for you, and I have completed My blessing upon you, and I have approved Islam for your religion.* (The Table, 3)

Again, if we pause for a moment to consider this matter impartially, we will see that never before in the history of man has there been any single person who accomplished what the Prophet Muhammad ﷺ has, nor has any been at all like him. This is clear beyond the shadow of a doubt. Compared to his achievement, the deeds of such great Prophets as Musa and 'Isa, as well as the deeds of the great Sahaba and close companions lag far behind in importance. Nobody has ever taken upon himself such a load, under such adverse conditions and hostile circumstances. The Noble Prophet ﷺ combined all these many roles in his person: he was at once teacher and religious instructor, spiritual advisor and counselor, political leader as well as judge and supreme commander; not a single moment of his life was idly spent.

What a remarkable assembly it was that gathered in the Holy Mosque in Madinah, in that simple building of four straight walls, which constituted this sublime maqam! In this Masjid, the Holy Prophet ﷺ personally conducted the ritual prayers, and stayed on every day after prayer preaching to the congregation, enlightening their thoughts through his counsel, guidance and teaching, and busying himself with arranging affairs for the common people. Whoever met him, would bring to him his problems and expect some solution and answer from him. He comforted the poor, assisted the destitute and lonely. It was the Holy Prophet 🏵 himself who provided for the Ashab-us-Safa.

It was only natural that the envious hypocrites hated the Prophet 🏵, who in the fires of holiness burnt the idol that man had made of himself. They prepared their own Hellfire.

The Holy Prophet 🏵, himself a personification of justice and guidance, exhibited such great tact and skill towards his friends and companions, that not one of them felt he had been treated to less favor than the other; thus their feeling of brotherhood was not undermined. For these Companions were constantly vying with each other to make themselves more agreeable and loveable to the Beloved of Allah 🏵.

In Hadith, which have been corroborated by hundreds of Sahaba, he foretold in great detail the fitna, dissent and division, which would befall his nation after his time, and as he had foretold, so it came to be. These are fixed facts of history that cannot be denied or altered.

For example, there is a Hadith approved by many sources, which tells of the martyrdom of 'Ammar bin Yasir by the Fi'at al-Baghiya (the party of rebellion), and which tells that his last drink would be some milk mixed with water. This Hadith is explicit in foretelling a future event and it is impossible to deny this. Had it been possible, not to have this name attached to their group, those who found ways of denying a great number of things would certainly have denied this too.

In addition to information of this category, the Prophet 🏵 also sketched the future of Islam in rough outlines. Examples of this are the foretelling of the conquests of the Roman and Iranian Empires, and the passing on of the treasures of Khosroes to Saraqa. Even if some of this can be explained away through a strained application of interpretative strategy, yet there is much that remains shining in the light of pure prophetic vision. There is little choice but to accept the prophethood of the Prophet Muhammad ﷺ. Beyond doubt, he has no equal and never will the likes of him be seen again.

The Holy Prophet's ﷺ Passing and Other Details of His life

A day or two after returning from the Farewell Pilgrimage, the Prophet ﷺ suffered from a state of great exhaustion. His blessed body was shaken by frequent fits of fever. His temperature rose to such a degree that Abu Said, paying a sick call to the Blessed Prophet ﷺ, withdrew his hand in amazement as soon as he touched him. When he had fallen ill with fever at other times, the Holy Prophet ﷺ had prayed for recovery, but this time he did not do so.

Even while he was so gravely ill, he could not but think about his nation. The Companions were terribly distraught. When his illness seemed to worsen, they gathered around the Holy Prophet's ﷺ presence. He spoke to them, saying, "Bring me pen and ink, so that I can write my will, that you might not fall into error after I am gone." But a disagreement arose among the Sahaba. The Bani Hashim and most of the Ansar wished for the pen and ink to be brought, while others said, "What need is there to write down a will or testament?" One of these was 'Umar who said, "It is not right to rob the Prophet ﷺ of his strength while he is so very weakened by disease." The Holy Prophet ﷺ requested of them to do their arguing elsewhere, saying, "It is not proper for the Companions to dispute in the presence of their Prophet."

He directed them to abandon the writing of a will. Three days before the Prophet's ﷺ passing, his uncle 'Abbas bin Abdul-Muttalib who was very keen on the disclosure of the future, met with 'Ali and suggested to him that he ask the Holy Prophet ❀ about the question of his succession. 'Ali replied, "If the Holy Prophet ❀ does not entrust it to us, he will entrust it to no other," thus avoiding the question, or rather, not seeing it fit to trouble the Holy Prophet ❀ once again in a matter the Prophet ❀ had already pronounced upon.

The Prophet's ❀ illness worsened. When he felt unable to lead the prayers in the mosque, he appointed Abu Bakr to be Imam in his stead. The first time Abu Bakr led the Sahaba in prayer was at the 'Isha' prayer on Thursday night. When Abu Bakr stood before the *Jama'at* (congregation), he began to weep. Somewhat later, the Beloved of Allah ❀ felt slightly better, so that he proceeded to the mosque for the morning prayer, supported by 'Ali and al-Fadl bin al-'Abbas, and followed Abu Bakr's lead while sitting down. After the prayer he made supplication for himself, for the whole community and for all of the Prophets. He praised Allah Almighty, and prayed for those who had fallen in His way and he exhorted people to cling to the faith.

Then he said, "Oh my people, have you heard of the Lord's servant who was asked by Him, 'What do you love more, this world or the world to come?' The man chose the afterlife. The Lord was pleased with him and promised him that He would admit him into His Almighty Presence.'" Nobody understood these words but Abu Bakr as-Siddiq who began to weep. "Oh my Prophet ❀," he said, "may my father and mother be your ransom." The Prophet ❀ knew that he had understood and turning to him said, "Oh Abu Bakr, you will be with me in the other world." And he went on to say, "If I was to take any friend other than Allah Almighty, I would have chosen Abu Bakr as my friend. Nobody has shown me such friendship as he, and no one's wealth has given me more benefit than his."

After this he spoke, "Oh my people, you must know that death must be, and that not one living thing can escape from it! But there will come a day after death, which will be the Day of Justice. The great in this world will seek retaliation from the low, and the lowly from the high born, and not one shall be wronged. If there is any one among you who has suffered

557

through me, let him now step forth and make good his claim. If there is any to whom I have spoken a rough word, let him retaliate now with rude speech, so that I might go home to my Lord in a blameless state, and nobody might have a right to claim of me."

The Deep Love of the Sahaba

Hearing these words, the people began to weep aloud and they cried, "Oh Rasulullah ❀, whoever has any right over you, let him now give up all claim!" But 'Ukkasha bin Mihsan rose to his feet and said, "Oh Rasulullah ❀! In a certain raid, I drove my camel alongside yours. You raised your whip to strike your camel and in doing so, you hit me and caused me great pain. For this I have a right of retaliation over you." The Holy Prophet ❀ answered, "Come, if you like, you may hit me now." 'Ukkasha replied, "Yes, I wish to do so." Now the Prophet ❀ had a whip and he ordered Bilal to go and fetch it, saying, "Go get the whip, but don't let my daughter Fatima know about it, for she won't be able to bear it."

The Companions all reproached 'Ukkasha bitterly, saying, "Are you not ashamed, do you not fear Allah? Will you not forego this matter of retaliation?" But the Prophet ❀ said, "Leave him, it is his right." 'Uthman bin 'Affan spoke up and said, "Oh 'Ukkasha, I will give you one hundred camels instead of this reprisal." 'Abd-ur-Rahman bin 'Awf made a similar offer, and all the Companions one by one offered to pay something to allay his claims, but 'Ukkasha accepted none of it. Finally, the whip was brought. 'Ali sprang to his feet and said, " 'Ukkasha, the Holy Prophet ❀ is ill and cannot bear such severe pain. If you really wish to strike, deal me a hundred lashes in his stead, if you have the strength." But 'Ukkasha would accept none of this; he rose and took the whip from the Prophet's ❀ hand.

The Prophet ❀ said to him, "Come closer," and when he drew near him, he said, "Do not strike me too hard, for I no longer have the strength to withstand a violent blow." Hearing these words, his companions feared for him and began to weep. 'Ukkasha said, "Oh Rasulullah ❀, the day you struck me with your whip, my back was bare, while you are now covered with your mantle." The Holy Prophet 🕮 immediately threw off his cloak.

Then 'Ukkasha laid the whip aside, knelt down by Muhammad's side and rubbed his face against the Prophet's 🕮 blessed skin, weeping loudly. Tears came to the Holy Prophet's 🕮 eyes, all the people wept and the mosque sighed and moaned, and such sounds rose to the heavens that all thought it must be an earthquake. For some time 'Ukkasha would not lift his face from the Holy Prophet's blessed person. Finally, the Prophet 🕮 asked him, "Oh 'Ukkasha, why have you done this?" 'Ukkasha answered, "I was afraid that I and these people might not see you again after this day, and I therefore wished to rub my face against your blessed person, so that Allah might spare me the fires of Hell." The Holy Prophet 🕮 then said, "He has made Hell forbidden to you," and he repeated it thrice.

After this, one person got up and said, "Oh my Prophet 🕮, one day a poor dervish came to you, asking something of you and you turned to me, saying, 'Give him whatever you have on you, until I repay you for it.' That day I had on me three silver coins and I gave them to the poor man. I ask now you to pray to the Lord for me that He might grant me the reward for this, and place it in the balance of my good deeds." The Holy Prophet 🕮 replied, "Those three coins are a debt that I owe you, and the reward for that gift of sadaqa is mine." He ordered Fadl bin al-'Abbas to give this man three silver coins, saying, "Now you may give these coins to a dervish and the reward will be yours."

Another person rose, saying, "Oh Rasulullah 🕮, in a certain battle, I stole three silver coins of the booty; what am I to do now?" The Prophet 🕮 replied, "Take those three coins and place them in the public treasury (Bayt-al-Mal)." Yet another man rose, saying, "I am a liar, and my tongue is abominably wicked, please pray for me." The Prophet 🕮 prayed for him. Then 'Umar bin al-Khattab said to the man, "Oh fellow, why have you disgraced yourself before all the people!" But the Prophet 🕮 said to him, "Oh 'Umar, disgrace in this world is better than disgrace in the next." 'Umar then said, "I have no doubt that this man is not a hypocrite, for had he been one, he would have hidden his defect and not feared Allah and placed his hopes in the Prophet's ✿ prayer." To that the Prophet ✿ said, "That is certainly true." Of 'Umar, the Holy Prophet ✿ said, "'Umar is always with the Truth, and the Truth is always with him, wherever he may be."

Advice of the Prophet ✿

After this the Holy Prophet ✿ repaired to his rooms, and the people saw him no more after this. His illness grew more severe and on the third day it became grave. When people asked 'Ali about the Prophet's ✿ state, he would reply, "He is well." "Then show him to us," they demanded. A group of Muhajirin and Ansar entered Aisha's room. The Holy Prophet ✿ looked up at them, his eyes brimming with tears and he had not the strength any more to sit up. He asked al-Fadl bin al-'Abbas to lift him and prop him up against a cushion. The Prophet ✿ gazed at his beloved companions and wished to address them, but he could not. He only made supplication for them, saying:

> "You have taken the trouble and come here to me, may Allah reward you for your kindness. May Allah help you and grant you high stations of Paradise. May He keep you on the straight path and keep you out of harm's way. May He give you eminence and draw you nigh to His Mercy. I urge you earnestly to fear God, for I am come to you both as a warner and a messenger of glad tidings. Do not seek quarrel with the Lord, and destroy not the cities and countries and peoples of the earth, for Allah says in His Holy Book:

> *That is the Last Abode, We appoint it for those who desire not exorbitance in the earth, nor corruption. The issue ultimate is to the Godfearing.* (The Story, 83)

> "I exhort you to keep away from rebellion and worshipping other than Allah, and to remain steadfast in the religion as you have been commanded, to and keep all its commandments. And expel the idolaters from Arabia. I have left you two things that you may hold on to firmly after I have gone. If you do so, you will not go astray. One of

these is the Quran, the other my beloved friends. And be good to the Ansar, for they, too, are my beloved friends and they are venerable companions, so give them proper respect and honor, for you will hear wise counsel from them in their houses. Dwell not on their shortcomings, but be generous with their mistakes. For I entreat the Lord Almighty for Mercy on myself and on my Beloved Companions."

When he had finished speaking, he sank back and his head fell upon his cushion. His Companions asked him, "Oh Prophet of Allah 🏵! When you have passed away, who shall wash you, and who shall lay you in your grave?" To both questions the Prophet 🏵 answered, "He who is the closest to me." Then they asked, "What shall we use as a winding sheet?" and he replied, "That which I am wearing." "And who shall conduct the funeral prayer for you?" He 🏵 replied:

"May the Almighty forgive you and grant you great reward in the path of His revealed religion, for that you suffer so much with me. Wash my body and wind it in its winding sheet and place it in its grave. First of all, Jibra'il will come and pray over me, then Israfil, the Mikha'il and finally Azra'il. After that it is your turn to come and pray for me, one group after the other, men and women, let them all come and pray over me and then go home. My greetings of peace upon you all, and peace and blessings on all those who follow my way and religion up to the Day of Judgment. I will be waiting for you by the side of the Bridge of Sirat for all my nation to cross over, entreating my Lord for forgiveness and mercy, and interceding on behalf of my entire nation."

When she came to see him in his room, his daughter Fatima's eyes overflowed with tears. He spoke to her and said, "Why are you aggrieved? Of all the people of my household you are to be the first to follow me, and it will be quite soon." And he gave 'Ali certain instructions.

When the Companions had all left his side, the Prophet's 🏵 wives entered the apartment. His blessed tongue had grown heavy and his eyes began to turn inward. The wives remarked that he was exhausted from his pain and thinking that medicine might benefit him, Asma with her own hand dropped some drops of a potion into his blessed nostril. When the Holy Prophet 🏵 recovered his senses he asked, "Who did this?" and the wives grew fearful and shy of saying, "We did it," so instead they said, "It was 'Abbas." The Holy Prophet 🏵 then called for 'Abbas and asked him, "Oh my uncle, why have you done this?" 'Abbas replied, "Oh my Prophet 🏵, I did not do this, it was the women." Then the wives confessed, saying, "We were worried about you, for your illness had overwhelmed you and you had passed from your senses." The Prophet 🏵 then said, "Whoever was in the house, let them all take this medicine, all except my uncle 'Abbas, so that they might remember never to do such a thing again." And it was done as he bade them.

The third day of his illness was a Jum'a, and the Prophet's 🏵 fever kept rising. There was near him a jug that he used to perform his ablutions, and they filled it and placed it by his side. From time to time he dipped his hand into it and cooled his forehead, saying, "Oh Allah, help me!" 'Abbas came and saw his condition, then he said to 'Ali, "Oh 'Ali, I know the signs of death and I can tell when they appear on the face of the sons of Abdul-Muttalib. Our blessed Prophet 🏵 is about to breathe his last. Go then and ask of him who shall succeed him in leadership of the nation, and learn this matter. Let us know if it be one of the Bani Hashim or one of the sons of Abdul-Muttalib, so that we may give him our support; or, if it should be a man of another tribe, that we might know well in advance." 'Ali replied, "Oh my uncle, there is no need to ask him this, for the Arabs will never consent to the leadership of a man other than Quraysh." 'Abbas then fell silent.

On Monday, the twelfth night of Rabi' al-Awwal of the eleventh year of the Hijra, the Holy Prophet 🏵 felt a slight improvement and slept till around the time of the night prayer ('Isha). He opened the door of his room and saw that the people were praying in the mosque, Abu Bakr leading them in the 'Isha payer. Seeing this, the Prophet 🏵 grew very glad in his heart and gave thanks, saying, "Alhamdulillah! After my time, my nation will go on to preserve my Sunna." He wished to rise from his bed, but he could not stand, so he sat on the side of his bed. Aisha came and asked, "Oh Rasulullah 🕌, do you wish for a miswak (tooth-stick)?" The Prophet 🕌 said, "Bring one," and Aisha gave him the miswak she had in her room after softening it for him. The Prophet 🕌 cleaned his blessed teeth with it, and Aisha said to him, "Oh Prophet of Allah 🕌, don't use it so vigorously, so as not to hurt your teeth." The Prophet 🕌 replied, "Oh Aisha, this is the way it must be done, for it is a part of my Sunna."

Aisha also said, "The Holy Prophet 🕌 spoke for such a long time about the rights of the neighbor and good neighborliness, that I began to worry that he would make the neighbors to be his heirs, and he spoke with such concern about the slaves that I began to fear that after their master's death they would be set free." (In fact, Islam introduced strict guidelines regarding the just and kind treatment of slaves, and elaborated on the merits of setting them free, as a charitable, pious act.)

When Abu Bakr had completed his prayer, they told him, "The Holy Prophet 🕌 has been watching from his room." Abu Bakr was very happy to hear that the Prophet's 🕌 condition admitted this, and he immediately came to his side. Seeing him sitting upright, he grew ever more pleased. In his joy, he spoke lightly and pleasantly to his daughter Aisha, and the Prophet 🕌 heard him and was pleased. He even laughed a bit and said jokingly, "Oh Aisha, today Rasulullah 🕌 is in a good state, and today it is the turn for me to go visit my other wives." Aisha replied, "As long as he is ill, the Prophet 🕌 shall stay in my house; when he is well he may go to his other wives." Thereupon the Holy Prophet 🕌 laughed, but he gave no reply.

Since the onset of the Holy Prophet's 🕌 illness, Abu Bakr had been staying in the mosque and had not visited his wife. Aisha then said to him, "Oh my father, for days you have not gone home; tonight the Prophet 🕌 is feeling better, so why do you not go to your home as well?" Abu Bakr then left the mosque and went to see his wife. All the people of Madinah were glad and relieved and gave each other the good news of the improvement. "He was not able to sit up or turn his head, now he is sitting upright and has returned to health," they said.

The Friend on High, the Exalted Companion of Paradise

Aisha held the Prophet ﷺ by the hand and placed his blessed head upon her chest, and for some time he lay there peacefully. Around the time of the forenoon, the agony of death set in, and in accordance with the station of the Beloved of Allah ﷺ it happened with great violence. The elements composing the human body of Muhammad ﷺ could not withstand the unveiled revelation of the Divine. His blessed countenance turned from red to black, while sweat poured from his brow. Those administering to him frequently dipped a rag into a cup of water to wipe his face and cool his brow. Around the noontide of the twelfth day of the month Rabi' al-Awwal, which was a Monday, he uttered his last words, which were *"Rafiq-al-'a'la, Rafiq-al-'a'la"* (the Friend on High, the Exalted Companion of Paradise) and departed from this world of woe to the world of Celestial Beauty.

'Ali stepped out of the room, weeping. 'Umar said to him, "Do not weep, for the hypocrites will believe and say that the Prophet ﷺ has died, whereas he has not died! He has gone to the Presence of the Lord! He will come again, just as Musa used to leave his people for a time to converse with his Lord, and return after some days. Likewise, Rasulullah ﷺ will come back to us." The Companions were in a state of great confusion and distress. 'Umar went around with his sword drawn, saying, "Whoever claims that the Holy Prophet ﷺ is dead, I shall strike his head from his neck."

Abu Bakr came as soon as he heard the news, and he entered the room and found Aisha there in tears. He stepped up to the Holy Prophet ﷺ and pulled back the mantle that covered his blessed face. He gazed upon his beauty that was preserved even in death, bent down and kissed him and replaced the mantle on his face. Then he stepped outside where 'Umar was still telling the people that the Prophet ﷺ had not really died, but would return to them after a while. Abu Bakr went to him and said to him, "Oh 'Umar, do not speak thus, for the Lord has revealed this verse concerning the Holy Prophet ﷺ when He says:

Thou art mortal; and they are mortal...   *(The Companies, 30)*

Such was Abu Bakr's dignity and authority that 'Umar quieted down and said, "By Allah, when I heard these verses from Abu Bakr, it was as though I had never heard them before."

It is related that Abu Bakr stepped out and addressed the people saying, "Oh people, if anyone worships Muhammad, Muhammad is dead; but if anyone worships Allah, He is alive and immortal." And he recited this verse:

Muhammad is naught but a Messenger; Messengers have passed away before him. Why, if he should die or is slain, will you turn about on your heels? If any man should turn about on his heels, he will not harm God in any way; and God will recompense the thankful. It is not given to any soul to die, save by the leave of God, at an appointed time. Whoso desires the reward of this world, We will give him of this; and whoso desires the reward of the other world, We will give him of that; and We will recompense the thankful.

(The House of Imran: 144, 145)

Then it was that people began to believe that the Prophet ❀ had truly passed away, and all folk began to weep. They went to the room where he lay and looked at him, then they returned to the mosque and wept. Abu Bakr then addressed them, comforting them and explaining that it was natural for Muhammad ❀ to pass into the world of the unseen.

Just at that time, Usama had returned with his troops and they were entering the city. Usama planted the banner before the Prophet's door. Everyone felt greater dismay and dread, for just as the city of Madinah had been drowned in light at the Holy Prophet's ❀ coming from the place of his birth, now the opposite effect was manifested: Madinah appeared filled with darkness.

'Ali and 'Abbas washed and dressed the blessed body of the Holy Prophet ❀, tears flowing down their cheeks. Abu Bakr remained in the Prophet's ❀ room. He emerged and offered everyone condolences, explaining that the very form of Muhammad ❀ was sure to pass into the hidden world.

Choosing a Successor

Outside voices were growing louder, saying, "Who will now be chosen as his successor?" Some of the Ansar submitted suggestions for candidates of their own choice. The tribe of 'Aws suggested Usayd bin Khudayri, while the tribe of Khazraj proffered Sa'd bin 'Ubada as successor to the Prophet ✸. Had either of these been elected, rivalry between the two tribes would have resulted and conditions would have reverted to the tribalism and feuding of pre-Islamic times, the unity of the 'La ilaha illAllah' would have been broken and tribal allegiance would again have taken the place of religious fervor.

Sa'd bin 'Ubada was inciting people with his fiery speeches and they were about to pledge their allegiance to him. Had this happened, the Muhajirin would have been sure to object, and thus fierce dissension would have arisen. It was at this moment of great danger that Abu Bakr stepped forth and counseled the assembled tribesmen with gentle words and reason. He took 'Umar and Abu 'Ubayda bin al-Jarrah each by a hand and told the assembly to chose either one of them for their leader.

Abu Bakr reminded them that although the Ansar were highly praiseworthy and had earned much merit for their support and hospitality to the Prophet ✸ in the early days of Islam, now that Islam had spread among all the tribes of Arabia, the question was one of an authority that would be accepted by the whole of Arabia. "You will always remain our treasured Ansar," he said, "but if you now decide to break the unity of the ranks of Islam, you will cause the whole religion will fall apart."

Thus he spoke to them and admonished the assembled Ansar. Then Sa'd bin Nu'man of the Khazraj rose and addressed his people, saying, "It is true that we as a people have fought much and earned much glory, but we did it only for the sake of Allah and His Prophet ✸. We expected no recompense in this world. Our Holy Prophet ✸ was of the clan of Quraysh, and therefore, it is only befitting that his successor should also be of that tribe." One by one, the men got up and spoke, each giving his opinion, until there was great uproar and confusion in the assembly hall. At last 'Umar could take no more, he sprang up and said, "Oh people of the Ansar, is it not known to you that the Prophet ﷺ appointed Abu Bakr to be Imam over us and that he led the prayers when the Prophet ﷺ himself was not able to? That is a sign that he intended him to succeed him as Khalifa." And, turning to Abu Bakr, he said, "Stretch out your hand, let me pledge my allegiance to you and give me the honor of being the first to do so." But Bashr bin Sa'id jumped in between and pledged his allegiance even before 'Umar and Abu 'Ubayda managed to do so.

After 'Umar and Abu 'Ubayda, the rest of the tribe of 'Aws took his hand. The Khazraj then also gave up their idea of electing Sa'd bin 'Ubada as their chief and they all pledged allegiance to Abu Bakr, and so did all the Muhajirin. There were some of the Companions of the clan of the Bani Hashim who would have chosen 'Ali as their Khalifa; among these were Zubayr ibn al-'Awwam, Miqdad bin 'Amr ibn al-Aswad, Salman al-Farsi, Abu Dharr al-Ghifari, 'Ammar ibn Yasir, 'Utayba bin Abi Lahab. At first they refused to pledge allegiance to Abu Bakr, but in the end they consented and all gave Bay'at.

Later, 'Ali said, "We know Abu Bakr to be the Close Companion of Allah's Messenger ﷺ and his Companion in the Cave, and we confirm his being Siddiq-al-Jalil. It is only that we felt aggrieved because of our own closeness and kinship with the Holy Prophet ﷺ and we felt we ought to have had a say in the matter." Abu Bakr replied to this, "It was never our intention to keep you outside of the decision-making process; on the contrary, it was because of our intimate acquaintance and because of the delicacy of the situation that we did not feel it necessary to ask for your separate counsel."

Oh Traveler on the Way to Truth! Let us explore the true meaning of this matter. While the Prophet's ﷺ daughter Fatima was still alive, 'Ali could not possibly have taken Bay'at with Abu Bakr, and it was only because of her that he did not do so. After her death some six months later he came to Abu Bakr and pledged his allegiance. But scholars who cling only to appearances and have not yet tasted of real faith cannot grasp the meaning of these statements; they chew only on dry bones and taste nothing but the chaff.

Even in the Holy Quran there are given clear signs and indications that show that Abu Bakr was meant to be the Prophet's ❁ first successor:

Whosoever obeys God and the Messenger – they are with those whom God has blessed, Prophets, just men, martyrs, the righteous; good companions they! (min an-nabi'ina wa-s-siddiqina wash-shuhada was-salihin, wa hasuna ulayka rafiqan.)

(Women, 69)

If this verse be interpreted, it goes to show that 'siddiq' can only apply to Abu Bakr, and 'shuhada' points to the three martyred Khalifas, i.e. 'Umar, 'Uthman and 'Ali. In another verse these lofty personalities are detailed by these description:

Muhammad is the Messenger of God, and those who are with him are hard against the unbelievers, merciful one to another. Thou seest them bowing, prostrating, seeking bounty from God and good pleasure. Their mark is on their faces, the trace of prostration.

(Victory, 29)

It was Abu Bakr who was very severe towards the unbelievers, 'Umar who turned away from no one and was very quick to forgive, and 'Uthman whose broken heart sought Divine Pleasure more than any and who spent more time in Sajda than any of the others.

The Battles of the Holy Prophet ❁

The traditionalists say that Rasulullah ❁ personally took part in twenty-seven battles and raids. These are:

The raids of al-Abwa, Buwat, 'Ushayra in the Yanbu' valley; the first fight at Badr; the great Battle of Badr; the raids on the Bani Sulaym, al-Sawiq, Ghatafan (which is the raid of Dhu Amarr), and Bahran; the Battle of Uhud; the raids on Hamra'ul-Asad, on the Banu Nadir, and Dhatul-Riqa' of

Nakhl; the last Battle of Badr; Dumatul-Jandal; the Battle of al-Khandaq; the raids on the Banu Qurayza, the Banu Libyan of Hudhayl, on Dhu Qurad, and the Banu Mustaliq of Khuza'a; al-Hudaybiyah; the Battle of Khaybar; the accomplished pilgrimage; the occupation of Mecca; the Battle of Hunayn; the raid on Ta'if; the Battle of Tabuk.

He actually fought in nine engagements: Badr; Uhud; al-Khandaq; Qurayza; al-Mustaliq; Khaybar; the occupation of Mecca; Hunayn and al-Ta'if. Apart from these, there were thirty-eight expeditions and raiding parties the Prophet ﷺ did not personally take part in.

There is general agreement that along his life, the Holy Prophet ﷺ performed the pilgrimage four times, twice before the Hijra. He also performed the 'Umra (the lesser pilgrimage) four times.

The Prophet's ﷺ Scribes

The Prophet's ﷺ scribes were these, some of whom wrote down the revelations, some of whom wrote letters and kept the books of the zakat collection. The first of these was 'Uthman bin 'Affan; the second was 'Ali bin Abi Talib; the third was Khalid bin Sa'id, the fourth his brother Aban bin Sa'id; the fifth 'Ala ud-Din bin al-Hadhrami; the sixth Adiy bin Ka'b; the seventh Zayd bin Thabit; the eighth Abdullah bin Ja'far; the ninth Mu'awiya bin Abi Sufyan; the tenth was Hanzala bin Abi 'Amir.

The Prophet's ﷺ Military Weaponry

The Holy Prophet ﷺ possessed seven swords. The first of these he wore the day he set out from Mecca to Madinah, its name was Ma'sur. He wore it also on the day of Badr. Another sword had belonged to al-'As, and it was a famous sword among the Arabs, called 'Dhul-Fiqar'. On the day of Badr it fell to him as booty and he left it to 'Ali. There were three other swords, which he took from the spoils of the Bani Qaynuqa: one was called Badbar, one was called Samsama and the third was called Qula'i. There were two more swords that Ali had taken from the temple of idols; one of these was called Muhzam and the other Rasub.

He had three bows, their names were Rawha and Safra and Bayda, and he had three spears, which were called Firta and Zirtra and Fafila. And he had one helmet and a shield, which had been sent to him by the Sultan of Egypt, the Muqawqis. It was covered all over with writing. The Holy Prophet ﷺ said, "It was pierced and it was not passed down to any man, but became undone of itself."

The Holy Prophet's ﷺ Blessed Description

Ali describes the Holy Prophet ﷺ thus:

> "He was of medium stature, had black eyes, a wheat colored skin color, pinkish complexion. His neck was white and his beard very curly, and pared to a rounded contour; his hair was black and beautiful and he wore it long, and from his throat to his chest there was a line of very fine hairs like a line drawn with a pen. Other than he had no hairs on his chest.

> "His blessed head was neither very great nor very small, his hands and feet were well-proportioned, and his chest was flat and wide; in the middle of his chest there were three hairs halfway grown together like a mole. He walked swiftly and energetically, as if he were descending downhill. His countenance was so beautiful that no one in his presence could bear to gaze at him. His nose was straight, his teeth were widely spaced and very white. He either wore his hair loose or braided, or hid it underneath his turban or let it hang out from.

> "He was sixty-three years old, and yet only a few hairs in his beard had turned white. Allah Almighty never created anyone better or more generous or more courageous than he, peace and blessings be upon him forever, Amin."

wa min Allah at-tawfiq.

And Allah knows best.

Holy Days of the Islamic Calendar

The following are the twelve months of the Islamic lunar calendar, in chronological sequence, including broadly observed holy days:

MUHARRAM	1st is Islamic New Year; 9th and 10th are days of fasting; 10th is Ashura.
SAFAR	
RABI' AL-AWWAL	12th Rabi' al-Awwal is the Prophet's birthday, known as mawlid; milad; mawlud; celebrated globally.
RABI' ATH-THANI	
JUMADI AL-AWWAL	
JUMADI ATH-THANI	
RAJAB	According to Hadith, the month of Allah. Mi'raj an-Nabi. Superogatory fasting and prayers.
SHA'BAN	According to Hadith, the month of the Prophet. 15th is Nifsu Sha'ban; 7th is Laylat ul-Raghaib. Superogatory fasting and prayers.
RAMADAN	According to Hadith, the month of the people. The month of fasting.
SHAWWAL	1st is Eid al-Fitr, the celebration marking the end of Ramadan, which is observed either two or three days.
DHUL-QADAH	
DHUL-HIJJAH	The month of Hajj. Standing at Mount Arafat is on the 9th and Eid al-Adha, the celebration commemorating hajj, is celebrated on the 10th.

Glossary of Terms

Abu – father.

Abu Bakr – the closest companion of the Prophet and first man to embrace Islam; father of Aisha, wife of the Prophet; migrated from Mecca to Madinah with the Prophet; first appointed successor of the Prophet; known as the most generous of the Companions.

Abu Talib – uncle of the Prophet; father of `Ali.

Abdul-Muttalib – the Prophet's paternal grandfather and an influential leader of the Quraysh tribe. Became the Prophet's guardian when his mother died.

Adab – etiquette; manners; propriety. Islamic teachings emphasize the application of adab to all actions. It has been said, "To know adab is to know Islam."

Ahl as-Sunnah, wal Jama`ah – People of the Sunnah, and Majority.

Ahl al-Bayt – People of the House, a term reserved for the Prophet's family.

Ahl al-Kitab – People of the Book, a reference to followers of the Torah (Old Testament) and the Injeel (New Testament), the divine books revealed to Prophets Moses and Jesus, respectively.

Aisha – daughter of Abu Bakr; wife of the Prophet; a respected jurist, teacher and narrator of Prophetic Traditions; known for her exceptional memory, sagacity and acumen.

Akhira – the Afterlife.

al – the

al-Amin – the Trustworthy; a name attributed to the Prophet.

Alayhim as-salam – "And upon them be peace", spoken upon mention of prophets and messengers; abbreviations include A.S., a.s. and (a).

Allah – The One True God, Who is independent of and Creator of all things, Who has no mother, son, or partner; The Supreme Deity and Universal God for all people, times and places, Who sent down a consistent message through His Prophets and Messengers, that humanity may be rightly guided.

Allahu Akbar – Allah is the Greatest.

Allahu Ahad – Allah is One.

`Ali, bin Abu Talib – first cousin of the Prophet and the first boy to embrace Islam; son of Abu Talib; husband of Fatimah, the Prophet's daughter; father of Hasan and Husayn; the fourth successor of the Prophet.

`Alim – scholar of Islam.

Alhamdulillah – *all Praise is due to Allah;* similar to "Praise the Lord"; hallelujah; alleluia.

Amir – leader.

Ansar – Helpers, Supporters; an honored title given to the people of Madinah, who swore allegiance to the Prophet and received him generously upon his migration from Mecca; who helped establish the Muslim nation, and shared all their possessions with those Muslims who had migrated and left all behind.

Aqeeda – doctrine.

As salamu alaykum - The greeting of Muslims meaning, "Peace be with you"; literally supplicating for the Almighty's peace to descend; a global custom which outwardly indicates the peaceful nature of Islam.

Ayah – a verse of Quran; plural, ayaah.

Azan, Adhan – the prescribed call to prayer (in Arabic), pronounced five times daily. The one who calls adhan is known as "mu`azzin".

Bid`a – innovation; an act not attributed to the Prophet. Innovation in religion must be examined for its merit and on the basis of cause and effect. For example, the Prophet did not say his prayers while traveling on a bus, or recite verses of Quran across phone lines, or use a microphone to broadcast the call to prayer, each of which are modern-day innovations that make Islam more accessible and/or easier to practice.

Bismillah – In the Name of Allah; a serious phrase of seeking God's Help, commonly uttered by Muslims prefacing any given act.

Bismillah ar–Rahman ar–Rahim – *In the Name of Allah, the Most Beneficent, the Most Merciful;* a highly eminent phrase that precedes all chapters of the Quran; often prefaces correspondence, speeches, declarations.

573

Caliph – successor; "khalifah" generally refers to the supreme leader of the Muslim nation.

Din, deen – way, religion; Dee*n al-Islam,* the Islamic Faith.

Du`a – supplication; most often comprised of verses of Quran or hadith; normally recited after the prescribed prayers although encouraged at any time, by raising hands and uttering the supplication either in Arabic or other languages.

Eid, `Id – festivity; the two annual Eids in Islam; Eid al–Fitr, the celebration marking the end of Ramadan; Eid al–Adha, the celebration commemorating hajj, the pilgrimage to Mecca.

Fatwa – legal ruling by a qualified jurist; plural, fatawa.

Fatiha – the opening; first chapter of the Quran.

Fatimah, az–Zahra – daughter of the Prophet; wife of `Ali; mother of Hasan and Husayn; acknowledged as one of the Perfect Women in Islam.

Fiqh – Islamic jurisprudence; faqih, a jurist; plural, fuqaha'.

Fir'aun – Pharoah; specifically, who challenged Prophet Moses and was drowned in the miraculous parting of the Red Sea.

Fisabil-illah – For the Sake of Allah (for God's Sake); connoting an act dedicated to the Almighty.

Four Imams, Four Caliphs – the four immediate successors of the Prophet to whom allegiance was obligatory throughout the Muslim world; namely, Abu Bakr as-Siddiq, `Omar ibn al-Khattab, `Uthman bin Affan, and `Ali ibn Abi Talib.

al–Furqan – the criterion; the Quran.

Ghusl – prescribed bath, requisite for prayer without which ablution is void; Must be performed after sexual relations, upon cessation of menstruation, forty days after childbirth, and before burial. Held as sunnah before many forms of worship, such as Friday congregational prayer, the Eid prayers, and performance of hajj.

Hadhrat, Hazrat – title of respect applied to Prophet Muhammad ﷺ as well as to other prophets and messengers, his family and companions, and great figures mentioned in Quran and Hadith; however the term is also used to address high persons who are present.

Hadith – authorized, recorded Prophetic Traditions on a host of topics, narrated by companions of the Prophet and transmitted down through time; plural, ahadith.

al-Hafiz – The Protector, an attribute of Allah; a hafiz of Quran has been tested by a board of scholars and certified as one who has memorized all of the Quran and can recite any verse or portion of it at random. Also a common Urdu salutation, "Khuda Hafiz" meaning "May God protect you."

Hajj – one of the five pillars of Islam; the pilgrimage at Mecca is incumbent on every Muslim in the world who has the financial means and the health to sustain the annual ritual at least once in their lifetime; male, hajji; female, hajjah; plural, hujjaj, hajeej.

Halal – lawful; permissible.

Haraam – unlawful; forbidden; prohibited.

Haram ash-Sharif – a term applied to three of the Muslim world's holiest sites, i.e. the Holy Ka`ba in Mecca; the Prophet's Mosque in Madinah; the al-Aqsa Mosque in Jerusalem.

Hasan – grandson of the Prophet; son of `Ali and Fatimah, who became a great leader and imam.

Husayn – grandson of the Prophet; son of `Ali and Fatimah, who also became a great leader and imam; martyred at Karbala in Iraq.

Hijra – migration; refers to the Islamic calendar which commences with the date when the Prophet migrated from Mecca to Madinah; (adj.) hijiri.

`Ibadat – worship.

Iftar – food or meal with which the fast is broken at sunset.

Ihsan – the state of divine proximity mentioned in the hadith, "To worship Allah as if you see Him…"

Ijma' – consensus of Muslim scholars.

Imam – one who leads the congregational prayer; also, an elite scholar; one responsible for the mosque, its leader.

Imam ash–Shafi`i – an eminent scholar and founder of one of the great schools of Islamic jurisprudence.

InshaAllah –*If Allah Wills,* spoken at the time of making a commitment, with recognition that nothing is granted without Allah's permission.

Iqamah – a lesser version of the adhan, recited just before the prayer commences.

Islam – the way of submission to the Divine Will.

Jannah – Heaven; Paradise.

Jahannam – Hell; hellfire.

Jihad – struggle; in a narrow sense, understood to mean "war" or military exercise or engagement. "Jihad al–Akbar, "the great struggle" refers to the highest level of self-discipline that brings one closest to the Almighty as a result of overcoming one's ego.

Jinn – beings which Allah created from fire, just as He created angels from divine light and mankind from clay. The Jinn community is comprised of believers as well as unbelievers.

Juma' – Friday; day of the Islamic weekly congregational prayer.

Kaba – also "Bayt Allah", Allah's House; originally built in Mecca by Prophet Abraham and his son as a tribute to The One God; the direction Muslims face when offering prayer; the site of the annual Muslim pilgrimage, hajj.

Kalimat ash-Shahadah – the Muslim Creed of Faith, namely, *Ash-hadu anla ilaha illallah, wa ash-hadu anna Muhammadan Abduhu wa Rasuluh* "I bear Witness that there is no God but Allah, and I bear Witness that Muhammad is the Servant and Messenger of Allah."

Khadijah, al–Kubra – first wife of the Prophet and mother of his children; respected member of the Quraysh tribe; the first woman to embrace Islam; commonly acknowledged as one of the perfect women in Islam.

Khatam, al-Mursaleen – final; finish; end; finality of messengerhood.

Khutba – the sermon which accompanies congregational prayer such as the Friday prayer or on holy days such as Eid.

Kiswah – the beautifully-decorated covering of the Kaba, usually made of rare velvet exquisitely embroidered in pure gold and silver thread.

Kufr – state of unbelief; kafir, one who does not believe in Allah.

La ilaha illallah – there is no God but Allah.

Laylat al-Qadr – Literally, "Night of Power"; a blessed occasion which occurs once a year on an odd night within the last ten days of Ramadan. On this occasion Muslims offer extra prayers, charity, and seek the Almighty's infinite blessings and forgiveness of past sins; it is said whoever attains the blessings of this holy night should attain high spiritual power.

Laylat al-Raghaib – The 7th of Rajab (on the 6th night) and a holy day for Muslims which commemorates a highly blessed occasion, reported as the night in which the blessed essence of Prophet Muhammad (s) was transferred from his father to his mother; she afterwards experienced many miracles.

Madinah – the city to where the Prophet migrated from Mecca and established the Muslim nation; burial place of the Prophet; second holiest place in the Muslim world.

Madhhab – a legal method or school of Islamic law; generally refers to Hanafi, Shafi'i, Maliki, Hanbali and Jafari schools.

Maghrib – sunset; west; evening prayer of the five daily prayers, offered when the sun sets; "al-Maghrib", common Arab reference to Morocco.

Muhajir, muhajireen – one who migrated away from a place or ruler that was religiously oppressive; a group who migrated. Those who migrated from Mecca to Madinah.

Makkah, Mecca – location of the Kaba; birthplace of the Prophet; see *Qiblah*.

Masjid al-Aqsa – the Haram Sharif (holy sanctuary) in Jerusalem, from where the Prophet ﷺ experienced the glorious Mi'raj (Divine Ascension to Heaven). This is the third holiest site in Islam, after Mecca and Madinah.

MashaAllah – This is what Allah has chosen, determined or willed; attributes the source of all good to Allah.

Mawlid, an-Nabi – the birthday of the Holy Prophet Muhammad ﷺ, namely the 12th Rabi' al-Awwal. Mawlid is observed with special prayers, fasting and celebrations and Salawat all over the world.

Mi'raj, an-Nabi – ascension; the heavenly ascension at divine invitation whereby the Prophet physically rode the heavenly transport Buraq from Mecca to Jerusalem, then ascended from this world through all the levels of Heaven. The occasion is broadly celebrated as a holy day throughout the world.

Muhammad bin `Abdallah – the Prophet; Muhammad son of Abdallah.

Muhammad ar-Rasulullah – Muhammad is the Messenger of God.

Mu'min – believer.

Mushrik – see *Shirk*.

Muslim – one who submits to Allah's Will; a follower of Islam; feminine, muslimah.

Nabi, nabi Allah – prophet; prophet of Allah; plural, anbiyya. Islam teaches that 124,000 prophets were sent to every nation and people as reinforcers of the Divine Message, that Allah is One and Muhammad is His Messenger. Some prophets were also messengers, such as Adam, Noah, Abraham, Moses, Jesus and Muhammad ﷺ.

Nafs; an-nafs al-ammara – the lower self from which base desires emanate.

Nifsu Sha'ban – Also referred to as "Laylat al-Bara`ah" (The night of freedom from Fire); occurring between 14th and 15th day of Sha`ban. Traditions of Prophet Muhammad (s) prove it is a meritorious night in which people of the earth are attended by special divine mercy.

Qibla – direction in which Muslims face to say their prayers, i.e. Mecca.

Qiblatain – "two qiblahs"; refers to Jerusalem, which was the first qiblah to which Muslims prayed, and Mecca, the city to which the qiblah was changed during the Prophet's lifetime.

Qira'at – recitation of Quran.

Qudsi Hadith – divine communication direct from Allah to the Prophet, which was other than a revealed verse of Quran.

Quran – Word of Allah Almighty; the divine book of Muslims revealed to the Prophet over twenty-three years, brought down by the Angel Gabriel; the core of Islamic law and comprehensive guidance which governs all aspects of life for Muslims.

Quraysh – an influential, pagan Arab tribe that held the reins of power at the advent of Islam; boycotted the Prophet and militarily opposed the Muslims.

Rabi' al-Awwal – the third month of the Islamic Lunar calendar.

Rabb, Rabbi – Lord; my Lord.

Rabbil Alameen – Lord of all the Worlds; a phrase included in al–Fatiha, the Lord's Prayer of Muslims and opening chapter of the Quran.

Radhi Allahu anhu – Allah be well pleased with him; anhu connotes "him"; anha connotes "her"; anhum connotes "them".

Rak`at – one complete cycle of the prescribed Muslim prayer, which is comprised of either two, three or four cycles.

Ramadan – the month of fasting; the ninth month of the Muslim calendar; the month the first revelation of Quran was brought down; in which the Night of power occurs; one full reading of Quran during Ramadan is highly praised.

ar-Rasheed – the Rightly Guided; a name attributed to the Prophet.

Rasul, Rasul Allah – messenger, Messenger of Allah; refers to Prophet Muhammad. Allah sent many messengers to deliver His Message to people of all regions and eras, such as Abraham, David, Moses, and Muhammad ﷺ.

Ruh – the soul; the spiritual self which separates from the physical self at the time death.

Sadaqa – charity; an act that has the power to deter evil and invoke spiritual well-being, benefit, and protection from harm.

as-Siddiq – the Truthful, a name associated with many prophets as well as Muhammad #; also a name of his dear companion, Abu Bakr.

Sahabah – Companions of the Prophet; those who saw or met the Prophet during his lifetime, or who were physically in his presence. The Sahabah narrated the greatest volume of Prophetic Traditions known as Hadith.

Sahur – pre-dawn food or meal specifically taken before the fast commences.

Sajdah – prostration, a prescribed component of prayer reserved exclusively for worship of Allah; also, sujud.

Salaf –reference to the Sahabah (Prophet's Companions), and the next few subsequent generations of Muslims.

Sallallahu alayhi was salam – May the Peace and Mercy of Allah be upon him; an expression applied exclusively to Prophet Muhammad. Abbreviated versions include p.b.u.h., s.a.w., s.a.w.s, and s.

Salat – prayer; also known as namaz (Urdu). The five compulsory daily prayers are known as Fajr (morning), Zuhur (midday), `Asr (afternoon), Maghrib (evening), and `Isha (night).

Salawat – any form of praising Prophet Muhammad #, but most typically in beautiful verses or chanting.

Sawm – fasting.

Sayyidina – title of great respect applied to Prophet Muhammad # as well as to other prophets and messengers, his family and companions, and great figures mentioned in Quran and Hadith; also Syedna, Syedina (masc.); Sayyidatuna, Syeda, Sayyida (fem.). When addressing one who is present with effective language connoting respect, the term Sayyid (masc.) and Sayyida (fem.) are also used.

Shaytan – Satan.

**Shi`a** – supporters of Ahlul Bayt; followers of the Ja`fari madhhab.

Shirk – associating partners with Allah; said to be the only sin Allah will not forgive; mushrik, one who associates partners with Allah.

Slavery – Islam introduced strict guidelines regarding the just and kind treatment of slaves, respecting their right of religious freedom, made their owners entirely responsible for their welfare, and elaborated on the merits of setting them free as a charitable, pious act, and their freedom was irreversible.

Subhanahu wa ta`ala – Glorified and Exalted, in exclusive reference to Allah.

Sunnah – example of the Prophet, illuminated by his words and deeds.

Sura, surat – a chapter of Quran; Surat al-Fatiha, meaning "Chapter the Fatiha".

Tabi`een – the third generation of the early Muslims, who lived after the passing of Prophet Muhammad.

Talbiya – the supplication uttered by pilgrims to Mecca, specifically: *Labbayk Allahumma, labbayk…* (Here I am Lord, at Your service).

Taqlid – to follow qualified, scholarly opinions.

Tasawwuf – the Islamic science that promotes human spirituality and helps one reach the state known as "ihsan".

Tasbih, tasabih, masbaha – rosary; prayer beads used to enumerate both prescribed and superogatory supplications.

Tazkiyyah, an-nafs – purification; the state of purifying and disciplining of the lower self, ego.

Umar ibn al-Khattab – close companion of the Prophet; father of Hafsa, the Prophet's wife; second Caliph who advanced Islam beyond the Arabian Peninsula and defeated both the Roman and Persian Empires – two oppressive superpowers; liberated Jerusalem from Roman control; it is said Satan feared him.

**`Ulama** – plural of `alim; scholars.

Umm – mother; ummi, my mother; ummul, mother of.

Ummat al-Mumineen – Mothers of the Faithful, a title reserved exclusively for the wives of the Prophet.

Umrah – the lesser hajj; includes all the rituals of hajj with the exception of the visit to `Arafat; pilgrimage performed at times other than days allocated for hajj; two umrahs are considered equal to one hajj.

Ummah – literally, "nation"; understood to mean the global body of Muslims.

Usool – principles; sciences; usool al-fiqh, principles of jurisprudence.

Uthman – Companion of the Prophet and his third successor; original compiler of the Quran in book form; distinguished as "Thu-noorayn", one with to sources of light, for marrying two of the Prophet's daughters.

Wahi – divine revelation intended for chosen prophets and messengers, which was completed with the revelation to Prophet Muhammad ﷺ and will not occur again.

Wudu – prescribed ablution; a requisite of prayer, and for reading the Quran.

Zakat – a pillar of the Islamic faith that binds adult Muslims to pay 2.5 percent of their annual wealth into a welfare fund that assists the needy.

Other titles available from

Islamic Supreme Council of America

The Honor of Women in Islam
Scholars in Islam Series
By Professor Yusuf da Costa
ISBN 1-930409-06-0
Suggested Retail Price: $10.99

Relying explicitly on Islamic source texts, this concise, scholarly work elucidates the true respect and love for women inherent in the Islamic faith. It examines the pre-Islamic state of women, highlights the unprecedented rights they received under Islamic Law, and addresses the prominent beliefs and prevailing cultures throughout the Muslim world regarding the roles of women. In addition, brief case studies of historical figures such as Mary, mother of Jesus and Hagar, slave maiden of Sarah are presented within the Islamic tradition. The Honor of Women in Islam is an excellent resource for academics, policymakers, theologians, laypersons, and service providers. Paperback. 90 pp.

In the Mystic Footsteps of Saints
Sufi Wisdom Series
By Shaykh Muhammad Nazim Adil al-Haqqani
Volume 1 – ISBN 1-930409-05-2
Volume 2 – ISBN 1-930409-09-5
Suggested Retail Price: $10.99

Narrated in a charming, old-world storytelling style, this highly spiritual series offers several volumes of practical guidance on how to establish serenity and peace in daily life, how to heal from emotional and spiritual scars, and how to discover the role we are each destined to play in the universal scheme. Written by Shaykh Nazim Adil al-Haqqani, a descendant of best-selling poet and Sufi mystic Jalaluddin Rumi and World Leader of the Naqshbandi-Haqqani Sufi Order. Paperback. Average length 175 pp.

For more available titles, please visit our Web site at
http://www.islamicsupremecouncil.org

Printed in the United States
80271LV00003B/19-45

9 781930 409118